SOMETHING ABOUT THE AUTHOR

Editor: Anne Commire

Associate Editors: Agnes Garrett, Helga P. McCue

Assistant Editors: Dianne H. Anderson, Kathryn T. Floch, Mary F. Glahn,
D. Jayne Higo, Linda Shedd, Susan L. Stetler

Consultant: Adele Sarkissian

Sketchwriters: Rosemary DeAngelis Bridges, Mark Eisman

Research Assistant: Kathleen Betsko

Editorial Assistants: Lisa Bryon, Susan Pfanner, Elisa Ann Sawchuk

Also Published by Gale

CONTEMPORARY AUTHORS

*A Bio-Bibliographical Guide to Current Writers in
Fiction, General Nonfiction, Poetry, Journalism,
Drama, Motion Pictures, Television,
and Other Fields*

(Now Covers More Than 60,000 Authors)

Library of Congress Catalog Card Number 72-27107

ISBN 0-8103-0053-2

SOMETHING ABOUT THE AUTHOR

Facts and Pictures about Authors

and Illustrators of Books for Young People

Anne Commire

VOLUME 20

GALE RESEARCH
BOOK TOWER
DETROIT, MICHIGAN
48226

Table of Contents

Introduction   vii   **Illustrations Index**   241

Acknowledgments   ix   **Author Index**   253

Introduction

Beginning with Volume 15, the time span covered by *Something about the Author* was broadened to include major children's writers who died before 1961, which was the former cut-off point for writers covered in this series. This change will make *SATA* even more helpful to its many thousands of student and professional users.

Authors who did not come within the scope of *SATA* have formerly been included in *Yesterday's Authors of Books for Children*, of which Gale has published two volumes.

It has been pointed out by users, however, that it is inconvenient to have a body of related materials broken up by an arbitrary criterion such as the date of a person's death. Also, some libraries are not able to afford both series, and are therefore denied access to material on some of the most important writers in the juvenile field.

It has been decided, therefore, to discontinue the *YABC* series, and to include in *SATA* at least the most outstanding among the older writers who had been selected for listing in *YABC*. Volumes 1 and 2 of *YABC* will be kept in print, and the listings in those two volumes will be included in the cumulative *SATA* index.

GRATEFUL ACKNOWLEDGMENT

is made to the following publishers, authors, and artists,
for their kind permission to reproduce copyrighted material.

ABINGDON PRESS. Illustration by Judith G. Brown from *Max and the Truffle Pig* by Judith G. Brown. Copyright © 1963 by Abingdon Press. Reprinted by permission of Abingdon Press.

ADDISON-WESLEY PUBLISHING CO., INC. Illustration by Jerry Pinkney from *Mildred Murphy, How Does Your Garden Grow?* by Phyllis Green. Copyright © 1977 by Phyllis Green./ Illustration by Susanna Natti from *The Downtown Fairy Godmother* by Charlotte Pomerantz. Text copyright © 1978 by Charlotte Pomerantz. Illustrations copyright © 1978 by Susanna Natti. Both reprinted by permission of Addison-Wesley Publishing Co., Inc.

AMERICAN BOOK CO. Sidelight excerpts from *The Wayside: Home of Authors* by Harriet Lothrop. Reprinted by permission of American Book Co.

AMERICAN HERITAGE PUBLISHING CO., INC. Sidelight excerpts from an article, "They Heard You in Cape Town!" by Dorothy Gordon, August, 1955, in *American Heritage*. Copyright 1955 by American Heritage Publishing Co., Inc. Reprinted by permission of American Heritage Publishing Co., Inc.

ANGUS & ROBERTSON PUBLISHERS. Illustration by Harold Thomas from *Tales Told to Kabbarli* by Daisy Bates, retold by Barbara Ker Wilson. Copyright © 1972 University of Adelaide for original collection. Reprinted by permission of Angus & Robertson Publishers.

ATHENEUM PUBLISHERS. Illustration by Dale Payson from *If You Listen* by Gunilla B. Norris. Copyright © 1971 by Gunilla B. Norris./ Illustration by Richard Cuffari from *The Top Step* by Gunilla B. Norris. Copyright © 1970 by Gunilla Norris./ Illustration by Warwick Hutton from *Noah and the Great Flood* by Warwick Hutton. Copyright © 1977 by Warwick Hutton. All reprinted by permission of Atheneum Publishers.

BLACKIE AND SON, LTD. Illustrations by Florence Harrison from *Poems* by Christina Rossetti. Reprinted by permission of Blackie & Son, Ltd.

THE BODLEY HEAD, LTD. Illustration by Edward Ardizzone from *The Little Train* by Graham Greene. Illustrations copyright © 1973 by Edward Ardizzone. Reprinted by permission of The Bodley Head, Ltd.

ALBERT BONNIERS FÖRLAG AB (Sweden). Illustration by Elsa Beskow from *Barnen på Solbacka* by Elsa Beskow. Copyright © 1974 by Albert Bonniers Förlag AB./ Illustration by Elsa Beskow from *Blommornas Bok* by Elsa Beskow. Copyright 1955 by Albert Bonnier Förlag AB. Both reprinted by permission of Albert Bonniers Förlag AB.

THE CARDAVON PRESS, INC. Illustration by Rockwell Kent from "Autumn Rivulets" in *Leaves of Grass* by Walt Whitman. Copyright 1936 by Doubleday, Doran & Co., Inc. Reprinted by permission of The Cardavon Press, Inc.

CHILDRENS PRESS. Photographs by Vince Streano from *Together* by June Behrens. Copyright © 1975 by Regensteiner Publishing Enterprises, Inc. Reprinted by permission of Childrens Press.

CITATION PRESS. Sidelight excerpts from *Books Are By People* by Lee Bennett Hopkins. Copyright © 1969 by Scholastic Magazine, Inc. Reprinted by permission of Citation Press, a division of Scholastic Book Services.

WILLIAM COLLINS & SONS CO., LTD. Autolithographs by Charles Mozley and Sidelight excerpts from *A Vicarage Family: An Autobiographical Story* by Noel Streatfeild. Copyright © 1963 by Noel Streatfeild./ All reprinted by permission of William Collins & Sons Co., Ltd.

WILLIAM COLLINS & WORLD PUBLISHING CO., INC. Illustration by Kurt Werth from *Noodles, Nitwits, and Numskulls* by Maria Leach. Copyright © 1961 by Maria Leach. Reprinted by permission of William Collins & World Publishing Co., Inc.

COLUMBIA UNIVERSITY PRESS. Sidelight excerpts from *Christina Georgina Rossetti* by Eleanor Water Thomas. Reprinted by permission of Columbia University Press.

CONCORDIA PUBLISHING HOUSE. Art by Dhimitri Zonia from *Journeys to Bethlehem, The Story of the First Christmas* retold by Dorothy Van Woerkom. Copyright © 1974 by Concordia Publishing House. Reprinted by permission of Concordia Publishing House.

COWARD, McCANN & GEOGHEGAN, INC. Illustration by Margot Tomes from *Those Foolish Molboes* by Lillian Bason. Text copyright © 1977 by Lillian Bason. Illustrations copyright © 1977 by Margot Tomes. Reprinted by permission of Coward, McCann & Geoghegan, Inc.

DELL PUBLISHING CO., INC. Illustration by Mercer Mayer from *More Adventures of the Great Brain* by John D. Fitzgerald. Text copyright © 1969 by John D. Fitzgerald. Illustrations copyright © 1969 by Mercer Mayer. Reprinted by permission of Dell Publishing Co., Inc.

THE DIAL PRESS. Illustration by Mercer Mayer from *The Return of the Great Brain* by John D. Fitzgerald. Text copyright © 1974 by John D. Fitzgerald. Illustrations copyright © 1974 by The Dial Press./ Illustration by Steven Kellogg from *Gustav the Gourmet Giant* by Lou Ann Gaeddert. Text copyright © 1976 by Lou Ann Gaeddert. Pictures copyright © 1976 by Steven Kellogg. Both reprinted by permission of The Dial Press, a division of Dell Publishing Co., Inc.

DODD, MEAD & CO. Sidelight excerpts from *Reluctant First Lady* by Lorena Hickok. Copyright © 1962 by Lorena A. Hickok./ Sidelight excerpts from *The Touch of Magic: The Story of Helen Keller's Great Teacher, Anne Sullivan* by Lorena Hickok. Copyright © 1961 by Lorena A. Hickok./ Illustration by Sam Savitt from *A Boy and a Pig, But Mostly Horses* by Sherman Kent. Copyright © 1974 by Sherman Kent./ Sidelight excerpts from *Robert Service: A Biography* by Carl F. Klinck. Copyright © 1976 by Carl F. Klinck./ Illustration by Maynard Dixon from *The Trial of '98* by Robert W. Service. Copyright 1910 by Dodd, Mead & Company./ Illustration by Nevin and Phyllis Washington from *Mahalia: Gospel Singer* by Kay McDearmon. Text copyright © 1976 by Katherine M. McDearmon. Illustrations copyright © 1976 by Nevin and Phyllis Washington./ Illustration by Ted Lewin from *Volunteer Spring* by Judy Long. Copyright © 1976 by Judy Long. All reprinted by permission of Dodd, Mead & Co.

DOUBLEDAY & CO., INC. Sidelight excerpts from the Introduction to *Reaching for the Stars* by Frederick C. Durant, III, book by Erik Bergaust. Copyright © 1960 by Erik Bergaust./ Illustration by Edward Ardizzone from *The Little Train* by Graham Greene. Illustrations copyright © 1973 by Edward Ardizzone./ Illustration by Albert Orbaan from *Cross Among the Tomahawks* by Milton Lomask. Copyright © 1961 by Milton Lomask./ Illustration by Lewis C. Daniel from *Leaves of Grass* by Walt Whitman. Copyright 1946 by Doubleday, Doran & Co./ Illustration by Edw. A. Wilson from *The Magnificent Idler, The Story of Walt Whitman* by Cameron Rogers. Copyright 1926 by Doubleday, Page & Co. All reprinted by permission of Doubleday & Co., Inc.

ELSEVIER-DUTTON PUBLISHING CO., INC. Pictures by Brinton Turkle from *The Boy Who Didn't Believe in Spring* by Lucille Clifton. Illustrations copyright © 1973 by Brinton Turkle./ Pictures by Lois Fisher and Karl Murr from *You and Democracy* by Dorothy Gordon. Copyright 1951 by E.P. Dutton and Co., Inc. Both reprinted by permission of Elsevier-Dutton Publishing Co., Inc.

ELSEVIER-NELSON BOOKS. Jacket painting by Lydia Rosier from *Once Upon Another Time* by Robert C. Lee. Copyright © 1977 by Robert C. Lee./ Illustration by Allan Davis from *The Treasure of Spanish Bay* by George Beardmore. Copyright © 1975 by George Beardmore. Both reprinted by permission of Elsevier-Nelson Books.

FARRAR, STRAUS & GIROUX, INC. Illustration by De Wolfe Hotchkiss from *Champions in Sports and Spirit* by Ed Fitzgerald. Copyright © 1956 by Edward Fitzgerald. Reprinted by permission of Farrar, Straus & Giroux, Inc.

LIBRARIE ERNEST FLAMMARION. Sidelight excerpts from *Saint-Exupéry* by Marcel Migeo, translated from the French by Herma Briffault. Copyright © 1959 by Flammarion. Reprinted by permission of Librarie Ernest Flammarion.

FOLCROFT LIBRARY EDITIONS. Sidelight excerpts from *H.G. Wells* by Geoffrey West. Reprinted by permission of Folcroft Library Editions.

FOLLETT CORP. Illustration by Marilyn Fitschen from *Rotten Snags! Rotten Hair!* by Dale Fitschen. Copyright © 1975 by Dale Fitschen and Marilyn Fitschen. Reprinted by permission of Follett Corp.

FOUR WINDS PRESS. Illllustration by Leigh Grant from *Mystery at Fire Island* by Hope Campbell. Text copyright © 1978 by Hope Campbell. Illustrations copyright © 1978 by Scholastic Magazines, Inc. Reprinted by permission of Four Winds Press, a division of Scholastic Book Services.

EDITIONS GALLIMARD. Sidelight excerpts from *A Sense of Life* by Antoine de Saint Exupéry. Copyright © 1956 by Editions Gallimard. Reprinted by permission of Editions Gallimard.

GARRARD PUBLISHING CO. Illustration by Cary from *Dragons, Ogres, and Scary Things* by Kathleen Arnott. Copyright © 1974 by Kathleen Arnott./ Illustration by Lou Cunette from *April Fool!* by Leland B. Jacobs. Copyright © 1973 by Leland B. Jacobs./ Drawings by Kelly Oechsli from *Hello, Pleasant Places,* poetry selected by Leland B. Jacobs. Copyright © 1972 by Leland Jacobs. All reprinted by permission of Garrard Publishing Co.

GROSSET & DUNLAP, INC. Illustration by Jo Polseno from *The Story of Helen Keller* by Lorena A. Hickok. Copyright © 1958 by Lorena A. Hickok./ Illustration by William Sharp from *Five Little Peppers and How They Grew* by Margaret Sidney. Copyright 1948 by Grosset & Dunlap, Inc. Both reprinted by permission of Grosset & Dunlap, Inc.

HARCOURT BRACE JOVANOVICH, LTD. (London). Photographs by Gil and Ann Loescher from *The Chinese Way* by Gil Loescher with Ann Dull Loescher. Copyright © 1974 by Gilbert Damian Loescher and Ann Dull Loescher. Reprinted by permission of Harcourt Brace Jovanovich, Ltd. (London).

HARCOURT BRACE JOVANOVICH, INC. Photograph from *The Way It Is* edited by John Holland. Copyright © 1969 by Harcourt Brace Jovanovich, Inc./ Photographs by Gil and Ann Loescher from *The Chinese Way* by Gil Loescher and Ann Dull Loescher. Copyright © 1974 by Gilbert Damian and Ann Dull Loescher./ Sidelight excerpts from *What the Woman Lived: Selected Letters of Louise Bogan, 1920-1970* edited by Ruth Limmer./ Illustration by Antoine de Saint Exupéry from *The Little Prince* by Antoine de Saint Exupéry. Copyright 1943 by Harcourt Brace and World, Inc. All reprinted by permission of Harcourt Brace Jovanovich, Inc.

HARPER & ROW, PUBLISHERS, INC. Illustration by Howard Knotts from *A Day in the Country* by Willis Barnstone. Text copyright © 1971 by Willis Barnstone. Pictures copyright © 1971 by Howard Knotts./ Illustration by Judith Gwyn Brown from *Mandy* by Julie Edwards. Text copyright © 1971 by Julie Edwards. Pictures copyright © 1971 by Judith Gwyn Brown./ Sidelight excerpts from *Reading, Writing and Remembering: A Literary Record* by E.V. Lucas./ Sidelight excerpts from *A Sense of Life* by Antoine de Saint Exupéry. Copyright © 1965 by Harper & Row Publishers, Inc. All reprinted by permission of Harper & Row, Publishers, Inc.

HAWTHORN BOOKS, INC. Sidelight excerpts from *Ouida: The Passionate Victorian* by Eileen Bigland. Reprinted by permission of Hawthorn Books, Inc., a division of Elsevier-Dutton Publishing Co., Inc.

A.M. HEATH & CO., LTD. Autolithographs by Charles Mozley and Sidelight excerpts from *A Vicarage Family* by Noel Streatfeild. Copyright © 1963 by Noel Streatfeild./ Sidelight excerpts from *Beyond the Vicarage* by Noel Streatfeild. Both reprinted by permission of A.M. Heath & Co., Ltd.

HERON BOOKS. Illustration by Anthony Colbert from *The Research Magnificent* by H.G. Wells. Reprinted by permission of Heron Books.

HOLT, RINEHART AND WINSTON, INC. Illustration from "The Barefoot Boy" by John Greenleaf Whittier in *The Open Road: A Book for Wayfarers* compiled by E.V. Lucas./ Frontispiece from *A Book of Verses for Children* by E.V. Lucas. Both reprinted by permission of Holt, Rinehart and Winston, Inc.

HORN BOOK, INC. Sidelight excerpts from *Illustrators of Children's Books, 1744-1945* compiled by Bertha E. Mahony and others. Copyright 1947, renewed © 1974./ Sidelight excerpts from an article, "The Album and the Artist," in April, 1964 *Horn Book*. Copyright © 1964 by The Horn Book, Inc./ Sidelight excerpts from *Illustrators of Children's Books, 1946-1956* by Bertha M. Miller and others, compilers. Copyright © 1958 by The Horn Book, Inc. All reprinted by permission of Horn Book, Inc.

HOUGHTON MIFFLIN CO. Illustration by Susan Meddaugh from *Good Stones* by Anne Merrick Epstein. Copyright © 1977 by Anne Merrick Epstein./ Illustration by W.E. How from *Shackleton and the Antarctic* by Margery and James Fisher. Copyright © 1957 by James Barrie Books, Ltd./ Illustration by Nicole Rubel from *Rotten Ralph* by Jack Gantos. Text copyright © 1976 by Jack Gantos. Illustrations copyright © 1976 by Leslie Rubel./ Illustration by Becky Gaver from *Fast & Slow* by John Ciardi. Copyright © 1975 by John Ciardi./ Illustration by

George Giguère from *The Five Little Peppers and How They Grew* by Margaret Sidney. Copyright 1909 by Harriett M. Lothrop./ Sidelight excerpts from *Walt Whitman, An American* by Seidel Canby. Copyright © 1971 by Edward T. Canby and Marion Canby. All reprinted by permission of Houghton Mifflin Co.

GERALD HOWE, LTD. Illustration by H.G. Wells from *H.G. Wells* by Geoffrey West. Reprinted by permission of Gerald Howe, Ltd.

JARROLD COLOUR PUBLICATIONS. Photographs from *Ouida: The Passionate Victorian* by Eileen Bigland. Reprinted by permission of Jarrold Colour Publications.

JUDSON PRESS. Illustration by Joan Orfe from *My Very Special Friend* by Lucille E. Hein. Copyright © 1974 Judson Press. Reprinted by permission of Judson Press.

JUNIOR DELUXE EDITIONS. Illustration by Tasha Tudor from *The Wind in the Willows* by Kenneth Grahame. Copyright © 1966 by The World Publishing Company. Illustrations copyright © 1966 by Tasha Tudor. Reprinted by permission of Junior Deluxe Editions.

ALFRED A. KNOPF. Photograph by Frank Pearsall and caricature from *Whitman: An Interpretation in Narrative* by Emory Halloway. Copyright 1926 by Emory Halloway./ Illustration by Fritz Wegner from *Jacob Two-Two Meets the Hooded Fang* by Mordecai Richler./ Text copyright © 1975 by Mordecai Richler. Illustration copyright © 1975 by Alfred A. Knopf, Inc. Both reprinted by permission of Alfred A. Knopf, a division of Random House.

LAMPLIGHT PUBLISHING, INC. Illustration by Trina Schart Hyman from *You've Come a Long Way, Sybil Macintosh* by Charlotte Herman. Copyright © 1974 by Charlotte Herman. Illustrations copyright © 1977 by Lamplight Publishing, Inc. Reprinted by permission of Lamplight Publishing, Inc.

LERNER PUBLICATIONS CO. Designs by Vicki Hall from *The Red Man in Art* by Rena Neumann Coen. Copyright © 1972 by Lerner Publications Co. Reprinted by permission of Lerner Publications Co.

THE LIMITED EDITIONS CLUB. Illustration by Charles Mozley from *The Invisible Man* by H.G. Wells. Special contents of this edition copyright © 1967 by The George Macy Companies, Reprinted by permission of The Limited Editions Club.

J.B. LIPPINCOTT CO. Illustration by Munro Leaf from *Turnabout* by Munro Leaf. Copyright © 1967 by Munro Leaf./ Illustration by Tasha Tudor from *A Little Princess* by Frances Hodgson Burnett. Illustrations copyright © 1963 by Tasha Tudor. Foreword copyright © by Phyllis McGinley./ Illustration by Tasha Tudor from *The Secret Garden* by Frances Hodgson Burnett. Copyright 1911 by F.H. Burnett. Copyright renewal 1938 by Verity Constance Burnett. Illustrations copyright © 1962 by J.B. Lippincott Co./ Sidelight excerpts from *Experiment in Autobiography,* Volume I and II, by H.G. Wells. Copyright 1934 by Herbert George Wells, renewal copyright © 1962 by George Philip Wells and Francis Richard Wells. All reprinted by permission of J.B. Lippincott Co.

LITTLE, BROWN AND CO. Illustration by Steele Savage from *Mythology* by Edith Hamilton. Copyright 1942 by Edith Hamilton. Reprinted by permission of Little, Brown and Co.

LOTHROP, LEE & SHEPARD CO. Illustration by Hermann Heyer from *Five Little Peppers Midway* by Margaret Sidney. Copyright 1890 and 1893 by D. Lothrop Company. Copyright 1918 by Harriett M. Lothrop. Reprinted by permission of Lothrop, Lee & Shepard Co.

THE LUTHERAN CHURCH IN AMERICA. Sidelight excerpts from an article, "I Love Life," February 26, 1964, in *The Lutheran.* Reprinted by permission of The Lutheran Church in America.

MACMILLAN, INC. Illustration by F.D. Bedford from *Another Book of Verses for Children* edited by E.V. Lucas. Copyright 1907 by The Macmillan Co./ Illustration by Eugene Karlin from *Puss in Boots, The Sleeping Beauty and Cinderella,* adapted by Marianne Moore. Text copyright © 1963 by Marianne Moore. Illustrations copyright © 1963 by The Macmillan Co./ Illustration by Nonny Hogrogian from *Paz* by Cheli Durán Ryan. Copyright © 1971 by Cheli Durán Ryan. Copyright © 1971 by Nonny Hogrogian./ Photos by Allyn Baum from *Antarctica: The Worst Place in the World* by Allyn Baum. Copyright © 1966 by Allyn Z. Baum and the Macmillan Co. All reprinted by permission of Macmillan, Inc.

MACMILLAN PUBLISHERS, LTD. (London). Photos by Allyn Baum from *Antarctica: The Worst Place in the World* by Allyn Baum. Copyright © 1966 by Allyn Z. Baum and the Macmillan Co. Reprinted by permission of Macmillan Publishers, Ltd. (London).

McGRAW-HILL, INC. Illustration by Don Miller from *Haji of the Elephants* by Willis Lindquist. Copyright © 1976 by Willis Lindquist./ Jacket illustration by Charles Lilly from *Pickles and Prunes* by Barbara Moe. Copyright © 1976 by Barbara Moe. Both reprinted by permission of McGraw-Hill, Inc.

McGRAW-HILL RYERSON, LTD. (Canada). Sidelight excerpts from *Robert Service: A Biography* by Carl F. Klinck. Copyright © 1976 by Carl F. Klinck. Reprinted by permission of McGraw-Hill Ryerson, Ltd. (Canada).

DAVID McKAY CO., INC. Sidelight excerpts from *The Winged Life: A Portrait of Antoine de Saint-Exupéry, Poet and Airman* by Richard Rumbold and Lady Margaret Stewart. Reprinted by permission of David McKay Co., Inc.

JULIAN MESSNER. Illustration by Janet and Alex D'Amato from *More Colonial Crafts, for You to Make* by Janet and Alex D'Amato./ Illustration by Charles Clement from *All the Better to Bite With* by Helen Doss with Richard L. Wells. Both reprinted by permission of Julian Messner, a division of Simon & Schuster.

WILLIAM MORROW AND CO. Illustration by Jay Hyde Barnum from *Buddy and the Old Pro* by John R. Tunis. Copyright © 1955 by Lucy R. Tunis./ Illustration by Susan Jeschke from *Busybody Nora* by Johanna Hurwitz. Illustrations copyright © 1976 by Susan Jeschke. Both reprinted by permission of William Morrow and Co.

THE NEW YORK TIMES CO. Sidelight excerpts from an article, "The Human Factor in Graham Greene," by V.S. Pritchett, February 26, 1978, in the *New York Times Magazine.* Copyright © 1978 by The New York Times Co. Reprinted by permission of The New York Times Co.

NEW YORKER MAGAZINE, INC. Sidelight excerpts from an article, "Humility, Concentration and Gusto," by W. Winthrop Sargeant, February 16, 1957, in *New Yorker./* Sidelight excerpts from an article, "Department of Amplification," April 13, 1957, in *New Yorker.* Both reprinted by permission of New Yorker Magazine, Inc.

W.W. NORTON & CO., INC. Sidelight excerpts and photos from *Edith Hamilton: An Intimate Portrait* by Doris Fielding Reid. Copyright © 1967 by W.W. Norton & Co., Inc. All reprinted by permission of W.W. Norton & Co., Inc.

PANTHEON BOOKS, INC. Illustration by Josef Scharl from *Rock Crystal* by Adalbert Stifter. Translated by Elizabeth Mayer and Marianne Moore. Copyright 1945 by Pantheon Books, Inc. Copyright © 1965 by Random House, Inc./ Illustration by Susan Detrich from *On the Path of Venus* by Lloyd Motz. Text copyright © 1976 by Lloyd Motz. Illustrations copyright © 1976 by Random House, Inc. Both reprinted by permission of Pantheon Books, Inc., a division of Random House, Inc.

PEGASUS. Sidelight excerpts from *Marianne Moore: The Cage and the Animal* by Donald Hall. Reprinted by permission of Pegasus.

CLARKSON N. POTTER, INC. Photograph and illustrations by James F. Sullivan and Stephen Lawrence from *The H.G. Wells Scrapbook,* edited by Peter Haining. Copyright © 1978 by Peter Haining. All reprinted by permission of Clarkson N. Potter, Inc.

PRENTICE-HALL, INC. Sidelight excerpts from *Norman Vincent Peale—Minister to Millions* by Arthur Gordon. Copyright © 1972, 1958 by Norman Vincent Peale and Arthur Gordon. Reprinted by permission of Prentice-Hall, Inc.

G.P. PUTNAM'S SONS. Photographs and Sidelight excerpts from *Antoine de Saint-Exupéry: His Life and Times* by Curtis Cate. Copyright © 1970 by Curtis Cate. All reprinted by permission of G.P. Putnam's Sons.

RAND McNALLY & CO. Illustration by Tasha Tudor from *The Night Before Christmas* by Clement Clarke Moore. Copyright © 1975 by Rand McNally & Co. Reprinted by permission of Rand McNally & Co.

RANDOM HOUSE, INC. Sidelight excerpts from *Generations: A Memoir* by Lucille Clifton./ Illustration by Peggy Fortnum from *Thursday's Child* by Noel Streatfeild. Copyright © 1970 by Noel Streatfeild./ Illustration by Valenti Angelo from *Leaves of Grass* by Walt Whitman./ Illustration by Judith Gwyn Brown from *When the Sirens Wailed* by Noel Streatfeild. Text copyright © 1976 by Noel Streatfeild. Illustrations copyright © 1976 by Random House./ Illustration by Edward Ardizzone from *The Magic Summer* by Noel Streatfeild. Copyright © 1967 by Noel Streatfeild./ Illustration by Edward Gorey from *The War of the Worlds* by H.G. Wells. Copyright © 1960 by Epstein and Carroll Associates, Inc. All reprinted by permission of Random House, Inc.

RUTLEDGE BOOKS. Illustration by Raul Mina Mora from *The Beginning Knowledge Book of Fossils* by Anne Orth Epple. Copyright © 1969 by Rutledge Books, Inc. Reprinted by permission of Rutledge Books, a division of Macmillan, Inc.

CHARLES SCRIBNER'S SONS. Illustration by Adrienne Adams from *Houses from the Sea* by Alice E. Goudey. Text copyright © 1959 by Alice E. Goudey. Pictures copyright © 1959 by Adrienne Adams./ Photograph from *Physical Fitness Through Sports and Nutrition* by Walter

H. Gregg. Copyright © 1975 by Dr. Walter H. Gregg. Both reprinted by permission of Charles Scribner's Sons.

THE SEABURY PRESS, INC. Illustration by Talivaldis Stubis from *The Cookie Book* by Eva Moore. Text copyright © 1973 by Eva Moore. Illustration copyright © 1973 by Talivaldis Stubis./ Jacket illustration by Mike Eagle from *Shelter from the Wind* by Marion Dane Bauer. Copyright © 1976 by Marion Dane Bauer. Both reprinted by permission of The Seabury Press, Inc.

MARTIN SECKER & WARBURG, LTD. Sidelight excerpts from an article, "The Art of Poetry: Marianne Moore," by Donald Hall in *Marianne Moore: A Collection of Critical Essays* edited by Charles Tomlinson. Reprinted by permission of Martin Secker & Warburg, Ltd.

SIMON & SCHUSTER, INC. Sidelight excerpts from *For My Own Amusement* by R.F. Delderfield. Copyright © 1972 by R.F. Delderfield./ Sidelight excerpts from *Graham Greene on Film, Collected Film Criticism 1935-1940* edited by John Russell Taylor./ Sidelight excerpts from *A Sort of Life* by Graham Greene. Copyright © 1971 by Graham Greene. All reprinted by permission of Simon & Schuster, Inc.

TIME, INC. Sidelight excerpts from an article, "Marianne Moore, 79 Keeps Going Like Sixty," by Jane Howard in *Life,* January 13, 1967. Copyright © 1967 by Time, Inc./ Sidelight excerpts from an article, "Greene, the 'Funny Writer,' on Comedy," January 23, 1970, in *Life* Magazine./ Sidelight excerpts from an article, "Aged Lover of Ancients," September 15, 1958, in *Life* Magazine. Copyright © 1958 by Time, Inc. All reprinted by permission of Time, Inc.

VICTOR BOOKS. Illustration by Robert G. Doares from *Sarah and the Pelican* by Margaret Epp. Copyright © 1977, 1968 by Margaret Epp. Reprinted by permission of Victor Books, a division of S.P. Publications, Inc.

THE VIKING PRESS INC. Illustration by Robert Lawson from *The Story of Ferdinand* by Munro Leaf. Copyright 1938 by Munro Leaf and Robert Lawson. Copyright renewed © 1964 by Munro Leaf and John W. Boyd./ Illustration by Robert Lawson from *Wee Gillis* by Munro Leaf. Copyright 1938 by Munro Leaf and Robert Lawson. Copyright renewed © 1966 by Munro Leaf and John W. Boyd./ Sidelight excerpts from an article, "The Dial: A Retrospect," by Marianne Moore in *Predilections.* All reprinted by permission of The Viking Press, Inc.

HENRY Z. WALCK, INC. Illustration by Tasha Tudor from *A Child's Garden of Verses* by Robert Louis Stevenson. Copyright 1947 by Henry Z. Walck, Inc. Reprinted by permission of Henry Z. Walck, Inc.

FREDERICK WARNE & CO., INC. Illustration by Randall Enos from *It's Not Fair* by Robyn Supraner. Illustrations copyright © 1976 by Randall Enos. Reprinted by permission of Frederick Warne & Co., Inc.

FREDERICK WARNE & CO., LTD. (London). Photograph from *A Young Person's Guide to Ballet* by Noel Streatfeild. Text copyright © 1975 by Noel Streatfeild. Reprinted by permission of Frederick Warne & Co., Ltd. (London).

A.P. WATT, LTD. Sidelight excerpts from *Experiment in Autobiography,* Volumes I and II, by H.G. Wells. Copyright 1934 by Herbert George Wells, renewal copyright © 1962 by George Philip Wells and Francis Richard Wells. Reprinted by permission of A.P. Watt, Ltd.

WEYBRIGHT AND TALLEY, INC. Sidelight excerpts from *Four Rossettis: A Victorian Biography* by Stanley Weintraub. Reprinted by permission of Weybright and Talley, Inc.

ALBERT WHITMAN & CO. Pictures from the Walt Disney production based on the original drawings by Robert Lawson from *Ferdinand the Bull* by Munro Leaf. Copyright 1936 by Munro Leaf and Robert Lawson. Copyright 1938 by Walt Disney Enterprises. Reprinted by permission of Albert Whitman & Co.

H.W. WILSON CO. Sidelight excerpts from an article, "Listening to Youth," by Dorothy Gordon, October, 1967, in *Wilson Library Bulletin.* Copyright © 1967 by The H.W. Wilson Co./ Sidelight excerpts from an article, "Munro Leaf," May, 1937, in *Wilson Library Bulletin.* Copyright 1937 by The H.W. Wilson Co. Both reprinted by permission of H.W. Wilson Co.

THE YANKEE PEDDLER BOOK CO. Illustration by Alexander D. "Sandy" Read from *Tony the Tuna* by S. Kip Farrington, Jr. Copyright © 1975 by S. Kip Farrington, Jr. Reprinted by permission of The Yankee Peddler Book Co.

Illustration by Elsa Beskow from *Barnen på Solbacka* by Elsa Beskow. Copyright © 1974 by Albert Bonniers Förlag AB. Reprinted by permission of the Estate of Elsa Beskow./ Illustration by Elsa Beskow from *Blommornas Bok* by Elsa Beskow. Copyright 1955 by Albert Bonniers Förlag AB. Reprinted by permission of the Estate of Elsa Beskow./ Photograph from *The Next 50 Years on the Moon* by Erik Bergaust. Copyright © 1974 by Erik Bergaust. Reprinted by permission of the Boeing Co./ Photograph from *Frozen Snakes and Dinosaur Bones* by

Margery Facklam. Copyright © 1976 by Margery Facklam. Reprinted by permission of The Buffalo Museum of Science./ Illustration by Arthur Rackham from *Goblin Market* by Christina Rossetti. Reprinted by the kind permission of Mrs. Barbara Edwards./ Sidelight excerpts from *Mama's Boarding House* by John D. Fitzgerald. Reprinted by permission of Ann Elmo Agency./ Sidelight excerpts from *Papa Married a Mormon* by John D. Fitzgerald. Reprinted by permission of Ann Elmo Agency./ Sidelight excerpts from *Harper of Heaven* by Robert Service. Reprinted by permission of Feinman and Krasilovsky./ Sidelight excerpts from *Ploughman of the Moon* by Robert Service. Reprinted by permission of Feinman and Krasilovsky./ Illustration by Steven Kellogg from *Gustav the Gourmet Giant* by Lou Ann Gaeddert. Text copyright © 1976 by Lou Ann Gaeddert. Pictures copyright © 1976 by Steven Kellogg. Reprinted by permission of Sheldon Fogelman./ Sidelight excerpts from an article, "The Conspicuous Service of Graham Greene: A New Honor and a New Novel," edited by George P. Hunt, in *Life* Magazine, February 4, 1966. Reprinted by permission of Graham Greene./ Sidelight excerpts from *Christina Rossetti: A Portrait with Background* by Marya Zaturenska. Reprinted by permission of Mrs. Marya Zaturenska Gregory./ Sidelight excerpts from an article, "An Interview with Marianne Moore," December, 1965, in *McCall's*. Reprinted by permission of Donald Hall and the Estate of Marianne Moore./ Sidelight excerpts from *For My Own Amusement* by R.F. Delderfield. Copyright © 1972 by R.F. Delderfield. Reprinted by permission of David Higham Associates, Ltd./ Sidelight excerpts from an article, "A Letter to Ezra Pound," by Marianne Moore in *Marianne Moore: A Collection of Critical Essays* edited by Charles Tomlinson. Reprinted by permission of the Estate of Marianne Moore./ Sidelight excerpts from an article, "Lucille Clifton: Making the World 'Poem-Up'," by Jackson Scarupa, October, 1976, in *Ms.* Copyright © by Ms. Foundation for Education, Inc. Reprinted by permission of *Ms./* Sidelight excerpts from an article, "The Staying Power and the Glory," by Michael Mewshaw, April 16, 1977, in *The Nation*. Reprinted by permission of *The Nation./* Sidelight excerpts from an article, "An Interview with M.E. Kerr," by Paul Janeczko, December, 1975, in *English Journal*. Reprinted by permission of the National Council of Teachers of English./ Photographs from *Robert Service: A Biography* by Carl F. Klinck. Copyright © 1976 by Carl F. Klinck. Reprinted by permission of the Provincial Archives of Alberta and Germaine Service./ Illustration by Moses Soyer from *The First Book of the Ballet* by Noel Streatfeild. Copyright © 1953 by Franklin Watts, Inc. Reprinted by permission of Moses Soyer./ Illustration by Grabianski from *Bible Stories* told by Norman Vincent Peale. Copyright © 1969 under the title "Bibelgeschichten" by Verlag Carl Verberreuter, [Wien-Heidelberg]. Reprinted by permission of Verlag Carl Verberreuter./ Sidelight excerpts and photographs from *Antoine de Saint-Exupéry: His Life and Times* by Curtis Cate. Copyright © 1970 by Curtis Cate. Reprinted by permission of Wallace & Shiel Agency.

PHOTOGRAPH CREDITS

Willis Barnstone: Ned Cunningham; Marion Dane Bauer: Daniels Studio; Kathryn Ewing: Bachrach; Munro Leaf: Margaret Leaf; Willis Lindquist: Atelier von Behr; E.V. Lucas: National Portrait Gallery, London; Marijane Meaker: Janet Berte; Marianne Moore: George Platt-Lynes; Charlotte Pomerantz: Helen Miljakovich.

SOMETHING ABOUT THE AUTHOR

ANGLE, Paul M(cClelland)   1900-1975

OBITUARY NOTICE: Born December 25, 1900, in Mansfield, Ohio; died May 11, 1975, in Chicago, Ill. American historian, historical society executive, and author and editor of books dealing mainly with Abraham Lincoln. Angle began his career with the American Book Company, but quickly went on to become an executive secretary for the Illinois State Historical Library, and was for many years director and secretary of the Chicago Historical Society. Angle was a leading authority on Abraham Lincoln and his *The Lincoln Reader,* a Book-of-the-Month Club selection, gained wide public acclaim. With Carl Sandburg he co-authored *Mary Lincoln, Wife and Widow,* and was one of the experts to dispute the authenticity of the "Lincoln the Lover" series of letters and memorandums published in the *Atlantic Monthly,* purportedly written by Lincoln, concerning his early romance with Ann Rutledge. *For More Information See: American Authors and Books, 1640 to the Present Day,* 3rd edition, Crown, 1972; *Contemporary Authors, Permanent Series,* Volume 2, Gale, 1978; *Current Biography,* 1955, H. W. Wilson, 1956; *Directory of American Scholars,* 6th edition, Volume 1, Bowker, 1974; *The New Century Handbook of English Literature,* revised edition, Appleton, Century, Crofts, 1967; *The Reader's Encyclopedia of American Literature,* Crowell, 1962; *Twentieth Century Authors,* 1st supplement, H. W. Wilson, 1955; *Who's Who in America,* 38th edition, Marquis, 1974. *Obituaries: Contemporary Authors,* Volume 57-60, Gale, 1976; *Current Biography,* 1975, H. W. Wilson, 1975; *New York Times,* May 13, 1975; *Washington Post,* May 15, 1975.

ARNOTT, Kathleen   1914-

PERSONAL: Born November 19, 1914, in London, England; daughter of William Thomas (a scientist) and Mabel (a school teacher; maiden name Horlock) Coulson; married David W. Arnott (a professor), September 1, 1942; children: Margaret (Mrs. Mark Beresford-Peirse), Rosemary (Mrs. Richard Davies). *Education:* Teacher Training College, Saffron Walden, Essex, England, diploma in education, 1935; attended Kingsmead Theological College, Birmingham, 1938-39. *Religion:* Presbyterian. *Residence:* Southwest Scotland. *Agent:* John Cushman, 25 West 43rd St., New York, N.Y. 10036; Curtis Brown, 1A Craven Hill, London W2 3EP, England.

CAREER: Elementary school teacher in Beckenham, Kent, England, 1935-38; United Missionary Teacher Training College, Ibadan, Nigeria, lecturer in education, 1939-43; teacher and worker in leper settlement in Nigeria, 1943-52; kindergarten teacher in Sevenoaks, Kent, 1956-72.

WRITINGS: Ayo (juvenile fiction), Oxford University Press, 1951; *Titi Goes Fishing* (juvenile picture book), Longmans, 1959; *Titi Goes to a Party* (juvenile picture book), Longmans, 1959; *Catching the Cattle Thief* (juvenile fiction), Longmans, 1960; *African Myths and Legends,* Walck, 1962, Oxford University Press, 1978; *Jane's New Dress* (juvenile reader), Longmans, 1962; *Peter Runs Away* (juvenile reader), Longmans, 1962; *Richard's Lucky Find* (juvenile reader), Longmans, 1962; *The Fire* (juvenile reader), Longmans, 1962; *Bola at School* (juvenile fiction), Oxford University

KATHLEEN ARNOTT

Press, 1965; (contributor) Jacynth Hope-Simpson, editor, *Book of Witches*, Hamish Hamilton, 1966; *Tales of Temba*, Walck, 1967; *African Fairy Tales*, Muller, 1967, Transatlantic, 1971; *Bola at College* (juvenile fiction), Oxford University Press, 1968; (contributor) Belle Becker Sideman, editor, *World's Best Fairy Tales*, Reader's Digest Services, 1969; *Animal Folk Tales Around the World*, Walck, 1970; *Auta the Giant Killer*, Clarendon Press, 1971; *Dragons, Ogres, and Scary Things*, Garrard, 1974; (contributor) Marguerite Henry, editor, *Stories from Around the World*, Hubbard Press, 1974; *Spider, Crabs, & Creepy Crawlers: Two African Folktales*, Garrard, 1978. Has also written scripts for BBC schools programmes.

WORK IN PROGRESS: A book of African folktales for younger readers and an autobiography entitled *A London Childhood Between the Wars.*

SIDELIGHTS: "I was born during the 1914-18 war in South London, and remember seeing the first German zeppelins passing overhead on their way to bomb central London. I had a happy childhood, with one sister and two younger brothers for whom I invented and told stories about magic.

"My father went blind when I was eight, and my mother went back to teaching to help family finances. I used to visit her infant school and tell long stories to her 45-50 poor, diffi-

cult children, while she prepared handwork materials, etc. I began teaching Sunday School when I was fourteen and went to Teacher Training College at eighteen.

"I taught in a Beckenham (London) infant school for four years, often inventing magic stories about the children themselves and sometimes writing them down.

"When appointed lecturer in infant method at a women's college in Ibadan, Nigeria, I discovered that my students, and also the children in local schools, had virtually no contemporary storybooks with a Nigerian background. So I wrote my first schoolgirl tale, *Ayo,* for Oxford University Press, and it was an instant success and is still in print. From then on, I alternated between writing fiction for African children and African folktales for British and American children. My stories have been used in Africa, New Zealand, Australia, the Philippines, Germany and many European countries, and translated into Japanese, Dutch, Portuguese, German and braille.

"I have a Scottish husband who has just retired from the University of London, and we have settled in a beautiful part of Southwest Scotland, where we both hope to continue writing. He is at present compiling a dictionary and grammar of the Fula (West Africa) language, and I am continuing my research into African folktales and beginning the story of my London childhood."

HOBBIES AND OTHER INTERESTS: Sketching, music, golf, travel.

**Just then,
the animals came racing
down the forest path.**
■ (From *Dragons, Ogres, and Scary Things* by Kathleen Arnott. Illustrated by Cary.)

BARNSTONE, Willis 1927-

PERSONAL: Born November 13, 1927, in Lewiston, Me.; son of Robert Carl (a businessman) and Dora (Lempert) Barnstone; married Helle Phaedra Tzapoulou (now a painter), June 1, 1949; children: Aliki, Robert, Anthony. *Education:* Bowdoin College, B.A. (cum laude), 1948; graduate study at University of Paris, 1948-49, and School of Oriental and African Studies, University of London, 1952-53; Columbia University, M.A. (with high honors), 1956; Yale University, Ph.D. (with distinction), 1960. *Residence:* Heritage Woods, Bloomington, Ind.

CAREER: American Friends Service Committees, social worker in Mexico, 1945-46; Anavrita Academy, Anavrita, Greece, instructor in French and English, 1949; Les Editions Skira, Geneva, Switzerland, translator of French art texts, 1951; Wesleyan University, Middletown, Conn., instructor, 1958-59, assistant professor of Romance languages, 1959-62; Indiana University, Bloomington, associate professor of Spanish, Portuguese, and comparative literature, 1962-66, professor, 1966—, professor of East Asian studies, 1973-76, professor of Latin American studies, 1976—; visiting professor, University of Massachusetts, summer, 1967, University of California, 1968-69; Colgate University, Hamilton, N.Y., O'Connor professor of literature, classics, and Spanish, 1973; Insituto Superior del Professor and Professor de Lenguas Vivas, Buenos Aires, Argentina, professor, 1975-76; University of Texas, Austin, visiting professor, 1977. *Military service:* U.S. Army, 1954-56. *Member:* Modern Language Association of America.

AWARDS, HONORS: Danforth summer grant, 1960; nomination for Pulitzer Prize in literature, 1960, for *From This White Island,* and 1977, for *China Poems;* Guggenheim fellowship, 1961-62; Cecil Hemley Memorial Award of the Poetry Society of America, 1968; ACLS (American Council of Learned Societies) senior fellowship, 1968-69; Fulbright teaching fellowship, 1975; nomination for National Book Award, 1977, for translation of *My Voice Because of You;* Lucille Medwick Memorial Award of the Poetry Society of America, 1978; NEH (National Endowment for the Arts) fellowship, 1979-80.

WRITINGS: Poems of Exchange, Institut Francais d'-Athenes, 1951; *Notes for a Bible* (poetry), Hermanos Hernandez (Malaga), 1952; *From This White Island,* Twayne, 1959; (translator) *Eighty Poems of Antonio Machado,* Las Americas, 1959; (translator from the Greek, with wife, Helle Barnstone) Margarita Liberaki, *The Other Alexander* (novel), Noonday, 1959.

(Editor with Hugh A. Harter) Miguel de Cervantes, *Rinconete y Cortadillo* (college text), Las Americas, 1960; (editor and translator) *Greek Lyric Poetry,* Bantam, 1962, enlarged edition, Indiana University Press, 1966; (translator and author of introduction) Ignacio Bernal, *Mexico Before Cortez: Art, History and Legend,* Dolphin Books, 1963; (translator) *Physiologus Theobaldi Episcopi de Naturis Duodecim Animalium,* Indiana University Press, 1964; *Sappho: Lyrics in the Original Greek with Translations,* Doubleday-Anchor and New York University Press, 1965; (editor and reviser) Luis de Gongora, *Soledades,* translated by Edward Wilson, Las Americas, 1965; (general editor) *Modern European Poetry* (anthology), Bantam, 1966; *A Sky of Days* (poetry), Indiana University Press, 1967; (translator and author of introduction) *The Poems of Saint John of the Cross,* Indiana University Press, 1967, reprinted, New Directions, 1972;

Aliki and Willis Barnstone.

(editor and author of introduction) Edgar Lee Masters, *New Spoon River,* Macmillan, 1968, Collier, 1968; (editor and co-editor, with Mary Ellen Solt, of introduction) *Concrete Poetry: A World View,* Indiana University Press, 1969.

(Editor) *Spanish Poetry from the Beginning Through the Nineteenth Century,* Oxford University Press, 1970; (translator) Shir Hashirim, *The Song of Songs,* Kedros (Athens), 1970; *A Day in the Country,* Harper, 1971; *Antijournal,* Sono Nis Press (Vancouver), 1971; (editor) *Eighteen Texts: Writings by Contemporary Authors,* Harvard University Press, 1972; (translator and author of introduction, with Ko Ching-po) *The Poems of Mao Tse-tung,* Harper, 1972; *New Faces of China* (poems and photographs), Indiana University Press, 1973; *China Poems,* University of Missouri Press, 1976; (translator and author of introduction) Pedro Salinas, *My Voice Because of You,* State University of New York Press, 1976; (translator and author of introduction) *The Poems of Fray Luis de León,* State University of New York Press, 1979; (editor with Aliki) *A Book of Women Poets from Antiquity to Now,* Schocken Books, 1980; *The Dream Below the Sun: Poems of Antonio Machado,* Crossing Press, 1980.

Contributor of translations: (Greek, Latin, and Portuguese sections) *The World's Love Poetry,* edited by Michael R. Martin, Bantam, 1960; *Anthology of Spanish Poetry,* edited by Angel Flores, Anchor Books, 1961; *Concise Encyclopaedia of Modern World Literature,* edited by Geoffrey Grigson, Hawthorn, 1963; (poetry sections) Nikos Kazantzakis, *Spain,* translated by Amy Mims, Simon and Schuster, 1963; *Language of Love* (short stories), edited by Michael R. Martin, Bantam, 1964; *Genius of the Spanish Theater* (plays),

**I woke in
a blue pool**
■ (From *A Day in the Country* by Willis Barnstone. Illustrated by Howard Knotts.)

edited by Robert O'Brien, Mentor Books, 1965; *Medieval Lyric Poetry*, edited by W.T.H. Jackson, Bantam, 1966.

Original poems included in *New Campus Writing, Number 3*, Grove, 1959. Other original poems have been published in more than fifteen periodicals, including *Yale Review, New Letters, The Nation, New York Book Review, Chicago Review, New Yorker, Antioch Review, Columbia University Forum, Prairie Schooner, Nine* (London), *Points* (Paris), and *Triad*. Contributor of verse translations, and occasional prose translations and articles to *Nation, Arizona Quarterly, Tulane Drama Review, Evergreen Review*, and other literary journals, and book reviews for the *New York Times Sunday Book Review*. Editor-in-chief, *Artes Hispanicas Hispanic Arts*, published jointly by Indiana University and Macmillan. Served on the editorial board of *Books Abroad* and *Mundus Artium*.

WORK IN PROGRESS: Antonio Machado, a study of the lyrical speaker in the poems.

SIDELIGHTS: Barnstone has spent extended periods in Mexico, Spain, France, England, Greece and Asia. He has written articles on Easter Island, Jorge Luis Borges, Peru, Egypt, and mainland China for *Holiday* (accompanied by photographs) and on Portugal for *Saturday Evening Post*. Barnstone's adaptation of *Joaquín Murieta* by Pablo Meruda was broadcast on BBC Third Programme in 1976.

BARNUM, Jay Hyde   1888(?)-1962

PERSONAL: Born about 1888(?), in Geneva, Ohio; married Hilma Charlotte Larsson (daughter of author and illustrator, Marjorie Flack); children: Timmie, Gregory, Amanda. *Education:* Attended the Cleveland Art School and the School of the Art Institute of Chicago; studied in Woodstock, New York, with Bellows, Speicher, and Kroll. *Home:* Hastings-on-Hudson, New York.

CAREER: Author and illustrator of books for children, commercial illustrator. Illustrator of the children's page, Newspaper Enterprise Association, Chicago, after high school; advertising drawings and fashion posters for the Marshall Field department store and others; began illustrating for various magazines, also doing their covers, early 1930's. His illustrations have appeared in *Collier's, Cosmopolitan* and *Good Housekeeping;* first book illustrations were for *The Kid from Tomkinsville*, by John R. Tunis, and later projects include illustrations for such classics as *The Adventures of Robin Hood* and *King Arthur and the Knights of the Round Table*. *Awards, honors:* Runner-up, Caldecott Medal, 1947, for *The Boats on the River*.

WRITINGS—All for children; all self-illustrated: *The New Fire Engine*, Morrow, 1952; *The Little Old Truck*, Morrow, 1953, reissued, E. M. Hale, 1966; *Motorcycle Dog*, Morrow, 1958.

Illustrator: John R. Tunis, *The Kid from Tomkinsville*, Harcourt, 1940; Tunis, *Champion's Choice*, Harcourt, 1940; Tunis, *World Series*, Harcourt, 1941; Marjorie Flack, *The Boats on the River*, Viking, 1946; Flack, *The Happy Birthday Letter*, Houghton, 1947; Eleanore M. Jewett, *Mystery at Boulder Point*, Viking, 1949; Carl L. Carmer, *Too Many Cherries*, Viking, 1949; Ruth Sawyer, *The Little Red Horse*, Viking, 1950; Bella Koral, *Abraham Lincoln* (illustrated with John A. Maxwell), Random House, 1952; Priscilla Carden, *Vanilla Village*, Ariel, 1952; Eleanor G. Vance, *The Adventures of Robin Hood*, Random House, 1953; Jane Thayer, *The Horse with the Easter Bonnet*, Morrow, 1953; Thayer, *Popcorn Dragon*, Morrow, 1953; Estelle B. Schneider, *King Arthur and the Knights of the Round Table* (adapted from Howard Pyle's *The Story of King Arthur and His Knights*), Random House, 1954; Tunis, *Buddy and the Old Pro*, Morrow, 1955; Gladys E. Brown, *Two-Bow Bill*, Morrow, 1955; Thayer, *Charley and the New Car*, Morrow, 1957.

SIDELIGHTS: One of Jay Hyde Barnum's most vivid childhood memories was going row-boating with his father, and it was a special pleasure if he could row. Another thrill in his

He was fast, but Carl was faster. ■(From *Buddy and the Old Pro* by John R. Tunis. Illustrated by Jay Hyde Barnum.)

early days was going for a canoe ride with the Soo Indians and shooting the rapids beside the Soo Canal.

His first book illustrations were for John R. Tunis' *The Kid from Tomkinsville*. Interestingly, he and Tunis, years before at Cannes, France, had played a tennis match against the King of Sweden and his partner. Barnum and Tunis lost!

Jay Hyde Barnum, besides illustrating the work of others, also wrote three children's books which he then illustrated. The *New York Times*, writing about *The New Fire Engine*, says, "This is a lively story with amusing pictures and a constant supply of well-balanced excitement. A wonderful vocabulary selection adds much to its appeal." To the *Saturday Review*, "[The Little Old Truck] is a story which rediscovers the warmth of personal relationship between man and the things of his making. Here are consideration and attachment for the tool tried and lived with."

FOR MORE INFORMATION SEE: New York Times, March 9, 1952; *Saturday Review*, August 22, 1953; Bertha Mahony Miller and others, compilers, *Illustrators of Children's Books, 1946-1956*, Horn Book, 1958; Martha E. Ward and Dorothy A. Marquardt, *Authors of Books for Young People*, Scarecrow, 1964; (obituary) *New York Times*, September 14, 1962.

BARR, Donald   1921-

PERSONAL: Born August 2, 1921, in New York, N.Y.; son of Pelham (an economist) and Estelle (a psychologist; maiden name, de Young) Barr; married Mary Margaret Ahern (a college teacher), April 22, 1946; children: Christopher James, William Pelham, Hilary Benedict Thomas, Stephen Matthew. *Education:* Columbia University, A.B., 1941, M.A., 1951. *Politics:* Republican. *Home:* Beech Hill Rd., Colebrook, Ct. 06021. *Office:* Hackley School, Tarrytown, N.Y. 10591.

CAREER: Columbia University, New York, N.Y., instructor in English, 1946-56, assistant to dean, School of Engineering, 1956-59, assistant dean, Faculty of Engineering and Applied Science, 1959-64, former director of Science Honors Program; Dalton School, New York, N.Y., headmaster, 1964-74; Hackley School, Tarrytown, N.Y., headmaster, 1975—. Associate program director, National Science Foundation, 1963-64. Member, New York County Republican Committee, 1952-63. *Military service:* U.S. Army, 1943-45; served in Office of Strategic Services, 1945.

WRITINGS: The How and Why Wonder Book of Atomic Energy, Grosset, 1961; *The How and Why Wonder Book of Primitive Man,* Grosset, 1961; (contributor) Nona Balakian and Charles Simmons, editors, *The Creative Present: Notes*

DONALD BARR

on Contemporary American Fiction, Doubleday, 1963; *The How and Why Wonder Book of Building*, Grosset, 1964; *Arithmetic for Billy Goats*, Harcourt, 1966; (with Darlene Geis and Martin L. Keen) *The Wonders of Prehistoric Life*, Grosset, 1966; *Who Pushed Humpty Dumpty?: Dilemmas in American Education Today*, Atheneum, 1971; *Space Relations: A Slightly Gothic Interplanatary Tale*, Charterhouse, 1973. Contributor of articles and reviews to *Saturday Review*, *Columbia University Forum*, *Commonweal*, *New York Times Book Review*, *Columbia Engineering Quarterly*, and other periodicals.

SIDELIGHTS: "When I was a young man, I always wrote anything anyone asked me to. How I loved to be published! I reviewed any book the *Times* or the *Saturday Review* sent me. I wrote—for nothing—a column for a little newspaper some former students of mine had started. When publishers wanted books about education, I wrote books about education. When asked for children's books on science and mathematics, I wrote those. (I enjoyed writing those, because in writing for children one writes to *be* enjoyed.)

"But nobody ever asked me to write stories. And what I secretly wanted to write was adventure stories. I was fifty-two before I got to write my first novel, a space opera.

"Since then, I have been too busy running the Hackley School to do much writing, but the desire to write adventure stories—thrillers, space operas, tales of war and politics—is getting stronger and stronger in me. Sometimes, while I am sitting in my office talking to a student or being talked to by a student's mother, a little bit of fiction—a good thing the hero might say, or an ingenious turn of plot, or a surprising place for a murder, or a planet of mutants or fanatics—will slip into my thoughts. It is getting harder and harder to chase these ideas out. . . . As a boy, I used to daydream. Now I plan stories. But of course, it's the same thing. It has to be. If you're ashamed of your daydreams, you'll never be a storyteller.

"My father, a little Englishman with high detachable collars and rimless *pince-nez* spectacles on a black string, taught me to write, not so much by sitting me down and giving me lessons as by the way he talked, by the way he responded to the way I talked, by the books he had and the way he talked about them, by the quiet helpful things he said about my 'compositions' for school. He taught me never to be lazy or self-indulgent about words, never to say *sort of* what I meant, never to use two words where one would do, never to bumble, never to write a sentence I could not comfortably read aloud, never to let my words get out in front of my ideas. He taught me that words should put sights, sounds, smells, tastes, touches, and above all *ideas* into the reader's mind. I was to get the reader to say, 'What a nightmarish thought!' or 'Yes, that's *just* the way it is!' or 'Ah, *that's* the explanation!'—not 'Oh, what pretty words!' My father called me 'Boy'—or when he was in an affectionate mood, 'Rat Poison.' 'Boy,' he would say, 'when you're writing about the villain, don't say, ''He was a bad man.'' Make the *reader* say, ''He's a bad man.'' You stay out of sight.'

"Our house was full of books. He sent me to G. K. Chesterton's books to learn how to argue and how to be playful and pictorial in arguing. He sent me to H. G. Wells' to learn how theories could become as vivid as adventure stories. After 'bedtime,' when the household was asleep, I would get my flashlight and read books under the covers. My father knew. 'Rat Poison,' he might murmur the next day, blinking, 'just don't ruin your eyes'."

Barr, who is alternately described as a conservative and iconoclastic educator, believes in both rigid discipline and internal motivation for students. He rejects mass testing, saying: "Everywhere schools and colleges ignore and starve the youngster's desire to learn; they find and exploit his desire to *pass*." He adds: "What youngsters, even adolescents, need to see is not a system grinding out decisions but a man making moral choices. How else will they learn to become men and to make moral choices?"

Barr also advocates strong control by parents. In *Who Pushed Humpty Dumpty?: Dilemmas in American Education Today*, Barr writes: "We offer very little resistance to our children. We tend to withhold reality from them by behaving as if there were no such notion as *earning* things. We thus keep them ignorant of the fundamental concept of human society, the concept of reciprocity . . . we feel that we are being gratuitously mean if we make a child wait for satisfaction we could just as easily grant at once. But it is by waiting that children learn what time is."

Jerrold K. Footlick commented on Barr's philosophy: ". . . He is not content merely to comment; he reports what works for him and recommends specific approaches in such areas as reading, mathematics and science. And now that the awesome educational reforms of the past decade are being retrospectively viewed with growing skepticism, men like Donald Barr will be heard from with greater frequency. It is no more possible to reach a conclusion on their wisdom now that it was possible to judge the progressives in the 1920's or the reformers in the 60s. But for those who fear that education has become too undisciplined, Barr's manifesto will provide an arsenal of thought and a manual of action. His book is by turns pedantic and stubborn, charming and daring. And a lot of it makes sense."

FOR MORE INFORMATION SEE: Eleanor Cameron, *The Green and Burning Tree*, Atlantic-Little, Brown, 1969; *Newsweek*, September 27, 1971.

BASON, Lillian   1913-

PERSONAL: Born October 17, 1913, in Albany, N.Y.; daughter of Victor and Gertrude (Nilson) Peterson; married Charles R. Bason, June 2, 1939; children: Frank, Christine Bason Becker, Roger. *Education:* Attended Adelphi College; New York University, B.A., 1938. *Religion:* Presbyterian. *Home address:* 2430 Iris, N.W., Albuquerque, N.M. 87104.

CAREER: New York Stock Exchange, New York, N.Y., secretary, 1932-39; writer, 1964—. Has worked as substitute teacher and volunteer story teller. Town historian of Lewisboro, N.Y., 1972—. *Member:* Authors Guild of Authors League of America, Forum of Writers for Young People, Lewisboro Historical Society (president, 1973-78), Rio Grande Writers Association.

WRITINGS—For children: *Isabelle and the Library Cat*, Lothrop, 1966; *Pick a Raincoat, Pick a Whistle*, Lothrop, 1966; *Eric and the Little Canal Boat*, Parents' Magazine Press, 1967; *Castles and Mirrors and Cities of Sand*, Lothrop, 1968; *Spiders*, National Geographic Society, 1974; (translator) *Those Foolish Molboes* (Danish folk tales), Coward, 1977. Writer and producer of radio scripts for Church Women United during the 1940's.

**And they returned home
with the little boat on their wagon.**
■ (From *Those Foolish Molboes* by Lillian Bason. Illustrated by Margot Tomes.)

LILLIAN BASON

WORK IN PROGRESS: Translating more Danish folk tales; nonfiction for children, about storks and white owls.

SIDELIGHTS: "I like to share my sense of wonder at the world and all it contains with young children. Wherever I travel, I find inspiration in the people, places, and stories of the countries I visit. My interest is equally in stories and non-fiction subjects that fascinate me.

"I grew up in a small town in New York State and began writing poems and stories when I was around ten. Reading was what I enjoyed most. During summer vacations I roller-skated to the town library and brought home an armful of books every week. Then I took them to my favorite tree that had fat curving branches. They were just right for climbing and sitting on, hidden from everyone."

BAUER, Marion Dane 1938-

PERSONAL: Born November 20, 1938, in Oglesby, Ill.; daughter of Chester (a chemist) and Elsie (a kindergarten teacher; maiden name, Hempstead) Dane; married Ronald Bauer (an Episcopal priest), June 25, 1959; children: Peter Dane, Elisabeth Alison. *Education:* Student at La Salle-Peru-Oglesby Junior College, 1956-58, and University of Missouri, 1958-59; University of Oklahoma, B.A., 1962. *Politics:* Democrat. *Religion:* Episcopalian. *Home:* 13908 McGinty Rd., Minnetonka, Minn. 55343. *Agent:* Ann Elmo Agency, Inc., 60 E. 42nd St., New York, N.Y. 10017.

CAREER: High school English teacher in Waukesha, Wis., 1962-64; Hennepin County Technical School, Minneapolis,

Minn., instructor in creative writing for adult education program, 1975-79; University of Minnesota Continuing Education, instructor of fiction writing, 1979—. *Member:* Authors Guild of Authors League of America, Society of Children's Book Writers. *Awards, honors:* Golden Kite Honor Book for the Society of Children's Book Writer for *Foster Child,* 1979.

WRITINGS: Shelter from the Wind (juvenile novel), Seabury, 1976; *Foster Child* (juvenile novel), Seabury, 1977; *Tangled Butterfly* (young adult novel), Houghton, 1980.

WORK IN PROGRESS: Sing, O Barren, an adult novel.

SIDELIGHTS: "For almost as long as I can remember, I have known, in some part of myself, that I wanted to be a writer. At first I thought I would be a poet, although my love was for stories. Stories seemed so *long,* not to create but to write out, and I have never, in all my life, won a battle with a pencil. In my hand, a pencil has always been an awkward tool, almost an enemy to be subdued, though in my struggle with points that break and a hand that quickly aches, I am always the loser. In high school, however, I learned to type, and the typewriter was to my fingers what wings would be to someone who could not walk—absolute freedom. From that time on my direction was clear.

"I wanted to write, and yet I wasn't sure I could trust myself to the forms meant for other's eyes. I spent many years writing letters, journals, an occasional poem, polishing my craft,

MARION DANE BAUER

(From *Shelter from the Wind* by Marion Dane Bauer. Illustrated by Mike Eagle.)

dreaming about the time when I would do more. They were busy years as a student, a teacher, a mother of young children, an active volunteer in community and church. And then the day came when I had to decide, am I going to do it, really do it, or am I only going to dream about it? I sat down to my faithful little typewriter and began.

"In the years that have followed, the typewriters have changed, grown more sophisticated, but the process remains much the same. I begin from some place in my life, some incident or idea which touches a feeling that is important to me. I begin with a character, a problem, add on the other characters who fill out that person's life, and I aim them in the general direction I want them to grow into. Then I come to my typewriter every day to see what they will do. I rewrite many times, in the later stages in response to thoughtful critiques from my editor. And when I am through, the novel never quite meets my own expectations, fulfills the dream of what I meant, so I begin on another.

"I hope to go on beginning for as long as I have life."

FOR MORE INFORMATION SEE: Horn Book, August, 1976.

BAUM, Allyn Z(elton) 1924-

PERSONAL: Born October 22, 1924, in Chicago, Ill.; son of Moses (an insurance broker) and Effie F. (Kaufman) Baum; married Pell Le Witt (an art historian), September 16, 1963. *Education:* Northwestern University, B.S. in Journalism, 1948. *Home:* The Barn, Box 371, East Canaan, Conn. 06024. *Office: Medical Economics,* Oradell, N.J. 07649.

CAREER: International News Photos, bureau chief in Berlin, Germany, 1948-49, general manager for Europe, Paris, France, 1949-50; United Press Photos, general manager for Germany, Berlin and Frankfurt, 1950-52; *American Daily,* London, England, photo editor and writer, 1953-55; *Coronet,* New York, N.Y., associate editor, 1955-57; *New York Times,* New York, N.Y., staff photographer, 1957-67; *Medical Economics,* Oradell, N.J., senior editor 1967—. *Military service:* U.S. Army Air Forces, 1943-46; became sergeant. *Member:* The Players (New York).

WRITINGS: Antarctica, the Worst Place in the World, Macmillan, 1966. Contributor of photographs and articles to newspapers and magazines throughout the world.

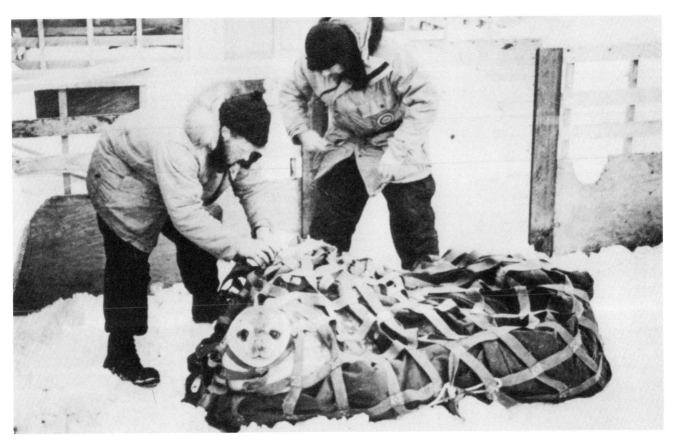

Webbed nets are used to transport seals without injury. ■ (From *Antarctica: The Worst Place in the World* by Allyn Baum. Photo by the author.)

ALLYN Z. BAUM

SIDELIGHTS: Baum's extensive travels have included two expeditions to Antarctica. He is competent in French and German.

HOBBIES AND OTHER INTERESTS: Eighteenth-century English furniture, opera, skiing.

BEARDMORE, George   1908-1979
(Cedric Beardmore, Cedric Stokes, George Wolfenden)

PERSONAL: Born May 18, 1908, in England, died December 1979; son of Frank (a potter) and Sissie (Bennett) Beardmore; wife deceased; children: Victoria Beardmore Knowles, Tiffa Beardmore Meadows. *Education:* Educated in England and Scotland. *Politics:* "Nil on all." *Religion:* Sufi. *Home:* Trim's Cottage, West Stour, Gillingham, Dorset, England.

CAREER: Writer.

WRITINGS: (Under pseudonym Cedric Beardmore) *Dodd the Potter,* Doubleday, 1931; (under pseudonym George Wolfenden) *The House in Spitalfields,* Hurst, 1937; (under pseudonym George Wolfenden) *The Undefeated,* Hurst, 1940; (under pseudonym George Wolfenden) *The Spy Who Died in Bed,* Hurst, 1941; (under pseudonym George Wolfenden) *The Little Doves of Destruction,* Hurst, 1942; (under pseudonym Cedric Stokes) *All Space My Playground*, Macdonald & Co., 1943; *Madame Merlin*, Macdonald & Co., 1946; *A Tale of Two Thieves*, Macdonald & Co., 1947; *Far Cry*, Macdonald & Co., 1947; *The Staffordshire Assassins*, Macdonald & Co., 1950; *A Thousand Witnesses*, Macdonald & Co., 1953; *Charlie Poccok's Indian Bride*, Macdonald & Co., 1967, Viking, 1968; *Waldo Rush 48%*, Macdonald & Co., 1968; *Arnold Bennett in Love* (biography), Bruce & Watson, 1972.

Books for young adults: *Going into the Country*, Phoenix House, 1948; *The Isle of Apes*, Macdonald & Co., 1950; *North Wind*, Macdonald & Co., 1952; *Belle of the Ballet's Gala Performance*, Hulton Press, 1956; *Belle of the Ballet's Country Holiday*, Hulton Press, 1957; *Jack O'Lantern and the Fighting Cock*, Hulton Press, 1958; *Lesley's Great Adventure*, Paul Hamlyn, 1967; *Islands of Strangers*, Macdonald & Co., 1968; *Expedition to Faollen*, Macdonald & Co., 1970; *The Maid of the Isles*, Macdonald & Co., 1974; *Ladies of Spain*, Macdonald & Co., 1975, published as *The Treasure of Spanish Bay*, Thomas Nelson, 1976.

Contributor of over ninety stories to *Eagle* and *Girl*.

WORK IN PROGRESS: A serious study of a child's life during World War I, "largely but not entirely autobiographical."

SIDELIGHTS: "As a child I remember much resentment being referred to as 'a child' and classed among children and boys. I was ME. As I grew up and looked round the class-

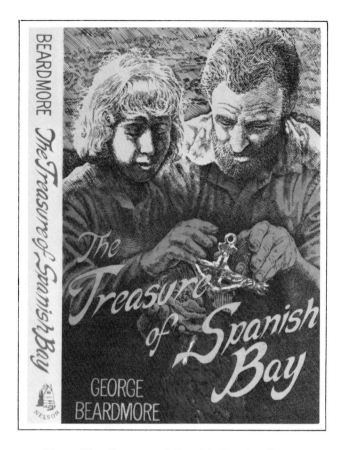

(From *The Treasure of Spanish Bay* by George Beardmore. Illustrated by Allan Davis.)

room I saw that we were all different animals, not 'boys' at all. One rarely smiled, another was a born clown, a third spent his time drawing devils, and a fourth became adept at calligraphy. When I grew up and became obsessed with writing, I remembered this observation, perhaps unconsciously, and NEVER referred to 'children,' 'young people,' 'boys,' 'girls,' etc., but gave each character his or her own individuality.

"My first whole book was written when I was fourteen, chiefly as an escape from a torrid domestic atmosphere. Alas, old age and a moderate serenity have overtaken me so that I no longer have to write."

Beardmore discussed his book *Arnold Bennett in Love:* "The biography of Arnold Bennett's marriage arose from the fact that I am Bennett's nephew and therefore had unique insight into his character. Outwardly, he gallantly endeavoured to be amiable, generous, of assistance to young writers. In this he succeeded. It would appear that I alone am left to know that *chez lui* he was arrogant and intolerant. Following the late war, I visited his French widow, Marie Marguerite, at her home near Montauban, France. Subsequently, she bequeathed to me all Arnold's letters to her (these are now in the library of Keele University, England), and I was thereby enabled to shed light on his private life and the burden he carried of a stern Victorian upbringing that he tried to amend. The book makes unpleasant reading, but was necessary in the interests of truth."

HOBBIES AND OTHER INTERESTS: Gardening, bee keeping, astronomy, and natural history.

GEORGE BEARDMORE

ERIK BERGAUST

BERGAUST, Erik   1925-1978

PERSONAL: Born March 23, 1925, in Baerum, Oslo, Norway; died March 1, 1978 in McLean, Virginia; came to the United States, 1949, naturalized, 1956, married Jean Cameron Somers, January 13, 1951; children: Christine, Erik, Paul, Jane. *Education:* Frogner Gymnasium, B.S., 1943; student, Oslo Handelgymnasium, 1944. *Home:* Falls Church, Virginia.

CAREER: Author, editor, and publisher. Editor and publisher of numerous publications concerning air and sea exploration, 1946; manager of airplane and helicopter services, 1948-52; free lance aviation writer, 1949-52; North Springs, Inc., president, 1962-64. Conducted a weekly radio program, "Washington Radio Features" and has been associated with the Voice of America. Chairman Republican Advisory Committee on space and aerospace, 1962—. *Military service:* Served with the Norwegian Resistance Movement, 1943, and the Norwegian Exile Army, 1944-45. *Member:* National Press Club, Aviation and Space Writers Association, Authors Guild, Environmental Writers Association of America (member of board of directors, 1972—), National Space Club (founder; president, 1957-59), American Helicopter Society, American Military Engineers, American Rocket Society, Convertible Aircraft Pioneers, Norsk Astronautisk Forening, Mason.

WRITINGS—All published by Putnam, except as noted: (With Gunnar Oxaal) *Reisen til Manen Blir Alvor,* Fabritius (Oslo), 1952; (with Bernt Balchen) *The Next Fifty Years of Flight,* Harper, 1954; (with William Beller) *Satellite!,* Hanover House, 1956; *Rockets and Missiles,* 1957; *Rockets Around the World,* 1958; (with Seabrook Hull) *Rocket to the Moon,* Van Nostrand, 1958; *Rockets of the Navy,* 1959; *Satellites and Space Probes,* 1959; *First Men in Space,* 1960; *Reaching for the Stars,* Doubleday, 1960; *Rockets of the Air Force,* 1960; *Rockets of the Army,* 1960; *Birth of a Rocket,* 1961; *Rocket Aircraft: U.S.A.,* 1961; *Rockets to the Moon,* 1961; *Rockets to the Planets,* 1961; (with Thorstein Thelle) *Romfartens ABC,* P. F. Steensballes boghandels (Oslo),

1961; (with William O. Foss), *Coast Guard in Action,* 1962; (with W. O. Foss) *Helicopters in Action,* 1962; *Our New Navy,* 1962; *Rocket Power,* 1962; *Saturn Story,* 1962; *Space Stations,* 1962; *Rocket City: U.S.A.,* Macmillan, 1963; *The Next Fifty Years in Space,* Macmillan, 1964.

(With W. O. Foss) *The Marine Corps in Action,* 1965; (with W. O. Foss) *Skin Divers in Action,* 1965; (editor) *Illustrated Space Encyclopedia,* 1965, revised edition published as *The New Illustrated Space Encyclopedia,* 1971; *Rockets of the Armed Forces,* 1966; *Aircraft Carriers in Action,* 1968; *Mars: Planet for Conquest,* 1968; *Murder on Pad 34,* 1968; (with W. O. Foss) *Oceanographers in Action,* 1968; *Convertiplanes in Action: The VTOL Success Story,* 1969; *The Russians in Space,* 1969; (with T. Thelle) *Havforsking,* B. H. Reenskaug (Oslo), 1970; (editor) *The Illustrated Nuclear Encyclopedia,* 1971; *National Outdoorsmen's Encyclopedia,* Remington & Ross, 1973; *The Next Fifty Years on the Moon,* 1974; *Rescue in Space: Lifeboats for Astronauts and Cosmonauts,* 1974; *Colonizing the Planets,* 1975; *Colonizing the Sea,* 1976; *Colonizing Space,* 1978.

SIDELIGHTS: **March 23, 1925.** Born in Baerum, Oslo, Norway and educated there. As a teenager, Bergaust had the tragic misfortune of seeing many of his friends and relatives sent to Nazi concentration camps from which they never returned. Frederick C. Durant, III, a personal friend, gave this biographical sketch of Bergaust during the war years: "On that September day in 1944, the day the first V-2 plummeted down upon Chiswick-on-Thames, Erik Bergaust was arrested by the Gestapo and thrown into jail. He had hoped to escape to 'Little Norway' in Canada for pilot training and return to Europe to fly Spitfires against the enemy. But by the time he was spirited from jail by the Underground and across the border to Sweden, it was too late to proceed to Canada. The war was almost over and he had to settle for service in the Norwegian exile army which moved into Norway for cleanup operations when Germany surrendered.

"In 1949, he immigrated to the U.S., sponsored by Colonel Balchen. Twenty-four years old, he had already become a successful aviation editor and reporter for Norway's largest newspaper. Settling in Washington, D.C., Erik became a free-lance aviation and space flight writer. Convinced that space flight would soon become a big business, he was instrumental in organizing, and became editor of, *Missiles and Rockets.* It is worth noting that he insisted on the subtitle: *Magazine of World Astronautics.* Later he founded *Space Business Daily,* *Ground Support Equipment* (for missile/space programs), and *Underwater Engineering.* At the same time he was writing seriously for the hard-cover book market...." [Frederick C. Durant, III, introduction to *Reaching for the Stars* by Erick Bergaust, Doubleday, 1960.[1]]

1952. Met Wernher von Braun, famous space scientist who became a close acquaintance.

1954. Wrote *The Next Fifty Years of Flight* with Bernt Balchen. "I had the pleasure of working under Bernt as a press officer and editor while he was the president of the federation of Norwegian flying associations, the Norwegian Aero Club. Also, I have had the opportunity of writing about him in newspapers and magazines, probably more than anybody else. From my experience I know that his vision (which gave the United States the lead in Arctic flying) is sound and clear, optimistic—but still conservative. Sometimes his prophecies sound fantastic—as when he suggested that the United States would need air bases in the cold wasteland

Lunar rover in operation. The 400-pound vehicle can transport two men at 10 mph. ■ (From *The Next 50 Years on the Moon* by Erik Bergaust. Photo courtesy of Boeing.)

close to the North Pole—but experience has taught that his predictions usually come true.'' [Erik Bergaust, introduction to *The Next Fifty Years of Flight* by Bernt Balchen and Erik Bergaust, Harper, 1954.[2]]

1960. Wrote an unauthorized biography of Wernher von Braun based on their personal acquaintance. ''Most of the information in this book was obtained over a period of ten years from personal talks and conversations with Wernher von Braun. But much background information and much of the material has been obtained from many other sources. Some of it is based on speeches, papers, or articles authored by von Braun himself and presented at meetings of the American Rocket Society or published in technical journals....'' [Erik Bergaust, introduction to *Reaching for the Stars,* Doubleday, 1960.[3]]

March 1, 1978. Died in McLean, Virginia.

Bergaust lived with his wife, Jean, and their four children in Falls Church, Virginia. He was the chairman of the Republican advisory committee on space and aerospace. Frederick Durant described him as ''. . . a brilliant innovator. He sparks ideas and specializes in techniques of communication. Probably the greatest number of people that ever heard of him for the first time was when a critical open letter to the President appeared as a signed full-page editorial ad in the New York *Times* shortly after Sputnik I.

''Erik drives himself at a merciless pace, working hard, and when there is a moment, playing just as hard. He loves a crusade and most people in the rocket and guided missile game recall his tireless fight a few years ago for recognition of the outstanding competence and accomplishments of the Army missile team at Redstone Arsenal. Such a personality

makeup naturally wins professional enemies as well as friends. Many of his detractors are unable to appreciate his hard-driving tactics and stubborn loyalty to a cause.''[1]

In its review of *The Next Fifty Years in Space, Library Journal* noted that ''Mr. Bergaust . . . explains his subject skillfully and simply, and he brings authority because of his proximity to the men behind the scenes. His is an engrossing book that goes beyond the original ideas of the first rocket pioneers and will undoubtedly clarify many ideas and concepts for the reader. . . .''

A more controversial book was *Murder on Pad 34,* about the deaths of Apollo-One astronauts, Virgil Grissom, Edward White, and Roger Chaffee. ''The title . . . ,'' according to a *Library Journal* reviewer, ''expresses [Bergaust's] conclusion after studying reports of the Apollo accident. . . . He gives much more detail on the accident itself than ever appeared in the press accounts, then reviews the work of NASA and its contractors on the Apollo and previous projects. . . . Whether his accusation of murder is valid, and if so, who is guilty, is left up to each reader to decide.''

FOR MORE INFORMATION SEE: Horn Book, August, 1974, June, 1975; (obituary) *Washington Post,* March 4, 1978.

BESKOW, Elsa (Maartman) 1874-1953

PERSONAL: Born February 11, 1874, in Stockholm, Sweden; died in 1953; daughter of a Norwegian businessman; married Dr. Nathaniel Beskow, a minister and headmaster, 1892; children: six sons. *Education:* Attended technical

(From *Blommornas Bok* by Elsa Beskow. Illustrated by the author.)

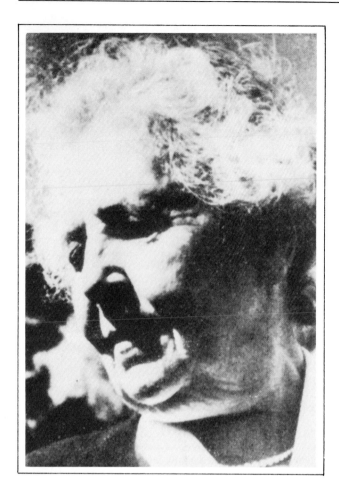

ELSA BESKOW

school and art academy in Sweden. *Home:* Djursholm, Sweden.

CAREER: Author and illustrator of books for children. Began sketching and telling stories at an early age; her first published books were a series of painting books for children; first children's book appeared in 1892.

WRITINGS—All children's books; all self-illustrated: *Tant Groen, Tant Brun, och Tant Gredelin*, 1924, published in America as *Aunt Green, Aunt Brown, and Aunt Lavender*, Harper, 1928; *Aunt Brown's Birthday*, Harper, 1930; *The Tale of the Wee Little Old Woman* (translated from the Swedish by Marion Woodburn), Harper, 1930, special edition, E. M. Hale, 1956; *Peter's Voyage* (translated from the Swedish by Rita Scherman), Knopf, 1931; *Buddy's Adventures in the Blueberry Patch* (translated from the Swedish by Siri Andrews), Harper, 1931 [another edition, adapted from the Swedish by Sheila LaFarge, published as *Peter's Adventures in Blueberry Land*, Delacorte, 1975]; *The Adventures of Peter and Lotta*, Harper, 1931; *Elf Children of the Woods* (translated from the Swedish by Zita Beskow), Harper, 1932 [another edition, adapted from the Swedish by William J. Smith, published as *Children of the Forest*, Delacorte, 1970].

Other children's books: *Olle's Ski Trip* (translated from the Swedish by S. Andrews), Harper, 1928; *Pelle's New Suit* (translated from the Swedish by M. Woodburn), Dreyers, 1929, Platt & Munk, 1930, reissued, Harper, 1961; *Hat House*, Harper, 1931; *The Sun-Egg* (translated from the

Swedish by Z. Beskow), Harper, 1933; *Ocke, Nutta och Pillerill*, Bonnier, 1939; *Aarets Saga* ("The Year's Tale"), Bonnier, 1939; (with Anna Warburg) *My Rainy-Day Book* (translated from the Swedish by Frances Harbord), Harrap, 1938, published in America as *Handwork Book for Children*, Bridgmen, 1940; *Det Hande en Gaang*, Bonnier, 1945; *Petters och Lottas Jul*, Bonnier, 1947; *Blomsterfesten*, Damm, 1947; *Onkel Blaas Nye Baat*, Damm, 1950; *ABC-Resan*, Bonnier, 1957; (with Herman Siegvald and Bo Beskow) *Vill Du Lasa?*, Svenska, 1955; *Sagan om den Nyfikna Abborren*, Bonnier, 1965; *The Little Elves of Elf Nook* (translated from the Swedish by Sonja Bergvall), Bonnier, 1966; *Elsa Beskows Sagor*, Bonnier, 1967.

Also author of *Kistan Paa Herrgaardsvinden*, 1932; *Duktiga Annika*, 1960; *Sessalatts Aventyr*, 1960; *Smaanissene; Blomsterfesten I Tappan* ("Flower Festival in the Little Garden"); *Goerans Bok* ("George's Book"); *Lasse-Litten I Tradgaarden* ("Little Larry in the Orchard"); *Lillebrors Segelfard* ("Little Brother's Sailing Trip"); *Resen Till Landet Langesen* ("Journey to the Land of Long Ago"); *Sagan Om Gnallmaans* ("Story of Cry Baby").

(From *Barnen på Solbacka* by Elsa Beskow. Illustrated by the author.)

(From *Mors Lilla Olle* by Elsa Beskow. Illustrated by the author.)

SIDELIGHTS: "I was born in Stockholm, Sweden, on the eleventh of February, 1874. There were six of us, five girls and a boy—a happy flock. The summers especially, which we spent on a country estate amidst beautiful surroundings and beside a sparkling lake, stand out for me in a hallowed light. The winters in town, with school and lessons and the gray streets, have not left many sunny memories."

"In summer time we led an extremely happy life in our country home, close to a small, idyllic lake surrounded by birch trees and dark pines. The house was old, with a tile roof under whose eaves the swallows built their nests, and was surrounded by a garden with big apple trees. There we children lived a glorious outdoor life, bathing, rowing, picking berries and wildflowers, and inventing all sorts of games.... I was allowed to go to my aunts' small kindergarten at the age of four. My grandmother lived with us, taught me to crochet, and told me many amusing stories...." [Bertha E. Mahony and others, compilers, *Illustrators of Children's Books: 1744-1945*, Horn Book, 1947.[1]]

"Like most small children, I developed an early passion for scribbling and painting on every scrap of paper I happened to come across. I remember how delighted I was, even at the age of four or five, every time I discovered a new and more correct way of drawing a face or figure. At the same age I learned to read and began with great enthusiasm to read fairy tales aloud to my sisters. Even before I had outgrown baby language, I used to make up tales and repeat them to my older brother. I studied with intense interest the simple drawings found in children's books at that time. When I was seven years old, I already had my future clearly planned. I had quite definitely made up my mind to 'write and draw fairy-tale books.'

"When I was fifteen, I began to study at the Technical School in Stockholm. Four years later I became engaged to a young artist and theologian, Nat[haniel] Beskow, and put aside further thoughts of an artistic education. The same year I obtained a position as technical teacher in a school and began to draw for children. When I married, I had completed my first book.

"Since then, a long line of books has come forth with my own six boys as models and critics. Most of the books have wandered out into the world...."

Beskow's books for children were created in the years between 1897 and 1952. Altogether she wrote and illustrated eight collections of fairy tales and thirty-three books. Her books have been translated into several languages, including Danish, Norwegian, English, German, French, Polish, and Russian. In Sweden more than three and a half million copies of Beskow's books have been sold. In the United States *Pelle's New Suit* has been the most popular of her books.

In the last year of her life, Beskow received the Nils Holgersson plaque as a tribute to her work. After her death in 1953 an award, similar to the American Caldecott medal, was instituted in her name. The first recipient of the Elsa Beskow plaque was Tove Jansson, who received the award in 1958.

Of Beskow's contribution to Swedish children's literature, Eva von Zweigbergk in her book, *Children's Books in Sweden 1750-1950*, said: "Subconsciously the Swede longs for the landscape of Elsa Beskow—because this landscape is real."

FOR MORE INFORMATION SEE: Bertha E. Mahony and others, compilers, *Illustrators of Children's Books, 1744-1945*, Horn Book, 1947; Stanley J. Kunitz and Howard Haycraft, editors, *Junior Book of Authors*, second edition revised, H. W. Wilson, 1951.

BROWN, Judith Gwyn 1933-

PERSONAL: Born October 15, 1933, in New York, New York. *Education:* Attended Cooper Union and Parsons School of Design; New York University, B.A. degree in Fine Arts History, 1956. *Home:* New York, New York.

CAREER: Children's author and illustrator, artist. Worked for a printer doing paste-ups and book jackets, where she learned technical part of book design and offset printing, 1958-60; illustrated first books, *Mr. DeLuca's Horse* and *It's Fun to Speak French*, 1962, and since then has been prolific, illustrating over fifty books and writing and illustrating four of her own. Has works in the permanent collection of the Metropolitan Museum of Art, New York, N.Y., the Kerlan Collection, University of Minnesota, and the Huntington Library, San Marino, Calif.

JUDITH GWYN BROWN

WRITINGS—All for children; all self-illustrated: *Max and the Truffle Pig*, Abingdon, 1963; *The Happy Voyage* (Junior Literary Guild selection), Macmillan, 1965; *Muffin*, Abelard, 1972; *Alphabet Dreams*, Prentice-Hall, 1976.

Illustrator: Marjorie Paradis, *Mr. DeLuca's Horse*, Atheneum, 1962; Katherine Dougherty, *A Street of Churches*, Abingdon, 1962; Margaret Hodges, *The Secret in the Woods*, Dial, 1963; Marilyn Sachs, *Amy Moves In*, Doubleday, 1964; Shyrle Hacker, *The Mystery of the Swan Ballet*, F. Watts, 1965; Padraic Colum, *The Stone of Victory and Other Tales* (ALA Notable Book), McGraw, 1966; Dale B. Carlson, editor, *The Brainstormers*, Doubleday, 1966; Scott Corbett, *Pippa Passes*, Holt, 1966; Helen M. Miller, *Janey and Friends*, Doubleday, 1967; Eileen Rosenbaum, *Two for Trouble*, Doubleday, 1967; Beatrice C. Brown, *Jonathan Bing*, Lothrop, 1968; Helene Hanff, *Butch Elects a Mayor*, Parents' Magazine Press, 1969.

Mira Lobe, *The Grandma in the Apple Tree*, McGraw, 1970; Mary Cockett, *Rosanna the Goat*, Bobbs-Merrill, 1970; Daniel Cohen, *Ancient Monuments: How They Were Built*, McGraw, 1971; Julie Edwards, *Mandy*, Harper, 1971; Barbara Robinson, *The Best Christmas Pageant Ever*, Harper, 1972; Wilma Yeo, *The Mystery of the Third Twin*, Simon & Schuster, 1972; Joan Tate, *Ben and Annie* (illustrated by Mary Dinsdale), Brockhampton, 1973, illustrated in the United States by Judith G. Brown, Doubleday, 1974; Elizabeth Coatsworth, *Daisy*, Macmillan, 1973; Wylly Folk St.

John, *The Secret of the Seven Crows*, Viking, 1973; Patricia Clapp, *King of the Dollhouse*, Lothrop, 1974; Andre Norton, *Lavender-Green Magic*, Crowell, 1974; Marden Dahlstedt, *Shadow of the Lighthouse*, Coward, 1974; Noel Streatfeild, *When the Siren Wailed*, Collins, 1974, published in the United States as *When the Sirens Wailed* (Junior Literary Guild selection), Random House, 1976; Marjorie F. Stover, *Chad and the Elephant Engine*, Atheneum, 1975; Miriam Schlein, *The Girl Who Would Rather Climb Trees*, Harcourt, 1975; Anatolii G. Aleksin, *My Brother Plays the Clarinet*, Walck, 1975; Mary E. Robertson, *Jemimalee*, McGraw, 1977; Edith Fowke, *Ring Around the Moon*, Prentice-Hall, 1977; S. E. Moore, *Secret Island*, Four Winds, 1977; Ida DeLage, *ABC Santa Claus*, Garrard, 1978; M. Schlein, *I Hate It*, Whitman Publishing, 1978; Jack Lovejoy, *The Rebel Witch*, Lothrop, 1978; Daniel Curley, *Hilarion*, Houghton, 1979; Lucile Watkins Ellison, *Butter on Both Sides*, Houghton, 1979.

WORK IN PROGRESS: Three portraits in oil and several book jackets.

SIDELIGHTS: "I consider myself primarily an illustrator, but the most pervasive phenomenon common to writers and artists, as I see it, is being alone."

"Do all them flars belong to Sir? I mean can 'e pick'm whenever he likes?" ■ (From *When the Sirens Wailed* by Noel Streatfeild. Illustrated by Judith Gwyn Brown.)

"Art on any level is not a collective effort, and the aloneness of it, often appearing early in life by circumstance, temperament, or both, is necessary.

"I was born in New York, an only child. I have always thought the city, with its enormous variety, magnificent, and yet I feel a sense of separateness from it. I think artists and writers, those who work full time at their craft, and sustain themselves by it, find that they must ultimately make a choice as to the greater importance of a complete life as we generally think of it, or the work itself.

"The working out of art on any level takes so much time: not just the *doing* of it, but the time spent thinking about it, and being concerned with the work of others. I try to read as much as I can and look at pictures of all kinds. I particularly enjoy 19th century fiction, and I make a point of reading poetry every day. I also go to the museums so that I might keep in mind what is truly imaginative, rare and great; and continually affirm to myself what is most important even when I am least sure of my own efforts.

Finally, the day came when Mandy awoke to discover that the world was no longer out of focus. She opened her eyes slowly and became aware of a soft pink room and watery sunlight shining gently through transparent curtains at a high window. ■ (From *Mandy* by Julie Edwards. Illustrated by Judith Gwyn Brown.)

"When I illustrate a book I consider each particular text as a complete world. The characters and settings for the illustrations come from this concern rather than from a conscious effort to draw in a given mode or style.

"After reading the manuscript I do sketches quite freely, and only for myself, of the people in the story. Sometimes as I work I think of other literary or pictorial connections—that is, the manuscript before me will bring to mind a line of verse or a descriptive passage from another book I have read. Or, in my mind's eye, I will have a glimpse of a picture I have seen at some past time. The two merge: the text on which I am working and the remembered passage or image I recall. In this way something more dramatic, or more deeply felt can be brought to the illustration, and the new picture has an added dimension.

"The next stage is the process of figuring out composition, and the more careful drawing of the characters in the setting. At this point I do research in the Picture Collection of the New York Public Library for historic or architectural background and for costumes, etc.

"The final putting together of the elements is almost like the first impulse, and has to do with getting down on paper in ink

Anthony heard a loud barking sound. A growling dog was rushing at him. It had leaped out of the doghouse that stood near the back porch—.... ■ (From *The Treasure of Alpheus Winterborn* by John Bellairs. Illustrated by Judith Gwyn Brown.)

Suddenly, a rustling sound in the branches above them made them look up. There was Jean, the shepherd, peering down through the leaves, looking very sad. ■(From *Max and the Truffle Pig* by Judith Gwyn Brown. Illustrated by the author.)

or paint the air and light, the emotion of the situation portrayed. The idea is to make the finished picture correspond as much as possible with the image as originally conceived.

"It is my feeling that an artist's life is lived for the most part in the mind. If this sounds severe I must also say that I do have friends, I like to talk and eat and walk my dog—a Hungarian sheepdog who, I think, is absolutely beautiful. I care very much for animals, and I am a member of several groups promoting animal protection.

"Apart from illustrating books, I also paint portraits, and subjects combining the real world with the world of the imagination; these done in oil on canvas."

Brown has been illustrating children's books almost continuously since she began this endeavor in 1960. Along with enhancing others' stories with her artwork she has also managed to write and illustrate four of her own, one of which, *Muffin,* was seen in this way by School Library Journal, "The straight-forward, uncomplicated story is endearing . . . ink drawings charmingly decorate the book." The *New York Times Book Review* said about *Jonathan Bing,* "Judith Gwyn Brown's illustrations and jacket are just about perfect, and the whole book demands to be given to a million children quickly."

Brown manages to keep her illustrating skills honed by drawing each day, and by keeping interested in the fine arts, both old and new. Through the reading of serious fiction and poetry she is able to keep herself seeing things in a literary way, which is helpful to her in her process of illustration.

FOR MORE INFORMATION SEE: Martha E. Ward and Dorothy A. Marquardt, *Authors of Books for Young People,* Scarecrow, 1967; Lee Kingman and others, compilers, *Illustrators of Children's Books, 1957-1966,* Horn Book, 1968; *Horn Book,* August, 1976; *Publishers Weekly,* November 8, 1976; *Who's Who in American Art,* 1978, 1980.

BURT, Jesse Clifton   1921-1976

OBITUARY NOTICE: Born August 29, 1921, in Nashville, Tenn.; died November 20, 1976. Educator, historian, and author of several books for children and one about the city of Nashville. Burt spent the majority of his career in the Tennessee higher education system. He was variously associated with Vanderbilt University, Lambuth College, where he was a dean, and at the University of Tennessee, Nashville Center, where he had been extension division instructor in history since 1956. For children he wrote several books on vocational choices as well as _Indians of the Southeast: Then and Now,_ a book dealing with Indian history, tradition, and culture. Burt was the recipient of the Danforth Award in 1954 for youth writings. _For More Information See: Contemporary Authors,_ Volume 9-12, 1st revision, Gale, 1974.

CAMPBELL, Hope
(G. McDonald Wallis)

PERSONAL: Born in Seattle, Wash.; daughter of Howard Roswell (a business manager) and Genevieve (Talbott) McDonald; married Charles Wallis (deceased); children: Christopher, John. _Education:_ Attended private schools in Hawaii, China, and California. _Home:_ 285 Riverside Dr., New York, N.Y. 10025.

CAREER: Actress, under names Cathy McDonald and Geraldine McDonald, in radio, stock companies, touring companies and on television, New York, N.Y., hospital shows, the West Coast Company of "Sabrina Fair," east and west coast shows for United Service Organization (U.S.O.) tour in European Theater of Operations with "Dear Ruth," radio and television commercials; script writer for church series, Los Angeles, Calif., for the "War Is the Enemy" series, New York, N.Y. _Member:_ Equity, AFTRA (American Federation T.V. and Radio Artists), Authors Guild.

WRITINGS: Liza, Norton, 1965; _Home to Hawaii,_ Norton, 1967; _Why Not Join the Giraffes?,_ Norton, 1968; _Meanwhile, Back at the Castle,_ Grosset, 1970; _No More Trains to Tottenville_ (ALA Best Young Adult Book), McCall Publishing, 1971; (with Mary Anderson) _There's a Pizza Back in Cleveland,_ Four Winds, 1972; _Peter's Angel: A Story About Monsters,_ Four Winds, 1976; _Mystery at Fire Island,_ Four Winds, 1978; _A Peak Beneath the Moon,_ Four Winds, 1979.

Under name G. McDonald Wallis: _The Light of Lilith,_ Ace Books, 1961; _Legend of Lost Earth,_ Ace Books, 1963, revised under name, Hope Campbell, Four Winds, 1977.

Under pseudonyms provided by Grosset & Dunlap; all published by Grosset, 1963: (Virginia Hughes) _Peggy Goes Straw Hat_ ("Peggy Lane Theater Stories"); (Helen Wells) _The Playhouse Mystery_ ("Cherry Ames Girls Annual"); _The Trouble with Sarah_ ("Cherry Ames Girls Annual").

ADAPTATIONS—Play: James Reach, _Why Not Join the Giraffes?_ (three acts), Samuel French, Inc., 1969.

SIDELIGHTS: "More than anything I have always loved water and boats. Water Rat could have been speaking to me when he said, in Kenneth Grahame's _Wind in the Willows,_ 'Believe me, my young friend, there is _nothing_—absolutely nothing—half so much work doing as simply messing about in boats.' As a child, 'messing about in boats' was precisely what I wished to do. But, since that first love was lost to me—careers at sea as sailors, or, preferably, ships captains were not open to little girls when I grew up—I had to choose a different profession.

"Therefore, I would become the greatest actress in the world! No doubt about it, I firmly believed, after seeing my first play at age five. It was in San Francisco, during one of our frequent trips there from Hawaii, where my parents and I lived in a paradise of nature and exotic surroundings. The play was _Peter Pan._ The theatre was the Geary. As so many

HOPE CAMPBELL

other children have dreamed, I, too, was convinced that now I could—and would—fly. I donned gym shorts and top, the closest approximation to 'Peter's' costume I could find, and sped to the window of our eleventh story hotel room. My mother averted an early and untimely end by racing to grab the seat of my shorts and pulled me back inside. I was already hanging more than halfway out, quite ready to leap and soar.

"'My, you were stubborn,' a former nurse-companion from Hawaii said recently. 'All you talked about was Peter Pan and acting. Acting, acting!'

"What she might not have known was another early decision. After acting, when I reached an ancient age, too feeble for treading the boards—well, then I would write books for children. For, if not outside, swimming, surfing, climbing trees, I was inside, devouring and re-reading my own children's books which I cherished, and in which, even as a child, I sensed a special value. Although I, too, wrote constantly; poems, compositions, stories, it seemed certain that I'd be ninety—at least—before embarking on this second profession in any serious way. It was a great surprise to find myself writing professionally at a far, far younger age.

"It was also startling, years later, after an acting career which began in Los Angeles in my early teens; took me to New York via an old-fashioned three ring traveling circus; on to radio, TV, various stock companies, and a USO tour of Europe—to find myself back in San Francisco in a play at the Geary Theatre, standing on the very stage where I'd first seen _Peter Pan._ Everything had come full circle, I thought.

"I have to take a shower," said Candy when she walked up the ramp. She was blue with cold. ■ (From *Mystery at Fire Island* by Hope Campbell. Illustrated by Leigh Grant.)

Why disturb this unusual symmetry? By then I'd also had my first son, still a baby, who required time and attention. Perhaps it was time to start writing.

"Back in New York, I awoke from a sound sleep one night, sat bolt upright in bed and wrote a science fiction story in one half hour, then went back to sleep. The next day I typed it in one half hour, sent it off, and then received a check in the mail—at which I stared. It had taken me only one hour to make more than very expensive MD's charge for a visit. This was it. What a wonderful, part-time creative, and possibly lucrative sideline to domesticity and motherhood.

"But I thought only of short stories, and was appalled when I was given an assignment to write a book. A whole book? It took more time to decipher how many words to a page, how many pages to a chapter, how many chapters to a book—than it did to write it. I also discovered, or thought, that I couldn't plot.

"A plot, to me, should be like a play; beginning, middle, end, cliff-hangers, strong curtains, and come to a full circle again. On the next book, however, not an assignment, but a science fiction idea of my own, I learned a personal, natural

way of plotting. And after many books for children, young adults, and adults, I begin to see how my books 'happen.' All start with a central idea containing the question, 'What if . . .?' And then progress, quite naturally, into further questions of, 'Now what would happen next?' Answers to these questions often come from lying down, eyes closed, to visualize the next probable sequence of events.

"People have sometimes complained, or congratulated, 'You never write the same book twice!' And that is quite true. All of my books are different, not only in age-range, but idea, content, even form and style. The most interesting complaint, or suggestion, or question, came recently from a friend who was referring to my life and varied experiences. She said, 'All those things you *haven't* written! Why not?' And she was quite right, too.

"Only rarely have I drawn upon my own experience, preferring flights of fancy or fantasy. I have not written the riches-to-rags story, when, after my father died, my mother and I were plunged from splendid, lavish living to near poverty. Nor have I written the circus story, the USO story, the China story, the how-to-become-a-successful-young-actress story—not one of them. But, having had children twelve years apart, I am once again raising a teen-age son who takes a lot of my time.

"Maybe, if I do reach ninety, that childhood dream will be realized. I'll become a writer, starting all over again. That is, if—now that it's possible—I don't return to my first love and just start 'simply messing about in boats'."

CARLEY, V(an Ness) Royal   1906-1976

OBITUARY NOTICE: Born August 14, 1906, in Bridgeport, Conn.; died August 15, 1976. Author and illustrator of children's books, poet, and owner of an art service. The Van Ness Service, dealing in advertising and promotional art, was the mainstay of Carley's career, but at the same time he wrote, produced, and appeared on television shows, and lectured to civic and religious groups. Carley's books for children range from the self-illustrated *The Lazy Cat* to a book of poetry, *Creation Poems.* He was the compiler-illustrator and the author of several books in the religious vein as well. *For More Information See: Contemporary Authors, Permanent Series,* Volume 2, Gale, 1978; *The Writers Directory, 1976-1978,* St. Martins, 1976.

CLIFTON, Lucille   1936-

PERSONAL: Born June 27, 1936, in Depew, N.Y.; daughter of Samuel L., Sr. (a laborer) and Thelma (a laborer; maiden name, Moore) Sayles; married Fred J. Clifton (an educator, writer, and artist), May 10, 1958; children: Sidney, Fredrica, Channing, Gillian, Graham, Alexia. *Education:* Attended Howard University, 1953-55, and Fredonia State Teachers College, 1955. *Home:* 2605 Talbot Rd., Baltimore, Md. 21216. *Agent:* Curtis Brown Ltd., 60 East 56th St., New York, N.Y. 10022. *Office:* Coppin State College, 2500 West North Ave., Baltimore, Md. 21216.

CAREER: New York State Division of Employment, Buffalo, claims clerk, 1958-60; U.S. Office of Education, Washington, D.C., literature assistant for CAREL (Central Atlantic Regional Educational Laboratory), 1969-71; Coppin State

College, Baltimore, Md., poet-in-residence, 1971—. *Member:* International P.E.N., Authors Guild of Authors League of America, Maryland State Committee for Black Art and Culture, Windsor Hills Association (member of board of directors, 1972). *Awards, honors:* Discovery Award from the New York YW-YMHA Poetry Center, 1969; National Endowment for the Arts awards, 1970, 1972.

WRITINGS—All for children, except as indicated: *Good Times* (poems for adults), Random House, 1969; *Some of the Days of Everett Anderson*, Holt, 1970; *The Black BC's* (alphabet poems), Dutton, 1970; *Good News About the Earth* (adult), Random House, 1972; *Everett Anderson's Christmas Coming*, Holt, 1972; *Good, Says Jerome*, Dutton, 1973; *All Us Come Cross the Water*, Holt, 1973; *Don't You Remember?*, Dutton, 1973; *The Boy Who Didn't Believe in Spring*, Dutton, 1973, Spanish edition, translated by Alma Flor Ada, *El Niño Que No Creía en la Primavera*, Dutton, 1976; *An Ordinary Woman* (adult), Random House, 1974; *Everett Anderson's Year*, Holt, 1974; *The Times They Used to Be*, Holt, 1974; *My Brother Fine With Me*, Holt, 1975; *Generations* (autobiography), Random House, 1976; *Everett Anderson's Friend*, Holt, 1976; *Three Wishes*, Viking, 1976; *Everett Anderson's 1-2-3*, Holt, 1977; *Amifika*, Dutton, 1977; *Everett Anderson's Nine Month Long*, Holt, 1978. Contributor of stories and poems to magazines, including *Redbook* and *Negro Digest*.

WORK IN PROGRESS: The Land of Chimes, a Black fairy tale, for Dutton; translating poems for an anthology; writing poems.

LUCILLE CLIFTON

SIDELIGHTS: **June 27, 1936.** Born in Depew, N.Y.. Clifton's father worked in the steel mills and her mother in a laundry. ''My mother bore two children, a boy and a girl. My father was the father of four. He had three daughters by three different women, his first wife who died when she was twenty-one years old, my mother who triumphed with a son, and my youngest sister's mother who had been my father's lover when my mother was a bride. Our mothers had all known each other, had been friends. We were friends. My sisters and I. And my Mama had raised us all.

''When I was born my father was thirty-five years old. The handsomest man in town, Mama always said. She was twenty-one, a plump brown girl who had never had a real boyfriend. He was always a wonder to her, like someone from a foreign place, and she would watch him and listen to his words as if they were commandments. He had been called Mr. Sayles Lord when he was young and thought he was some kind of a God man. Once I asked him why he was so sure that he was going to heaven. God knows me, he said. God understands a man like me. Mama didn't really understand such a man. But she loved him. She cleaned his mess and fed him and took his abuse and called him 'your crazy Daddy' in a voice thick with love until the day she dropped dead at forty-four years old.

'''When you was born we was going to name you Georgia,' Daddy told me once. 'Because my mother's name was Georgia and your Mama's mother was named Georgia too. But when I saw you there you was so pretty I told your Mama I wanted to name you Thelma for her. And she said she didn't like her name and for me to give you another name with the Thelma. So I looked at you and you looked just like one of us and I thought about what Mammy Ca'line used to say about Dahomey women and I thought this child is one of us and I named you Lucille with the Thelma. Just like my sister Lu-

cille and just like my real Grandmother Lucy. Genie, my Daddy's mother. First Black woman legally hanged in the state of Virginia.'

''Depew is where I was born. Depew New York, in 1936. Roosevelt time. It was a small town, mostly Polish, all its life turned like a machine around the steel mill. We lived in a house on Muskingum Street, and my Mama's family lived on Laverack. My grandparents lived in this big frame house on Laverack Street with one toilet. And in that house were my Mama's family, the Moores, and a lot of other people, lines of people, old and young.

''There was an old man who was a deacon, a pillar of the church. I remember once in prayer meeting, he was praying and the lights went out . . . a blackout, you know, in the second world war. And he was deep in the middle of his best praying. He was a very religious man, a deacon, and all of a sudden the lights went out and he looked up and shouted 'Dammit, now, God!' then went on with his prayer. A good prayer too.

''Our whole family lived there. In Depew. All the Moores, I mean. All around the steel mill. My grandfather and Daddy and uncles and all our men. Turning around the plant.

''Depew. One of the earliest things I remember was the goat in the backyard. Our house was on top of a big hill and across the yard and down the hill in the back were the Moores. And Grandma kept a goat back there. Depew.

''The closest big city was Buffalo, twelve miles away.'' [Lucille Clifton, *Generations: A Memoir*, Random House, 1976.[1]]

Tony stopped and made believe his sneaker was untied to see what King was going to do. King stopped and blew on his shades to clean them and to see what Tony was going to do. ■ (From *The Boy Who Didn't Believe in Spring* by Lucille Clifton. Pictures by Brinton Turkle.)

Early 1940's. Family moved to Buffalo. "When we moved to Buffalo, we were moving to the big city. I was six or seven, maybe even five, and we moved to Buffalo one night in a truck. We thought it was the biggest place in the world. The lady who owned the house had left a doll for me in the attic, and that doll and that attic and that whole house smelled like new days. Purdy Street."[1]

Late 1940's. "I remember when my uncle came home from the second world war, my Mama's baby brother. He belonged to the ninety-second division, which was the colored infantry, I think, and they had been in Italy. Oh we were all so proud of him, and one afternoon my Grandma was sitting by the window looking out, and my aunt came into the kitchen from getting the mail and said 'Mother, we got a letter from Buddy . . . and Here It Is!' And my uncle come grinning through the door with his soldier's suit on and oh my Grandma Moore laughed and cried and laughed again. I always remember how my Grandma Moore just sang out 'Oh here's my Buddy Buddy Buddy Buddy!'

"She was my grandmother that called me Genius. My Mama's mother. The Moores moved to Buffalo a while after we did, and they moved to downtown. She believed that I was twelve years old until the day she died, and I was married and pregnant. Always thought I was twelve, and she called me Genius because she knew I went to college."[1]

1953. Entered Howard University on a full scholarship. "When I went away to college, well, that was some time. People couldn't get it straight that I was going to Howard and not Harvard. Nobody in our family had graduated from high school at that time, and at that time no member of our church had ever gone to college. I had won this scholarship, you know, and they gave me this big party at the church. The Baptist church.

"Now we didn't know a thing about going to college. I remember I took my Grandma's wedding trunk, all held together with rope. Me and Mama went over to Peoples' and bought me a black silk skirt and a red see-through blouse and we packed Grandma Moore's wedding trunk. When they delivered it at Howard, all those ritzy girls from Chicago and Texas, oh I was so embarrassed I went down at night to pick it up. This old trunk with thick rope around it and Georgia Moore written in ink. Anyway, I went away to college, and before I left I had to go and say goodby to everybody.

"And we went to see Grandma and she was watching for us, and when we started down her block, she ran out on the porch hollering 'Everybody, Everybody, Here come my Genius!' And all her neighbor people come running out on the porch. And here I come, here I come.

"My Grandma Moore told me to behave myself away from home, and I promised that I would. I had never been away from home and my own people before and let me tell you I was scared but I didn't let on. Then she asked me 'Where was Moses when the lights went out?' and I said 'Grandma, I just don't know,' and she said 'Well, that's all right, just keep your dress tail down,' and I said 'Yes, ma'am,' because I understood that part.

"I was sixteen years old and went away to college and I had never slept a night away from my Mama and when me and my friend Retha and my friend Betty got to Washington they had this huge train station. I had never seen a place like that and I started to almost cry and I said to Retha as soon as I ate I was going back home. Then a Howard man came up to us and looked at Betty all little and cute with her college clothes and her name tag on and said, 'You'll love it here, and we'll love you,' and he turned to me and asked me if I was her mother. From that moment I knew I wouldn't last. And I didn't. Two years. That was all.

"But what a two years it was! What a time! I was from New York, so that was a big deal, and I was a drama major, so that was a big deal too. At that time, at Howard, if you weren't light-skinned or had long hair you had to have something pretty strong going for you. Well, I was a drama major from New York. They didn't know that Buffalo is a long way from New York City, and for them that did know, I could lay claim to Canada, so it worked out well enough.

"My Daddy wrote me a letter my first week there, and my Daddy could only write his name. But he got this letter together and it said 'Dear Lucilleman, I miss you so much but you are there getting what we want you to have be a good girl signed your daddy.' I cried and cried because it was the greatest letter I ever read or read about in my whole life. Mama wrote me too and her letter said, 'Your daddy has written you a letter and he worked all day.'

"Being away from home, I didn't even know how to do it. I used to think I was going to starve to death. Nobody had any notion of what I needed or anything. One time Mama sent me a box full of tuna fish. I hid it under my bed and at night I would take it out and open can after can of tuna fish. And I was always afraid I'd make a mistake and Daddy would find out. I knew he'd know whatever I did. Whatever I did. But I was proud. The first Thanksgiving I went back home and now I had only been gone since September but when I stepped off the train Daddy and my sister Jo were there and Jo said 'Oh, she don't look so different,' but I started talking with a Washington accent and I even had to try to remember the way home. I was a mess. I thought everything seemed so little.''[1]

1955. Left Howard University. ''I left Howard after two years. Lost my scholarship because I didn't study. I didn't have to, I thought. I didn't have to know about science and geography and things that I didn't want to know. I was a Dahomey woman. And so I came home to a disappointed and confused Mama and a Daddy who was furious and defensive and sad.

''Feet of clay, he said to me. My idol got feet of clay. God sent you to college to show me that you got feet of clay.

''Daddy, I argued with him, I don't need that stuff, I'm going to write poems. I can do what I want to do! I'm from Dahomey women!''[1]

Attended Fredonia State Teachers College near Buffalo. Joined a group of black intellectuals who read and performed plays, and met Fred Clifton, then teaching philosophy at the University of Buffalo. ''It was in Buffalo that I began finding my own voice as a writer. But I still never thought about publishing. What I was writing was not like the poems I'd been reading.'' [Harriet Jackson Scarupa, ''Lucille Clifton: Making the World 'Poem-Up','' *Ms.* Magazine, October, 1976.[2]]

May 10, 1958. Married Fred Clifton, an educator, writer, and artist.

1959. Mother died. ''My Mama dropped dead in a hospital hall one month before my first child was born. She had gone to take a series of tests to try to find out the cause of her epilepsy. I went to visit her every day and we laughed and talked about the baby coming. Her first grandchild. On this day, Friday, February 13, it was raining but I started out early because I had not gone to see her the day before. My aunt and my Uncle Buddy were standing in the reception area and as I came in they rushed to me saying 'Wait, Lue, wait, it's not visiting hours yet.' After a few minutes I noticed other people going on toward the wards and I started up when my aunt said 'Where you going, Lue?' and I said 'Up to see my Mama,' and they said all together 'Lue Lue your Mama's dead.' I stopped. I said 'That's not funny.' Nobody laughed, just looked at me, and I fell, big as a house with my baby, back into the telephone booth, crying 'Oh Buddy Oh Buddy, Buddy, Buddy.'

''One month and ten days later another Dahomey woman was born, but this one was mixed with magic.''[1]

1969. Received the prestigious Discovery Award from the YW-YMHA Poetry Center in New York City. First book, *Good Times,* published and chosen by the *New York Times* as one of the ten best books of the year.

Father died. ''When Mama died they said he wouldn't last long. He'll have a hard time without Thel, they whispered, he can't make it without Thel. Even the widows and old girlfriends that gathered like birds nodded to each other. He needed Thel, he'll be gone soon.

'But he fooled them. He was a strong man, a rock, and he lived on for ten years in his house, making a life. He took one of Mama's friends for his girlfriend, just as easily as he had married Mama when Edna Bell, his first wife and my sister Jo's mother, had died at twenty-one. And Mama's friend took care of him just as Mama had done, cooking and cleaning and being hollered at so much that once my children had asked me Is that lady Papa's maid or what? And I had answered No, not really, she's like my Mama was.

''He lived on ten years in that house after Mama died, but my Mama lingered there too. His friend said she could hear her in the mornings early when it was time to get up and get his breakfast, and she would roll over and jump out of bed and run toward the kitchen, calling I'll get it, Thel, I'll get it. She was tough as a soldier, my father would say of my dead mother. She wasn't a Dahomey woman, but she was the Mama of one.

''Smoke was hanging over Buffalo like judgment. We rode silently through shortcuts we knew, and came at last into my father's street. It was night. There were no children playing. In the middle of the block the door to my father's house stood open and lighted as it had when my mother had died. Fred parked the car and we unstuck ourselves from the seats, tired and limp.... My husband and my brother took my hands and we walked slowly toward the family we had tried to escape.

''We are orphans, my brother whispered. Very softly.''[1]

1970-1979. Continued to write poetry books and books for children in her Baltimore home. The Cliftons have six children. ''I write in spurts. I'm completely undisciplined. I never do all the things you're supposed to, like write at a set time every day. And I can't write if it's quiet.

''It's important for my children to know there are some things I need to do for myself, for them to know I'm a woman who's thinking things, that I have days when I get tired of them. But they actually help with my writing, especially the children's books. They keep you aware of life. And you have to stay aware of life, keep growing to write.

''They also keep me sane. I did this reading at the Library of Congress once. It was a great honor. Next day, I was ironing and I said, 'What is this great *poet* doing ironing?' The kids laughed, said, 'Are you crazy?' and I came back to earth.''[2]

FOR MORE INFORMATION SEE: Redbook, November, 1969; *Black World,* July, 1970; *Horn Book,* June, 1970, December, 1971, June, 1974, February, April, October, December, 1975, October, 1976; April, 1978; Selma G. Lanes, *Down the Rabbit Hole,* Atheneum, 1971; *New York Times Book Review,* November 4, 1973; Harriet Jackson Scarupa, ''Lucille Clifton—Making the World 'Poem Up','' *Ms.* Magazine, October, 1976; Lucille Clifton, *Generations,* Random House, 1977.

"Wild Rice Harvest" (1969) by Patrick Des Jarlait. ■ (From *The Red Man in Art* by Rena Neumann Coen. Designed by Vicki Hall.)

COEN, Rena Neumann 1925-

PERSONAL: Born February 22, 1925, in New York, N.Y.; daughter of Joshua H. (a professor) and Tamar (Mohl) Neumann; married Edward Coen (a professor of economics), June 26, 1949; children: Deborah, Joel, Ethan. *Education:* Barnard College, B.A., 1946; New York University, graduate study, 1946-47; Yale University, M.A., 1948, graduate study, 1947-49; University of Minnesota, Ph.D., 1969. *Politics:* Democrat. *Religion:* Jewish. *Home:* 1425 Flag Ave., S., Minneapolis, Minn. 55426.

CAREER: Minneapolis Institute of Arts, Minneapolis, Minn., research assistant and lecturer, 1961-66; St. Cloud State College, St. Cloud, Minn., assistant professor, 1969-72, associate professor of art history, 1973—. Docent, Jewish Museum, New York, summer, 1948. Organizer, Bicentennial Exhibition of ''Painting and Sculpture in Minnesota,'' University of Minnesota Gallery, 1976. *Member:* American Association of University Professors, College Art Association of America, The Society for Values in Higher Education (fellow), Minnesota Historical Society, Minneapolis Society of Fine Arts, Phi Kappa Phi. *Awards, honors:* Danforth fellowship, 1966-69; Smithsonian post-doctoral fellowship, 1976-77.

WRITINGS—All published by Lerner, except as noted: *Kings and Queens in Art,* 1965; *Farms and Farmers in Art,* 1965; *American History in Art,* 1966; *Medicine in Art,* 1970; *The Old Testament in Art,* 1970; *The Black Man in Art,* 1970; *The Red Man in Art,* 1972; *Painting and Sculpture in Minnesota, 1820-1914,* University of Minnesota Press, 1976. Contributor to art and historical journals.

WORK IN PROGRESS: Research in nineteenth century American painting and its iconography.

SIDELIGHTS: Coen has lived abroad for varying periods, including three years' residence in England, 1949-52. Her works are included in the Kerlan Collection at the University of Minnesota.

D'AMATO, Alex 1919-

PERSONAL: Born February 4, 1919, in Italy; son of Luigi (a stone cutter) and Raffaela D'Amato; married Janet Potter (a writer and artist), February 28, 1949; children: two daughters. *Education:* Attended art schools and special graphic design courses. *Home and office:* 32 Bayberry St., Bronxville, N.Y. 10708.

CAREER: Graphic designer. Designer of books, book jackets, records and Christmas ornaments.

WRITINGS—With wife, Janet D'Amato; all self-illustrated: *Animal Fun Time* (juvenile), Doubleday, 1964; *Cardboard Carpentry,* Lion Press, 1966; *Handicrafts for Holidays,* Lion Press, 1967; *Indian Crafts,* Lion Press, 1968; *African Crafts for You to Make,* Messner, 1969; *African Animals Through African Eyes,* Messner, 1971; *American Indian Craft Inspirations,* M. Evans, 1972; *Gifts to Make for Love or Money: A How-to Book of Imaginative Ideas for Fun-Giving or Fund-Raising,* Golden Press, 1973; *Colonial Crafts for You to Make* (juvenile), Messner, 1975; *Quillwork: The Craft of Paper Filigree,* M. Evans, 1975; *Italian Crafts: Inspirations from Folk Art,* M. Evans, 1977; *More Colonial Crafts for You to Make,* Messner, 1972; *Woodland Indians Crafts,* Messner, 1979; *Galaxy Games,* Doubleday, 1980.

Illustrator—with Janet D'Amato: Mary Elting, *Water Come, Water Go,* Harvey House, 1964; Mary Elting, *Aircraft at Work,* Harvey House, 1964; Evelyn L. Fiore, *The Wonder Wheel Book of Birds,* Thomas Nelson, 1965; Arthur Liebers, *Fifty Favorite Hobbies,* Hawthorn Books, 1968; Iris Vinton, *The Folkways Omnibus of Children's Games,* Stackpole, 1970.

FOR MORE INFORMATION SEE: Horn Book, February, 1970.

(From *More Colonial Crafts for You to Make* by Janet and Alex D'Amato. Illustrated by the authors.)

DELANO, Hugh   1933-

PERSONAL: Born December 14, 1933, in Cranford, N.J.; son of Philip Ingalls (a mechanical engineer) and Margaret (Hawks) Delano; married Marylou Lyons (a registered nurse), April 9, 1958; children: Hugh P., Jonathan, Peter, Craig. *Education:* Attended Washington College, Chestertown, Md. *Religion:* Presbyterian. *Home:* 6 Manor Ave., Cranford, N.J. 07016. *Office: New York Post,* 210 South St., New York, N.Y. 10002. *Agent:* Matt Merola, Mattgo Enterprises, 185 E. 85th St., New York, N.Y. 10028.

CAREER: Plainfield Courier-News, Plainfield, N.J., news writer, sports writer, and author of column "Sports Slants," 1956-64; *Newark News,* Newark, N.J., sports writer and author of columns "Over the Blue Line" and "College Chatter," 1964-71; *New York Post,* New York, N.Y., sports writer and author of columns "Working Press" and "Hockey Beat," 1971—. His sports writing concentrates on major league baseball, professional hockey, football, basketball, and college sports; he has appeared on television and radio programs. Selector for National Hockey League All-Star teams; former member of Heisman Football Trophy selection committee. *Military service:* U.S. Marine Corps, 1953-56; served in Philippines; became sergeant.

MEMBER: Professional Hockey Writers Association (president of New York chapter; member of board of directors of national association), Baseball Writers Association of America, National Sportscasters and Sports Writers Association, Overseas Press Club of America, Sigma Delta Chi, Pro Football Writers Association of America, National Football Foundation, and National Football Hall of Fame. *Awards, honors:* Sports reporting award from New Jersey Sports Writers Association, 1965; sports column award from New Jersey Press Association, 1971, for "College Sports Chatter"; sports story selected by Dutton, 1977, for *Best Sports Stories,* edited by Irving T. Marsh and Edward Ehre.

WRITINGS: (With Ken Hodge and Don Awrey) *Power Hockey,* Atheneum, 1975; *Eddie: A Goalie's Story* (biography of Eddie Giacomin), Atheneum, 1976; *The Book of Sports,* Pinnacle Books, 1980. Contributor to *Complete Handbook of Pro Hockey* and to sports magazines and newspapers.

SIDELIGHTS: "As a former high school and college athlete of modest skill, I have always believed that sports' participation is more vital than winning or achieving stardom for young people, and that the lessons of teamwork, self-discipline, self-sacrifice, and dedication have a carry-over value in later life. At a time when professional sports have been marred by greed and individualism, I prefer to write about the human drama and positive points in sports. In twenty years of sports writing my newspaper writing has run the gamut of sports—from dog shows and rowing to the World Series and the Super Bowl, and from high school sports to professional sports."

FOR MORE INFORMATION SEE: Stan Fisher, *Slashing!,* Crowell, 1974; *Best Sports Stories,* Dutton, 1977.

HUGH S. DELANO

DE LA RAMÉE, (Marie) Louise 1839-1908
(Ouida)

PERSONAL: Surname was originally Ramé; born January 1, 1839 (or 1840, according to some sources), in Bury St. Edmunds, England; died January 25, 1908, in Viareggio, Italy; buried in Lucca, Italy; daughter of Louis (a French instructor) and Susan (Sutton) Ramé.

CAREER: Novelist and author of children's stories. Contributor to *Bentley's Miscellany,* 1859-60.

WRITINGS—All under pseudonym Ouida; novels: *Held in Bondage; or, Granville de Vigne,* [London], 1863, Lippincott, 1864; *Strathmore; or, Wrought by His Own Hand,* [London], 1865, Lippincott, 1866; *Chandos,* [London], 1866, Lippincott, 1875; *Idalia,* Lippincott, 1867; *Under Two Flags: The Story of the Household and the Desert,* [London], 1867, Lippincott, 1876, reissued, A. Blond, 1967; *Cecil Castlemaine's Gage, and Other Novelettes,* [London], 1867, Lippincott, 1877, reprinted, Books for Libraries, 1970; *Tricotrin: The Story of a Waif and Stray,* Lippincott, 1869; *Puck: His Vicissitudes, Adventures, Observations, Conclusions, Friendships, and Philosophies,* Lippincott, 1870; *Folle-Farine,* Lippincott, 1871; *Pascarel,* [London], 1873, Lippincott, 1874; *Signa,* Lippincott, 1875; *In a Winter City,* Chapman & Hall, 1876; *Ariadne: The Story of a Dream,* Lippincott, 1877; *Friendship: A Society of Society,* Lippincott, 1878.

Moths, Lippincott, 1880, reissued, C. Chivers, 1966; *A Village Commune,* G. Munro, 1881; *In Maremma,* Lippincott, 1882; *Wanda, Countess Von Szalras,* J. W. Lovell, 1883; *Princess Napraxine,* J. W. Lovell, 1884; *A Rainy June,* J. W. Lovell, 1885; *Othmar,* Lippincott, 1885; *Don Gesualdo,* G. Munro, 1886; *A House Party,* J. W. Lovell, 1886, reprinted, Scholarly Press, 1977; *Guilderoy,* J. W. Lovell, 1889; *The Tower of Taddeo,* W. Heinemann, 1890, Hovendon, 1892; *Two Offenders,* Lippincott, 1893; *The Silver Christ [and] A Lemon Tree,* Macmillan, 1894; *An Altruist,* F. T. Neely, 1897; *The Massarenes,* R. F. Fenno, 1897; *Waters of Edera,* R. F. Fenno, 1899; *Syrlin,* Chatto & Windus, 1899; *Findelkind,* Ginn, 1900 [another edition illustrated by E. B. Barry, L. C. Page, 1901]; *Helianthus,* Macmillan, 1908.

Stories: *Randolph Gordon, and Other Stories,* Lippincott, 1867; *A Leaf in the Storm, and Other Stories,* Lippincott, 1872; *A Dog of Flanders* (for children: illustrated by E. Mazzanti), [London], 1872, Nims & Knight, 1892 [other editions illustrated by Edmund H. Garrett, Lippincott, 1893; Angus MacDonall and Hugo D. Pohl, Rand McNally, 1910; Maria L. Kirk, Lippincott, 1915; Gustav Tenggren, Macmillan, 1925; Frances Brundage, Saalfield, 1926; Harvey Fuller, A. Whitman, 1927; John Fitz, Jr., J. C. Winston, 1928]; *Two Little Wooden Shoes* (for children), Chapman & Hall, 1874 [another edition published as *Bebee; or, Two Little Wooden Shoes* (illustrated by E. B. Barry), J. Knight, 1896]; *Beatrice Boville, and Other Stories,* G. Munro, 1877; *Pipistrello, and Other Stories,* G. Munro, 1880; *Bimbi: Stories for Children,* Lippincott, 1882 [other editions illustrated by E. H. Garrett, Lippincott, 1892; M. L. Kirk, Lippincott, 1910]; *Afternoon, and Other Sketches,* G. Munro, 1884.

Ruffino, and Other Stories, United States Book Company, 1890; *Santa Barbara, and Other Stories,* United States Book Company, 1891; *The Nuremberg Stove* (for children), J. Knight, 1892, reissued, Macmillan, 1952 [other editions illustrated by M. L. Kirk, Lippincott, 1916; F. Brundage, Saalfield, 1927; Frank Boyd, Macmillan, 1928; Edwin J. Prittie, J. C. Winston, 1929]; *Rinaldo, The Halt, [and] The Stable-Boy,* G. Munro, 1892; *A Provence Rose,* J. Knight, 1894; *Toxin: A Story of Venice* (illustrated by Louise L. Heustis), F. A. Stokes, 1895, *Muriella; or, La Selve,* L. C. Page, 1897; *La Strega, and Other Stories,* D. Biddle, 1899, reprinted, Books for Libraries, 1969; *The Little Earl* (illustrated by E. B. Barry), D. Estes, 1900; *Two New Dog Stories, and Another* (illustrated by Ivan P. Thompson), D. Biddle, 1909; *Moufflou, and Other Stories* (illustrated by M. L. Kirk and E. H. Garrett), Lippincott, 1917.

Essays: *Views and Opinions,* Methuen, 1895; *Critical Studies,* T. F. Unwin, 1900.

ADAPTATIONS—Movies and filmstrips: "Under Two Flags" (motion pictures), Biograph, 1915, Fox Film Corp., 1916, Universal Films, 1922, Twentieth Century-Fox Films, 1936; "Her Greatest Love" (motion picture), adaptation of *Moths,* Fox Film Corp., 1917; "A Boy of Flanders" (motion picture), adaptation of *A Dog of Flanders,* starring Jackie Coogan, Metro Pictures, 1924; "Flames of Desire" (motion picture), adaptation of *Strathmore,* Fox Film Corp., 1924; "A Dog of Flanders" (motion picture), RKO Radio Pictures, 1935; "Favorite Children's Books: A Dog of Flanders" (filmstrip; color, with a phonodisc and a user's guide), Coronet Instructional Films, 1969.

Play: Geraldine B. Siks, *The Nuremberg Stove,* Children's Theatre Press, 1956.

SIDELIGHTS: The woman Ouida (as she was to become known in the literary world) was born on **New Year's Day, 1839** on the outskirts of Bury St. Edmunds. She was christened Maria Louisa Ramé. The name Ouida evolved from her infant attempts to pronounce her name Louisa. Given to great mood swings, she was a precocious, intelligent child and a voracious reader.

She was reared by her mother, Susan Sutton, and the maternal side of her family. Her father, a mercurial Frenchman named Louis Ramé, absented himself before her birth and saw her only sporadically (to her great despair).

In *Friendship*, the most autobiographical of her novels, she described the father of her heroine as patterned after her own father. "He was a man of many ambitions, of no achievement. A political gamester, a political conspirator, his life was spent in the treacherous seas of political intrigue, and he at the last perished in their whirlpool. Little was known of him—by his daughter almost nothing.... Her father had come and gone, come and gone, as comets do.... He would kiss her carelessly, bid her do a problem or write a poem, stay a few days, and go.... He ceased to come.... His death was mysterious, like his life. He passed away and made no sign." [Eileen Bigland, *Ouida: The Passionate Victorian*, Duell, Sloan, and Pearce, 1951.[1]]

It was her father, however, who taught her history and mathematics, who inspired in her a real love for literature, and who gave her an enduring affection for flowers, trees, animals and birds.

At age eleven, she wrote in her diary: "I must have perseverance to excell in anything.... I must study or I shall know nothing by the time I am a woman:"[1] While on her twelfth birthday she made the following resolution: "I hope as I grow in years I may grow in goodness and in cleverness.... I hope I shall possess Patience, Industry, and Perseverance."[1]

1850. A highlight of her early life was an invitation to visit her father at Boulogne for a summer holiday. "You can have a ball any night you please they dance every night but Mondays Wednesday and Fridays are the regular ball days when they have the band.... We have been introduced to and have called upon the Princess Lettitia Bonaparte, she has a daughter about my age a very nice little girl or rather big girl for she is much taller than I am...."[1]

Another entry reads: " ... I went last Wednesday to the ball, I danced a great deal, I had five beaux 2 of their names were Victor de Croquenoire and Albert de Courcy and 2 of the Leveriers and the other little boy's name I don't know, it was very full ... I went to the theatre with the dear Mdlles de Lagorgette and Mme de Lagorgette Mr. O'Hara papa and mama, a nephew of Mr. Peter's was there so handsome!"[1]

Upon her departure for home, she wrote: "Monday. Finish packing up. Sad, very sad breakfast, Mme Genau gave me a bottle of Cassé, and a beautiful bouquet of flowers, went to the office for a permet, got on board, said a sorrowful goodbye to dear Papa, laid down and floated from the shores of dear Beautiful France."[1]

1851. Suffered a mild attack of smallpox. "I might have died, but thank God I recovered and without being pitted which of course I don't care about so much as my life but still I shouldn't have liked it."[1]

Louise de la Ramée, 1878. Drawing by Alice Danyell.

The same year Ramée visited the Great Exhibition in London. " ... I admire the nave much more than the transept I declare when the organs are playing and you hear them and look from the gallery it is beautiful, exquisite, I could not put down all the things I liked if I would.... What do I mean by saying I like the nave better than the transept, certainly the latter is much more beautiful, the building far more, but the nave is so fairy-paradisy-like a looking place that when you gaze from the top to the bottom down the immense length it seems surely this cannot be built by men.... Oh, it was Eden itself, I wished all the people away no-one to jostle against and I should have thought among those beautiful works of art that I had dropped from the earth onto the abode of fairies and Peries, oh, that silver and ebony inkstand with a deer and a fawn and the inkstands formed of stumps of trees all in chased silver—it did not look at all like what it was, it was lovely."[1]

"The treasures of scholarship are sweet to all who open them. But they are perhaps sweetest of all to a girl that has been led both by habit and by nature to seek them. The soul of a girl whilst passions sleep, desires are unknown, and self-consciousness lies unawakened, can lose itself in the impersonal as no male student can. The mightiness and beauty of past ages become wonderful and all-sufficient to it, as they can never do to a youth beset by the stinging fires of impending manhood. The very element of faith and of imagination, hereafter its weakness, becomes the strength of the girl-scholar. The very abandonment of self, which later on will fling her to Sappho's death, or mure her in the cell of Heloise, will make her find a cloudless and all-absorbing happi-

"'OH! MY NECKLACE!' SHE CRIED."—*Page* **1.**

(From *Toxin: A Story of Venice* by Ouida. Illustrated by Louise L. Heustis.)

ness in the meditations of great minds, in the myths of heroic ages, in the delicate intricacies of language, and in the immeasurable majesties of thought.''[1]

1857. Moved to London with her mother and grandmother.

1863. *Held in Bondage,* published in three volumes, was an enormous success.

The literary critics of the day deluged her books with annihilating comments . . . frowned and scribbled ''bogus Shelley'' in the margin. All this increased rather than lessened the sale of her books.

Ramée gained the reputation as a difficult hostess, and a menacing guest completely devoid of social sense. William Allingham, the poet, described his meeting with Ouida: ''Ouida in green silk, sinister, clever face, hair down, small hands and feet, voice like a carving-knife.''[1]

Lady Paget, wife of the Ambassador to Italy became one of her few friends and admirers. She wrote of their first meeting. '' . . . When this little person was introduced I rubbed my eyes with wonder. A frail, diminutive creature stood before me, clad in trailing damask of black and pale blue. Long brown hair hung down her back, adding to the straight-

downness of her appearance. A pair of large, innocent, dark blue eyes gazed earnestly at me and the smallest of gloved hands met mine. But oh! the rest was too fearful. The nose, the contour of the face and the complexion all justified the Duc de Dion's cutting criticism. A harsh voice grated on my ear and my first thought was: 'What must not a woman suffer who, with such a thirst for beauty, has been treated thus by nature? Much ought to be forgiven her.'

''I cannot join in the silly abuse of her books on the count of immorality, because she happens to call a spade a spade, but she never makes vice attractive. Her love of nature and her sympathy for everything helpless and oppressed she clothes in beautiful and pathetic language. Her knowledge of the world was always nil, for an ungovernable imagination held the place of reality.''[1]

In Ramée's odd view of herself and the world as she perceived it, myriad fancies abound. She described her heroine in *Friendship* as patterned after herself. ''She was a beggar's brat found on a doorstep; she was a cardinal's daughter; she was a princess's *petite faute;* she was a Rothschild's mistress; she was a Cabinet Minister's craze; she was poor de Morny's daughter; she had been a slave in Circassia; she had been a serf in White Russia; she had been found frozen, a tambourine in her hand, outside the gates at Vincennes; her

(From *A Dog of Flanders* by Louise de la Ramée. Illustrated by Hiram P. Barnes.)

father was at the galleys, her mother kept an inn. No, they were both Imperial spies and very rich; no, they were both dead; no, nobody ever said that, they said this. The poor Emperor knew, beyond doubt; and the secret had died with him. She was quite out of society; she was not received anywhere, she was received everywhere. Oh, that was not true, but this was. Well, the less said the better."[1]

1874. Moved into the Villa Farinola, which commanded one of the loveliest views in Tuscany. "The villa was high up on the mountain side—vast, dusky, crumbling, desolate without, as all such places are, and within full of that nameless charm of freedom, space, antiquity, and stillness that does no less perpetually belong to them.

"Where these old villas stand on their pale olive slopes, those who are strange to them see only the peeling plaster, the discoloured stones, the desolate courts, the grass-grown flags, the broken statues, the straying vines, the look of loneliness and of decay.

"But those who know them well, love them and learn otherwise; learn the infinite charm of those vast silent halls, of those endless echoing corridors and cloisters, of those wide wind-swept, sun-bathed chambers, of those shadowy loggie,

Reproduction of book jacket.

where the rose glow of the oleander burns in the dimness of the arches; of those immense windows wreathed with sculpture and filled with the glistening silver of olive woods, and mountain snows, and limitless horizons; of those great breadths of sunlight, of those white wide courts, of those tangled gardens, of those breezy open doors, of those wild rose-trees climbing high about the Aetrurian torso, of those clear waters falling through acanthus leaves into their huge red conches; of that sense of infinite freedom of infinite solitude, of infinite light, and stillness, and calm. . . . "[1]

Ramée set about stuffing the scant elegance of this treasured rented villa with jungle plants, white bearskin rugs and a glut of miniatures, she, alas, had no knowledge of objets d'art. She did, however, have an unerring eye for outdoor beauty and under her care the gardens of the Villa Farinola became breathtaking. "The delights of an Italian garden are countless. It is not like any other garden in the world. It is at once more formal and more wild, at once greener with more abundant youth and venerable with more antique age. It has all Boccaccio between its walls, all Petrarca in its leaves, all Raffaelle in its skies. And then the sunshine that beggars words and laughs at painters!—the boundless, intense, delicious, heavenly light! What do other gardens know of that, save in the orange-groves of Granada and the rose-thickets of Damascus?"[1]

...She sat on the edge of the roof with one foot on the highest rung of the ladder. ■ (From *Two Little Wooden Shoes* by Louise de la Ramée. Illustrated by Edmund H. Garrett.)

(From the movie "A Dog of Flanders," starring David Ladd. Copyright © 1959 by Twentieth Century-Fox Film Corp.)

(From the movie "Under Two Flags," starring Claudette Colbert and Ronald Colman. Copyright 1936 by Twentieth Century-Fox Film Corp.)

Wrapped in her dreams, absorbed in the romances she wrote, she regarded herself as a goddess, a being apart from the ordinary world.

Henry James's estimate of Ramée. "She was *curious,* in a common, little way . . . of a most uppish or dauntless little spirit of arrogance and independence . . . a little terrible and finally pathetic *grotesque.*"[1]

1873-1876. *In a Winter City, Ariadne* and *Pascarel* were published. She wrote lovingly of Italy: "Where lies the secret spell of Florence?—a spell that strengthens, and does not fade with time?

"It is a strange, sweet, subtle charm that makes those who love her at all love her with a passionate, close-clinging faith in her as the fairest thing that men have ever builded where she lies amidst her lily-whitened meadows.

"Perhaps it is because her story is so old and her beauty is so young?

"The past is so close to you in Florence. You touch it at every step. Every line, every road, every gable, every tower, has some story of the past present in it. In the winding, dusky, irregular streets, with the outlines of their loggie and arcades and the glow of colour that fills their niches and galleries, the men who 'have gone before' walk with you. The beauty of the past goes with you at every step in Florence. Everywhere there are flowers, and breaks of songs, and rills of laughter, and wonderful eyes that look as if they too, like their poets, had gazed into the heights of heaven and the depths of hell. And then you will pass out at the gates beyond the city walls, and all around you there will be a radiance and serenity of light that seems to throb in its intensity and yet is divinely restful, like the passion and the peace of love when it has all to adore and nothing to desire.

"'As for the people—the dear people!—the more I dwelt amongst them the more I loved them. There is no other people on the face of the earth so entirely lovable, even with their many faults, as the Italians. But what is known of them by other nations?—hardly anything at all.'"[1]

September 10, 1893. Ramée's mother who had been the mainstay of her existence died. Ouida was fifty-four and terrified at the thought of facing life alone. "I shall miss her as long as I live, and if the knowledge that all are dead who cared for me be bracing, I have that tonic.

"I cannot tell you how much I miss my mother, nor how I am haunted by the remembrance of all her great sufferings after her fall. Her eyes were so beautiful to the last, and like those of a woman of twenty. Her little dog Rex is still very unhappy, though none of his habits are changed, and he is fond of me."[1]

A few years later she wrote to console a friend. "I am so sorry you have lost your mother. It is a loss one feels more, not less, with each succeeding year. I lost mine some years ago. She gave me the happiest childhood ever led on earth; and I know now that I was always utterly ungrateful. A Florentine peasant said once to me: 'Whilst one's mother lives one is never old, for there is always someone for whom one is young.'"[1]

1894. Ramée was evicted from her villa. With her life and fortunes falling asunder, she turned her back on Florence and went to Lucca. "I am weary of everything except my dogs."[1]

"I *don't* like Lucca . . . I don't think I shall ever like anything ever again . . . I should not like to live and die here; it does not seem Italy at all, and one never sees a flower."[1]

Her publishers had given up soothing and coaxing her and told her bluntly, her days as a novelist was done.

April 21, 1900. Wilfrid Scawen Blunt visited Ramée. "We went, Cockerell and I, to call on Ouida at her villa at S. Alessio. Our driver did not know the house or understand who it was that we wanted to visit, but at last suggested, in answer to our questions, 'The lady with the many dogs.' 'Oh, yes,' we said, 'the lady with the dogs.' And so, sure enough, it was. Arrived there, we found it to be a nice old villa, with trees and a high garden wall, and an eighteenth-century iron gate, towards which, from inside, seven or eight dogs, poodles and nondescripts, came at us open-mouthed. The noise was deafening, and it was some time before we could make our ringing heard. At last the bell was answered by a portly man-cook in cap and apron, who, after some delay consequent on my sending in my card, admitted us. At the end of ten minutes we were shown into a front hall, and there found the lady of the house, seated at a small table (as one finds in the opening scene of a play)—a little old lady, dressed in white, who rose to meet us and to reprove her dogs, who were yelping at us still in chorus. A mild reproof it was, nor did it save us from their caresses. The largest poodle placed his paws upon my knees, and another took my hat in his mouth. 'They do not often bite,' she explained, 'except beggars.'

"We sat down and talked. I had been prepared, by the violence of some of her writings and by what I had just heard of her, to find her somewhat loud and masculine; but she proved the reverse of this. In face Ouida is much more French than English; her father, she told us, was French, M. Ramé, and her mother an Englishwoman. She is small-featured, soft and distinguished, though she can never have been pretty, with a high forehead, rather prominent blue eyes, dulled and watery with age, almost white hair, and that milk-and-roses complexion which old people sometimes get, and which gives them a beatified look. It was difficult to understand her capable of such malevolence as *Friendship.* She can never, I think, have been a sensual woman or have inspired a sensual affection, whatever passions she may display in her writings. Her conversation is good, intellectual, but not affected or the talk of a blue stocking; it gives one the impression of a woman who has thought out her ideas and has the courage still of her opinions. We talked about the inhumanity of modern Europe, and especially of modern England, and the rage for slaughter which is its chief feature. We talked also about Italy and Crispi, who is her *bête noire* here, as Chamberlain is in England. She talks English perfectly, as she says she does French and Italian, and she complained to us of the slip-shod writing of the day. It was evidently a pleasure to her to talk and to find us such good listeners. She was greatly taken with Cockerell, perhaps for his modesty, and was curious as to who he could be, for I had not introduced him. 'Who is he?' she said to me in private, 'who is he *really?*'

"When at the end of a couple of hours we moved to go, she would have detained us and made us both promise to come again. She cannot go now to England on her dogs' account, for these monopolise her life. Altogether she is a somewhat pathetic figure, condemned to solitude, not by choice but by

Bust of Ouida by Giuseppi Norfini.

necessity, and regretting the cheerful society of Florence. The exile from it has, I fancy, been the work of her books, for she has had a bitter pen. 'The world tries its revenge on us,' she said, 'for having despised it.' We both left her with feelings of respect, almost of affection, certainly of sympathy.''[1]

1903. Evicted once again, this time bodily, she fled by cart, eighteen miles in wind and rain, to the Hotel de Russie in Viareggio. There she collapsed for seven months in a state of nervous exhaustion.

She started legal proceedings against her evictors which led her to further diminish her energies.

''December 1, 1903.
''I have left S. Alessio and have been vilely treated by the Grosfils, though I do not owe them a centime. What money and years wasted!

''December 18.
''I find this *brouillon* of what the Grosfils (did) and think you may like to read it.

''My lawyer here tells me it will be imprisonment and fines for them.

''December 22.
''The matter is in the hands of the law already. Thanks all the same. The name is Grosfils. Her son broke open my box in

her presence with a chisel! The *broullion* I sent you was for your own reading; a more detailed copy had already gone to Rennell Rodd. I would not live in Viareggio if you gave me the town. Except the sea, it is everything I abhor. D'-Annunzio's *villino* is a mere cotton-box with a dirty, dreary waste around it. The pines are nearly all cut down. The house has no view of the sea. By road it is four miles through an ugly flat country. He took it for six months and only stayed two. The contadino said that he '*piangeva tanto.*' I understand his tears in that howling desert! From the back the place looks charming.''[1]

She wrote to Sir Sydney Cockerell who had just visited Tolstoy in Russia.

''January 2, 1904
''I am glad indeed to see your beautiful and minute handwriting once more; but regret indisposition from which you have suffered. Did you get it in Russia? To me, Tolstoy has not much *intellect*. Many of his doctrines are absolutely foolish. He has little judgement of literature and not much, surely, of men. His admiration of Dickens proves the non-intellectual fibre of his mind; and his morality and monogamy are against common-sense and Nature. . . .

''It is very injurious to my interests not to come to England, but (money apart) I have no one whom I can trust with my dogs. My maid likes them, and has been with me twenty-three years, but I should not be sure of her if I were absent. You cannot trust Italians out of sight.

''January 6, 1904
''Thanks for the Tolstoys. But I know all his views and arguments. When he says that 'any rational being requires to believe in a God' he shows how limited his mind is. Probably if he had not been a Russian he would have been a much greater man. In many ways he is absolutely silly. In vulgar parlance his doctrines 'will not wash.' Observe too how he ignores the fact that fighting is *natural* to man. See a little child's rage before it can speak; its angry gestures, its inflamed face, its dumb fury. Men would not live in peace together if armies were abolished. Tolstoy does not realise that man is a very rudimentary imperfect creature occupying a very small place in an immense and unknown universe.

''January 23, 1904
''Do not mistake me; I think Tolstoy a great novelist, a great character for courage and self-sacrifice; but I cannot think a man who believes in Christianity is a man of great intellect, and his logic is sadly defective in many other ways. He judges the rest of the world by Russia. . . .

''I mean to take the *Westminster Gazette*. It is the best of the English papers, I think. . . .

''Surely the infants of today will be the men of twenty years hence; I do not believe the human race will ever be much altered; and it degenerates physically. War, as we know it, may end, because armies will mutually blow each other into space; but something equally bad will come in its stead, until the earth vanishes, as a scientist forsees, by the combustion of the atmosphere by electricity.

''P.S. There is a country beginning with an I which still cherishes the views that once were Iceland's.

"Here a few days ago, a father and son were sweeping up snow; they differed as to where they should put it; the son killed the father.

"In Lucca a cook and an ostler quarreled about frying; the latter ripped open the former's abdomen. In front of my villa at S. Alessio a girl sat on a wall, plaiting; she chaffed a peasant passing by; he shot at her with a revolver. The bullet entered her brother's thigh; he was three months in hospital. These are everyday occurrences. No one blames them; and unless the offender is a socialist or anarchist, they are seldom punished.

"January 28, 1904
"If you do not believe in the divinity of Christ what remains? What of course was always there, a poor man of fine instincts sore troubled by the suffering and injustice which torment Tolstoy today. He drew the poor after him, naturally, by his assurances that the future would compensate them for their painful labour. But I have never been able to understand how theories so crude, so illogical, so uneducated, and unsupported, could ever attract or satisfy intellectual minds.

"'One must believe something,' I am told. Why? Why should one need a belief? The whole of existence is a mystery; and science does not explain it more than ignorance. Tolstoy must know as well as I do that numbers of people are born vile and bad; was Whittaker Wright tempted by poverty? The mere sentimental 'do unto others' etc. etc. cannot restrain the passions, or rein in the appetites, or solve the problems of life. Tolstoy is dangerous because he is misleading. He is an educated Christ. If he had been born in France he would have been a very great man, but the frightful life of Russia has disturbed his brain.

"June 7, 1904
"I see nothing in that nation (Japan) to be desired as a future influence. Their stupid superstitions, their grovelling Emperor-worship, their rejection of love to the lowest plane, their savage murders and suicides, seem to me to embody all which we most desire to eliminate from our own lives. Men who suffer so little physically as the yellow races must be cruel. They go to slaughter like a horde of ants; and their war-craze is not heroism but a repetition of their suicidal mania. Patriotism is not what we want in Europe and America. It is a much wider, finer, more impersonal feeling. Some years ago men seemed to be approaching this ideal, but ever since the Franco-German War they have deteriorated everything except mechanics; and the bicycle and autocar are ruining them physically. You call this view pessimism; it seems to me common-sense.

"June 26, 1904
"Europe and the U.S.A. are horribly vulgar in all their ways and thoughts and actions; how much gentler, calmer, more graceful, and more courteous were the people of my childhood?

"July 7, 1904
"I am this time wholly in accord with Tolstoy. But it is a pity he brings in the Deity in various forms, because the continuance of war through thousands of years is inconsistent with the direction of a beneficent and omnipotent God. I think, as I have always done, that Tolstoy is a great genius but not a great intellect. The two are distinct. . . .

"It is so true that the intellect is powerless against the passion for bloodshed.

OUIDA, 1872

"July 8, 1904
"What is the use of art or literature? The world is choked with over-production and the earth is soaked with blood. I think it must have been better in Etruscan times. They were so fond of their dogs! So were the Romans. And they were honest about their human slaves."[1]

January 25, 1908. Died of pneumonia in Via Zanardelli, Viareggio. She rests at Bagni di Lucca, under a bier which carries a recumbent figure of herself with a dog lying at her feet.

She had written of her earlier childhood countryside during her last bitter days of loss and confusion in Bogni di Lucca. "Give my love to the blackbirds and hawthorns of Hardwick. . . . Tell the trees, the flowers, the birds, I do not forget the beauty of their home. Would it have been better with me if I had stayed near them? *Si jeunesse savait!* But, alas! all that youth thinks of is to flee away into the sunrise light of what it believes to be the glory of the future. We are but unwise dreamers at our wisest."[1]

Mr. Norman Douglas provided this epitaph: "The last, almost the last, of our lady authors."[1]

FOR MORE INFORMATION SEE: G. S. Street, "An Appreciation of Ouida," in his *Quales Ego,* Merriam, 1896; Max Beerbohm, *More,* J. Lane, 1899; Carl Van Vechten, *Excavations,* A. Knopf, 1926; Malcolm Elwin, *Victorian Wallflowers,* P. Smith, 1934; Yvonne Ffrench, *Ouida: A*

Study on Ostentation, Appleton-Century, 1938; Elizabeth R. Montgomery, *Story Behind Great Stories,* McBride, 1947; Eileen Bigland, *Ouida: The Passionate Victorian,* Duell, 1951; "Story of Ouida," *Newsweek,* November 26, 1951; Monica Stirling, *The Fine and the Wicked: The Life and Times of Ouida,* Coward-McCann, 1958; "Lady on a Plush Pegasus," *Time,* March 24, 1958.

DELDERFIELD, R(onald) F(rederick) 1912-1972

PERSONAL: Born February 12, 1912, in Greenwich, London, England; died June 24, 1972; married May Evans, 1936; children: one son, one daughter. *Education:* Attended West Buckland School. *Residence:* Sidmouth, Devon, England.

CAREER: Author, playwright, and newspaperman. Worked in various capacities on the country newspaper that his father owned, 1929-40. *Military service:* Served in the Royal Air Force, 1940-45, as a public relations officer in Europe.

*WRITINGS—*Plays: (With Basil Thomas) *This Is My Life* (three-act), C. H. Fox, 1944; *Peace Comes to Peckham* (three-act), Samuel French, 1948; *All Over Town* (three-act), Samuel French. 1948; *Worm's Eye View* (three-act), Samuel French, 1948; *The Queen Came By* (three-act), Baker, 1949; *Sailors Beware* (one-act), H.F.W. Deane, 1950; *Waggon-load o' Monkeys* (three-act), H.F.W. Deane, 1952; *The Old Lady of Cheadle* (one-act), H.F.W. Deane, 1952; *Misow! Misow!* (one-act), Samuel French, 1952; *Made to Measure* (one-act), Samuel French, 1952; *The Bride Wore an Opal Ring* (one-act), Samuel French, 1952; *Absent Lover* (one-act), Samuel French, 1953; *Smoke in the Valley* (one-act), Samuel French, 1953; *Spark in the Juice* (three-act), F. de Wolfe & R. Stone, 1953; *The Testimonial* (one-act), Samuel French, 1953; *The Orchard Walls* (three-act), Samuel French, 1954; *And Then There Were None* (one-act), Samuel French, 1954; *The Guinea-Pigs* (one-act), H.F.W. Deane, 1954; *Home Is the Hunted* (one-act), Samuel French, 1954; *Where There's a Will* (three-act), Samuel French, 1954; *The Rounderlay Tradition,* H.F.W. Deane, 1954; *Ten till Five* (one-act), F. de Wolfe & R. Stone, 1954; *Musical Switch* (one-act), F. de Wolfe & R. Stone, 1954; *The Offending Hand* (three-act), H.F.W. Deane, 1955; *Uncle's Little Lapse* (three-act), F. de Wolfe & R. Stone, 1955; *Flashpoint* (three-act), Samuel French, 1958; *The Mayerling Affair* (three-act), Samuel French, 1958; *Wild Mink* (one-act), Samuel French, 1962; *Once Aboard the Lugger* (three-act), Samuel French, 1962.

Histories: *Napoleon in Love,* Hodder & Stoughton, 1959, Little, Brown, 1960, reissued, Pan Books, 1974; *The March of the Twenty-Six: The Story of Napoleon's Marshals,* Hodder & Stoughton, 1962; *The Golden Millstones: Napoleon's Brothers and Sisters,* Weidenfeld & Nicolson, 1964, Harper, 1965; *Napoleon's Marshals,* Chilton Books, 1966; *The Retreat from Moscow,* Atheneum, 1967; *Imperial Sunset: The Fall of Napoleon, 1813-14,* Chilton, 1968.

Other writings: *These Clicks Made History,* Raleigh Press, 1946; *Seven Men of Gascony* (novel), Bobbs-Merrill, 1949, reissued, Simon & Schuster, 1973; *Farewell the Tranquil,* Dutton, 1950 (published in England as *Farewell the Tranquil Mind,* Hodder & Stoughton, 1950, reissued, 1974); *Nobody Shouted Author* (autobiographical), W. Laurie, 1951; *Bird's Eye View* (autobiographical), Constable, 1954; *The Adven-*

tures of Ben Gunn (based on Robert Louis Stevenson's *Treasure Island;* illustrated by William Stobbs), Hodder & Stoughton, 1956, published in America as *The Adventures of Ben Gunn: A Story of the Pirates of Treasure Island,* Bobbs-Merrill, 1957; *The Avenue Goes to War,* Hodder & Stoughton, 1958, Ballantine, 1964, reissued, Pocket Books, 1976; *The Dreaming Suburb,* Ballantine, 1958, reissued, Pocket Books, 1976; *Diana,* Putnam, 1960, reissued, Pocket Books, 1975 (published in England as *There Was a Fair Maid Dwelling,* Hodder & Stoughton, 1960); *Stop at a Winner,* Hodder & Stoughton, 1961; *The Unjust Skies,* Hodder & Stoughton, 1962; *Mr. Sermon* (novel), Simon & Schuster, 1963, reissued, Pocket Books, 1975 (published in England as *The Spring Madness of Mr. Sermon,* Hodder & Stoughton, 1963, reissued, 1972); (editor) *Tales Out of School: An Anthology of West Buckland Reminiscences, 1895-1963,* H. E. Warne, 1963; *Under an English Sky,* Hodder & Stoughton, 1964; *Too Few for Drums,* Simon & Schuster, 1964, reissued, Pocket Books, 1975; *The Avenue* (originally published separately as *The Avenue Goes to War* and *The Dreaming Suburb*), Simon & Schuster, 1964, reissued, Hodder, 1972.

The Horseman Riding, Hodder & Stoughton, 1966, Simon & Schuster, 1967; *Post of Honor,* Ballantine, 1966, reissued, 1974; *Return Journey,* Simon & Schuster, 1967, reissued, Pocket Books, 1975 (published in England as *Cheap Day Return,* Hodder & Stoughton, 1967, reissued, Corgi Books, 1972); *For My Own Amusement* (autobiographical), Hodder & Stoughton, 1968, Simon & Schuster, 1972; *The Green Gauntlet,* Simon & Schuster, 1968, reissued, Pocket Books, 1975; *Come Home Charlie and Face Them,* Hodder & Stoughton, 1969, published in America as *Charlie Come Home,* Simon & Schuster, 1976; *God Is an Englishman,* Simon & Schuster, 1970; *Overture for Beginners* (autobiographical), Hodder & Stoughton, 1970; *Theirs Was the Kingdom,* Simon & Schuster, 1971; *To Serve Them All My Days,* Simon & Schuster, 1972; *Give Us This Day,* Simon & Schuster, 1973.

SIDELIGHTS: **February 12, 1912.** Born in Greenwich, London, England. ". . . It seems my arrival caused something of a stir in the family, my father, a fanatical radical, revering Abe Lincoln as the Skipper-next-to-God. It was a fortunate day on which to be born in our house. Busts and pictures of Abe occupied all corners of the house, and every bookcase was stuffed with Civil War memoirs. Perhaps this circumstance alone was responsible for what I can only regard as a special relationship with America, for I never did see it as a foreign country, in the sense that France, Switzerland and even Australia are repellently alien." [R. F. Delderfield, *For My Own Amusement,* Simon & Schuster, 1968.[1]]

1916-1917. Attended his first school. "At the infants' department the cane was in the offing (for five-year-olds!) but I never saw it used, although I am quite sure it was.

"Discipline, however, was rigidly maintained. We were compelled to sit with arms folded on the desk and chatterboxes were silenced by having sticking-plaster slammed across mouths. Slow learners were exhibited as fools. There were dunces' caps and frequent banishments 'to the corner,' but I do not look back on that red-brick building with horror, notwithstanding the gloomy, cavernous impression it made upon me, or the memory of the hysterical efforts of an ageing spinster to control a class of sixty children. As long as one behaved as a robot one was not punished."[1]

April, 1918. Family moved to the rural suburb of South Croyden. "The impact of my transition from central London to what was then a semi-rural suburb was considerable. All my very earliest impressions were of drab streets, strident Cockney voices, khaki, naphtha flares, Zeppelin raids and fog, of maroons exploding neighbors into panic, of pinched, wartime expressions in butter queues and of the firelit security of a home dominated by a noisy, extrovert father. But on a showery day . . . all this disappeared as though banished by a fairy godmother's wand and in its place were rows of trim terrace houses lurking behind hedges of clipped privet, flocks of rosy-faced children who inhabited them, clumps of towering elms and meadows bordered by flowering hawthorn but, above all, acres of buttercups and daisies, with here a rash of bluebells and there a rank for foxglove.''[1]

1918. Attended a private school called a "college." "There were thousands of such establishments in those days, when a private education (inferior in every way to a state education) was reckoned the only reliable passport to a white-collar occupation. My 'college' was as seedy and pretentious as most such schools—seventy boys and four underpaid ushers, presided over by a jovial gentleman who wore blue serge and sang 'When you come to the end of a perfect day' at the annual prizegiving. Everything about that school was dog-eared, even the split-bamboo cane the Head used on occasion, but for me it was as rich in character as Tom Brown's Rugby.

"From here I moved to a grammar school where, for the first time, I met a few schoolmasters who were neither clowns nor bullies but men with a genuine interest in the practice of their profession. I have used them all at one time or another, sometimes compounding three or four into a single character—the mild and courteous Bentley, who ruled like a cultured King René of the Two Sicilies, the informative Scott, who had a way of making English words perform the tricks of circus dogs, the grave and kindly Parkinson, the ironic and candid Barlow, and above all, the tempestuous Mr. Ferguson, who taught French. . . . I learned more French from Ferguson in six months than from a succession of other teachers in ten years, and when adrift in France in 1944 and thrown upon my own inadequate resources, I often summoned his spirit to my side.''[1]

1929. After attending a commercial college, joined the staff of his father's country newspaper. ". . . With the world slump just over the horizon, I joined the staff of *The Exmouth Chronicle*, my father's weekly newspaper, as general reporter and spare-time ledger clerk. Times were hard, and my starting salary was five shillings a week, plus a withheld thirty more for board and lodging at home.

"It seems, looking back, a modest sum, even for those pinch-penny days, but my father had not learned the knack of adjusting to the passage of years. To him the value of money was static and had he owned a vineyard he would have paid for labor at the rate of a penny a day, citing Holy Writ as a precedent. I was seventeen then, and he had gone out to work at twelve for about the same weekly sum as I received. His views concerning money survived another world war. Even in the early fifties it was difficult to persuade him that five pounds a week did not put a man in the supertax bracket.

"At that time, Father was fifty-five, and his obsession with the game of bowls coincided with a conviction that forty-three years of steady toil is as much as can be expected from a human being. He opted out, transferring the paper to me as though it had been a bicycle that required to be kept in rea-

sonable running order, and I like to think this was a manifestation of faith in my latent ability as a journalist. Doubts regarding this, however, continue to linger in the mind. More probably he never gave a thought to the dangers and complexities of placing his destiny in the hands of a youth so utterly lacking in experience. The prospect of a libel suit had never cost him a moment's sleep. He had been walking hand-in-hand with libel and slander ever since he entered local politics at the age of twenty-one. By 1929 he and they were boon companions.

"I learned by trial and error—the only way anyone can learn to be a newspaperman—and sometimes the element of error brought me within hailing distance of disaster. More often, however, it brought me into conflict with the local mandarins; for, whereas it was easy to learn the rules of evidence whilst attending sessions at the local Magistrates' Court, it was very difficult indeed to acquaint myself with the sensitive areas of the fifty-odd individuals who ranked as mandarins. They all had an Achilles' heel, and it was essential when interviewing them or reporting their speeches to know what would enlist them as patrons and what would incur their wrath. I soon learned to identify them and set about studying them in detail, a technique now discernible among stalwarts who interview national mandarins on television. In those days, however, there was little in common between Fleet Street men and small-town provincials like myself. The Fleet-Streeter could be, and often was, very cavalier with human material, basing his style on story value. The province-based reporter had to live with the sober face to London news editors, who sometimes employed me on local stories that made national headlines.''[1]

1936. Married May Evans. The couple had two adopted children, Veronica and Paul.

1940-1945. Served in the Royal Air Force. "I carried five books in my kit bag through six years of war, and I am seldom to be found without at least two of them within easy reach. They are an odd and contrasting company and the only thing they have in common is their devotee, myself. They have shared every crisis point in my life, and because of this I shall try to make it my business to see that they are on hand when the lights go out. They are Stevenson's *Treasure Island*, the second volume of Carlyle's *French Revolution*, Mark Twain's *Huckleberry Finn*, Baron de Marbot's *Memoirs*, translated by A. J. Butler, and Helen Ashton's *Doctor Serecold*. I am partial to the Bible, to John Betjeman's collected verse, and to the *Oxford Book of English Verse*, but could, I feel, survive a year's isolation on a desert island without them. On the other hand I should feel very deprived without my standbys. I must have read each of these five books a score of times. . . .''[1]

Mid 1940's. After success of his first play, began a full career as an author and a playwright. ". . . The money came in dribs and drabs, subject to all kinds of deductions and penal taxation. For every shilling grossed, eightpence slipped between the floor boards. In my case there was ten percent for the agent, ten percent for the Wolverhampton initiators, a backlog of outlay to be recovered by the promoter, and several expensive trips to town to attend to various matters arising out of the production. All the same it was far more money than I had ever thought to earn, and I set about spending it. Before the run was two months old we adopted another child, this time a week-old boy. We bought a better car and began attending country house sales and replacing all our furniture with antiques.

". . . We bought a detached house on the cliffs at Budleigh and commissioned builders to do extensive repairs to it, the Americans having occupied it during the war and burned doors and banisters to keep themselves warm. Cautiously our lives as well as our possessions began to expand.

"We enjoyed it all immensely but success, and the relative affluence it brought, had disturbing undercurrents. I never had felt and never learned to feel at ease with theater folk, except when interviewing them as a journalist. I did not see them as real people. To become one of them enlisted me, against my will, in a band of gypsies, who lived from hand to mouth, selling their skills like clothes pegs and painting their faces in anticipation of riotous assembly round the campfire. In habits of thought, and standards of social conduct, they were foreign to all the people I had known and consorted with over the years. Their gaiety was as brittle as their promises, and I saw their frequent bouts of melancholy as unconscious rehearsals for parts they might be called upon to play later on. Their comradeship was lightly bestowed and as lightly discarded. Above all, I had learned the hard way not to believe a single word they uttered, even when they were sober.

"This was one thing, but another was more fundamental and had to do with our future habitat. Were we to up stakes and go and live among the gypsies? Or would we be better advised to do what Warwick Deeping and his wife did when the overnight success of *Sorrell and Son* engulfed him in the twenties; that is, sit down and pretend that it had never happened?

"For it was in these terms that I began to see myself, not as a creative artist, with some undefined role to play in the theater, but as a stay-at-home entertainer, someone who turned out three- and one-act plays much as a cabinet maker makes something practical from a stock of seasoned timber. I saw playwriting as a kind of extended journalism, better-paid certainly, but not nearly so interesting or so vital, because it was contrived and made to fit a pattern imposed on it by custom and fashion. I had always thought of everything I wrote as worth the passing attention of an audience but I had not (and still have not) an urge to compose moral symphonies, or to project fashionable or political themes over the footlights. I have never had much sympathy with the notion that the theater should be used for any means other than diverting people, and this is not to say that I was obsessed with comedy. A play, to me, was a prolonged charade. If one sought enlightenment or mental enlargement then one went to a book and turned the pages slowly, pondering the wisdom therein. It was this detached approach to the stage that determined my course from 1946 onward. I stayed where I was, among the people I knew and liked and trusted, and on terrain with which I was thoroughly familiar, continuing to write plays—a whole spate of them—but never letting them engage more than the surface of the mind and thinking of them, always, as a means of livelihood and nothing else."[1]

1950-1970. Wrote novels and histories—became known as a chronicler of English life. "I did many other things apart from writing. For more than two years I ran a small farm, learning how to milk cows and rear pigs, fowls and ducks. May became an expert at making Devonshire cream and butter, and we ultimately acquired a T.T. license from the Ministry of Agriculture. Later on I ran a brace of antique shops, but all these activities, I soon realized, were no more than field work in preparation for what I really wanted to do. On January 1, 1956, almost exactly ten years from the time *Worm's Eye View* began its run, I cut the painter and did it,

settling down to write the first section of *The Avenue Story*, a long saga that aimed at projecting the English way of life in a London suburb from the end of World War One to the reconstruction period of the late nineteen-forties.

"The abrupt change of direction involved us in considerable financial readjustments. I had published three or four books by then but the theater had claimed by far the greater part of my time. In that first year as a novelist my income dropped seventy percent, but so did my expenses, and once the backlog of taxation was paid off I was no worse off. Although my standard of living fell, and we moved from house to cottage, I enjoyed a sense of liberation that had evaded me since the day H. E. Bates and I drew our civvy kit as the demob center. At last I could write what I wanted to write, and not what fashion and the advice of professional actors dictated.

"In the next decade I completed three two-volume sagas, four histories of aspects of the Napoleonic Empire, and half a dozen shorter novels. The three plays I wrote during this period were historical dramas, specially written for Pitlochry Festivals. Everything I knew and felt and had experienced over the past forty-odd years went into the characters I created and came to life as they grew from a few sentences on a blank sheet into three-dimensional, flesh-and-blood men and women. In most cases I used the West Country backdrop, where the sky and seascape are never the same for more than ten minutes and the landscape, apparently unchanging, puts on a brand-new costume for each of the four seasons. From going to London once a fortnight I went there about twice a year, and after half a dozen brief and very depressing expeditions to the Continent, I threw the travel brochures in the wastepaper basket and settled for more familiar scenes, the Welsh hills, the Lakes, the moorland country of the North Riding, the Cheviots, and, above all, the pine, bracken and granite outcrop country of the West. I can never be absent from Britain for more than twelve hours before I begin to suffer the pangs of homesickness, and the older I grow the more mulishly insular I become. One of the postwar trends that continue to amaze me is the annual summer trek to countries like Spain and Italy where, as I see it, a majority of people are still grappling with social and political problems solved by British liberal governments in the late nineteenth century. They may have more sun, and they may be temporarily solvent, but they are amateurs in the essentials of democratic practice, particularly those of maintaining public order and sharing what there is to be shared. Some day I hope history will acknowledge this.

"Which brings me, more or less, up to date, a balding, unrepentant, stay-at-home, content to sit here weaving home-grown garments, at peace with most people (except gibbering enthusiasts who strap men and monkeys into capsules and send them spinning round space), and content to accept at its face value the farewell tag stage directors toss at young actresses after an unsuccessful audition—'Don't ring us. We'll ring you..' "[1]

June 24, 1972. Died at the age of sixty. Delderfield's panoramic family sagas have been compared to Hardy, Galsworthy, and Dickens. His juvenile, *The Adventures of Ben Gunn* (written as a "pre-sequel" to Stevenson's *Treasure Island*), has been called a minor classic of modern-day children's literature. "I have always seen myself as a lineal descendant of the medieval minstrel who trudged from castle to castle telling tales for his supper. Not that I am complaining. I am a compulsive teller of tales, a really chronic case. Give me a pen and some blank sheets of paper, and I am content to ply my craft in a hogshead, of the kind Huck Finn inhabited. Deny me the privilege and I would die of boredom and frustration in the Palace of the Doge set in the Garden of Eden.''[1]

One of Delderfield's earliest novels was *Seven Men of Gascony,* a historical novel set during the Napoleonic wars. The *Christian Science Monitor* review said, ''Well-conceived and well-executed, Mr. Delderfield's story of Napoleon's last six years pulses with the devotion of unnamed hundreds of thousands and the horrors of a Continent at war—all expressed in realistic terms of ordinary, naturally decent men.'' The *New York Herald Tribune* added, ''The author has achieved a war chronicle of breadth and vigor admirably more devoted to the sources of human behavior than to the mechanics of warfare.''

The Adventures of Benn Gunn: A Story of the Pirates of Treasure Island was an attempt by the author to settle unanswered questions about Stevenson's *Treasure Island* through the use of a supplementary story centered on the pirate life of the marooned Ben Gunn. *Library Journal* commented, ''May be read and enjoyed by 12-15-year-old boys who like an exciting story of adventure or piracy; may also be read to learn the answers to many questions left by Stevenson—answers logically and vividly presented.'' *Horn Book* noted, ''For the boy who reads and rereads the original story, this will give real pleasure. For it is no second *Treasure Island,* although a good plot fills in the old tale and the writing captures its style and atmosphere remarkably well.''

Diana tells of the romance between a Cockney orphan and a wealthy heroine. *Kirkus* described it as ''a romantic story which should appeal to women who seek in fiction the undevious, tasteful, and gently nostalgic. . . .'' The *New York Times* added, ''The author, one of England's popular novelists and playwrights, recaptures with refreshing simplicity the awkwardness, excitement, and delights of youth. . . . This is a charming novel both in its understanding of the ironic predicaments of the lovers and in their identification with an enchanted setting.'' On the other hand, *New Yorker*'s comments included, ''A very long and romantic English novel with a run-of-the-mill air that does not really detract from its pale but solid virtues; it is a carefully written work, and has not only a plot that unravels smoothly but enough logic to leave the reader without anything to wonder about.''

Delderfield also wrote several historical studies of Napoleon. *Napoleon in Love* details the emperor's quest for romantic fulfillment. A *Kirkus* review included, ''Neither a book for scholars nor sensation hunters, this is a sober investigation of Napoleon, a man of formidable energy, immense shrewdness, and where women were concerned, childlike ingenuity.'' *Library Journal* commented, ''Authentic and painstaking, it is still essentially a popular, readable account for the general public. Despite the sensational possibilities of the theme . . . it is presented in good taste and provides considerable insight into Napoleon's personality. It reveals much, too, of the color of life in the Napoleonic era.'' Of *Napoleon's Marshals, Library Journal* commented, ''[This] volume lies halfway between a collective biography and a military panorama. . . . R. F. Delderfield attempts to concentrate on the personalities involved—their friendships, loves, and hatreds—but it is difficult to cope with 26 individual backgrounds. Some portraits are sharper than others. . . . The total result, however, falls short of either collective biography or military panorama. Acceptable, but supplemental material for the average reader of history.''

God Is an Englishman was one of Delderfield's last novels. The *New York Times* observed, ''A cheerful anachronism in the world of letters, Mr. Delderfield writes with vigor, unceasing narrative drive and a high degree of craftsmanship. At his best he may remind one of Trollope, at his worst of Hugh Walpole. . . . He is a storyteller, which is no small thing to be. But he is not a novelist who can create characters so individual or so universal that they linger in the memory. . . . Although difficult to take seriously, [this book] provides a good bird's-eye view of Victorian England and contains numerous snippets of social history. . . . There is a place for the conventional, traditional, lively and amusing sort of fiction.''

Delderfield's books have sold at least a million copies in the United States alone. According to Simon & Schuster, *God Is an Englishman* and *Theirs Was the Kingdom* have each sold over 65,000 copies in hard cover.

FOR MORE INFORMATION SEE: R. F. Delderfield, *Nobody Shouted Author,* Laurie, 1951; R. F. Delderfield, *Bird's Eye View: Autobiography,* Constable, 1954; Brian Doyle, editor, *Who's Who of Children's Literature,* Schocken Books, 1968; R. F. Delderfield, *Overture for Beginners,* Hodder & Stoughton, 1970; R. F. Delderfield, *For My Own Amusement,* Simon & Schuster, 1972.

Obituaries: *New York Times,* June 27, 1972; *Washington Post,* June 28, 1972; *National Observer,* July 8, 1972; *Newsweek,* July 10, 1972; *Publishers Weekly,* July 17, 1972.

DOSS, Helen (Grigsby) 1918-

PERSONAL: Born August 9, 1918, in Sanderstead, Surrey, England; daughter of Owen Eugene and Maude (Menely) Grigsby; married Carl M. Doss (a Methodist minister), June 20, 1937; children: Donald, Richard, Dorothy, Elaine, Ted, Laura, Susan, Rita, Diane, Tim, Alex, Gregory. *Education:* Eureka College, student, 1934-35; Santa Ana Junior College, A.A., 1936; University of Redlands, B.A., 1954. *Religion:* Protestant. *Home:* Tucson, Arizona.

CAREER: Free-lance writer. *Member:* Society of Southwestern Authors.

WRITINGS: The Family Nobody Wanted, Little, Brown, 1954; *A Brother the Size of Me,* Little, Brown, 1957; *If You Adopt a Child,* Holt, 1957; *All the Children of the World,* Abingdon, 1958; *The Really Real Family,* Little, Brown, 1959; *Friends Around the World,* Abingdon, 1959; *Jonah,* Abingdon, 1964; *King David,* Abingdon, 1967; *Young Readers Book of Bible Stories,* Abingdon, 1970; (with Richard L. Wells) *All the Better to Bite With,* Messner, 1976; *Your Skin Holds You In,* Messner, 1978.

SIDELIGHTS: ''As far back as I can remember, I wanted to be a writer. At Girl Scout camp I wrote plays, skits, and camp songs. At Maine Township High School, in an Illinois suburb of Chicago, my favorite subjects were English and journalism. I was a voracious reader and read everything: newspapers, classics of literature, mysteries, essays, and almost anything on science. Then I went on to college in Southern California, and I looked forward to graduating and becoming a full-time writer. Already I'd started to write articles for the *American Girl* Magazine, but I really wanted to write novels.

"My career took a temporary detour, and my college was interrupted mid-stream, when I fell in love and married Carl Doss. 'Raise a family of children,' Carl told me. 'Let your ideas mature, and then you'll have something to write about!'

"Of course I never dreamed that my family would be so unusual; it would be the subject of my first book! It was written from notes jotted down about funny things the children said, and some of the experiences happened while I was still writing *The Family Nobody Wanted*. While washing out diapers, putting new knee patches on jeans, and baking bread, I also studied at home, took a summer school course, and finally received my college degree—with twelve small children cheering for me in the front row.

"I continued to write many books for children, while my own children were growing up. Now that all twelve are long grown and gone, and I live alone, I still write books for children now and then. After all, I now have twenty-six grandchildren to write for! But my real, long-suppressed desire has been to write long novels, especially historical fiction with an accurately researched background. I am now finishing one with an Old Testament background, full of adventure, action, and romance; and I have five other historical novels already planned. For some of them I hope to travel, and live awhile in a foreign country doing research and gathering background material. The future looks very exciting to me!

"In the meantime, I am what I've always been, an outdoor person who loves to hike, camp, swim, and explore—as long as I can manage to do those things without getting sunburned, or catching a poison-ivy rash, both of which I am susceptible to. I am still fascinated by science, the world of

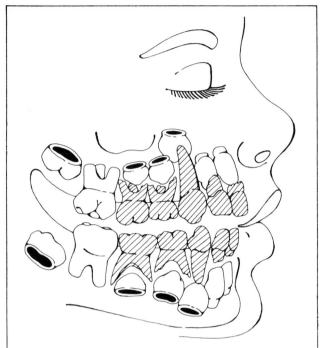

HOW TEETH GROW. Baby teeth are shown in stripes. The permanent teeth are growing under them and are shown all white. The first permanent molars at the left have already erupted.

(From *All the Better To Bite With* by Helen Doss with Richard L. Wells. Illustrated by Charles Clement.)

nature, children, and all kinds of people. I really enjoy living—and writing."

The Dosses were the parents of twelve adopted children—six boys and six girls—of minority and mixed racial backgrounds. The ancestries of the children include strains of Japanese, Chinese, Filipino, Hawaiian, Mexican, American Indian, East Indian, and various European nationalities. The story of this unusual family is told in *The Family Nobody Wanted*, *A Brother the Size of Me*, and *The Really Real Family*.

HELEN DOSS

EPP, Margaret A(gnes) (Agnes Goossen)

EDUCATION: Graduate of Bethany Bible Institute, Hepburn, Saskatchewan, Canada; additional study at Prairie Bible Institute, Three Hills, Alberta. *Home:* P.O. Box 178, Waldheim, Saskatchewan, Canada.

CAREER: Writer, mainly of books for juniors and teenagers.

WRITINGS: Peppermint Sue, Moody, 1955; *North to Sakitawa*, Moody, 1955; *Light on Twin Rocks* [and] *Music in the Wapawekkas*, Moody, 1956; *The Long Chase* [and] *Budworms and Tepees*, Moody, 1956; *Vicki Arthur*, Moody, 1956; *The Sign of the Tumbling T*, Moody, 1956; *Come Back, Jonah* [and] *The Secret of Larrabie Lake*, Moody, 1956; *Sap's Running*, Moody, 1956; *Thirty Days Hath September*

MARGARET A. EPP

(story collection), Moody, 1956; *Canadian Holiday,* Moody, 1956; *Shades of Great Aunt Martha,* Moody, 1956; *Anita and the Driftwood House,* Moody, 1957; *All in the April Evening* (story collection), Moody, 1959; *No Hand Sam* (missionary stories), Mennonite Publishing House, 1959.

(Under pseudonym Agnes Goossen) *Mystery at Pony Ranch,* Moody, 1963; *But God Hath Chosen: The Story of John and Mary Dyck,* Mennonite Publishing House, 1963; *Come to My Party* (nonfiction), Zondervan, 1964; *A Fountain Sealed,* Zondervan, 1965; *The Brannans of Bar Lazy B,* Moody, 1965; *Trouble on the Flying M,* Moody, 1966; *Jungle Call,* Beacon, 1966; *The North Wind and the Caribou,* Moody, 1966; *Search Down the Yukon,* Moody, 1967; *Walk in My Woods* (autobiography), Moody, 1967; *Prairie Princess,* Moody, 1967; *No Help Wanted,* Moody, 1968; *The Princess and the Pelican,* Moody, 1968; *This Mountain Is Mine* (biography), Moody, 1969; *The Princess Rides a Panther,* Moody, 1970; *Call of the Wahoa and Other Adventures,* Moody, 1971; *Great Frederick and Friends,* Moody, 1971; *Runaway at the Running K,* Moody, 1972; *Into all the World,* Moody, 1973; *The Earth is Round,* Christian Press, 1974; *Proclaim Jubilee!,* Bethany Bible Institute, 1976; *Tulpengasse,* Christian Press, 1978; *Sarah and the Mystery of the Hidden Boy,* Victor Books, 1979.

SIDELIGHTS: "I was born August 1, 1913, in a farmhouse, near Waldheim, Saskatchewan, the fourth—of nine—children to Henry and Agnes (Goossen) Epp. Spent six years of my childhood in Honan and Shantung, China, where my parents served as missionaries under the China Mennonite Mission Society. Shortly before my ninth birthday the family returned to Canada, due to health problems. For the next forty-two years—except for occasional absences, the farmhouse—my birthplace—was to be my home base. My pres-

ent home is in the town of Waldheim, where I've been living, and writing—between trips to various parts of the globe—for fifteen years.

"Unconsciously or consciously, I've been a nut-gatherer for most of my life. Since I began writing in earnest, thirty years ago, I've been a squirrel with a purpose. The nut-gathering has taken me to many parts of the world—the United States, Central and South America, the Carribeans, Africa, the Middle East, the Orient, and Europe—though some of the most prized nuts were found in my own back yard. And invariably I have returned to my home to turn out a new batch of 'nut-bread.'

"When and how and where did it all begin? No doubt with a father who was original in all his thinking, and a mother who was a born story teller and the daughter of another. But consciously for me, the thing began one magic moment when I was seven, a first-grader, and enrolled in a boarding school in Shantung, China. The most exciting hour of each week came on Saturday nights, when 'Auntie' Mary DeGarmo collected the boys and girls around her to read to us. Books were not for touching, but for being read too. The seven-year-old stood one day, facing the glassed-in bookcase,

Just as if this was proper threshingtime chore for a girl. "Fences will be down today, at both places. And we cannot risk the cows getting into the grain."
■ (From *Sarah and the Pelican* by Margaret Epp. Illustrated by Robert G. Doares.)

gloating in the rich, rich reading hours to come. Suddenly, the Flash! One day I would write books—and boys and girls all over the world would delight in them as I delighted in our Saturday night readings. It was an exciting secret between God and me. I never spoke of it, but I never forgot.

"Five years later, in a little Saskatchewan schoolhouse, I thought of my secret dream with deep despondency, having just come to realise that the English spoken in our tight little Mennonite community, was not the English of living literature. How was I to acquire English ears? At the moment—and for years afterwards—my ethnic and cultural background seemed a hopeless burden to me, which was nonsense, of course. There's not an aspect of it that has not yielded rich returns or a bit of purposeful nut-gathering. But at the moment I made a solemn promise to myself, and that too was of utmost importance. I would be on the lookout for books that could teach me things about the English language. I would read them rapidly first, so the story could no longer distract me. Then I would immediately begin a careful re-reading, paying attention to words and phrases, sentences and paragraphing, absorbing the language as I went along. I smile today when I'm told that my conversational English is somewhat bookish in tone. Of course. Quite natural. Books have been my tutors.

"I count over my 'advantages' today—factors that helped shape me. My setting in a large, hard-working family, where play-time and privacy and money were rare—and in an intimate community where everyone knew everyone else, yet where each had liberty to be himself, different from everyone else. The writer in me delights in the world of colourful individualists I knew—and make use of today.

"My need to share my good things with brothers and sisters. I never owned a pet, rarely owned a toy. We manufactured playthings out of scraps and a dab of flour paste or two. We wrote our own nonsense rhymes, and clowned our way through made-up stories.

"Poverty was a daily companion, and so was work. Not *make-work*. We did essential chores, and knew the whole family would suffer if we fell down on our jobs. Granted, we would gladly have seen less of these grim-faced friends, but they gave us a certain dignity too, and a sense of worth. And when the Great Depression struck—I was sixteen that year—we had little left to learn about how to live without money. Wheat that might have sold at over a dollar in fall, sold in spring at twenty-nine cents per bushel. Yet that was only the beginning of hard times the Canadian west endured. Seven years of crop failure followed, owing to drought conditions. And to finish off our scanty crops, came the hordes of grasshoppers. I'll never forget the metallic whirr and march of the invaders, nor the sound of millions of mandibles chewing their way through our standing grain, nor the sight of fields left starkly black in their wake. There went the slightest hope that I'd be able to go to high school!

"We spoke of the three dread D's—depression, drought, and the destroyer. In spite of them I was able to attend—and graduate from—Bethany Bible Institute at Hepburn, twelve miles from home. Fees were kept low, teachers teaching for next to nothing—to give the jobless young people something purposeful to do through the long winters. To give them anchorage for the hard times, and set their priorities straight. A spinal injury gave me time and leisure after that to finish my high school studies by government correspondence course.

"For thirty years and more now I've been a full-time writer—and there's not an aspect of the rather austere conditions that shaped me which has not proved a blessing in the end.

"'But how can *you* write for *children*?' I frequently hear people exclaim. 'You've never been a *mother*!'

"Why, I've been surrounded by children all my life. I mothered my younger siblings, haunted the nursery in church, baby-sat with the thirty-four nephews and nieces that came along, and am on good terms with the forty-odd grand-nephews and nieces. Not to mention the hundreds of children I've taught in Sunday school, and Vacation Bible school, and summer camps. I've lacked no opportunity to practise story-telling arts.

"Besides, I write as readily for adults as for the various ages of juveniles. In the past twelve years I have written five full-length adult books, all non-fiction, five teen-slanted fiction books, and five junior-slanted books—also fiction. This human squirrel is still busily collecting informational nuts, and turning out new loaves.

"*The Earth Is Round* was written on assignment to celebrate the centenniel of the coming of Mennonites to Manitoba from Russia, 1874-76. My maternal grandparents were part of that migration, as teen-agers, though they were part of the 8,000 that settled in South Dakota, Nebraska and Kansas. Ten thousand settled in Manitoba.

"The three Princess books have become the Sarah Scott books now that Victor Books, of Wheaton, Ill. have taken up the option to publish them. *Prairie Princess* became *Sarah and the Magic Twenty-Fifth*. *The Princess and the Pelican* now is *Sarah and the Pelican*. *The Princess Rides a Panther* goes under the title of *Sarah and the Lost Friendship*. A fourth in the series is due to come off the press soon. It will be titled *Sarah and the Hidden Boy Mystery*. Books five and six have been written—and a seventh (and last) is in the planning. It will take several years before they appear."

EPPLE, Anne Orth 1927-

PERSONAL: Born February 9, 1927, in Tuckahoe, N.Y.; daughter of Albert (a fireman) and Anna (Ritter) Orth; married Lewis E. Epple (an electrical engineer), July 17, 1949; children: Lee Scott, Douglas Craig. *Education:* Attended high school in Eastchester, N.Y. *Religion:* Lutheran. *Home:* 336 Wickham Rd., Glastonbury, Ct. 06033. *Agent:* Lenniger Literary Agency, Inc., 437 Fifth Ave., New York, N.Y. 10016.

CAREER: Bronx Zoo, Bronx, N.Y., assistant in education department and school lecturer, 1946-52. *Member:* National Wildlife Federation, National Geographic Society, Evergreen Garden Club.

WRITINGS: Nature Quiz Book, Platt, 1955; *Modern Science Quiz Book*, Platt, 1958; *The Beginning Knowledge Book of Ants*, Crowell-Collier, 1969; *The Beginning Knowledge Book of Fossils*, Crowell-Collier, 1969; *The Lookalikes*, St. Martin's, 1971; *Nature Crafts*, Chilton, 1974; *Something from Nothing Crafts*, Chilton, 1976. Also ghost writer of another nature book. Contributor to *Ranger Rick's Nature Magazine*, and to other publications.

Rhamphorynchus, another flying reptile, was two feet long. Unlike Pteranodon, it had a long tail. ■ (From *The Beginning Knowledge Book of Fossils* by Anne Orth Epple. Illustrated by Raul Mina Mora.)

WORK IN PROGRESS: Several nature books and a house-plant book.

HOBBIES AND OTHER INTERESTS: Hiking, backpacking, tent-trailering, birding, photography, and all aspects of nature study. "Most recently became a National Council Flower Show student judge and am studying to become an accredited Flower Show Judge."

EPSTEIN, Anne Merrick 1931-

PERSONAL: Born October 3, 1931, in Alplaus, N.Y.; daughter of Albert William (a metallurgist) and Katherine (Walker) Merrick; married David Epstein (a musician, conductor, and composer), June 21, 1953; children: Eve, Beth. *Education:* Antioch College, A.B., 1953; graduate study at Columbia University and Art Students League of New York, 1954-56, and Wilberforce University, 1957. *Residence:* Lexington, Mass. *Agent:* Marilyn Marlow, Curtis Brown Ltd., 575 Madison Ave., New York, N.Y. 10022.

CAREER: Look, New York City, assistant in circulation promotion department, 1956-57; teacher of art and music in Enon, Ohio, 1957-61; writer. *Member:* American Society of Composers, Authors and Publishers (Writer Division). *Awards, honors:* Ford Foundation recording grant, 1976, for "Night Voices."

WRITINGS: Stone Man, Stone House, Doubleday, 1972; *Good Stones,* Houghton, 1977. Author of poetic narration for "Night Voices" (for narrator, orchestra, and children's chorus), Carl Fischer, Inc., 1979.

WORK IN PROGRESS: A novel based on a true sixteenth-century survival story.

SIDELIGHTS: "I cannot say why I began to write. I only know that reading was very important to everyone in my family. It was not unusual for me, my mother and father, as well as several of my sisters, to spend our evenings quietly reading our books. This must have given special pleasure to my mother, whose own childhood was spent in a setting where reading was considered a waste of time, if not downright sinful. I always liked to hear her describe the intricate steps she had to take in order to read a favorite book. It must have appeared to my young mind that reading (and by inference, writing) was almost a privilege.

"In my early years we had no neighbors with young children. I spent many hours alone, sometimes amusing myself by telling stories to imaginary friends. This rather lonely childhood was followed by the years of World War II, when stories of survival were told and retold, sometimes in our home by the survivors themselves. Perhaps this is why I return to themes of self-sufficiency and survival in some of my writing."

ANNE MERRICK EPSTEIN

(From *Good Stones* by Anne Merrick Epstein. Illustrated by Susan Meddaugh.)

"Camping and wilderness living seem to loom large as idea storehouses for me. Once on a family camping trip I watched my two daughters amusing themselves by building little houses out of twigs and pine cone chips. This small incident in our family's life was the seed that led to my writing *Stone Man, Stone House,* my first published book.

"Much of the setting of *Good Stones* has its source in camping trips taken in the northeast mountains when I was a child. One summer, while helping to buy supplies at a small store in a mountain town, I heard people discussing an old hermit who lived on one of the mountains. He showed himself only in the winter, they said, when he rode his toboggan into the valley and bought supplies for the year. The memory of this conversation endured for some thirty years, forming the basis for an important character in *Good Stones.*

"I would give an incorrect impression if I did not emphasize the importance of music in my life. In fact, my earliest childhood ambition was to be an opera singer! To entertain my imaginary friends I made up songs as well as stories. (It's just as well these early friends were imaginary—certainly real friends would not have put up with my 'entertainments' for long.) And so it was with special pleasure that I wrote the narration for 'Night Voices,' a commission my husband and I received from the Boston Symphony Orchestra Young People's Concerts. As I listened to my husband composing the music after I'd written the narration—an idea that just seemed to arrive, but not before I'd thrown away many pieces of scribbled paper—it was exhilarating to hear my own imagination being expanded and reshaped at the piano.

"Much of my family's life revolves around the world of music, both in our enjoyment in making and hearing music at home, and in traveling and living in Europe, where my husband conducts. During our sojourns in Europe there have been long periods when we've had only each other to rely upon. Thus we've learned to call on one another for many things, not the least of which is my request for final approval before daring to call a manuscript 'finished.'"

"Night Voices" was recorded by Vox Records in 1979.

FOR MORE INFORMATION SEE: Horn Book, August, 1977.

EWING, Kathryn 1921- (Kathryn Douglas)

PERSONAL: Born April 12, 1921, in Jenkintown, Pa.; daughter of Richard and Kathryn (Heger) Jockers; married A. Paul Webster, June 13, 1958 (died September 13, 1965); married Douglas H. Ewing (a physicist), May 15, 1969. *Education:* Studied dance privately in Philadelphia and New York City, attended drama school in Philadelphia. *Address:* Box 109, Solebury, Pa. 18963.

CAREER: Heger School, Jenkintown, Pa., teacher of dance, 1937-58; real estate broker in Bucks County, Pa., 1965-69. Member of summer stock productions, 1946-50; teacher of speech and drama at Rosemont College, 1947; writer and actress in television commercials, 1948-50.

WRITINGS: A Private Matter (novel), Harcourt, 1975; (under pseudonym Kathryn Douglas) *Cavendish Square Trilogy* (novel), Ballantine, 1976; (under pseudonym Kathryn Douglas) *The Cavendish Chronicles* (novel), Ballantine, 1979; *Things Won't be the Same* (novel), Harcourt, 1980.

KATHRYN EWING

"First, when I get an idea, I never try to make it into a story immediately. I set it to simmer on a back burner and every now and then I stir in a few questions, such as: Do I really like this idea so much that I can't stop thinking about it? Can I sort of see in my mind's eye the way the characters look? The kind of house they live in? The things they do?

"Can I sort of hear how they sound when they talk? Do I, in fact, even know a few of the things they are likely to say? Do I have some glimmer of how it will all end? And have I a strong, deep feeling about what I hope the story will mean; what it will say?

"Asking questions like the above turns up the heat a bit on that back burner. After a while things start to percolate so I stir in more questions. What, I ask, do you story people want most in the whole world? What do you hate? Whom do you love? What do you fear?

"This tends to get things bubbling like fury and just when it's about to boil over I sit down and place a big fat #1 at the top of a nice clean empty white page. And if my idea is really a good one, and if I've answered the questions as best as I can and, oh, yes, I almost forgot! if I'm a little bit lucky . . . why, lo and behold, I find I'm writing a book."

FACKLAM, Margery Metz   1927-

PERSONAL: Born September 6, 1927, in Buffalo, N.Y.; daughter of Eduard Frederick (a civil engineer) and Ruth (Schauss) Metz; married Howard F. Facklam, Jr. (a high school biology teacher), July 9, 1949; children: Thomas, David, John, Paul, Margaret. *Education:* University of Buffalo, B.A., 1947; State University College at Buffalo, M.S., 1976. *Home:* 9690 Clarence Center Rd., Clarence Center, N.Y. 14032.

The savings on most items were astonishing. Marcy always looked first for the saving earned by the extra Super Bonus coupon. But as she worked away with the scissors, she gave close attention to all the coupons.... ■ (From *A Private Matter* by Kathryn Ewing. Illustrated by Joan Sandin.)

WORK IN PROGRESS: Under pseudonym Kathryn Douglas, a novel in the "Cavendish Square series," for Ballantine.

SIDELIGHTS: "Many times a girl or boy will ask me, 'How do you get your ideas?' But of course they really know how. The answer is, just the way everyone else does, from something I see or read or hear, or perhaps OVERHEAR for I'm a shameless eavesdropper.

"Everyone gets ideas. Some lucky people get lots of good ones. I seem to get many scrawny little things scarcely worth thinking twice about. But everyone in the world recognizes that exciting moment when something connects in the brain and, like a light snapped on, THERE is an idea.

"So I think what is meant is not 'How do you get your ideas?' but 'Once you get an idea, how do you turn it into a story?' And since it's possible to go about this in several ways, I'll tell my way.

MARGERY METZ FACKLAM

This exhibit of woodland animals shows not only what a skunk looks like, but also where it lives.
■ (From *Frozen Snakes and Dinosaur Bones* by Margery Facklam. Photograph courtesy of the Buffalo Museum of Science.)

CAREER: Erie County Department of Social Welfare, Buffalo, N.Y., caseworker, 1948; high school teacher of science in Snyder, N.Y., 1949-50; Buffalo Museum of Science, Buffalo, N.Y., assistant administrator of education, 1970-74; Aquarium of Niagara Falls, Niagara Falls, N.Y., curator of education, 1974-76; Buffalo Zoo, Buffalo, N.Y., curator of education, 1976-77; free-lance children's writer, 1977—. *Member:* National League of American Pen Women, Niagara Falls Association of Professional Women Writers.

WRITINGS: Whistle for Danger, Rand McNally, 1962; *Behind These Doors,* Rand McNally, 1968; (with Patricia Phibbs) *Corn Husk Crafts,* Sterling, 1973; *Frozen Snakes and Dinosaur Bones* (Junior Literary Guild selection), Harcourt, 1976; *Wild Animals, Gentle Women* (Junior Literary Guild selection), Harcourt, 1978; (with husband, Howard Facklam) *From Cell to Clone: The Story of Genetic Engineering,* Harcourt, 1979. Contributor of articles to magazines, including *Redbook* and *Guideposts.*

SIDELIGHTS: "Some people know when they are very young that they want to be writers. I didn't, although I did love books. And one summer I edited the *Junior Journal* in our small town neighborhood. One of the things I remember best is the weekly trip to the big Victorian downtown library every Friday evening to get our reading for the week. My mother and my aunts were avid readers and I caught the bug early.

"I worked my way through college by taking care of a colony of porcupines, a job that was to open interesting jobs for me much later. I married right after college and we began to raise a family of five. I started to write when my houseful of children settled in for naps. At first, I wasn't very successful. I sold a few articles and some funny poems. Then, with our last child and only daughter crawling under the table as I typed, I wrote my first book, *Whistle for Danger,* a fictionalized account of a summer I spent working at the zoo in the reptile house.

"Then I was hooked. I was a writer. Now I write about the things that fascinate me, mostly animals and nature. When our oldest son was starting college, I returned to work, first at a science museum and then at an aquarium and a zoo. Those jobs were motherlodes of material for new books. I met people and animals I could hardly wait to write about.

"*Frozen Snakes and Dinosaur Bones* was written because I was sure that children were missing the best part of the museum, behind the scenes where the exhibits are made, skeletons put together and animals mounted.

"I love to teach and write. They are similar. When you write, you teach, only you have a bigger classroom and you reach only the people who want to know what you have to tell them.

"Writing is hard work, but it is exciting, fun, exasperating, and the most wonderful job in the world."

HOBBIES AND OTHER INTERESTS: Sailing, nature in general, animals in particular.

FOR MORE INFORMATION SEE: Buffalo Courier Express, September 16, 1962; *Junior Literary Guild Bulletin,* March, 1976, Spring, 1978.

FARRINGTON, Benjamin   1891-1974

OBITUARY NOTICE: Born July 10, 1891, in Cork, Ireland; died November 17, 1974. Classicist and author. Farrington spent twenty years as professor of classics at the University of Wales, and he was professor emeritus there for the twenty following years. Earlier university posts included Queen's University in Belfast, Northern Ireland, the University of Cape Town, and the University of Bristol. Farrington wrote extensively, among other topics, about the ancient Greek and Roman worlds, especially in their connection with the sciences. *Greek Science: Its Meaning for Us* is perhaps his most well-known work. *For More Information See: Contemporary Authors,* Volume 65-68, Gale, 1977. *Obituaries: AB Bookman's Weekly,* December 16, 1974; *Contemporary Authors,* Volume 53-56, Gale, 1975.

FARRINGTON, Selwyn Kip, Jr.   1904-

PERSONAL: Born May 7, 1904, in Orange, N.J.; son of Selwyn Kip and Josephine (Taylor) Farrington; married Sara Houston Chisholm, August 9, 1934. *Education:* Educated in New Jersey. *Politics:* Republican. *Religion:* Episcopalian. *Residence:* East Hampton, Long Island, N.Y.

CAREER: Author, lecturer, and sportsman. Worked in advertising with Kelly Nason, Inc., New York, N.Y., during 1940's; has appeared in seven motion pictures on salt water fishing. *Member:* American Society of Ichthyologists. *Awards, honors:* Order of Al Merito from Republic of Chile, 1943.

WRITINGS: Atlantic Game Fishing (illustrated by Lynn Bogue Hunt; introduction by Ernest Hemingway), Kennedy Bros., 1937; *Bill, the Broadbill Swordfish* (illustrated by Hunt), Coward-McCann, 1942; *Pacific Game Fishing* (illustrated by Hunt), Coward-McCann, 1942; *Railroading from the Head End,* Doubleday, Doran, 1943; *Giants of the Rails* (illustrated by Glen Thomas), Garden City Publishing, 1944; *Railroads at War,* Coward-McCann, 1944; *The Ducks Came*

After three weeks in the beautiful and very flat sound between these two lovely countries, Denmark and Sweden, it was not surprising that Theodora fell in love. ▪(From *Tony the Tuna* by S. Kip Farrington, Jr. Illustrated by Alexander D. "Sandy" Read.)

Back (illustrated by Hunt), Coward-McCann, 1945; *Interesting Birds of Our Country* (illustrated by Hunt), Garden City Publishing, 1945; *A Book of Fishes* (illustrated by Hunt), Blakiston, 1946; *Railroading from the Rear End,* Coward-McCann, 1946; *Ships of the U.S. Merchant Marine* (illustrated by Jack Coggins), Dutton, 1947; *Fishing the Atlantic, Offshore and On* (illustrated by Hunt), Coward-McCann, 1949; *Railroads of Today,* Coward-McCann, 1949; *Sports Fishing Boats,* W. W. Norton, 1949.

Railroading the Modern Way, Coward-McCann, 1951; *Fishing the Pacific, Offshore and On* (illustrated by Hunt), Coward-McCann, 1953; *Railroading around the World,* Coward-McCann, 1955; *Fishing with Hemingway and Glassell,* McKay, 1971; *Skates, Sticks, and Men: The Story of Amateur Hockey in the United States,* McKay, 1971; *The Santa Fe's Big Three: The Life Story of a Trio of the World's Greatest Locomotives,* McKay, 1972; *The Trail of the Sharp Cup: The Story of the Fifth Oldest Trophy in International Sports,* Dodd, 1974; *Labrador Retriever: Friend and Worker,* Hastings House, 1976; *Tony the Tuna,* Yankee Peddler, 1976; *Railroading Coast to Coast,* Hastings House, 1977.

Contributor: Eugene Virginius Connet, editor, *American Big Game Fishing,* Derrydale Press, 1935; *Fishing and Vacation Yearbook,* Garden City Publishing, 1942; *British Book of Sporting Fish,* 1947; *The Great Outdoors,* 1947.

Contributor to periodicals, including *Collier's, Cosmopolitan, Sportsman,* and *Reader's Digest.*

SIDELIGHTS: An expert fisherman, Farrington helped design the emergency fishing kits used by the U.S. Army, Navy, and Coast Guard. Farrington has held several world fishing records, and in 1937 served as captain of the U.S. team in international fishing matches in England and Cuba. During the same year, Farrington wrote his first book, *Atlantic Game Fishing.* A critic for *Saturday Review* commented that the book "is of interest to the novice as well as to the expert. . . . We feel certain that anyone who reads this book will not only enjoy its contents, but will wish to have it with him at all times, as a ready reference on the subject of big and small game fishing."

Farrington's great enthusiasm for railroads inspired him to write numerous books on the subject. In his *Railroading around the World,* Farrington examined the railroading systems outside the United States. A reviewer for the *Chicago Sunday Tribune* noted, "The author, who has written six other rail books, has a good grasp of engineering and mechanical principles. With knowledge of foreign railroading scanty in our country, his book goes a long way towards filling the gap."

HOBBIES AND OTHER INTERESTS: Saturday Review, January 1, 1938; *Chicago Tribune,* July 24, 1955.

FATCHEN, Max   1920-

PERSONAL: Born August 3, 1920, in Adelaide, South Australia; son of Cecil William (a farmer) and Isabel (Ridgway) Fatchen; married Jean Wohlers (a teacher), May 15, 1942; children: Winsome Genevieve, Michael John, Timothy James. *Education:* Attended high school in South Australia. *Religion:* Methodist. *Home address:* Jane St., Smithfield, South Australia. *Agent:* Winant, Towers Ltd., 1 Furnival

MAX FATCHEN

St., London E.C.4, England. *Office address:* c/o *Advertiser,* 121 King William St., Adelaide, South Australia.

CAREER: Adelaide News and *Sunday Mail,* Adelaide, South Australia, journalist and special writer, 1946-55; *Advertiser,* Adelaide, South Australia, special writer, 1955-71, literary editor, 1971—. *Military service:* Royal Australian Air Force, World War II. *Awards, honors: The River Kings* received a commendation and *The Spirit Wind* was a runner-up in annual book-of-the-year award of Australian Children's Book Council.

WRITINGS—Juveniles: *The River Kings,* Methuen, 1966, St. Martins, 1968; *Conquest of the River,* Methuen, 1970; *The Spirit Wind,* Methuen, 1973; *Chase Through the Night,* Methuen, 1976; *The Time Wave,* Methuen, 1978. Contributor of light verse to *Denver Post.*

WORK IN PROGRESS: A book of children's verse for Penguin, *Songs for My Dog and Other People;* a children's book about a boy's reaction to war for Methuen, *Closer to the Stars.*

SIDELIGHTS: "I was born on a hay farm at Angle Vale in South Australia. My early life revolved around the farm; I was an only child and I day-dreamed a good deal as I learnt to drive a team of eight Clydesdale horses. I liked ploughing best; the singing sound as the furrows turned, the warm Australian day, the hawks hovering as if pinned to the sky.

"Life revolved around our small church; there were tea meetings, where the tables groaned with cakes and pastries, where big men expounded their faith, and tea came from large coppers fired by logs of wood. It was this beginning that made me aware of the feeling and mood of landscape.

"Later, as a journalist I travelled in remote areas of Australia—with surveyors among the islands of the Gulf of Carpenteria, or flying with helicopter pilots across swamps where the geese rose in living carpets or past muddy estuaries, where the seagoing crocodiles, drawn up like small canoes, lifted their heads as we came down low to buzz them as we passed. But what impressed me were some of the songmen of the Aboriginal tribes I met—old men who knew the legends and who talked about them to me as we sat at night by the moonlit rivers of Arnhem Land. They taught me about the way landscape has its poetry and meaning, and when I came to write my book, *The Spirit Wind,* about a young boy who escapes from an old sailing ship in a South Australian gulf, I based the character of Nunganee (the Aboriginal who helps him) on the Aboriginal men I had met on those northern nights.

"When I travelled along the Australian river, the Murray, with old riverboat men, again the feeling of the landscape, the movement of the river, the birds that congregated in small families on the long sandspit, and the river towns tucked around the bends all found their way into my books. When I was at sea with the trawlermen, getting more stories for my paper, I watched the conflict between men and the sea, enjoyed the yarns in the fo'castle, wedged myself in the corner of the wheelhouse as the great grey-bearded waves went roaring past in the Australian bight.

"I have always liked my contact with people; the railway men on the slow outback trains, where the heat can buckle the rails; the cattle men along the Birdsville track in Australia's interior, where, at night, while your campfire flickers, you are aware of the immense, brooding land out there in the darkness under its lonely stars and its remote moon. There is a feeling of great space and light in Australia; if most of us are crowded into our cities there still remains the effect of the wide land beyond it.

"So it comes spilling out my fingers when I write. It possesses me like a spell. I like to write in images; to make pictures with words so that you can see them as I can see them.

"I want the reader to be standing beside me or running beside me, breathless with interest as we clamber up some old riverbank or hang onto a rail in the wild sea. A book is a voyage and I don't just want my readers to be passengers anxious to get off because they feel seasick with all the words, but eager members of the crew shouting, 'land ho' when we sight the islands of imagination.

"Books can deal in sad things, in bright things; stories must be honest, and honest stories are not always happy, but they can be moving, vivid, arresting, so that you never want to put them down.

"That's what I want my stories to be. Come aboard my book. We're sailing in five minutes!"

Fatchen has made two writing trips to the United States for the *Advertiser,* is "very fond of America and Americans," [and] has "warm links with Denver and the *Denver Post.*" He explains that his light verse first found its way into the

Post through a long friendship with that newspaper's former cartoonist, Pulitzer Prize-winner Pat Oliphant, who began his career on the Adelaide *Advertiser* illustrating Fatchen's lighter pieces.

FISHER, Margery (Turner)   1913-

PERSONAL: Born in 1913, in Camberwell, London, England; married James Fisher (an author, naturalist, and publisher); children: three sons, three daughters. *Education:* Attended Amberley House, Christchurch, New Zealand, and Somerville College, Oxford, holds B.Litt. and M.A. degrees. *Home:* Ashton, Northampton, England.

CAREER: Author and critic. Teacher of English at Oundle School, 1939-45; organizer of courses on reading and writing for pleasure for the National Federation of Women's Institutes. *Awards, honors:* Eleanor Farjeon Award, 1967.

WRITINGS: Field Day, Collins, 1951; (with husband, James Fisher) *Shackleton*, Barrie, 1967, published in America as *Shackleton and the Antarctic*, Houghton, 1958; (editor) *A World of Animals* (illustrated by Maurice Wilson), Brockhampton Press, 1962; *John Masefield*, H. Z. Walck, 1963; *Intent upon Reading: A Critical Appraisal of Modern Fiction for Children*, Brockhampton Press, 1961, F. Watts, 1962, revised and enlarged edition, Brockhampton Press, 1964; (editor) *Open the Doors*, World Publishing, 1965; (editor) Richard H. Horne, *Memoirs of a London Doll*, André Deutsch, 1967, Macmillan, 1968; *Henry Treece*, Bodley Head, 1969; *Matters of Fact: Aspects of Non-Fiction for*

The sturdy little *Nimrod* was to meet a more serious danger in the next few days than any she might meet on the homeward voyage. ■ (From *Shackleton and the Antarctic* by Margery and James Fisher. Illustrated by W.E. How.)

Children, Crowell, 1972; *Who's Who in Children's Books*, Holt, 1975.

Also editor, sole writer, and publisher of a periodical of continuing reviews of children's books, *Growing Point*, beginning, 1962.

SIDELIGHTS: "I have always been determined to be a writer since I made magazines for my teddy bears when I was six, but initially thought of myself as a novelist. Publishers thought otherwise. I am an obsessive reader and only exert myself physically in the garden because I like growing vegetables. Music is my chief interest outside books—listening, singing and playing the piano. Eleven grandchildren keep me in touch with children's tastes up to a point."

One of Fisher's most noteworthy contributions to literature is her book, *Intent upon Reading: A Critical Appraisal of Modern Fiction for Children*. A reviewer for the *New York Herald Tribune* commented that within the text "... Mrs. Fisher's enthusiasm for the finest books is very evident and no one interested in children's books can afford to miss her perceptive comments...." The reviewer, however, did criticize Fisher for the book lists she compiled at the end of each chapter, suggesting, "It would have been better to list only those books enthusiastically presented...." The history and criticism of nonfiction children's books was covered in one of the author's latest pieces of work, *Matter of Fact: Aspects of Non-Fiction for Children*. A *Horn Book* reviewer wrote, "The ... chapters are ... ample and alive with enthusiasm, sharp opinions, judicious comparisons, and pertinent quotations."

FOR MORE INFORMATION SEE: Brian Doyle, editor, *Who's Who of Children's Literature*, Schocken Books, 1968; *Horn Book*, April, 1970, February, 1973, June, 1976.

MARGERY FISHER

But the bees went around the house and started flying through the window into her room, all waiting for their turn to get at her petals. ∎(From *Rotten Snags! Rotten Hair!* by Dale Fitschen. Illustrated by Marilyn Fitschen.)

FITSCHEN, Dale 1937-

PERSONAL: Born October 13, 1937, in St. Louis, Mo.; son of Jacob J. and Flora (Freihaut) Fitschen; married Marilyn Olsen (an artist and illustrator), February 10, 1962; children: Romy, Jean-Claire, Samantha. *Education:* Washington University, St. Louis, Mo., B.A., 1960; also attended Roosevelt University, 1960-62, and University of Chicago, 1962-65. *Home:* 1029 South Clinton, Oak Park, Ill. 60304. *Office:* Regional Transportation Authority, Marina City, Chicago, Ill. 60601.

CAREER: Victor Rouse Associates, Chicago, Ill., urban planner, 1972-73; Chicago Transportation Authority, Chicago, transportation planner, 1973-75; Regional Transportation Authority, Chicago, transportation planner, 1975—. Founder of local Co-Op Kindergarten, 1970; president and founder of Co-Op Elementary School #3, 1971-78; member of South Shore Food Co-Op and Co-Op Gardens, both 1974—.

WRITINGS: (Illustrated by wife, Marilyn Fitschen) *Rotten Snags, Rotten Hair!* (juvenile), Follett, 1975.

WORK IN PROGRESS: Five children's books.

SIDELIGHTS: Fitschen commented that he has been reading and telling stories to his children for ten years and they were the ones who persuaded him and their mother to write books.

HOBBIES AND OTHER INTERESTS: Literature, the outdoors, gardening, game playing.

FITZGERALD, Edward Earl 1919-

PERSONAL: Born September 10, 1919, in New York, N.Y.; son of Francis J. and Mary Leona (Morgan) Fitzgerald; married Libuse P. Ostruk, June 6, 1942; children: Eileen Frances, Kevin Paul. *Home:* 26 Claudet Way, Eastchester, N.Y. 10709. *Office:* 280 Park Ave., New York, N.Y. 10017.

CAREER: Author and editor. Reporter, Westchester County Publications, Inc., 1937-42; editor, Macfadden Publications, Inc., 1946-60; *Sport* magazine, editor-in-chief, 1951-60, editorial director men's group, 1952-60, assistant to the president, 1958-60; editor-in-chief, Literary Guild of America, 1960-64; Doubleday & Co., vice-president, general manager of book club division, 1964-68; president, chief executive officer, McCall Publishing Co., 1968-71; vice-president, Book-of-the-Month Club, Inc., 1971—. *Military service:* U.S. Army, 1942-46. *Member:* Overseas Press Club.

WRITINGS: (With Lou Boudreau) *Player-Manager,* Little, Brown, 1949, revised edition, 1952; *College Slugger,* A. S. Barnes, 1950; *Yankee Rookie,* A. S. Barnes, 1952, reprinted, Grosset & Dunlap, 1961; *Champions in Sports and Spirit* (illustrated by De Wolfe Hotchkiss), Farrar, Straus, 1956; *The Ballplayer,* A. S. Barnes, 1957; *More Champions in Sports and Spirit* (illustrated by H. Lawrence Hoffman), Vision Books, 1959; *Johnny Unitas: The Amazing Success Story of Mr. Quarterback,* Nelson, 1961; (with Yogi Berra) *Yogi: The Autobiography of a Professional Baseball Player,* Doubleday, 1961; (with Mel Allen) *You Can't Beat the Hours: A Long, Loving Look at Big-League Baseball, Including Some*

(From *Champions in Sports and Spirit* by Ed Fitzgerald. Illustrated by De Wolfe Hotchkiss.)

Yankees I Have Known, Harper, 1964; (with John Unitas) *Pro Quarterback: My Own Story,* Simon & Schuster, 1965.

Editor: *Tales for Males,* Cadillac, 1945; *Kick-Off!,* Bantam Books, 1948; *The Turning Point,* A. S. Barnes, 1948; *The Story of the Brooklyn Dodgers* (with an introduction by Red Barber), Bantam Books, 1949; *The Book of Major League Baseball Clubs,* A. S. Barnes, 1952; *A Treasury of Sport Stories,* Bartholomew House, 1955; *The National League,* Grosset & Dunlap, 1959, revised edition, 1966; *The American League,* Grosset & Dunlap, 1959, revised edition, 1966.

SIDELIGHTS: The *New York Times* review of Edward Fitzgerald's *Yankee Rookie* included, "This young rookie, with his love for his parents, his over-eagerness at bat, his desire not to be thought high-hat, acts and talks like a real person. Swift action, tense situations and personal crises combine to make this an exciting story." The *San Francisco Chronicle* noted, "Filled with baseball lore, the book also paints a vivid picture of a young man's struggles to reach the top in the sport he loves."

FOR MORE INFORMATION SEE: New York Times, November 16, 1952; *San Francisco Chronicle,* November 16, 1952, March 31, 1957; *New Yorker,* March 30, 1957; *New York Times Book Review,* June 7, 1964.

FITZGERALD, John D(ennis) 1907-

PERSONAL: Born in 1907, in Utah.

CAREER: Author. His career includes stints as a foreign correspondent and jazz drummer; his first book, *Papa Married a Mormon,* was published in 1955, and it is primarily a reminiscence of his life in Utah when it was still a territory. It was received widely enough to have been published in England and Germany, and several more such books followed. In 1967 the first of his "Great Brain" series, stories based on his own Utah boyhood with his brother Tom, was published. *Awards, honors:* Pacific Northwest Library Association Young Readers' Choice Award, 1976, for *Great Brain Reforms;* Surrey School Book of the Year Award, 1976, for *Me and My Little Brain.*

WRITINGS—For children: *The Great Brain* (illustrated by Mercer Mayer), Dial, 1967; *More Adventures of the Great Brain* (illustrated by Mayer), Dial, 1969; *Me and My Little Brain* (illustrated by Mayer), Dial, 1971; *The Great Brain at the Academy* (illustrated by Mayer), Dial, 1972; *Brave Buffalo Fighter (Waditaka Tatahka Kisisohitika)* (illustrated by John Livesay), Independence Press, 1973; *The Great Brain Reforms* (illustrated by Mayer), Dial, 1973; *Private Eye,* T. Nelson, 1974; *The Return of the Great Brain* (illustrated by Mayer), Dial, 1974; *The Great Brain Does It Again* (illustrated by Mayer), Dial, 1975.

Other: *Papa Married a Mormon* (memoir), Prentice-Hall, 1955; *Mamma's Boarding House* (memoir), Prentice-Hall, 1958; *Uncle Will and the Fitzgerald Curse* (memoir), Bobbs-Merrill, 1961; (with Robert C. Meredith) *The Professional Story Writer and His Art,* Crowell, 1963; (with Meredith) *Structuring Your Novel: From Basic Idea to Finished Manuscript,* Barnes & Noble, 1972.

SIDELIGHTS: **1907.** Born in Utah. "As a child I feared and resented Papa before I loved him. My earliest recollection of him was a tall man with black curly hair who came home at a certain time on week days and remained home all day on Sundays. I was afraid of him because he always picked me up and tossed me toward the ceiling, catching me as I came down. I was certain that one day he would miss and I'd get hurt. I resented him because when he came home we had to share Mama with him. She was always there to love us, settle our little quarrels, doctor our bruises, kiss away our tears and no matter what she was doing would stop to listen to anything we had to say.

"But the minute Papa came home everything changed. She'd meet him with a kiss. They would hold hands while they talked for a few minutes. She would walk with him to his rocking chair and fuss over him, lighting his pipe or cigar. She'd sit on his lap or the arm of the rocking chair and stroke his hair while they whispered and laughed.

"She'd ignore us children while this was going on. I remember I pretended to fall one time and let out a lusty cry of pain. If Papa hadn't been home, Mamma would have taken me in her arms, inspected my bruise and made me well with a kiss. Instead she merely said, 'John D., you aren't hurt and you know it. Now be quiet.'

"In time I learned to tolerate Papa, then enjoy him, and later to love him very much.

"We children called two people Aunt and Uncle who weren't related to us. One was Uncle Mark, who was Marshal of West Adenville; the other was Aunt Bertha. She came into our lives the day she walked into the office of *The Advocate* [father's newspaper], plunked down her carpetbag and introduced herself in a thick New England accent.

"'Name's Bertha Tuttle. The widow Tuttle. You be Tom Fitzgerald, I reckon.' As Papa got up from his desk, she continued, 'Hail from down Vermont way. Been cooking in the camp boarding house at Castle Rock, nigh on to four years now. Jest buried my husband—that be Mr. Tuttle—t'other day.'

"Papa shook his head. 'I'm sorry to learn of your bereavement, Mrs. Tuttle.'

"''Twas God's will. 'Twere jest a question of time afore God called him. Mr. Tuttle was a consumptive. That's how I brung him out here. Doc Brayton, that be young Doc Brayton, Old Doc died some time ago, 'lowed as how Mr. Tuttle might live a little longer if I brung him out West. I did and I cared fer him. And now the good Lord has called him.'

"Papa was perplexed. 'I'm sorry about your husband's death. Do you want me to print Mr. Tuttle's obituary?'

"''Twould be right nice of you, but t'aint the reason I'm here. Mr. Tuttle and I aren't blessed with any young 'uns. Now he's passed away, a mining camp ain't a fit place fer a respectable widow. Bertha, I says to myself, find yourself a good family that needs you as much as you need them. Mr. Tuttle used to read that paper of your'n and he'd say, "Bertha, the man who wrote that editorial is a good man." So I asks around and found you to be a Catholic married to a Mormon. And I says to myself, t'ain't no never mind if a Methodist joins a family like that.'

"'But—' Papa tried to protest.

"'Ain't no other way, Mr. Fitzgerald. Ain't got kith nor kin back East. Can't live alone in a mining camp. Ain't no place for a respectable widow. If it be money, fergit it. It ain't dignified to be a servant. All I be wantin' is a home and be makin' myself useful.'

"'But my wife might object,' Papa said, though he couldn't help smiling.

"'Ain't no woman in her right mind objects havin' help around a house, especially when there's four young 'uns. I ain't the imposin' kind, Mr. Fitzgerald, but I already told them to send my trunk from the railway station to your house. I'll stay one month. Then if you or your Missus be of a mind I should leave, there won't be nary an argument.'

"And that was how Aunt Bertha came to live at our house, where she remained until she died at the age of seventy-nine. During all that time she refused to accept any wages. She would charge material for clothes to Papa's account at the General Store. When she needed cash she'd take it from the extra sugar bowl in the kitchen cabinet and tell Mamma how much she'd taken.

"Aunt Bertha was a hulking woman who towered over Mamma. She had big hands and big feet like a man's, soft grey eyes, and big lips from which, strangely for a big woman, came a high pitched voice. She had the first false teeth I'd ever seen and was often misplacing them. Then the whole family would have to hunt until they were found before we could sit down to eat.

''The only quarrel Mamma ever had with Aunt Bertha was shortly after the big woman came to live with us. Mamma really laid down the law to Aunt Bertha that day and they were devoted to each other the rest of their lives. To understand the quarrel it is necessary for me to explain my childhood recollections of God and religion. I remember well the Sunday evenings after supper when Papa read from the Bible and Mamma read to us from the Book of Mormon. I remember the singing of the hymns and the fact that I was very partial to the Mormon hymns because to me the louder you sang them, the better they sounded. I remember Papa saying the Rosary and how all of us would then say the Latter-Day Saint version of the Lord's Prayer. I remember the Mormon Primary, where simple Bible stories were read to us and we were taught to make little gifts for our parents. I do not recall a single instance during the years I went to Primary when any Latter-Day Saint religious beliefs or tenets were introduced into the lessons.

''To me, Jesus Christ and Christmas were synonymous. The cutting of the tree, the stringing of popcorn and cranberries, the pink stockings Mamma made for us pinned to the tablecloth around our dining-room table, and all the wonder of it. Each year Papa would read to us the story of the Nativity and it always made me cry as I thought of the little Jesus in the manger. Christ to me was all things beautiful, like the snow on the ground, the birds singing in the trees, the petal of a rose, the sunset, the rainbow after a storm.

''But God was difficult for me to understand. The God that Papa and Mamma told me about was a friendly, kind, generous God who loved everybody because God was love. God loved all children so much he sent a personal Guardian Angel to watch over each one. When Papa told me about my Guardian Angel, he pointed at my left shoulder and said, 'He is sitting right there on your shoulder, J. D., where he can hear and watch everything you do. He knows everything you think. He will tell you without speaking when you are doing something that will make God cry. He'll report every good thing you do and every bad thing you do to God, who will write it all down in a big book. God sent him to watch over you. He will guard you from harm. And if you are good, when you die, he will show you the way to Heaven.'

''And even today when I say or do something I know God wouldn't approve, I find myself glancing with anxiety and embarrassment at my left shoulder.

''I found my Guardian Angel very tolerant with little boys. He didn't say a word when I gleefully entered into the conspiracy of driving Old Lady Miller [a neighbor] crazy. Later, when she became one of our family's dearest friends, I realized that my Guardian Angel had known all along how it would turn out.

''The God my parents told me about gave me a warm and cozy feeling deep inside. He was the Father of all the people. When I said or did anything I knew God wouldn't approve, I felt the same way as I did when I said or did anything that would hurt Mamma or Papa. The God I loved was very compassionate and would forgive me if I prayed to Him. I was never afraid of Him. I couldn't understand when I'd hear some kid's mother say to him, 'If you do that again, God will punish you.' I asked Mamma about this and she told me that God never punished anyone because God was love.

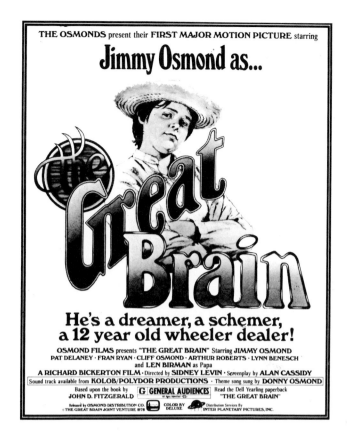

A 1978 advertisement for the movie, "The Great Brain."

''My brother Tom was the cause of the first and only quarrel Mamma and Aunt Bertha ever had. Katie, who was afraid to sleep alone and had always slept with Mamma until Aunt Bertha came, was terribly afraid of harmless little garter snakes. Aunt Bertha caught Tom putting a garter snake in the bed she shared with Katie. She grabbed Tom by the ear and shouted so loud that Mamma could hear downstairs, 'Do you want to burn in everlasting Hell? God will punish you if you ever do the likes of that again.'

''Mamma rushed upstairs. 'Don't you ever dare speak to my children that way. Don't you ever dare to threaten any of my children with God's punishment. I've taught my children to believe that God is love and not some terrible monster that goes around punishing little children.'

''Tom received three days' silent treatment for punishment. I remember the many times I wished that Papa and Mamma would just give us a good whipping and get it over with instead of the terrible silent treatment. The punishment might last for one day or even a week. During this time neither Papa nor Mamma would speak to us. They would pretend that we didn't exist. Even while we were eating, if we asked one of them to pass something, they pretended they didn't hear.

''I remember I was confused about Heaven and Hell until I asked Papa about it. He leaned back in his rocking chair and puffed on his pipe for a moment. 'Try to remember the happiest and most joyful moment in your life, J. D. When you go to Heaven, you feel that way all the time. Now, try to remember the unhappiest and saddest moment in your life. That is the way it is in Hades all the time.'

"I didn't question Papa's description of Heaven and Hell, because when I got a little older, I'd hear people say, 'This is heavenly,' when they were happy; and they always said, 'This is Hell,' when they were unhappy or sad.

"I remained confused about God even after Aunt Cathie came out West to make us into good Catholics. She began teaching us the Cathechism and told us that God was Three Persons. For a long time, I thought of the Father as being the Father of all the people, and the Son as being the Father of good people like us, and the Holy Ghost as being the God of the people who said he'd punish their children.

"I enjoyed the Mormon Primary on Saturday afternoons, until Aunt Cathie arrived. I liked listening to the Bible stories, making things, being with my playmates, and the ice cream, cookies, homemade candy, popcorn balls and other treats they used to serve us. I had lots of fun acting in the plays and taking part in some of the portrayals of Bible stories.

"Sweyn was baptized a Mormon when he was eight years of age and had reached the age of reason. Tom was also baptized a Mormon. Katie and I never were baptized as Mormons, because Katie was so terribly afraid of water she got hysterical when they tried to get her down to the creek. As for me, my Aunt Cathie came West before I was eight years old.

"A Sunday dinner with fewer than five guests was a novelty in our house. In those days we called the meal dinner, and it was eaten at two o'clock sharp in the afternoon. The extra leaves for the big oak dining table would accommodate eighteen people. The children always ate first with Mamma's everyday dishes. After the table was cleared, Mamma would put on her real Irish linen tablecloth with napkins to match; remove the cut-glass tumblers from the dining-room buffet, with the matching water pitcher and bowls; open the china closet and take out her set of Haviland china. Last she'd place a bowl of fruit in the center of the table.

"They were a strange mixture of people who sat beneath the chandelier with its multi-colored pieces of glass which used to tinkle when there was a draft in the room.

"Mamma never knew and Papa would forget how many people he'd invited during the week to come for Sunday dinner. We children liked it when Henry Dussiere, his wife and their son Pierre came, because Mr. Dussiere would bring his accordion, and he and his wife would sing lilting songs in their native Basque. We could not understand a word but we would laugh and laugh because they sounded so funny. The sheepmen and cattlemen would always ask us children to get out the leather sacks containing our gold pieces. They would have us pile the gold pieces up on the floor with the two-dollar-and-a-half pieces in one pile, the five-dollar pieces in another pile. Then they would say that one pile looked a little low and give each of us a gold piece to place upon it.

"Sometimes Papa would bring the Chief of an Indian tribe to the house. Mamma would insist she be warned in advance because the Chiefs thought that because they were invited as guests they could have anything in the house. They would go around and point and grunt and pick up anything that struck their fancy.

"Uncle Will, Hal Gentry, Judge Baker, Uncle Mark and sometimes Windy Davis came regularly for Sunday dinner.

We would watch out the front window, and when Tom saw Judge Baker coming, he'd shout: 'Here comes old cherry nose. If the Indians cut off his nose all he'd have to do would be to stick a cherry on it and nobody would know the difference.'

"How I loved it when Uncle Mark, Uncle Will, Marshal Gentry and Judge Baker came. That meant we could listen to them talk about the ghost town of Silverlode and all the bad men who had lived there.

"After dinner we'd often change back into our everyday clothes. We'd keep looking at Uncle Will until finally he'd say, 'Marshal Gentry and Marshal Trainor, I believe there's a band of outlaws headed this way.'

"Tom, Sweyn and I, our arms loaded with empty bottles and cans, would lead the parade to the creek. We'd place the bottles and cans on logs and in the crotches of trees. Then we'd get behind a log and start screaming. 'Thar's Blackie Dalton sticking his head over that thar log.' Uncle Will's pearl-handled pistol would boom, and the can or bottle representing the outlaw would go flying through the air. 'Look out, Marshal,' I'd scream, 'Lefty Lammons is hidin' in that thar tree.' Either Uncle Mark or Marshal Gentry would draw their guns and another outlaw would bite the dust. We'd remain until the cans and bottles representing the outlaw band had been decimated. When we returned, Mamma would gently scold Uncle Will. He'd smile at her and say, 'I'm sorry, Princess, but that gang of desperadoes meant to take over the town. We barely stopped in time.'

"Once I asked Uncle Will why he called Mamma Princess. 'Your father,' he said, 'like any Irishman worth his salt, claims to be descended from the Kings of Ireland, though between you and me, John, this is pure blarney. But your mother is descended from the Kings of Denmark who beat the pants off the English, which was something the Irish never did do.'

"For many years after, I thought that wars were fought by soldiers beating other soldiers with sticks until their pants fell off.

"I remember how I couldn't believe the miracle when faucets were put into our sink and the water pump removed. To be able to get water without pumping was a mystery to me. An even greater miracle was the big twelve-foot kitchen range Papa bought, and hooked the water tank into it. To be able to get hot water right out of the tap instead of heating it in the big copper-bottomed wash tubs was unbelievable.

"One day I entered the bathroom from the back porch right after Grandma had left it after taking a bath. I'd been playing cowboys and Indians, and when I saw Grandma's wig on the chair, I picked it up and ran into the kitchen screaming, 'Poor Grandma, the Indians done scalped her.'

"Mamma stopped stirring some cake batter and took the wig from me. 'John D.,' she said firmly, 'you must promise me you'll never tell anyone about this.'

"Grandma came into the kitchen with a towel wrapped around her head. 'Grandma Elizabeth,' I blurted out in breathless admiration, 'were you really scalped by the Indians?'

(From the movie "The Great Brain," starring Jimmy Osmond. Released by Osmond Distribution Co., 1978.)

"She laughed and tousled my hair with her fingers. 'Let me put it this way, John, I lost all my hair crossing the plains.'

"I knew she was just being modest. 'Can I see the scars, Grandma, please?'

"She laughed again. 'I'm afraid they are all healed. It was a long, long time ago.' She removed the towel and bent over so I could see her bald head, as Mamma said, 'Mother, please! How could you?'

"I stared in fascination at Grandma's bald head. Finally I summoned the courage to reach out and touch it. 'Gee,' I said with admiration, 'I'll betcha there isn't anybody got a Grandma who's been scalped by the Indians, like me.'

"'John D.,' Mamma said severely, 'please refrain from using the word "betcha." And, young man, you listen very carefully to what Mamma is going to say. You must promise never to tell anyone that Grandma wears a wig.'

"I promised, but I broke my word at my next birthday party.

" . . . All my playmates came to our house. There were cakes, cookies and ice cream. I opened all my presents. It was winter time and so we began playing games in the house like Heavy, heavy hangs over my poor head; Button, button whose got the button; Hide the thimble, and other childhood amusements which seemed so much fun then. When we grew tired of playing games, we began what to most of us was the best game of all, bragging about our families and possessions.

"I was a little jealous of Frank Davis, who was about a year older than I. The other kids including the girls acted as if he was some kind of a hero. 'There ain't a smarter sheep dog than my dog Shep,' he said. Nobody could deny it.

"I said, 'Don't say "ain't," Frank. You should say "isn't." My Papa is the best educated man in Adenville and has a college diploma to prove it.'

"But my friends weren't interested in academics. 'My Paw,' Frank boasted, 'is the best sheep shearer in the world.'

''Harold McKnight spoke up. 'My Paw's the best bronco buster in the world.'

''Eddie Andrews the son of the blacksmith threw out his chest. 'My Paw is the strongest man in the world.'

''The girls entered the bragging contest. Jane Prudy said her mother made the best pies in the world and that was why she won all the blue ribbons at the county fair.

''It was my birthday and I felt cheated. I was desperate. I held up my hands for attention. 'My Grandma Elizabeth was scalped by Indians,' I said defiantly.

''I gloried in their open-mouthed astonishment.

''Finally Frank Davis challenged me, 'You're fibbing, John and you know it.'

'''I am not,' I shouted back at him. 'I saw and felt Grandma's head. She hasn't got a hair on it. She was scalped by the Indians when crossing the plains and I'll prove it next time she visits us.'

''They all crowded around me. I had become the most envied and popular boy in West Adenville by virtue of Grandma's bald head.

''I enjoyed my new-found fame for weeks, but I began to worry about it as the weather got better and I knew Grandma and Grandpa Neilsen would soon be coming to visit us. The skeptics among my friends kept asking my brothers when Grandma and Grandpa Neilsen were coming. They knew almost as soon as I did when the news reached Mamma that my grandparents would arrive the following Saturday.

''In desperation, I took my problem to Tom, who consented to devote his great brain to conceiving a plan that would get me off the hook providing I paid his price. The price was high. I had to promise to do all his chores for a month, give him my braided leather whip and fifteen cents in cash.

''The day Grandpa and Grandma Neilsen drove into town a dozen kids followed them right up to the gate of our corral. My friends all crowded around me and demanded to know when I'd prove Grandma had been scalped by the Indians. I ran into the barn and hollered up to the loft to Tom. He came down the rope ladder. 'Stop worrying, J. D.,' he said. 'My great brain will save the day for you. Listen carefully.'

''I was wide-eyed with admiration for my brother's great brain. I am afraid I let my enthusiasm run away with me. I not only challenged the skeptics to be on hand for Grandma's unveiling, but also issued invitations to almost every kid in town. Long before curtain time, kids began lining up along the picket fence across our front yard.

''Grandpa and Grandma Neilsen were right on schedule. Since they always came out and sat on our front porch for about an hour before supper time, my brother's great brain had to figure out a way of allaying any suspicions they might have had concerning the large number of kids along the fence. Pete Hanson, who was the best squaw wrestler in town for his age, was on our front lawn. One by one he was challenging all the kids to wrestle him. At the count of one they would raise their right legs, while lying on their backs. At the count of two they would lock legs. At the count of three they would see who could push his opponent's leg down. Pete won every time.

''My brother Tom opened the screen on our upstairs window and crept to the edge of our front porch. When he was ready he gave me the signal by whistling like a whippoorwill. The sight of my brother on the roof over our porch and the kids lined up against the fence attracted the attention of several adults.

''I walked over and challenged Pete to wrestle. At the count of one we raised our legs, at the count of two we locked them, at the count of three, Pete following instructions put all his strength into the move and sent me tumbling head over heels. I immediately grabbed my leg and began to bawl. 'It's broke. My leg is broke.'

''Grandma Elizabeth was out of the porch swing at the first yelp. As she came running from the porch, my brother Tom on the roof expertly swung a fish line with a hook on it and snatched Grandma's wig right off her head. She was so intent on her supposedly injured grandchild she didn't even know it.

''My brother beat a hasty retreat back through the window, out the back window, down a tree and to the barn where he expected to establish a perfect alibi.

''All the kids along the fence began screaming, 'Look! Look! It's true. She's been scalped by the Indians.'

''I shivered with fright as I saw Grandpa coming, the wig in his hands. Then I heard Grandma laugh. She'd found there was nothing wrong with me and had seen Grandpa holding the wig. She pulled me to my feet. 'I hope, John, that the childhood treasures you charged for this exhibition were worth it.'

'''But Grandma,' I protested, 'I didn't charge anything. Honest Injun, I didn't. They wouldn't believe me when I told them you had been scalped by the Indians.'

''Grandma took the wig from Grandpa. 'You boys asked for proof, now you've seen it,' she said to the kids lining the fence.

''Frank Davis jumped up and down waving his arms and shouting, 'Hurrah for Grandma Neilsen!' The rest of the kids took up the cheering.

''Grandma bowed to them and said, 'Thank you, boys.' Swinging the wig by her side she walked back and into the house with the cheers of the audience ringing in her ears. What she said gave me a place in the hall of fame for years to come. I looked at Grandpa, who was now smiling, and placed my hand in his.

'''Gosh Grandpa,' I said reverently, 'I'll betcha I got the most wonderful Grandma in the world.'

''Grandpa squeezed my hand. 'I'll betcha you have, John. At least I have thought so for many, many years.'

''When Mamma heard about it, she knew that only Tom's great brain could have conceived the plan. But Grandma wouldn't let her punish my brother or me.

''For the remainder of my childhood whenever my playmates began to brag about their parents or relatives, I just remained quiet. I knew that sooner or later some kid would say, 'Shucks, that ain't nothing. John's Grandma was scalped by real Indians.'

"I carried my fame with dignity. I'd nod my head and modestly admit that while Grandpa Neilsen was killing twenty Indians, other Indians grabbed Grandma and tied her to the stake. They scalped her before Grandpa could kill twenty-seven more Indians and rescue her.

"I was eight years old when I made my first Holy Communion. We set out for Castle Rock one Saturday morning so we could go to Confession. Mamma didn't go with us, but she prepared three shoe boxes filled with fried chicken, hard boiled eggs, sandwiches, cookies and cake.

"Castle Rock was a big disappointment to me. The buildings, the vegetation, even the people, all seemed to be covered with coal dust. Everything looked dirty except the inside of the church. On one side of the altar was a life-sized statue of the Blessed Virgin and Child. On the opposite side was a statue of the patron saint of the church, St. Joseph. I was frightened when I entered the confessional, but under Father Caffarella's guidance I got along fine. I fell asleep on the ride back to West Adenville. Mamma and Aunt Bertha had a big supper waiting for us because we couldn't eat anything from midnight until after Holy Communion the next morning.

"At five o'clock in the morning we got up and dressed in our new clothes. Katie had a white dress Mamma made for her and she looked like an angel in it with her long white lace veil. Sweyn had already made his first Holy Communion. Aunt Cathie wanted Tom, Earnie [adopted brother], Katie and me to make ours together.

"During the drive to Castle Rock I wasn't aware of my own thirst and hunger until Tom started complaining. Aunt Cathie kept shushing him, but he just kept on complaining that he was slowly and surely dying of thirst and hunger. Remembering how they always gave us ice cream and cake at the Mormon Primary, Tom finally blurted out, 'I know now what the difference is between the Mormons and the Catholics.'

"'And what is that, Thomas?' Aunt Cathie asked, no doubt expecting Tom to speak of the advantages of Catholicism.

"'The Mormons feed you and the Catholics starve you,' my brother replied. Papa laughed, but Aunt Cathie was quite angry.

"My first Holy Communion seemed the most wonderful and inspiring thing that ever happened to me. The pageantry, the glory, the sacredness of the Mass and Communion brought me extreme ecstasy. My childish mind kept comparing the austerity of the Mormon services with the pomp and ceremony of the Catholic Mass. I cried when it was all over.

"Papa treated us to a surprise by taking us all to the town's only restaurant for breakfast. On the way back home, Sweyn, Katie, Earnie and I kept talking about how beautiful and wonderful the Mass and Communion had been. Tom just sat staring at the road.

"Mamma had a big chicken dinner waiting for us when we returned. After eating, we had to take a nap because of the early hour we'd got up. When we woke up we went out to play until supper time, except Tom, who sat in the parlor reading his almanac.

"Mamma and Aunt Bertha washed the supper dishes. Aunt Cathie never helped with any of the dishes or housework.

When Mamma and Aunt Bertha came into the parlor, Tom walked over to Mamma.

"'Mamma,' he said looking up at her, 'let's sing some hymns like we used to on Sunday nights before Aunt Cathie came.'

"Aunt Cathie spoke quickly. 'You're a Catholic now, Junior, and soon you will learn how to sing Catholic hymns in Latin as well as English.'

"Tom ignored her. 'Please Mamma, let's sing "Come, Come Ye Saints."'

"'Your Aunt Cathie was speaking to you, Tom D.,' Mamma said.

"Tom shrugged. 'You must be mistaken, Mamma. My name isn't Junior. And she's got no right to tell me what to do and what not to do. She isn't my Mamma. I don't like her and I wish she'd go back where she came from and leave us alone.'

"Aunt Cathie got up and marched across the room. 'If you can't teach your children manners, Tena,' she said sharply,

"Did you say something?" Sally Anne asked. Again they went through that did you say something, no, I didn't say anything, did you say something, business.
■ (From *The Return of the Great Brain* by John D. Fitzgerald. Illustrated by Mercer Mayer.)

'I will.' She grabbed Tom by the ear and spun him around. It was a silly thing to do because Tom drew back his foot and kicked her on the shins.

"Aunt Cathie let out a shriek. She pointed at Tom. 'This is the Godless one. This is the lost one of this generation. Just like Uncle Sean and brother Will. I demand that you punish him, Thomas.'

"Before Papa could answer, Mamma spoke up. 'Cathie, if you ever lay a hand on any of my children or Earnest again, you'll have to leave my house. That the boy kicked you was wrong, but you provoked him into it. I have consented to your supervising the spiritual upbringing of my children, but I, and I alone, shall supervise their moral and physical upbringing.'

"Papa seemed to grow suddenly very old and weary. Finally he spoke, 'Tena is right, Cathie.' Then he motioned to Tom. 'Come here, T. D.'

"Tom squared his shoulders and walked over to Papa. 'There is something that you and you alone can decide, T. D.,' Papa said. 'Your mother and I agreed that we would let each child choose his or her own religion. You are old enough to think for yourself. Think hard, T. D. Would you rather not become a Catholic?'

"'That's insane,' Aunt Cathie shouted, 'allowing a mere boy to make a decision like that.'

"Papa looked sternly at Aunt Cathie. 'Be quiet, please,' he said. Then he looked at Tom.

"Tom didn't flinch. 'I want to be a Mormon like Mamma and all my friends,' he said.

"'Would you mind telling me why, T. D.?' Papa asked.

"Tom didn't hesitate. 'There's a lot of reasons, Papa. If being a Catholic makes people like Aunt Cathie, I don't want to be like her. I don't like not being able to understand what the priest is saying. In the Latter-Day Saints church I can understand everything Bishop Aden says. I don't like the Catholic God as much as I do the Mormon God.'

"'But T. D.,' Papa protested, 'there is only one God.'

"Tom shook his head. 'The Mormon God doesn't get angry at people who laugh and have fun, but Aunt Cathie's God gets mad if you even smile.' He stepped back and pointed his finger at Aunt Cathie. 'Before she came here we were happy. Even Aunt Bertha was happy, and she's a Methodist. We read the Bible and the Book of Mormon on Sundays. We sang all kinds of hymns and nobody said you could only sing one kind. We weren't afraid of God and we believed that He loved us all. We prayed to God and didn't have to worry about saying only certain words. Now Aunt Cathie has brought her nasty old God here and He gets mad at anybody who dares to smile. Nobody sings, or laughs in our house any more. Mamma and Aunt Bertha used to always be singing, laughing and happy. Now nobody dares because Aunt Cathie's God will get mad if they do. You can do what you want with me, Papa, but I'm not going to be a Catholic. I'm going to the Latter-Day Saint Sunday school and I'm going to be a Mormon.'

"Aunt Cathie pointed at Mamma. 'Tena has poisoned the boy's mind against me.'

"Papa looked at Aunt Cathie. I'd never seen him so angry. 'That is the cruelest and most unjust remark I have ever heard.' Papa stood up, and this time he pointed at Aunt Cathie. 'How dare you say such a lie about my wife! Go to your room. Pray to God to forgive you for the manner in which you have distorted His divinity to a child. I'll never permit you to force religion upon my children. Their faith in religion must come from within.'

"Aunt Cathie's eyes blazed. 'How dare you speak to your own sister in this manner? All the boy needs is a good old-fashioned whipping.'

"Papa's voice was hoarse as he said, 'Go to your room, Cathie, before I say things I may later regret.'

"Aunt Cathie left the room and Papa sat down again. He looked at Tom. 'My son,' he said and must have been very moved to call Tom anything but T. D., 'I have been very unjust to you and your mother. I just want to impress on you two things. First, that there is only one God and He is the Father of all the people. Second, that you do not judge all Catholics by your Aunt Cathie. I am a Catholic. Now,' Papa looked around the room, 'we will spend our Sunday evening as we did before Aunt Cathie came here. The first hymn we will sing will be "Come, Come Ye Saints."'

"And that was how my brother Tom decided to be a Mormon. Sweyn, Katie, Earnie and I remained Catholics.

"I cannot remember a time during my childhood when we had fewer than four dogs, and sometimes we had as many as ten. Every time any bitch in town had a litter of pups you could almost bet that one or more would end up at our home. Mamma found homes for the dogs with sheepmen and cattlemen and ranchers who visited us.

"I learned a very important lesson about dogs when I was a child. I was being punished for trampling down some of Mamma's flowers when I had carelessly run through her flower bed. I was feeling sorry for myself and perhaps that was why I tried to take it out on one of our dogs. While I was sitting on our back porch playing with him, I grabbed his ear and twisted it. The dog yelped with pain. I twisted the ear again, and again the dog yelped. Mamma opened the back door but didn't say a word.

"That night right in the middle of supper, Mamma got up from her place and walked around behind me. She grabbed my ear and twisted it until tears came into my eyes. Papa and the rest looked at Mamma with astonishment; but she didn't say a word, just went back to her place and resumed eating.

"After supper, when I was sitting on the parlor floor playing, Mamma laid aside her embroidery work, leaned over, grabbed my ear and twisted it until I cried: 'Please, Mamma. I'm getting the silent treatment. Isn't that enough punishment for ruining your flowers?'

"Papa put down the book he was reading and looked at Mamma. 'The boy deserves an explanation, Tena girl.'

"Mamma merely shook her head. 'I know what I'm doing.'

"I went over and laid my head in Mamma's lap. 'Please Mamma, forgive me for trampling on your flowers.'

"To my consternation she grabbed my ear and twisted it again. I rushed over to Papa.

"'Holy Jupiter!' Papa shouted. 'What is this nonsense?'

"Mamma beckoned to me. I approached her cautiously with my hands over my ears.

"She smiled at me. 'You know I love you, don't you, John D.?'

"When I nodded, she continued. 'Then perhaps you'll understand how Spot felt this afternoon. He knew you loved him and couldn't understand why you hurt him by twisting his ear. The first time he thought you'd just made a mistake. But when you did it the second time, the poor dog couldn't understand why his master who loved him was hurting him. Now, if you'll promise never to hurt another animal, I'll forgive you.'" [John D. Fitzgerald, *Papa Married a Mormon*, Prentice-Hall, 1955.[1]]

After the death of Fitzgerald's father, the *Advocate* was sold to Mr. Hackett. "'. . . I went to see Mr. Hackett. He was sitting at the roll top desk in the *Advocate* office, with the inevitable cigar in his mouth. Pushing a green eyeshade to the top of his head, he looked up at me.

"'Mr. Hackett,' I said earnestly, 'Dr. LeRoy told Mamma and me that Papa was going to die a year before he died. Instead of going to school I stayed home that year and worked with Papa every day. Papa also knew he wouldn't live long. He tried to teach me all he could about the newspaper and printing business during that year. I've told Mamma I'm not going back east to college. I came to ask you for a job.'

"He seemed a little embarrassed as he answered. 'I don't see how I can give you a job, John. First there is your mother to consider. She sold me the *Advocate* to get money to send you to college. And then there is the fact—and remember journalists must deal with facts—that I doubt if I could afford to hire you, even if your mother did give her consent.'

"'There was plenty of work for both Papa and me,' I persisted.

"'That may well be,' he admitted, 'but I am not your father. I won't be able to keep the circulation your father had, and I probably won't get so much printing.'

"'I'm sure you will,' I encouraged him. 'We'll work hard and build up the circulation and the printing.'

"'Just what can you do to help?' he asked.

"I was quick to press my advantage. 'I can set type. I can do the makeready on all hand bills and printing. I can run the hand press and the Washington press. I can take either one apart and put it together again. I can solicit advertising and new subscribers. I can gather the social news. I can sweep the place out. I can—'

"'Just a minute,' he laughed as he held up his hand. 'All right, John, providing your mother consents and if you are willing to work for a very small salary, until we see how things work out. Bishop Aden told me that your father wanted you to be a journalist. You will never get rich in this business, but if you've got printer's ink in your veins, you'll be a newspaper man the rest of your life and love it.'

"I never did find out whether Mr. Hackett persuaded Mamma to let me take the job, or if Mamma realized she

He had no sooner got the words out of his mouth when the ghost of Tinker came right up out of its grave behind its headstone. He was dressed in a white sheet just like a ghost is supposed to be. ■ (From *More Adventures of the Great Brain* by John D. Fitzgerald. Illustrated by Mercer Mayer.)

couldn't get me to change my mind." [John D. Fitzgerald, *Mamma's Boarding House*, Prentice-Hall, 1958.[2]]

Fitzgerald went into the newspaper field, eventually spending four years abroad as a foreign correspondent. Returning to the States, he began writing articles and short stories but didn't have much luck selling them. Newspaper work was hard to find, so he became a purchasing agent and continued to submit stories to magazines. The stories began to sell so consistently that he quit his job to concentrate on freelance writing. In the years before 1950 he had more than three hundred stories published.

"Everything went along beautifully until the bottom fell out of the short-story market. It got down to one Thanksgiving Day when my wife and I had pancakes without syrup or sugar for our Thanksgiving dinner. I hocked my typewriter, swore I'd never write again, and got a job in a bank. Then one Christmas my wife gave me a typewriter. She had never lost confidence. I told her the short-story market was shot. She said to write a novel. I wrote an autobiographical novel entitled *Papa Married a Mormon*, and was dumbfounded when it was accepted by Prentice-Hall and even more dumbfounded when it became a best seller, a selection of two book clubs, and was published in seven foreign countries.

"I had never thought about writing a juvenile novel until one evening when some friends dropped in and we got to talking about our childhood. I told them some true stories about my brother Tom and his great brain, which made them laugh so much my wife suggested I write a book about Tom. The memories of childhood are either elusive or vivid. My memories of Tom are very graphic because he swindled me so many times when I was a boy. I wrote *The Great Brain* based upon actual experiences I had with Tom and his great brain as a boy. It was my first juvenile novel and I was both surprised and delighted when it was accepted by Dial Press. This was followed by two more books in the Brain series. Meanwhile I received hundreds of letters from boys and girls wanting to know what happened to the Great Brain at the Catholic Academy in Salt Lake City. And that is how I came to write *The Great Brain at the Academy*."

Of *The Great Brain*, the first book in this series, the *New York Times Book Review* has written, "Tom [the oldest brother] would be enough to send most younger brothers stuttering off to the psychiatrist. But not J. D. The plucky youth is a willing Watson to his brother's Holmes, a Tonto to his Lone Ranger, and, as this charming memoir testifies, a Boswell to his Johnson. The subtlety of the author's characterizations as well as the tone of the background are captured by [the] pen and ink drawings."

A later book, *Me and My Little Brain*, was written about in this way by *The Horn Book Magazine*, "Lively, humorous, suspenseful, it derives much of its appeal from the author's perceptive, conversational style, which is as indicative of adolescent ambivalence as the sudden voice change." And according to *Children's Book Review*, "[*Me and My Little Brain*] is Tom Sawyer country—we are some miles further west and a decade or two later but the feeling's just the same. . . . Mr. Fitzgerald has humour, ingenuity and a light touch with character and situation; he also has sympathy, insight and depth."

FOR MORE INFORMATION SEE: New York Times, November 13, 1955; *San Francisco Chronicle*, November 10, 1955; *New York Times Book Review*, November 19, 1967; *The Horn Book Magazine*, April, 1972; *Children's Book Review*, Autumn, 1974.

GAEDDERT, Lou Ann (Bigge) 1931-

PERSONAL: Surname is pronounced *Ged*-ert; born June 20, 1931, in Garden City, Kan.; married Orlan M. Gaeddert; children: Andrew, Martha. *Education:* Attended Phillips University; University of Washington, B.A., 1952; attended Radcliffe College. *Politics:* Republican. *Religion:* Protestant. *Residence:* Jackson Heights, N.Y. *Agent:* Curtis Brown, Ltd., 575 Madison Ave., New York, N.Y. 10022.

CAREER: Author. *West Seattle Herald,* Seattle, Wash., writer and editor, 1952-54; worked in publicity departments of T. Y. Crowell, 1954-55, and Doubleday, 1956-61.

WRITINGS: Noisy Nancy Norris (illustrated by Gioia Fiammenghi), Doubleday, 1965; *The Split-Level Cookbook: Family Meals to Cook Once and Serve Twice,* Crowell, 1967; *Too Many Girls* (illustrated by Marylin Hafner), Coward, McCann, 1972; *Noisy Nancy and Nick* (illustrated by Fiammenghi), Doubleday, 1970; *All-in-All: A Biography of George Eliot,* Dutton, 1976; *Gustav the Gourmet Giant* (illustrated by Steven Kellogg), Dial, 1976; *Your Night to Make Dinner* (illustrated by Ellen Weiss), Watts, 1977.

SIDELIGHTS: Gaeddert's first book, *Noisy Nancy Norris,* grew out of her concern and experience with raising children in an apartment building. In 1967, the Communications Laboratory of Bank Street College of Education produced a mo-

(From *Gustav the Gourmet Giant* by Lou Ann Gaeddert. Illustrated by Steven Kellogg.)

LOU ANN GAEDDERT

When Sarah practices ballet
Ralph makes fun of her.
■ (From *Rotten Ralph* by Jack Gantos. Illustrated by Nicole Rubel.)

tion picture which was based on *Noisy Nancy Norris* and was narrated by Shirley MacLaine.

FOR MORE INFORMATION SEE: Lee Bennett Hopkins, *Books Are by People,* Citation, 1969; *Horn Book,* December, 1976.

JACK GANTOS

GANTOS, John (Bryan), Jr. 1951-
(Jack Gantos)

PERSONAL: Born July 2, 1951, in Mount Pleasant, Pa.; son of John (a construction superintendent) and Elizabeth (Weaver) Gantos. *Education:* Emerson College, B.F.A., 1976. *Home:* 304 Marlborough St., Boston, Mass. 02116.

CAREER: Has held a variety of jobs, including apprentice electrician, construction foreman, electric saw-blade sharpener, shortorder cook, beach sweeper, and x-ray technician; full-time writer, 1976—.

WRITINGS—All published by Houghton; all illustrated by Nicole Rubel: *Rotten Ralph,* 1976; *Sleepy Ronald,* 1976; *Fair Weather Friends,* 1977; *Aunt Bernice,* 1978; *Worse Than Rotten Ralph,* 1978.

WORK IN PROGRESS: An adult novel.

SIDELIGHTS: "I write everyday and I read at least three times as much as I write. I write for children because they enjoy my work. One day I was passing in front of a book store window where *Rotten Ralph* (my first) was being displayed. Several children were chanting 'rotten Ralph . . . rotten Ralph . . . rotten Ralph . . .' over and over. For a writer to receive such sincere attention is rare. They are a good audience and deserve good books.''

FOR MORE INFORMATION SEE: Horn Book, June, 1976; *Publishers Weekly,* February, 1977.

REBECCA GAVER

GAVER, Rebecca   1952- (Becky Gaver)

PERSONAL: Born October 11, 1952, in Oakland, Calif.; daughter of Harry Lawrence (a retired navy officer) and Ellease (Hopson; a hospital receptionist) Gaver. *Education:* University of Florida, Gainesville, Fla., B.F.A., 1974. *Politics:* Registered Democrat. *Home:* The Peacock Inn, 4752 E. Fort Lowell Rd., Tucson, Az. 85712. *Office:* P.O. Box 3565, Tucson, Az. 85722.

CAREER: Free-lance illustrator and designer. Institute of Food & Agricultural Sciences, University of Florida, Gainesville, Fla., illustrator, 1974-78. Speaker at Children's Book Fair, Gainesville, Fla., 1975, 1976; guest lecturer, children's literature seminar, University of Florida, 1977; sporadic artwork on programs, posters and set design for Hippodrome Theatre, Gainesville, Fla. *Exhibitions:* Hogtown Graphics' 1st Annual Show; The Frame Factory, Gainesville, Fla., 1974; Hogtown Graphics' 2nd Annual Show; Center of Modern Art, Micanopy, Fla., 1975; (one woman show) Campus Credit Union, 1975. *Member:* Hogtown Original Graphics, Inc. (secretary-treasurer, 1976), Organization of Professional Printmakers in Gainesville, Southeastern Graphics Council, Regional Printmakers Association. *Awards, honors:* Second in poster contest for *Seventeen* Magazine, 1972; Creative Achievement Award, Phi Beta Kappa, 1973.

ILLUSTRATOR: John Ciardi, *Fast & Slow: Poems for Advanced Children and Beginning Parents,* Houghton, 1975; *Two Dozen Drawings,* privately printed, 1977; *Drawings: A Season with the Hippodrome Theater,* privately printed, 1979. Illustration has appared in *Seventeen* Magazine.

SIDELIGHTS: "I've been drawing since I was a child—when my mother went shopping, I used to while away the time sketching cartoons on a pad I dragged around with me. I've also been very aware of lettering—I would follow the lines of words on billboards and neon signs, and retrace them in the air the way I thought they should be. My family moved every two or three years, so I had a fragmented childhood with no single place where I grew up. Instead, I had a polyglot of experiences, including, among other things, the initiation of Hawaii into statehood. I got to do a little speech (at age eight) while a tree was planted in the schoolyard.

"My interests range throughout all phases of the graphic arts. In drawing, my natural tendency is toward representative detail, which easily lends itself to illustration. My formal schooling included both commercial and fine art. But I became disenchanted with advertising art, and turned toward prints and illustration as an outlet for my energies. I now do free-lance illustration design, layout, and calligraphy. My personal work includes paintings, drawings and a variety of prints—I've done etchings, silkscreen prints, lithographs, and woodcuts, and I experiment with any new processes I find. Using an offset printing press, I have printed two small books of my own work. I did all the production work—typesetting, layout, camerawork, printing and binding—personally.

"*Fast and Slow* is the only book I've had the chance to illustrate so far. It was a coincidence that the author, John Ciardi, was in Gainesville as a guest lecturer at the same time that I was about to graduate from college and look for work. We met, he saw my art, and prompted Houghton-Mifflin to hire me. As it was my first 'big-time' experience, the job was both exhilarating and exhausting. I ended up doing more than just the illustrations, once I got going. I did a dummy of the layout (because I wanted to know just how the pictures would fit with the words, rather than leave it up to the publisher), and I designed and rendered the lettering of the title.

"I especially enjoy illustrating for (and talking to) children, for they are intuitively curious and observant. Their reactions are honest and immediate: they are quick to point out mistakes, and appreciate authenticity. For this reason I try to carefully research anything with which I am not already familiar. For instance, I went to a pet store to draw a live boa constrictor for the illustration of 'Pets' from *Fast and Slow.* And the children I've met are hungry for any new or novel experience, anxious to learn, to become more involved with their visual world.

"Pen-and-ink is my favorite illustrative medium, partly out of necessity. Commercially, line work is easiest—and cheapest—to reproduce. Also, it is easier to render with clarity in pen-and-ink than with some other media. However, this by no means restricts me to this medium alone.

"I greatly admire work of Maurice Sendak, Edward Gorey, Tomi Ungerer and many other illustrators. I've also learned much from Todd Walker, a photographer-printer with whom I work. My two books were printed on his private press."

FOR MORE INFORMATION SEE: Horn Book, October, 1975.

If it starts to squeeze, will you phone me please? I'd hate not to say goodbye. ■ (From *Fast & Slow* by John Ciardi. Illustrated by Becky Gaver.)

GERGELY, Tibor   1900-1978

OBITUARY NOTICE: Born August 3, 1900, in Budapest, Hungary; died January 13, 1978, in New York, N.Y. Illustrator of children's books, painter, and graphic artist. Gergely worked during his years in Europe with various newspapers and periodicals, doing illustrations and cartoons. In the same period he also painted murals, illustrated books, and designed stage decorations; he had exhibitions of his paintings in Europe and America. In 1939 Gergely came to the United States to live, his time being spent mainly in commercial art and book illustration. He illustrated a great number of Golden Books, in which he created worlds populated with baby wild animals and barnyards, fire engines, and taxis. Gergely illustrated a host of other children's books, including Margaret Wise Brown's *Wheel on the Chimney*, which was a runner-up for the Caldecott Medal in 1955. *For More Information See: American Picturebooks from Noah's Ark to The Beast Within*, Macmillan, 1976; *Illustrators of Books for Young People*, 2nd edition, Scarecrow, 1975; *Illustrators of Children's Books, 1744-1945*, Horn Book, 1945, reprinted, 1970; *Illustrators of Children's Books, 1946-1956*, Horn Book, 1958. *Obituaries: Publishers Weekly*, January 30, 1978.

GORDON, Dorothy   1893-1970

PERSONAL: Born April 4, 1893, in Odessa, Russia; daughter of Leo (an international lawyer) and Rose (Schwarz) Lerner; married Bernard Gordon (a lawyer), June 28, 1910; children: Frank, Lincoln. *Education:* Hunter College (now of the City University of New York), B.A.; graduate study at the Sorbonne, University of Paris. *Politics:* Independent. *Home:* Chetwood, George's Mills, N.H.

CAREER: Writer; radio and television moderator. Concert folksinger, 1923-29; producer of programs for children for the British Broadcasting Corp. (BBC) in London, 1929; director of music programs for the "American School of the Air" on Columbia Broadcasting Co. (CBS), 1931-38; producer of "The Children's Corner," 1936-38; member of the Mutual Broadcasting System staff, 1938-39; consultant for children's programs on NBC, and director and actress for "Yesterday's Children," 1939-40; producer of a news program for children on station WQXR, 1940-42; director of children's radio programs for the Office of War Information, 1942-44; moderator for the "New York Times Youth Forum," 1944-61. Consultant for youth activities for the *New York Times. Member:* Overseas Press Club.

AWARDS, HONORS: National Conference of Christians and Jews award, 1948-55; School Broadcast Conference award, 1949; Institute of Education by Radio award, 1949-51; New York State Mother of the Year award, 1951; McCall's Gold Mike award, 1951; George Foster Peabody award, 1951, 1964, 1966; Federation of Jewish Women's Organizations award, 1952; Town Hall award, 1953; Columbia University Scholarship Press gold key, 1954; Ohio State University award for education on radio and TV, 1955; General Federation of Women's Clubs award, 1955; LL.D., 1959, from Fairleigh Dickinson University; Thomas Alva Edison award for scientific information to youth through the mass media; Williamsburg Settlement award for developing youth interest in world affairs; Governor's Award, Academy of Television Arts and Sciences, 1965.

WRITINGS: (Editor) *Sing It Yourself* (illustrated by Alida Conover), Dutton, 1928; *Around the World in Song* (illustrated by Conover), Dutton, 1930; *Dorothy Gordon's Treasure Bag of Game Songs* (illustrated by Veronica Reed), Dutton, 1939; *Come to France* (illustrated by Reed), American Book Co., 1940; *Knowing the Netherlands* (illustrated by Reed), American Book Co., 1940; *All Children Listen*, G. W. Stewart, 1942; *You and Democracy* (illustrated by Lois Fisher and Karl Murr), Dutton, 1951; *Who Has the Answer: An Inquiry into the Behavior of Today's Teenagers*, Dutton, 1965.

SIDELIGHTS: Born in Odessa, Russia, the youthful Gordon traveled throughout the Balkan countries in the company of her mother, attending village festivals which displayed colorful costumes, dances and songs which she learned to sing. Fluent in seven languages, Gordon could sing in fourteen. Her parents discovered that she had a singing voice worthy of training, and sent her to Italy where she studied with Gabriel Sibella, Roberto Moranzoni, and Gabriel Gills.

As a singer of folk songs, she gave many concerts. Her own children encouraged her to sing for other children and after the first concert at the Princess Theatre, she appeared throughout the United States and Canada between 1923 and 1929. "I started my concerts in 1923 over WEAF. At the station there was a glass window that separated the studio from a sort of waiting room outside.

"My announcer was Graham McNamee. We were having a great deal of fun together before I went on the air because I was so frightened of this thing. There was this little tiny round instrument in front of me. I said, 'Well, what happens?,

It takes care of the aged and seeks constantly to protect children from being hired for labor.
■ (From *You and Democracy* by Dorothy Gordon. Pictures by Lois Fisher and Karl Murr.)

"He said, 'Well, you just stand right there—and you just sing.'

"I said, 'Oh no, I just can't. There's no audience, no people.'

"I think a stage person always needs that relationship between audience and artist.

"I was frightened to death—scared as scared could be, and I said, 'But nothing will happen. Don't tell me that I sing into this thing, and then it goes out and someone hears it!'

"He laughed at me. He said, 'Of course you will be heard. You'll be heard by more people than you realize.'

"All I could think of was that my boys, little youngsters, were up in our apartment with wires across the whole ceiling of the nursery and earphones on their ears desperately trying to listen to me. I didn't know at that time what they got. I found out later. They said they heard nothing but squawks and curious sounds that didn't sound at all like mother.

"Suddenly I saw a great deal of excitement outside of the glass window which separated the studio from the waiting room. People running back and forth and signaling to one another. Graham McNamee, who wanted to know what it was all about, opened the door and went out. Being an artist I knew the show must go on so I went right on singing this soft beautiful little Brittany lullaby. All the time I was wondering what in the world was going on—whether the place was on fire. My accompanist got worried but I went on nevertheless.

"Out there in the waiting room was my husband whose face would sort of light up, and he had a grin from ear to ear, so I knew that there was no catastrophe of any kind. Something very pleasant seemed to be happening.

"When I finished and got off the air, Graham McNamee walked in and said to me, 'I have a very interesting thing to tell you. We had word that they heard *you* in Cape Town.'

"That did something to me which has never left me. . . .

"As I traveled about the country, the various radio stations would invite me to sing and to perform in relation to my concert program. I wasn't paid. I would just go to a station and sing fifteen minutes or so and talk about the concert that was coming. I did that in a number of the cities throughout the country.

"I have tramped up more stairs and gone into more old buildings and I became increasingly more and more astonished at the crudeness of some of these places—and to think that in spite of that, music personality could come out on the air, it was quite amazing!" [Dorothy Gordon, "They Heard You in Cape Town!," *American Heritage*, August, 1955.[1]]

After a year in London (1929), Gordon returned to America to direct the music programs on CBS' "American School of the Air." She penned many of the scripts for these dramas, and often played some of the roles.

One of her most popular programs was "Yesterday's Children" which ran from 1939 to 1940. It consisted of famous men and women telling why they enjoyed reading a favorite book of theirs.

From 1944 to 1961 Gordon was the moderator for the "New York Times Youth Forum." "When the Youth Forums were conceived in 1943, my mind was so filled with the image of the concentration on six-year-olds in Germany, Russia, and Japan that I wanted to start with young children, as young as possible. We compromised and began with youngsters ranging in age from nine to twelve. 'What Does the War Mean to Me?' was the first Forum subject. 'Will they talk?' I was asked. I didn't know, but I was determined to find out. Having established a close relationship with the schools over many years through my stage and radio programs, I contacted several educators from public, private, and parochial schools to get a cross section of the youth. I suggested speaking to an assembly to outline what I had in mind and to ask the children such questions as: What does the war mean to you? What do you think started the war? What do you think lies ahead?

"The adults were skeptical. They were certain the children would not speak or were so young that they couldn't possibly know what was going on. Well, the adults were wrong. There was great astonishment when little hands flew up and, when called upon, the children spoke easily, fluently, thoughtfully. Principals, teachers, headmasters gasped at the clear, well-formulated opinions expressed by the children, some of whom had always chosen to remain in the background. That was the beginning. A panel of children representing a cross section of youth from different schools was selected and the Youth Forum swung into action. From the very beginning the programs evoked great interest in the adult world. In order to have the children participate as much as possible, I asked them to send in questions for discussion. Responses came quickly.

"Then, in 1945, the war was over. The world was in a state of change. The United Nations came into being. A devastated Europe was being rehabilitated. New threats were looming—Soviet Russia, China, and the greatest challenge of all, atomic energy. The time had come to move into wider areas of discussion. A new world was in the making and the young people felt they were a big part of it. With increasing frequency requests came in that we use secondary school students as panel members. We opened the discussions not only to high school students but to college and university students as well. And to keep the stimulus alive we continued to hold occasional programs featuring the younger children and we encouraged questions from them when they were in the audience." [Dorothy Gordon, "Listening to Youth," *Wilson Library Bulletin*, October, 1967.[2]]

Gordon also wrote several books for and about children and compiled twenty-two singing games for children. "In my book *You and Democracy* I wrote: 'Man does not come by his democratic conscience overnight in his manhood. He is not born in it. Instead it must be instilled into his thinking from his alphabet days on in order to make him fit for liberty.'

"The threat of totalitarian ideology could best be met, it seemed to me, by a reaffirmation of faith in our democracy. I knew that the greatest hope for a lasting democracy lay in an awareness of the principles of freedom, which could best be realized through one of the strongholds of democracy—freedom of speech. Our young people live in a free society. They must be given every opportunity to inquire, to

DOROTHY GORDON

learn, and to express opinions and beliefs. Young people with clear, well-formulated opinions on today's issues are likely to emerge as the leaders of tomorrow."[2]

Gordon was also consultant on youth activities for the *New York Times* and the recipient of several awards and honors including the Governor's Award from the Academy of TV Arts and Sciences in 1965. She was married to a lawyer, Bernard Gordon, and had two sons. Her home was in George's Mills, New Hampshire. On May 11, 1970 she died at the age of seventy-seven. In 1967 she wrote: "In the more than two decades since I started the Youth Forums I have never lost the excitement engendered by the young people involved in the programs. They are so alert, knowledgeable, challenging, provocative. At times one finds muddled thinking which seems to clear as the discussion moves along. The very essence of the free exchange of ideas is the answer to the tactics of the unscrupulous spellbinder who too often reaches out to our youth. There are many forces challenging our freedom and world peace. The irresponsible dissidents, the hippies, the negative elements, the youths who make the headlines are in most cases not the peace builders of tomorrow. Indeed not. It is the large number of thinking youth moving in constructive rather than destructive action upon whom we can set our hopes. So, give them a platform, these citizens of tomorrow, and guide them into expressing their opinions, hopefully based on knowledge and facts."[2]

FOR MORE INFORMATION SEE: Time, July 13, 1942; *Parents' Magazine,* February, 1948; *American Heritage,* August, 1955; *Wilson Library Bulletin,* October, 1967; (obituary) *New York Times,* May 12, 1970.

ALICE E. GOUDEY

GOUDEY, Alice E. 1898-

PERSONAL: Born January 3, 1898, in Junction City, Kansas; daughter of John West and Elizabeth (Poland) Edwards; married Wayne G. Martin, Jr., August 29, 1918 (divorced, 1945); married Earl S. Goudey, June 2, 1947; children: (first marriage) Dorothy (Mrs. William Sheeham, Jr.); (stepchildren) Pelton Goudey, Joyce Goudey (Mrs. William Smykal). *Education:* Student at Columbia University, 1946, New School of Social Research, and New York University, 1947-48. *Home:* Morrill, Maine.

CAREER: Author of books for children. Teacher in Kansas elementary schools, 1915-18; editorial work for *Western Grain Journal,* Kansas City, Missouri, 1919. *Member:* Authors Guild. *Awards, honors:* Runner-up for the Caldecott Medal, 1960, for *Houses from the Sea,* and 1962, for *The Day We Saw the Sun Come Up* (both illustrated by Adrienne Adams).

WRITINGS: The Good Rain (illustrated by Nora S. Unwin), Dutton, 1950; *The Merry Fiddlers* (illustrated by Bernard Garbutt), Aladdin Books, 1951; *Danny Boy, the Picture Pony* (illustrated by Paul Brown), Scribner, 1952; *Smokey, the Well-Loved Kitten* (illustrated by Meg Wohlberg), Lothrop, 1952; *Jupiter and the Cats* (illustrated by P. Brown),

Scribner, 1953; *Here Come the Bears!* (illustrated by Garry MacKenzie), Scribner, 1954; *Here Come the Deer!* (illustrated by G. MacKenzie), Scribner, 1955; *Here Come the Elephants!* (illustrated by G. MacKenzie), Scribner, 1955; *Here Come the Whales!* (illustrated by G. MacKenzie), Scribner, 1956; *Here Come the Lions!* (illustrated by G. MacKenzie), Scribner, 1956; *Here Come the Seals!* (illustrated by G. MacKenzie), Scribner, 1957; *Here Come the Beavers!* (illustrated by G. MacKenzie), Scribner, 1957; *Here Come the Wild Dogs!* (illustrated by G. MacKenzie), Scribner, 1958; *Houses from the Sea* (ALA Notable Book; illustrated by Adrienne Adams), Scribner, 1959; *Here Come the Raccoons* (illustrated by G. MacKenzie), Scribner, 1959; *Here Come the Bees!* (illustrated by G. MacKenzie), Scribner, 1960; *The Day We Saw the Sun Come Up* (ALA Notable Book; illustrated by A. Adams), Scribner, 1961; *Here Come the Dolphins!* (illustrated by G. MacKenzie), Scribner, 1961; *Here Come the Squirrels!* (illustrated by G. MacKenzie), Scribner, 1962; *Sunnyvale Fair* (illustrated by Paul Galdone), Scribner, 1962, reissued, 1972; *Butterfly Time* (*Horn Book* honor list; illustrated by A. Adams), Scribner, 1964; *Graywings* (illustrated by Marie Nonnast), Scribner, 1964; *Here Come the Cottontails* (illustrated by G. MacKenzie), Scribner, 1965; *Red Legs* (illustrated by M. Nonnast), Scribner, 1966.

SIDELIGHTS: Alice E. Goudey began writing children's stories as supplementary reading material for her students while teaching in Kansas. That was her main goal throughout her writing career.

Her first published book, *Good Rain,* was reviewed by a *New York Herald Tribune* critic who commented, "This is a charming idea for a small child's picture book, and Miss Unwin has interpreted it happily, with pictures full of feeling."

Of *Butterfly Time,* the *New York Times* said, "Poetic words and delicate full-color illustrations evoke the wonder and beauty of butterflies without any sacrifice of accuracy...." *New Yorker* commented that "The drawings are so good that one can't help wishing that the text, a dialogue between brother and sister, were a little less wooden. But, this is not, perhaps, important, since the intention—to make butterflies irresistible—has been accomplished...."

The *Horn Book* review of *Graywings* said, "Simple, poetic text conveys the rhythm in nature's cycles, while illustrations, warmed by the greens in grass and water, show the grace and design in a gull's motions. One of the all-too-few instances where scientific concept is presented for the younger reader with literary and artistic style."

Saturday Review described *Here Come the Cottontails!* as "authentic information about animals [which projects] a warm feeling about the creatures without personification...." The *New York Times* said "... there is an intimacy and lucidity to the prose throughout that even the youngest ... will find as satisfying as the fine ink sketches splashed in spring greens."

Alice E. Goudey's last book was *Red Legs,* a story of the grasshopper. The *New York Times* said, "The illustrations are delicate in detail and color. The typographical layout will be helpful to a young reader, tedious to a more experienced one."

**When friends come in
to play on rainy days
we show them all our shells.**

■ (From *Houses from the Sea* by Alice E. Goudey.
Illustrated by Adrienne Adams.)

Goudey's works are included in the Kerlan Collection at the
University of Minnesota.

HOBBIES AND OTHER INTERESTS: Reading, gardening,
sewing, and painting.

FOR MORE INFORMATION SEE: Horn Book, August,
1964, June, 1966; Doris de Montreville and Donna Hill, editors, *Third Book of Junior Authors,* H. W. Wilson, 1972.

GREEN, Phyllis   1932-

PERSONAL: Born June 24, 1932, in Pittsburgh, Pa.; daughter of Victor Geyer (a plumbing contractor) and Phyllis (a
teacher; maiden name, Sailer) Hartman; married Robert Bailey Green (an insurance executive), August 15, 1959; children: Sharon Ann, Bruce Robert. *Education:* Westminster
College, New Wilmington, Pa., B.S. in Ed., 1953; University
of Pittsburgh, M.Ed., 1955. *Residence:* Madison, Wis.

CAREER: Elementary and special education teacher in
Dormont, Pa., and Newark and Wilmington, Del., 1953-59;
free-lance writer, 1959—. Former band vocalist and actress
in summer theater. *Member:* Detroit Women Writers, Pen

Women (Madison branch), Society of Children's Book Writers.

WRITINGS: The Fastest Quitter in Town, Addison-Wesley,
1972; *Nantucket Summer,* Thomas Nelson, 1974; *Ice River,*
Addison-Wesley, 1975; *Mildred Murphy, How Does Your
Garden Grow?,* Addison-Wesley, 1977; *Wild Violets,*
Thomas Nelson, 1977; *Grandmother Orphan,* Thomas Nelson, 1977; *Walkie-Talkie,* Addison-Wesley, 1978; *Nicky's
Lopsided, Lumpy But Delicious Orange,* Addison-Wesley,
1978; *A New Mother for Martha,* Human Sciences Press,
1978; *The Empty Seat,* Thomas Nelson, 1979; *Bagdad Ate It,*
Watts, 1980; *Gloomy Louie, The Doom King,* A. Whitman,
1980. Contributor of short stories, poems, and articles to national magazines.

Plays: "By the Beautiful Sea," first read at the off off Broadway theater, St. Clements, January, 1978; "Deer Season,"
produced at St. Clements, January, 1980; author of two radio
plays produced on Wisconsin public radio stations, "I'll Be
Home for Christmas" and "Acapulco Holiday."

WORK IN PROGRESS: Stage play, radio play, and a novel
for young people.

SIDELIGHTS: "In my senior year of college I decided that I
wanted to write a book for mice. On the first page it stated
that only mice were allowed to read the book and if you wer-
en't a mouse, you had to close the book and stop reading it.
Fortunately I never got beyond that first page, but I was on
my way to being a writer.

PHYLLIS GREEN

We will be able to see Mt. Tamalpais one way and Novato the other way. I wish we could see New Jersey. I miss it so. ■ (From *Mildred Murphy, How Does Your Garden Grow?* by Phyllis Green. Illustrated by Jerry Pinkney.)

"I tried writing about two stories a year until 1968 when I got serious and took a creative writing course at the College of Marin in California. My teacher was Mr. Lawrence Hart. I sold a story to a literary magazine before the semester was over.

"I was ecstatic over this first sale for three days. Then I got so nervous! I was going to be published! I would wake up at night and start to cry. I told my husband I had the terrible feeling I was going to be famous. This made him laugh and then I laughed too because we both knew it was so remote. Still, I could not bear to break into print so I had to telephone the editor and ask to have my story returned and I returned their $35 check. He was a very kind editor.

"After that I was able to have two other stories published by using pseudonyms. But when I sold my first book for children, *The Fastest Quitter in Town,* I became brave and used my own name. In the story there is a great-grandfather who loses his precious ring. My own grandmother lost her wed-

ding ring once and that is how I got the idea for the story. The part about the boy quitting the baseball game came in a revision and I got the idea from some neighbor children in Michigan who played ball in the school field behind our house.

"I wanted to write about a place where we vacationed and a teen-age girl who gives up her favorite doll. Thus, came the story *Nantucket Summer.* My childhood doll was also called Dorothy.

"The idea for *Ice River* came from a newspaper article about two boys skating on thin ice.

"We moved once from New Jersey to California and our daughter was lonely for her old friends, especially when she heard 'soft, slow, sad music' on the radio. And that was the beginning for *Mildred Murphy, How Does Your Garden Grow?*

"*Wild Violets* takes place at a time when I was in school. Some of the things that happened in school were as I remembered them, but most of the main story is made up.

"Hearing about girls who shoplifted gave me the start of the story of Christy in *Grandmother Orphan.* The idea of having a family of waifs came out of my imagination.

"As for *Nicky's Lopsided, Lumpy But Delicious Orange,* there was an 'Ernestine Ring' in my childhood who conned me all the time!

"I grew up in the country, ten miles north of Pittsburgh, Pennsylvania. I had very nice parents and a very nice brother which is probably why I like to write about pleasant families. Now I live in Madison, Wisconsin with some other very nice people: my husband (we are still laughing) and our daughter and son. My family is always as happy as I am when I sell a book. It makes it all great fun."

HOBBIES AND OTHER INTERESTS: "I like to read books for young people and books about plays and playwrights."

GREENE, Graham   1904-

PERSONAL: Born October 2, 1904, in Berkhamsted, Hertfordshire, England; son of Charles Henry (headmaster of Berkhamsfed School) and Marion Raymond (Greene) Greene; married Vivien Dayrell Browning, 1927; children: one son, one daughter. *Education:* Attended Berkhamsted School; attended Balliol College, Oxford, 1922-25. *Religion:* Catholic convert, 1926. *Home address:* 9 Bow St., London W.C. 2, England.

CAREER: Times, London, England, sub-editor, 1926-30; film critic for *Night and Day* during the thirties; *Spectator,* London, England, film critic, 1935-39, literary editor, 1940-41; with Foreign Office in Africa, 1941-44; Eyre & Spottiswoode Ltd. (publishers), London, England, director, 1944-48; Indo-China correspondent for *New Republic,* 1954; Bodley Head (publishers), London, England, director, 1958-68. *Awards, honors:* Hawthornden Prize, 1940, for *The Labyrinthine Ways (The Power and the Glory);* James Tait Black Memorial Prize, 1949, for *The Heart of the Matter;* Catholic Literary Award, 1952, for *The End of the Affair;* Boys' Clubs of America Junior Book Award, 1955, for *The Little Horse*

Bus; Pietzak Award (Poland), 1960; Litt.D., Cambridge University, 1962; Balliol College, Oxford, honorary fellow, 1963; Royal Society of Literature Prize; Companion of Honour, 1966; D.Litt., University of Edinburgh, 1967; Legion d'Honneur, chevalier, 1969.

WRITINGS—Fiction, except as indicated: *Babbling April* (poems), Basil Blackwell, 1925; *The Man Within*, Doubleday, 1929; *The Name of Action*, Heinemann, 1930, Doubleday, 1931; *Rumour at Nightfall,* Heinemann, 1931, Doubleday, 1932; *Orient Express,* Doubleday, 1932 (published in England as *Stamboul Train,* Heinemann, 1932); *It's a Battlefield,* Doubleday, 1934, reissued with new introduction by author, Heinemann & Bodley Head, 1970; *Basement Room, and Other Stories,* Cresset, 1935 ("Basement Room" revised and entitled "The Fallen Idol" published in *The Third Man* [and] *The Fallen Idol,* Heinemann, 1950); *England Made Me,* Doubleday, 1935, reissued as *The Shipwrecked,* Viking, 1953, reissued under original title with new introduction by author, Heinemann & Bodley Head, 1970; *The Bear Fell Free,* Grayson & Grayson, 1935; *Journey Without Maps* (travel), Doubleday, 1936, 2nd edition, Viking, 1961; *This Gun for Hire,* Doubleday, 1936 (published in England as *A Gun for Sale,* Heinemann, 1936); *Brighton Rock,* Viking, 1938, reissued with new introduction by author, Heinemann & Bodley Head, 1970; *The Confidential Agent,* Viking, 1939, reissued with new introduction by author, Heinemann & Bodley Head, 1971; *Another Mexico,* Viking, 1939 (published in England as *The Lawless Roads,* Longmans, Green, 1939).

The Labyrinthine Ways, Viking, 1940 (published in England as *The Power and the Glory,* Heinemann, 1940), reissued under British title, Viking, 1946, reissued under British title with new introduction by author, Heinemann & Bodley Head, 1971; *British Dramatists* (nonfiction), Collins, 1942; *The Ministry of Fear,* Viking, 1943; *Nineteen Stories,* Heinemann, 1947, Viking, 1949, later published with some substitutions and additions as *Twenty-one Stories,* Heinemann, 1955, Viking, 1962; *The Heart of the Matter,* Viking, 1948, reissued with new introduction by author, Heinemann & Bodley Head, 1971; *The Third Man,* Viking, 1950; *The Lost Childhood, and Other Essays,* Eyre & Spottiswoode, 1951, Viking, 1952; *The End of the Affair,* Viking, 1951; *The Living Room* (play in two acts), Heinemann, 1953, Viking, 1957; *The Quiet American,* Heinemann, 1955, Viking, 1956; *Loser Takes All,* Heinemann, 1955, Viking, 1957; *The Potting Shed* (play in three acts; first produced, 1957), Viking, 1957; *Our Man in Havana,* Viking, 1958, reissued with new introduction by author, Heinemann & Bodley Head, 1970; *The Complaisant Lover* (play; first produced, 1959), Heinemann, 1959, Viking, 1961; *A Visit to Moran* (short story), Heinemann, 1959.

A Burnt-Out Case, Viking, 1961; *In Search of a Character: Two African Journals,* Bodley Head, 1961, Viking, 1962; *Introductions to Three Novels,* Norstedt (Stockholm), 1962; *The Destructors, and Other Stories,* Eihosha Ltd. (Japan), 1962; *A Sense of Reality,* Viking, 1963; *Carving a Statue* (play in two acts; first produced, 1968), Bodley Head, 1964; *The Comedians,* Viking, 1966; (with Dorothy Craigie) *Victorian Detective Fiction: A Catalogue of the Collection,* Bodley Head, 1966; *May We Borrow Your Husband? And Other Comedies of the Sexual Life,* Viking, 1967; (with Carol Reed) *The Third Man: A Film* (annotated filmscript), Simon & Schuster, 1968; *Travels With My Aunt,* Viking, 1969; *Collected Essays,* Viking, 1969; (author of introduction) Al Burt and Bernard Diederich, *Papa Doc,* McGraw, 1969; *A Sort of Life* (autobiography), Simon & Schuster, 1971; *Graham*

GRAHAM GREENE

Greene on Film: Collected Film Criticism, 1935-1940, Simon & Schuster, 1972 (published in England as *The Pleasure Dome,* Secker & Warburg, 1972); *The Portable Graham Greene,* includes *The Heart of the Matter,* with a new chapter, *The Third Man,* sections from eight other novels, six short stories, nine critical essays, and ten public statements, Viking, 1972; *The Honorary Consul,* Simon & Schuster, 1973; *Collected Stories,* Viking, 1973.

Omnibus volumes: *3: This Gun for Hire; The Confidential Agent; The Ministry of Fear,* Viking, 1952, reissued as *Three by Graham Greene: This Gun for Hire; Confidential Agent; The Ministry of Fear,* 1958; *Three Plays,* Mercury Books, 1961; *The Travel Books: Journey Without Maps* [and] *The Lawless Roads,* Heinemann, 1963; *Triple Pursuit: A Graham Greene Omnibus,* includes *This Gun for Hire, The Third Man, Our Man in Havana,* Viking, 1971.

Juvenile books: *This Little Fire Engine,* Parrish, 1950, published as *The Little Red Fire Engine,* Lothrop, Lee & Shepard, 1952; *The Little Horse Bus,* Parrish, 1952, Lothrop, Lee & Shepard, 1954; *The Little Steamroller,* Lothrop, Lee & Shepard, 1955; *The Little Train,* Parrish, 1957, Lothrop, Lee & Shepard, 1958.

Editor: *The Old School* (essays), J. Cape, 1934; H. H. Munro, *The Best of Saki,* 2nd edition, Lane, 1952; (with brother, Hugh Greene) *The Spy's Bedside Book,* British Book Service, 1957; (author of introduction) Marjorie Bowen, *The Viper of Milan,* Bodley Head, 1960; *The Bodley Head Ford Madox Ford,* Volumes I and II, Bodley Head, 1962.

Contributor: *24 Short Stories,* Cresset, 1939; *Alfred Hitchcock's Fireside Book of Suspense,* Simon & Schuster, 1947; *Why Do I Write?,* Percival Marshall, 1948. Contributor to *Esquire, Commonweal, Spectator, Playboy, Saturday Eve-*

ning Post, New Statesman, Atlantic, London Mercury, New Republic, America, Life, and other publications.

SIDELIGHTS: **October 2, 1904.** Born in Berkhamsted, Hertfordshire, England. "If I had known it, the whole future must have lain all the time along those Berkhamsted streets.

"Our home until I reached the age of six was a house called St. John's, one of the boardinghouses of Berkhamsted School. My father was housemaster there.

"As children we used to go down to the drawing room for about an hour after tea, from 5:30 to 6:30, to play with our mother, and I remember the fear I felt that my mother would read us a story about some children who were sent into a forest by a wicked uncle to be murdered, but the murderer repented and left them to die of exposure and afterwards the birds covered their bodies with leaves. I dreaded the story because I was afraid of weeping. I would infinitely have preferred quick murder to the long-drawn-out pathos of their end. My tear ducts in childhood, and indeed for many years later, worked far too easily, and even today I sometimes slink shamefaced from a cinema at some happy ending that moves me by its incredibility. (Life isn't like that. Of such courage and such fidelity we dream only, but in my distress I wish them true.)

"I think that my parents' was a very loving marriage; how far any marriage is happy is another matter and beyond an outsider's knowledge. Happiness can be ruined by children, by financial anxieties, by so many secret things; love too can be ruined, but I think their love withstood the pressure of six children and great anxieties." [Graham Greene, *A Sort of Life,* Simon and Schuster, 1971.[1]]

1910. Family moved to the School House when Greene's father, Charles Henry, became headmaster of Berkhamsted School. The School House remained their home until the father's retirement in the twenties. "It was after I was six and we had all moved to the School House, but before I went to school, that I began regularly to steal currants and sultanas out of the big biscuit tins in the School House storeroom, stuff my pockets full with them, currants in the left, sultanas in the right, and feast on them secretly in the garden. The meal ended always with a sensation of nausea, but to be secure from detection I had to finish them all, even the strays which had picked up fluff from the seams of the pockets. There is a charm in improvised eating which a regular meal lacks. . . .

"I shared my bed with a multitude of soft animals of which I can remember a teddy bear (the most loved), a glove bear (it came second in my affection because it could not stand alone) and a blue plush bird (it was the age of Maeterlinck). I kept the bird, I think, only for the sake of filling the bed, because I disliked the feel of plush and . . . [possessed a] terror of birds. When quiet had fallen on the house, the fear of fire would emerge like smoke and I would imagine I had been deserted by all my family. I would drop the teddy bear out of bed and shout for the nurse or nursery maid to pick it up. When one of them came, I felt assured again that all was normal, and I could sleep, though once I remember getting out of bed and sitting on the top of the stairs in order that I might hear the voices from the dining room below, the low comforting drone of dull adult conversation which told me that the house was not yet ablaze."[1]

As the son of a headmaster, Greene developed an early background in children's literature. Very important when he was a boy were books of adventure and romantic travel. "The books on the nursery shelves which interested me most were *The Little Duke* by Charlotte M. Yonge (the memory of this book returned to me when I was writing *The Ministry of Fear* and when I revised the novel after the war I inserted chapter headings from *The Little Duke*), *The Children of the New Forest* by Captain Marryat, the Andrew Lang Fairy Books, the E. Nesbits, of which I liked best *The Enchanted Castle, The Phoenix and the Carpet, Five Children and It* (the less fantastic *The Would-Be-Goods* and *The Treasure Seekers* never meant much to me). Two incidents from these books have always remained vivid to me, one of terror and one of joyful excitement: the Ugly Wugglies made of masks and umbrellas in *The Enchanted Castle* who suddenly came alive and applauded the children's play from their roofless mouths, clapping empty gloves, and the end of *The Phoenix,* when the magical bird has gone and a great box arrives full of everything the children have ever desired: 'toys and games and books, and chocolate and candied cherries, and paint-boxes and photographic cameras'—Brownies they would have been in those days. I think I read alone, but perhaps it was read aloud to us, Kipling's *Baa Baa, Black Sheep,* which was like a warning not to take happiness in childhood for granted. At an earlier period of course there was Beatrix Potter. I have never lost my admiration for her books and I have often reread her, so that I am not surprised when I find in one of my own stories, 'Under the Garden,' a pale echo of Tom Kitten being trounced up by the rats behind the skirting board and the sinister Anna-Maria covering him with dough, and in *Brighton Rock* the dishonest lawyer, Prewitt, hungrily echoes Miss Potter's dialogue as he watches the secretaries go by carrying their little typewriters.

"Toward the end of this period in my life I came on Henty. We had on the nursery shelves a long run of Henty, and I particularly liked the dull historical parts. 'The XIVth Hussars proceeded in close order to the top of the ridge. On the right flank were the Second Ghurkas . . .' Rider Haggard I discovered after Henty. My favorite, of course, was *King Solomon's Mines,* but the later adventures of Quatermain bored me. I fell fast in love with Nada the Lily, and because of his savagery I admired Chaka, the great King of Zululand. Later I read *The Brethren* (about the Crusades), from which a great phrase remains in my mind to this day, 'So they went, talking earnestly of all things, but, save in God, finding no hope at all,' *The Wanderer's Necklace* (a romance of Byzantium in which the hero is blinded by the woman he loves), and *Ayesha,* the sequel to *She.* I didn't at all care for romantic *She,* and found the metaphysical love story sloppy as I find it today (I have always preferred Freud to Jung). But the scene in *Ayesha* when the mad Khan goes hunting with bloodhounds the lord who had courted his wife held me with the strange attraction of suffering and cruelty. 'What followed I will not describe, but never shall I forget the scene of those two heaps of worrying wolves, and of the maniac Kahn, who yelled in his fiendish joy, and cheered on his death-hounds to finish their red work.' *Montezuma's Daughter* led me to read and reread a history of Mexico in the school library; the dark night of Cortez's retreat from Mexico City along the narrow causeways haunts me still. What a happy chance it seemed in those days to be the son of the headmaster, for in the holidays all the shelves of the library were open to me, with thousands of books only waiting to be explored.

"The influence of early books is profound. So much of the future lies on the shelves: early reading has more influence

He would just come to a stop, until someone came and pushed him into a siding where he would get older and older and rustier and rustier and nobody would remember him. ■(From *The Little Train* by Graham Greene. Illustrated by Edward Ardizzone.)

on conduct than any religious teaching. I feel certain that I would not have made a false start, when I was twenty-one, in the British-American Tobacco Company, which has promised me a post in China, if I had never read Captain Gilson's *Lost Column,* and without a knowledge of Rider Haggard would I have been drawn later to Liberia? (This led to a wartime post in Sierra Leone. At Oxford I had made tentative inquiries about the Nigerian Navy as a future career.) And surely it must have been *Montezuma's Daughter* and the story of the disastrous night of Cortez's retreat which lured me twenty years afterwards to Mexico. *The Man-eaters of Tsavo* on the other hand fixed in me a boring image of East Africa which even Hemingway was powerless to change. Only an assignment to report the Mau-Mau rebellion in 1951 and the sense of continuous danger on the Kikuyu roads was able to remove it.''[1]

Fall, 1912. Attended Berkhamsted School. ''I went to school just before I was eight, as my birthday came in October, after term had started. My form master in the bottom form was called Frost. [He] had the reputation of getting on well with very small boys, but I was a little afraid of him. He used to sweep his black gown around him in a melodramatic gesture, before he indulged his jovial ogrish habit of screwing a fist in one's cheek till it hurt.

''Of my first day at school I can remember nothing except that I had to read a passage from *Captain Cook's Voyages,* the set English book that term. I found the formal eighteenth-century prose very dull, and I still do. History was my favorite subject, and when I was about twelve a rather foolish master whom we all despised stated in my annual report, otherwise given up to laconic statements—'Satisfactory,' 'Tries hard,' 'Weak' and suchlike—that I 'had the makings of an historian.' I was pleased,

but considered rightly that it was an attempt to pander favor with my father.

''The only class I actively hated was held in the gym. I was very bad at gymnastics and all life long my instinct has been to abandon anything for which I have no talent; tennis, golf, dancing, sailing, all have been abandoned, and perhaps it is only desperation which keeps me writing, like someone who clings to an unhappy marriage for fear of solitude. I particularly disliked trying to vault or to climb a rope. I suffered in those days, like a character of mine, Jones, in *The Comedians,* from flat feet, and I had to wear supports inside my shoes and have massage from a gym mistress. The massage tickled a little and my soles sometimes ached, but on the whole I found the treatment agreeable, perhaps because it was given by a woman. This must have been between the age of ten and twelve, for it was the war of 1914 which brought a number of mistresses to the school in place of the masters who had joined the Army.''[1]

1917. At thirteen, Greene was sent to live in the house where he had spent his earliest years. He was now a boarder at St. John's. ''I had passed thirteen and things were worse even than I had foreseen. I lay in bed in the dormitory of St. John's, listening to the footsteps clatter down the stone stairs to early prep and breakfast, and when the silence had safely returned I began trying to cut my right leg open with a penknife. But the knife was blunt and my nerve was too weak for the work.

''I was back in the house of my early childhood, but the circumstances had changed. The garden across the road, France across the Channel, was now closed to me: I could no longer set foot in the chintzy drawing room where my mother had read aloud to us and where I had wept over the story of the children buried by the birds. In those early days I had not even been aware that there existed in the same house such grim rooms as those I lived in now. Even the door by which I entered the house was a different one, a side door like a service entrance, though no servant would have endured the squalor we lived in. There was a schoolroom with ink-stained nibbled desks insufficiently warmed by one cast-iron stove, a changing room smelling of sweat and stale clothes, stone stairs, worn by generations of feet, leading to a dormitory divided by pitch-pine partitions that gave inadequate privacy—no moment of the night was free from noise, a cough, a snore, a fart. Years later when I read the sermon on hell in Joyce's *Portrait of the Artist* I recognized the land I had inhabited. I had left civilization behind and entered a savage country of strange customs and inexplicable cruelties: a country in which I was a foreigner and a suspect, quite literally a hunted creature, known to have dubious associates. Was my father not the headmaster? I was like the son of a quisling in a country under occupation. My elder brother Raymond was a school prefect and head of the house—in other words one of Quisling's collaborators. I was surrounded by the forces of the resistance, and yet I couldn't join them without betraying my father and my brother.

"I endured that life for some eight terms—a hundred and four weeks of monotony, humiliation and mental pain. It is astonishing how tough a boy can be, but I was helped by my truancies, those peaceful hours hidden in the hedge. At last came the moment of final decision. It was after breakfast one morning in the School House dining room, on the last day of the summer holidays, that I made my break for liberty. I wrote a note, which I placed on the black oak sideboard under the whisky tantalus, saying that instead of returning to St. John's, I had taken to the Common and would remain there in hiding until my parents agreed that never again should I go back to my prison. There were enough blackberries that fine autumn to keep me from hunger, and I prided myself on knowing every hidden trench.

"It was time I looked at my exposed flank—a steep clay path between oaks and beeches above Kitchener's Fields. I moved rashly out beyond the cover of the bushes and began to descend, until, turning a corner, I came face to face with my elder sister, Molly. I could have run, of course, but that hardly suited the dignity of my protest, and so I went quietly home with her. It was a tactical defeat, but it proved all the same a strategical victory. I *had* changed my life; the whole future was decisively altered."[1]

1920. After Greene's abortive attempt to run away, his father sent him to London for psychoanalysis. "I don't know by what process of elimination my father and brother chose Kenneth Richmond to be my analyst, but it was a choice for which I have never ceased to be grateful, for at his house in Lancaster Gate began what were perhaps the happiest six months of my life.

"Often of an evening I found myself in the company of authors. Richmond himself was one, if only of a book, which I found rather dull reading, on educational theory. Walter de la Mare came to the house—the poet I admired most at that time—and wrote his spidery signature in my new-bought copy of *The Veil*. One evening we played a game in which each guest in turn had to imitate a vegetable, and I remember how we all simultaneously recognized De la Mare's stick of asparagus. Such evenings were far away from the hours of prep in St. John's musty schoolroom. My only duties were to

read history of a morning in Kensington Gardens and at eleven o'clock to go in for an hour's session with the analyst."[1]

After his stay in London, Greene returned, "repaired—to the world of school. It was a life transformed. I was no longer a boarder at that hated brick barracks called St. John's, which had become so mysteriously changed from the home of a happy childhood, and I had no fear of the old routine of classes. Classes, when once I had outwitted and outgrown the gym, I had never hated, and I returned to them with the proud sense of having been a voyager in very distant seas. Among the natives whom I had encountered there, I had been the witness of strange rites and gained a knowledge of human nature that it would take many years for my companions to equal, or that was what I believed.

"I had left for London a timid boy, anti-social, *farouche:* when I came back I must have seemed vain and knowing. Who among my fellows in 1920 knew anything of Freud or Jung? That summer I invited Walter de la Mare to a strawberry tea in the garden with my parents. He had come to lecture in Berkhamsted and I posed proudly as the poet's friend, though I wished my father had been more impressed by his poetry. 'It lacks passion,' he argued with me, and to refute him I showed him a poem in *The Veil*.

"I found it easy now to make friends. . . . A school has many backwaters, but I was at last in the mainstream. Instead of those petty gangsters of St. John's there were Eric Guest (later a distinguished Metropolitan magistrate), Claud Cockburn, Peter Quennell."[1]

1922. Attended Balliol College, Oxford until 1925. "I went up to Oxford for the autumn term of 1922 to Balliol with nothing resolved—a muddled adolescent who wanted to write but hadn't found his subject, who wanted to express his lust but was too scared to try, and who wanted to love but hadn't found a real object."[1]

It was during his time at college that the youthful Greene, bored with the reality of his uneventful, teenage years, played Russian roulette with his elder brother's revolver. "I can remember very clearly the afternoon I found the revolver in the brown deal corner cupboard in a bedroom which I shared with my elder brother. It was the early autumn of 1923. . . . I knew what to do with it because I had been reading a book (I think Ossendowski was the author) which described how the White Russian officers, condemned to inaction in southern Russia at the tail end of the counterrevolutionary war, used to invent hazards with which to escape boredom. One man would slip a charge into a revolver and turn the chambers at random, and his companion would put the revolver to his head and pull the trigger. The chance, of course, was five to one in favor of life.

"I put the muzzle of the revolver into my right ear and pulled the trigger. There was a minute click, and looking down at the chamber I could see that the charge had moved into the firing position. I was out by one. I remember an extraordinary sense of jubilation, as if carnival lights had been switched on in a dark drab street. My heart knocked in its cage, and life contained an infinite number of possibilities. It was like a young man's first successful experience of sex—as if among the Ashridge beeches I had passed the test of manhood. I went home and put the revolver back in the corner cupboard.

"This experience I repeated a number of times. At fairly long intervals I found myself craving for the adrenalin drug, and I took the revolver with me when I returned to Oxford. There I would walk out from Headington toward Elsfield down what is now a wide arterial road, smooth and shiny like the walls of a public lavatory. Then it was a sodden unfrequented country lane. The revolver would be whipped behind my back, the chamber twisted, the muzzle quickly and surreptitiously inserted in my ear beneath the black winter trees, the trigger pulled.

"Slowly the effect of the drug wore off—I lost the sense of jubilation, I began to receive from the experience only the crude kick of excitement. It was the difference between love and lust. And as the quality of the experience deteriorated, so my sense of responsibility grew and worried me. I wrote a bad piece of free verse (free because it was easier in that way to express my meaning clearly without literary equivocation) describing how, in order to give myself a fictitious sense of danger, I would 'press the trigger of a revolver I already know to be empty.' This verse I would leave permanently on my desk, so that if I lost the gamble, it would provide incontrovertible evidence of an accident, and my parents, I thought, would be less troubled by a fatal play-acting than by a suicide—or the rather bizarre truth. (Only after I had given up the game did I write other verses which told the true facts.)

"It was back in Berkhamsted during the **Christmas of 1923** that I paid a permanent farewell to the drug. As I inserted my fifth dose, which corresponded in my mind to the odds against death, it occurred to me that I wasn't even excited: I was beginning to pull the trigger as casually as I might take an aspirin tablet. I decided to give the revolver—since it was six-chambered—a sixth and last chance. I twirled the chambers round and put the muzzle to my ear for a second time, then heard the familiar empty click as the chambers shifted. I was through with the drug.... One campaign was over, but the war against boredom had got to go on. I put the revolver back in the corner cupboard, and going downstairs I lied gently and convincingly to my parents that a friend had invited me to join him in Paris."[1]

1924. Boredom, Greene's name for an enemy that has stalked him all his life, led him to engage in many unorthodox endeavors at Oxford. "It was an odd schizophrenic life I lived during the autumn term of 1924. I attended tutorials, drank coffee at the Cadena, wrote an essay on Thomas More, studied the revolution of 1688 'from original sources,' read papers on poets to the Ordinary and the Mermaid, attended debates at the Union, got drunk with friends; then 'Cross a step or two of dubious twilight, come out on the other side, the novel.' There another life began, where I exchanged last letters with the woman I loved, who was engaged to another man, wrote a first novel never to be published, the unhappy history of a black child born to white parents...."[1]

1925. "Perhaps, until one starts at the age of seventy to live on borrowed time, no year will seem again quite so ominous as the one when formal education ends and the moment arrives to find employment and bear personal responsibility for the whole future. My parents had given me everything they could possibly owe a child and more. Now it was my turn to decide and no one—not even the Oxford Appointments Board—could help me very far. I was hemmed in by a choice of jails in which to serve my life imprisonment, for how else at twenty can one regard a career which may last as long as life itself, or at the best until that sad moment is reached

when the prisoner is released, in consideration of good behavior, with a pension?"[1]

Greene attempted to get a job in China, dreamed of becoming a consul or joining "the Nigerian Navy." In the end, he fell to tutoring and writing a romantic novel that was never finished. "I had a horror of becoming involved in teaching. It was a profession into which you could so easily slip, as my father had done, by accident. A widowed lady living at Ashover, a village in Derbyshire, required someone to look after her son of eight during the holidays. I would not be asked to live in the house: I would have a room in a private hotel with all my meals, but there was no salary attached....

"The position suited me, for I had the evenings free when I could work at my novel.... The widow was undemanding. She didn't want her son to be overworked. A little mathematics perhaps in the morning (I had forgotten all I ever knew), a quarter of an hour of Latin (equally forgotten), some games after lunch.... I had what I thought the bright idea of teaching him a little carpentry, though I had never practiced it myself. There was a large shady garden which reminded me of my uncle's at Harston with lots of outhouses in which I discovered wooden crates, nails, hammers. I suggested we should build a toy theater. My pupil agreed readily enough: he was a boy without initiative: he was quite ready to stand around holding the nails. Unfortunately the toy theater failed to take even a rudimentary shape, so that after two days' work I decided that what we had been making without knowing it was a rabbit hutch. He was quite satisfied, even though there was no rabbit; he was as undemanding as his mother."[1]

1926-30. Employed as a sub-editor for the London *Times*.

February, 1926. Converted to Roman Catholicism. Not from conviction at first, but because he had fallen in love with a girl who was Catholic. "I met the girl I was to marry after finding a note from her at the porter's lodge in Balliol protesting against my inaccuracy in writing, during the course of a film review, of the 'worship' Roman Catholics gave to the Virgin Mary, when I should have used the term 'hyperdulia.' I was interested that anyone took these subtle distinctions of an unbelievable theology seriously, and we became acquainted. Now it occurred to me, during the long empty mornings, that if I were to marry a Catholic I ought at least to learn the nature and limits of the beliefs she held. It was only fair, since she knew what I believed—in nothing supernatural. Besides, I thought, it would kill the time."[1]

1927. Married Vivien Dayrell Browning. The couple had two children: one son, one daughter. After twenty years, the marriage broke-up. Precisely why—Greene thinks—is his private business.

1929. *The Man Within* published. On December 31, 1929 Greene resigned his position at the *Times*. "So I left the coal grate and the faces under the green eyeshields, faces which remain as vivid to me now when the names of their owners are forgotten as those of close friends and women I have loved. In the years to come I was bitterly to regret my decision. I left *The Times* the author of a successful first novel. I thought I was a writer already and that the world was at my feet, but life wasn't like that. It was only a false start."[1]

1930. *The Name of Action*, an adventure story and Greene's second published novel, was a failure. "Now I can see quite clearly where I went wrong. Excitement is simple: excitement is a situation, a single event. It mustn't be wrapped up in thoughts, similes, metaphors.''[1]

1935-39. Employed as a film critic for the London *Spectator*. ''Four and a half years of watching films several times a week. . . . I can hardly believe in that life of the distant thirties now, a way of life which I adopted quite voluntarily from a sense of fun. More than four hundred films—and I suppose there would have been many many more if I had not suffered during the same period from other obsessions—four novels had to be written, not to speak of a travel book which took me away for months to Mexico, far from the Pleasure-Dome—all those Empires and Odeons of a luxury and a bizarre taste which we shall never see again. How, I find myself wondering, could I possibly have written all these reviews? And yet I remember opening the envelopes, which contained the gilded cards of invitation, for the morning Press performances (mornings when I should have been struggling with *Brighton Rock* and *The Power and the Glory*) with a sense of curiosity and anticipation. These films were an escape—escape from that hellish problem of construction in Chapter Six, from the secondary character who obstinately refused to come alive, escape for an hour and a half from the melancholy which falls inexorably round the novelist when he has lived for too many months on end in his private world.

''From film-reviewing it was only a small step to script-writing. That also was a danger, but a necessary one as I had a family to support and I remained in debt to my publishers until the war came. I had persistently attacked the films made by Alexander Korda and perhaps he became curious to meet his enemy. He asked my agent to bring me to Denham and when we were alone he asked if I had any film story in mind. I had none, so I began to improvise a thriller—early morning on Platform 1 at Paddington, the platform empty, except for one man who is waiting for the last train from Wales. From below his raincoat a trickle of blood forms a pool on the platform.

'''Yes? and then?'

'''It would take too long to tell you the whole plot—and the idea needs a lot more working out.'

''I left Denham half an hour later to work for eight weeks on what seemed an extravagant salary, and the worst and least successful of all Korda's productions thus began. So did our friendship which endured and deepened till his death, in spite of two bad screenplays and my reviews which remained unfavourable. Year later, after the war was over, I wrote two more screenplays for Korda and Carol Reed, 'The Fallen Idol' and 'The Third Man,' and I hope they atoned a little for the prentice-scripts of which I prefer to forget even the titles.'' [*Graham Greene on Film, Collected Film Criticism 1935-40*, edited by John Russell Taylor, Simon & Schuster, 1962.[2]]

1937-38. Made a trip to southern Mexico to write a study on the persecution of the Church and to escape a libel suit brought against him by Twentieth Century-Fox on behalf of the child star, Shirley Temple. The studio charged that Greene, who was then a film critic, had accused Twentieth Century-Fox of procuring Miss Temple for immoral purposes in his review of the movie ''Wee Willie Winkie.'' During his Mexican exile the idea for his novel, *The Power and the Glory*, which was published in 1940, was formulated.

1941-44. During World War II Greene served with the Foreign Office in Africa. ''During the Blitz one loved London particularly. Awful as the war was, one is nostalgic for the feeling of that period. The city became a series of villages. During a blackout you could see the stars and the moon, even on Oxford Street, and flares dropping like chandeliers. In the morning there was the sound of broken glass being swept up. It wasn't white, as you'd think, but blue-green.'' [''The 'Conspicuous Service' of Graham Greene, a New Honor and a New Novel,'' *Life*, edited by George P. Hunt, February 4, 1966.[3]]

1948. *The Heart of the Matter*, which won the James Tait Black Memorial Prize for 1949, was published. The book established him as a complex and Catholic writer. ''It's my most popular book, but I don't like it any longer. Scobie is too self-pitying. I don't like many English Catholics. I don't like conventional religious piety. I'm more at ease with the Catholicism of Catholic countries. I've always found it difficult to believe in God. I suppose I'd now call myself a Catholic atheist. The English Catholic I admire is Alexander Pope.

''And Newman, of course. As a writer I have often been criticized by the pious. Cardinal Newman answers them.'' [V. S. Pritchett, ''The Human Factor in Graham Greene,'' *The New York Times Magazine*, February 26, 1978.[4]]

1954. Traveled to Vietnam as the Indochina correspondent for *New Republic*. Greene has oftened traveled on assignments from newspapers in England, for French publicatios' and sometimes for the BBC.

1955. *The Little Horse Bus* won the Boys' Clubs of America Junior Book Award. Although Greene is primarily known for his adult fiction, he wrote several books for children in the fifties.

1961. *A Burnt-Out Case* published. For the background material for this book, Greene paid an extended visit to a leper colony. ''Leper colonies aren't horrible at all. I'm much more nauseated by hospital scenes in films, which make me put my head down and tie up my shoelaces.''[3]

1962. Awarded a Litt.D. from Cambridge University. In reply to a comment that his books were personal with the author using his characters to verbalize his own opinions, Greene stated: ''A novelist can easily unself himself. He can write as a woman or a child. The opinions in my novels are not mine: They are the opinions of my characters. Readers are very stupid about this. I do not take people straight from real life in my novels. A novel is not a work of travel or autobiography. Even these are re-creations. I shall never write my own reminiscences because I have a poor memory. Real people are crowded out by imaginary ones, that is why I have to stare at them for so long. There has once or twice been a little straight reporting in my novels—there was some in *The Quiet American*, but no real people. Real people would wreck the design. The characters in my novels are an amalgam of bits of real people; one takes the isolated traits from many; they are fused by the heat of the unconscious. Real people are too limiting.''[4]

1963. Made an honorary fellow of Balliol College, Oxford.

1966. Awarded the Companion of Honour.

1973. *The Honorary Consul* published. When Greene is not traveling, he lives in a modern apartment house in Antibes, France overlooking a busy marina. ''I'm in that ugly block

(From the movie "The Power and the Glory," starring Laurence Olivier. Copyright © 1961 by Paramount-Talent Associates.)

near the marina. The old harbor used to come right up to the walls when I took the place. It was very nice until they built this monstrous basin for the luxury yachts and cruisers. We used to be quiet."[4]

1978. Greene's latest book, *The Human Factor,* published. "I'm usually awake by six and keep going until I have a hundred words. That means about five hours. I have to be strict with myself or I'd never get anything done. I used to write 500 words a day, but as I got older, I found that was too much. So I cut down to 300, then to 100, just to keep my hand in. I never lose track of where I am. Sometimes I stop smack in the middle of a paragraph.

"Of course I used to work much faster. Back when I was young I liked to bring out a new book every year. It was a conscious reaction against the Bloomsbury people, most of whom seemed content to do a few things, build a huge reputation, and rest on it. But even then I always had to revise my novels again and again to get them right. Now it takes me years to finish a book and sometimes it still isn't right." [Michael Mewshaw, "The Staying Power and the Glory," *The Nation,* April 16, 1977.[5]]

When asked if experience and practice with the writer's craft didn't develop confidence in the writer's talent, Greene replied: "One has no talent. I have no talent. It's just a question of working, of being willing to put in the time."[5]

In 1970, film rights were purchased for "May We Borrow Your Husband?," and, in 1971, *The End of the Affair* was filmed for television.

ADAPTATIONS—Screenplays based on his books and stories: "Orient Express," 1934; "This Gun for Hire," 1942; "The Ministry of Fear," 1944; "The Confidential Agent," 1945; "The Smugglers," 1948; "Brighton Rock," 1948; "The Fallen Idol," screenplay by Greene, 1949; "The Third Man," screenplay by Greene, 1950; "The Heart of the Matter," 1954; "The End of the Affair," 1955; "Loser Takes All," 1957; "The Quiet American," 1958; "Across the Bridge," 1958; "Our Man in Havana," screenplay by Greene, 1960; "The Power and the Glory," 1962; "The Comedians," screenplay by Greene, 1967; "The Living Room," 1969; "The Shipwrecked," 1970; "Travels with My Aunt," 1973; "England Made Me," 1973; "A Burned-Out Case," 1973.

Filmstrips: "The Little Train" and "The Little Fire Engine" in "Popular Picture Books—Set I," Random House, 1977.

FOR MORE INFORMATION SEE: America, January 25, 1941; *Living Writers,* Sylvan Press, 1947; Henry Reed, *The Novel Since 1939,* Longmans, Green, 1947; Paul Rostenne, *Graham Greene: Temoin des temps tragiques,* Julliard, 1949; Kenneth Allott and Miriam Farris, *The Art of Graham Greene,* Hamish Hamilton, 1951, Russell & Russell, 1965; P.

H. Newby, *The Novel: 1945-1950,* Longmans, Green, 1951; Orville Prescott, *In My Opinion,* Bobbs-Merrill, 1952; Francois Mauriac, *Great Men,* Rockliff, 1952; Maire-Beatrice Mesnet, *Graham Greene and the Heart of the Matter,* Cresset, 1954; Francis Wyndham, *Graham Greene,* Longmans, Green, 1955; Sean O'Faolain, *The Vanishing Hero,* Atlantic Monthly Press, 1956; Morton Dauwen Zabel, *Craft and Character in Modern Fiction,* Viking, 1957; John Atkins, *Graham Greene,* Roy, 1958; William R. Mueller, *The Prophetic Voice in Modern Fiction,* Association Press, 1959; Francis L. Kunkel, *The Labyrinthine Ways of Graham Greene,* Sheed, 1959; Frank Kermode, *Puzzles and Epiphanies,* Chilmark, 1962; John Russell Taylor, *Graham Greene on Film, Collected Film Criticism 1935-40,* Simon & Schuster, 1962; R. O. Evans, editor, *Graham Greene: Some Critical Considerations,* University of Kentucky Press, 1963; Philip Stratford, *Faith and Fiction,* University of Notre Dame Press, 1964; L. A. DeVitis, *Graham Greene,* Twayne, 1964; Walter Allen, *The Modern Novel,* Dutton, 1965; *New York Times Book Review,* January 23, 1966; *Times Literary Supplement,* January 27, 1966; *Life,* February 4, 1966; *New York Review of Books,* March 3, 1966; David Lodge, *Graham Greene,* Columbia University Press, 1966; Graham Green, *A Sort of Life,* Simon & Schuster, 1971; Carolyn Riley, editor, *Contemporary Literary Criticism,* Gale, Volume I, 1973, Volume III, 1975; *Horn Book,* October, 1974; *The Nation,* April 16, 1977; *New York Times Magazine,* February 26, 1978.

If you want to condition your body for vigorous sports competition, you will need to increase your food intake, because the longer and harder you work the more energy you need. ■ (From *Physical Fitness Through Sports and Nutrition* by Walter H. Gregg, Ed.D. Photo courtesy of Evanston Township High School.)

GREGG, Walter H(arold)   1919-

PERSONAL: Born April 7, 1919, in Columbus, Ohio; son of Herbert L. (a building contractor) and Lula B. (Pettibone) Gregg; married Betty Louise Harrold, March 28, 1942; children: Sue Ellen Gregg Roupas, Jay Harrold. *Education:* Ohio State University, B.Sc., 1941, M.A., 1947; Columbia University, Ed.D., 1952. *Home:* 828 Glenview Rd., Glenview, Ill. 60025. *Office:* Department of Health and Physical Education, Northwestern University, Evanston, Ill. 60201.

CAREER: Franklin High School, New Athens, Ohio, teacher of mathematics, health, and physical education, and athletic coach, 1941-42; Penn. State College, Slippery Rock, Pa., instructor in education and coach of football, swimming, and baseball, 1947-51; Miami University, Oxford, Ohio, 1951-57, began as assistant professor, became associate professor of health, physical education, and recreation, also health coordinator and director of graduate studies; Northwestern University, Evanston, Ill., professor of health and physical education, 1957—. Member of Illinois governor's advisory committee for Division of Alcoholism, Department of Mental Health. Spokesperson for California Raisin Advisory Board. *Military service:* U.S. Naval Reserve, lieutenant, Air Force, active duty, 1942-46. *Member:* American School Health Association (fellow), College Physical Education Association.

WRITINGS: A Boy and His Physique (booklet), National Dairy Council, 1961, revised edition, 1970; *Physical Fitness Through Sports and Nutrition* (juvenile), Scribner, 1975. Contributor to health and education journals.

WORK IN PROGRESS: Preparing books on eating patterns of high school athletes and developing a guide for curriculum development in physical education.

SIDELIGHTS: "I have a long background in sports' participation and an intense interest in the health and welfare of young people."

HOBBIES AND OTHER INTERESTS: "Refinishing and building colonial furniture—I have built two houses of my own. I play handball and golf, regularly." Gregg also enjoys gardening.

GRIFFITHS, G(ordon) D(ouglas)   1910-1973

OBITUARY NOTICE: Born July 19, 1910, in Wallasey, Cheshire, England; died in July, 1973. Griffiths was a farmer before the onset of World War II, during which he served with the British Army Intelligence Corps. Afterwards he taught French, Latin, and Greek in several Devonshire prep schools, and was a publisher's reader and free-lance writer. With his wife, Griffiths authored *History of Teignmouth*, but it was as a children's writer that he made his mark. His three books for children are animal narratives, with the locale of each of them being the Dartmoor region of Devon, England. The animals he focuses on, in natural settings, are as varied as a hedgehog, wild ponies, and an abandoned cat. Griffiths also contributed many fishing articles to periodicals. *For More Information See: The Author's and Writer's Who's Who*, 6th edition, Burke's Peerage, 1971; *Contemporary Authors, Permanent Series*, Volume 2, Gale, 1978; *Twentieth Century Children's Writers*, St. Martin's, 1978.

Edith Hamilton at Bryn Mawr College.

HAMILTON, Edith   1867-1963

PERSONAL: Born August 12, 1867, in Dresden, Germany, of American parents; died May 31, 1963; raised in Fort Wayne, Ind.; daughter of Montgomery and Gertrude (Pond) Hamilton. *Education:* Studied at Bryn Mawr College, receiving both B.A. and M.A. degrees in 1895. *Religion:* Presbyterian. *Residences:* Washington, D.C., and Mt. Desert Island, Me.

CAREER: Bryn Mawr School, Baltimore, Md., headmistress, 1896-1922; full-time writer, beginning, 1922. *Member:* National Institute of Arts and Letters, American Academy of Arts and Letters, P.E.N. *Awards, honors:* Mary E. Grant European fellow at the Universities of Leipzig and Munich, 1895-96; National Achievement Award, 1950; Constance Lindsay Skinner Award, 1958; D.Litt. from the University of Rochester, 1949, the University of Pennsylvania, 1953, and Yale University, 1959; was named an honorary citizen of Athens, Greece, and received the Greek Golden Cross of the Order of Benefaction, 1957.

WRITINGS: The Greek Way, Norton, 1930, reissued, Avon, 1973, enlarged editions published as *The Great Age of Greek Literature,* Norton, 1942, and *The Greek Way to Western Civilization,* New American Library, 1948; *The Roman Way,* Norton, 1932, reissued, Avon, 1973; *The Prophets of Israel,* Norton, 1936, a new edition published as *Spokesmen for God: The Great Teachers of the Old Testament,* 1949, reissued, 1962; *Mythology* (illustrated by Steele Savage), Little, Brown, 1942, reprinted, New American Library, 1971; *Witness to the Truth: Christ and His Interpreters,* Norton, 1948; *The Echo of Greece,* Norton, 1957; *The Ever-Present Past,* Norton, 1964; *A Treasury of Edith Hamilton* (selections; edited by Doris Fielding Reid), Norton, 1969.

Other: (Translator) *Three Greek Plays: Prometheus Bound, Agamemnon, The Trojan Women,* Norton, 1937, reissued, 1965; (editor) Plato, *The Collected Dialogues of Plato, Including Letters,* Pantheon Books, 1961; (translator) Euripides, *The Trojan Women,* Bantam Books, 1971.

Contributor of articles to periodicals, including *Atlantic Monthly, Saturday Review of Literature,* and *Theatre Arts Monthly.*

SIDELIGHTS: **August 12, 1867.** Born of American parents in Dresden, Germany. Raised in Fort Wayne, Indiana. Hamilton's father, a cultivated man, began teaching her Latin when she was seven. Her younger sister, Alice, wrote of Hamilton's phenomenal verbal memory as a child: "Edith, the first born, though only eighteen months older than I, seemed much more mature, partly because she was a passionate reader. . . . Edith read everything she could lay her hands on. She was a natural storyteller, and on the long walks my mother insisted on our taking every day, Edith would give us résumés of Scott and Bulwer-Lytton and De Quincey. She could not understand my childish taste in books and she would stop at an exciting spot, such as Amy Robsart's death in *Kenilworth,* and say, 'Now you've got to finish it yourself.' Sometimes I did, but sometimes I slipped back to the 'Katy' books, to her infinite disgust. She also loved to learn poetry by heart, and as we walked to and from our daily music lesson, she would recite to me Macaulay's *Lays of Ancient Rome,* 'Naseby,' and 'Ivry' till I knew them by heart. Then came Shelley, Keats, and Byron. I am sure I learned 'The Eve of St. Agnes' just by listening to her recite it." [Doris Fielding Reid, *Edith Hamilton: An Intimate Portrait,* Norton, 1967.[1]]

Attended her first school, Miss Porter's School in Farmington, Conn., as a teenager. Years later, when asked what she was taught there, Hamilton replied, "Oh, we weren't *taught* anything."[1]

1895. Received her B.A. and M.A. degrees from Bryn Mawr College, where she majored in the classics. Awarded the European fellowship from Bryn Mawr and spent a year in Germany studying the classics at the Universities of Leipzig and Munich. Hamilton was the first woman to enroll at the University of Munich. "The head of the University used to stare at me, then shake his head and say sadly to a colleague, 'There, now you see what's happened? We're right in the midst of the woman question'."[1]

1896. Returned to the United States and became the first headmistress of Bryn Mawr School in Baltimore. ". . . I was very young and very ignorant when I first came to Baltimore and, I may say, very, very, frightened. I remember vividly saying to myself as I traveled down here, 'If I were put in

charge of running this train, I could hardly know less how to do it than I know how to run the Bryn Mawr School.'"[1]

". . . How very hard it was for me to live up to the school's sins! By that I mean I had to take them terribly seriously, because the only punishment ever inflicted on any of the girls was an interview with me; and very often they were the kind of thing you just want to laugh over. One illustration I am going to allow myself. . . . I think we would all consider her a person with an original and adventurous turn of mind. One morning she got up very early and went to the school house long before anybody else was there and occupied herself in the main study room. . . . During prayers everything was as orderly as possible. But then—prayers ended, the desk lids were raised, and out leaped from every one a lot of very lively and very longlegged grasshoppers! I couldn't possibly describe the scene to you—it couldn't be described. I am sure none of you could ever guess how long it was before the school building was completely purified of these creatures. Well, the terrible perpetrator of this deed was brought down to me to be convicted of sin. And what I had to do my best to do was not to burst out laughing. You can see that was a duty that often was very hard on me.

"And another thing I see as very difficult; it was up to me, even though my teachers were so good, to keep the atmosphere of the school one where real life and book learning were in the same world. It is so easy to get them apart. I remember once, going into a classroom where a small girl was beginning her recitation with 'Achilles came out of his tent on the seashore in front of a Greek camp and stood looking over the main.' It was so smooth I was suspicious. At last I said, 'and what was the main, Emma?' She answered, 'A ship blown up in the Spanish war.' I got a very clear idea of how possible it was to learn words by heart without ever thinking of their making sense.

"I can't say, though, that I myself ever thought much of college professors as educational guides for school girls. I know that is heresay, but I really think that. I fought a battle royal with the History Department of Bryn Mawr College because they wanted me to drop all history from the school. Don't send us any girls, they said, with silly stories in their heads about Alfred and the cakes, or George Washington and his little hatchet. We can teach them much better if you just leave it all to us. Well, that dreadful education idea was defeated because the English Department at Bryn Mawr College sided with me. But all the same, I still remember with bitterness a Greek entrance examination where my girls, who had learned their Greek as Bryn Mawr College told them to, by reading Xenophon's *March of the 10,000* and the *Iliad*'s battles of gods and men on the ringing plains of windy Troy, were asked to turn into Greek one of Aesop's fables about a frog! It was terrible and I still am angry when I think about it!

"What I prized about the close connection of the school with the college was that it made hard work necessary. I can see myself sitting on the back stairs in the school building, telling a girl that she had failed her college entrance examination, and I can feel the heavy silence that got between us, and then I see her looking at me firmly and saying, 'Well, I've got to put off making my debut at the Bachelors' Cotillion for a year.' The Bryn Mawr School taught me that failure had its good side as well as its bad side. It did not need to create a complex; it could create courage. . . . Plato spoke for them all when he said with finality, 'Hard is the good'."[1]

Besides administrative duties, Hamilton taught senior Latin. "I loved teaching far and away more than anything else I did. I got a great deal of fun out of teaching Virgil. I remember once translating to my class the description in the *Aeneid* of the exhausted oarsmen after the great boat race. In the next number of the school magazine there appeared: 'One whose words we always revere tells us that *Anhelitus quatit memba* should be translated, Their limbs shook from their pants'."[1]

June, 1922. Retired from Bryn Mawr. "There is a bit of Aristotle I always like to quote. He says it is a definition of happiness. It is that, but I think it also is what education should strive for: 'the exercise of vital powers along lines of excellence, in a life affording them scope'."[1]

Bought a house at Sea Wall, Mt. Desert Island, Maine where she spent almost every summer for the next forty years. "The air is so stimulating. The island is not only beautiful, it has vitality. There is nothing tame about this ocean."[1]

Autumn, 1924. Moved to 24 Gramercy Park in New York City with her lifelong friend, Doris Reid. Began a writing career.

1929. First trip to Greece and Egypt. Of the pyramids, Hamilton wrote: "They look to be nothing made by hands but part of the basic structure of the earth. Where the wind lifts the sand into shapes of gigantic geometry—triangles which, as one watches, pass into curves and break again into sharp-pointed outlines, a cycle of endless change as fixed as the movement of the stars against the immensity of the desert which never changes—the pyramids, immutable, immovable, are the spirit of the desert incased in granite."[1]

1930. Wrote first book, *The Greek Way.* Hamilton never wrote anything for publication which was not accepted.

1942. Retold the stories of classical mythology in her book, *Mythology,* which sold well over one and a half million copies. The book was an exhaustive task which took three years to complete. "A book on Mythology must draw from widely different sources. Twelve hundred years separate the first writers through whom the myths have come down to us, from the last, and there are stories as unlike each other as *Cinderella* and *King Lear.* To bring them all together in one volume is really somewhat comparable to doing the same for the stories of English literature from Chaucer to the ballads, through Shakespeare and Marlowe . . . and so on, ending with, say, Tennyson and Browning. . . .

"Faced with this problem, I determined at the outset to dismiss any idea of unifying the tales. That would have meant either writing *King Lear,* so to speak, down to the level of *Cinderella*—the vice versa procedure being obviously not possible—or else telling in my own way stories which were in no sense mine and had been told by great writers in ways they thought suited their subjects. I do not mean, of course, that a great writer's style can be reproduced. . . . My aim has been nothing more ambitious than to keep distinct for the reader the very different writers from whom our knowledge of the myths comes. For example, Hesiod is a notably simple writer and devout; he is naive, even childish, sometimes crude, always full of piety. Many of the stories in this book are told only by him. Side by side with them are stories told only by Ovid, subtle, polished, artificial, self-conscious, and the complete skeptic. My effort has been to make the reader see some difference between writers who were so different. After all, when one takes up a book like this, one does not

She had to know what was in the box. One day she lifted the lid—and out flew plagues innumerable, sorrow and mischief for mankind. In terror Pandora clapped the lid down, but too late. One good thing, however, was there—Hope. It was the only good thing the casket had held among the many evils, and it remains to this day mankind's sole comfort in misfortune. ■ (From *Mythology* by Edith Hamilton. Illustrated by Steele Savage.)

ask how entertainingly the author has retold the stories, but how close he has brought the reader to the original."[1]

1943. Moved to 2448 Massachusetts Ave., Washington, D.C., where she lived for the next twenty years with Doris Reid.

1956. Second trip to Greece. Visited Italy.

1957. Completed her seventh book. Besides her books, Hamilton contributed numerous articles and reviews to magazines and translated ancient classics.

August, 1957. Recognized as the greatest woman classicist, Hamilton was made an honorary citizen of Athens. On the stage of the ancient theater of Herodes Atticus at the foot of the Acropolis she accepted the award. ". . . I am a Citizen of Athens, of the city I have for so long loved as much as I love my own country. This is the proudest moment of my life. And yet as I stand here . . . under the very shadow of the Acropolis a deeper feeling rises. I see Athens, the home of beauty and of thought. Even today among buildings, the Parthenon is supreme, Plato's thought has never been transcended; of the four great tragedians, three are Greek. We are here to see a performance of the *Prometheus*. In all literature, Prometheus is the great rebel against tyranny. It is most fitting that he should be presented to the world now, in this period of the world's history, and here, in the city of Athens. For Athens, truly the mother of beauty and of thought, is also the mother of freedom. Freedom was a Greek discovery. The Greeks were the first free nation in the world. In the *Prometheus* they have sent a ringing call down through the centuries to all who would be free. Prometheus, confronted with the utmost tyranny, will not submit. He tells the tyrant's messenger, who urges him to yield, 'Go and persuade the sea-wave not to break. You will persuade me no more easily.' That is the spirit Greece gave to the world. It challenges us and we need the challenge. Greece rose to the very height not because she was big, she was very small; not because she was rich, she was very poor; not even because she was wonderfully gifted. She rose because there was in the Greeks the greatest spirit that moves in humanity, the spirit that makes men free. It is impossible for us to believe that, of all the nations of the world, Greece was the only one that had the vision of what St. John in the Gospels calls 'the true light' which, he adds, 'lightest every man who cometh into the world'; but we know that she was the only one who followed it. She kept on—on what one of her poets calls 'the long and rough and steep road.' Therefore her light was never extinguished. Therefore we are met tonight to see a play which has lived for twenty-five hundred years. In those years the Greeks have been outstripped by science and technology, but never in the love of the truth, never in the creation of beauty and freedom.''[1]

August 12, 1957. Returned to New York on her ninetieth birthday. Spent the remainder of the summer at Sea Wall in Maine. When asked if she had any writing in mind, she replied: ". . . I am not going to do it now. I am going up to my summer home on Mt. Desert and lie on the rocks and watch the tide.''[1]

January, 1958. Lectured at the Institute of Contemporary Arts. ". . . How honored I feel that I, a woman of ninety, should be asked to speak before the Institute of *Contemporary* Arts.''[1]

Spring, 1958. Returned to Washington, D.C. after a guest appearance on a New York radio program. "I will be ninety-one years old this summer and I have done all the work I am ever going to do. From now on I mean to enjoy myself. Nothing more.''[1]

Began editing the *Dialogues of Plato*. Presented the Constance Lindsay Skinner Award in New York.

Travelled to Spain. "I write while we wait at the airport for the plane which is to take us to Malaga. We have been in Madrid less than a day but long enough to have lost our hearts to the Ritz, the nicest hotel I have ever been in. The dinner the best I have had in years. . . . We get back to Madrid and the Prado in about two weeks. Lovely weather, very warm.''[1]

April, 1958. Wrote from Caceres: "We left Seville Saturday morning and stayed the night at this place [Caceres], a tiny town on the top of a little hill and unbelievably medieval and charming, and flower bedecked. No postcards of them. The next day, yesterday, we went up to Guadalupe, but the Virgin was a poor show compared to Seville's and I did not care to go and look at her jewelry. But we stepped out of the church into a dining room—part of the church—where we had a most amusing lunch served by nuns with a lot of priests often smoking cigarettes and helping the nuns. They were a jolly laughing lot. Peals of laughter especially at one priest.''[1]

June, 1960. Travelled to France. "Old people who do not get out into the air to exercise soon cannot even get out of bed to work and I do not want that to happen to me. I have a lot of work to do yet and there is no end to the reading and thinking I must do before I can finish it." ["Aged Lover of Ancients," *Life*, September 15, 1958.[2]]

1960-1961. Gave four public lectures.

August 12, 1962. Celebrated her ninety-fifth birthday at Sea Wall in Maine. "I think I'm a little better off in this century. In Greece then women were allowed in the theater, but that's about the only public place. There were a lot of men in the market place you would not want your daughter to run up against.''[2]

May 31, 1963. Died. A week before her death, Hamilton remarked with characteristic vigor: "You know I haven't felt up to writing but now I think I am going to be able to finish that book on Plato.''[1]

Hamilton's theories of education were modeled on the beliefs of the greatest civilization before ours—the Greeks. Whereas we believe in the mass education of all young—a view that Miss Hamilton described as "magnificent," but also criticized for its tendency to produce similar minds—the Greeks emphasized differences, and thus, a kind of educational freedom which enabled each individual to develop his own specific talents independently. Hamilton pointed to television as one factor contributing to the "deadly commonplace" nature of our education—millions of children see the same thing at the same time.

Many of these same ideas can be expanded to include the whole of society. In her acceptance speech for the Constance Lindsay Skinner Award, reprinted in *Publishers Weekly*, Hamilton explained: "The picture which Thucydides gives of the age of Pericles is of a nation of independent individuals, wanting to be let alone to do their own work but closely bound together by a love of country. . . . A great . . . , good and enduring republic it must be along such lines. The Athenians kept their eyes fixed on the individual boy growing up . . . to meet life's changes with grace. Only an ideal, [but] . . . not the way I look at it. Ideals have tremendous power. When ideals are low they fade out and are forgotten; great ideals have had power of persistent life."

Hamilton's first book was published after her retirement from her position as headmistress at age 63. *The Greek Way* was an interpretation of the Greek mind and spirit, and applied the Greek ideal to civilization today. The comments of reviewers were mixed. *Outlook* wrote, "The book is delightful reading throughout—and good sense, too. Of the greater writers who have discussed the Greek way of life and thought, none has expressed himself in a manner more likely to appeal to the common reader. The atmosphere of ponderous erudition which hangs over the usual work of scholarship on the Greek period is absent from Edith Hamilton's work.'' Added *Saturday Review:* ''Miss Hamilton makes little demands on any sort of special knowledge of antiquity in her readers, but she succeeds in conveying an atmosphere and getting us to share in her admiration of the Greek spirit.'' Negative comments included a review in *New Statesman,* which read, ''This book is an American interpretation of Greek civilisation. It is written in a sustained, but deadly vein of enthusiasm. . . . The style is that of the direct statement with 75 per cent of the statements unsupported by documentation.'' Five new chapters were added when the book was published as *The Great Age of Greek Literature* in 1942. *Churchman* described it as ''. . . a treasury of inspiration for those who would appreciate the contribution of ancient Greece to the civilization of the world.'' *The Greek Way* enjoyed a long popularity, proven when it was chosen by the Book-of-the-Month Club in 1957—27 years after its first publication. The sequel to *The Greek Way, The Echo of Greece* was published in 1957—the author's ninetieth year.

In a like manner, *The Roman Way* described a way of life as it was presented in the works of ancient poets such as Plautus and Virgil, and attempted to apply these thoughts to the modern world. A *Theatre Arts Monthly* critic commented: ''*The Greek Way* established Miss Hamilton's reputation as a scholar and as an interpreter to the modern mind of Greek civilization. . . . Her pen here is more pliant, her choice of phrase and epithet more sure, and her ability to point her argument just as persuasive. The fact that her preference is always for the Greek way has put her on her mettle among these brilliant Romans, and she does them all full justice.''

Hamilton retold the stories of classical mythology in her book, *Mythology.* A review of the book in *Nation* included the following remarks: ''. . . In a prose at once edged and colorful, she has thrown the whole of even familiar Greek and Norse mythology into a fresh and luminous context. She has never overpressed suggestions and intimations. She has distilled into incidental observations the whole meaning of mythology itself to the modern scholar. . . .'' The *New York Times* added: ''. . . Its merit is largely derived from the author's interest in Greek and Roman myths, which she sees not merely as outworn fancies of dead antiquity, but as living fables not wholly deprived of meaning for our time. Created when the world was young, there is in them, as in most things engendered in humanity's youth, a quality of timelessness, inherent, and unforgettable.''

John Mason Brown, in his book, *Seeing More Things,* described Hamilton as a citizen of both the ancient and the modern worlds, ''equally at home with the best of both.'' He called her a woman ''who would be unusual in any period; in ours she is unique.'' In a speech reprinted in *Publishers Weekly,* Virginia Matthews added, ''As she distilled and interpreted to us what was the finest and best of the world two thousand years ago, so have her own books represented what is best in American literature today.''

FOR MORE INFORMATION SEE: Outlook, May 28, 1930; *New Statesman,* September 20, 1930; *Saturday Review,* November 15, 1930; *Theatre Arts Monthly,* March, 1933; *New York Times,* May 24, 1942; *Nation,* September 19, 1942; *Churchman,* March 15, 1943; John Mason Brown, *Seeing More Things,* Whittlesey House, 1948; *Publishers Weekly,* March 17, 1958; ''Aged Lover of Ancients,'' *Life,* September 15, 1958; J. M. Brown, ''Heritage of Edith Ham-

EDITH HAMILTON

ilton: 1867-1963,'' *Saturday Review,* June 22, 1963; Doris F. Reid, *Edith Hamilton: An Intimate Portrait,* Norton, 1967; Hope Stoddard, *Famous American Women,* Crowell, 1970.

Obituaries: *New York Times,* June 1, 1963; *Time,* June 7, 1963; *Newsweek,* June 10, 1963; *Publishers Weekly,* June 10, 1963; *Current Biography,* July, 1963; *Americana Annual,* 1964.

HANE, Roger   1940-1974

OBITUARY NOTICE: Born in 1940, in Bradford, Penn.; died June 14, 1974, in New York, N.Y. Hane was fatally beaten by six youthful bicycle thieves while testing his new bike in Central Park. Advertising designer and illustrator. Hane did work for a great many periodicals and corporations, including *Time, McCall's, Fortune,* Columbia Records, and Exxon Corporation. For children he illustrated *Mohawk: The Life of Joseph Brant.* Hane was the recipient of an Award of Excellence from the Society of Illustrators in 1975, and was chosen Artist of the Year by the Artist Guild. *For More Information See:* J. Snyder, ''Roger Hane,'' *Graphis,* 29, Number 167, 1973-1974; (obituary) *New York Times,* June 21, 1974.

MARGARET HARMON

HARMON, Margaret   1906-

PERSONAL: Born January 4, 1906, in Philadelphia, Pa.; daughter of Arthur C. and Laura (Blake) Morgan; married Arthur R. Harmon (a mechanical engineer, August 22, 1945). *Education:* Bryn Mawr College, A.B., 1928. *Home:* 1549 Canterbury Rd., St. Petersburg, Fla. 33710.

CAREER: Has worked as an editor for a publisher and for scholarly journals, and as a technical writer for industry.

WRITINGS: Stretching Man's Mind: A History of Data Processing, Mason/Charter, 1975; *The Engineering Medicine Man: The New Pioneer* (on careers in bioengineering), Westminster, 1975; *Working with Words: Careers for Writers,* Westminster, 1977; *Ms. Engineer* (on careers for women in engineering), Westminster, 1979.

SIDELIGHTS: "My books are really a fall-out from my work as a technical writer. Three are vocational books for high school students. I especially enjoyed writing *Ms. Engineer* and being able to tell young women about the great opportunities that have recently opened up in this field for them. Women should aspire to more diversified and difficult jobs than they have in the past. Some of the prejudice they think they encounter may actually be their own hang-ups and lack of confidence in themselves."

HEIN, Lucille Eleanor   1915-

PERSONAL: Born June 11, 1915, in Chicago, Ill.; daughter of Ernest and Sena (Midthun) Hein. *Education:* University of Wisconsin, B.A., 1937, M.A., 1938, graduate study, 1938-40; summer study at University of Leiden, the Sorbonne, and in England at University of London and University of Birmingham. *Religion:* Lutheran. *Home:* 33 Central Ave., Staten Island, N.Y. 10301.

CAREER: Wagner College, Staten Island, N.Y., instructor in English, 1940-44; Camp Fire Girls, Inc., New York, N.Y., program executive, 1945-50; free-lance writer, 1950—. Occasionally teaches, mainly as volunteer, in educational programs, in-service courses for teachers, community recreation and adult education programs, nursery schools, clubs for teen-agers, Sunday School classes, and youth organization, 1940—.

WRITINGS: Enjoy Your Children, Abingdon, 1959; *One Small Circle,* Abingdon, 1962; *Enjoying the Outdoors with Children,* Association Press, 1966; *We Talk With God: Devotions for Family and Group Use,* Fortress, 1968; *Thinking of You,* Association Press, 1969; *I Can Make My Own Prayers,* Judson Press, 1971; *Entertaining Your Child,* Harper, 1971; *Prayer Gifts for Christmas,* Augsburg, 1972; *Walking In God's World,* Judson Press, 1972; *My Very Special Friend,* Judson Press, 1974; *A Tree I can Call My Own,* Judson Press, 1974; *From Sea to Shining Sea,* Judson Press, 1975; *That Wonderful Summer,* Judson Press, 1978.

Editor: La Rue Thurston, *The Complete Book of Campfire Programs,* Association Press, 1958; Robert H. Loeb, Jr., *She-Manners: The Teen Girl's Book of Etiquette,* Association Press, 1959; Charles Merrifield, *Leadership in Voluntary Enterprises,* Oceana Publications, 1961; Gunnar Peterson and Harry Edgren, *The Book of Outdoor Winter Activities,* Association Press, 1962; Claire Cox, *Rainy Day for Kids,* Association Press, 1962. Contributor of articles to about fifty magazines, and of a weekly story to *Lutheran,* 1958-62.

SIDELIGHTS: **June 11, 1915.** Born in Chicago, Illinois and raised in Madison, Wisconsin where her family owned a bakery business. Began writing at eight years old and continued writing and publishing through her teens. "I have kept journals since I was eight or nine. I seldom look at them. But when I do, I note that almost every entry begins with a reference to weather or season or sunrise or sunset or some natural scene.

"Nature. Weather. I notice this on first arising and as I go late to bed. We are creatures of a business and industrial world, yet we still inhabit the world of weather and seasons and natural surroundings. Nature still rules the universe. It rules my life." [Lucille E. Hein, "I Love Life," *The Lutheran,* February 26, 1964.[1]]

1933-1940. Attended the University of Wisconsin where she received her B.A. and M.A. degrees. Hein spent two years of further study on her Ph.D. Major fields of academic study were: English, comparative literature, and classical and modern languages (Greek, Latin, Sanskrit, French, German and others).

1940. Became one of the first two women on the faculty of the Grymes Hill campus of Wagner College in New York. "I was younger than some of my students. Some of these were

I miss my mother and daddy and brother. But I have made Great Grandmother my very special friend while I am here. ■ (From *My Very Special Friend* by Lucille E. Hein. Illustrated by Joan Orfe.)

refugees from Germany and others were advanced students going in for the ministry.''[1]

1945-1950. Program specialist for Camp Fire Girls, Inc.

1950—. Free-lance writer. Besides books, Hein writes stories for children, youth, and adults; fiction and non-fiction; business and industrial pamphlets, public relations materials, reports, magazine articles, poetry translations, and personal interviews. ''I love people. I love this sometimes infamous, sometimes inspirational planet, this tragic-comic planet. I want to live. What is so desirable about death? I will enjoy life while I have it.

''I love. And I am loved. Perhaps that is why I am so seldom discontented. Love has many variations. In my life I have known many loves. Love for dear family. Love for close friends. Love for the casual social encounters, neighbors, co-workers. Love for the stranger sitting beside me at the concert hall. Almost unbearable love for the one held closely, sometimes secretly in my heart. Generous love for mankind—those people of the planet whom I will never meet.

''When I love, I am loved. When I love, I have everything.

''Love for people enables me to laugh at man's caprices, weep for man's sorrows. It enables me to meet new people and go new places with a sense of curiosity and expectation, rather than with distrust of the new and ridicule of the different. The world changes. But people do not change. I love people. I am at home in the world.

''Call me Pollyanna. You do not offend me. There is value in being a Pollyanna. When Pollyanna has only one slice of cake, she cuts it in half and shares it with a friend. For her, a half-loaf is better than none. For her, the cup is always half full, never half empty. She can eat her cake and have it too.

''Like Pollyanna . . . I get a kick out of life. What else is there but life and death? My faith has taught me that I need not fear death. But, until death comes, I am going to enjoy life.

''I prefer to be with those who look on the world as worth living in and worth living for and worth saving for the future. I listen to the prophets of gloom and doom. But I have not yet succumbed to the expectation that I will be blown up by the Big Bomb or be left with a few hundred others on a devastated planet.

''I have great excitement in my heart each morning as I awake. I cannot wait to rise from bed and start the day. Sleep is a waste of time. My heart beats in expectation and high hope for this day. I run (not walk) from window to window of my apartment to exclaim at the dawn. The world is waiting.''[1]

Hein's papers are in the archives of the State Historical Society of Wisconsin.

HOBBIES AND OTHER INTERESTS: Travel, outdoor life, hiking, the theater, music and art.

FOR MORE INFORMATION SEE: Staten Island Advance, October 5, 1954, March, 1959; *The Lutheran*, February 26, 1964; *Staten Island Sunday Advance*, December 14, 1975.

HERMAN, Charlotte 1937-

PERSONAL: Born June 10, 1937, in Chicago, Ill.; daughter of Harry (a mattress manufacturer) and Leah (Kossof) Baran; married Melvin Herman (an attorney), January 27, 1957; children: Sharon, Michael, Deborah, Karen. *Education:* University of Illinois, student, 1955-57; Roosevelt University, B.A., 1960. *Residence:* Lincolnwood, Ill.

CAREER: Teacher in the public schools of Chicago, Ill., 1960-63. *Member:* Children's Reading Round Table, Off-Campus Writers' Workshop, Society of Midland Authors, Authors Guild. *Awards, honors:* Society of Midland Authors Children's Book Ward, 1978, for *Our Snowman Had Olive Eyes*.

WRITINGS—Juveniles: String Bean, J. Philip O'Hara, 1972; *The Three of Us*, J. Philip O'Hara, 1973; *You've Come a Long Way, Sybil Macintosh*, Lamplight, 1974; *The Difference of Ari Stein*, Harper, 1976; *Our Snowman Had Olive Eyes*, Dutton, 1977.

WORK IN PROGRESS: Two juveniles, *On the Way to the Movies* and *My Mother Didn't Kiss Me Goodnight*, for Dutton.

SIDELIGHTS: ''Sometimes I don't know if I'm writing for children or for myself.

''I have found that writing, especially children's stories, has put me in touch with myself—my thoughts and feelings, both past and present. I have never completely grown up, it

Tear up that letter too. You can do better. ■ (From *You've Come a Long Way, Sybil Macintosh* by Charlotte Herman. Illustrated by Trina Schart Hyman.)

CHARLOTTE HERMAN

seems, and it's easy for me to become a child again, or an adolescent. I hope I'm a better writer because of this and can write about people that readers can identify with and believe in and care about.

"I want very much to write *good books*, books of value. That's always my intention. Young readers are the best people around, and I want to give them my best."

HOBBIES AND OTHER INTERESTS: "I enjoy bicycling and love to take long bike rides through the forest preserves and along Lake Michigan. I am also attempting to relearn how to roller skate. When I'm indoors and not writing I like to play piano."

FOR MORE INFORMATION SEE: Horn Book, April, 1978.

HEY, Nigel S(tewart)   1936-

PERSONAL: Born June 23, 1936, in Morecambe, Lancashire, England; son of Aaron and Margery (Kershaw) Hey; married Miriam Lamb, October 13, 1960 (divorced, 1977); married Sue Ann Gunn, July 23, 1978; children: Brian, Jocelyn. *Education:* University of Utah, B.A., 1958. *Home:* 12 Briston Grove, London N8 9EX, England.

CAREER: United Press International, newsman in Salt Lake City, Utah, 1958; *Kentish Express* (weekly newspaper), Ashford, Kent, England, copy editor, 1959-60; *Bermuda Mid-Ocean News* (daily newspaper), Hamilton, Bermuda, associate editor, 1958-59, 1960-61; Weltech College, Salt Lake City, Utah, director, 1962-64; Newspaper Printing Corp., Albuquerque, N.M., editor, 1964-66; Sandia Laboratories (research and development lab), Albuquerque, N.M., information specialist, 1966-72; IMSWORLD Publications, London, editorial director and deputy publisher, 1972—. New Mexico Conference on Social Welfare, member of board of directors, 1966-70. *Member:* American Institute of Aeronautics and Astronautics, National Association of Science Writ-

ers, International Association of Science Writers, Association of British Science Writers, American Association for Advancement of Science (AAAS). *Awards, honors:* New Mexico State Press Association awards for editorial writing and feature writing in weekly newspapers; Royal Society of Health, fellow, 1978.

WRITINGS—Youth books: *The Mysterious Sun,* Putnam, 1971; (with Science Book Associates editors) *How Will We Feed the Hungry Billions?* Messner, 1971; *How Will We Explore the Outer Planets,* Putnam, 1977. Writer of film, "The Space Age and You," and short television film clips on science; co-writer of other full-length science films.

WORK IN PROGRESS: Science, Communication, and the Public, a book on the provision of science and technology information to the general public.

SIDELIGHTS: Hey, who has speared barracuda off Bermuda and driven a tunnel into a Greek mountain, looks on research for books as another, semi-vicarious, type of adventure. He writes: "We must . . . learn to think of technology as the farmer thinks of his plow—as a means of husbanding the finite fields of earth. Most vital subject? Easy—it's the race between population, the preservation of ecological balances, and the humanitarian management of world food, water and energy resources."

HICKOK, Lorena A.   1892(?)-1968

PERSONAL: Born in East Troy, Wisc.; died May 3, 1968 in Rhinebeck, N.Y. *Education:* Attended University of Minnesota. *Politics:* Democrat. *Residence:* Hyde Park, N.Y.

CAREER: Writer. Reporter for *Minneapolis Tribune* in the early 1920's; became reporter for Associated Press in New York, N.Y., in mid-1920's; served as aide to head of Works Projects Administration; member of staff of president of New York World's Fair, 1939-40; served in women's division of Democratic National Committee until her retirement in 1945.

WRITINGS: (With Eleanor Roosevelt) *Ladies of Courage,* Putnam, 1954; *The Story of Franklin D. Roosevelt* (illustrated by Leonard Vosburgh), Grosset, 1956; *The Story of Helen Keller* (illustrated by Jo Polseno), Grosset, 1958, reissued, 1974; *The Story of Eleanor Roosevelt* (illustrated by William Barss), Grosset, 1959; *The Touch of Magic: The Story of Helen Keller's Great Teacher, Anne Sullivan Macy,* Dodd, 1961; *The Road to the White House,* Chilton, 1962; *Reluctant First Lady,* Dodd, 1962; (with Jean Gould) *Walter Reuther: Labor's Rugged Individualist,* Dodd, 1972.

SIDELIGHTS: **About 1892.** Born in East Troy, Wisconsin. Hickok's father was an itinerant butter maker.

1908. After the death of her mother, moved to Battle Creek, Michigan, where she finished high school in three years. ". . . The best teacher I ever had, Miss Alicent Holt . . . taught me Latin, Greek and manners in Battle Creek, Michigan, High School many years ago." [Lorena A. Hickok, *The Touch of Magic: The Story of Helen Keller's Great Teacher, Anne Sullivan Macy,* Dodd, 1961.[1]]

About 1911. Worked for the Battle Creek *Evening News.* Attended the University of Minnesota. "'Hick' is a nickname I acquired while in college, and it has clung to me ever since." [Lorena A. Hickok, *Reluctant First Lady,* Dodd, 1962.[2]]

Hickok later worked for the Minneapolis *Tribune,* where she eventually became its Sunday editor. Also reported on politics and football for the *Tribune.* Hickok worked for the New York *Mirror* as well.

1928. Joined the Associated Press in New York. "... Like many other women reporters those days, struggling to gain a solid footing in their profession, I had a strong aversion to what we called 'women's page stuff....'

"During the years Franklin Roosevelt was Governor of New York, I covered him whenever he was in New York City, followed him on several trips around the state and worked as a correspondent on some of his campaigns. Since I was always the only woman in the group of political writers, I came in for a good deal of good-natured ribbing from him. Mrs. Roosevelt says I was the only woman reporter she and Louis Howe knew when Franklin Roosevelt became President. She is probably right, for women covering politics were something of a novelty those days. As a person, I enjoyed him, but I did not take his ideas very seriously. All politicians looked alike to me those days."[2]

October, 1932. Assigned to report on Eleanor Roosevelt during Franklin Roosevelt's presidential campaign. "I began covering Mrs. Roosevelt about a month before the election in 1932.

"I did not seek the assignment for myself and did not want it. Interested as I was in Mrs. Roosevelt, I much preferred the job I was doing, covering her husband. But I had felt for some time that Mrs. Roosevelt would be different from other candidates' wives, and that the AP ought to assign someone to cover her.

"It wasn't easy to convince the AP. Candidates' wives those days were supposed, like children, to be seen and not heard. They went along on their husbands' trips, but their activities were limited to teas and luncheons in their honor—at which, of course, they did not utter a word for the public to hear...."[2]

November 9, 1932. "The news appeared in big black headlines all over the country on Wednesday morning....

"He [Roosevelt] had won by what the politicians call 'a landslide,' carrying all but six of the forty-eight states, with a total of 472 electoral votes against 59 for Herbert Hoover. Nobody was very much surprised, at least nobody among the correspondents who had been covering the two candidates.

"The night before the election Franklin Roosevelt spoke at a rally in Poughkeepsie, not far from Hyde Park....

"He spoke late in Poughkeepsie, at 10:45 P.M. It was well after eleven when he finished.

"After the speech Mrs. Roosevelt announced that she was driving down to New York. She would be teaching as usual the next morning at the Todhunter School.

"Her husband objected. He did not like to have her drive any long distance alone, especially at night, for she was apt to get drowsy behind the wheel. It was seventy-five miles to

New York. It was a rainy night, too, and the blacktop roads—most of the roads were blacktop those days—would be slippery.

"'Well, all right,' he finally agreed, 'if you'll take Hick along to keep you awake.'

"... For weeks we had been together almost constantly, the reporter dogging her footsteps day in and day out. It had been a little difficult at first, for Mrs. Roosevelt was extremely shy, especially with reporters. Not with the political writers, who covered her husband, but with the reporters who covered her—or tried to. The fact that this particular reporter had been a political writer covering her husband before she was assigned to take on Mrs. Roosevelt might help some, I had hoped. Thrown together as we were, we would have become mortal enemies or very good friends. We had become very good friends. I was now fairly well aware of how Mrs. Roosevelt felt about what lay ahead of her, although she had never talked so frankly about it before.

"'For him, of course, I'm glad—sincerely,' Mrs. Roosevelt added after a pause. 'I couldn't have wanted it to go the other way. After all, I'm a Democrat, too.

"'Now I shall have to work out my own salvation. I'm afraid it may be a little difficult. I know what Washington is like. I've lived there.'

"For eight years, during the administration of President Wilson, her husband had been Assistant Secretary of the Navy. They had not been very happy years for Mrs. Roosevelt.

"Almost defiantly, she continued:

"'I shall very likely be criticized. But I can't help it.'"[2]

March 1, 1933. "The last night before the Roosevelts went to Washington, she [Eleanor Roosevelt] came to have dinner with me in my apartment. Her husband, as usual, was tied up in conferences with his advisers. So she ordered dinner for them and left.

"She referred to that evening as her last night out of captivity."[2]

March 2, 1933. On inauguration eve Hickok spent the evening with Eleanor Roosevelt. Their friendship had developed to a point where Hickok could no longer objectively report on the Roosevelts. "In the late afternoon ... the Roosevelts left for Washington and the inauguration.

"They went down from New York on a special train, with members of their family, Louis Howe, some of Franklin Roosevelt's 'Brain Trust,' as the newspapermen called it, a number of Secret Service men and the reporters.

"Although I'd not be covering Mrs. Roosevelt any more—on her arrival in Washington she would become Bess Furman's responsibility—I, too, was aboard that train. For a very special reason.

"Arrangements had been made for me to interview Mrs. Roosevelt immediately upon her arrival at the White House following the inauguration. To get that interview, I had obtained not only her permission, but that of her husband, and I had volunteered to let Louis Howe read the story before I turned it in. It was supposed to be the first time the wife of a President was ever interviewed by a newspaper reporter in the White House. It would be the last newspaper story I'd ever write about Mrs. Roosevelt.

"We had dinner sent up, but neither of us felt much like eating. As the evening wore on, we kept moving restlessly about, pacing the floor. . . .

"Late in the evening her husband sent in the final draft of his inaugural address for her to read before it went to the mimeographers. She read it aloud to me.

"We tried to map out the interview I was to have with her the following day—the reactions to watch for in the crowd. I'd not be up at the Capitol to hear the inaugural address. I'd be waiting for her at the White House. But we got nowhere. The story just didn't seem very important, not even to me.

"It did not even occur to me at the time, but I could have slipped out to a telephone after she read the inaugural address to me and could have given the AP the gist of it, with a few quotations. And I could have told about the reports coming in from around the country to the room next door. I knew who was there, who was coming and going. If I had, it would have been a scoop—the biggest scoop of my career. But scoops and my career did not seem important that night, even to me.

"My suffering, my sense of guilt came later. One day I talked about it to Louis Howe. But he did not give me any comfort.

"'A reporter,' he commented drily, 'should never get too close to the news source.'

"I never discussed it with anyone else. But while I did not realize it at the time and remained with the AP several months longer, that night Lorena Hickok ceased to be a newspaper reporter."[2]

Summer, 1933. Motor tour with Eleanor Roosevelt throughout New England, Quebec, and the Gaspé Peninsula. "I had left the AP and the newspaper business when we started on our trip. Upon our return to Washington a month later I took a job with Harry Hopkins, who had become head of the newly organized Federal Emergency Relief Administration, which the newspaper headline writers called FERA.

"Mrs. Roosevelt and I started out from New York on July 6. . . .

"Our quarters in Quebec were in marked contrast to those we occupied on some other stops on that trip. We had a gorgeous suite at the Château Frontenac.

"After the lovely scenery along the Gaspé Peninsula, our drive down through New Brunswick to Maine was depressing. The whole countryside had been ravaged by forest fires, and we drove mile after mile through stark, charred trees without any branches.

"Our last night in Canada we stayed in a tourist camp—something else Mrs. Roosevelt had always wanted to do. It was a very comfortable tourist camp, with clean, attractive log cabins, each with a huge stone fireplace. The food was excellent, and, to her great satisfaction, Mrs. Roosevelt was able to buy a Maine newspaper. It was the first newspaper she had seen since we left Quebec.

LORENA A. HICKOK

"The rest of our trip was uneventful, and enjoyable. Nobody bothered us at all. We spent a couple of nights near Skowhegan, Maine, where my actress friend Jean Dixon, who later became Mrs. Ely, was appearing in summer stock. We drove up to Campobello. . . .

"I sometimes think I may be the only person who ever visited Campobello when there was no fog. The weather while we were there was clear and cool, and the scenery had a kind of unearthly beauty."[2]

Fall, 1933. Appointed confidential observer for Harry L. Hopkins, the Federal Emergency Relief Administrator. In that capacity, Hickok travelled about the country reporting on local relief efforts and on the conditions of relief recipients. "Immediately after our return, I started out on my new job with Harry Hopkins. I had been hired to travel about the country, watching what was happening to people on relief—physically, mentally, and emotionally—and trying to find out when the husbands were going to get back their jobs. I wrote long confidential reports to Mr. Hopkins, which he sent to the President, who would pass them on to members of his Cabinet and to other department heads who might be interested. I held the job for three years, and I think I probably talked with more people on relief than anyone else in the world ever did. I learned to drive, acquired an automobile and motored most of the time, alone. Very few of the relief clients I met ever knew I was from Washington.

"I took the job partly because Mrs. Roosevelt wanted me to take it. She was, even in those early days of her husband's administration, probably one of the best informed and most understanding citizens in the country on the plight of the unemployed. . . .

"Harry Hopkins was an experienced and highly respected social worker, but he had an understanding of people on relief that many social workers never were able to acquire. They had been taught to deal with 'problem families.' But in the FERA and, later, the WPA, we were not dealing with 'problem families.' The great majority of the people on relief were respectable citizens, who, through no fault of their own, were obliged to have help from the government. Some of them had been very prosperous before the Great Depression set in.

"One day just before I started on my first trip, Harry Hopkins said to me:

"'When you are talking with a relief client, just say to yourself: "But for the grace of God, I'd be sitting on the other side of this table." '

"I found out later that he said that to all his field representatives before they started out.

"The Great Depression had never really hit me personally at all—not as it had those people. At the AP I had had to take a salary cut, along with everybody else, but it hadn't really hurt.

"In southwestern Pennsylvania I found towns in which there was no merchandise in the stores, and nobody would have been able to buy it if there had been. The steel mills were shut down, and the coal mines operating only one or two days a week—if at all.

"But when I arrived in West Virginia, I decided that those people in Pennsylvania were prosperous by comparison—even the men near Uniontown, whom I had found living in abandoned coke ovens!"[2]

1934. Trip with Eleanor Roosevelt to Puerto Rico and the Virgin Islands. Also toured the American West with Roosevelt. The Roosevelt-Hickok friendship was an intimate one which lasted thirty years until the death of Eleanor Roosevelt. Their correspondence consisted of more than 3,000 letters.

1936. Resigned from the Federal Emergency Relief Administration.

1939-1940. Director of promotion for the New York World's Fair.

1940. Publicity director for the Democratic National Convention. Often stayed at the White House during that time. Hickok helped Eleanor Roosevelt with writing projects and wrote a number of books, including several on Roosevelt.

1954. Co-author with Eleanor Roosevelt of *Ladies of Courage*. Moved to Hyde Park, where Hickok lived until her death.

1958. Wrote *The Story of Helen Keller*. "Most authors will tell you that writing a book is a lonely business. It is. But very few books—if any—fiction or non-fiction, were ever written whose authors did not receive help from someone.

"First, there is the research, interviews, reading and studying the work of other writers, manuscripts, letters. In this case, the interview was with Helen Keller and the late Polly Thomson. The writer was then working on a book for children about Miss Keller, but Teacher, as they affectionately called her, inevitably came into the conversation. She always did."[1]

1958. Donated all of her letters from Eleanor Roosevelt to the Franklin D. Roosevelt Library in Hyde Park with the proviso that they remain closed until ten years after her death.

1961. Wrote *The Touch of Magic,* a biography of Anne Sullivan Macy, Helen Keller's teacher. ". . . No author ever finished a book with greater regret. During the months I worked on this book she became as real to me as a living person—a warm, very human, greatly loved friend. I miss her. Not as Miss Keller must miss her always. But nevertheless I miss her."[1]

1962. Death of Eleanor Roosevelt.

Wrote *Reluctant First Lady*. "The story in this book is a very personal one. It had to be. For it was written largely out of the memories of two persons—Mrs. Roosevelt's and mine. This is especially true of our vacation motor trips, since on those trips we were alone or with strangers most of the time. Neither of us ever kept any notes or diaries."[2]

May 3, 1968. Died in Rhinebeck, N.Y.

1978. Letters between Roosevelt and Hickok became accessible to researchers. The letters are the subject of a book by Doris Faber, *The Life of Lorena Hickok,* scheduled for publication by William Morrow & Company.

About the Roosevelt-Hickok book, *Ladies of Courage,* a reviewer for the *Christian Science Monitor* wrote, "Though the authors are Democrats, *Ladies of Courage* covers woman politicians from Elizabeth Cady Stanton to Oveta Culp Hobby. Personal weaknesses are disclosed, but these only add to the down-to-earth character of the book. . . ." *Library Journal* commented, "The political experience of both authors gives the book a practical, authoritative ring. It ought somehow to reach every woman in the country." *New Republic* added, "The material of the book is heartening as it submits the proof of how many women in this country have overcome even these God-imposed and man-sustained handicaps. . . . There is a separate chapter on Mrs. Roosevelt for which Miss Hickok alone is responsible. It is a warm and often moving account of a life. . . . The style is of a sort often called 'breezy,' which usually means that a steady wind moans through the holes in the prose."

Hickok later expanded the chapter on Mrs. Roosevelt to a book, *The Story of Eleanor Roosevelt. Library Journal* called it a "Very warm and readable biography. Mrs. Roosevelt's childhood is particularly well handled. . . . Passages concerning her relations with her father are most moving. Background scenes and characters support the heroine in a most satisfactory manner. Will be adored by girls in elementary grades and possibly junior high, especially those who like 'a sad story with a happy ending.' " *Saturday Review* noted, "If this story . . . only skims the surface in order to reach young readers, nevertheless it supplies numerous interesting details and has an appealing simplicity."

They went to Cape Cod, not far from Boston. Helen wanted to "see" the ocean and play in the waves.
■ (From *The Story of Helen Keller* by Lorena A. Hickok. Illustrated by Jo Polseno.)

The *New York Times* review of *The Story of Franklin D. Roosevelt* said, "The author has succeeded in capturing much of the personality and strength of spirit of the man with the warm, winning smile." *Library Journal*, however, commented, "A lively, smoothly-written, but two-dimensional biography in which the complexity of Roosevelt's personality and his effect upon his time have been so treated as to produce a hero-myth. . . ."

The *New York Times* called *Walter Reuther: Labor's Rugged Individualist*, "An attractive biography of the United Automobile Workers leader. Begun by the late Lorena Hickok, it has been 'completed' . . . by Jean Gould. . . . Although [Miss Gould] writes objectively, not ignoring Reuther's faults (among them a large ego), the book does not really penetrate Reuther's character, but is mainly a description of his career and the battles he fought for his many and firmly held ideals."

FOR MORE INFORMATION SEE: Christian Science Monitor, May 27, 1954; *New Republic*, June 14, 1954; *New York Times*, January 27, 1957; *Saturday Review*, February 21, 1960; Lorena A. Hickok, *The Touch of Magic; The Story of Helen Keller's Great Teacher, Anne Sullivan Macy*, Dodd, 1961; Lorena A. Hickok, *Reluctant First Lady*, Dodd, 1962; *Horn Book*, February, 1963; *New York Times Book Review*, July 30, 1972; Deirdre Carmody, "Letters by Eleanor Roosevelt Detail Friendship with Lorena Hickok," *New York Times*, October 21, 1978. Obituary: *Washington Post*, May 4, 1968.

HOLLAND, John L(ewis)   1919-

PERSONAL: Born October 21, 1919, in Omaha, Neb.; son of Edward Lewis (in advertising business) and Ellen (Dean) Holland; married Elsie M. Prenzlow, August 30, 1947; children: Kay E., Joan E., Robert D. *Education:* University of Omaha (now University of Nebraska at Omaha), B.A., 1942; University of Minnesota, M.A., 1947, Ph.D., 1952. *Office:* Department of Social Relations, Johns Hopkins University, Baltimore, Md. 21218.

CAREER: Western Reserve University (now Case Western Reserve University), Cleveland, Ohio, instructor and director of counseling center, 1950-53; U.S. Veterans Administration Hospital, Perry Point, Md., chief of vocational counseling service, 1953-56; National Merit Scholarship Corp., Evanston, Ill., director of research, 1957-63; American College Testing program, Iowa City, Iowa, vice-president for research and development, 1963-69; University of Iowa, Iowa City, professor of education and psychology, 1963-69; Johns Hopkins University, Baltimore, Md., professor of social relations, 1969—, professor of education and director of Center for Study of Social Organization of Schools, 1969-75. Fellow, Center for Advanced Study in the Behavioral Sciences, 1965-66. *Member:* American Psychological Association (fellow), American Educational Research Association. *Awards, honors:* Research award, American Personnel and Guidance Association, 1960.

Angel's dog's name is Negrita—that means Blackie. He takes her on the roof because the kids on the street tease her and she bites them. ■ (From *The Way It Is* edited by John Holland.)

WRITINGS: Manual for the Holland Vocational Preference Inventory, Consulting Psychologists Press, 1958, 6th edition published as *Manual for the Vocational Preference Inventory,* 1967; *Explorations of a Theory of Vocational Choice,* Part V, Chronical Guidance Press, 1964; *The Psychology of Vocational Choice: A Theory of Personality Types and Model Environments,* Blaisdell, 1966; *Making Vocational Choices: A Theory of Careers,* Prentice-Hall, 1973.

Contributor: *Creativity: Its Assessment and Measurement,* Educational Testing Service, 1962; H. Borow, editor, *Man in a World of Work,* Houghton, 1964; C. W. Taylor, editor, *Widening Horizons in Creativity,* Wiley, 1964; J. M. Whiteley, editor, *Perspectives on Vocational Development,* American Personnel & Guidance Association, 1972. Writer of research reports for American College Testing Program. Contributor of more than one hundred articles to psychology and education journals. Consulting editor, *Journal of Applied Psychology,* 1961-69, and *Journal of Vocational Behavior,* 1971-77.

WORK IN PROGRESS: Revising theory of personality and occupational classification.

FOR MORE INFORMATION SEE: Horn Book, August, 1969.

HORNOS, Axel   1907-

PERSONAL: "H" in surname is silent; born July 3, 1907, in Buenos Aires, Argentina; became American citizen, 1958; son of Claudio B. (a diplomat) and Rosa (Valle) Hornos; married Mary A. Wassington, May 10, 1930; children: Maribel Hornos Gotzmer, Serge. *Home:* 177 Long Meadow Circle, Pittsford, N.Y. 14534.

CAREER: Eastman Kodak Co., International Markets Division, Rochester, N.Y., worked in creative advertising in several photographic areas, 1944-68, retired, 1968. Association for Teen-Age Diplomats (affiliate of American Field Service), president, 1954, 1955, 1957.

WRITINGS: Argentina, Paraguay, Uruguay (youth book), Thomas Nelson, 1969.

Translator into Spanish: John Hodgson Bradley, *Autobiography of the Earth,* Editorial Sudamericana (Buenos Aires), 1939; G. Russell Harrison, *Atoms in Action,* Editorial Sudamericana, 1942; David Dietz, *The History of Science,* [Buenos Aires], 1943; Jerry Mangione, *Mount Allegro,* Editorial Futuro (Buenos Aires), 1944. Contributor to *Atlantic, Saturday Review, American Mercury, Dance, Rochester Democrat and Chronicle, Smithsonian, Mankind, Antioch Review,* and *New York Times* (travel section).

WORK IN PROGRESS: Three juveniles, *Storm over the Pampas, The Gauchos, Superhorsemen of the Pampas,* and *Shadows in the Forest;* an adult book on Argentina, tentatively titled *The Silver Land;* research for a book on Guidobaldo and Elisabetta di Montefeltro, Duke and Duchess of Urbino.

SIDELIGHTS: "I have my grandchildren, and felt dutybound to write for their generation. Although I have ceased to be active in the ATAD (Association for Teen-Age Diplomats), I am still an ardent believer in its motto: 'Be together, work together, oh ye peoples of the earth'."

Hornos was a resident of Europe for ten years, living in France, Italy, Spain, and Switzerland. He still travels a great deal in South America and Europe, mostly for research purposes.

HOBBIES AND OTHER INTERESTS: Biography, the visual arts, classical music, sociology, world politics.

FOR MORE INFORMATION SEE: Best Sellers, August 1, 1969.

HURWITZ, Johanna   1937-

PERSONAL: Born October 9, 1937, in New York, N.Y.; daughter of Nelson (a journalist and book seller) and Tillie (a library assistant; maiden name, Miller) Frank; married Uri Levi Hurwitz (a college teacher and author), February 19, 1962; children: Nomi, Beni. *Education:* Queens College (now of the City University of New York), B.A., 1958; Columbia University, M.L.S., 1959. *Home:* 10 Spruce Pl., Great Neck, N.Y. 11021.

CAREER: New York Public Library, New York, N.Y., children's librarian, 1959-63; Queens College of the City University of New York, Flushing, N.Y., lecturer on children's literature, 1965-68; Calhoun School, New York City, children's librarian, 1968-75; Manor Oaks School, New Hyde Park, N.Y., children's librarian, 1975-77; Great Neck Library, Great Neck, N.Y., children's librarian, 1978—. *Member:* American Library Association, Amnesty International, Beta Phi Mu, Authors Guild, P.E.N.

WRITINGS—Juveniles: *Busybody Nora,* Morrow, 1976; *Nora and Mrs. Mind-Your-Own Business,* Morrow, 1977; *The Law of Gravity,* Morrow, 1978; *Much Ado About Aldo,* Morrow, 1978; *New Neighbors for Nora,* Morrow, 1979; *Aldo Applesauce,* Morrow, 1979; *Once I Was a Plum Tree,* Morrow, 1980; *Superduper Teddy,* Morrow, 1980.

WORK IN PROGRESS: More Nora stories; a book about an older girl.

SIDELIGHTS: "My parents met in a bookstore and there has never been a moment when books were not important in my life. Some of my happiest early memories are of being read to by my parents. I can remember my mother reading *Stuart Little* to me and my father reading aloud from Chaucer's *Canterbury Tales.* The walls of our apartment were lined with books. Once when I was five years old, an accident resulted in a head injury and a lot of blood. My mother telephoned for an ambulance. When the medical attendants arrived at our apartment, they gaped in amazement at our books. 'Hurry, hurry!' my mother shouted. She was afraid I would die. But they just stared speechless at the number of books. 'Gee lady, you must like to read,' said one of the men without moving. And it was true, we all did.

"As soon as I was old enough, I got a library card so that I would have access to even more volumes. I loved the library so much that I made the firm decision by age ten that someday I would become a librarian. And I also planned that I would write books too.

"I started working for the New York Public Library when I was still in high school and became a full fledged librarian in 1959. But it was not until 1976 that my first book for children

After the cake was finished, Mommy helped them to make chocolate frosting, which luckily was Daddy's favorite as well as theirs. ■ (From *Busybody Nora* by Johanna Hurwitz. Illustrated by Susan Jeschke.)

JOHANNA HURWITZ

was published. In between, I married and had two children. And I wrote hundreds of letters to friends and relatives.

"When I write a letter, it is usually long and has bits of conversation and perhaps a humorous incident or two recorded in it. I am sure the letter writing that I do has been the best type of training for my book writing.

"I took a poetry writing course with Louise Bogan at New York University. When the class ended a group of my fellow classmates and I decided to meet regularly and read and critique one another's writing efforts. Gradually, the group grew as friends who were interested in literature and writing joined us. It was in this way that I met my husband. He was a friend of a friend of a friend of an original member of the writing group.

"I get angry when people ask me when am I going to write a book for adults. I do not feel that my writing for children is practice for that. I write for children because I am especially interested in that period of life. There is an intensity and seriousness about childhood which fascinates me. I can remember my own childhood in great detail and also the childhood of my daughter and son (who are both rapidly outgrowing this period). It is from my memories and also my observations of the children with whom I work, that I get my ideas for writing.

"When I am not writing, I like to cook and sometimes I play the piano (poorly) or the phonograph (excellently). Both food and music have crept into my stories. In fact all my friends know that they may find themselves or their pets or their hobbies or their foibles described in a story. Even my cat has appeared in one book, although his name was given to a dog in another book.

"My children are both great readers. As their father is also a writer, I suspect in time they will be writers too. After all, what do you expect? Their grandparents met in a bookstore."

FOR MORE INFORMATION SEE: Horn Book, June, 1976, December, 1976.

HUTTO, Nelson (Allen)   1904-

PERSONAL: Born December 12, 1904, in Nuevo Laredo, Mexico; son of John Renfroe (a teacher) and Rebecca (Nelson) Hutto; married Pauline Hardesty, June 4, 1928; children: Emily (Mrs. J. W. Frederick), Nell (Mrs. D. K. Usiak). *Education:* Hardin-Simmons University, B.A., 1925; Columbia University, M.S., 1927. *Politics:* Democrat. *Religion:* Baptist. *Agent:* Lenninger Literary Agency, 11 West 42nd St., New York, N.Y. 10036.

CAREER: Hardin-Simmons University, Abilene, Tex., associate professor of journalism and director of publicity, 1927-35; Abilene (Tex.) High School, journalism adviser, 1935-36; Sunset High School, Dallas, Tex., journalism adviser, 1936-69.

WRITINGS: Breakaway Back, Harper, 1963; *Goal Line Bomber,* Harper, 1964; *Victory Volley,* Harper, 1967. Author of short history of Dallas, *From Buckskins to Top Hat,* 1953. Contributor of more than eighty short stories and novelettes to magazines.

HOBBIES AND OTHER INTERESTS: Sports, music (listening to good music and playing the piano).

HUTTON, Warwick   1939-

PERSONAL: Born July 17, 1939; son of John (an artist) and Helen (Blair) Hutton; married Elizabeth Mills, August 26, 1965; children: Hanno, Lily. *Education:* Colchester Art School, N.D.D., 1961. *Politics:* None. *Religion:* None. *Residence:* Cambridge, England.

CAREER: Illustrator, painter, and glass engraver. Visiting lecturer, Cambridge College of Art and Technology, 1972—, Morley College, 1973-75. *Member:* Cambridge Society of Painters and Sculptors.

Then the fountains of the great deep were released, and the windows of heaven were opened, and the waters increased, but the ark was borne up and floated above the land. ■ (From *Noah and the Great Flood* by Warwick Hutton. Illustrated by the author.)

WARWICK HUTTON

WRITINGS—All self-illustrated: *Making Woodcuts* (adult), St. Martin's, 1974; *Noah and the Great Flood* (juvenile), Atheneum, 1977; *The Sleeping Beauty* (juvenile), Atheneum, 1979.

WORK IN PROGRESS: More children's picture books, *Beauty and the Beast* and others.

SIDELIGHTS: "I am a full time artist. Although I am primarily a painter, most of my time at present is taken up with teaching and producing picture books. I like to write my own texts, and then spend some months drawing and painting my way into the story; each of my picture books seems to take about a year to produce, because the early planning and background work has to be rather thorough. I use models and real objects and landscapes to draw from as much as possible. I like to enter the story I am working on as much as possible, and I thoroughly enjoy the process. My picture books are not really just for children, I hope adults will enjoy them too.

"When I am not occupied with painting and woodcuts, I carry out commissioned glass engravings for civic buildings, churches, homes, etc."

FOR MORE INFORMATION SEE: Horn Book, December, 1977.

INGRAMS, Doreen 1906-

PERSONAL: Born January 24, 1906, in London, England; daughter of Edward (a member of Parliament and privy councillor) and Isabella (Scott) Shortt; married Harold Ingrams (a political officer with service in Arabia), June 3, 1930; children: two daughters. *Education:* Privately educated in London, England, and in Switzerland. *Home:* 3 Westfield House, Tenterden, Kent, England.

CAREER: British Broadcasting Corp., London, England, senior assistant in Arabic Service, 1956-68. Lecturer for Central Office of Information. Member of executive committee, Council for the Advancement of Arab-British Understanding. *Member:* United Nations Association (vice-chairman of Tenterden branch). *Awards, honors:* Co-winner with her husband of Founders Medal of Royal Geographical Society and of Lawrence of Arabia Medal of Royal Central Asian Society.

WRITINGS: A Survey of Social and Economic Conditions in the Aden Protectorate, H.M.S.O., 1949; *A Time in Arabia,* J. Murray, 1970; *Palestine Papers 1917-1922: Seeds of Conflict,* J. Murray, 1972; *The Arab World* (booklets and film strip), EMC Corp., 1974; *Mosques & Minarets,* EMC Corporation, 1974; *New Ways to Ancient Lands,* EMC Corp., 1974; *Tents to City Sidewalks,* EMC Corporation, 1974. Contributor to *Middle East Handbook,* 1971, to *Gulf Handbook,* 1976-77, and to geographical and political journals.

WORK IN PROGRESS: Research for a book about women in the Arab world.

SIDELIGHTS: "I was born in London, England, and from a very early age took part in my father's political life. I was only four when my sister and I drove in a carriage and pair round the city of Newcastle in the north of England with a large placard saying 'Vote for Daddy.' When I was twelve, my father became Chief Secretary of Ireland, and we went to live in a lovely house in Phoenix Park, Dublin, now the residence of the United States ambassador. But it was a time of unrest, and wherever we went we were followed by a detective. When we returned to London, I attended a day school, but our holidays were nearly always spent abroad, and I think my taste for travel dates from those early visits to France, Germany, and Italy.

"My chief interest, however, was acting and going to the theatre. I was determined to go on the stage, and I spent five years in the provinces and in London, not achieving anything very spectacular, but enjoying almost every moment of it.

"When I married, I began a fascinating life of travel and exploration, shared with my husband. He encouraged me to keep a diary of our life in South Arabia, and when I retired, after working for a number of years with the British Broadcasting Corporation, I brought out those old diaries and tried to make something of them. The result was a book called *A Time in Arabia.*

"Since retiring, I have been busy writing or speaking, and of course, travelling, mostly to Arab countries but also to the United States. Although I am a good age now, I shall not feel old until I can no longer pack my bags and fly off on another exploration, for to me every journey is an exploration."

FOR MORE INFORMATION SEE: Listener, December 31, 1970.

JACOBS, Leland Blair 1907-

PERSONAL: Born 1907, in Tawas City, Michigan. *Education:* Michigan State Normal College, A.B.; University of Michigan, M.A.; Ohio State University, Ph.D. *Office:* Teachers College, Columbia University, New York, N.Y. 10027.

CAREER: Began teaching in a one-room schoolhouse; worked as an elementary education, Teachers College, College University; author and editor of books for children. *Member:* International Reading Association, National Conference on Research in English, National Council of Teachers of English, International Association for Childhood Education. *Awards, honors:* Received the Distinguished Teacher Award from Mills College, New York; was chosen as a distinguished alumnus of the Ohio State College of Education in their centennial year, 1970; elected to the Reading Hall of Fame, 1979; elected a charter member, New Jersey Literary Hall of Fame, 1979.

WRITINGS: Good Night, Mr. Beetle (illustrated by Gilbert Riswold), Holt, 1963; *Just Around the Corner* (illustrated by John E. Johnson), Holt, 1964; *Old Lucy Lindy* (illustrated by Ed Renfro), Holt, 1964; (with Allan D. Jacobs) *Behind the Circus Tent,* Lerner, 1967; *Is Somewhere Always Far Away?* (illustrated by J. E. Johnson), Holt, 1967; *Alphabet of Girls* (illustrated by J. E. Johnson), Holt, 1969; *The Monkey and the Bee,* Western Publishing, 1969; *The Stupid Lion, and Other Stories* (illustrated by Karl Stuecklen), L. W. Singer, 1969; *I Don't, I Do* (illustrated by Frank Carlings), Garrard, 1971; *What Would You Do?* (illustrated by F. Carlings), Garrard, 1972; *April Fool!* (illustrated by Lou Cunette), Garrard, 1973; *Teeny-Tiny* (illustrated by Marilyn Lucey), Garrard, 1976.

Editor: (And reteller) *Belling the Cat, and Other Stories* (illustrated by Harold Berson), Golden Press, 1960; (with Eleanor Murdoch Johnson) *Treat Shop,* enlarged edition, C. E. Merrill, 1960; *Delight in Numbers* (illustrated by Kiyoaki Komoda), Holt, 1964; (with Sally Nohelty) *Poetry for Young Scientists* (illustrated by Ed Young), Holt, 1964; *Using Literature with Young Children,* Teachers College Press, 1965; (with E. M. Johnson and Jo Jasper Turner) *Adventure Lands,* C. E. Merrill, 1966; (with E. M. Johnson) *Enchanted Isles,* C. E. Merrill, 1966; (with J. J. Turner) *Happiness Hill,* C. E. Merrill, 1966; (with Shelton L. Root) *Ideas in Literature,* C. E. Merrill, 1966; *Poetry for Autumn* (illustrated by Stina Nagel), Garrard, 1968; *Poetry for Chuckles and Grins* (illustrated by Tomie de Paola), Garrard, 1968.

Poetry for Bird Watchers (illustrated by Ted Schroeder), Garrard, 1970; *Poetry for Summer* (illustrated by Joann Stover), Garrard, 1970; *Poetry for Winter* (illustrated by Kelly Oechsli), Garrard, 1970; *Poetry of Witches, Elves, and Goblins* (illustrated by Frank Aloise), Garrard, 1970; *All about Me: Verses I Can Read* (illustrated by Hertha R. Depper), Garrard, 1971; *Animal Antics in Limerick Land* (illustrated by Edward Malsberg), Garrard, 1971; (with A. D. Jacobs) *Arithmetic in Verse and Rhyme* (illustrated by K. Oechsli), Garrard, 1971; *Funny Folks in Limerick Land* (illustrated by Raymond Burns), Garrard, 1971; *Playtime in the City* (illustrated by K. Oechsli), Garrard, 1971; *Poems about Fur and Feather Friends* (illustrated by F. Aloise), Garrard, 1971; *Poetry for Space Enthusiasts* (illustrated by F. Aloise), Garrard, 1971; *The Read-It-Yourself Storybook,* Golden Press, 1971; *Hello, People!* (illustrated by E. Malsberg), Garrard, 1972; *Hello, Pleasant Places* (illustrated by K. Oechsli), Garrard, 1972; *Hello, Year!* (illustrated by F. Aloise), Garrard, 1972; *Holiday Happenings in Limerick Land* (illustrated by E. Malsberg), Garrard, 1972; *Funny Bone Ticklers in Verse and Rhyme* (illustrated by E. Malsberg), Garrard, 1973; (with Allan D. Jacobs) *Sports and Games in Verse and Rhyme,* Garrard, 1975. Author of textbooks, text and educational materials, and contributor of articles to *Elementary English, Childhood Education, Education, The Reading Teacher, The Instructor, Today's Child, Early Years,* and *Day Care.*

SIDELIGHTS: Jacobs first began teaching in a one-room schoolhouse. By 1949 he was assistant professor of elementary education at Ohio State University, where he taught courses in children's literature, the language arts, and early childhood. He served as consultant to the Ohio School of the Air for radio programs designed for grade school children. He later became professor of elementary education at Teachers College of Columbia University and served as a consultant to *Junior Libraries.*

Jacobs has lectured at numerous universities and colleges on language arts, the teaching of reading, children's literature, and elementary school curriculum and teaching. A consultant and lecturer for many state educational associations, national organizations, and school systems, Jacobs is also a member of the selection committee for the *Weekly Reader* book club.

"Many people are involved in teaching a child to read, and every one of them in his own way is an educator. Before the child is old enough to go to school, he receives rudimentary lessons in reading.

". . . The persons in the home are, in many ways, the first educators in the complicated act of learning to read. When the child reaches the age where typically his schooling begins, there are three other people who may markedly influence his progress in learning to read: the classroom teacher,

"Nancy, my girl,"
said the pirate.
"Come and get
your present."
"Is it gold?"
Nancy asked.
■(From *April Fool!* by Leland B. Jacobs. Illustrated by Lou Cunette.)

We watched
How a shy
Little bird had come
To picnic
On each
Sandwich crumb.

Jay Lee

(From *Hello, Pleasant Places,* poetry selected by Leland B. Jacobs. Drawings by Kelly Oechsli.)

the school librarian, and the children's librarian in the public library. If these three people work together compatibly, the child is fortunate indeed in getting from each the kind of help which he needs to refine his competencies in reading skills and to influence his total reading behavior.

"Let us hope that in every community in America this trio would practice together and, through the discipline of playing as a group, would learn to respect the individual role and contribution of each as well as the common bond and contribution of all as one.

"The children's librarian, the school librarian, and the teacher actually gain in prestige when they pool their individual resources and are articulate about their common purposes and responsibilities." [Leland B. Jacobs, "Three to Teach Reading," *Junior Libraries*, September 15, 1955.[1]]

A leading authority on children's literature, Jacobs believes that parents should read aloud to their children. "Surely our children do learn much from what we read to them. They can't help it, for books deal with ideas, feelings, and values. A book is a record of what has moved a man, what he has felt was worth cherishing and struggling for. Anyone who opens one of these records is bound to learn from it. We learn from books not because they contain 'lessons' as such but because they are rooted in the sense and sensibilities of living.

"Even after children are able to read well on their own, there is still a place for reading aloud in the family circle. . . . We can choose stories and poems and nonfiction that have the same appeal as the books the children read to themselves but that are on somewhat higher levels of taste. We can choose books that cry out for oral interpretation.

"Thus in our home reading, we make a gradual shift from the total dependence of the very young child to a shared independence on the part of the reading child. At this point the child may even take his turn reading aloud, becoming a truly active participant in this delightful family enterprise.

"The best experiences in shared reading at home come when children and parents alike are truly engrossed in the ideas and feelings that emerge from the printed page. Only when a writer fully captures both adult and child can great literature be fully appreciated. [Leland B. Jacobs, "What Shall We Read to Our Children?," *National Parent-Teacher Magazine*, November, 1956.[2]]

Jacobs retold three fairy tales in his first book, written in 1960. A decade later he wrote poetry books for young readers. "What . . . shall we read to our children? Prose and poetry that charm them magically or tickle their funny bones. Books that let them walk in the shoes of others and thus come to know life intimately and well. Books that bring an occasional honest tear, books that make them ponder and wonder and believe and know. Books that go beyond the real world as well as those that confirm and extend everyday experiences. In this way, with our help, our children can learn that

> 'A book is a pony with magic feet,
> Bearing its rider on high adventures.'[2]

Gearing most of his works to the interests of young children, Jacobs wrote about the country, the city, the world of make-believe, and home in his book, *Is Somewhere Always Far Away?*. "He writes about such common things as traffic

lights and country roads, bees and busstops, and manages to make them very special. . . . It is a nicely designed attractive book which will amuse and delight young children," observed a critic for *Young Readers' Review*. A reviewer for *Library Journal* noted, "Four- and five-year-olds will be carried along by the rhythm of the lines . . . and first-graders will identify with the 'I' of the verses. This is an appealing book of poems for young children."

FOR MORE INFORMATION SEE: *Publishers Weekly*, March 26, 1949; *Junior Libraries*, September 15, 1955; *National Parent-Teacher Magazine*, November, 1956; *Senior Scholastic*, October 10, 1958; *Library Journal*, September 15, 1963.

JOHNSON, Evelyne 1932-

PERSONAL: Born January 20, 1932, in New York, N.Y.; daughter of David (a mathematician, inventor, and professor) and Rose (a musician; maiden name, Geiger) Levow; married Frank A. Johnson, Jr. (an artist's representative), October 10, 1950; children: Barry. *Education:* Attended New York University, National Academy of Design, and New School for Social Research. *Politics:* Liberal Democrat. *Religion:* Jewish. *Residence:* New York, N.Y.

CAREER: Free-lance artist and copy writer. Evelyne Johnson Associates, New York City, proprietor, 1965—. *Member:* Society of Illustrators, Society of Photographers and Artists Representatives, Graphic Artists' Guild.

WRITINGS: The Elephant's Ball (juvenile), McGraw, 1977; *The Cookie Cookbook*, Dell, 1979.

Series of juvenile cloth books; all published by Elsevier-Dutton, 1979: *My Animal Friends, Baby's Farm, My Favorite Toys, Beddybye Baby, Peek-a-boo Baby, Fun in the Tub, I am a Baby*.

WORK IN PROGRESS: Children's books and cookbooks.

SIDELIGHTS: "I want to write children's books and other fiction stories in a humorous way, to show how people, no matter how different, can enjoy life together and share each other's customs. My cookbooks are written to reflect my years of study and interest in good nutrition combined with gourmet cooking."

HOBBIES AND OTHER INTERESTS: Ecology, art, music, gourmet cooking, and travel.

JOHNSON, Siddie Joe 1905-1977

OBITUARY NOTICE: Born August 20, 1905, in Dallas, Tex.; died July 27, 1977, in Corpus Christi, Tex. Librarian, author of children's books, and book reviewer. Miss Johnson was for many years the head of the children's department of the Dallas Public Library where she later became coordinator of children's services. In connection with her library work, she received the first Grolier Award in 1954, and the Texas Librarian of the Year Award in 1964. Miss Johnson's books for children often deal with her native Texas, her first book, *Debby*, dealing with the Texas of her youth. Miss Johnson was a noted children's book reviewer for the *Dallas Morning News* for thirty years. *For More Information See: Authors of Books for Young People,* 2nd edition, Scarecrow, 1971; *A Biographical Directory of Librarians in the United States and Canada,* 5th edition, American Library Association, 1970; *Childhood in Poetry,* Supplement 1, Gale, 1972; *The Junior Book of Authors,* 2nd edition, revised, H. W. Wilson, 1951; *Texas Writers of Today,* Gryphon Books, 1971. *Obituaries: School Library Journal,* January, 1978.

KENT, Sherman 1903-

PERSONAL: Born December 1, 1903, in Chicago, Ill.; son of William and Elizabeth (Thacher) Kent; married Elizabeth Gregory, December 20, 1934; children: Serafina Kent, Bathrick, Sherman, Tecumseh. *Education:* Yale University, Ph.B., 1926, Ph.D., 1933. *Home:* 2824 Chain Bridge Rd. N.W., Washington, D.C. 20016.

CAREER: Yale University, New Haven, Conn., instructor, 1928-30, 1933-36, assistant professor, 1936-44, associate professor, 1944-47, professor of history, 1947-53; U.S. Office of Strategic Services, Washington, D.C., chief of African section, 1941-43, chief of Europe-Africa division, 1943-45; U.S. Department of State, Washington, D.C., acting director of Office of Research and Intelligence, 1946; National War College, Washington, D.C., member of resident civilian staff, 1946; Central Intelligence Agency (CIA), Washington, D.C., director of Office of National Estimates, 1952-68. *Awards, honors:* Guggenheim fellowship, 1947; National Civil Service Award, 1961; President's Award for Distinguished Civilian Federal Service, 1967.

WRITINGS: Electoral Procedure under Louis Philippe, Yale University Press, 1937; *Writing History,* Appleton, 1942, revised edition, 1967; *Strategic Intelligence for American World Policy,* Princeton University Press, 1948, Shoestring Press, 1966; *A Boy and a Pig, but Mostly Horses* (children's book), Dodd, 1974; *The French Election of 1827,* Harvard University Press, 1975.

WORK IN PROGRESS: An edition of the 1827 diary of Comte Joseph de Villele; and a boys' adventure story, as yet untitled.

SIDELIGHTS: "I wrote the book, *A boy and a Pig, but Mostly Horses,* at my wife's urging. The idea was to put down some stories and incidents of my own youthful days. The book is essentially autobiographical and almost all of it is non-fiction. My principal intended audience was my own four grandchildren, three of whose names I borrowed for the three boys I write about. 'Jason' of the book is really my brother Roger, 'Simon' is me, and 'Brendan' is a boyhood friend named Wilmer Webb."

They headed into the low hills that lay between Rock Creek and Sonoma Mountain. ■ (From *A Boy and a Pig, But Mostly Horses* by Sherman Kent. Illustrated by Sam Savitt.)

SHERMAN KENT

KER WILSON, Barbara   1929-

PERSONAL: Born September 24, 1929, in Sunderland County, Durham, England; daughter of William and Margaret Ker Wilson; married Peter R. Tahourdin (a composer), December 15, 1956; children: Julia, Sarah. *Education:* Attended North London Collegiate School. *Religion:* Christian. *Home:* 109 Darling Point Rd., Darling Point, New South Wales, 2027, Australia.

CAREER: Oxford University Press, London, England, children's assistant editor, 1949-54; The Bodley Head Ltd., London, England, children's editor, 1954-59; William Collins Sons and Co. Ltd., London, England, children's editor, 1959-62; Angus & Robertson Ltd., Sydney, Australia, children's editor, 1965-72; Hodder & Stoughton, Australia, children's editor, 1972-76; currently condensed books' editor, *The Reader's Digest,* Australia. Former editorial consultant, Blackie & Son Ltd., London, England. *Member:* P.E.N., National Book League, Australian Society of Authors.

WRITINGS: Scottish Folk-Tales and Legends, Oxford University Press, 1954; *Path-Through-the-Woods,* Criterion, 1958, S. G. Phillips, 1960; *The Wonderful Cornet,* Hamish Hamilton, 1959; *Fairy Tales of England,* and similarly titled books for France, India, Mexico, Ireland, Germany, Persia, and Russia (all published by Dutton, 1959-61).

The Lovely Summer, Dodd, 1960; *Look at Books,* Hamish Hamilton, 1960; *Noel Streatfeild: A Monograph,* Bodley Head, 1960, Walck, 1964; *Writing for Children,* Boardman, 1960, Watts, 1961; compiler, *The Young Eve,* Blackie & Son, 1960; *Last Year's Broken Toys,* Constable, 1962, published

in America as *In Love and War,* World Publishing, 1962; (editor) B. S. Gottlieb, *What a Boy Should Know About Sex,* Constable, 1962; (editor) B. S. Gottlieb, *What a Girl Should Know About Sex,* Constable, 1962; *A Story to Tell,* J. G. Miller, *Ann and Peter in Paris,* Muller, 1963; (editor) Emily Bronte, *Wuthering Heights,* Blackie & Sons, 1964; *Ann and Peter in London,* Muller, 1965; *Beloved of the Gods,* Constable, 1965, published in America as *In the Shadow of Vesuvius,* World Publishing, 1965.

Greek Fairy Tales, Muller, 1966, Follett, 1968; *Legends of the Round Table,* Hamlyn, 1966; *Animal Folk Tales,* Hamlyn, 1966; *A Family Likeness,* Constable, 1967, published in America as *The Biscuit-Tin Family,* World, 1968; *Australian Kaleidoscope,* Collins, 1968, Meredith, 1969; *Australia, Wonderland Down Under,* Dodd, 1969.

Hiccups, J. G. Miller, 1970; *Tales Told to Kabbarli,* Crown, 1972; *The Magic Fishbones,* Angus & Robertson, 1974; *The Magic Bird,* Angus & Robertson, 1974; *A Handful of Ghosts,* Hodder & Stoughton, 1976; *Alitji: In the Dreamtime* (Aboriginal Pitantjatjara version of *Alice in Wonderland*), Adelaide University, 1976; *The Turtle and the Island,* Hodder & Stoughton, 1978; *The Willow Pattern Story,* Angus & Robertson, 1978.

SIDELIGHTS: "I knew that I wanted to write from an early age, and began to write plays at primary school—they were performed in class, much to my delight. My father wrote erudite scholarly works on engineering science, and I used to accompany him on visits to his publisher, from time to time.

BARBARA KER WILSON

Wommainya died of grief for his two drowned boys. And now they are all up in the sky. ■ (From *Tales Told to Kabbarli* by Daisy Bates. Retold by Barbara Ker Wilson. Illustrated by Harold Thomas.)

This was how I became interested in publishing, as well, from an early age.

"Eventually I pursued a double career as a writer and a publisher's editor. Folklore has always held an irresistible appeal for me: I regard it as the universal well-spring of all imaginative writing. From my collection of Scottish, Australian Aboriginal (*Tales Told to Kabbarli*) and New Guinea (*The Turtle and the Island*) folklore, I derived particular inspiration and satisfaction. My teenage novels (*Path-Through-the-Woods, The Lovely Summer, Last Year's Broken Toys,* and *Beloved of the Gods*) have backgrounds of social history, and *Last Year's Broken Toys* draws on my own deeply impressed experience of being a schoolgirl during the second world war, at a school on the outskirts of London all through the Blitz. *Path-Through-the-Woods* and *The Lovely Summer* are also concerned with the position of women in society—as, to an extent, is *Beloved of the Gods,* in which I also tried to give an impression of the way of life of slaves in an important household of ancient Rome. I enjoy turning sudden ideas into short stories for young children (*A Story to Tell* and *Hiccups*), many of the tales in these two books were written for my own daughters.

"Like a number of other publisher's editors who are also authors, I am never sure which facet of this double career should come first! As a writer, my primary interest is to tell a story, and time and again I find myself returning to the refreshing vigour of the world's oldest stories, folk tales, the springboard for all fiction, including the most sophisticated

modern novel. As a publisher's editor, it is often very satisfactory to be able to suggest ideas which are not right for my own style of authorship to other writers, and see them used successfully.

"Both as a children's writer and as an editor, I see children's literature as a great force for international understanding, and I have participated in arranging numerous multi-language editions of books orginally published in English. My work with children's writing has taken me all over the world, and I have seen this branch of literature grow and develop significantly in extent and depth. The experience of leaving the country of my birth, England, to emigrate to another land, Australia, has provided me with much material which I hope to use in the future as a basis for further books."

FOR MORE INFORMATION SEE: Horn Book, June, 1963; *Publishers Weekly,* May 28, 1973.

KNIGHT, Ruth Adams   1898-1974

OBITUARY NOTICE: Born October 5, 1898, in Defiance, Ohio; died July 4, 1974, in South Pasadena, Calif. Author, editor, and radio scriptwriter. Ruth Knight began her writing career as a reporter, then drama and literary editor with the *Toledo Daily Times,* in which she had a daily column, and the *Toledo Sunday Times.* During radio's prime Knight wrote radio sketches for, among others, "Death Valley Days," "Show Boat," and "Cavalcade of America," and had her own program, "Brave Tomorrow." She was the author of a variety of historical novels, and her books for young people included *Valiant Comrades*, a dog story. She wrote others in this same genre, along with several which deal with the problems of young people. One of Knight's short stories, "What a Darling Little Boy!," was included in *O. Henry Memorial Award Prize Stories of 1944*. *For More Information See: Authors of Books for Young People*, 2nd edition, Scarecrow, 1971; *Contemporary Authors*, Volume 5-8, 1st revision, Gale, 1969; *Current Biography*, H. W. Wilson, 1943, and 1955; *Foremost Women in Communications*, Bowker, 1970; *More Junior Authors*, H. W. Wilson, 1963; *Ohio Authors and Their Books*, World Publishing, 1962. *Obituaries: Contemporary Authors*, Volume 49-52, Gale, 1975. *New York Times*, July 7, 1974.

KOHLER, Julilly H(ouse) 1908-1976

OBITUARY NOTICE: Born October 18, 1908, in Cincinnati, Ohio; died December 24, 1976, in Sheboygan, Wis. Author of books for children. Julilly Kohler used the Kentucky of her childhood as the setting for several of her books, including *The Sun Shines Bright* and *The Boy Who Stole the Elephant*. The latter was dramatized in 1971 for the "Disney Hour" television show. Kohler was a trustee for Wellesley College and Ripon College, and was awarded the Sears Roebuck Civic Development Medal for her efforts in saving Wisconsin Indian mounds. *For More Information See: American Authors and Books, 1640 to the Present Day*, 3rd edition, Crown, 1972; *Contemporary Authors*, Volume 77-80, Gale, 1979; *Ohio Authors and Their Books*, World Publishing, 1962. *Obituaries: AB Bookman's Weekly*, February 14, 1977; *Contemporary Authors*, Volume 69-72, Gale, 1978.

KOMROFF, Manuel 1890-1974

OBITUARY NOTICE—See sketch in *Something About the Author*, Volume 2: Born September 7, 1890, in New York, N.Y.; died December 10, 1974, in Kingston, N.Y. Novelist, editor, and author of books for children. Komroff began his career as a newspaper reporter in New York City, and was variously a movie critic for *Film Daily*, a Modern Library editor at Boni & Liveright Publishing, founder and editor of the Library of Living Classics at Dial Press, and an instructor at Columbia University. Komroff wrote many historical novels, for children as well as for adults, which deal with historical figures from *Julius Caesar* to *Disraeli*. *Coronet*, a two-volume adult historical novel, sold widely and was a Literary Guild selection. Komroff edited new editions of such classic works as Dostoyevsky's *The Brothers Karamazov* and Tolstoy's *War and Peace*, and was the author of works of fiction, both in novel and short story form. *For More Information See: American Authors and Books, 1640 to the Present Day*, 3rd edition, Howe, 1972; *American Novelists of Today*, Greenwood Press, 1976; *Authors of Books for Young People*, 2nd edition, Scarecrow, 1971; *Concise Dictionary of American Literature*, Greenwood Press, 1969; *Contemporary Authors*, Volume 1-4, 1st revision, Gale, 1967; *The New York Times Biographical Service*, Volume 5, Arno, 1974; *The Oxford Companion to American Literature*, 4th edition, Oxford University Press, 1965; *The Reader's Encyclopedia of American Literature*, Crowell, 1962; *Something About the Author*, Volume 2, Gale, 1971; *Twentieth Century Authors: A Biographical Dictionary of Modern Literature*, H. W. Wilson, 1942; *Twentieth Century Authors*, 1st supplement, H. W. Wilson, 1955; *Who's Who in America*, 38th edition, Marquis, 1974; *Who's Who in the World*, 2nd edition, Marquis, 1973. *Obituaries: AB Bookman's Weekly*, January 20, 1975; *Contemporary Authors*, Volume 53-56, Gale, 1975; *New York Times*, December 11, 1974.

LEAF, (Wilbur) Munro 1905-1976
(John Calvert, Mun)

PERSONAL: Born December 4, 1905, in Hamilton (now part of Baltimore), Md.; died, December 21, 1976 in Garrett Park, Maryland; son of Charles Wilbur and Emma India (Gillespie) Leaf; married Margaret Butler Pope, December 29, 1926; children: Andrew Munro, James Gillespie. *Education:* University of Maryland, B.A., 1927, Harvard University, M.A., 1931. *Address:* 11121 Rokeby Ave., Garrett Park, Md. 20766.

CAREER: Teacher and football coach, Belmont Hill School, Belmont, Mass., 1929-30, Montgomery School, Wynnewood, Pa., 1931; Bobbs-Merrill Co., New York, N.Y., manuscript reader, 1932-33; F. A. Stokes Co., New York, N.Y., editor and director, 1933-39; author and illustrator, 1934—. *Military service:* Served in the United States Army during World War II, 1942-46; became major. *Member:* Kappa Alpha, Cosmos Club (Washington, D.C.), The Players Club, Dutch Treat Club, Century Association (New York City). *Awards, honors:* Runner-up for the Caldecott Medal, 1939, for *Wee Gillis*.

"Yes," said the Tiger softly, "your trial for BEING CRUEL TO ANIMALS," and he smiled again.
■(From *Turnabout* by Munro Leaf. Illustrated by the author.)

WRITINGS—All for young people, except as noted: (Under pseudonym Mun) *Lo, the Poor Indian* (illustrated by the author), Lead, Mahony, 1934; *Grammar Can Be Fun* (illustrated by the author), F. A. Stokes, 1934, reissued, Lippincott, 1962; *Robert Francis Weatherbee* (illustrated by the author), F. A. Stokes, 1935; *Manners Can Be Fun* (illustrated by the author), F. A. Stokes, 1936, revised edition, Lippincott, 1958; *The Story of Ferdinand* (illustrated by Robert Lawson), Viking, 1936, reissued, 1969; *Noodle* (illustrated by Ludwig Bemelmans), F. A. Stokes, 1937, reissued, Four Winds, 1969; *Wee Gillis* (illustrated by R. Lawson), Viking, 1938, reissued, 1967; *Safety Can Be Fun* (illustrated by the author), F. A. Stokes, 1938, revised edition, Lippincott, 1961; (for adults) *Listen, Little Girl, Before You Come to New York* (illustrated by Dick Rose), F. A. Stokes, 1938; *Fair Play*, F. A. Stokes, 1939, reissued, Lippincott, 1967; *The Watchbirds: A Picture Book of Behavior*, F. A. Stokes, 1939.

More Watchbirds: A Picture Book of Behavior, F. A. Stokes, 1940; *John Henry Davis*, F. A. Stokes, 1940; *Fly Away, Watchbird! A Picture Book of Behavior*, F. A. Stokes, 1941; *The Story of Simpson and Sampson* (illustrated by Lawson), Viking, 1941; (reteller) *Aesop's Fables* (illustrated by Lawson), Heritage, 1941; *A War-Time Handbook for Young Americans* (illustrated by the author), F. A. Stokes, 1942; *Health Can Be Fun* (illustrated by the author), F. A. Stokes, 1943; *Three and Thirty Watchbirds: A Picture Book of Behavior*, Lippincott, 1944; *Gordon the Goat*, Lippincott, 1944; *Let's Do Better*, Lippincott, 1945; (under pseudonym John Calvert) *Gwendolyn the Goose* (illustrated by Garrett Price), Random House, 1946; *How to Behave and Why*, Lippincott, 1946; *Flock of Watchbirds*, Lippincott, 1946; (for adults; with William C. Menninger) *You and Psychiatry*, Scribner, 1948; *Boo, Who Used to Be Scared of the Dark* (illustrated by Frances T. Hunter), Random House, 1948; *Sam and the Superdroop* (illustrated by the author), Viking, 1948; *Arithmetic Can Be Fun*, Lippincott, 1949.

History Can Be Fun, Lippincott, 1950; *Geography Can Be Fun*, Lippincott, 1951, revised edition, 1962; *Reading Can Be Fun*, Lippincott, 1953; *Lucky You*, Lippincott, 1955; *Three Promises to You*, Lippincott, 1957; *Science Can Be Fun*, Lippincott, 1958; *The Wishing Pool*, Lippincott, 1960; *Being an American Can Be Fun*, Lippincott, 1964; *Turnabout*, Lippincott, 1967; *Who Cares? I Do* (illustrated by the

Then came the bull, and you know who that was, don't you?—Ferdinand. ■ (From *Ferdinand the Bull* by Munro Leaf. Pictures from the Walt Disney production based on the original drawings by Robert Lawson.)

(Lobby poster for the movie "Ferdinand the Bull." Copyright 1938 by Walt Disney Enterprises.)

author), Lippincott, 1971; *Metric Can Be Fun!* (illustrated by the author), Lippincott, 1976.

Also author, with Dr. Seuss, of an army field manual on malaria, *This is Ann* (short for anopheles mosquito), 1934, and of a booklet, *I Hate You! I Hate You!*, 1968.

ADAPTATIONS—Movie: "Ferdinand and the Bull," adapted from *The Story of Ferdinand,* Walt Disney Enterprises, 1938.

SIDELIGHTS: **December 4, 1905.** "I was born . . . just outside of Baltimore at Hamilton, Maryland. My mother and father were both born in Maryland, both their mothers and fathers were born in Maryland and both—well anyway it had been going on long enough, so I moved to Washington, D.C., before I was two months old.

"I had a very happy childhood and, as far as I am able to detect, didn't pick up any serious complexes along the way." ["Munro Leaf," *Wilson Library Bulletin,* May, 1937.[1]]

1923-1927. "I went to school in Washington and then there I was right back where I started, in Maryland at the state university. That went on for four pleasant years with me studying a little of this and a little of that. In 1927 I got my varsity letter in lacrosse and an A.B. degree."[1]

1927-1931. ". . . I went up to Harvard to the graduate school and took a Master of Arts degree in English literature—just why, I'll never know. I very definitely did not want to teach.

"The following year I went back to Harvard. This time I had a wife, Margaret Pope of Washington—a very nice wife, I might add, and I liked her so well that I still have the same one.

"Well I never became a Doctor of Philosophy because I did some special research work at Harvard on the early novel and coached football at the Roxbury Latin School until Harvard gave me an assistantship in an English course and sent me to England the following summer to buy books for the Widener Library.

Then he set out walking and crawling, running and creeping all over the hills stalking stags.
■ (From *Wee Gillis* by Munro Leaf. Illustrated by Robert Lawson.)

"Then I took a job in the fall of 1929 to teach and coach at the Belmont Hill School. I stayed there two pleasant years, then went to the Montgomery School in Wynnewood, Pa., to spend one more delightful year in teaching and coaching."[1]

1932-1939. Worked as a manuscript reader for Bobbs-Merrill Company. Later became an editor and director for the F. A. Stokes Company in New York. ". . . I had begun to suspect that what I had always hazily been wanting was crystalized in book publishing. We came to New York in the fall of 1932 and I read occasional manuscripts for the Bobbs Merrill Company's New York office until the spring of 1933 when I went to the Frederick A. Stokes Company. There I am still, thoroughly enjoying myself doing a little of this and that. In fact I believe that it was because they didn't know in quite what capacity I was working for them that they last year [1936] made me a director, so that I would have some consistent title."[1]

1934. Began writing books—a career which became his lifework. ". . . I wrote a book for children called *Grammar Can Be Fun* in which I tried to take some of the dullness out of the really painful business of correcting children's slips of

the tongue. I drew some scratchy pencil indications of what an artist was supposed to draw in the book and finally wound up by doing them myself. If anybody would dignify them by calling them illustrations, it was not for me to argue about it. Some people bought the book, so then I was a full fledged author and illustrator all in one lump.

"The next year I did a little story called *Robert Francis Weatherbee* and in 1936 *Manners Can Be Fun.*"[1]

1936. Became famous as the creator of Ferdinand the Bull. The children's story has been translated into sixteen languages and has sold 2.5 million copies. "I wrote *The Story of Ferdinand* . . . in 25 minutes on a rainy Sunday afternoon. I wrote it for Rob (Robert Lawson, a late author-illustrator). I had known Rob for about two years. He was doing illustrations for children's books but was unhappy having to conform to publishers' ideas. I gave him *Ferdinand* and told him, 'Rob, cut loose and have fun with this in your own way.' I picked the story of a bull 'cause dogs, cats, rabbits, and mice had been done thousands of times. I thought out the plot—bull, Spain, bullfight, no fight. The bee became a mechanical device for the book to have a plot. The bull needed a name, of course a Spanish name, so, I took it right out of a fourth-grade textbook. Ferdinand was the name of the husband of Isabella, the queen who financed Chris Columbus's expedition in 1492. You can't get a more Spanish name than that!'' [Lee Bennett Hopkins, *Books Are By People,* Citation, 1969.[2]]

1937. Collaborated with Ludwig Bemelmans on another successful children's book. ''My wife, Margaret, ran the children's section in Brentano's book store in New York City. There was a young girl there who was employed to paint murals. Margaret thought she was quite good. 'Write a story for her to illustrate,' Margaret told me. I wrote about my neighbor's 11-year-old dachshund. [He was the basis of the story *Noodle.* . . . (His neighbor was Hendrik Van Loon, author of *The Story of Mankind* . . . Mr. Van Loon was the first author to win the John Newbery Medal.] I gave the story to this young girl to illustrate, but I did not like what she did with it. I threw the whole thing up on the shelf. One day Ludwig came into Brentano's to see how his book *Hansi* . . . was selling. My wife chatted with him. One night he and his wife, Madeline, came to dinner. I told him, 'Ludwig, I've got a story for you.' I gave him *Noodle,* and we were a team!''[2]

1939. Son, Andrew Munro Leaf, was born.

1941. Second son, James Gillespie, was born.

1942-1946. Enlisted in Army April, 1942 as lieutenant and left in January, 1946 as major, having served in U.S. and European Theatre.

MUNRO LEAF

He liked to sit just quietly and smell the flowers.
■ (From *The Story of Ferdinand* by Munro Leaf. Illustrated by Robert Lawson.)

1960. Invited by the United States Department of State to serve as a global ''Everyman.'' From 1961 to 1964 Leaf and his wife traveled in over twenty countries, speaking with children, editors, publishers, and librarians. ''. . . The number one mission of the American specialist abroad is to be a decent American. . . . We have yet to find in any of the 24 countries we visited the man or woman who does not wish for his or her child a chance for a better life.

''Since no such thing as an illiterate democracy can exist, books, as the backbone of education, are vitally important abroad.'' [''Nickle Words for a Golden Mission,'' *Wilson Library Bulletin,* September, 1964.[3]]

1968. Wrote a self-illustrated booklet, *I Hate You! I Hate You!* as a result of his three cultural and educational exchange program tours for the State Department. ''It took me 62 years to think this up and it is my most satisfying work.''[2]

December 21, 1976. Died of cancer in Garrett Park, Maryland at the age of seventy-one. The author-illustrator believed that today's children would shape tomorrow's world, and that writing for the young was his contribution to a better future. ''Early on in my writing career I realized that if one found some truths worth telling they should be told to the young in terms that were understandable to them. Some 200 translations have seemed to bear me out.'' [*Who's Who in America,* 39th edition, Volume 2, Rand McNally, 1976.[4]]

Leaf's best known book is *The Story of Ferdinand,* hailed by many as a juvenile classic. Two separate *Library Journal* reviewers wrote: ''One of the funniest books of the year. . . . The strong black and white drawings are done with humor and a feeling for Spain. The text is almost rhythmical in its simplicity . . .'' and ''. . . It is impossible to think how Robert Lawson's drawings could be improved. He uses caricature but it is not distorted, there is gusto in the action, and real comic drama in the characterization.''

FOR MORE INFORMATION SEE: Library Journal, November 1, 1936; New York Times, September 19, 1937; Wilson Library Bulletin, May, 1937, September, 1964; J. K. Hutchens, "On an Author," New York Herald Tribune Book Review, November 13, 1949; Kunitz and Haycraft, editors, Junior Book of Authors, second edition revised, H. W. Wilson, 1951; Stanley J. Kunitz, editor, Twentieth Century Authors, first supplement, H. W. Wilson, 1955; Brian Doyle, editor, Who's Who of Children's Literature, Schocken Books, 1968; Lee B. Hopkins, Books Are By People, Citation, 1969; Donnarae MacCann & Olga Richard, The Child's First Books, H. W. Wilson, 1973; Who's Who in America, 39th edition, Volume 2, Rand McNally, 1976.

Obituaries: New York Times, December 22, 1976; New York Times Biographical Service, December, 1976; Time, January 3, 1977; Publishers Weekly, January 17, 1977; School Library Journal, February, 1977; A. B. Bookman's Weekly, March 7, 1977.

LEE, Robert C.   1931-

PERSONAL: Born December 21, 1931, in Brooklyn, N.Y.; son of Robert Corwin (a business executive) and Elsie (Calder) Lee; married Marilyn Superak (a trainer of horses), March 27, 1951, divorced, July, 1974; married Gaye Hamby Lee (a librarian), May 31, 1975; children (first marriage): Robert III, Christopher, Scott. Education: Stanford University, A.B., 1956; San Jose State College, M.A., 1962. Home: P.O. Box 894, Warsaw, Mo. 65355. Office: Warsaw R-9

ROBERT C. LEE

School District, Warsaw, Mo. 65355. Agent: Philip Sadler, 206 Broad St., Warrensburg, Mo.

CAREER: Teacher in Aptos Unified School District, Aptos, Calif., 1956-60, in Corralitos Unified School District, Watsonville, Calif., 1960-65; Pajaro Valley Unified School District, Watsonville, Calif., federal project coordinator, 1965-67; Buffalo High School, Buffalo, Mo., teacher, 1967-73, high school principal, 1973-75; Warsaw R-9 School District, Warsaw, Mo., director of elementary education, 1975—. Military service: U.S. Army, 1953-56; became sergeant. Member: National Education Association, Missouri State Teachers Association. Awards, honors: It's a Mile from Here to Glory received the Mark Twain Award, 1974 and was runner-up for the 1974 Dorothy Canfield Fisher children's book award.

WRITINGS—For young people: The Iron Arm of Michael Glenn, Little, Brown, 1965; The Day It Rained Forever, Little, Brown, 1968; I Was a Teenage Hero, McGraw, 1969; It's a Mile from Here to Glory, Little, Brown, 1972; Once Upon Another Time, Thomas Nelson, 1977.

Writes a regular weekly column for the Bolivar Herald-Free Press and The Buffalo Republican-Reflex.

WORK IN PROGRESS: Summer of the Green Star and Time for the Tiger.

SIDELIGHTS: "I am a storyteller—I pretend to be nothing more. I believe very strongly that children should read fictional material to develop insights and understandings, to stimulate the imagination that will eventually produce creativity, to overcome the awful and deadening effect of television.

"My wife and I traveled to Germany, Scandinavia and Russia to pursue our interests in children's literature."

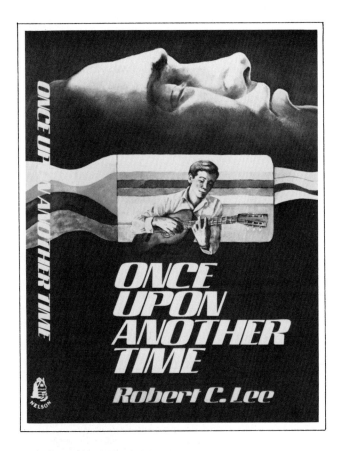

(From Once Upon Another Time by Robert C. Lee. Jacket painting by Lydia Rosier.)

LEWIS, E. M.
(Mary Melwood)

PERSONAL: Born in Carlton in Lindrick, Nottinghamshire, England; daughter of John Burtwistle (a landowner) and Mary Agres (a town registrar; maiden name, Justice) Hall; married Morris Lewis; children: Robert Hall, Roderick Alan. *Education:* Attended schools in England. *Politics:* "Nil." *Religion:* "Nil." *Home:* 5 Hove Lodge Mansions, Hove St., Hove, Sussex, England.

CAREER: Has been an elementary school teacher; playwright and author. *Awards, honors:* Arts council awards, 1964, for "Tuesday Bird," and 1965, for "Five Minutes to Morning."

WRITINGS: (Under pseudonym Mary Melwood) *Nettlewood* (novel), Deutsch, 1974, Seabury, 1975.

Plays: "Tuesday Bird," first produced, 1964; "Five Minutes to Morning," first produced, 1966; "Masquerade," first produced in Nottingham, England, at Nottingham Playhouse, 1974; "The Small Blue Hopping Stone," first produced in Detroit, Mich., at Southfield Repertory Theatre, 1976. Plays are also represented in anthologies, including *All the World's a Stage*, Delacorte.

WORK IN PROGRESS: Another play.

SIDELIGHTS: Lewis wrote and produced her first full-length play while she was twelve or thirteen. Interested in drama since her early childhood, she was involved in town musicals and helped establish a small company in 1936.

E.M. LEWIS

LEWIS, Hilda (Winifred)   1896-1974

OBITUARY NOTICE: Born about 1896 in London; died in February, 1974, in England; educator, historical novelist, and author of books for children. One of Britain's foremost historical novelists, Hilda Lewis was well-known for her exhaustively researched studies such as her trilogy including: *I Am Mary Tudor, Mary the Queen,* and *Bloody Mary. The Ship That Flew,* an historical fantasy, is the highlight of her work for children. *For More Information See: The Author's and Writer's Who's Who,* Hafner, 1971; *Twentieth Century Children's Writers,* St. Martin's Press, 1978. *Obituaries: A B Bookman's Weekly,* July 15, 1974; *Contemporary Authors,* Volume 49-52, Gale, 1975.

LINDQUIST, Willis   1908-

PERSONAL: Born June 5, 1908, in Winthrop, Minn. *Education:* Attended the University of Minnesota and George Washington University Law School.

CAREER: Following admission to the bar, became a tax lawyer with the U.S. Internal Revenue Service; author of books for children. *Military service:* Served in the Merchant Marine for three years during World War II. *Awards, honors: Haji of the Elephants* was selected as a "Children's Book of the Year," 1976, by the Child Study Association.

WRITINGS: Burma Boy (ALA Notable Book; illustrated by Nicholas Mordvinoff), Whittlesey House, 1953; *The Golden Stamp Book of Boats and Ships* (illustrated by Robert Doremus), Simon & Schuster, 1956; *Animals from All Over the World* (illustrated by James G. Irving and Sy Barlowe), Simon & Schuster, 1956; *Call of the White Fox* (illustrated by P. A. Hutchison), Whittlesey House, 1957; *The Red Drum's Warning* (illustrated by Harper Johnson), Whittlesey House, 1958; *Alaska, the Forty-Ninth State* (illustrated by P. A. Hutchison), McGraw, 1959; Irwin Shapiro, editor, *Christianity & Byzantium,* Western, 1966; *Folktales from Many Lands* (illustrated by Gordon Laite), L. W. Singer, 1969; *Stone Soup* (illustrated by Bob Shein), Western Publishing, 1970; *Haji of the Elephants* (illustrated by Don Miller), McGraw, 1976.

Contributor of articles and photographs to various periodicals, including *National Geographic.*

SIDELIGHTS: "As a boy in Minnesota I had among other things a cat, and a dog that went with me to school, rabbits and also a small owl. When I was in high school I raised bees and sold the honey. One time while taking some bees from a roof I got stung twenty-two times and was in bed for one day.

"While I was at the University some friends and I ran two plays. While attending school at the George Washington University, I earned my living by working at the Library of Congress. After becoming a lawyer, I spent my summers in going to Denmark and Sweden. At both places I did articles for *National Geographic* Magazine.

"On another occasion in Costa Rica I had a terrible experience at a bull fight; I had my head and shoulders in a bull ring and my feet on the outside of the corrida; a bull got loose outside and came storming along the outer rail. I did not know he was there until he was almost upon me, then I lifted my feet up and into the bull-ring itself; at the same instant the bull on the outside made a stab at my legs but I was inside by then.

"After the war I decided to live in New York City. My interest in birds led me to join the Boy Scouts of America. I interested many boys in birding and took them to many places of interest for birding in the New York City area.

"As a scout leader I did many things for the scouts. I helped them to make wildlife shelters for birds and animals. Over a period of years we made many birdhouses and put them up. We also got many owl-boards and pellets from many different kinds of owls. At this time I became interested also in taking care of different types of birds that needed help in some form. The biggest I ever handled was about three feet tall; the smallest I ever handled was a humming bird, I had quite a few of those. Because of all this work I was given a medal by the scouts for distinguished conservation.

"I should say that most of my time has been spent with birds of one kind or another or other animals. In Burma, for example, I became interested in the elephants and spent quite a bit of time learning more about them. Home in New York City I have often gone to the zoo to see the different animals and birds they have there."

During his vacations, Willis Lindquist traveled extensively in foreign countries. His first book, *Burma Boy,* was written after a visit to Burma. In reviewing the book, a *Chicago Sunday Tribune* critic wrote, "Boys and girls will thrill to Haji's adventures in this beautifully written and stirring tale of a boy whose love for his elephant outweighed all fear and whose courage won him his heart's desire. The author's skill

By now the leaders had lost his scent and could no longer see him or hear him ahead of them. He knew they would not turn back to search for him. That was not the way of charging elephants. ■(From *Haji of the Elephants* by Willis Lindquist. Illustrated by Don Miller.)

in conveying the feel and the spell of the jungle is equally matched by superbly dramatic illustrations." The *New York Times* added, "Willis Lindquist knows Burma at first-hand and gives us a vivid impression of the teak forests, the jungle, the native villages, all of which is repeated in Nicolas Mordvinoff's illustrations."

Horn Book's comments on *Call of the White Fox* included, "Although the book as a whole does not have the poetic beauty of the author's *Burma Boy*, it is nevertheless a very good story, well-written and lively...." The *New York Herald Tribune Book Review* noted, "The beauty of the little Arctic fox, Kali, lingers in your mind long after you read this swift and mysteriously exciting story of a thirteen-year-old American boy at a trading post in far northern Alaska.... Although Paula Hutchison's black and white sketches illustrate the text very well indeed, this is not a thin, handsome picture book like *Burma Boy*. It is primarily an adventure and mystery story in fairly large print...."

WILLIS LINDQUIST

FOR MORE INFORMATION SEE: Better Homes and Gardens, May, 1948; *New York Times,* August 16, 1953; *Chicago Sunday Tribune,* September 6, 1953; *Horn Book,* April, 1957, April, 1977; *New York Herald Tribune Book Review,* May 12, 1957; Muriel Fuller, editor, *More Junior Authors,* H. W. Wilson, 1963; *School Library Journal,* January, 1977.

LOESCHER, Ann Dull 1942-

PERSONAL: Born November 11, 1942, in Rutherford, N.J.; daughter of Floyd N. and Ann (maiden name, Spence) Dull; married Gilburt Damian Loescher (a university professor), September 25, 1971; children: Margaret Madeline. *Education:* Colby-Sawyer College, A.A., 1962; University of Connecticut, B.A., 1965; Southern Connecticut State College, M.A., 1968. *Home:* 844 Park Ave., South Bend, Ind. 46616; and 23 South Hill Park Gardens, London NW3 2TD, England. *Agent:* Marilyn Marlow, Curtis Brown Ltd., 575 Madison Ave., New York, N.Y. 10022.

CAREER: Elementary school teacher in Niantic, Conn., 1965-68; American Community Schools, London, England, elementary school teacher, 1968-75, assistant principal, 1973-75. *Member:* Amnesty International.

WRITINGS—All with husband, Gilburt Damian Loescher: *The Chinese Way: Life in the People's Republic of China,* Harcourt, 1974; *Human Rights: A Global Crisis,* Dutton, 1979.

SIDELIGHTS: "In the summer of 1968, I took a leave of absence from the school where I taught in a small Connecticut town and went to London. I intended to stay one year but stayed seven. This move proved to be of the greatest importance to me. Not only did I meet Gil there but I travelled extensively in China, the Soviet Union, and most of Europe, came to enjoy teaching more, and gained a much broader view of the world in general. While living abroad, I developed new interests. Among them are travel and photography. Walking became a preferred means of transport rather than an imposition! Through Gil, I came to realize that writing and publishing a book is actually possible. Now we have done a second one together, and look forward to others.

"Having taught upper elementary and junior high kids for ten years, I have become aware of the great need for books on international issues and on other cultures and peoples for school children. In particular, there seems to be little attention given to providing interesting non-fiction books for junior high school students. I think it is important for older children to have access to books which demonstrate the need for social justice in the world today. I find writing books to fill this gap most rewarding.

"Now that we have a small daughter, I have also become interested in books for the very young and hope to put together some picture stories which will appeal to them."

HOBBIES AND OTHER INTERESTS: Photography (especially black and white), hiking, reading, and cooking.

LOESCHER, Gil(burt Damian) 1945-

PERSONAL: Born March 7, 1945, in San Francisco, Calif.; son of Burt G. (a rancher) and Helene (Aachen) Loescher; married Ann Dull (a teacher), September 25, 1971; children: Margaret Madeline. *Education:* St. Mary's College of California, B.A., 1967; Monterey Institute of Foreign Studies, M.A., 1969; London School of Economics and Political Science, Ph.D., 1975. *Religion:* Roman Catholic. *Home:* 844 Park Ave., South Bend, Ind. 46616; and 23 South Hill Park Gardens, London NW3 2TD, England. *Agent:* Marilyn Marlow, Curtis Brown Ltd., 575 Madison Ave., New York, N.Y. 10022. *Office:* Department of Government and International Studies, University of Notre Dame, Notre Dame, Ind. 46556.

CAREER: American Community School, London, England, principal, 1969-71; University of Notre Dame, Notre Dame, Ind., assistant dean of College of Arts and Letters and assistant professor of international studies and Department of Government, 1975—. *Member:* Amnesty International (London), Amnesty International Adoption Group (founder and group leader, South Bend, Ind.), International Studies Association, Indiana Consortium for International Programs (board of directors), Association for Asian Studies, American Political Science Association. *Awards, honors:* Dorothy Danforth Compton fellow, Institute for the Study of World Politics, 1978-79; Centre for International Studies, London School of Economics (visiting fellow), 1978-79.

WRITINGS: (With wife, Ann Dull Loescher) *The Chinese Way: Life in the People's Republic of China,* Harcourt, 1974; (with Donald Kommers), *American Foreign Policy and Human Rights,* University of Notre Dame Press, 1979; (with wife) *Human Rights: A Global Crisis,* Dutton, 1979. Contributor of articles to *The World Today* (London), *Europa,* and *Archiv* (Bonn), and of reviews to *The China Quarterly, The Review of Politics, Survey, The Round Table, Yearbook of World Affairs,* and *Jahrbuch des Öffenlichen Rechtes.*

ANN DULL LOESCHER

WORK IN PROGRESS: Books for young people on China and on disarmament. Books for adults on American foreign policy and human rights and on the Sino-Vietnamese conflict.

SIDELIGHTS: "My most recent book [*Human Rights: A Global Crisis*] is about human rights. To write a book about human rights in the world is to undertake a task more necessary than pleasant. The struggle for human rights today is almost everywhere a defensive one. Thirty years after the adoption of the Universal Declaration of Human Rights, an international order of peace, justice, and the rule of law is still a dream. Torture, terrorism, violence, political repression, and hunger continue. Human rights should be the common property of mankind. However, they are not readily available to the majority of the world's people.

"Americans have tried to deal with the complex problem of human rights (mainly civil rights) in this country but like people elsewhere, they hardly have begun to face the international dimensions of the issue. Human rights is rapidly emerging as a political issue of enormous moral force. One of the main purposes of this book is to appeal to the humanity in young people by presenting them with facts about human rights violations, for the first step to solving the problem is to bring its existence into the open. Secondly, this book exam-

GIL LOESCHER

ines what international organizations, both governmental and non-governmental, are doing to reduce and ultimately to eliminate at least the most flagrant human rights violations.

"The study of international human rights is especially significant for young people now. Every young person should have the opportunity to learn about the principles and issues of international human rights to enable him or her to understand the problem and ultimately help contribute to its solution. A global perspective on human rights should be part of the basic education of everybody, particularly for those who are going to live in the 21st century.

"Research for this book was conducted in London and New York. The institutions which provided the most useful information were Amnesty International, the United Nations, the International Commission of Jurists, the International League for Human Rights, Minority Rights Group, and P.E.N. International.

"More generally, I am interested in international affairs. I teach international relations at university level and have travelled extensively in several foreign countries. I lived in England for six years and used London as a base to travel to such places as China, the Soviet Union, most of Eastern and Western Europe, and parts of Northern Africa. Most recently, I travelled to Cuba. During these trips, I do free-lance photography and my pictures have been published in major international newspapers, magazines and encyclopedias such as the *New York Times, London Times, London Daily Telegraph, Newsweek, Nova,* and *Encyclopaedia Britannica.* I try to combine academic interest in international politics with practical experience and first hand observation gained through travel and writing.

"Authors of books for young people have an important but unrealized potential for influencing students' international orientation. It is important that authors acquaint young peo-

Students are encouraged to admit any failures and short comings they might have in school and in their relationships with other students. ■ (From *The Chinese Way* by Gil Loescher with Ann Dull Loescher. Photographs by Gil and Ann Loescher.)

ple with other nations and cultures and prepare them to deal with the problems of tomorrow. There is a great need for books for students about international events because the problems of tomorrow will be more global both in terms of their implications and solutions than are the problems of today. This is the first step towards preparing our young people for not only national citizenship but also global citizenship.

"My wife and I maintain a residence in London and spend as much time there as possible. We enjoy the quality of life in England and it gives us peace of mind and a cross-cultural perspective so vital to our work and interests. Most of all, we enjoy walking in the English countryside and the Highlands of Scotland."

HOBBIES AND OTHER INTERESTS: Reading, writing, biking, the theatre, and most sports.

LOMASK, Milton   1909-

PERSONAL: Born June 26, 1909, in Fairmont, W.Va.; son of Samuel Josiah and Clara (Reinheimer) Lomask. *Education:* University of Iowa, A.B., 1930; Northwestern University, A.M., 1941. *Religion:* Roman Catholic. *Home and office:* 6758 Towne Lane Rd., McLean, Va. 22101.

CAREER: Des Moines Register, Des Moines, Iowa, reporter, 1930-35; *St. Louis Star-Times,* St. Louis, Mo., copy edi-

MILTON LOMASK

tor, 1936-37; *New York Journal-American,* copy editor, 1938-39; New York University, instructor, 1950-60. Lecturer at Catholic University of America, 1964—, Georgetown University, 1964—. Writer, 1950—. *Military service:* U.S. Army, four years, became captain. *Member:* Authors League, American Historical Association, Children's Book Guild of Washington. *Awards, honors: Vanguard: A History* won the American Institute of Aeronautics and Aeronautics history award in 1971.

WRITINGS—Adult: (With Leonard Hawkins) *The Man in the Iron Lung,* Doubleday, 1956; *Andrew Johnson: President on Trial* (History Book Club selection), Farrar, Straus, 1961; *Seed Money: The Guggenheim Story,* Farrar, Straus, 1964; (with Constance M. Green) *Vanguard: A History,* Smithsonian Institution Press, 1971; *A Minor Miracle: An Informal History of the National Science Foundation,* National Science Foundation, 1976; *Aaron Burr: The Years from Princeton to Vice-President,* Farrar, Straus, 1979.

Juvenile: *St. Isaac and the Indians,* Vision Books, 1956; *John Carroll: Bishop and Patriot,* Vision Books, 1956; *My Eskimos,* Vision Books, 1957; *St. Augustine and His Search for Faith,* Vision Books, 1957; (with Brendan Larnen) *St. Thomas Aquinas and the Preaching Beggars,* Vision Books, 1957; *The Cure of Ars: The Priest Who Outtalked the Devil,* Vision Books, 1958; *The Secret of Grandfather's Diary,* Ar-

Oomah was the most famous of the Huron medicine men. He was a crafty old man, sharp-voiced and high-tempered. Many Hurons suspected him of being a fraud, but for years he had somehow managed to keep them under his spell. ■ (From *Cross Among the Tomahawks* by Milton Lomask. Illustrated by Albert Orbaan.)

iel Books, 1958; *The Secret of the Marmalade Cat,* Ariel Books, 1959; *Ship's Boy with Magellan,* Doubleday, 1959; *Charles Carroll and the American Revolution,* Kenedy, 1959.

General Phil Sheridan and the Union Cavalry, Kenedy, 1960; *The Secret of the One-Eyed Moose,* Ariel Books, 1960; *Andy Johnson: The Tailor Who Became President,* Ariel Books, 1961; *Cross Among the Tomahawks,* Doubleday, 1961; (with Ray Neville) *The Way We Worship,* Vision Books, 1961; *A Bird in the Hand,* Bruce, 1964; *John Quincy Adams: Son of the American Revolution,* Ariel Books, 1965; *Rochambeau and Our French Allies,* Kenedy, 1965; *Assignment to the Council,* Doubleday, 1966; *I Do Solemnly Swear,* Ariel, 1966; *This Slender Reed: A Life of James K. Polk,* Ariel, 1966; *Beauty and the Traitor: The Story of Mrs. Benedict Arnold,* Macrae Smith, 1967; *Old Destiny: A Life of Alexander Hamilton,* Farrar, Straus, 1968.

Robert H. Goddard: Space Pioneer, Girrard, 1972; *The First American Revolution* (ALA Notable Book), Farrar, Straus, 1974; *The Spirit of 1787: The Making of Our Nation,* Farrar, Straus, 1980. Contributor to *America, American Heritage, Barron's Weekly, Better Homes and Gardens, Catholic Digest, Catholic Layman,* and other periodicals.

WORK IN PROGRESS: Aaron Burr: The Years of Exile (adult).

SIDELIGHTS: ''I have been a full-time writer since 1950—write fiction, history and biography for both adults and young readers. I prefer writing for the young. They send you letters so that you know that they are out there. Recently a fifth-grader paid me a great compliment. 'I used to think,' she wrote, 'that I had more imagination than anyone in the world. Then I read your book *The Secret of Grandfather's Diary.* Now I think you have the most.'

''I work in a large office in my home, accompanied by a collie named Muffin and a calico cat named Scoot. When the work is history or biography I scribble my notes on huge rolls of butcher paper, slice them into their various categories and hang the pieces on the wall for easy reference. The historian who taught me this trick called it 'the butcher-paper method of doing research.'

''I'm a great believer in travel. When I'm working on a biography it helps in understanding your hero or heroine by going wherever he or she went. One of my present subjects is that mysterious scamp, Aaron Burr. Burr made two trips down the Ohio and Mississippi Rivers, so I have persuaded an oil barge company to let me travel down the two rivers on one of those tow boats that push oil-carrying barges from Pittsburgh to New Orleans.

''I like writing about scamps and underdogs. Most American biography deals with successful people. Who knows, perhaps we can all learn something from the failures like Aaron Burr.''

LONG, Judith Elaine   1953-
(Judy Long)

PERSONAL: Born April 20, 1953, in Norfolk, Va.; daughter of David Pershing and Mildred Maxene Taylor. *Education:* DePauw University, B.A., 1975. *Residence:* Carlstadt, N.J.

(From *Volunteer Spring* by Judy Long. Illustrated by Ted Lewin.)

CAREER: Atheneum Publishers, New York, N.Y., executive editor, 1975—.

WRITINGS: (Under name Judy Long) *Volunteer Spring* (novel for young adults), Dodd, 1976.

WORK IN PROGRESS: Another novel for young adults.

LOTHROP, Harriet Mulford Stone   1844-1924
(Margaret Sidney)

PERSONAL: Born June 22, 1844, in New Haven, Connecticut; died August 2, 1924, in San Francisco, California; daughter of Sidney Mason (an architect) and Harriet (Mulford) Stone; married Daniel Lothrop (founder of the Lothrop publishing company), October 4, 1881 (died, 1892); children: Margaret. *Education:* Attended private school in New Haven, Connecticut. *Home:* ''The Wayside'' (former home of Louisa May Alcott and later of Nathaniel Hawthorne), Concord, Massachusetts.

CAREER: Author of children's books. Began writing at an early age; became a contributor to *Wide Awake* magazine, 1878; took over her late husband's publishing firm, 1892-94; involved in patriotic activities later in life, founding the Concord chapter of the Daughters of the American Revolution and the National Society of the Children of the American Revolution, 1895, president, 1895-1901.

WRITINGS—All under pseudonym Margaret Sidney; "Five Little Peppers" series, all published by Lothrop, except as noted: *Five Little Peppers and How They Grew*, 1881, reissued, 1976 [other editions illustrated by William Sharp, Grosset, 1948; Barbara Cooney, Junior Deluxe Editions, 1954; Sari (pseudonym of Ann Fleur), A. Whitman, 1955; Reisie Lonette, Grosset, 1963]; *Five Little Peppers Midway* (illustrated by W. L. Taylor), 1890; *Five Little Peppers Grown Up* (illustrated by Mente), 1892; *Phronsie Pepper: The Youngest of the Five Little Peppers* (illustrated by Jessie McDermott), 1897; *The Stories of Polly Pepper Told to the Five Little Peppers* (illustrated by J. McDermott and Etheldred B. Barry), 1899; *The Adventures of Joel Pepper* (illustrated by S. Gallagher), 1900; *Five Little Peppers Abroad* (illustrated by Fanny Y. Cory), 1902; *Five Little Peppers at School* (illustrated by Hermann Heyer), 1903; *Five Little Peppers and Their Friends* (illustrated by Eugenie M. Wireman), 1904; *Ben Pepper* (illustrated by E. M. Wireman), 1905; *Five Little Peppers in the Little Brown House* (illustrated by H. Heyer), 1907; *Our Davie Pepper* (illustrated by Alice Barber Stephens), 1916.

Fiction, except as noted; all published by Lothrop: (With others) *Tressy's Christmas*, 1880; *Half Year at Bronckton*,

HARRIET LOTHROP

1881; *So as by Fire*, 1881; *Ballad of the Lost Hare*, 1882; *The Pettibone Name: A New England Story*, 1882; *How They Went to Europe*, 1884; *Ringing Words and Other Sketches*, 1885; *On Easter Day* (poem), 1886; *The Golden West as Seen by the Ridgeway Club* (nonfiction), 1886; *Hester, and Other New England Stories*, 1886; *The Minute Man: A Ballad of "The Shot Heard Round the World,"* 1886; *Two Modern Little Princes and Other Stories*, 1886; *A New Departure for Girls* (illustrated by F. Childe Hassam), 1886; *Dilly and the Captain* (illustrated by F. C. Hassam), 1887; *How Tom and Dorothy Made and Kept a Christian Home*, 1888.

Old Concord: Her Highways and Byways (nonfiction), 1888; *St. George and the Dragon: A Story of Boy Life, and Kensington Junior*, 1888; *The Little Red Shop*, 1889; *Our Town: Dedicated to All Members of the Y.P.S.C.E.*, 1889; *An Adirondack Cabin: A Family Story*, 1890; *Rob: A Story for Boys*, 1891; (with others) *The Kaleidoscope*, 1892; *Little Paul and the Frisbie School*, 1893; (editor) *Lullabies and Jingles*, 1893; *Whittier with the Children* (nonfiction), 1893; *The Old Town Pump: A Story of East and West*, 1895; *The Gingham Bag: The Tale of an Heirloom*, 1896; *A Little Maid of Concord Town: A Romance of the American Revolution* (illustrated by Frank T. Merrill), 1898; *The Judges' Cave: Being a Romance of the New Haven Colony in the Days of the Regicides* (illustrated by C. M. Relyea), 1900; *Sally: Mrs. Tubbs*, 1903; *Two Little Friends in Norway* (illustrated by H. Heyer), 1906; *A Little Maid of Boston Town* (illustrated by F. T. Merrill), 1910.

He left her sitting straight up among her parcels.
■(From *The Five Little Peppers and How They Grew* by Margaret Sidney. Illustrated by George Giguère.)

ADAPTATIONS—Movies; all produced by Columbia Pictures: "Five Little Peppers and How They Grew," 1939; "Five Little Peppers at Home," 1940; "Five Little Peppers in Trouble," 1940; "Out West with the Peppers," 1940.

Mrs. Pepper, as audience, was seated in her big rocking chair that Ben had brought out from the kitchen and placed in the best spot on the grass to see it all... ■ (From *The Adventures of Joel Pepper* by Margaret Sidney. Illustrated by Sears Gallagher.)

SIDELIGHTS: **June 22, 1844.** Born in New Haven, Connecticut. Lothrop's background was distinguished—Sidney Mason Stone, her father, was one of New Haven's greatest architects. "One of the first things that I call from my childish book of remembrance is that I played with the children of my imagination. I had 'lots' (as the children say) of girl and boy friends, and I was an out-of-door little creature as far as restricted city life would allow. But I dearly loved to get away and curled up in a big chair in the Library, or under a large table where the ample cloth fell down and successfully hid me from the children 'tagging' me, then it was that I peopled my world with all sorts of playmates that real life did not afford. . . .

"Well, it is impossible to say when the 'Peppers' [Lothrop's fictional family] really began. At any rate, when [as] a slip of a girl I would be taken to ride in the country I always longed to find a little brown house, well settled down at the back, and a good bit from the road. I knew exactly how the little path ran up to the big green door, and the grass tried to grow in the front yard. And around it all was the glorious expanse of real country fields. Oh, how I longed for that to be my

home. I could not understand how my father who was a most successful architect, ever had been so foolish as to live in a big city and not in this place, where I might have hens and chickens, and scratch the back of the pigs. A little girl friend had once harrowed my very soul by telling me of that bliss once when she spent a day in the country, and I couldn't speak to her for a week without tears of envy and vexation.

"Then as I couldn't find the counterpart of my little brown house, I said 'I will make one for myself.' So that began 'the little brown house in Badgertown' that all children love." [Margaret M. Lothrop, *The Wayside: Home of Authors,* American Book Co., 1940.[1]]

1878. Submitted her first stories to *Wide Awake,* a magazine published by D. Lothrop Company of Boston. Used the initials, "H.M.S." for her first literary contributions. Eventually adopted the pen name "Margaret Sidney." "I chose my penname 'Sidney' because it was my father's first name. He was a splendid man, strong and true, & that made me like 'Sidney' which I had always liked from 'Sir Philip' down. Besides I wanted something a good deal different from the lackadaisical soubriquets that were frequently selected in the 'seventies,' when I chose mine. 'Margaret' was my favorite name for a girl *not* because it means 'Pearl' and 'Daisy' but because it means *Truth.* So there you have it—Truth and justice or chivalry, or whatever you call the broad helpful influence diffused by 'Sidney.'

...For times were hard with them now. The father had died when Phronsie was a baby, and since then Mrs. Pepper had had hard work to scrape together money enough to put bread into her children's mouths and to pay the rent of the Little Brown House. ■ (From *Five Little Peppers and How They Grew* by Margaret Sidney. Illustrated by William Sharp.)

"I chose to write under a penname just as thousands of others do I suppose. I was not going to be good game for derision if I failed."[1]

January, 1880. Chapters I and II of *Five Little Peppers and How They Grew* appeared in *Wide Awake*. The author, then thirty-six, had created the "Pepper" family from remembrances of her childhood imagination. ". . . There was Mrs. Pepper. *Unconsciously* I put into her character some of my mother's qualities. Unconsciously I say, for I never copied any one, nor any sayings of people in my stories.

"Now my judgment told me that I must eliminate Mr. Pepper, because the whole *motif* 'to help Mother' would be lost, if the father lived. It hurt me dreadfully. He was a most es-

He clung to his pear with both hands and ate away with great satisfaction, regardless of his new resting-place. ■ (From *Five Little Peppers Abroad* by Margaret Sidney. Illustrated by Fanny Y. Cory.)

timable man, and I loved my own father so much, it seemed the most wicked thing to do. I went around for days, feeling droopy and guilty. But it had to be done. . . .

"Well all the above came on gradually, as I thought and played with the Peppers. . . . I never had an idea of printing my brain children. It was one thing to 'yarn' to the other children . . . but quite another to realize that anybody really wanted to know them, thinking and writing, and having awfully good times with all the creatures of my imagination, till, and I was as much surprised as any one, they simply had to get between book covers. It was this way: I sent one of the Pepper 'yarns' to the *Wide Awake*. It was 'Polly Pepper's Chicken Pie'—This was followed by 'Phronsie Pepper's New Shoes'—The Editor wrote asking me to fill out a year with Pepper Stories. . . ."[1]

"The little girl'll be killed!" said others with bated breath, as a powerful pair of horses whose driver could not pull them up in time, dashed along just in front of her! With one cry, Phronsie sprang between their feet, and reached the opposite curbstone in safety! ■ (From *Five Little Peppers and How They Grew* by Margaret Sidney.)

1881. Dedicated her first book, *Five Little Pepper and How They Grew,* to her mother.

> "TO THE MEMORY OF
> MY MOTHER;
> wise in counsel—tender in judgment, and in all charity—
> strengthful in Christian faith
> and purpose—
> I dedicate, with reverence, this simple book."

[Margaret Sidney, *Five Little Peppers and How They Grew,* Lothrop, 1902.[2]]

October 4, 1881. Married the founder of the Lothrop Publishing Company, Daniel Lothrop, who had encouraged her to publish her stories.

1883. Purchased "The Wayside" in Concord, Massachusetts, the former home of Nathaniel Hawthorne and, before that, of the Louisa May Alcott family.

1885. Daughter, Margaret, born. Continued to write books about the "Pepper" family. Years later, her daughter recalled how her mother created her stories: "The Peppers became as real to me when I was a little girl, as they were to Mother, although I did not have a creative imagination, and was therefore obliged to wait for a new book, in order to learn about their latest adventures. I realized that Mother, however, seemed to commune with them when she was writing a book. When I was a young girl, she and I would often sit in front of the open fire in the old sitting room. She would be rocking in her comfortable brown wicker chair, and I, wanting to read yet hesitating to do so for fear she might be lonely, would ask her if I couldn't bring her a book and a lamp. She would say, 'No'; then seeing my hesitancy, would turn with that charming smile of hers, and reassure me. 'Oh, no, Margaret. I am happy; I am just thinking of the Peppers.' Quietly she would continue her rocking and I, content, would open my book. Once in a while I would look up to see how she was, and often I would catch a little smile stealing across her face, just as if she were listening to an amusing story being told her by someone I could not see—one of the Pepper children, I knew.

"I could almost see them clustered around Mother and her chair, they seemed so real to me. The mental picture is as vivid today as it was then. Polly, dark eyes dancing, and brown hair encircling her eager face, stood close against Mother's right elbow. Phronsie, with the golden hair, leaned on Mother's right knee, gazing into her face—I knew that expression of earnest interest. Sturdy old Ben hung over the back of the chair, while Davie almost breathless with excitement, stood a little way off. Joel was jumping up and down with eagerness; he would joggle Mother's left arm and I felt I could hear him say, his dark head nodding to give his words the proper emphasis: 'You haven't heard about this!'" [Elizabeth Johnson, "Margaret Sidney vs. Harriet Lothrop," *Horn Book,* April, 1971.[3]]

"...If we can only keep together, dears, and grow up good, so that the little brown house won't be ashamed of us, that's all I ask." ■ (From *Five Little Peppers and How They Grew* by Margaret Sidney. Illustrated by Hermann Heyer.)

1895. Founded the Concord Chapter of the Daughters of the American Revolution and the National Society of the Children of the American Revolution.

1898. Besides her popular "Pepper" series, Lothrop wrote several other children's stories. *A Little Maid of Concord Town,* a romance about her beloved, adopted, Massachusetts home, was published. "Some dozen years or so ago, the author of this volume planned to write an historic story of Old Concord, dealing with the months and the years prior to 1775, to show the natural sequence of events that gave to the old town her opportunity 'to fire the shot heard round the world,' and made her so large a factor in shaping the destiny of the American Republic.

"It was no mere chance that set apart the Old North Bridge at Concord as the arena where was enacted the opening scene of that struggle for independence that made the Colonies a free nation. Old Concord had long been preparing for what God in his providence was preparing for her; and the brilliant episode on the 19th of April, 1775, was but the natural result of that long and faithful preliminary work. Marvellous indeed in the eyes turned backward to that April morning, is the outcome!

"The fact and fiction of the story contained in these pages can be easily separated in the mind of the reader, and yet preserve a harmony of action. . . . The picturesque and dramatic episode in the life of beautiful Meliscent Barrett so attracted the author these dozen years ago, that she was impelled to use it as a central force around which to adjust her story. Tradition and fireside tales are, after all, much of the warp and woof of our Colonial and Revolutionary history; such annals inspire and lead, perchance, swifter to the true spirit of those epochs, than the labored art of the historian." [Margaret Sidney, preface to *A Little Maid of Concord Town,* Lothrop, 1898.[4]]

1900-1924. Continued to write and pursue an active interest in historical preservation. In her own book, *The Wayside: Home of Authors,* Lothrop's daughter recalled her mother's later years: "As the years had passed, books had continued to come from Mother's pen, in all some thirty or forty; the series about the Five Little Peppers had grown to twelve volumes; there had been other favorites, such as *The Little Maid of Concord Town* and its companion volume about Boston. She had remembered her birthplace, New Haven, Connecticut, in *The Judge's Cave, a Romance of the Regicides.* Perhaps even more interesting was the chatty semi-guidebook, *Old Concord: Her Highways and By-ways.*

"In her later years Mother spent a good deal of time in travel, taking trips of some duration to Egypt and Palestine as well as to England, Norway, and the Continent. She found particular joy in such out-of-the-way spots as Spitzbergen and in places with literary associations. The last nine winters of her life she spent in California where she had many friends and where she could work with greater ease than in the more

"This doll is for you," she said gravely, putting a doll attired in a wonderful pink satin costume into Jane's arms. "I've told her about your dog, and she's a little frightened, so please be careful."
▪ (From *Five Little Peppers Midway* by Margaret Sidney. Illustrated by Hermann Heyer.)

(From the movie "Five Little Peppers at Home" based on the novel *Five Little Peppers and How They Grew.* Copyright 1940 by Columbia Pictures Corp.)

(From the movie "Five Little Peppers and How They Grew." Copyright 1939 by Columbia Pictures Corp.)

rigorous climate of New England. The breadth of the continent, however, did not separate her spirit from Concord and the home which was filled for her with associations.''[1]

August 2, 1924. Died, at the age of eighty, in San Francisco. Shortly before her death she had completed an article on Edgar Allan Poe in connection with a proposal to name a square in his honor. Years before, Lothrop had worked out a personal philosophy of action which she strove to follow throughout her lifetime.

          "PROMISE YOURSELF

''To be strong that nothing can disturb your peace of mind.

''To talk of health, happiness and prosperity to every person you meet.

''To make all your friends feel that there is something to them.

''To look on the sunny side of everything and make your optimism come true.

''To think only of the best, to work only for the best, and to expect only the best.

''To be just as enthusiastic about [the] success of others as you are about your own.

''To forget the mistakes of the past and press on to the greater achievements of the future.

''To wear a cheerful countenance at all times, and to have a smile ready for [every] living creature you meet.

''To give so much time to the improvement of yourself that you have no time to criticise others.

''To be too large for worry, too noble for anger, too strong for fear, and too happy to permit the presence of trouble.

''To think well of yourself and to proclaim this fact to the world—not in loud words, but in great deeds.

''To live to the faith that the world is on your side so long as you are true to the best that is in you.''[1]

FOR MORE INFORMATION SEE: Margaret M. Lothrop, *The Wayside: Home of Authors,* American Book Company, 1940; Laura Benét, *Famous Storytellers for Young People,* Dodd, 1968; Elizabeth Johnson, ''Margaret Sidney vs. Harriet Lothrop,'' *Horn Book,* April, 1971.

LUCAS, E(dward) V(errall)   1868-1938

PERSONAL: Born June 12, 1868, in Eltham, Kent, England; died June 26, 1938, in London, England; son of Alfred and Jane Lucas; married Elizabeth Griffin, 1897; children: Audrey. *Education:* Attended University College, London.

CAREER: Novelist, poet, essayist, and author and editor of books for children. After being apprenticed to a bookseller at the age of sixteen, Lucas worked for many newspapers and periodicals, including the *Sussex Daily News,* 1889-92, as a

E.V. LUCAS, 1931

reporter, the London *Globe,* 1893-1900, the *Academy,* 1896-1901, and *Punch* as an assistant editor and later its film reviewer; chairman of Methuen & Co., publishers, beginning 1924. Served on the Royal Commission on Historical Monuments, 1928-38, and on the Crown Lands Advisory Committee, 1933. *Member:* Athenaeum, Beefsteak, and Garrick Clubs. *Awards, honors:* Companion of Honor, 1932; LL.D., St. Andrews University; D.Litt., Oxford University.

WRITINGS—Essays: *Fireside and Sunshine,* Methuen, 1906, reprinted, Books for Libraries, 1968; *Character and Comedy,* Macmillan, 1907; *One Day and Another,* Macmillan, 1909; *Good Company: A Rally of Men,* Methuen, 1909; *Old Lamps for New,* Macmillan, 1911; *Loiterer's Harvest,* Macmillan, 1913, reprinted, Books for Libraries, 1971; *Cloud and Silver,* Doran, 1916, reprinted, Books for Libraries, 1971; *A Boswell of Baghdad,* Doran, 1917, reprinted, Books for Libraries, 1970; *'Twixt Eagle and Dove,* Methuen, 1918; *Mixed Vintages: A Blend of Essays Old and New,* Methuen, 1919; *The Phantom Journal, and Other Essays and Diversions,* Methuen, 1919, reprinted, Books for Libraries, 1970; *Adventures and Enthusiasms,* Doran, 1920; *Urbanites: Essays New and Old* (illustrated by George L. Stampa), Methuen, 1921, reprinted, Books for Libraries, 1970; *Giving and Receiving: Essays and Fantasies,* Doran, 1922, reprinted, Books for Libraries, 1971; *You Know What People Are* (illustrated by George Morrow), Methuen, 1922; *Luck of the Year: Essays, Fantasies, and Stories,* Doran, 1923, reprinted, Books for Libraries, 1969; *Encounters and Diversions,* Methuen, 1924, reprinted, Books for Libraries, 1972.

The sweet Misses Lillies of the Valley could not be tempted from their retreat. ■ (From "The Rose's Breakfast" in *Forgotten Tales of Long Ago* by E.V. Lucas. Illustrated by F.D. Bedford.)

Events and Embroideries, Methuen, 1926, Doran, 1927; *A Founded Isle, and Other Essays*, Methuen, 1927, reprinted, Books for Libraries, 1968; *The More I See of Men: Stray Essays on Dogs*, Methuen, 1927; *Out of a Clear Sky: Essays and Fantasies about Birds*, Methuen, 1928; *A Rover I Would Be: Essays and Fantasies*, Methuen, 1928; *Turning Things Over: Essays and Fantasies*, Dutton, 1929, reprinted, Books for Libraries, 1970; *Traveller's Luck: Essays and Fantasies*, Methuen, 1930; *Visibility Good: Essays and Excursions*, Lippincott, 1931, reprinted, Books for Libraries, 1968; *Lemon Verbena, and Other Essays*, Lippincott, 1932, reprinted, Books for Libraries, 1969; *At the Sign of the Dove*, Methuen, 1932; *Saunterer's Rewards*, Methuen, 1933, Lippincott, 1934, reprinted, Books for Libraries, 1970; *Pleasure Trove*, Lippincott, 1935, reprinted, Books for Libraries, 1968; *Only the Other Day: A Volume of Essays*, Methuen, 1936, reprinted, Books for Libraries, 1967; *All of a Piece: New Essays*, Lippincott, 1937, reprinted, Books for Libraries, 1968; *Adventures and Misgivings*, Methuen, 1938, reprinted, Books for Libraries, 1970.

Novels: *Listener's Lure: A Kensington Comedy*, Macmillan, 1906; *Over Bemerton's: An Easy-Going Chronicle*, Macmillan, 1908; *Mr. Ingleside*, Macmillan, 1910; *London Laven-* der: *An Entertainment*, Macmillan, 1912; *Landmarks*, Macmillan, 1914; *The Vermilion Box*, Doran, 1916; *Verena in the Midst: A Kind of a Story*, Doran, 1920; *Rose and Rose*, Doran, 1921; *Genevra's Money*, Methuen, 1922, Doran, 1923; *Advisory Ben*, Methuen, 1923, Doran, 1924; *Windfall's Eve*, Methuen, 1929, Lippincott, 1930; *Down the Sky: An Entertainment*, Lippincott, 1930; *The Barber's Clock: A Conversation Piece*, Methuen, 1931, Lippincott, 1932.

Poems: *Songs of the Bat*, W. P. Griffith, 1892; *All the World Over* (illustrated by Edith Farmiloe), G. Richards, 1898; *The Book of Shops* (illustrated by Francis D. Bedford), G. Richards, 1899; *Four and Twenty Toilers* (illustrated by F. D. Bedford), E. Dalton, 1900; *The Visit to London* (illustrated by Bedford), Methuen, 1902; *Mr. Punch's County Songs* (illustrated by Ernest H. Shepard), Methuen, 1928; *The Pekinese National Anthem* (illustrated by Persis Kirmse), Methuen, 1930; *No-Nose at the Show* (illustrated by P. Kirmse), Methuen, 1931.

Travel: *Highways and Byways in Sussex* (illustrated by Frederick L. Griggs), Macmillan, 1904 [excerpts published as *Mid-Sussex: Highways and Byways* and *East Sussex: Highways and Byways*, Macmillan, 1937]; *A Wanderer in Holland* (illustrated by Herbert Marshall), Macmillan, 1905; *A Wanderer in London* (illustrated by Nelson Dawson), Macmillan, 1906; *A Wanderer in Paris* (illustrated by Walter Dexter), Macmillan, 1909; *A Wanderer in Florence* (illustrated by Harry Morley), Macmillan, 1912; *A Wanderer in Venice* (illustrated by Morley), Macmillan, 1914; *More Wanderings in London* (illustrated by H. M. Livens), Doran, 1916 (published in England as *London Revisited*, Methuen, 1916); *Roving East and Roving West*, Doran, 1921; *Introducing London* (illustrated by Ernest Coffin), Doran, 1925; *Zigzags in France*, Methuen, 1925; *Wanderings and Diversions*, Putnam, 1926; *A Wanderer in Rome* (illustrated by H. Morley), Doran, 1926; *Introducing Paris*, Methuen, 1928; *French Leaves*, Methuen, 1931; *English Leaves*, Lippincott, 1933, reprinted, Books for Libraries, 1969; *London Afresh*, Methuen, 1936, Lippincott, 1937.

Biographical: *Bernard Barton and His Friends: A Record of Quiet Lives*, E. Hicks, 1893; (editor) *Charles Lamb and the Lloyds*, Smith, Elder, 1898, Lippincott, 1899; *The Life of Charles Lamb*, Putnam, 1905, reprinted, R. West, 1973; *A Swan and Her Friends*, Methuen, 1907; *David Williams: Founder of the Royal Literary Fund*, J. Murray, 1920; *Letters to the Colvins*, Anderson Galleries, 1928; *The Colvins and Their Friends*, Methuen, 1928, reprinted, R. West, 1973; *Reading, Writing, and Remembering: A Literary Record*, Harper, 1932, reprinted, Scholarly Press, 1971; *At the Shrine of St. Charles*, Dutton, 1934; *The Old Contemporaries*, Methuen, 1935.

Art: *British Pictures and Their Painters: An Anecdotal Guide to the British Section of the National Gallery*, Macmillan, 1913 (published in England as *The British School: An Anecdotal Guide to the British Painters and Paintings in the National Gallery*, Methuen, 1913); *Edwin Austin Abbey, Royal Academician: The Record of His Life and Work*, Scribner, 1921; *Vermeer of Delft*, Methuen, 1922; *John Constable, the Painter*, Minton, Balch, 1924; *A Wanderer among Pictures: A Companion to the Galleries of Europe*, Doran, 1924; *Vermeer the Magical*, Methuen, 1929, reprinted, Books for Libraries, 1971.

"Little Books on Great Masters" series: *Chardin and Vigée-Lebrun*, Doran, 1924; *Rembrandt*, Doran, 1924; *Michael Angelo*, Doran, 1924; *Velasquez*, Doran, 1926; *Giorgione*,

Doran, 1926; *Leonardo da Vinci*, Doran, 1926; *Frans Hals*, Doran, 1926; *Van Dyke*, Doran, 1926.

For children: (Editor) *The Dumpy Books for Children*, G. Richards, 1897; *The Flamp, The Ameliorator, [and] The Schoolboy's Apprentice* (illustrated by Olive Crane), G. Richards, 1897, F. A. Stokes, 1927; (editor) *A Book of Verse for Children*, G. Richards, 1897, reprinted, Books for Libraries, 1970; (with wife, Elizabeth Lucas) *Three Hundred Games and Pastimes; or, What Shall We Do Now?*, Macmillan, 1903; (editor) *Old Fashioned Tales* (illustrated by F. D. Bedford), Wells, Gardner, 1906; (editor) *Another Book of Verses for Children* (illustrated by Bedford), Macmillan, 1907, reprinted, Books for Libraries, 1971; *Anne's Terrible Good Nature, and Other Stories for Children* (illustrated by A. H. Buckland), Macmillan, 1908, reissued, Gollancz, 1970; *The Slowcoach: A Story of Roadside Adventure* (illustrated by M. V. Wheelhouse), Wells, Gardner, 1910; *Playtime and Company: A Book for Children* (illustrated by E. H. Shepard), Doran, 1925; *A Cat Book* (illustrated by Pat Sullivan), Harper, 1927; *If Dogs Could Write: A Second Canine Miscellany*, Lippincott, 1930.

Other: (With Charles Larcom Graves) *The War on the Wenuses* (a skit based on H. G. Wells' *The War of the Worlds*), [London], 1898, reprinted, Arno, 1975; (author of introduction) Jane Austen, *Pride and Prejudice*, Methuen, 1900; (author of introduction) Austen, *Northanger Abbey*, Methuen, 1901; (author of introduction) Charles Lamb, *The Essays of Elia*, Methuen, 1902; (author of introduction) Lamb, *The King and Queen of Hearts*, Methuen, 1902; (with C. L. Graves) *England Day by Day* (illustrated by G. Morrow), Methuen, 1903; (with Graves) *Wisdom While You Wait*, Inside-Britt, 1903; (with Graves) *Signs of the Times; or, The Hustlers' Almanack for 1907* (illustrated by G. Morrow), A. Rivers, 1906; (with C. L. Graves) *Hustled History; or, As It Might Have Been* (illustrated by G. Morrow), I. Pitman, 1908; (author of introduction) James Russell Lowell, *Fireside Travels*, H. Frowde, 1909; (with George Morrow) *What a Life! An Autobiography*, Methuen, 1911, reprinted, Dover, 1975; *A Group of Londoners*, [Minneapolis], 1913; (adaptor) *Swollen-Headed William: Painful Stories and Funny Pictures after the German*, Dutton, 1914; (with C. L. Graves) *All the Papers: A Journalistic Revue* (illustrated by G. Morrow), I. Pitman, 1914; (translator) Hun Svedend, *In Gentlest Germany* (illustrated by Morrow), J. Lane, 1915; *Outposts of Mercy*, Methuen, 1917; (author of introduction) George Morrow, *George Morrow: His Book*, Methuen, 1920; *The Same Star* (three-act comedy), Methuen, 1924.

Editor: *The Open Road: A Little Book for Wayfarers*, Holt, 1901, reprinted, Books for Libraries, 1970; *The Works of Charles and Mary Lamb*, five volumes, Putnam, 1903, reprinted, Scholarly Press, 1971; *The Original Poems and Others by Ann and June Taylor and Adelaide O'Keefe* (illustrated by F. D. Bedford), Wells, Gardner, 1903; *The Friendly Town: A Little Book for the Urbane*, Methuen, 1905, reprinted, Books for Libraries, 1971; *Forgotten Tales of Long Ago* (illustrated by F. D. Bedford), F. A. Stokes, 1906; *The Gentlest Art: A Choice of Letters by Entertaining Hands*, Macmillan, 1907; *The Ladies Pageant*, Macmillan, 1908; *Runaways and Castaways* (illustrated by F. D. Bedford), Wells, Gardner, 1908; *Some Friends of Mine: A Rally of Men*, Macmillan, 1909; *The Second Post*, Macmillan, 1910; *William Cowper's Letters: A Selection*, Oxford University Press, 1911; Charles Lamb, *The Best of Lamb*, Methuen, 1914, reprinted, 1962; *Methuen's Annual*, Methuen, 1914; *Remember Louvain! A Little Book of Liberty and War*, Methuen, 1914; G. K. Chesterton, *A Shilling for My Thoughts*,

(From *A Book of Verses for Children* by E.V. Lucas.)

Methuen, 1916; Mary, Queen Consort of George V, King of Great Britain and Ireland, *The Book of the Queen's Doll House*, Volume II, Methuen, 1924; G. K. Chesterton, *A Gleaming Cohort: Being Selections from the Writings of G. K. Chesterton*, Methuen, 1926; *The Joy of Life: An Anthology of Lyrics Drawn Chiefly from the Works of Living Poets*, Methuen, 1928; *Post-Bag Diversions*, Harper, 1924; *The Letters of Charles Lamb, to Which Are Added Those of His Sister, Mary Lamb*, Methuen, 1935, reprinted, AMS Press, 1968; *A Hundred Years of Trent Bridge*, [Worcester, England], 1938.

Collections and selections: *A Little of Everything*, Macmillan, 1912; *Harvest Home*, Macmillan, 1913; *Specially Selected: A Choice of Essays* (illustrated by G. L. Stampa), Methuen, 1920, reprinted, Books for Libraries, 1970; *The Minerva Edition of the Works of E. V. Lucas*, Library Press, 1926; *And Such Small Deer*, Lippincott, 1931; *As the Bee Sucks* (illustrated and edited by E. H. Shepard), Methuen, 1937.

SIDELIGHTS: **June 12, 1868.** Born in Eltham, Kent, England of Quaker parents in a house they named *Villa Stresa* to commemorate their Italian honeymoon, Lucas was the second of seven children. "... My maternal grandmother, *née* Pattison, however, I knew well, for her long and useful life continued after I was grown up. There must be many left in Luton to remember Mrs. Drewett's treatments and cures. She was celebrated there and in the neighbourhood as an unqualified doctor, and three of her remedies were famous; her cough medicine, her rhubarb mixtures (amazingly unpleasant), and, above all, her ointment—Grandma's Ointment as we called it.... I remember very clearly my grand-

**Blessings on thee, little man,
Barefoot boy, with cheek of tan!**

■ (From "The Barefoot Boy" by John Greenleaf Whittier in *The Open Road: A Book for Wayfarers* compiled by E.V. Lucas.)

mother in her black dress and white shawl and her quiet, unhastening, efficient way; always doing something, baking her wonderful brown bread, making a pork pie (shaped like a turnover and completely obsolete in these inferior days of juiceless meat and plaster of Paris crust), mixing with secret rites her ointment.

"My grandmother, whom I used to visit until I was in the late twenties, had an old servant named Ann, with a high Bedfordshire voice, with whom like so many elderly mistresses with elderly maids, she was continually bickering; but never to any real loss of temper. Ann, I must admit, was very trying, for her memory was short where my grandmother's was exact; but she was not spared.

"At breakfast my grandmother would suddenly ring the bell—a copper bell with a loose handle.

"Enter Ann, a little flustered.

"'Look at the table, Ann,' her mistress would say, 'and see what thee have forgotten.'

"Ann would look and look, while I was longing to prompt her. 'Ann, you old duffer, the salt,' I wanted to say.

"After a while Ann would give it up. 'I'm sorry, m'm, but I don't miss nothing.'

"'If thee look in the cupboard, Ann, thee'll find the salt.'

"Although Mrs. Drewett preferred Josephus to the Bible, she was no rebel, and indeed the simplicity of her trust in verbal scripture often perplexed me. She believed, for example, as her daughter, my mother, did, that on that distant reuniting day we should actually and physically reassemble for judgment, and this macabre idea struck her as 'nice.' 'Nice' was indeed one of her favourite words. She thought certain articles of food 'nice'; she also, I remember, thought it 'nice' that Jesus Christ should have been crucified between two thieves." [Audrey Lucas, *E. V. Lucas: A Portrait*, Kennikat Press, 1969.[1]]

His father, considered an incredibly spoiled and selfish man, always put his own needs before those of his wife and children. For this reason Lucas was sent to nine different schools and removed from most because of controversy about the bill. "I got from my father very little but knowledge of what to avoid. I may have got much that I could not help, but, consciously, from his self-protectiveness I learned something different, and from his piety without works to be too much the unbeliever."[1]

1884. Apprenticed to a Brighton bookseller at the age of sixteen. "Except for school terms elsewhere, I was destined to be a Brightonian for more than twenty years, for when at last, just after my sixteenth birthday, a broken scholastic career, which included nine schools of varying merit, came to an end, I was apprenticed to a Brighton bookseller and thus lost the years in which the ordinary youth has most fun and learns most. And when I had finished with that, I spent two years more gaining experience as a member of the staff of the *Sussex Daily News*, a Brighton paper.

"The bookshop had a circulating library with an enormous stock of works no longer in circulation, many of them dating from the eighteenth century, so that I was able to make explorations in reading not easy for ordinary boys, while the work later, on the *Sussex Daily News*, taught me to keep my thoughts in easily accessible pigeon-holes; but I used to look with envy on those contemporaries who were still at good schools or at the university, with playing-fields at their service. Nor did it decrease my dissatisfaction to have to be, as part of my regular duty, every day at noon in the porter's lodge of Brighton College to see what new guides to knowledge the young barbarians were needing.

"Most of all I now regret the loss of a classical education. The world no doubt is the best or most serviceable schoolmaster; but the world's curriculum does not include Latin and Greek. If it were any consolation, I would remind myself that Frederick the Great and Cecil Rhodes were equally without the dead languages; but it is not.

"Although during that apprenticeship I spent most of my spare time, and some of my employer's, in reading, I was trying to write, too; always verse. I seem to have written no prose before I was twenty-one. The productions of these early years are collected in three or four manuscript books, one of which, *Verrallana*, 1888, begins with the following appeal to the reviewer:

'Were I to seek publicity in print
The Critic's heart I'd soften, if I could,
("The Critic's heart," say I? The Critic's flint)
With this decree of Arnold's gentle Budh:
"Kill not, for Pity's sake, and lest ye slay
The meanest thing upon its way."''

"The verses are all serious. No love poems, but plenty of polemics and inquiries into the anomalies of life, with anxious views on the next world. In fact, a sceptic's commentary.

"I seem very early to have doubted and denied. In fact all my life I have been without belief in any guiding purpose behind the veil and with too quick a consciousness of the world's inequality, injustice, cruelty and of the waste and frustration that are continually evident. This is why almost all my writing has been concerned with the pleasant things, and why I have laid so much emphasis on what I found to be beautiful or worthy of honour. Perhaps I was thus concentrating for fear that I might weep." [E. V. Lucas, *Reading, Writing and Remembering: A Literary Record*, Harper, 1932.[2]]

1889-1892. Worked as a reporter on the *Sussex Daily News*. "As a member of the staff of the *Sussex Daily News*, I had to be prepared at a moment's notice to be sent anywhere—to police courts, inquests, theatres, charity meetings, music-halls, flower-shows, meets of hounds, shipwrecks, weddings, funerals, concerts, entertainments, billiard matches—everything, in short, where shorthand, which I never learned, was not essential. In my spare time at the office I wrote paragraphs, criticisms, descriptive articles and reviews of books. The quality of the work may have been low, but the practice was useful, and every day I spent less time in getting ready to begin.

"For two years I led this strange hand-to-mouth existence—in exchange not for salary, but for pocket money—beginning each morning at eleven, when I had to be in the Hove Police Court, and ending between 2 and 3 a.m., when the paper went to bed. Apart from the useful training acquired, I value those two years for the companionship of the only other non-shorthand writer on the staff, Vincent Brown, a fine critic of literature, a fearless talker and the author of some powerful novels of peasant life, all on the tragic side but filled with pity and understanding. *My Brother* was perhaps his best work. Brown's greatest literary heroes, Thomas Hardy and Dostoievsky, soon became mine.

"An early instance of the choice of words—how one epithet can be better than another—occurred during one of my assignments (as the American journalistic stories say), while I was on the Brighton paper. Buffalo Bill brought his Wild West Show to the town, and his advertising representative, Major Burke, who also had a wide felt hat and long shining locks, invited the press to his tent, where whisky was not inconspicuous. In the course of conversation, I remarked that there would naturally be a procession. He was shocked and even pained. 'Young man,' he said, 'ours is not a procession; ours is a cavalcade. . . .'"[2]

1892. Attended University College in London. Lucas also contributed verses and articles to the *Globe*, which he later joined permanently, remaining on the staff for many years. "I might have remained on the *Sussex Daily News* for ever had not still another of my uncles acquired a 'concern,' as Quakers say, for my future and produced a sum of two

Charles Graves and E.V. Lucas at Froghole.

hundred pounds in order that I might go to London and attend lectures at University College for as long as the money lasted.

"In January, 1892, therefore, I found lodgings in Harrington Square, Camden Town—opposite Mornington Crescent, where Tennyson once had rooms, in a cupboard in one of which he left the MS. of 'In Memoriam,' and only a few yards beyond the house in the Hampstead Road with a tablet on it saying that George Cruikshank lived there. Cruikshank, who had illustrated *Oliver Twist* and *Harrison Ainsworth* and whose great teetotal satire, 'The Triumph of Bacchus,' I had known in a maple frame ever since I could remember. My bed-sitting-room was on the top floor; I had breakfast in a little back room on the ground floor, with a plaster bust of Dante as its sole decoration, not impossibly a replica of the one which Eckermann once discovered Goethe scrutinizing as he also ate.

"One doesn't hear the phrase 'good talkers' so much as one used to, but in my early days in London there were many men famous for their conversation. It was the thing to talk well. I don't know that I cared much about meeting them, for everything they said sounded as if they had said it before, and what I enjoy is the offspring of the moment; but they were informative enough. At one of the houses to which I carried an introduction soon after arriving in London in 1892—Richard Whiteing's in St. Mary Abbot's Terrace—many well-known talkers were in the habit of meeting.

"Whiteing had not then written his novel *No. 5 John Street*, which brought him his fame (and which, as Reader for Grant Richards, I was to discover), but he was an active journalist, and the author of a delicate satirical fantasy called *The Island*, and was prepared at a moment's notice to converse wittily, whimsically or oracularly on any theme that occurred.

"I had a standing invitation to Sunday's evening meal, and as other people were similarly on the free list there used to be plenty to listen to. I say listen, for I was much too shy to take part; nor am I what is called a talker: indeed, I have been accused of ruining much good conversation by interjecting nonsense. In consequence of this shyness I must confess to having allowed several Sundays to pass before I could collect enough courage to ring the bell. I went all the way down to Kensington, on a bus, starving, and then daren't face the ordeal of meeting strangers. No one who is not shy can have any notion of the odds with which the shy have to contend and what bitter struggles they pass through. I have often gone without lunch or dinner wholly through a reluctance, amounting to an inability, to enter a restaurant alone. I don't pretend to be as shy as that now, but am still more of a claustrophil than a claustrophobe."[2]

1893-1900. Reporter on the London *Globe*.

1896. Worked on the reconstructed *Academy* until 1901.

1897. Married Elizabeth Griffin.

At their various homes in London they were visited by people in the literary world—Joseph Conrad, James Barrie, G. K. Chesterton, John Galsworthy, Hugh Walpole and A. A. Milne.

1899. Compiled the best selling anthology, *The Open Road*.

Early 1900's. Assistant editor of *Punch*. Later becoming its film reviewer.

1905. Began a series of travel books—the first, *A Wanderer in London*.

E.V. Lucas, painting by Robin Guthrie.

His travels to Florence, Italy produced this opinion in a letter to his mother: "I don't like it. Indeed I hate it. The streets are intolerably noisy and dangerous, the people are hard and grasping. Everything is dirty and neglected and I am bitten anew by corrupt insects every few hours."[1]

Of Paris, he recorded: "Every one who has made a stay in Paris or in any French town, and has been at all observant, must have noticed, either singly or in little groups, that prettiest of the flora and fauna of Roman Catholic countries, a 'first communicant' in her radiant and spotless attire—from white shoes to white veil, and crown of innocence over all. One sees them usually after the ceremony, soberly marching through the streets, or flitting from this friend to that like runaway lilies. Prinking and preening a little in the shop windows, too; and no wonder, for it is something to be thus clad and thus important; and never will such clothes be worn by these wearers again. Meanwhile the younger children envy, and little attendant bodies of proud relations somewhere in the vicinity admire and exult."[1]

He spoke of his country house which had formerly been a shepherd's cottage: "Sometimes when I'm having dinner here, I imagine the shepherd's ghost coming back to have a look round. I suppose if he peeped in and saw me sitting here alone, in a dinner jacket, drinking champagne and being waited on by Watkins, he would think it a disgusting spectacle. As indeed it is."[1]

1919. Traveled around the world and later wrote his impressions in *Roving East and Roving West*.

1924. Became chairman of Methuen's Publishing Company.

1932. Made a Companion of Honour.

(From *Another Book of Verses for Children* edited by E.V. Lucas. Illustrated by F.D. Bedford.)

June 26, 1938. Died in London, England. "For the greater part of my literary life I have been able to choose my own subjects and write nothing that I did not want to write or that I did not believe. Hence I have driven the quill with no less contentment than other men drive ponies or Bogatti cars. Few authors can have been so lucky as I in blending recreation with livelihood."[2]

After his death A. A. Milne wrote: "One would save for him the little gleanings of the week; ridiculous things, odd things, damnable things: heard, read, discovered: thinking, 'I must tell E. V. that,' knowing that his comment would give just that extra flavour to one's own emotion."[1]

James Agate wrote of Lucas: "I have an idea that the serenity of the writer was a mask hiding the torments of a man knowing as much about hell as any of Maupassant's characters, or even Maupassant himself."[1]

FOR MORE INFORMATION SEE: Grant M. Overton, "That Literary Wanderer, E. V. Lucas," in his *Cargoes for Crusoes,* Appleton, 1924; E. W. Gosse, "Essays of Mr. Lucas," in *Essays of Today,* edited by Francis H. Pritchard, Little, Brown, 1924; Arthur St. John Adcock, "E. V. Lucas," in his *Glory That Was Grub Street,* F. A. Stokes; 1928; E. V. Lucas, *Reading, Writing and Remembering: A Literary Record,* Harper, 1932; Audrey Lucas, *E. V. Lucas: A Portrait,* Methuen, 1939, reprinted, Kennikat, 1969; Frank A. Swinnerton, *Georgian Literary Scene,* sixth edition, Farrar, Straus, 1951; Swinnerton, *Figures in the Foreground,* Doubleday, 1964; Brian Doyle, editor, *Who's Who of Children's Literature,* Schocken Books, 1968.

MARTIN, Rene   (?)-1977

OBITUARY NOTICE: Born in Paris, date uncertain; died August 14, 1977. Artist, illustrator of books for children. Specializing in natural and scientific subjects, Rene Martin illustrated several books for children including Rachel Carson's *The Sea Around Us,* Herbert S. Zim's *Blood,* and David C. Knight's *Let's Find Out About Weather. For More Information See: Illustrators of Children's Books,* Scarecrow, 1975.

McDEARMON, Kay

PERSONAL: Born in San Francisco, Calif.; daughter of John (an engineer) and Mary (Gavin) Healy; married James R. McDearmon (a college professor), July 26, 1954. *Education:* University of California, Berkeley, B.A. *Home:* 2160 Julie, Turlock, Calif. 95380.

CAREER: High school teacher in Oakland, Calif., 1948-51; high school teacher of business education in Lafayette, Calif., 1951-54; writer, 1955—. *Member:* Soroptimists International. *Awards, honors: Polar Bear* and *Cougar* were named outstanding science books for children by National Science Teachers Association, 1976 and 1977, respectively.

WRITINGS—All for children: *A Day in the Life of a Sea Otter* (Junior Literary Guild selection), Dodd, 1973; *The Walrus: Giant of the Arctic Ice,* Dodd, 1974; *Mahalia: Gospel Singer,* Dodd, 1976; *Polar Bear,* Dodd, 1976; *Cougar,* Dodd, 1977; *Gorillas,* Dodd, 1979. Contributor of about twenty-five articles to magazines.

WORK IN PROGRESS: Biographies; animal books.

She became a voice of freedom as well. An admirer called her "the single most powerful black woman in the United States." ■ (From *Mahalia: Gospel Singer* by Kay McDearmon. Illustrated by Nevin and Phyllis Washington.)

SIDELIGHTS: "I have always liked to write; in fact, in high school I often wrote two themes when only one was required. In college I worked on the university daily. I am interested primarily in people; did a bit of '*Roots*' study on a three-week trip to Ireland."

HOBBIES AND OTHER INTERESTS: Travel, golfing, bicycling, ". . . pleased that neighborhood girls sometimes ask me to bicycle around with them."

MEAD, Margaret   1901-1978

OBITUARY NOTICE: Born December 16, 1901, in Philadelphia, Pa.; died November 15, 1978, in New York, N.Y. Anthropologist, educator, lecturer, and author of works in her field. A world renowned humanitarian and respected leader in the field of cultural anthropology, Margaret Mead held a number of prominent positions. At the time of her death, she was serving as special lecturer in anthropology at Columbia University and as curator of the American Museum of Natural History. Over the years, the popular lecturer and outspoken social critic received many awards and honors including several honorary degrees, the Chi Omega National Achievement Award, 1940, and the Lehmann Award of the New

York Academy of Sciences, 1973. The author of more than 25 books and innumerable articles, Margaret Mead will long be remembered for such works as *Coming of Age in Samoa, Culture and Commitment,* and *Male and Female.* For young people she wrote *People and Places* and *Anthropologists and What They Do. For More Information See: The Author's and Writer's Who's Who,* 6th edition, Hafner, 1971; *Authors of Books for Young People,* 2nd edition, Scarecrow, 1971; *Contemporary Authors,* Volume 1-4 revised, Gale, 1967; *Current Biography,* Wilson, 1940, 1951; *Encyclopedia of American Biography,* Harper, 1974; *International Who's Who,* Europa, 1978; *Who's Who,* 130th edition, St. Martin's, 1978. *Obituaries: A B Bookman's Weekly,* December 4, 1978; *Chicago Tribune,* November 16, 1978; *Contemporary Authors,* Volume 81-84, Gale, 1979; *Newsweek,* November 27, 1978; *New York Times,* November 16, 1978; *Publishers Weekly,* November 27, 1978; *Time,* November 27, 1978; *Washington Post,* November 16, 1978.

MEAKER, Marijane 1927-
(M. J. Meaker; pseudonyms, Ann Aldrich, M. E. Kerr, Vin Packer)

PERSONAL: Born May 27, 1927, in Auburn, New York. *Education:* Studied at the University of Missouri; Columbia University, B.A., 1949. *Home:* East Hampton, New York.

CAREER: E. P. Dutton, New York, assistant file clerk; freelance writer, 1949—. *Awards, honors: Dinky Hocker Shoots Smack* was an American Library Association Notable Book, one of *School Library Journal*'s Best Books of the Year, 1972, and winner of the Media and Methods Maxi Awards, 1974; *If I Love You, Am I Trapped Forever?* was chosen as an honor book in the Children's Spring Book Festival, 1973;

MARIJANE MEAKER

Is That You, Miss Blue? was among the ALA's Notable Books for Children and Best Books for Young Adults, 1975.

WRITINGS: Game of Survival, New American Library, 1968; *Shockproof Sydney Skate,* Little, Brown, 1972.

Under name M. J. Meaker: *Sudden Endings,* Doubleday, 1964; *Hometown,* Doubleday, 1967.

Under pseudonym Ann Aldrich: *We Walk Alone,* Gold Medal Books, 1955; *We Too Must Love,* Gold Medal Books, 1958; *Carol, in a Thousand Cities,* Gold Medal Books, 1960; *We Two Won't Last,* Gold Medal Books, 1963; *Take a Lesbian to Lunch,* MacFadden-Bartell, 1972.

Under pseudonym M. E. Kerr; all for young people: *Dinky Hocker Shoots Smack* (ALA Notable Book), Harper, 1972; *If I Love You, Am I Trapped Forever?,* Harper, 1973; *The Son of Someone Famous,* Harper, 1974; *Is That You, Miss Blue?* (ALA Notable Book), Harper, 1975; *Love Is a Missing Person,* Harper, 1975; *I'll Love You When You're More Like Me,* Harper, 1977; *Gentlehands,* Harper, 1978.

Under pseudonym Vin Packer; all published by Gold Medal Books except as indicated: *Dark Intruder,* 1952; *Spring Fire,* 1952; *Look Back to Love,* 1953; *Come Destroy Me,* 1954; *Whisper His Sin,* 1954; *The Thrill Kids,* 1955; *Dark Don't Catch Me,* 1956; *The Young and Violent,* 1956; *Three-Day Terror,* 1957; *The Evil Friendship,* 1958; *5:45 to Suburbia,* 1958; *The Twisted Ones,* 1959; *The Damnation of Adam Blessing,* 1961; *The Girl on the Best Seller List,* 1961; *Something in the Shadows,* 1961; *Intimate Victims,* 1962; *Alone at Night,* 1963; *The Hare in March,* New American Library, 1967; *Don't Rely on Gemini,* Delacorte Press, 1969.

SIDELIGHTS: **May 27, 1927.** Born in Auburn, New York. Reading and writing were early formed habits for Meaker, and everything about writing or writers fascinated her. ''My reading experience began at home. Our living room was four walls of books and my father was a great reader. I caught the habit from him. I also went to the library with him often. He was always studying something; a period in history, a science, a famous person. I hung around libraries waiting for him to do his research. He was in no way connected with literary matters. He manufactured mayonnaise. But he spent a great deal of time reading. Also, there was no television when I grew up, either. My writing experience began when my reading experience did. I was always writing something, wanting to tell my own story.'' [Paul Janeczko, ''An Interview with M. E. Kerr,'' *English Journal,* December, 1975.[1]]

Meaker attended Stuart Hall in Staunton, Virginia. A rebellious teenager, she was suspended in her senior year for throwing darts at pictures of faculty members. Fortunately, her mother's intervention resulted in her reinstatement and graduation from the Virginia school.

Following study at the University of Missouri (majored in English Literature), Meaker moved to New York City where she worked for the E. P. Dutton Publishing Company. She sold her first short story to *Ladies' Home Journal* for eight hundred and fifty dollars, left the publishing company, and began her career as a free-lance writer.

In 1972 her first book for young adults, *Dinky Hocker Shoots Smack!* was published and Meaker began to write for a new reading audience. ''Paul Zindel's *The Pigman* inspired me to write my first YA [Young Adult] novel. I loved that story, and then wanted to tell one as well as he did. I am very aware of the 'competition,' and I'm competitive. It is like being in a room with good storytellers. I want to participate and tell my own.

"My 'job' as a writer of books for young people is to entertain them, hope they will want to come back for more.

"I think there is a very valid distinction between writing for young adults and writing for adults. I'm speaking of fiction, and I've published novels for both age groups.

"First, let me say I think it is an individual thing, and has to do with an author's style. When I'm writing for the adult market, I assume, rightly or wrongly, that my reader is bringing many more years of experience to the material. I assume that this experience allows him to pick up on certain subtleties that might not yet be obvious to a youngster of eleven or twelve (roughly the age I believe I write for). For example, if I want to present a very prejudiced person in an adult novel, I would probably paint him with far fewer strokes than in a YA novel. I would hope my readers would perceive him as a bigot, having known many people like him, getting the familiar ring of the bigot rather more effortlessly than someone with less living experience.

"As an adult novelist, I am by nature more economical in description and examples. I like a tight, subtle story, to write and to read. But I feel that that kind of glib shorthand can often be misinterpreted when talking with a youngster. And because I don't think in either adult or YA novels I ever present a pure villain, or a totally negative character, I want to be sure my YA audience understands exactly what kind of person I'm drawing.

"I've always thought you get from a book what you bring to it, but when I'm writing for the YA audience, I'm aware that they are still being formed. I'm helping to form them, in a small way. I am conscious of that.

"I was very much formed by books when I was young. I was a bookworm and a poetry lover. I think of myself, and what I would have liked to have found in books those many years ago. I loved Ezra Pound, but I was confused by his bigotry, for example. I also remember being depressed by all the neatly tied-up, happy-ending stories, the abundance of winners, the theme of winning, solving, finding—when around me it didn't seem that easy. So I write with a different feeling when I write for young adults. I guess I write for myself when I was that age, which happily is no longer the same person.

"I also think an adult reader has, for better or worse, come to grips with problems the young adult might not yet have come to grips with. So my subject matter is different. Just as I no longer concentrate at all on what impression I'm making on adults or parents, I don't write adult novels about that. My pains are different now. It is a less transient world than the world of young adults, where one is still making and losing friends, wondering what to do with their lives. The material in the adult novels is less basic, from my point of view, perhaps more cynical. I find idealism easier to present in young adult novels, and allow for more helpful themes.

"I don't censor myself, but I'm a little more selective with young adults in what kind of story I want to tell."[1]

(From *I'll Love You When You're More Like Me* by M.E. Kerr. Illustrated by Fred Marcellino.)

Meaker continues to devote much of her spare time to reading. "I read everything I can get a chance to read, from mysteries to modern novels to non-fiction. I don't read many classics anymore, nor many history books or biographies. I'm a bit centered on the modern world. I also read many newspapers and magazines.

"I don't have many interests that I cultivate anymore, really. They are there, and they are mostly to do with books and publishing. I like to gossip about people I know, and I love animals."[1]

Meaker is probably best known as M. E. Kerr and under that name has successfully written novels for young adults. In all of these novels, according to Mary Kingsbury, writing in *Horn Book*, "The author is concerned with love, its presence and, more commonly, its absence in the lives of her characters. . . . With style, wit, and compassion she describes adolescents coming to the realization that those they love will more often than not, fail to live up to their expectations." The first of these books, *Dinky Hocker Shoots Smack*, was critiqued in the *New York Times Book Review:* "The writer is sensitive not only to the dialogue, but to the themes of today's preoccupations. . . . This is a brilliantly funny book that will make you cry. It is full of wit and wisdom and an astonishing immediacy that comes from spare, honest writing. Many writers try to characterize the peculiar poignancy and the terrible hilarity of adolescence. Few succeed as well as M. E. Kerr in this timely, compelling, and entertaining novel." Added *Horn Book:* "Writing about contemporaneity with humor and insight requires unusual talents. In a first book, the author demonstrates such talent and

(From the television film "Dinky Hocker," based on *Dinky Hocker Shoots Smack,* starring Wendie Jo Sperber. Courtesy of Learning Corporation of America.)

presents a plethora of vivid characters who act and interact in believable, yet comic, ways. . . . The author has pulled all of this material together in a narrative that underscores the process of growing and changing in the teenage years. This low-key and funny book is a refreshing contrast to the many didactic and dismal books written for older readers."

In reviewing *Is That You, Miss Blue?*, Mary M. Burns, writing in *Horn Book*, commented: ". . . Much of the novel's power is derived from its delineation of character while consistently maintaining the young narrator's perspective. As seen through Flanders' eyes, the conflicting personalities are Dickensian types, skillfully limned but exaggerated. And the author achieves a balance between pathos and humor in documenting Miss Blue's disintegration. In a spare, wryly funny, genuinely moving book, M. E. Kerr surpasses all of her previous achievements."

FOR MORE INFORMATION SEE: New York Times Book Review, February 11, 1973; *Horn Book*, February, 1973, and August, 1975; Paul Janeczko, "An Interview with M. E. Kerr," *English Journal*, December, 1975; Mary Kingsbury, "The Why of People: The Novels of M. E. Kerr," *Horn Book*, June, 1977; Doris de Montreville and Elizabeth D. Crawford, editors, *Fourth Book of Junior Authors and Illustrators*, H. W. Wilson, 1978.

MOE, Barbara 1937-

PERSONAL: Born October 10, 1937, in Cincinnati, Ohio; daughter of Gerrit W. (a physician) and Martha (a nurse; maiden name, Radtke) Raidt; married Paul G. Moe (a physician), April 10, 1959; children: Steve, Susan, Danny, David, Amy, Rosemary. *Education:* University of Cincinnati, B.S., 1959; Ohio State University, M.S., 1961. *Politics:* Democrat. *Religion:* Protestant. *Home:* 1770 Hudson, Denver, Colo. 80220. *Agent:* Theron Raines, 475 Fifth Ave., New York, N.Y. 10017.

CAREER: Peace Corps volunteer in Shiraz, Iran, 1965-67; *Denver Post*, Denver, Colo., zone writer, 1976—. *Member:* Society of Children's Book Writers, Colorado Authors League. *Awards, honors:* Top Hand Award from Colorado Authors League, 1976, for *Pickles and Prunes*.

WRITINGS: The Ghost Wore Knickers (juvenile), Thomas Nelson, 1975; *Pickles and Prunes* (juvenile), McGraw, 1976.

WORK IN PROGRESS: My Cousin, The Vampire and *The Turtle who Loved my Father*, both juveniles.

SIDELIGHTS: "Swimming and writing keep me more or less sane."

BARBARA MOE

(From *Pickles and Prunes* by Barbara Moe. Illustrated by Charles Lilly.)

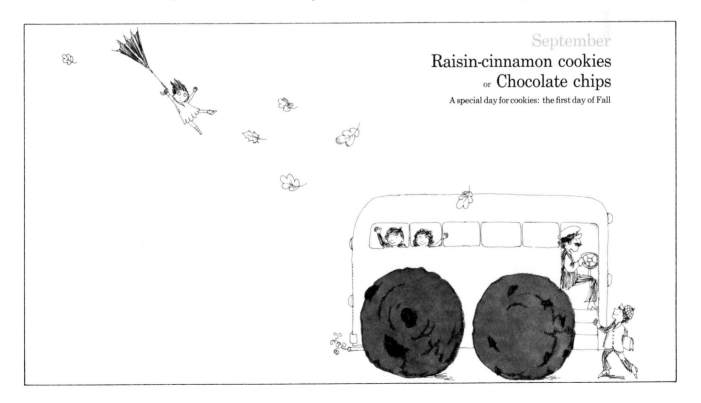

(From *The Cookie Book* by Eva Moore. Illustrated by Talivaldis Stubis.)

MOORE, Eva   1942-

PERSONAL: Born April 16, 1942, in Rome, N.Y.; daughter of Carlton Edward and Margaret (Agan) Moore. *Education:* Studied at secretarial school. *Office:* Scholastic Magazines, Inc., 50 West 44th St., New York, N.Y. 10036.

CAREER: Scholastic Magazines, Inc., New York, N.Y., secretary, 1962-63, editorial assistant, 1963-65, assistant editor, 1965-67, associate editor of children's books, 1967—. *Member:* Authors Guild.

WRITINGS: The Lucky Book of Riddles, Scholastic Book Services, 1964; *Johnny Appleseed,* Scholastic Book Services, 1964; *The Fairy Tale Life of Hans Christian Andersen,* Scholastic Book Services, 1969; *The Lucky Cook Book for Boys and Girls,* Scholastic Book Services, 1969, reissued as *The Seabury Cook Book for Boys and Girls,* Seabury, 1973; (editor with Beatrice S. de Regniers and Mary M. White) *Poems Children Will Sit Still For,* Citation Press, 1969; *The Story of George Washington Carver,* Scholastic Book Services, 1971; *The Cookie Book,* Seabury, 1973; *Dick Whittington and His Cat,* Scholastic Book Services, 1974.

SIDELIGHTS: "I write books for children just beginning to read—2nd- and 3rd-grade reading level. (*The Cookie Book* is for slightly older children.) I remember the great joy and excitement I felt at the age of six years when for the first time I held in my hands a book I could read myself—my first-grade primer, I think it was. And now it gives me great pleasure to think that seven and eight year olds might feel the same kind of joy in the books I write for them."

FOR MORE INFORMATION SEE: Horn Book, October 1973.

MOORE, Marianne (Craig)   1887-1972

PERSONAL: Born November 15, 1887, in Kirkwood, near St. Louis, Mo.; daughter of John Milton and Mary (Warner) Moore. *Education:* Bryn Mawr College, A.B., 1909; attended Carlisle Commercial College, 1910. *Religion:* Presbyterian. *Home:* 35 West Ninth St., New York, N.Y.

CAREER: United States Indian School, Carlisle, Pa., teacher, 1911-15; New York Public Library, New York, N.Y., assistant, 1921-25; *Dial,* New York, N.Y., acting editor, 1926-29. *Member:* National Institute of Arts and Letters, American Academy of Arts and Letters, Bryn Mawr Club.

AWARDS, HONORS: Collected Poems, published in 1952, received all three of the major American prizes for poetry—the 1952 National Book Award for poetry, the Bollingen Prize in poetry (awarded 1953 for work in 1952), and the 1952 Pulitzer Prize for poetry; she received the National Institute of Arts and Letters Gold Medal and the M. Carey Thomas Award in 1953, as well as the following awards in other years: National Institute of Arts and Letters grant in literature, 1946; Guggenheim Fellowship, 1945; Harriet Monroe Poetry Award, 1944; Shelley Memorial Award, 1941; *The Dial* Award, 1924. Honorary degrees: Litt.D. degrees from Mount Holyoke College, 1950, University of Rochester, 1951; L.H.D. degrees from Rutgers, The State University, 1955, Smith College, 1955, Pratt Institute, 1959, and others; Brandeis Award for Poetry, 1963; *A Festschrift for Marianne Moore's Seventy-Seventh Birthday,* edited by T. Tambimuttu, 1965; 1965 fellowship ($5,000) of Academy of

American Poets, for distinguished poetic achievement over a period of more than four decades.

WRITINGS—Poetry: *Poems,* Egoist Press, 1921; *Observations,* Dial Press, 1924 (a reprint, with additions, of the earlier *Poems*); *Selected Poems,* introduction by T. S. Eliot, Macmillan, 1935; *Pangolin, and Other Verse: Five Poems,* Brendin, 1936; *What are Years?, and Other Poems,* Macmillan, 1941; *Nevertheless* (poems), Macmillan, 1944; *Collected Poems,* Macmillan, 1951; *Like a Bulwark,* Viking, 1956; *O to be a Dragon,* Viking, 1959; *A Marianne Moore Reader,* Viking, 1961; *The Arctic Ox* (poems), Faber, 1964; *Tell Me, Tell Me: Granite, Steel, and Other Topics* (poetry and prose), Viking, 1966; *The Complete Poems of Marianne Moore,* Macmillan, 1967; *Selected Poems,* Faber, 1969; *Unfinished Poems,* P. H. & A.S.W. Rosenbach Foundation, 1972.

Other works: (Co-translator) A. Stifter, *Rock Crystal,* Pantheon, 1945; (translator) *Selected Fables of La Fontaine,* Faber and Faber, 1955, new edition published as *The Fables of La Fontaine,* Viking, 1965; *Predilections* (essays and reviews), Viking, 1955; *Letters from and to the Ford Motor Company,* Pierpont Morgan Library, 1958 (first appeared in *New Yorker,* April 13, 1957); (compiler, with others) *Riverside Poetry Three: An Anthology of Student Poetry,* Twayne, 1958; *Idiosyncrasy and Technique; Two Lectures,* University of California Press, 1958; *The Absentee; A Comedy in Four Acts* (play based on Maria Edgeworth's novel of the same name), House of Books, 1962; *Puss in Boots; The Sleeping Beauty; Cinderella* (a retelling of three fairy tales based on the French of Charles Perrault), Macmillan, 1963; *The Accented Syllable* (first published in the *Egoist,* October, 1916), Albondocani Press, 1969; (contributor) *Homage to Henry James* (essays; first appeared in the *Horn and the Hound,* 1934), P. P. Appel, 1971. Formerly editor of *The Dial.* Contributor of articles, essays, and verse to magazines.

ADAPTATIONS—Recordings: "Marianne Moore Reads from Her Own Words," Yale University Sound Recordings, 1975.

SIDELIGHTS: **November 15, 1887.** Born in Kirkwood, a suburb of St. Louis, Missouri. Shortly after her birth her father, John Milton Moore, suffered a nervous breakdown (from which he never fully recovered) and was sent to live with his parents in Ohio. "My father was an engineer, with his brother as consulting engineer—both graduates of Stevens Institute. Our mother lost him early, and we never saw him." ["An Interview with Marianne Moore," *McCall's,* December, 1965.[1]]

Moore's mother, Mary Warner Moore, took her infant daughter and son, John, who was seventeen months older than his sister, to live with her father, the Reverend John Riddle Warner, a Presbyterian minister. "[My mother, brother and I were close and] always were. And my grandfather was a most affectionate person.

"In St. Louis, I was given an alligator, called him Tibby, and tended him as if he were a little deity, caught flies for him, could hardly bear it when he died. We had some cats and kittens, cloth ones and sometimes real ones. I put oval stones along the fence where they were buried, which had roses growing on the wire between our yard and the neighbor's. And white clematis. They had fragrant graves, certainly and plenty of flowers. I couldn't bear that shoe box."[1]

1894. When her maternal grandfather died Moore moved to Carlisle, Pennsylvania with her mother and brother. Her mother supported them on a small inheritance and by teaching English at the Metzger Institute, a girl's school. "I took piano lessons for years. My mother also had me take singing lessons—in Carlisle—not because I had a good voice, but because I didn't. She wanted me to know about it at least."[1]

1896-1905. Educated at Carlisle's Metzger Schools. "[I remember] especially an art teacher, Miss Foster, who became Mrs. Beitzel. She taught German and drawing; made us think we liked teasels and milkweed pods, jointed grasses and twigs with buds that had died on the stem."[1] Moore retained an interest in painting and drawing throughout her life.

"There was Miss MacAllen, with a Latin class of two—Anna Hammond and me. I thought I was being killed with twenty lines of Latin as an assignment. When I got to college, it was pages—the most unjust thing I'd ever known, I felt; dogged along and then did fairly well."[1]

1905. Entered Bryn Mawr College. "I was hand reared. I got almost too much individual attention. We weren't made to take enough responsibility. But lonely? If anyone ever was homesick, *I* was in college. I didn't know how to work. I liked to discuss everything with someone and be corrected, phrase by phrase. It was very painful. I was at sea two years. All I could do was elect courses in biology—the professors in that department were very humane, also exacting, detailed and pertinacious. Doctor Warren, head of the department and secretary of the faculty, favored me with terrifying advice. He said, 'You have to stop going away on weekends and cutting classes.' I said, 'Why, Doctor Warren, I'm in deadly fear of missing something, never have been away for a weekend, never yet cut a class, ever. I'm just not grown up enough for these assignments; everyone is ahead of me. I seem a kind of juvenile.'

"Doctor Ashley came over from Columbia to give courses in law. I took torts, just because he was giving the course, as a relief from some of the more ferocious instructors. He was compassion itself. I seemed to need very humane handling, mothering by everyone—the case all my life, I think.

"Doctor Wheeler, at Bryn Mawr, gave me one credit—equivalent to about eighty in a standard of one hundred—but I didn't have a stand high enough in English entitling me to choose electives until my senior year. Then all that was left for me to elect was seventeenth-century imitative writing with Georgiana Goddard King—Bishop Andrewes, Francis Bacon, Jeremy Taylor and others. People say, 'How terrible.' It wasn't at all; was the very thing for me. Somewhat as Mr. Churchill acquired a love of well-shaped sentences from Gibbon and Macaulay. I was really fond of those sermons and the antique sentence structure."[1]

1907. While Moore was having academic trouble she began to write poetry. Her poems were printed in the Bryn Mawr literary magazine, *Tipyn O'Bob* and in the alumnae magazine, *The Lantern.* "But I didn't feel that my product was anything to shake the world." [Donald Hall, "The Art of Poetry: Marianne Moore," *Marianne Moore: A Collection of Critical Essays,* Charles Tomlinson, editor, Prentice-Hall, 1969.[2]]

1909. Received her A.B. from Bryn Mawr.

1910. Secretarial course at Carlisle Commercial College.

MARIANNE MOORE

1911-1915. Taught typing, bookkeeping, stenography, commercial law and commercial English at the United States Industrial Indian School in Carlisle. Moore found the subjects uninspiring. "I was half good. I could fix typewriters, but rapid calculating and bookkeeping were just too much for me. It was a necessary financial adventure, and I would have much preferred to sit by the fire and read." [W. Winthrop Sargeant, "Humility, Concentration and Gusto," *New Yorker,* February 16, 1957.[3]]

One of her students at the Indian School was Jim Thorpe, the famous Indian athlete. "He was liked by all—*liked* in italics, rather than venerated or idolized—unless perhaps privately admired by 'Pop' Warner, he was such an all-round phenomenon—'Jim.' He was off-hand, modest, casual about anything in the way of fame or eminence achieved. This modesty, with top performance, was characteristic of him, and no back-talk. The charge of professionalism was never popular in the Olympic world; everyone felt it should not be held against him, since any violation was accidental rather than intentional.

"I used to watch football practice on the field after school sometimes; signals for passes; little starts with the ball; kicks for goal; and often watched track sports in spring—throwing the hammer, at which James was adept, taking hurdles—the jump." [Marianne Moore, "Ten Answers—Letter from an October Afternoon, Part II," *Harper's,* 1964.[4]]

1915. First poem, "To the Soul of Progress," published in *The Egoist* (London). Gained a reputation as a "new" poet. Began contributing to *Poetry* magazine. "Originally, my work was refused by the *Atlantic Monthly* and other magazines...." [Marianne Moore, "A Letter to Ezra Pound," *Marianne Moore: A Collection of Critical Essays*, Charles Tomlinson, editor, Prentice-Hall, 1969.[5]]

1916. Moved to Chatham, New Jersey with her mother when her brother, an ordained Presbyterian minister, was assigned there.

1918. Moved to a basement apartment on St. Luke's Place in New York's Greenwich Village with her mother. Briefly employed as a secretary and as a private teacher. "I like New York, the little quiet part of it in which my mother and I live. I like to see the tops of the masts from our door and to go to the wharf and look at the craft on the river."[5]

1921. First book, *Poems*, published in England without Moore's knowledge. "To issue my slight product—conspicuously tentative—seemed to me premature. I disliked the term 'poetry' for any but Chaucer's or Shakespeare's or Dante's. I no longer feel my original instinctive hostility to the word, since it's a convenient, almost unavoidable term for the thing—although hardly for me:—my observations, experiments in rhythm, or exercises in composition. What I write ... could only be called poetry because there is no other category in which to put it."[2]

1921-1925. Library assistant at the Hudson Park branch of the New York Public Library. "Some of my elegant English friends—not T. S. Eliot—looked on my library tasks as menial work; felt I ought to be secretary to a potentate or doing something rather enviable, instead of charging books and answering reference questions. Actually, I never did reference work—I was completely incompetent. How many women garment workers are there? In what year was so-and-so mayor? To find things like that, I consulted the assistant librarian.

1924. *Observations* published. Received the Dial Award and $2,000 prize money. "Nor was a gift ever more complete and without victimizing involvements." [Marianne Moore, "The Dial: A Retrospect," *Predilections*, Viking, 1955.[6]]

July, 1925. Became acting editor of *The Dial*.

1926. Assumed full editorship of *The Dial*. "I think of the compacted pleasantness of those days at 152 West Thirteenth Street; of the three-story brick building with carpeted stairs, fireplace and white-mantelpiece rooms, business office in the first story front parlor, and in gold-leaf block letters, *THE DIAL*, on the windows to the right of the brownstone steps leading to the front door."[6]

July, 1929. *The Dial* ceased publication, thus ending Moore's professional editing. Returned to writing poetry, occasional essays and book reviews. She moved from her Greenwich apartment to a fifth floor Brooklyn apartment on Cumberland Street (a dignified address in those days) with her mother. Moore remained in her Cumberland Street apartment for almost forty years. "Decorum marked the life on Clinton Hill... An atmosphere of privacy with a touch of diffidence prevailed, as when a neighbor in furred jacket, veil, and gloves would emerge from a four-story house to shop at grocer's or meat-market....It was not unusual in those days, toward teatime, to catch a glimpse of a maid with starched cap and apron, adjust-

ing accessories on a silver tray...." [Donald Hall, *Marianne Moore: The Cage and the Animal*, Pegasus, 1970.[7]]

1932. Received the Helen Haire Levinson Prize for Poetry.

1935. *Selected Poems* published in London and New York. Received the Ernest Hartsock Memorial Prize. To the new book Moore added a postscript rather than a dedication which alluded to her mother, one of her most important critics. "Dedications imply giving, and we do not care to make a gift of what is insufficient; but in my immediate family there is one 'who thinks in a particular way'; and I should like to add that where there is an effect of thought or pith in these pages, the thinking and often the actual phrases are hers."[7]

1936. *Pangolin and Other Verse* published in London.

1940. Received the Shelley Memorial Award. Moore had a reverence for language and a disdain for imprecise words, verbal affections and digressions. "Always, in whatever I wrote—prose or verse—I have had a burning desire to be explicit; beset always, however carefully I had written, by the charge of obscurity." [Barbara Howes, "Miss Moore Herself," *New Republic*, 1966.[8]]

1941. *What are Years?* published. The title poem in the volume was one of Moore's favorites. "I think 'What Are Years?' is one of my solider compositions. I like 'His Shield' and 'The Buffalo'—the managing of the rhythms. I think 'What Are Years?' is the best done, best written."[1]

1942. Taught composition at the Cummington School in Massachusetts. She was subsequently a visiting lecturer at poetry seminars and readings at such diverse universities as Vassar, Harvard and the University of California. Moore felt uncomfortable at these readings. "I always have misgivings, for fear I'll be a disappointment. Am in dread of experts, at Harvard, say—or John Hopkins, Bryn Mawr and Radcliffe—because they know so much. It oughtn't to be that way. One thing does impress me: People who have a whole cosmos in their heads seem to have an equiforce that doesn't hurry you or themselves, take lots of time for things, becoming lost in the topic. They aren't tied in knots; appear very gentle."[1]

1944. *Nevertheless* published. Received the Contemporary Poetry's Patrons' Prize and the Harriet Monroe Poetry Award.

1945. Received a Guggenheim Fellowship. Translated with Elizabeth Mayer, Albert Stifter's *Rock Crystal, A Christmas Tale*.

1946. Received a joint grant from the American Academy of Arts and Letters and the National Institute of Arts and Letters. Began translating La Fontaine's *Fables*, a task which took over eight years to finish. "I worked practically all the time. I'd wake up at six and get right to work, and I'd keep at it all day and all evening, except for an occasional brief stop to eat, or maybe I'd have to go to the market and buy a few odds and ends. Then back to the job again. I did the whole thing over completely four times."[3]

1947. Mother and lifelong companion died. "My brother says that on my mother's birthday years ago, he remembered asking her, 'Do you feel well?' And she said, 'Yes, very well, but I don't want to live to a great old age.' I feel that way, too. I can't imagine complete helplessness. I'm not

Attempting to evade the curse, the King issued a proclamation, making it unlawful, upon pain of death, for anyone to use a spindle. ■ (From *Puss in Boots, The Sleeping Beauty and Cinderella,* adapted by Marianne Moore. Illustrated by Eugene Karlin.)

thought likely to die of a heart attack. I rather wish I could, but my heart is supposed to be good.''[1]

That same year Moore was elected to the National Institute of Arts and Letters.

1949. ''A Face'' was published separately. Awarded the first of many honorary degrees, a Litt.D. from Wilson College. ''... When I wrote 'A Face,' I had written something first about 'the adder and the child with a bowl of porridge,' and [my mother] said, 'Well, it won't do.'

'''All right,' I said, 'but I have to produce something.' Cyril Connolly had asked me for something for *Horizon*. So I wrote 'A Face.' That is one of the few things I ever set down and it didn't give me any trouble. And [my mother] said, 'I like it.' I remember that.''[2]

1950. Awarded honorary degrees from Mount Holyoke College and from Smith College.

1951. *Collected Poems* published. Received an honorary degree from the University of Rochester.

1952. Won the National Book Award, the Pulitzer Prize for poetry and the Bollingen Prize. Received an honorary degree from Dickinson College and the Youth Oscar Award from Brooklyn's Youth United for a Better Tomorrow as an inspiration to the young people enrolled in the agency's settlement houses. Upon receiving her award from the National Book Committee, she remarked: ''To be trusted is an ennobling experience; and poetry is a peerless proficiency of the imagination. I prize it, but am myself an observer.... In poetry understatement is emphasis. In poetry metaphor substitutes compactness for confusion and says the fish moves 'on winglike foot.' It also says—and for *it* I had better say Confucius—'If there be a knife of resentment in the heart, the mind will not attain precision.' That is to say, poetry watches life with affection.''[7]

1953. Visiting lecturer at Bryn Mawr. Received the Gold Medal for poetry from the National Institute of Arts and Letters, the M. Carey Thomas Award and an honorary degree from Long Island University.

1954. Completed the translation of *The Fables of La Fontaine,* which was dedicated to her brother for ''fixed confidence on his part in the auspiciousness of my efforts.''[7]

''... The only reason I know for calling my work poetry at all is that there is no other category in which to put it. I'm a happy hack as a writer. When I was translating La Fontaine's version of Aesop's fables I didn't strike while the iron was hot, but *till* it was hot. I never knew anyone with a passion for words who had as much difficulty in saying things as I do. I seldom say them in a manner I like. Help is needed: you need a horse, a boat, to help you.'' [Jane Howard, ''Marianne Moore, 79 Keeps Going Like Sixty,'' *Life,* January 13, 1967.[9]]

October 21, 1955. When asked by the Ford Motor Company to suggest a name for their important new car, she replied: ''I am complimented to be recruited in this high matter.

''I have seen and admired 'Thunderbird' as a Ford designation. It would be hard to match; but let me, the coming week, talk with my brother, who would bring ardor and imagination to bear on the quest.'' [''Department of Amplification,'' *New Yorker,* April 13, 1957.[10]]

October 27, 1955. Submitted some suggestions to the Ford Company which included:

''THE FORD SILVER SWORD''

November, 1955. After seeing some general sketches of the ''top secret'' new Ford model, Moore submitted more suggestions. ''The sketches: They are indeed exciting; they have quality, and the toucan tones lend tremendous allure—confirmed by the wheels. Half the magic—sustaining effects of this kind. Looked at upside down, furthermore, there is a sense of fish buoyancy. Immediately your word 'impeccable' sprang to mind. Might it be a possibility? The Impeccable. In any case, the baguette lapidary glamour you have achieved certainly spurs the imagination. Car-innovation is like launching a ship—'drama.'

''I am by no means sure that I can help you to the right thing, but performance with elegance casts a spell. Let me do some thinking in the direction of impeccable, symmechromatic, thunderblender.... (The exotics, if I can shape them a little.) Dearborn might come into one....

And, as his wife, he dressed her not only better than any of the women of Gschaid and of the valley were dressed, but better even than she had been at home...
■ (From *Rock Crystal* by Adalbert Stifter. Translated by Elizabeth Mayer and Marianne Moore. Illustrated by Josef Scharl.)

"Some other suggestions . . . for the phenomenon:

"THE RESILIENT BULLET
or Intelligent Bullet
or Bullet Cloisonné or Bullet Lavolta.

"(I have always had a fancy for THE INTELLIGENT WHALE—the little first Navy submarine, shaped like a sweet potato; on view in our Brooklyn Yard.)"[10]

December 8, 1955. Moore submitted one further suggestion. "May I submit UTOPIAS TURTLETOP? Do not trouble to answer unless you like it."[10]

The Ford Motor Company responded with a huge bouquet of roses and a Christmas card addressed to their "favorite turtletopper."

November 8, 1956. The name for the new car was finally decided. The company wrote Moore: "Because you were so kind to us in our early days of looking for a suitable name, I feel a deep obligation to report on events that have ensued.

"We have chosen a name. . . . It fails somewhat of the resonance, gaiety, and zest we were seeking. But it has a personal dignity and meaning to many of us here. Our name, dear Miss Moore, is—Edsel."[10]

The Edsel, the most pedestrian of Ford products, was a classic failure, but not to Miss Moore. "Nothing was wrong with that Edsel! I thought it was a very handsome car. It came out the wrong year."[7]

1963. Translated and adapted three tales by Charles Perrault: *Puss in Boots, The Sleeping Beauty,* and *Cinderella.*

A baseball fan, particularly of the Dodgers, Moore was escorted to the second game of the World Series for that year. "One of the handsomest things about the game, I think, is accuracy that looks automatic in fielding fast balls. I never tire of a speedy ball from the catcher finding the glove of the pitcher, when half the time he isn't even looking at it."[4]

1964. Visited Ireland and England. On this trip she had dinner with T. S. Eliot shortly before his death. "Nothing somber about this dinner—punctuated by esprit such as 'Wensleydale is not the Mozart of cheeses.'"[1]

1967. *The Complete Poems of Marianne Moore* published. At seventy-nine she was regarded as one of America's greatest living poets.

Her appearance was a personal source of discomfort to her although her contemporaries regarded her as a stylish woman famous for her tricorn hats. "I'm all bone, just solid, pure bone. I'm good-natured, but hideous as an old hop toad. I look like a scarecrow. I'm just like a lizard, like Lazarus awakening. I look permanently alarmed, like a frog. I *aspire* to be neat, I try to do my hair with a lot of thought to avoid those explosive sunbursts, but when one hairpin goes in, another seems to come out.

"Look at those hands: they look as if I'd died of an adder bite. A crocodile couldn't look worse. My physiognomy isn't classic at all, it's like a banana-nosed monkey. Well, I do seem at least to be awake, don't I?"[9]

1968. Received the National Medal for Literature.

February 6, 1972. Died in her sleep in her Greenwich Village apartment at the age of eighty-four. "I certainly never intended to write poetry. It never came into my head to think of it. And now, too, I think each time I write that it may be the last time; then something takes my fancy. Everything I have written is the result of reading or of interest in people, I'm sure of that. I had no ambitions to be a writer."[2]

HOBBIES AND OTHER INTERESTS: Painting and drawing.

FOR MORE INFORMATION SEE: Poetry, April, 1925, May, 1960; Elizabeth Drew, *Directions in Modern Poetry,* Norton, 1940; *Quarterly Review of Literature,* LV, 1948; Randall Jarrell, *Poetry and the Age,* Knopf, 1953; *New York Times Book Review,* May 16, 1954, October 4, 1959, December 3, 1961, December 25, 1966; *Western Review,* autumn,

1954; *New Yorker*, February 16, 1957, April 13, 1957, November 28, 1959; E. P. Sheehy and K. A. Lohf, *The Achievement of Marianne Moore* (bibliography), New York Public Library, 1958; *Saturday Review*, September 19, 1959, January 6, 1962; *Time*, September 21, 1959; *Commonweal*, November 20, 1959, January 26, 1962.

New Republic, January 4, 1960; *New York Herald Tribune Books*, November 26, 1961; *Atlantic*, February, 1962; *Esquire*, July, 1962; Bernard F. Engel, *Marianne Moore*, Twayne, 1964; Thurairajah Tambimuttu, editor, *Festschrift for Marianne Moore's Seventy-Seventh Birthday*, Tambimuttu & Mass, 1964; Jean Garrigue, *Marianne Moore*, University of Minnesota Press, 1965; *New York Times*, June 3, 1965, July 13, 1965; M. L. Rosenthal, *The Modern Poets*, Oxford University Press, 1965; *McCall's*, December, 1965; *Newsweek*, January 2, 1967; *Life*, January 13, 1967; Mary Brannum, *When I Was Sixteen*, Platt, 1967; Sister Therese, *Marianne Moore: A Critical Essay*, Eerdmans, 1969; Charles Tomlinson, editor, *Marianne Moore: A Collection of Critical Essays*, Prentice-Hall, 1969; *Current Biography Yearbook, 1968*, H. W. Wilson, 1969; Rosemary Sprague, *Imaginary Gardens*, Chilton, 1969; J. Durso, "Marianne Moore: Baseball Fan," *Saturday Review*, July 12, 1969.

Emery Kelen, *Fifty Voices of the Twentieth Century*, Lothrop, Lee, 1970; J. Garrigue, "Marianne Moore," in Allen Tate, editor, *Six American Poets*, University of Minnesota Press, 1971; Gary Lane, editor, *A Concordance to the Poems of Marianne Moore*, Haskell House, 1972; Louis Untermeyer, editor, *Fifty Modern American and British Poets*, McKay, 1973; George Plimpton, "Sporting Poets," *Harper's*, May, 1977.

Obituaries: *New York Times*, February 6, 1972; *Detroit News*, February 6, 1972; *Washington Post*, February 7, 1972; *Newsweek*, February 14, 1972; *Time*, February 14, 1972; *Publishers Weekly*, Feburary 14, 1972; *National Review*, March 3, 1972; *Current Biography Yearbook, 1972*; *Britannica Book of the Year, 1973*.

MOTZ, Lloyd

PERSONAL: Born in Susquehanna, Pa.; married; children: Robin Owen, Julie. *Education:* College of City of New York, B.S. (magna cum laude), 1930; University of Gottingen, Naumberg Fellow, 1929; Columbia University, Ph.D., 1936. *Home:* 815 West 181st St., New York, N.Y. 10033. *Office:* Columbia University, Box 57 Pupin, New York, N.Y. 10027.

CAREER: College of City of New York, New York, N.Y., instructor in physics, 1931-40; Columbia University, New York, N.Y., professor of astronomy, 1940—; Polytechnic Institute of Brooklyn, Brooklyn, N.Y., adjunct professor of physics, 1960—. Fellow: American Physical Society, Royal Astronomical Society. *Member:* American Astronomical Society, American Association for the Advancement of Science, American Federation of Scientists, Phi Beta Kappa (chapter secretary). *Awards, honors:* First prize for essay, Gravity Research Foundation, 1960; president of the New York Academy of Sciences, 1970; New York Academy of Sciences Award for overall contributions to physics and astronomy, 1972.

Illustrating how the force of gravity decreases with distance from the particle M. At the distance "d" the force is concentrated over the area ABCD. At twice the distance (2d) the force is spread over the area A'B'C'D' which is four times larger than ABCD. At three times the distance (3d) the same force is spread over the ninefold area A"B"C"D" which is the square of 3.

(From *On the Path of Venus* by Lloyd Motz. Illustrated by Susan Detrich.)

WRITINGS: What is Astronomy All About, Alumni Press, 1953; (with Enrico Fermi) *Thermodynamics*, Dover, 1956; *History of Time*, Gerrault-Perroux, 1957; *This is Astronomy*, McBride, 1959; *This is Outer Space*, Archer, 1960; *Astronomy—A to Z*, Grosset, 1964; *Essentials of Astronomy*, Columbia University Press, 1966, second edition, 1977; (with Enrico Fermi) *Molecules, Crystals, Statistical Mechanics*, Benjamin, 1966; *World of the Atom*, Basic Books, 1966; *Astrophysics and Stellar Structures*, John Wiley, 1970; *The Universe, Its Beginning and End*, Scribner, 1975; *On the Path of Venus* (juvenile), Pantheon, 1976. Author of introductions to Dover reprints of books of famous astronomers and physicists.

WORK IN PROGRESS: Astronomy textbook, for Nostrand.

HOBBIES AND OTHER INTERESTS: Music, tennis, chess, folk dancing.

ALBERT J. NEVINS

NEVINS, Albert J.   1915-

PERSONAL: Born September 11, 1915, in Yonkers, N.Y.; son of Albert J. and Bessie L. (Corcoran) Nevins. *Education:* Studied at Venard College, 1932-36, Maryknoll Noviate, Bedford, Mass., 1936-37, Maryknoll Seminary, Maryknoll, N.Y., 1937-42. *Religion:* Catholic. *Address:* Box 920, Huntington, Ind. 46750.

CAREER: Worked in editorial departments of Yonkers newspapers before studying for priesthood. Ordained Roman Catholic priest at Maryknoll, N.Y., June 21, 1942; assigned to editorial work, with headquarters at Maryknoll, 1942-69, as director of mass communications, 1945-69, director of World Horizon Films, 1947-69, director of Social Communications Department, 1958-69, editor of *Chinese-American Bulletin,* 1942-45, associate editor of *Maryknoll* Magazine, 1945-52, business manager, 1950-69, editor, 1952-69, editor, *World Campus,* 1958-67; Our Sunday Visitor, Inc., Huntington, Ind., vice-president, publisher, editor-in-chief, 1969—. Civil Air Patrol, lieutenant colonel served as group commander.

MEMBER: Catholic Institute of the Press (founder, member of executive board), Catholic Press Association (has been vice-president, treasurer, president, member of board of directors), Catholic Association for International Peace, Gallery of Living Catholic Authors, Africa Studies Association, Overseas Press Club, Inter American Press Association (board of directors and Freedom of the Press Committee),

IAPA Technical Center (treasurer). *Awards, honors:* Catholic Press Association, certificates of outstanding achievement for editorials, 1955, 1957, 1960, 1961, most distinguished contribution to Catholic journalism award, 1961; Catholic Institute of the Press, special citation, 1957; National Conference of Christians and Jews, certificate of recognition for editorial writing, 1957, national brotherhood award for editorial writing, 1958; International Film Festival, Lille, France, premier prix for films, "Story of Juan Mateo," 1957, "The Problem of People," 1961; Maria Moors Cabot prize for interhemispheric journalism advancing friendship, Columbia University, 1961; St. Augustine Award, Villanova University, 1962; Committee on International Non-Theatrical Events Golden Eagle award for "The Gods of Todos Santos," 1966; honorary LL.D., St. Benedict's College, Atchison, Kan. and the Catholic University, San Juan, Puerto Rico.

WRITINGS—Books: *The Catholic Year,* Essential Books, 1949; *Adventures of Wu Han of Korea,* Dodd, 1951; *Adventures of Kenji of Japan,* Dodd, 1952; *Adventures of Pancho of Peru,* Dodd, 1953; *Adventures of Ramon of Bolivia,* Dodd, 1954; *St. Francis of the Seven Seas,* Farrar, Straus, 1955; *Adventures of Duc of Indochina,* Dodd, 1955; *The Meaning of Maryknoll,* McMullen Books, 1956; (editor) *The Maryknoll Golden Book: An Anthology of Mission Literature,* Book Treasures, 1956; *Adventures of Men of Maryknoll,* Dodd, 1957; *The Making of a Priest,* Newman, 1958; *Away to East Africa,* Dodd, 1959; *The Maryknoll Book of Peoples,* Crawley, 1959.

The Young Conquistador, Dodd, 1960; *Away to the Lands of the Andes,* Dodd, 1962; (editor) *The Maryknoll Catholic Dictionary,* Grosset, 1964; *Away to Mexico,* Dodd, 1965; *The Story of Pope John XXIII,* Grosset, 1965; *Away to Central America,* Dodd, 1967; (editor) *Maryknoll Book of Treasures,* Maryknoll, 1968; *Away to Venezuela,* Dodd, 1969.

The Prayer of the Faithful, O.S.V. (Our Sunday Visitor), 1970; *Our American Catholic Heritage,* O.S.V., 1972; *The Way* (Catholic Edition), Tyndale, 1976; *General Intercessions,* O.S.V., 1978; *Questions Catholics Ask,* O.S.V., 1978. Also writer of pamphlets and articles.

Films written and produced: "The Miracle of Blue Cloud County," "Kyoto Saturday Afternoon," "The Kid Down the Block," "Indian Street."

Films written, photographed, and produced: "The Story of Juan Mateo," "Adan of the Andes," "Men of Tomorrow," "School for Farmers," "Light up the Jungle," "The Royal Road," "A Boy of the Bakuria," "Bride of Africa," "Land of the Twelve Tribes," "New Day in Africa," "The Training of a Maryknoller," "The Maryknoll Brother," "The Problem of People," "The Golden Kimono," "Man With a Mission," "Dateline Orient," "The Gods of Todos Santos," "Children of the Dust," "The Quiet Revolution."

WORK IN PROGRESS: An American Catholic Martyrology, a biographical work of all those who died for their faith within the United States, plus Americans who died for their religious beliefs outside the United States; *Felipe* (tentative title), concerns the life of Philip of Jesus, a Mexican youth who became one of the twenty-six martyrs of Nagasaki (Japan).

SIDELIGHTS: "When my first article about the day in the life of a chipmunk was published in a local newspaper when I was seven years old, I was bitten by the writing bug and have not recovered to this day. In high school I began regular work for a newspaper and writing has been a career ever since.

"I began writing books for young people quite by accident. One day during the Korean War, Dorothy Bryan, the children's editor for Dodd, Mead, called and asked if I could get someone to write a book on Korea that would explain its people and customs to American young people who knew very little about that country. After a number of phone calls, I finally found an author, experienced in things Korean, who agreed to write the book. Miss Bryan was delighted. However, after thinking it over, the author called me a few days later and said she could not go ahead with the project. Having committed myself, there was nothing left to do but write the book myself. After a lot of interviews and research, *The Adventures of Wu Han of Korea* came into being. The book met with success, was translated into a number of languages, and became the first of a series of adventure stories.

"I have two purposes in writing a book. One is to entertain which an author must do if she or he is to hold the reader. The second is to teach, not in a schoolroom way, but to make the reader aware of the world in which we live and particularly its people. It is surprising how much education and information will be accepted by the reader if the story is well told and interesting."

NEWBERY, John   1713-1767
(Abraham Aesop, Tom Telescope)

PERSONAL: Born in 1713, in Waltham St. Lawrence, Berkshire, England; died December 22, 1767, in Islington, England; buried at the parish of Lawrence Waltham, England; son of Robert Newbery (a farmer); descendant of the sixteenth century publisher, Ralph Newbery; married Mary Carnan; children: John, Mary, Francis; stepchildren: John, Thomas, Anna-Maria (Mrs. Christopher Smart). *Education:* Briefly attended a village school in England; mostly self-taught. *Religion:* Anglican. *Home:* Canonbury House, Islington, England.

CAREER: Publisher, printer, and author of children's literature. Assistant to William Carnan, owner and editor of the *Reading Mercury,* 1729-37; took over Carnan's firm (a shop for medicine and miscellaneous goods as well as a printing establishment), 1737; opened a warehouse in London, 1744; moved his business to the "Bible and Sun" in St. Paul's Churchyard, 1745; published the first children's periodical, *The Lilliputian Magazine,* 1751; founded several newspapers and magazines, including the *Universal Chronicle or Weekly Gazette,* 1758, the *Public Ledger,* 1760, and *The Christian Magazine,* the first periodical devoted entirely to religious matters; commissioned Oliver Goldsmith, Samuel Johnson and many other authors to write for him throughout his publishing career. *Awards, honors:* John Newbery Medal has been awarded since 1922 to the author of the most distinguished children's book of the year published in the United States.

WRITINGS—Original editions published by the author, except as noted: (Editor) *Letters on the Most Common, as Well as Important, Occasions in Life,* 1756; *A New History of England,* 1761; *The Art of Poetry on a New Plan,* 1762, reissued, Garland Publishing, 1970; *A Compendious History of the World from the Creation to the Dissolution of the Roman Republic,* two volumes, [London], 1763.

For children: *A Little Pretty Pocket-Book,* 1744, reprinted, facsimile edition, Harcourt, 1967; (editor) *The Circle of Sciences,* seven volumes, 1745-46; (editor) *A Spelling Dictionary* (supplement to *The Circle of Sciences*), third edition, P. Wilson, 1752; (under pseudonym Abraham Aesop) *Fables in Verse,* 1758; (supposed author with others) *Mother Goose's Melody,* circa 1760, Isaiah Thomas, circa 1785, facsimile edition reprinted as *The Original Mother Goose's Melody,* Singing Tree Press, 1969; (under pseudonym Tom Telescope) *The Newtonian System of Philosophy,* 1761; (supposed author) *The Renowned History of Giles Gingerbread,* circa 1765; (supposed author) *The History of Little Goody Two-Shoes,* circa 1766, reprinted, facsimile edition, Singing Tree Press, 1970.

SIDELIGHTS: **1713.** Born in Waltham St. Lawrence, Berkshire, England. In 1801 the village of young Newbery was described as follows: "Though now reduced to a few scattered houses, it is said to have been a place of remote antiquity and of much importance. Some of the buildings wear the appearance of having flourished in better times, and the ruins of many more are visible. The inhabitants assert that the houses were formerly very numerous; that they extended a considerable way on each side of the road, which, at the entrance of the village, passes under an arched gateway composed of large oak timbers. In a spacious field near was a Roman fortress, the site of which is still called Castle Acre, and it commands a delightful view over a very large extent of country." [Charles Welsh, *A Bookseller of the Last Century,* Augustus M. Kelley, 1972.[1]]

July 19, 1713. Baptised. Newbery was a descendent of the distinguished sixteenth-century publisher, Ralph Newbery and the son of a small village farmer, John Newbery. Though his formal education was limited, Newbery was primarily self-educated through extensive reading.

1729. Left his father's farm. Moved to nearby Reading where he was apprenticed to William Carnan, the proprietor of *The Reading Mercury* newspaper. Years later, Newbery's son, Francis, recalled his father's youthful ambitions. "By his talents and industry, and a great love of books, [he] had rendered himself a very good English scholar. His mind was too excursive to allow him to devote his life to the occupation of agriculture. He was anxious to be in trade, and at about the age of sixteen, as he was a very good accountant, and wrote an excellent hand, he engaged himself as an assistant in the house of one of the principal merchants in Reading, where his diligence and integrity soon established his character, while his agreeable manners and conversation, and information (for he pursued his studies in all his leisure hours) raised him into notice and esteem."[1]

1737. Carnan died and left his property equally to his brother and Newbery. Shortly thereafter, Newbery married Carnan's widow who was six years his senior and the mother of three children. His son commented on this union: "His love of books and acquirements had peculiarly fitted him for conducting such a concern as the newspaper and printing business at Reading, and rendered him doubly acceptable to the object of his affections, who was indeed a most amiable and worthy woman. They were in due time united in wedlock, and what a field now opened to his active and expanded mind!"[1]

1740. Toured England to obtain knowledge and experience about the book trade business. An account of this trip was faithfully recorded in a diary. "Going from this place

The great U.

HEre's great Q, and R,
Are both come from far,
To bring you good News
About the *French* War.

q, r.

so

(From *A Little Pretty Pocket-Book* by John Newbery.)

[Grantham] to Lincoln you cross a delicious plain, in length about 22 miles, the breadth I know not: in the whole 22 miles there is but one village (called Ancaster), and that just at the entrance of the town. Here we were almost famished for want of liquour, being obliged to travel upwards of 20 miles on a sultry summer's day without a drop. The spirit moved my brother traveller to ask the Shepard (*sic*), but the inhospitable wretch would not spare one spoonful.

"At almost every parish in this country [Lancashire] there is a very useful instrument called a Ducking Stool, where the women are cured of scolding, &c.

"Some time ago the cookmaid of this Inn (The 3 Cranes) being married was delivered of 2 children, which the good unexperienced women took for boys, and therefore at ye christening named them John and Joseph, but since ye said christening *Nature* has suffer'd a surprising change or ye *wise ones* were out in their Judgment, for the two boys are become two girls."[1]

Fire engines were a rarity as Newbery recorded: "Going from Leicester to Coventry we pass by . . . two Engine

Houses which are wrought by fire and throw a great quantity of water out of the pits."[1]

Newbery recorded things to be done, purchases and enquiries to be made on the journey, and various other private and business records, suggestions, and memoranda. "At my return advertize all sorts of the haberdashery and cutlery goods that I keep to be sold wholesale as cheap as in the country where made, only paying 2½ per cent. commission from the makers per John Newbery & Co., for ready money only, *and so excuse one's self from trusting.*

"Get a note in the following manner to secure Mr Collier's debt, viz., let Mr Collier give a promissory note of his hand to Mr Morsham, then Mr Morsham indorse it to Mrs Blackhead, and Mrs Blackhead indorse it to me. *This is better than any joint note, because all ye indorsers are liable.*"[1]

March, 1740. Daughter, Mary, born.

September, 1741. Son, John, born.

July, 1743. Son, Francis, born.

1744. Established a London branch of his publishing business, eventually settling his family and business in St. Paul's Churchyard. Engaged in the rapid expansion of his book publishing, printing, and selling enterprises, as his son, Francis, noted: "[He was] in the full employment of his talents in writing and publishing books of amusement and instruction for children. The call for them was immense, an edition of many thousands being sometimes exhausted during the Christmas holidays. His friend, Dr Samuel Johnson, who, like other grave characters, could now, and then be jocose, had used to say of him—'Newbery is an extraordinary man, for I know not whether he has read, or written, most books.'"[1]

Published his first children's book. A pioneer in children's publishing, Newbery was the first to produce a series of little books intended for amusement. "A *Little Pretty Pocket-Book*, intended for the Instruction and Amusement of Little Master Tommy and Pretty Miss Polly, with an agreeable Letter to read from Jack the Giant Killer, as also a Ball and Pincushion, the use of which will infallibly make Tommy a good Boy, and Polly a Good Girl. To the whole is prefixed a letter on education humbly addressed to all Parents, Guardians, Governesses, &c., wherein rules are laid down for making their children strong, healthy, virtuous, wise, and happy."[1]

1751. Published the first children's periodical, the *Lilliputian Magazine.* "The *Lilliputian Magazine;* or, The Young Gentleman and Lady's Golden Library. Being an attempt to amend the World, to render the Society of Man more amiable, and to re-establish the Simplicity, Virtue, and Wisdom of the Golden Age. No. 1. To be continued monthly."[1]

Oldest son, John, died as a result of a fall. The poet, Christopher Smart, who was a business associate and family friend, eulogized the young Newbery in a funeral poem:

"Henceforth be every tender fear supprest,
Or let us weep for joy, that he is blest;
From grief to bliss, from earth to heav'n remov'd,
His mem'ry honour'd, as his life belov'd,

"That heart o'er which no evil e'er had pow'r,
That disposition sickness could not sour;
That sense, so oft to riper years denied,
That patience heroes might have own'd with pride!
His painful race undauntedly he ran,
And in the eleventh winter died a man.''[1]

1753. Anna Maria Carnan, Newbery's step-daughter, married Christopher Smart. A frequent visitor at Newbery's home in St. Paul's Churchyard, Smart recalled the kindness his father-in-law exuded: "The author of these pages gives his testimony with peculiar pleasure to the merits of a gentleman whose friendship and civilities he experienced in early life, and whose beneficence indeed, to say nothing of his intellectual powers, suffered no object within the sphere of their exertions to be uncheered by his kindness.''[1]

1755. Newbery's medicine business, in which he sold many popular remedies, flourished as well as his even larger publishing business.

1758. Commissioned Oliver Goldsmith, to whom Newbery lent financial support, to write for him. Newbery commissioned many famous authors, including Smollett and Samuel Johnson. The latter immortalized Newbery in *The Idler* in the humorous character, Jack Whirler, "...whose business keeps him in perpetual motion, and whose motion always eludes his business; who is always to do what he never does, who cannot stand still because he is wanted in another place, and who is wanted in many places because he stays in none. Jack has more business than he can conveniently transact in one house, he has therefore one habitation near Bow Church and another about a mile distant. By this ingenious distribution of himself between two houses, Jack has contrived to be found at neither. Jack's trade is extensive, and he has many dealers; his conversation is sprightly, and he has many-companions; his disposition is kind, and he has many friends. Jack neither forbears pleasure for business nor omits business for pleasure, but is equally invisible to his friends and his customers; to him that comes with an invitation to a club and to him that waits to settle an account....

"But, overwhelmed as he is with business, his chief desire is to have still more. Every new proposal takes possession of his thoughts; he soon balances probabilities, engages in the project, brings it almost to completion, and then forsakes it for another, which he catches with the same alacrity, urges with the same vehemence, and abandons with the same coldness.''[1]

1758. Published a weekly newspaper, *The Universal Chronicle* or *Weekly Gazette*, which first printed Johnson's *Idler*.

January, 1760. Published the *Public Ledger*, a daily "register of commerce and intelligence.''

"We are unwilling to raise expectations which we may perhaps find ourselves unable to satisfy; and therefore they have no mention of criticism or literature, which yet we do not professionally exclude; nor shall we reject any political essays which are apparently calculated for the public good.''[1]

Goldsmith wrote "The Chinese Letters" for the *Ledger* which Newbery later published as *The Citizen of the World*.

June, 1762. Entered his son, Francis, in Trinity College, Oxford. In his autobiography Francis gave the following

Little Goody Two-Shoes

(From *The History of Little Goody Two-Shoes* by John Newbery.)

account of an incident involving his father. "At the Angel Inn [we] had apartments. While there, Mr Warton and two of young Newbery's schoolfellows at Merchant Taylor's School, who had been a twelvemonth before him at that college, dined with [us] on the first day. The party, who were all naturally cheerful and well acquainted, were soon at their ease. In the course of the evening Mr Warton took out of his pocket a linen cap, striped, which terminated in a point, and pulling off his wig, popped it on his head. The oddity and singularity of his appearance excited a burst of laughter, and a curiosity to know of what this was the symbol, when he informed [us] that a party of wags had established a club called 'The Jelly Bag Society,' of which this was worn as the token at their meetings, and that it had originated from the following epigram written by his friend there, Mr Newbery:—

'One day in Chelsea Meadows walking,
Of poetry and such things talking,

Says Ralph—a merry wag—
"An epigram, if smart and good,
In all its circumstances shou'd
    Be like a Jelly Bag!"

"Your simile I own is new;
But how wilt make it out?" says Hugh.
    Quoth Ralph: "I'll tell thee, friend:
Make it at top both large and fit
To hold a budget-full of wit,
    And point it at the end.'"'

"The old gentleman blushed, and said he did not know how they should have discovered him as the writer, but acknowledged that it was so. Mr Warton observed that the epigram had been ascribed to himself and others of the club, and that any of them would have been proud to own such a production. This was truly *'laudari a laudato viro.'*"[1]

October 2, 1765. Either because of laxity in the copyright laws at that time or a failure of Newbery's to renew his licenses, many of his books were pirated by printers in surrounding towns. Newbery protested these acts in an ad in an evening newspaper. "As several persons in the printing and book-selling business have, without the least regard to property, honour, or conscience, pirated this Dictionary, and others of Mr Newbery's little books, he hopes all parents and guardians, as well as the young gentlemen and ladies, for whose emolument they were written, will do him the favour and the justice to ask for his books, and observe that his name is prefixed to those they buy, that he, who has entered so heartily into their service, and been ever studious of their improvement, may, at least, reap some of the fruits of his labour."[1]

In another ad, Newbery showed an advanced concept of a kindergarten which was then unheard of. "*A sett of fifty-six squares,* with cuts and Directions for playing with them, newly invented for the use of Children. By which alone, or with very little assistance, they may learn to Spell, Read, Write, Make Figures and cast up any common sum in Arithmetick, before they are old enough to be sent to school, and that by the way of Amusement and Diversion.

"The whole so contrived as to yield as much entertainment as any of their Play Games usually do. By which means a great deal of Time, commonly idled away by Children, will be profitably as well as pleasantly employed.

"Upon the plan of the learned Mr Locke, who in his excellent Treatise of Education hath the following words on this method of teaching Children:—'Thus children may be coz-en'd into a knowledge of the Letters, be taught to Read, without perceiving it to be anything but a Sport, and play themselves into that which others are whipped for.'

"To which is added a Collection of Moral and Prudential Maxims intended to instil [sic] into their young minds the principles of Virtue, and the knowledge of Mankind."[1]

One of his improvements in the actual "dress" of books was his binding "in the vellum manner." "The Purchasers of Books bound in the Vellum manner are desired to observe that they are sewed much better than the Books which are bound in Leather; open easier at the Back, and are not so liable to warp in being read. If by any Accident the Covers should be stained or rubbed they may be new covered for a Penny, an advantage that cannot be remedied in Leather; so that this method of Binding is not only cheaper, but it is presumed will be found more useful.

"The only Motive for trying this Experiment was to adopt a Substitute for Leather which was greatly enhanced in its price, either by an increased Consumption, or of Monopoly; how far that purpose will be answered, must be submitted to the Determination of the Reader."[1]

1766. *Little Goody Two Shoes* was published. Newbery wittily advertised its first edition. "*The History of Little Goody Two Shoes,* otherwise called, Mrs. Margery Two Shoes, with the means by which she acquired her Learning and Wisdom, and in consequence thereof her Estate; set forth at large for the Benefit of those

'Who from a state of Rags and Care,
And having Shoes but half a pair;
Their fortune and their Fame would fix,
And gallop in a Coach and Six.'

"See the original manuscript in the Vatican at Rome, and the Cuts by Michael Angelo. Illustrated with the Comments of our great modern Critics. Third Edition, London.

"Printed for J. Newbery at the Bible and Sun, in St Paul's Churchyard, 1766. Price Sixpence."[1]

Goldsmith's *The Vicar of Wakefield* was published. In it Newbery was immortalized as ". . . the philanthropic bookseller in St Paul's Churchyard, who has written so many little books for children. He called himself their friend, but he was the friend of all mankind. He was no sooner alighted but he was in haste to begone, for he was ever on business of the utmost importance. . . ."[1]

December 22, 1767. Died at the zenith of his fame and prosperity at the age of fifty-four at his country home at Canonbury House, Islington, England. "I desire I may be Buried as private as possible in the Church Yard of the parish of Lawrence Waltham near my late ffather and mother and in the day time if it be convenient and I desire that my Corps[e] may be carried from the Hearse to the grave by six very poor men of the said parish and that six other poor old men of the said parish do support the pall and that each and every of them be paid half a guinea for their trouble and attendance. . . ."[1]

Buried by his own request, in the churchyard of his birthplace in Waltham St. Lawrence. On his tomb he is described simply as a "writer of children's stories."

Since 1922 his name has been commemorated by the famous Newbery Medal award presented annually by the American Library Association for the best children's book of the year. Newbery Medal books now carry his name everywhere.

FOR MORE INFORMATION SEE: Josephine Blackstock, *Songs for Sixpence: A Story about John Newbery,* Follett, 1955; A. B. Chrisman, "John Newbery: The Father of Children's Books," *Newbery Medal Books: 1922-1955,* edited by Bertha E. Miller and E. W. Fields, Horn Book, 1955; Brian Doyle, editor, *Who's Who of Children's Literature,* Schocken, 1968; Mary F. Thwaite, "John Newbery: Two Centuries After," *Horn Book,* April, 1968; W. Noblett, "John Newbery: Publisher Extraordinary," *History Today,* April, 1972; Charles Welsh, *A Bookseller of the Last Century: Being some Account of the Life of John Newbery, and of the Books he Published, with a Notice of the later Newberys,* Griffith, Farran, Okeden & Welsh, 1885, reprinted by Augustus M. Kelley Publishers, 1972.

NORRIS, Gunilla B(rodde) 1939-

PERSONAL: Born in 1939, in Argentina; daughter of a Swedish father (in the diplomatic service); married Reverend David A. Norris; children: Jennifer, John. *Education:* Sarah Lawrence College, B.A. *Residence:* Riverside, Connecticut.

CAREER: Children's author. Career has included being a counselor for a Girl Scout camp, a settlement house day camp, and a church camp. Her first book was published in 1965, and since then she has been prolific, producing a total of twelve books.

WRITINGS—All for children: The Summer Pastures (illustrated by Nancy Grossman), Knopf, 1965; *A Feast of Light* (illustrated by N. Grossman), Knopf, 1967; *Lillan* (illustrated by Nancie Swanberg), Atheneum, 1968; *The Good Morrow* (illustrated by Charles Robinson), Atheneum, 1969; *A Time for Watching* (illustrated by Paul Giovanopoulos), Knopf, 1969; *Take My Waking Slow* (illustrated by John Gundelfinger), Atheneum, 1970; *The Top Step* (illustrated by Richard Cuffari), Atheneum, 1970; *Green and Something Else* (illustrated by C. Robinson), Simon & Schuster, 1971; *If You Listen* (illustrated by Dale Payson), Atheneum, 1971; *Josie on Her Own,* Scholastic Book Services, 1972; *The Friendship Hedge* (illustrated by D. Payson), Dutton, 1973; *Standing in the Magic* (Junior Literary Guild selection; illustrated by R. Cuffari), Dutton, 1974.

SIDELIGHTS: "Born in Buenos Aires, Argentina, I learned Spanish as my first language. Then came an abrupt change when the family moved back to Sweden. I not only had to learn how to read and write but I had to learn Swedish as well. That no sooner conquered than the family was off to the U.S.A. and English was added. It was a challenge, and how!

"I suppose English really became a part of me when I discovered in junior high school that I liked to write. I liked to make sense out of all that was happening to me—to spell out what it was like to be foreign and often a little forlorn. From that time I had two loves: the theater and writing. And they are still my two loves. Both feel like a kind of marvelous magic. I know it is because both the theater and fiction are about people. And people are the most magic and important part of my life.

"One day I got to thinking about why there are some people who sparkle like firecrackers on a dark night. It is as if they have a glow on, a secret, magical way about them. I wanted to capture that quality, in a story. And that is how *Standing in the Magic* began. The book is about Brady Gladenough, a city boy, who has the special aliveness that makes a humdrum day go zing! And it is about his friend Joel. Their story is a real story and a magic story both."

Norris received her B.A. from Sarah Lawrence College and had additional training in the theatre. She has been a teacher in improvisational theatre for children and adults as well as a camp counselor. She is married to Reverend David Norris,

He wasn't going to think about how far it was. He'd jump from the fifth step, and then there'd be only two more. ■ (From *The Top Step* by Gunilla B. Norris. Illustrated by Richard Cuffari.)

has two children, and lives in Riverside, Connecticut. "Being a writer and an actress gives you a special way of looking at the world. You are always noticing how people strike you, how they do things, how they speak. You notice places, sounds, smells, and colors. And if you are lucky, you find a story among all that you've noticed.

"I am fortunate in my family because they are all noticers, too. My husband is a therapist and has to really listen to be good at his job. My daughter, Jennifer, is a musician and brings all she notices into her music. My son, John, is an avid naturalist with a special love for snakes. To catch one you have to be really awake and watching. I don't like catching snakes, but I do love catching stories and they are all around us if we are only alive to the magic of people."

Norris' works are included in the Kerlan Collection at the University of Minnesota.

"I got you a nosegay," repeated Sue-Ellen, planting a hasty kiss on the old woman's wrinkled cheek. Granny smiled. "Well, thank you, child." ■ (From *If You Listen* by Gunilla B. Norris. Illustrated by Dale Payson.)

FOR MORE INFORMATION SEE: Horn Book, December, 1968, April, 1969, April, 1971, April, 1975; *Library Journal,* May 15, 1969; *Bulletin of the Center for Children's Books,* March, 1975.

PEALE, Norman Vincent   1898-

PERSONAL: Born May 31, 1898, in Bowersville, Ohio; son of Charles Clifford (a physician-turned-Methodist minister) and Anna (DeLaney) Peale; married Loretta Ruth Stafford, June 20, 1930; children: Margaret Ann (Mrs. Paul F. Everett), John Stafford (an ordained minister and philosophy professor), Elizabeth Ruth (Mrs. John M. Allen). *Education:* Ohio Wesleyan University, B.A., 1920; Boston University, M.A., 1924, S.T.B., 1924. *Politics:* Republican. *Address:* 1030 Fifth Ave., New York, N.Y. 10028 and "Quaker Hill," Pawling, N.Y. 12564. *Office:* 1025 Fifth Ave., New York, N.Y. 10028.

CAREER: Reporter, *Morning Republican,* Findlay, Ohio, 1920, *Detroit Journal,* Detroit, Mich., 1920; ordained to the Methodist ministry, 1922; pastor, Berkeley, R.I., 1922-24, Kings Highway Church, Brooklyn, N.Y., 1924-27, University Church, Syracuse, N.Y., 1927-32, Marble Collegiate Reform Church, New York, N.Y., 1932—; author, 1937—. Chaplain, American Legion, Kings County, N.Y., 1925-27;

editor of *Guideposts,* an inspirational magazine; host of a weekly radio program on station WOR, and television programs, "What's Your Trouble," and "Guideposts Presents Norman Vincent Peale." Trustee, Ohio Wesleyan University and Central College; member of the executive committee of the Presbyterian Ministers Fund for Life Insurance; member of the Mid-Century White House Conference on Children and Youth, and the President's Commission for Observance of the Twenty-fifth Anniversary of the United Nations; president of the National Temperance Society, the Protestant Council, New York, N.Y., 1965-69, and the Reformed Church of America, 1969-70; lecturer on public affairs and personal effectiveness.

MEMBER: American Foundation of Religion and Psychiatry (president), Ohio Society of New York (president, 1952-55), Episcopal Actors Guild, American Authors Guild, Sons of the American Revolution, Alpha Delta, Phi Gamma Delta, Rotary Club, Masons, Metropolitan Club, Union League. *Awards, honors:* Freedom Foundation award, 1952, 1955, 1959, 1973, 1974; Horatio Alger award, 1952; American Education award, 1955; Government Service award for Ohio, 1956; National Salvation Army award, 1956; Distinguished Salesman's award from New York Sales Executives, 1957; Salvation Army award, 1957; International Human Relations award from the Dale Carnegie Club International, 1958; Clergyman of the Year award, 1964; Paul Harris Fellow award from Rotary International, 1972; Distinguished Patriot award from Sons of the American Revolution, 1973; Order of Aaron and Hur, Chaplains Corps, U.S. Army, 1975; D.D. from Syracuse University, 1931, Ohio Wesleyan University, 1936, Duke University, 1938, and Central College, 1964; L.H.D. from Lafayette College, 1952, and University of Cincinnati, 1968; LL.D. from William Jewell College, 1952, Hope College, 1962, and Brigham Young University, 1967; S.T.D. from Millikin University, 1958; Litt.D. from Jefferson Medical College, 1955, Iowa Wesleyan University, 1958, and Eastern Kentucky State College, 1964.

WRITINGS—All adult books concerning self-improvement or religion, except as noted: *The Art of Living,* Abingdon, 1957, new edition published as *The New Art of Living,* Worlds Work, 1975; *You Can Win,* Abingdon, 1938; (with Smiley Blanton) *Faith Is the Answer: A Psychiatrist and a Pastor Discuss Your Problems,* Abingdon-Cokesbury, 1940, enlarged and revised edition, Guideposts, 1955; *A Guide to Confident Living,* Prentice-Hall, 1948, reissued, Fawcett World, 1975; (with S. Blanton) *The Art of Real Happiness,* Prentice-Hall, 1950, revised edition, Fawcett World, 1976; *The Power of Positive Thinking,* Prentice-Hall, 1952, reissued, Fawcett World, 1976, abridged edition published as *The Power of Positive Thinking for Young People,* Prentice-Hall, 1954, reissued, Worlds Work, 1964; *Inspiring Messages for Daily Living,* Prentice-Hall, 1955, reissued, Worlds Work, 1963; *The Coming of the King: The Story of the Nativity* (for children; illustrated by William Moyers), Prentice-Hall, 1956; *He Was a Child* (for children; illustrated by Rafaello Busoni), Prentice-Hall, 1957; *Stay Alive All Your Life,* Prentice-Hall, 1957, reissued, Fawcett World, 1975; *The Amazing Results of Positive Thinking,* Prentice-Hall, 1959, reissued, Fawcett World, 1976; *The Tough-Minded Optimist,* Prentice-Hall, 1961, revised edition published as *Positive Thinking for a Time Like This,* 1975; *Adventures in the Holy Land,* Prentice-Hall, 1963; *Sin, Sex, and Self-Control,* Doubleday, 1965, reissued, Fawcett World, 1975; *Jesus of Nazareth: A Dramatic Interpretation of His Life from Bethlehem to Calvary,* Prentice-Hall, 1966; *The Healing of Sor-*

row, Doubleday, 1966, reissued, Gibson, 1975; *Enthusiasm Makes the Difference,* Prentice-Hall, 1967; *Bible Stories* (for children; illustrated by Grabianski), Watts, 1973; *You Can If You Think You Can,* G. K. Hall, 1974; *The Story of Jesus* (for children; illustrated by Robert Fujitani), Gibson, 1976; *The Positive Principle Today: How to Renew and Sustain the Power of Positive Thinking,* Prentice-Hall, 1976.

Other: (Editor) *Guideposts: Personal Messages of Inspiration and Faith,* Prentice-Hall, 1948; (editor) *New Guideposts,* Prentice-Hall, 1951; (editor) *The Guideposts Anthology,* Guideposts Associates, 1953; (author of introduction) Guideposts editors, *What Prayer Can Do,* Doubleday, 1953; (editor) *Faith Made Them Champions,* Guideposts Associates, 1954; (author of introduction) *The Sermon on the Mount,* World Publishing, 1955; (editor) *Unlock Your Faith-Power,* Guideposts Associates, 1957; (editor) *Guideposts to a Stronger Faith,* Guideposts Associates, 1959; (author of foreword) S. Blanton, *The Healing Power of Poetry,* Crowell, 1960; (editor) *Norman Vincent Peale's Treasury of Courage and Confidence,* Doubleday, 1970.

Author of the newspaper columns, "Positive Thinking," and "Confident Living," appearing in many papers; also writer for various secular and religious periodicals, including *Look, Reader's Digest,* and the *Christian Herald.*

SIDELIGHTS: **May 31, 1898.** Born in the rural Ohio town of Bowersville. His father, the Reverend Charles Clifford Peale, a former physician, was then the Methodist pastor of Bowersville. When, at the age of four months, Peale was photographed in his christening gown, his mother exclaimed: "He looks like a bishop already!" [Arthur Gordon, *Norman Vincent Peale: Minister to Millions,* Prentice-Hall, 1958.[1]]

1900. Father was transferred to Highland, a town not far from Bowersville, where his brother, Robert Clifford, was born.

1902. Family moved to Asbury Methodist Church in Cincinnati. Peale was a sensitive child, thin for his age and shy in groups.

1910-1916. Family was transferred to Greenville and then to Bellefontaine, Ohio. As a teenager, Peale delivered papers, worked in a grocery store, and sold pots and pans, door to door. A third son, Leonard, was born into the Peale family during this time. In high school the reticent Peale overcame his shyness to become a star debater.

Autumn, 1916. Entered Ohio Wesleyan University as a liberal arts major. At college Peale became president of his fraternity, Phi Gamma Delta, served in the students' army training corps until the end of World War I and was associate editor of the campus newspaper, the *Transcript.*

1920. Received a B.A. degree from Ohio Wesleyan. During college, Peale was torn between a career in journalism and the vocation to ministry. After graduation, having decided on journalism, he took a job with the *Morning Republican* in Findlay, Ohio. After a few months on the *Republican,* he accepted a position on the *Detroit Journal.*

Autumn, 1921. After a year in the newspaper world, Peale applied to the School of Theology at Boston University and was accepted. He preached his first sermon in a small church in a town on the outskirts of Boston—it was only twelve minutes long and simply explained what Christ had done for

NORMAN VINCENT PEALE

him and could do for others. "We came from God. He is our home, and there is a deep homesickness for Him in all of us. He is in our bloodstream, in the meshes of our minds, in the intricacies of our souls. We are His and He is ours. We can't get away from God; even if we deny Him, He haunts us. In our conflicts, our misery, we must turn back to Him for peace. A carrier pigeon, released in the air, instinctively turns home. Birds in their migrations unerringly go back to the same bush from which they came. Every river feels the lure of the sea. Every human life feels the tug of God."[1]

Summer, 1922. At home with his family in Ohio, Peale had a second opportunity to preach in a small Ohio town when the minister of the country church became ill. "I can remember it all as if it were yesterday. The church stood at the intersection of two roads that ran between the endless fields of corn and wheat. Back of the church, visible through the pulpit window, was a cool and inviting grove where the shade of the great trees was broken by long shafts of sunlight. The church was quiet and restful; some one had put a bunch of summer flowers on the communion table. Soon an organist arrived and began softly to play a medley of hymns while the people gathered. Most arrived in buggies, although there were a few Model T Fords and a Willys Knight or two that came chugging up to stop in the spacious yard.

"The peace and quiet, the radiantly fresh morning, the Sunday-go-to-meeting atmosphere moved me deeply. I felt a rush of gratitude at the thought that I was privileged to share my faith with these people—simple country people, and the salt of the earth. . . .

(From the movie "One Man's Way," starring Don Murray. Copyright © 1964 by United Artists Corp., Inc.)

"When time came for the sermon, I heeded my father's advice and gave a simple sermon based entirely on my own spiritual experience. I tried to use plain, everyday language and homey illustrations to drive home what Jesus Christ could do for my hearers. I described some of my own conflicts, and made the sermon a personal testimony of what Christ had done for me.

"While I was preaching, I suddenly became aware of the stillness that sometimes comes over a congregation when something very near to the heart of life creates a unity of understanding between the preacher and the people. It was a depth of feeling that seemed to tremble in the still summer air. There was something in it that made me think of a phrase that I had heard somewhere: 'An impingement like the hush of eternity.'

"I noticed then the strange look on people's faces that in the years that followed I was to see so often whenever that mystic hush comes as it does now and then. It is a kind of wonder, a look of blissful gratitude and goodness that appears when Jesus Christ is talked about and related to the simplicities of human lives. . . . It was one of the great formative experiences of my early ministry, deeply impressive and never forgotten."[1]

1922. Ordained into the Methodist Episcopal Church. Became pastor of a church in Berkeley, a small, impoverished mill town in Rhode Island. Peale continued his theological studies at Boston University during the week and returned to Berkeley every weekend.

1924. Received the Bachelor of Sacred Theology and Master of Arts in social ethics degrees from Boston University. Appointed minister of a small congregation with forty members in Brooklyn, New York. During his three-year pastorage, membership in the congregation rose to nine hundred. A new church was built. Years later, he remarked: "I was always lucky, lucky enough to be assigned to churches that were down. In every case, when I came along, attendance was low and morale was lower. There was no place to go but up!"[1]

Summer, 1926. First trip to Europe. He directed a tour of men and women and thus was given free passage. In Geneva, wanting desperately to see the United Nations in session but having no visitor's ticket, he spotted a door marked *Foreign Minister's Only.* "I'm a minister from the United States!"[1] he announced and was led to one of the best seats.

1927. Called to the University Methodist Church in Syracuse, New York.

June 20, 1930. Married Loretta Ruth Stafford. The couple eventually had three children: Margaret Ann, John Stafford and Elizabeth Ruth. In a letter to his wife he wrote: "I have discovered depths in my own heart that I did not know were there. Only you could bring them forth. . . . How wonderful it will be when I can look down every Sunday and see you there! . . . The faith you express in me will always hold me true. I want to be a good man and a great preacher, and you will be and are a great help. I love and honor you with my whole being. . . ."[1]

1932. Became the pastor of the Marble Collegiate Church on Fifth Avenue, New York City. Founded in 1628, the church claimed to be the oldest continuous Protestant pastorate in the United States and listed a membership of five hundred. By 1970 it had grown to four thousand—Peale's fame and "down-to-earth" sermons filled the church to overflow, regularly.

1936. Awarded an honorary Doctorate of Divinity.

1938-1939. Received an honorary Doctorate from Duke University. His first two books, *The Art of Living* and *You Can Win* were published.

Summer, 1939. Beloved mother, Anna Peale, died. "The night before my mother's funeral when all the others had retired, I felt I would like to be alone with her for a few moments. I went into the room where she lay, and gazed upon her face. Her hands were folded. My mother's hands were very beautiful, soft and graceful; I can feel their touch, and shall as long as life lasts.

"Very tenderly I put out my hand and touched hers. It was cold, like stone. I drew back and said, 'This is not my mother. What is this transformation? This is not my mother!' And there went through my heart a terror that struck to the center of my being, a terror and a horror of death.

"I went to my bedroom and walked to the window. Moonlight was bathing the hills in silvery radiance. I had always loved the moonlight, finding in it mystery and romance. But now it seemed cold and hateful, and the hills themselves seemed to mock, and the stars were sharp and bright, like points of hard steel. The whole universe seemed like a stone wall—cold, vast, utterly silent. It was death, death, everywhere the stark finality of death, and that night I slept a troubled sleep.

"The next morning, early, I went down into the garden. Dew was on the grass, birds were singing, the sky was blue, the world was bathed in sunshine. Life was speaking to me, and I found a measure of peace.

"But after a few weeks, as autumn came, I wanted to feel my mother's presence once again; I wanted to go where she sleeps in a little cemetery in southern Ohio. So I took the train, and as it rolled through the night I became impatient, as I used to be when I went home in happier times and eagerly awaited those breakfasts where we all laughed and talked at once in the spirit of family reunion.

"So I came back, and pushed open the gate of the old cemetery and stood by her grave. Then, all at once, I had one of those experiences that I shall treasure all my life, because suddenly, like a burst of light, it came to me; 'She isn't here. Why seek ye the living among the dead? She isn't here!' And I knew that she was not there in the grave, for I felt her with me, closer and dearer than ever. Something warm and peaceful, a deep joy, was in my heart."[1]

1941. During World War II Peale had wanted to join the armed forces as a chaplain, but his family and friends encouraged him to stay with his New York congregation. His attitude toward war never faltered: "We can't have international barbarism in the world and it is necessary that we strike it down. But after we have done so, and while we are doing so, we shall love these enemies of ours. We'll love them, finally, back into the family of nations for the redemption of the world."[1]

1943. Bought a sprawling farmhouse on 225 acres in Pawling, New York. The Peale family divided their time between their Fifth Avenue apartment and their Pawling home.

Late 1940's. Began editing *Guideposts,* a spiritual newsletter for businessmen. By the 1950's, *Guideposts* had grown to a monthly magazine and in the 1970's had approximately 2,-000,000 subscribers. In 1957 Peale's wife became co-editor.

1948. First best seller, *A Guide to Confident Living,* was published. The book was a combination of psychiatry and religion.

1952. Believing that the key to happiness is the cultivation of a positive attitude, Peale wrote *The Power of Positive Thinking.* The book became the third best-selling inspirational book of all time and its success made Peale one of the most sought after clergymen in the country. With success came criticism. Many regarded Peale's answers to everyday living too simple. "Maybe I *have* made it all sound too easy. That certainly wasn't my intention, because Christianity isn't easy; it's so tough that nobody lives up to it fully. I always tried to emphasize that fact. And maybe I *have* stressed the tangible, visible rewards of faith too much. But here again, it wasn't because I was trying to appeal to selfishness. It was because I've seen fantastic transformations take place in people who, through self-surrender and the agony of spiritual change, find themselves and become integrated personalities. I've seen these things happen over and over again. I wanted everyone to know about them, to experiment and find out for themselves."[1]

1954. The first of several inspirational books for children, *The Power of Positive Thinking for Young People,* was published. The prolific author-clergyman has participated in television advice programs and has written regular newspaper and magazine columns. Peale firmly believes in the power of mass media to achieve his work for Christ. "In this life we only get back what we give. Give hate to the world and the people around you, and you'll receive hatred. Cultivate an attitude of superiority, and you'll be treated with the same sort of contempt. Practice feelings of ill will and prejudice and anger, and that's what you'll get back. The whole universe is an echo-cavern. What you send out reverberates back to you. In order to have the love, esteem, and affection of other people, you must give them affection and esteem and love."[1]

1965-1969. Became President of the Protestant Council of New York, president of the National Temperance Association and the Reformed Church of America, and served on the White House conference on children and youth and on the

So Adam and his new companion, Eve, began an existence in which there were none of the thorns of life as we know it. No guilt. No shame. No disappointment. No disease. No fear of death, for there was no death. ■ (From *Bible Stories* told by Norman Vincent Peale. Illustrated by Grabianski.)

President's commission for the observance of the twenty-fifth anniversary of the U.N. He held numerous honorary degrees and was given several awards for his services.

1976. Latest book for children, *The Story of Jesus,* was published when the author-clergyman was seventy-eight. Peale continues to be active in his ministerial duties and displays a vigor which belies his age. "It's exciting to be alive—and to serve God and people."[1]

In 1941, Peale served as technical adviser for the Warner Brothers film, "One Foot in Heaven," concerning the life of a minister. Arthur Gordon's biography of Peale, *Minister to Millions,* was produced in 1963 by United Artists. "One Man's Way" starred Don Murray, Diana Hyland, and William Windom.

FOR MORE INFORMATION SEE: C. Woodbury, "God's Salesman," *American Magazine,* June, 1949; "America's Twelve Master Salesmen," *Forbes,* 1952; "Dr. Peale: An Articulate Leader of Christianity," *Newsweek,* December 28, 1953; L. M. Miller and J. Monahan, "Pastor of Troubled Souls," *Reader's Digest,* February, 1954; "Dynamo in the Vineyard," *Time,* November 1, 1954; E. E. White and C. R. Henderlider, "What Norman Vincent Peale Told Us about His Speaking," *Quarterly Journal of Speech,* December, 1954; Margaret Peale and others, "We Like Our Parents," *Good Housekeeping,* January, 1956; Arthur Gordon, *Norman Vincent Peale: Minister to Millions,* Prentice-Hall, 1958; Elisabeth L. Davis, *Fathers of America,* Revell, 1958; Clarence Westphal, *Norman Vincent Peale: Christian Crusader,* Denison, 1964; *Publishers Weekly,* January 14, 1974, July 12, 1976; George R. Plagenz, "Gloom Spurs Peale Revival," *Cleveland Press,* March 9, 1974, reprinted in *Authors in the News,* Volume 1, Gale, 1976; D. T. Miller, "Popular Religion of the 1950's: Norman Vincent Peale and Billy Graham," *Journal of Popular Culture,* Summer, 1975.

PELLOWSKI, Anne 1933-

PERSONAL: Born June 28, 1933, in Pine Creek, Wis.; daughter of Alexander (a farmer) and Anna (Dorava) Pellowski. *Education:* College of St. Teresa, Winona, Minn., B.A., 1955; Columbia University, M.S.L.S. (with honors), 1959; additional graduate study at University of Minnesota, summer, 1955, University of Munich, 1955-56, and New School for Social Research, 1965. *Religion:* Roman Catholic. *Office:* U.S. Committee for UNICEF, 331 East 38th St., New York, N.Y. 10016.

CAREER: College of St. Teresa, Winona, Minn., instructor in English, 1956-57; Winona Public Library, Winona, Minn., children's librarian, 1957; New York Public Library, New York, N.Y., children's librarian, 1957-59, researcher, 1960-65, senior children's librarian, 1961-62, assistant storytelling and group work specialist, Office of Children's Services, 1963-65; University of Maryland, Overseas Branch, Munich, Germany, instructor in English, 1959-60; U.S. Committee for the United Nations Children's Fund, New York, N.Y., director of Information Center on Children's Cultures, 1967—. University of Maryland, adjunct lecturer, 1965-66; summer lecturer at University of Wisconsin, 1966, and Columbia University, 1967. *Member:* American Library Association. *Awards, honors:* Fulbright fellow in Germany, 1955-56; Grolier Award, 1979.

WRITINGS: The World of Children's Literature, Bowker, 1968; *Have You Seen a Comet,* John Day, 1971; *The World of Storytelling,* Bowker, 1977; *Nine Crying Dolls,* Collins, 1980. Records stories for children under CMS label. Contributor to library journals.

ANNE PELLOWSKI

WORK IN PROGRESS: "I am writing a series of novels for children, based on my family, that will trace five generations of Polish-American children on a Wisconsin farm."

SIDELIGHTS: Researcher on children's literature at International Youth Library, Munich, 1955-56, 1959-60, 1966, at International Board on Books for Young People, Vienna, summer, 1963, and at U.S. Library of Congress, 1965-66. Speaks, reads, and writes German, French, Spanish; speaks Polish; can work in several other languages.

FOR MORE INFORMATION SEE: Horn Book, February, 1972.

PEPE, Phil(ip) 1935-

PERSONAL: Born March 21, 1935, in Brooklyn, N.Y.; son of Michael P. (an accountant) and Lillian (Martini) Pepe; married Adele Sbaratta, October 28, 1961; children: Jayne, David, James, John. *Education:* St. John's University, Jamaica, N.Y., B.A., 1956. *Politics:* Democrat. *Religion:* Roman Catholic. *Home:* 83 Hampshire Hill Rd., Upper Saddle River, N.J. 10016. *Agent:* Theron Raines, 244 Madison Ave., New York, N.Y. 10016. *Office: New York Daily News,* New York, N.Y.

CAREER: New York World-Telegram & Sun, New York, N.Y., sports writer, 1957-66; *New York News,* New York, N.Y., sports writer, 1968—. *Military service:* National Guard.

WRITINGS: Winners Never Quit, Prentice-Hall, 1967; *No-Hitter,* Four Winds, 1968; (with Bob Gibson) *From Ghetto to Glory,* Prentice-Hall, 1968; *Greatest Stars of the NBA,* Prentice-Hall, 1970; *Incredible Knicks,* Popular Library, 1970; *Stand Tall: The Lew Alcindor Story,* Grosset, 1970; (with Willis Reed) *A View from the Rim: Willis Reed on Basketball,* Lippincott, 1971; *Come Out Smokin': The Joe Frazier Story,* Coward, 1972; *Great Comebacks in Sports,* Hawthorn, 1973; *The Wit and Wisdom of Yogi Berra,* Hawthorn, 1975; (with Rick Wolff) *What's a Nice Harvard Boy Like You Doing in the Bushes?,* Prentice-Hall, 1976; (with Zander Hollander) *The Book of Sports Lists,* Pinnacle, 1979.

SIDELIGHTS: "I consider myself a journalist first, an author second. Most of my books have been written as an adjunct to my newspaper work or out of the necessity caused by strikes and a newspaper that folded.

"My first recollection that I may possess any writing skill came when I was in eighth grade. An English teacher assigned us to write a composition of Abraham Lincoln. When I submitted my composition, the teacher refused to believe I had written it without help.

"My mother soothed my hurt by suggesting that the teacher was actually complimenting my writing. I can trace to that incident the thought of writing for a living and combining my love for sports with this newly-discovered skill.

"My newspaper career has taken me all over the world covering the biggest sporting events, including two Olympics (Rome and Montreal), more than a dozen heavyweight championship fights (including a visit to Tokyo with Muhammad Ali), every World Series since 1961, three Super Bowls, the U.S. Open Golf championship, the Kentucky Derby.

"Sports excite me, but the people interest me more than the games. The most fascinating people I have met in sports are Muhammad Ali, Billy Martin, Reggie Jackson, Andre Thornton, and Bill Bradley."

POMERANTZ, Charlotte

PERSONAL: Born in New York, New York; married Carl Marzani (a writer), November 12, 1966; children: Gabrielle Rose, Daniel Avram. *Education:* L'Institut des Sciences Politiques, student; graduated from Sarah Lawrence College. *Residence:* New York, N.Y.

CAREER: Children's author, editor. Her first published work, *A Quarter-Century of Un-Americana, 1938-1963*, is a collection of "tragico-comical memorabilia of the House Un-American Activities Committee." Since then her attention has turned to writing for children, completing twelve books in the past fourteen years. *Awards, honors: New York Times* Outstanding Book of the Year award for *The Day They Parachuted Cats on Borneo* and for *The Piggy in the Puddle,* 1972 and 1974, respectively; *The Day They Parachuted Cats on Borneo* was chosen by the International Board on Books for Young People (IBBY) as one of the ten books from the United States for the International Year of the Child, 1977-78.

WRITINGS—For children: *The Bear Who Couldn't Sleep* (illustrated by Meg Wohlberg), Morrow, 1965; *The Moon Pony* (illustrated by Loretta Trezzo), Young Scott, 1967; *Ask the Windy Sea* (illustrated by Nancy Grossman and Anita Siegel), Young Scott, 1968; *Why You Look Like You Whereas I Tend to Look Like Me* (illustrated by Rosemary Wells and Susan Jeffers), Young Scott, 1969; *The Day They Parachuted Cats on Borneo* (illustrated by Jose Aruego), Young Scott, 1971; *The Piggy in the Puddle* (illustrated by James Marshall), Macmillan, 1974; *The Princess and the Admiral* (illustrated by Tony Chen), Addison-Wesley, 1974; *The Ballad of the Long-Tailed Rat* (illustrated by Marian

...He was often late for work. ■(From *The Downtown Fairy Godmother* by Charlotte Pomerantz. Illustrated by Susanna Natti.)

CHARLOTTE POMERANTZ

Parry), Macmillan, 1975; *Detective Poufy's First Case: or, The Missing Battery-Operated Pepper Grinder* (illustrated by Marty Norman), Addison-Wesley, 1976; *The Mango Tooth* (Junior Literary Guild selection; illustrated by Marylin Hafner), Greenwillow, 1977; *The Downtown Fairy Godmother* (illustrated by Susanna Natti), Addison-Wesley, 1978; *The Tamarindo Puppy and Other Poems* (illustrated by Byron Barton), Greenwillow, 1980.

Editor: (Special editorial assistant) *Einstein on Peace,* Simon & Schuster), 1960; *A Quarter-Century of Un-Americana, 1938-1963,* Marzani & Munsell, 1963.

SIDELIGHTS: From an early age writing was a favorite pastime for Pomerantz. "When I was nine, I wrote a children's story about a trio named Tommy, Lulu, and Dee Dee Dum Dum. Fortunately, it has been lost."

In high school she wrote for the newspaper and at Sarah Lawrence College wrote stories for the literary magazine. "In the course of these years I also wrote a long children's story about the hierarchy of personnel in a zoo which roughly paralleled Stern's department store, where I worked as a salesperson. Some years later, a friend suggested I submit it to a publisher and, after drastic cutting, it was published. This encouraged me to write and submit other stories for children. It never occurred to me to submit stories prior to this, and I still think one should write for a long time for the pleasurable pain of it before worrying about publication.

"Although I wrote children's books before I was married or had children, I find increasingly that the children provide rich raw material, with the emphasis on *raw*. Some years back my son, then four, was heard to mumble, 'Fee fi fo fum, I smell the blood of an English muffin.' That started me thinking about writing a detective story. It finally became *Detective Pouty's First Case*, published in 1976. *The Mango Tooth* would not have been written had my little girl not been at the age where the tooth fairy was making frequent visits. But the story is fiction."

Pomerantz lives with her husband and two children in New York City.

In general, Pomerantz' books have been favorably reviewed. Of *The Piggy in the Puddle*, the *Library Journal* thinks her "lively, tongue-twisting verse is marvelously complimented by Marshall's ... humorous illustrations." According to *Horn Book*, "This piffle about pigs is marvelous to read aloud and should delight small readers...."

FOR MORE INFORMATION SEE: Saturday Review, May 10, 1969; *Library Journal*, July, 1969, May 15, 1974; *Horn Book*, October, 1969, June, 1974, August, 1975, December, 1975; *Christian Science Monitor*, May 1, 1974; *New York Times Book Review*, May 5, 1974.

ROSS, David   1896-1975

OBITUARY NOTICE: Born July 7, 1896, in New York, N.Y.; died November 12, 1975, in New York, N.Y. Editor, poet, radio announcer, and commentator. David Ross, the popular radio broadcaster of the 1930's and 1940's and award winning poet, also edited two anthologies of poetry, *Poet's Gold*, and *The Illustrated Treasury of Poetry for Children*. *For More Information See: Contemporary Authors*, Volume 65-68, Gale, 1977. *Obituaries: A B Bookman's Weekly*, December 8, 1975; *Contemporary Authors*, Volume 61-64, Gale, 1976; *New York Times*, November 14, 1975.

ROSSETTI, Christina (Georgina)   1830-1894
(Ellen Alleyn)

PERSONAL: Born December 5, 1830, in London, England; died December 29, 1894, in London; buried in Highgate Cemetery, London; daughter of Gabriele Rossetti (an Italian political refugee who was a professor of Italian); sister of Dante Gabriel Rossetti (the poet and artist). *Education:* Educated entirely at home by her mother. *Religion:* Anglican. *Home:* 30 Torrington Square, London, England.

CAREER: Poet. Led an active literary and devoutly religious life; assisted her mother in schoolteaching, 1853-54, and in establishing day schools in London and Somersetshire, neither of which was successful.

CHRISTINA ROSSETTI

*WRITINGS—*Poetry: *Verses by Christina G. Rossetti, Dedicated to Her Mother*, privately printed, 1847; *Goblin Market, and Other Poems* (for children; illustrated by Dante Gabriel Rossetti), Macmillan, 1862 [other editions illustrated by Laurence Housman, Macmillan, 1893; Arthur Rackham, Lippincott, 1933, reprinted, F. Watts, 1969]; *The Prince's Progress, and Other Poems* (illustrated by D. G. Rossetti), Macmillan, 1866; *Poems*, Roberts Brothers, 1866; *Commonplace: A Tale of Today, and Other Stories*, Roberts Brothers, 1870; *Sing-Song: A Nursery Rhyme Book* (for children; illustrated by Arthur Hughes), Roberts Brothers, 1872, reprinted, Dover, 1968 [another edition illustrated by Marguerite Davis, Macmillan, 1924, reissued, 1966]; *Annus Domini: A Prayer for Each Day of the Year*, [London], 1874; *Goblin Market, The Prince's Progress, and Other Poems* (illustrated by D. G. Rossetti), Macmillan, 1875; *A Pageant, and Other Poems*, Roberts Brothers, 1881; *Called to Be Saints: The Minor Festivals Devotionally Studied*, Society for Promoting Christian Knowledge (S.P.C.K.), 1881; *Time Flies: A Reading Diary*, S.P.C.K., 1885; *The Face of the Deep: A Devotional Commentary on the Apocalypse*, E. & J. B. Young, 1892; *New Poems*, Macmillan, 1896; *Maude: A Story for Girls*, H. S. Stone, 1897, reissued, Archon Books, 1976; *Monna Innominata: Sonnets and Songs*, T. B. Mosher, 1899.

**"I've seen a hundred pretty things,
And seen a hundred gay;
But only think: I peep by night
And do not peep by day!"**

■ (From *Sing-Song* by Christina Rossetti. Illustrated by Arthur Hughes. Engraved by the Brothers Dalziel.)

Prose: *Speaking Likenesses* (illustrated by A. Hughes), Macmillan, 1874; *Seek and Find: A Double Series of Short Studies of the Benedicite*, Pott, Young, 1879; *A Strange Journey; or, Pictures from Egypt and the Soudan*, Harper, 1882; *Letter and Spirit: Notes on the Commandments*, S.P.C.K., 1883.

Collections and selections: *Poems*, Macmillan, 1891; *Verses*, E. & J. B. Young, 1895; *Reflected Lights from The Face of the Deep*, Dutton, 1899; *The Poetical Works of Christina G. Rossetti*, Little, Brown, 1902; *Redeeming the Time: Daily Musings for Lent*, E. & J. B. Young, 1903; *The Poetical Works of Christina Georgina Rossetti* (with a memoir and notes by her brother, William Michael Rossetti), Macmillan, 1906, reprinted, Adler's Foreign Books, 1970; *Poems for Children* (selected by Melvin Hix), Educational Publishing, 1907; *The Family Letters of Christina Georgina Rossetti* (edited by W. M. Rossetti), Scribner, 1908, reprinted, Folcroft, 1973; *Poems* (illustrated by Florence Harrison), Blackie, 1910; *Selected Poems of Christina G. Rossetti* (edited by Charles B. Burke), Macmillan, 1913; *Poems* (edited by Kathleen Jarvis), Mowbray, 1955, Philosophical Library, 1956; *Poems* (edited by Naomi Lewis), E. Hulton, 1959; *What Is Pink? A Poem* (illustrated by Margaret A. Soucheck), Holt, 1963 [another edition illustrated by Jose Aruego, Macmillan, 1971]; *Doves and Pomegranates: Poems for Young Readers* (edited by David Powell; illustrated by Margery Gill), Bodley Head, 1969, Macmillan, 1971; *A Choice of Christina Rossetti's Verse* (edited by Elizabeth Jennings), Faber, 1970; *Selected Poems of Christina Rossetti* (edited by Marya Zaturenska), Macmillan, 1970; *The Poetical Works of Christina Georgina Rossetti*, Adler's Foreign Books, 1972.

Contributor, under pseudonym, Ellen Alleyn, to *The Germ*, a Pre-Raphaelite magavine founded by her brother, Dante Gabriel Rossetti.

SIDELIGHTS: **December 5, 1830.** Born in London, England; one of four children—sister, Maria and brothers, Dante Gabriel, and William. One of Rossetti's early poems reflected on her childhood.

"Sing; that in thy song I may
　Dream myself once more a child
In the green woods far away,
　Plucking clematis and wild
Hyacinths, till pleasure grew
Tired, yet so was pleasure too,
Resting with no work to do.

"In the thickest of the wood
　I remember long ago
How a stately oaktree stood
　With a sluggish pool below
Almost shadowed out of sight;
On the waters dark as night
Water-lilies lay like light.

"There, while yet a child, I thought
　I could live as in a dream;
Secret, neither found nor sought;
　Till the lilies on the stream,
Pure as virgin purity,
Would seem scarce too pure for me:—
Ah but that can never be!

"I yet am well content in my shady crevice: which crevice enjoys the unique advantage of being to my certain knowl-

**Christina Rossetti and her mother.
Photo taken by Lewis Carroll.**

edge the place assigned me. And in my small way I have my small interests and small pleasures. . . .'' [Marya Zaturenska, *Christina Rossetti: A Portrait with Background*, Macmillan, 1949.[1]]

1842. Earliest known verse, ''To My Mother on Her Birthday.''

Among her great childhood pleasures were visits to the cottage of her grandfather Gaetano Polidori at Holmer Green in Buckinghamshire. ''So in these grounds, perhaps in the orchard, I lighted upon a dead mouse. The dead mouse moved my sympathy; I took him up, buried him comfortably in a mossy bed, and bore the spot in mind.

''It may have been a day or two afterwards that I returned, removed the moss coverlet, and looked . . . a black insect emerged. I fled in horror, and for long years ensuing I never mentioned this ghastly adventure to anyone.'' [Mackenzie Bell, *Christina Rossetti: A Biographical and Critical Study*, Roberts Brothers, 1898.[2]]

But this episode sank deep in her mind and made a melancholy music in her verse. ''The mystery of life, the mystery of death I see,''[1] she wrote in after years; and no poet has sought with keener, more desperate will to pierce these secrets.

Her journal notes on an encounter in the same garden, where frightened by a frog, she jumped, and so startled a second frog: ''Is it quite certain that no day will ever come, when even the smallest, weakest, most grotesque, *wronged* crea-

Seldom "can't,"
   Seldom "don't";
Never "shan't,"
   Never "won't."
■ (From *Sing-Song* by Christina Rossetti. Illustrated by Arthur Hughes. Engraved by the Brothers Dalziel.)

ture will not in some fashion rise up in the Judgment with us to condemn us, and so frighten us effectually once for all?''[2]

Educated at home, in constant association with her brothers and sister. ''My dear sister used to say that *she* had the good sense, William the good nature, Gabriel the good heart, and I the bad temper of our much-loved father and mother.''[2]

Rossetti was early acquainted with Shakespeare and Sir Walter Scott—nonetheless, her brother William said: ''As compared with the rest of the family, she read very little, and only what hit her fancy. . . . From 9 to 14 one of her most constant companions was Metastasio, the operatic poet.''[2]

1847. Privately printed collection of early poems from the press of grandfather Polidori who wrote the introduction:

''A Few Words to the Reader

''The Authoress of these pages was born in 1830, and her first composition, that on her mother's birthday, was written in 1842. These verses have therefore been composed from the age of twelve to sixteen.

''As her maternal grandfather, I may be excused for desiring to retain these early spontaneous efforts in a permanent form, and for having silenced the objections urged by her modest diffidence, and persuaded her to allow me to print them for my own gratification, at my own private press; and

My baby has a mottled fist,
   My baby has a neck in creases;
My baby kisses and is kissed,
   For he's the very thing for kisses.
■ (From *Sing-Song* by Christina Rossetti. Illustrated by Arthur Hughes. Engraved by the Brothers Dalziel.)

"THAT·WITH·THE· POOR·&·STRICKEN· SHE·MIGHT ∘∘∘ MAKE·A·HOME·

(From *Poems* by Christina Rossetti. Illustrated by Florence Harrison.)

"Remember me when no more day by day
   You tell me of our future that you planned;
   Only remember me; you understand
It will be late to counsel then, or pray.
Yet if you should forget me for a while
   And afterwards remember, do not grieve;
   For if the darkness and corruption leave
   A vestige of the thoughts that once I had,
Better by far you should forget and smile
   Than that you should remember and be sad.''

[Dorothy Margaret Stuart, *Christina Rossetti*, Macmillan and Co., 1930.[4]]

Broke off engagement for religious reasons.

1850. Seven poems published in *The Germ*, a literary magazine of the Pre-Raphaelite Brotherhood under the *nom-de-plume* Ellen Alleyn.

Since the brief flush of praise when her poems were published in *The Germ*, praise had become rare . . . a letter written about this time to the editor of the *Athenaeum* makes that clear. "I am not unaware, Sir, that the editor of a magazine looks with dread and contempt upon the offerings of a nameless rhymester and that the feeling is in 19 cases out of 20, a just and salutary one. It certainly is not for me to affirm,

though I am ready to acknowledge that the well-known partial affection of a grandparent may perhaps lead me to overrate the merit of her youthful strains, I am still confident that the lovers of poetry will not wholly attribute my judgment to partiality." [Eleanor Water Thomas, *Christina Georgina Rossetti*, Columbia University Press, 1931.[3]]

December, 1847 or **January, 1848.** William Bell Scott related his first meeting with Rossetti. "By the window was as a high narrow reading-desk, at which stood writing a slight girl, with a serious regular profile, dark against the pallid wintry light without. This most interesting to me of the two inmates turned on my entrance, made the most formal and graceful curtsey, and resumed her writing, and the old gentleman signed to a chair for my sitting down."[2]

October 14, 1848. *The Last Hope* (afterwards called *Hearts' Chill Between*) published in the *Athenaeum*. *Death's Chill Between* appeared a week later.

1849. Engaged to James Collinson.

"Remember me when I am gone away,
   Gone far away into the silent land,
   When you can no more hold me by the hand
Nor I half turn to go, yet turning stay;

...They all came clustering like a swarm of wasps round astonished Maggie. ■ (From *Speaking Likenesses* by Christina Rossetti. Illustrated by Arthur Hughes. Engraved by the Brothers Dalziel.)

that I am the one twentieth in question, but speaking as I am to a poet, in hope I shall not be misunderstood as guilty of egotism or foolish vanity when I say that my love for what is good in the works of others, teaches me that there is something not despicable in mine; that poetry is with me not a mechanism, but an impulse and reality, and that I know my aims in writing to be pure and directed to what is true and right."[1]

1851. Taught in a day school started by her mother to help support the family. Rossetti in ill-health was a chronic sufferer from bronchial and pulmonary trouble and believed herself to be dying of consumption. "I am not very robust, nor do I expect to become so; but I am well content with the privileges and immunities which attach to semi-invalidism." [Stanley Weintraub, *Four Rossettis: A Victorian Biography*, Weybright & Talley, 1977.[5]]

April 28, 1853. Grandmother died. "Thank God indeed that dear Grandmamma died without pain. . . . I am very glad she mentioned me, but hardly hope she understood my love. I have managed to put on nothing contrary to mourning today, and shall be glad to have the proper things, . . ." [William Michael Rossetti, editor, *The Family Letters of Christina Georgina Rossetti*, Haskell House, 1968.[6]]

1854. Father died.

(From *Goblin Market, and Other Poems* by Christina Rossetti. Illustrated by Dante Gabriel Rossetti.)

> **...Grunting and snarling.**
> **One called her proud,**
> **Cross-grained, uncivil;**
> **Their tones waxed loud,**
> **Their looks were evil.**
> ■ (From *Goblin Market* by Christina Rossetti. Illustrated by Arthur Rackham.)

1859. Wrote *Goblin Market and Other Poems* (published in 1862; illustrated by Dante Gabriel). Rossetti's publisher, Macmillan, wrote: "I took the liberty of reading *Goblin Market* aloud to a number of people belonging to a small working-men's society here (Cambridge). They seemed at first to wonder whether I was making fun of them; by degrees they got as still as death, and when I finished there was a tremendous burst of applause. I wish Miss Rossetti could have heard it."[3]

1861. Traveled to France accompanied by mother and brother, William Michael.

1862-1866. Fell in love with Charles Bagot Cayley, a scholar, author and linguist. Rossetti once again declined a proposal of marriage based on some religious ground, apparently that he was not a Christian of an orthodox type.

Rossetti offered her own concept of love: "If we analyze love, what is it we love in our beloved? Something that is lovable, . . . something that kindles admiration, attracts

**"...I wish you were a pleasant wren
And I your small accepted mate."**

■ (From *Poems* by Christina Rossetti. Illustrated by Florence Harrison.)

fondness, wins confidence, nourishes hope, engrosses affection. If love arises from a mere misreading of appearances, then deeper insight may suffice to annul it. But if it arises from a genuine, though alas! transitory cause, then a transference of the endearing grace to another might seem the remedy. On earth the hollow semblance or the temporary endowment is believed in and preferred; in heaven the perpetual reality. Crown and love together are transferred from Vashti to Esther; the satisfied heart accepts Jacob as 'very' Esau.''[1]

1871. At the request of her brothers and the editor, Rossetti had sent a poem sometime in 1871 to the *University Magazine,* a lively new literary paper that contained the most "advanced" names of the period. When she looked over the *University* magazine a hasty and courteous note went off at once to the editor:

"Dear Sir

"Your letter puts me in an embarrassment, not from any defect in it but (let me hope) from a misapprehension on my own part.

"No. 1 of your new series is the only no. of the *University Magazine* which I have seen, therefore my impression is based upon *it* alone. Allow me to speak from that impression, to express my apprehension that my one—no. [*sic*] colleagues are of a school of thought antagonistic to my own. If so, I am sure you will kindly set me free from my quasi-engagement to write on demand for the Magazine: for I never could be at my ease or happy in literary company with persons who look down upon what I look up to. I have not *played* at Xtianity, and therefore I cannot play at unbelief.

"Yet if I am making a mistake in my judgement it will require no slight forgiveness on your part to forgive me: may I ask so much?''[1]

1872. *Sing-Song,* a cycle of child poems, published. Acclaimed by *Athenaeum* review as the sweetest verse of the time.

"My baby has a mottled fist,
    My baby has a neck in creases,
My baby kisses and is kissed,
    For he's the very thing for kisses.''[4]

1882. Dante Gabriel died.

1883. Cayley died.

1885. *Time Flies,* a book of both poetry and prose, published. "Faith discerns, embraces; Hope anticipates, aspires; Fear curbs, spurns; Love curbs, spurns, anticipates, aspires, discerns, embraces, cleaves into, unites. Love is the panoply of graces.''[4]

Her brother, William wrote: "Christina's habits of composition were eminently of a spontaneous kind. I question whether she ever once deliberated with herself whether or not she would write something or other, and then, having thought out a subject, proceeded to treat it in regular spells of work. Instead of this, something impelled her feelings, or 'came into her head,' and her hand obeyed the dictation.''[2]

1886. Mother died.

1891. Developed cancer for which she was operated the following year. The malignancy, however, returned.

A friend, Grace Gilchrist, wrote of Christina Rossetti's work, life and personality: "My first recollection of Christina Rossetti hovers in the sunny dreamland of earliest childhood, and in this, it may be, the ethereal grace of her rare poet's nature finds its most appropriate setting. For then it is that I have a vivid impression of playing a game of ball with her one summer afternoon upon a sloping lawn, under the branches of an old apple tree in the garden of a tiny hamlet among the Surrey hills. It was in the June of 1863 that Miss Christina Rossetti came upon her first memorable visit to my home there; she was then a dark-eyed, slender lady, in the plenitude of her poetic powers, having already written some of her most perfect poems—*Goblin Market* and *Dream Land.*

"To my child's eyes she appeared like some fairy princess who had come from the sunny south to play with me. In appearance she was Italian, with olive complexion and deep hazel eyes. She possessed, too, the beautiful Italian voice all the Rossettis were gifted with—a voice made up of strange, sweet inflexions, which rippled into silvery modulations in sustained conversation, making ordinary English words and phrases fall upon the ear with a soft, foreign, musical intonation, though she pronounced the words themselves with the purest of English accents. Most of all I used to wonder at and admire the way in which she would take up, and hold in the hollow of her hand, cold little frogs and clammy toads, or furry many-legged caterpillars, with a fearless love that we country children could never emulate. Even to the individual whisk of one squirrel's tail from another's, or the furtive scuttle of a rabbit across a field or common, nothing escaped her nature-loving ken; yet her excursions into the country were as angels' visits, 'few and far between'; but when there, how much she noted of flower and tree, beast and bird!

"As a quaint instance of her shyness which was wholly charming, I can recall one little incident of her first visit to my mother.

"Upon her arrival she was shown to her room, to prepare for the simple meal of the household. She arrived by an afternoon train, and it must have been a late tea-supper. My mother, finding after the lapse of some time that she did not appear in the drawing-room circle, went upstairs in search of her, and, tapping at her door, found Miss Rossetti ready, but waiting, in some trepidation, too shy to venture down alone, or to be formally announced by the servant, into the expectant group in the drawing-room." [2]

December 29, 1894. Died at 30 Torrington Square. "Let us look up to heaven full of mansions rather than down to earth full of graves." [2]

"The day of judgment when we must all stand face to face not only with our Judge, but equally with each other. . . . It is no light offence to traduce the dead, to blacken recklessly their memory, to cultivate no tenderness for them, helpless and inoffensive as they now lie, with all their sins of omission or commission on their heads, . . . to court and blaze abroad every title of evidence which tells against them, to turn a dull ear, and lukewarm heart, to everything which tells in their favor. . . . Charity rejoiceth not in iniquity, but rejoiceth in the truth." [1]

Christina Rossetti, 1877. Drawing by her brother, Dante.

FOR MORE INFORMATION SEE: Ellen A. Proctor, *A Brief Memoir of Christina G. Rossetti*, S.P.C.K., 1895, reprinted, Folcroft, 1972; Mackenzie Bell, *Christina Rossetti: A Biographical and Critical Study*, Roberts Brothers, 1898, reprinted, Scholarly Press, 1976; William Michael Rossetti, editor, *Family Letters of Christina Georgina Rossetti*, Scribner, 1908, reprinted, Folcroft, 1973; Dorothy M. Stuart, *Christina Rossetti*, Macmillan, 1930, reprinted, Folcroft, 1974; Edith Birkhead, *Christina Rossetti and Her Poetry*, G. G. Harrap, 1930, reprinted, AMS Press, 1972; Freregond Shove, *Christina Rossetti: A Study*, Cambridge University Press, 1931, reprinted, Octagon Press, 1969; Frank L. Lucas, *Ten Victorian Poets*, Macmillan, 1948; Chauncey B. Tinker, *Essays in Retrospect*, Yale University Press, 1948; Marya Zaturenska, *Christina Rossetti: A Portrait with Background*, Macmillan, 1949.

Helen S. N. K. Cournos and John Cournos, *Famous British Poets*, Dodd, Mead, 1952; Margaret Sawtell, *Christina Rossetti: Her Life and Religion*, Mowbray, 1955, reprinted, Folcroft, 1974; Edith Deen, *Great Women of the Christian Faith*, Harper, 1959; Louis Untermeyer, *Lives of the Poets*, Simon & Schuster, 1959; Lona M. Packer, *Christina Rossetti*, University of California Press, 1963; Margaret B. Cropper, *Shining Lights*, Darton, 1963; Laura Benét, *Famous Poets for Young People*, Dodd, Mead, 1964; Georgina Battiscombe, *Christina Rossetti*, Longmans, Green, 1965; Sister Mary Joan, "Christina Rossetti: Victorian Child's Poet," *Elementary English*, January, 1967; Rebecca W. Crump, *Christina Rossetti: A Reference Guide*, G. K. Hall, 1976; Ralph A. Bellas, *Christina Rossetti*, Twayne, 1977.

Balthazar Paz built his whitewashed cottage in Spain and in France. The kitchen stove was in Spain, and the table was in France...When Balthazar Paz's wife, Thérèse, gave birth, he fitted wagon wheels to their bed, so the midwife could wheel her out of France and into Spain and out of Spain and into France. ■ (From *Paz* by Cheli Durán Ryan. Illustrated by Nonny Hogrogian.)

RYAN, Cheli Durán

PERSONAL: Born in New York City. *Education:* Has studied at the University of Barcelona; graduated from Trinity College, Dublin.

CAREER: Editor, writer. This author of children's books has also been employed as an editor of children's books by a New York publishing firm. Has translated Spanish poetry. *Awards, honors:* A finalist for the National Book Award in the Children's Book Category and an honor book for the Randolph J. Caldecott Medal, *Hildilid's Night* was also included in the Children's Book Showcase and the American Institute of Graphic Arts Children's Book Show, all in 1972.

WRITINGS: Hildilid's Night (ALA Notable Book; illustrated by Arnold Lobel), Macmillan, 1971, reissued, 1974; *Paz* (illustrated by Nonny Hogrogian), Macmillan, 1971; (editor and translator) *The Yellow Canary Whose Eye Is So Black* (poems), Macmillan, 1977.

SIDELIGHTS: Hildilid's Night has received several honors and a great deal of favorable attention from the critics. Much of its appeal stems from the fact that, as stated by *Library Journal,* "youngsters who are leery of the dark will sympathize with Hildilid." In addition to the empathy it inspires, the *New York Times Book Review* claims that *Hildilid's Night* will enchant readers because it is "a curious, furious tale told in rich considered language that begs to be read aloud."

FOR MORE INFORMATION SEE: New York Times Book Review, November 7, 1971; *Horn Book,* December, 1971; *Library Journal,* January 15, 1972; *Christian Science Monitor,* May 1, 1974; Margaret E. Ward and Dorothy A. Marquardt, editors, *Authors of Books for Young People,* 2nd edition supplement, Scarecrow, 1979.

SAINT EXUPÉRY, Antoine de 1900-1944

PERSONAL: Born June 29, 1900, in Lyons, France; reported "missing in action," July 31, 1944, in Southern France; son of Cesar de Saint Exupéry; married wife, Consuelo, the former Countess Manuelo. *Education:* Attended the College de Fribourg, Switzerland.

CAREER: Novelist and essayist. Commercial air pilot from 1926 until the beginning of World War II. *Military service:* Served in the French Army Air Force, 1921-26, and during World War II. *Awards, honors*—Military: Received a citation and the Croix de Guerre for his courage on reconnaissance flights during the Battle of France, May 1940; Other: Prix Femina-Vie Heureuse, 1931; Grand Prize of the French Academy, 1939.

WRITINGS—Novels: *Courrier Sud,* Gallimard, 1929, translation by Stuart Gilbert published as *Southern Mail* (illustrated by Lynd Ward), H. S. Smith & R. Haas, 1933 [another translation by Curtis Cate, Harcourt, 1972]; *Vol de Nuit,* Gallimard, 1931, translation by S. Gilbert published as *Night Flight* (with a preface by Andre Gide), Century, 1932, reprinted, Harcourt, 1974.

Essays: *Terre des Hommes,* Gallimard, 1939, translation by Lewis Galantiere published as *Wind, Sand, and Stars,* Reynal & Hitchcock, 1939, reissued, Heinemann, 1970 [another edition illustrated by John Cosgrave, II, Harcourt, 1949, reissued, 1968]; *Pilote de Guerre,* Gallimard, 1942, translation by L. Galantiere published as *Flight to Arras* (illustrated by Bernard Lamotte), Reynal & Hitchcock, 1942, reissued, Harcourt, 1969; *Lettre à un Otage,* Brentano's, 1943, translation by Jacqueline Gerst published as *Letter to a Hostage,* Heinemann, 1950; *Citadelle,* Gallimard, 1948, translation by S. Gilbert published as *The Wisdom of the Sands,* Harcourt, 1950.

For children: *Le Petit Prince* (illustrated by the author), Reynal & Hitchcock, 1943, translation by Katherine Woods published as *The Little Prince,* Harcourt, 1943, reprinted, 1971.

Other: *Airman's Odyssey* (selections), Reynal & Hitchcock, 1943, reissued, Harcourt, 1959; *Oeuvres Completes,* Gallimard, 1950; *Carnets,* Gallimard, 1953; *Lettres de Jeunesse, 1923-1931,* Gallimard, 1953, also published as *Lettres a l'-Amie Inventee,* Plon, 1953; *Lettres à Sa Mere,* Gallimard, 1955; *Un Sens à la Vie,* Gallimard, 1956, translation by Adrienne Foulke published as *A Sense of Life,* Funk & Wagnalls, 1965; *Lettres,* Club du Meilleur Livre, 1960.

ADAPTATIONS—Movies: "Night Flight," Metro-Goldwyn-Mayer, 1933; "The Little Prince," Paramount, 1975 (screenplay and lyrics by Alan Jay Lerner; music by Frederick Loewe).

Recordings: "The Little Prince," read in English by Peter Ustinov, Argo, 1972; "Le Petit Prince," read in French by Gerard Phillipe and Georges Poujouly, Everest, 1973.

Saint Exupéry at Cape Juby.

SIDELIGHTS: **June 29, 1900.** Born in Lyons, France, one of five children—(his full name being Antoine Marie Reger de Saint-Exupéry). "Nightfall would find us [children] dreaming in the vestibule. We were waiting for the passage of the lamps: they were carried like clumps of flowers and each moved beautiful shadows across the walls like palms. Then the mirage wheeled and the bouquet of light and dark palms was locked into the drawing-room. For us the day was now over and in our children's beds we were launched towards another day.

"Mama, you would lean over us, over this flight of angels, and so that the journey might be peaceful, so that nothing would disturb our dreams, you would smooth the sheet of this rumple, this shadow, this wave.... For a bed is smoothed as a divine finger smoothes the sea." [Curtis Cate, *Antoine de Saint-Exupéry,* Putnam, 1970.[1]]

"When I was a child, my sisters had a way of giving marks to guests who were honoring our table for the first time. Conversation might languish for a moment, and then in the silence we would hear the sudden impact of 'Sixty!'—a word that could tickle only the family, who knew that one hundred was par. Branded by this low mark, the guest would all unknowing continue to spend himself in little courtesies while we sat inwardly screaming with delight." [Marcel Migeo, *Saint-Exupéry,* translated from the French by Herma Briffault, McGraw-Hill, 1960.[2]]

1904. His father, Cesar de Saint-Exupéry, died, leaving his family in tight financial straits. Through the kindness of his maternal grandmother, Saint-Exupéry spent half his years at the Château de la Môle, in the Var. He loved this sunlit region of France—"the only corner of the world, apart from Greece, where even the dust has a fragrance." [Richard Rumbold and Lady Margaret Stewart, *The Winged Life: A Portrait of Antoine de Saint-Exupéry, Poet and Airman,* David McKay Co., 1955.[3]]

He recalled the stately cupboards of his house. "They opened to display heaps of frozen stores, piles of linen as white as snow. And the old housekeeper trotted like a rat from one cupboard to the next, forever counting, folding, unfolding, re-counting the white linen; exclaiming, 'Oh, good Heavens, how terrible!' at each sign of wear which threatened the eternity of the house; running instantly to burn out her eyes under a lamp so that the woof of these altar clothes should be repaired, these three-master's sails be mended, in the service of something greater than herself—a god, a ship."[3]

He and his sisters "would take refuge among the attic's beams. Enormous beams defending the house against God knows what. But yes, against time. For there was the enemy. We kept it at bay with traditions and the cult of the past. But only we, among those enormous beams, knew that this house was launched like a ship. Only we, visiting the holds, and the bulwarks, knew just where she was leaking.

(From the movie "The Little Prince," starring Stephen Warner and Gene Wilder. Copyright © 1974 by Stanley Donen Films, Inc. and Paramount Pictures Corp.)

We knew by which holes the birds crept in to die. We knew each crack in the timbering. Down below the guests conversed and the pretty ladies danced. What a deceptive security! No doubt liqueurs were being passed around. By black-clad waiters with white gloves. While we, up above, watched the blue night pour in through the cracks in the rooftop and saw a star, just one lonely star, drop on us through a tiny hole."[1]

Autumn, 1909. His mother, Marie Boyer de Fonsconlombe, left their home at Saint Maurice de Rémens and moved with her five children to Le Mans. There Saint-Exupéry was sent to Notre-Dame de Sainte-Croix, a Jesuit school. "And when the moon rose, [mother] would take our hands and tell us to listen, for those were the sounds of the earth and they were reassuring and they were good. You were so well sheltered by this house, with its sweeping robe of earth. You had concluded so many pacts with the lindens and the oaks and the flocks that we called you their princess. Gradually your face softened as the world was laid to rest for the night. 'The farmer has brought in his beasts.' You knew it from the distant lights of the stables. A hollow sound—'they're closing the sluices.' All was in order. Finally the seven o'clock express stormed through the twilight and disappeared, cleaning your world of all that is anxious and mobile and uncertain—like a face at the window of a sleeping-car. And dinner followed in a dining room that was too large and ill-lit and where—for we were watching you like spies—you became the Queen of Night.

"[My mother was] the only consolation when [I was] sad. When I was a child I used to come home with my heavy satchel on my back, in tears at being punished . . . and simply by taking me in [her] arms and kissing me [she] made me forget everything."[1]

1909-1914. Since many vacations were spent at Amberieu near Bugey and a large aviation field, he longed, from an early age, to become an aviator.

Summer, 1912. Given his first airplane ride by Jules Védrines, a popular aviator of the time. The airfield was not far from his home in Saint Maurice de Rémens. "I've been up in an aeroplane. You can't imagine what it's like. *C'est formidable!*

"I adore this profession. You can't imagine the calm, the solitude one finds at twelve thousand feet in a *tête-á-tête* with one's motor. And then the charming camraderie down below, on the field. You cat-nap on the grass, waiting for your turn. You follow your friend's gyrations with your eyes, waiting for your turn to go up in the same plane, and you swap stories. They're all marvellous. Stories of engine failures in mid-country close to unknown little villages where a flustered and patriotic mayor invites the airmen to dinner . . . and fairy tale adventures. . . ."[1]

1914. Sent to Collége de Fribourg in Switzerland.

1917. Admitted to Naval School. "Paris is, I've come to the conclusion, a less pernicious city than many provincial dumps, in the sense that certain of my fellow students who were really sowing their wild oats in their home towns have grown relatively sedate here because of the danger to one's health of playing around in Paris."[1]

1919. Failed the final examination at Naval School—probably intentionally.

1921. Joined the French Army Air Force. "This evening, by the peaceful light of a lamp, I learned to steer by compass. The maps spread out before him on the table, Sergeant Boileau explains: '. . . When you get this far' (and our studious foreheads bend over the crisscrossing lines) 'you veer 45° west. . . . There, you see, a village—leave it well to your left, and don't forget to correct the wind drift with the movable needle of your compass. . . .' I begin to dream. He wakes me. 'Pay more attention . . . now 180° west, unless you'd rather cut across here . . . but there are fewer landmarks to go by . . . the road here, you see, is easy to follow.'

"Sergeant Boileau offers me some tea. I drink the cup in tiny sips. If I lose my way, I think, I'll land in rebel territory. How often have I been told: 'If you climb out of your tin-trap and find yourself in front of a woman and kiss her on the breast, from then on you're sacred. She'll treat you like a mother, they'll give you oxen, a camel, and they'll marry you off. It's the only way of saving your life.'

"My trip is still too simple for me to hope for such surprises. Still, this evening I am full of dreams. . . ."[1]

"I fly because it releases my mind from the tyranny of petty things; it gives me a sense of the wider horizons."[3]

1923. Worked in a tile factory and, later, as a truck mechanic. "I have lived eight years of my life, day and night, with working-men. I have found myself sharing their ta-

On the morning of his departure he put his planet in perfect order. He carefully cleaned out his active volcanoes. ■ (From *The Little Prince* by Antoine de Saint Exupéry. Illustrated by the author.)

ble. . . . I know very well what I am talking about when I speak of working-class people, and I love them."[3]

"What is obscure is more tempting than what is clear. Between two explanations of a phenomenon people will instinctively go for the occult. Because the other, the true one, is dull and simple and doesn't make one's hair stand on end. A paradox is more tempting than a veritable explanation and people prefer it. Men of the world use science, art, philosophy as they use sluts. . . . Society people say: 'We have stirred up a few ideas' . . . and they disgust me. I like people whose need to eat, feed their children, and finish out the month have bound more closely to life. They know more about it."[1]

1926. Became a commercial pilot on the Toulouse, France-Dakar, West Africa run. ". . . I was enrolled as student airline pilot by the Latécoère Company, the predecessors of Aéropostale (now Air France) in the operation of the line between Toulouse, in southwestern France, and Dakar, in French West Africa. I was learning the craft, undergoing an apprenticeship served by all young pilots before they were allowed to carry the mails. We took ships up on trial spins, made meek little hops between Toulouse and Perpignan, and had dreary lessons in meterology in a freezing hangar. We lived in fear of the mountains of Spain, over which we had yet to fly, and in awe of our elders." [Antoine de Saint-Exupéry, *Airman's Odyssey*, Reynal & Hitchcock, 1942.[4]]

"We flew open ships, thrusting our heads round the windshield to take our bearings: the wind that whistled in our ears was a long time clearing out of our heads. Nor could a pilot trust the engines of these ancient biplanes . . . which would suddenly cut out in mid-air, or even occasionally drop out without warning with a great rattle like the crash of crockery.''[3]

"When you are flying the mail from Dakar to Casablanca, around two in the morning, you inch the black nose of your plane into a cluster of stars—I don't know their names, but they ride a bit to the right of the cusp of the Big Dipper. As they mount the curve of the sky, you exchange them for others, choose a new guidepost, so that you need not crane your neck. The night washes the visible world clear of all but the stars that reign over the black sands of the desert, and little by little it also cleanses your heart. The trivial worries that had seemed so urgent, the anger, the clouded desires and the jealousies are erased, and the real anxieties emerge. Then, as you slowly descend the stairway of the stars toward the dawn, you feel purged." [Antoine de Saint Exupéry, *A Sense of Life*, Funk & Wagnalls, 1965.[5]]

1927. Grounded as the commander of the airport at Juby in Rio de Oro on the treacherous West African coast. "I don't know when I shall be back [in Paris]; I have had so much to do for several months, searching for lost airmen, salvage of planes that have come down in hostile territory, and some flights with the Dakar mail. I have just pulled off a little exploit; spent two days and nights with eleven Moors and a mechanic, recovering a plane. Alarums and excursions, varied and impressive. I heard bullets whizzing over my head for the first time.''[3]

"Our life here is jolly. We live outside a Spanish fort on the beach and can go without fear down to the sea—a distance of less than twenty yards. . . . But if we go farther than that, we risk getting shot at. If we go farther than fifty yards, we risk being sent to rejoin our forefathers or being taken captive—it depends on the time of year. In Spring, if one happens to be attractive, one has the chance of being taken and kept as some chieftain's 'favorite,' which is better than being dead. But there's always the risk of becoming the chieftain's head eunuch instead!''[2]

"Never have I landed or slept so often in the Sahara, nor heard more bullets whine. And yet sometimes I dream of an existence where there is a tablecloth, fruit, walks under the lindens, perhaps a wife, where one greets people amiably instead of shooting at them, where one doesn't lose one's way at 200 kilometres an hour in the mist. . . .''[1]

1928. Wrote his first novel, *Courrier Sud* ("Southern Mail"), in which a wildly romantic French aristocrat copes with the realities of life and an unhappy love affair through the discipline of flying. "I have begun a novel. You are going to be amused. I've already done a hundred pages, but am doubtful about them. I'm always running up against the abstract in myself. I have an appalling tendency towards the abstract. It comes perhaps from my eternal loneliness. . . .''[3]

"I still believe in men to whom the airplane means more than a collection of parameters, for whom it is an organism whose breathing and heartbeat they listen to. They bring the plane down. They walk quietly around it. With the tip of their fingers, they stroke the fuselage, tap a wing. They are not calculating; they are meditating. Then they turn to the mechanic and say simply, 'There you are. . . . Stabilizer needs to be shortened a bit.'

"I admire Science, of course. But I also admire Wisdom.''[5]

1929. Won Legion of Honor Award for his work of patient reconciliation amongst the Spaniards and Moors at Juby.

October, 1929. Assigned to establish an air-mail route in South America from Brazil to Patagonia. "In my mind's eye I can still see the first night flight I made in Argentina. It was pitch-dark. Yet in the black void, I could see the lights of man shining down below on the plain, like faintly luminous earthbound stars. Each star was a beacon signaling the presence of a human mind. Here a man was meditating on human happiness, perhaps, or on justice or peace. Lost among this flock of stars was the star of some solitary shepherd. There, perhaps, a man was in communication with the heavens, as he labored over his calculations of the nebula of Andromeda. And there, a pair of lovers. These fires were burning all over the countryside, and each of them, even the most humble, had to be fed. The fire of the poet, of the teacher, of the carpenter. But among all these living fires, how many closed windows there were, how many dead stars, fires that gave off no light for lack of nourishment.''[5]

"I'm waiting to meet some young girl who is pretty and intelligent and full of charm and gaiety and relaxing and faithful . . . and so I shall not find her. And I go on monotonously courting the Colettes, the Paulettes, the Suzys, the Daisys, the Gabys who are all mass produced and bore the life out of one after a couple of hours. They're waiting-rooms, no more.''[1]

1931. Married Consuelo Gomez Carrillo. "I believe one should always be a little uneasy. . . . And for that reason I fear marriage. But of course it depends upon the wife.''[2]

Wrote his second novel, *Vol de nuit* ("Night flight"), which contrasted the rigors of night flying with the safety of marriage and domesticity. ". . . Those who . . . spend their lives glued to their lace-curtain windows. With the same eternal decoration adorning the mantlepiece in their rooms. Their lives are composed of habits. A prison. I have such a fear of habits. . . .''[1]

"Two people whom I know dropped over to see me: a confident young married couple whose domestic life, though doubtless a happy one, seemed to me terribly sour. You know the peevishness of people who enjoy too much security. The meaningless outbursts of spite, in the midst of all their contentment. I liked them very much, yet when they went off I breathed again; there is a certain lulling kind of peace which is hateful to me.''[3]

"Because I wrote that wretched book [*Night Flight*] I have been made to suffer. My comrades have ostracized me. Mermoz will tell you what things have been said about me by those whom I have not seen for ages but whom I was once fond of. They will tell you that I am pretentious! And there's not a soul from Toulouse to Dakar who doesn't believe it.''[2]

December 4, 1931. Received the Prix Femina-Vie Heureuse for *Vol de nuit*. "One mustn't learn to write but to see. Writing is a consequence. When the vision is absent the epithets applied are like layers of paint: they add arbitrary ornaments but they don't bring out what is essential. . . . One must ask oneself: 'How am I going to render the impression?' And the objects come to life through the reaction they evoke in us, they are described in depth. . . .''[1]

(From the half-hour television special "Night Fever," starring Trevor Howard and Bo Svenson. Presented by the Singer Company. Photo courtesy of Mr. Warren Lipton.)

1933. Tested sea planes at Perpignan after a long period of abject poverty while living in Paris. "One of my gravest worries has been my debts, and I haven't always been able to pay my gas bills, and I am still wearing the old clothes I had three years ago.

"I have just returned from the hydroplane base where I have been carrying out trials; my ears are still buzzing and my hands are still smeared with oil. And I am drinking all alone on the terrace of a little café, while it is growing dark but I don't feel like going anywhere for dinner . . . I am here on my own because I go backwards and forwards between Toulouse, Perpignan and Saint Raphaël. I spend most of my time beside a lake which is neither sea nor lake, but a flat, lifeless stretch of water—don't like it at all. . . . And when at nightfall I return to Perpignan, such an evening as this drags out interminably. I don't know anyone here and I don't even want to."[3]

"I trace my little provincial path. I pass to the right of this lamp-post and at the café I sit down in this chair. I buy my paper at the same kiosk and each time I get off the same phrase to the woman vendor. And the same companions . . . until . . . I feel an immense need to escape and to be new."[1]

May, 1935. Became a foreign correspondent and covered the May Day celebration in Moscow. "It was a long halt. Very likely other streets had opened like locks into Red Square, so

that these people had to wait. They waited in a glacial cold, for it had snowed again the night before. And all of a sudden a kind of miracle happened.

"The miracle was a return to the human. This unified, solid mass suddenly melted into single human beings. Accordions struck up along the street. Several male choruses with their brass instruments were in the line of march; now they grouped themselves in circles and began to play. Partly to get warm, partly for the fun of it, partly perhaps to celebrate the holiday, people started to dance. Here on the threshold of Red Square, thousands upon thousands of men and women, their faces suddenly unfrozen and smiling, danced in circles. The whole street took on a festive, familial air, like any Paris suburb on a July 14 night.

"A stranger spoke to me, offered me a cigarette. Another man proffered a light. The crowd was in high good spirits. . . .

"Then, up ahead, figures began to eddy about. The chorusers tucked their instruments under their arms, banners were raised, and the lines reformed. A group leader tapped one woman demonstrator lightly on the head with his stick to bring her into line. It was the last individual, personal gesture. People became grave again as they resumed their march toward Red Square. They were reabsorbed into the crowd as one ready to appear before Stalin."[5]

1936. Attempted a long-distance flight from Paris to Africa, but was forced down in the desert and rescued three days later. "A terrific crash rocked our world to its foundations. One second, two seconds passed. The plane quivered, and I waited with a grotesque impatience for the forces within it to burst like a bomb.... Five, six seconds. And we were seized by a spinning motion, a shock which jerked our cigarettes out of the window, pulverised the starboard window—and then nothing, nothing but a frozen immobility. I shouted to Prévot: 'Jump!' And we dived together through the wrecked window and found ourselves standing, side by side, sixty feet from the plane.

"Our prospects were by no means cheerful. Our reserves of water had been destroyed and we had no idea of our position within about two hundred miles. We set out at once, having indicated our plans, in letters thirty feet high, on the ground. We had just over a pint of coffee and we had to reach help before thirst overtook us.

"That day we covered roughly forty miles, including the trudge back to the aircraft. About twenty miles away, from the top of a ridge, we were unable to sight anything, except mirages which dissolved at our approach. We thought it best to return in the hope that an aircraft might have spotted us. That day we finished our last dregs of coffee.

"At dawn on the second day we collected about half a pint of dew from the wings and the fuselage, but it was mixed with paint and oil and was not a great deal of help to us.

"I decided on another plan and left Prévot behind with the plane. His job was to prepare and light fires (with magnesium flares which give a beautiful white light, and not with non-existent vegetation, as we had been told to do), to serve as a beacon for searching aircraft. Meanwhile I set off alone, still without water, on further explorations.

"That day I walked for about eight to nine hours at a brisk pace, and it was the more exhausting inasmuch as, even when the ground was hard, I had to mark my tracks for the return. Darkness overtook me before I got back, but the fires which Prévot had lighted helped me during the last few miles.

"Up till now, no aircraft had flown over us, and so we decided that we must be outside the range of help. Also, we were beginning to feel dreadfully the lack of water. We resolved to leave at dawn, abandoning the machine, and to go on walking until we collapsed altogether. It seemed useless to return again to the aircraft since no one was looking for us here. I remembered how Guillaumet was saved in this way in the Andes, and I decided to follow his example.

"That night we counted upon collecting a little dew on a parachute which we spread on the ground. Unfortunately, we were made to pay dearly for the first mouthful of water, vomiting bile most violently for half an hour afterwards; it may have been due to the coating on the parachute, or to the fact that there were deposits of salt at the bottom of the reserve tank of petrol, in which we had previously wrung out our clothes.

"We left, consequently, an hour late, still convulsed by nausea, and not thinking we should get very far. We had decided to go north-east, simply because we had not yet been in that direction, but we did not have much hope of that either.

"Next morning we were so exhausted that we could only advance about two hundred yards at a time, and then we came upon a track in the desert, and there we were picked up."[3]

That same year Saint-Exupéry covered the outbreak of the Spanish Civil War. "The morning the revolt started, armed with nothing but knives, they charged a combination of artillerymen and machine gunners. They captured the artillery. Then they seized the supplies of guns and ammunition in the barracks and proceeded, naturally enough, to turn the city into a small fortress.

"They control the city's water, gas, electricity, and transportation. On my morning walk, I see them busily putting the finishing touches to their barricades. You find all kinds, from simple walls of paving stones to double-ringed ramparts.

"I glanced over one wall. There they were. They had dragged furniture belonging to some board of directors from the building next door, and comfortably ensconced in red leather chairs, were preparing for their civil war.

"I am quite convinced of the sincerity of people who say: 'Terror in Barcelona? Nonsense. That great city in ashes? A mere twenty houses wrecked. Streets heaped with the dead? A few hundred killed out of a population of a million. Where did you see a firing line running with blood and deafening with the roar of guns?'

"I agree that I saw no firing line. I saw groups of tranquil men and women strolling on the avenue. When, on occasion, I ran against a barricade of militiamen in arms, a smile was often enough to open the way before me. I did not come at once upon the firing line. In a civil war the firing line is invisible; it passes through the hearts of men."[5]

"... No, it is not death that makes me shudder. It seems almost sweet to me when it is linked to life; and I like to think that in a cloister a death is celebrated like a feast day.... But this monstrous forgetfulness of the quality of man, these algebraic justifications, this is what I cannot accept.

"... In Spain the mobs are on the move, but the individual—that solitary universe—cries out in vain for help from the depths of his mine pit."[1]

April, 1937. Covered the siege of Madrid. "Each shell in the air threatened them all. I could feel the city out there, tense, compact, a solid. I saw them all in the mind's eye—men, women, children, all that humble population crouching in the sheltering cloak of stone.... Again I heard the ignoble crash and was gripped and sickened by the downward course of the torpedo.

"This same afternoon I witnessed a bombardment in the town itself. All the force of this thunderclap had to burst on the Gran Via in order to uproot a human life. One single life. Passers-by had brushed rubbish off their clothes; others had scattered on the run; and when the light smoke had risen and cleared away, the betrothed, escaped by miracle without a scratch, found at his feet his *novia*, whose golden arm a moment before had been in his, changed into a blood-filled sponge, changed into a limp packet of flesh and rags.

"I do not care a curse for the rules of war and the law of reprisal. Who was the first to begin? Retort calls forth retort always, and the first murderer among us has slipped away long since into the night of time. . . .

"As for the military advantage of such a bombardment, I simply cannot grasp it. I have seen housewives disemboweled, children mutilated; I have seen the old itinerant market crone sponge from her treasures the brains with which they were spattered. . . .''[5]

1938. Attempted a flight from Canada to South America, but suffered severe injuries when his plane crashed in Guatemala.

1939. Wrote "Terre des Hommes," a personal essay, suggested by Andre Gide, his literary admirer. That same year he won the Grand Prize of the French Academy.

Assigned to a post as flying instructor in Toulouse at the start of World War II. "I implore you with all my strength to persuade Chassin to get me on to fighters. I suffocate more and more. The atmosphere of this place is unbreathable. . . . If I cannot get into action, I shall suffer a moral breakdown. I feel I have got a lot to say about things; and I can only express myself as an active combatant and not as an onlooker. . . . Here they want to make me an instructor, both in navigation and as a pilot on heavy bombers. . . . Save me. You know I have no taste for war, but it is impossible to remain in the background and not to take a share of the risks. . . .

"It is a terrific sophistry to pretend that people should be relegated to a safe spot because they 'have a value.' It is only when one plays a part in things that one becomes truly effective. If those who 'have a value' are the salt of the earth, then let them mingle with the earth; one cannot say 'we' if one cuts oneself off—or, if one does say 'we' in those circumstances, one is a swine!''[3]

Made a captain in the Air Corps Reserve. "Ineffectiveness weighed us all down, all of us in the uniform of France, like a sort of doom. It hung over the infantry that stood with fixed bayonets in the face of German tanks. It lay upon the aircrews that fought one against ten. It afflicted those very men whose job it should have been to see that our guns and controls did not freeze and jam. . . .''[3]

May, 1940. Received Croix de Guerre for his courage on reconnaissance flights during the Battle of France.

Left for the United States and New York City after the fall of France. "True, we were already beaten . . . but I was filled with a sense of my responsibility. And what man can feel himself at the same time responsible and hopeless?''[3]

"I am living on the twenty-fifth floor of a hotel of stone, and I hear through my window the voices of a new city. And that voice has a harrowing sound. . . . It reminds me of the tumult in mid-ocean, the hubbub of a ship in distress. Never before have I felt so strongly this piling up of men in their stone pyramids and making all these sounds of departure, of traffic, of shipwreck, an embarkation of men without a captain, making them know not what voyage between their planet and the stars. . . . All these crowds, these lights, these spires of the buildings seem to state, overwhelmingly, the problem of Destiny. No doubt it's idiotic, but I feel here, more than elsewhere, as if I were on the high seas.''[2]

He was dismayed by the mechanization of American culture. ". . . But no one seems alarmed by this frightful freedom, which is freedom only not to be. Real freedom consists in the creative act. The fisherman is free when his instinct guides

Antoine de Saint Exupéry, as a young man.

his fishing. The sculptor is free when he sculpts a face. But it is nothing but a caricature of freedom to be allowed to choose between four types of General Motors' cars or three of Mr. Z's films . . . or between eleven different drugstore dishes. Freedom is then reduced to the choice of a standard item in a range of a universal similitude.''[1]

1941. Wrote *Flight to Arras,* which gave literary expression to the valiant French resistance. ". . . Our friends in the United States should not get a false picture of France. Some regard Frenchmen as a little like a basket of crabs. This is unjust. Only the controversialists talk. One does not hear those who keep still.''[5]

1942. Wrote *Pilote de Guerre* ("War Pilot"), a testimony to French valor.

1943. Wrote and illustrated *The Little Prince* while living in New York. "Just think, they're now asking me to write a book for children! . . . Accompany me to the stationer's would you? I want to buy some coloured pencils.''[1]

Later, a friend suggested he alter one of the many drawings he created for the book. "Impossible, *mon vieux.* If this were a written text, all right—I would agree to modify it, for after all I'm a writer. That's my job. But I can't do better than this drawing. It's quite simply a miracle. . . .

"We are all part of the same tribe. And this world of children's memories with our language and the games we invented, will always seem to me desperately truer than the other.

"... But the intellect, which takes apart and juxtaposes pieces, when not playfully muddling the arrangement to gain in picturesqueness, loses sight of the essential. When one analyses states, one grasps nothing of man. I am neither old nor young. I am he who is passing from youth to old age. I am something which is being formed. I am a process of ageing. A rose is not something which buds, opens, and fades. That is a pedagogical description, an analysis which kills the rose. A rose is not a series of successive states, a rose is a somewhat melancholy fête ... I am sad because of this strange planet I am living in. Because of all I fail to understand. . . ."[1]

April, 1943. Rejoined his old flying squadron in North Africa. Grounded due to his age, he worked as an instructor. "I tell you all this by way of explaining to you how herdlike our existence is here in the heart of this American air base. We wolf our food, standing, in a matter of minutes; 2600-horse-power planes buzz incessantly overhead; we are boxed into sleeping cubicles, three to a cell—but what really matters is that we live in a frightful human desert. Nothing here lifts the heart. Back in 1940, we flew missions that we knew had no purpose and we ourselves had little hope of getting back; it was a kind of illness that had to be lived through, and so is this. I shall be 'ill' in this sense for an undetermined period of time. I don't see that I have any right to refuse to endure the illness. That's all there is to it. But I am sad, sad to the depths of my being—not for myself but for my generation, which is so miserably impoverished. It is a generation that has known bars, calculating machines, and Bugattis exclusively as the forms of spiritual life, and now it finds itself caught up in herdlike action that has lost all human meaningfulness."[5]

"I've just had a few flights on a P.38. It's a fine machine. I should be happy to have had this as a present at the age of twenty, but I acknowledge with some gloom that today, at the age of 43, after 6,500 hours of flying in all the skies of the world, I can't find very much pleasure in the game. It's a way of getting around—that is all. And if I submit myself to this speed and altitude at a patriarchal age for the job, it's more so as not to escape any of the cares and vexations of my generation than from any hope of finding the satisfactions of the past."[3]

Summer, 1944. Assigned to make lone reconnaissance flights from Italy over Southern France. "You can't imagine what a thrill it is to approach the land of France when one hasn't seen one's country for three years, and to say to oneself: 'I'm overflying my country. I'm mocking the occupying power. I'm seeing things I'm forbidden to see.' My mission required me to hit the coast east of Marseille and to photograph the seaboard all the way to the east of Toulon. But from that height the earth looked naked and dead. . . . Our long-range cameras act like microscopes. I looked down and nothing stirred. Not a sign of life. I was deeply disappointed and overcome by a great melancholy. France is dead, I said to myself, growing more and more melancholic. Suddenly little grey puff-balls began framing my plane. I was being fired upon! France was alive! I was happy."[1]

"Once again I am experiencing the joys of high-altitude flights. They are like a diver's plunges into the depths of the sea: one enters forbidden territory, decked out in barbarous equipment, encased in a framework of dials and instruments and gauges; and high above one's country one breathes oxygen manufactured in the United States. The air of New York in the skies of France—isn't it odd? At the controls of this light, fleet monster, this Lightning P.38, there is no feeling of movement, but, rather, of being fixed and immobile at one and the same moment, over a whole continent.

"The photographs one brings back are submitted to stereoscopic analysis, as organisms are examined under a microscope; the interpreters of these photographs work exactly like the bacteriologists. They seek on the vulnerable body of France traces of the virus which devours her. One can die from the effects of these enemy strongholds and depots and convoys which, under the lens, appear like tiny bacilli.

"And then those hours of poignant meditation as one flies over France—so near and yet so far. One feels separated from her as though by centuries. All one's tender memories and associations, indeed one's very raison-d'être, are to be found there, stretched out, as it were, 35,000 feet below, in the clear glint of the sun; and yet, more inaccessible than the treasures of the Pharaohs under the glass-cases of a museum.

"I am sad for my generation, empty as it is of all human content (de toute substance humaine). One cannot live any longer on refrigerators, on politics, on balance-sheets and cross-word puzzles. One cannot live any longer without poetry, colour and love. My impression is that we are approaching the blackest period in the whole of human history."[3]

"The possibility that I may be killed in this war is not important. It is not important that I fly into a rage over these new airborne torpedos. (It is nonetheless true that they have nothing to do with planes or with flying and that they transform a pilot, all hemmed around by push buttons and dials, into a kind of head bookkeeper. Flying is also a matter of a certain ordering of connections.) But if I do come back alive from the thankless job that must be done, it will be to face only one challenge: What can one, what must one, say to men?"[5]

July 31, 1944. Reported "missing in action." Believed shot down over Southern France.

FOR MORE INFORMATION SEE: Antoine de Saint Exupéry, *Airman's Odyssey,* Reynal & Hitchcock, 1942; E. G. Fay, "Saint Exupery in New York," *Modern Language Notes,* November, 1946; Lewis Galantiere, "Antoine de Saint Exupery," *Atlantic Monthly,* April, 1947; Richard Rumbold and Margaret Vane-Tempest-Stewart, *Winged Life: A Portrait of Antoine de Saint Exupery, Poet and Airman,* McKay, 1955; John Pudney, *Six Great Aviators,* H. Hamilton, 1955; Maxwell A. Smith, *Knight of the Air: The Life and Works of Antoine de Saint Exupery,* Pageant, 1956, revised and enlarged edition, Cassell, 1959; L. Galantiere, "Most Unforgettable Character I've Met," *Reader's Digest,* December, 1957; Marcel Migeo, *Saint Exupery* (translation from the French by Herma Briffault), McGraw, 1960, V. S. Pritchett, "Lost in the Stars," *New Yorker,* March 18, 1961; Antoine de Saint Exupéry, *A Sense of Life,* Funk & Wagnalls, 1965; Andre Maurois, *From Proust to Camus,* Doubleday, 1966; Henri Peyre, *French Novelists Today,* Oxford University Press, 1967; Curtis Cate, *Antoine de Saint Exupery,* Putnam, 1970; Adele Breaus, *Saint Exupery in America, 1942-1943: A Memoir,* Fairleigh Dickinson University Press, 1971.

Saint Exupéry in the cockpit of his "Lightning."

Movie: "Saint Exupery" (20 minutes, sound, black & white; with a user's guide), McGraw-Hill, 1964.

SCHROEDER, Ted 1931(?)-1973

OBITUARY NOTICE: Born about 1931, in Peoria, Ill.; died August 9, 1973, in Ossining, N.Y. Illustrator, publishing company executive. Mr. Schroeder once served as the art director of the Champaign unit of Spencer Press. He became the art director of Garrard Publishing Company in 1962. Ted Schroeder illustrated several books for children including Patricia M. Markun's *First Book of Politics,* Wyatt Blassingame's *Pecos Bill Rides a Tornado,* and Adele DeLeeuw's *Paul Bunyan and His Blue Ox. Obituaries: Publishers Weekly,* October 1, 1973.

SEEGER, Elizabeth 1889-1973

OBITUARY NOTICE: Born about 1889; died November 2, 1973, in Bridgewater, Conn. Teacher, author of books for young people. Elizabeth Seeger taught for a time at the Dalton School of New York. She wrote several books for young readers aimed at acquainting them with the history, philosophy, legend, and ritual of Eastern religions such as Hinduism, Buddhism, Taoism, and Shintoism. Her works include *The Ramayana, The Five Sons of King Pandu, Eastern Religions,* and *Pageant of Chinese History* which received notice as an honor book for the John Newbery Medal in 1935. *Obituaries: Contemporary Authors,* Volume 45-48, Gale, 1974; *Publishers Weekly,* November 26, 1973.

SERVICE, Robert W(illiam) 1874(?)-1958

PERSONAL: Born January 16, about 1874, in Preston, Lancashire, England; emigrated to Canada, late 1890; died September 11, 1958, in Lancieux, Brittany, France; son of Robert and Emily (Parker) Service; married Germaine Bourgoin in 1913; children: Iris. *Education:* Glasgow University, student.

CAREER: Author and poet. Bank clerk, Commercial Bank of Scotland, Glasgow, 1889; after emigrating to Canada, was variously employed on a farm near Duncan, British Columbia, worked odd jobs while travelling along the Pacific Coast, and was with the Canadian Bank of Commerce, Victoria, British Columbia, which transferred him to Kamloops, British Columbia, later to Whitehorse in the Yukon Territory, then to Dawson in 1908; travelled eight years in the Yukon and sub-arctic; Balkan War correspondent for the *Toronto Star* in the Balkans. Ambulance driver, American Red Cross, World War I. *Military service:* Intelligence officer, Canadian Army, World War I.

WRITINGS—Poetry: The Spell of the Yukon, and Other Verses, Barse & Hopkins, 1907, reissued (illustrated by Gaylord Bennitt), C. F. Braun, 1967, published in Canada as *Songs of a Sourdough,* W. Briggs, 1907, reprinted, Ryerson, 1962; *Ballads of a Cheechako,* Barse & Hopkins, 1909, reissued, Ryerson, 1962; *Rhymes of a Rolling Stone,* Dodd, 1912, reissued, McGraw, 1977; *Rhymes of a Red Cross Man,* Barse & Hopkins, 1916; *Ballads of a Bohemian,* Barse & Hopkins, 1921; *Twenty Bathtub Ballads,* Francis, Day, & Hunter, 1939; *Barroom Ballads,* Dodd, 1940; *Songs of a Sun-Lover,* Dodd, 1949; *Rhymes of a Roughneck,* Dodd, 1950; *Lyrics of a Lowbrow,* Dodd, 1951; *Rhymes of a Rebel,* Dodd, 1952, *Songs for My Supper,* Benn, 1953, Dodd, 1955; *Carols of an Old Codger,* Dodd, 1954; *Rhymes for My Rags,* Dodd, 1956; *Songs of the High North,* Benn, 1958; *The Song of the Campfire* (illustrated by Richard Galaburr), Dodd, 1978.

Novels: *The Trail of '98* (illustrated by Maynard Dixon), Dodd, 1911; *The Pretender,* Dodd, 1914; *The Poisoned Paradise,* Dodd, 1922; *The Roughneck,* Barse & Hopkins, 1923; *The Master of the Microbe,* Barse & Hopkins, 1926; *The House of Fear,* Dodd, 1927.

Other: *Why Not Grow Young?,* Barse & Hopkins, 1928; *Ploughman of the Moon* (autobiography), Dodd, 1945; *Harper of Heaven* (autobiography), Dodd, 1948.

Collections: *The Complete Poems of Robert Service,* Dodd, 1940, reissued as *Collected Poems of Robert Service,* Dodd, 1964; *The Best of Robert Service,* Dodd, 1953, reissued, Benn, 1978; *Collected Verse,* Dodd, 1961-1965; *Yukon Poems of Robert Service,* Filter Press, 1967; *The Shooting of Dan McGrew and The Cremation of Sam McGee* (illustrated by Rosemary Wells), Young Scott, 1969.

ADAPTATIONS—Movies and filmstrips: "My Madonna" (motion picture), adaptation of *The Spell of the Yukon, and Other Verses,* Metro Pictures, 1915; "The Song of the Wage Slave" (motion picture), adaptation of *The Spell of the Yukon, and Other Verses,* Metro Pictures, 1915; "The Lure of Heart's Desire" (motion picture), adaptation of "The Spell of the Yukon," Metro Pictures, 1916; "The Spell of the Yukon" (motion picture), Popular Plays and Players, 1916; "The Law of the Yukon" (motion picture), adaptation of "The Spell of the Yukon," Mayflower Photoplay, 1920;

ROBERT W. SERVICE

"The Shooting of Dan McGrew" (motion pictures), Metro Pictures, 1915, Metro Pictures, 1924; "The Shooting of Dan McGoo" (animated cartoon), Loew's, 1945; "Poisoned Paradise" (motion picture), B. P. Schulberg, 1924; "The Trail of '98" (motion picture), Metro-Goldwyn-Mayer, 1929; "Clancy of the Mounted" (series of twelve motion pictures), Universal Pictures, 1933.

SIDELIGHTS: **January 16, 1874.** Born in Lancashire, England.

1878. Moved to Scotland where he lived with his aunts and his grandfather. "My three aunts sat round the glowing fire. Aunt Jeannie was reading *Good Words*, Aunt Bella the *Quiver*, and Aunt Jennie *Sunday at Home*. The only reading I was allowed was Fox's *Book of Martyrs*, whose pictures of burning saints gave me a gruesome delight. My aunts wore black silk skirts, and in front of the fire they drew them up over their knees. I was supposed to be too young to notice, but the fatness of their legs disgusted me. Grandfather would doze on the sofa till his snores awoke him. He had a crinkly white beard, and for long my idea of God was a grandiose edition of Grandfather.

"I lived with him and my three aunts in the little Ayrshire town. Grandfather was postmaster; Aunt Bella sold stamps, while Aunt Jennie jiggled a handle that in some inconceivable way sent off telegrams. Aunt Jeannie ran the house and looked after the garden and the hens. . . .

"Aunt Jeannie was housekeeper; Aunt Bella liked to scrub and work in the open air; but Aunt Jennie was accounted the literary one of the family, because she read books. The others only read papers. She encouraged me to learn poetry from the school primers. These selections were mostly from Campbell and Longfellow. So standing on a chair I would spout: 'The boy stood on the burning deck,' or 'It was the schooner Hesperus.' The more I ranted and gestured, the more they applauded. In those days I was not troubled by an inferiority complex, and to outsiders must have been an egregious little pest. I was undoubtedly precocious, but if they spoiled me it was not my fault. There was, in fact, quite a literary tradition in our family. My great-grandfather had been a crony of Robert Burns and claimed him as a second cousin. One of our parlour chairs had often been warmed by the rump of the Bard; for, besides being a rhymster, my ancestor had been a toper; so I expect if that chair could have talked it could have told of wild nights with John Barleycorn. To my folks anything that rhymed was poetry, and Robbie Burns was their idol.

"Perhaps something of this atmosphere affected me; but poetry attracted me from the first—largely, I suppose, because of the rhyming. So one day I astonished the family by breaking into verse. It was the occasion of my sixth birthday and the supper table was spread like a feast. The centrepiece was a cold boiled ham, a poem in coral and ivory. Flanking it in seductive variety were cookies, scones and cakes. For a high tea it was a tribute even to a pampered brat like myself. As I looked at it in eager anticipation, an idea came into my head. Grandfather was sharpening the knife to cut the ham, when suddenly he remembered he had forgotten to say grace. It was then I broke in.

"'Please, Grandpapa, can I say grace this time?'

"All eyes turned to me, and I could see disapproval shaping in their faces. But I did not give them a chance to check me. Bowing my head reverently I began:

> 'God bless the cakes and bless the jam;
> Bless the cheese and the cold boiled ham;
> Bless the scones Aunt Jeannie makes,
> And save us all from belly-aches. Amen.'

"I remember their staring silence and my apprehension. I expected to be punished, but I need not have feared. There was a burst of appreciation that to-day seems to me incredibly naive. For years after they told the story of my grace till it ended by enraging me.

"This was my first poetic flutter, and to my thinking it suggests tendencies in flights to come. First, it had to do with the table, and much of my work has been inspired by food and drink. Second, it was concrete in character, and I have always distrusted the abstract. Third, it had a tendency to be coarse, as witness the use of the word 'belly' when I might just as well have said 'stomach.' But I have always favoured an Anglo-Saxon word to a Latin one, and in my earthiness I have followed my kinsman Burns. So, you see, even in that first bit of doggerel there were foreshadowed defects of my later verse.

"Rather than join the boys in the street I would amuse myself alone in the garden, inventing imagination games. I would be a hunter in the jungle of the raspberry canes; I would be an explorer in the dark forest of the shrubbery; I would squat by my lonely campfire on the prairie, a little grass plot where the family washing was spread. I was absorbed in my games, speaking to myself or addressing imaginary companions. No wonder the others thought me a queer one. I looked forward to bedtime; for then, about half an hour before dropping off to sleep, I had the most enchanting visions. Shining processions of knights and fair ladies passed before my eyes: warriors, slaves and pages emerged and faded. I did not seem to imagine them. They just presented themselves, a radiant pageantry. They gave me a rare delight, and I was loath to fall asleep. But all at once this gift of visioning left me, and, alas! it has never returned.'' [Robert Service, *Ploughman of the Moon,* Dodd, 1945.[1]]

1880. While attending parish school, Service discovered his gift for telling stories and his facility in rhyming. ''My memories of the Long Grey Town are sunshine memories. No doubt there were dark days but they left no impression. One remembers the good and forgets the evil. And my last summer there was notably radiant. I discovered a woodland glade, with a stretch of greensward and a spring bubbling up from a bed of water-cress. The Fairy Dell and the Magic Spring I christened them, and they became our favourite haunt. . . . I had been reading Grimm and Andersen, and it was easy to invent on similar lines. . . .

''This was my discovery of my story-telling gift. It came so easily to me I was amazed other boys listened avidly. I never believed in fairy tales, but I could make others do so. While I talked with my tongue in my cheek, they hearkened goggle-eyed. Silly stuff, but if they liked it, it was all right with me. . . .''[1]

1885. Moved to Glasgow where his mother, father, brothers and sisters lived. Attended Hillhead School. ''Ah, those Saturdays in the Public Library, and my joy as I trudged three miles of streets to my city of books! At noon I would go to an eating place and have cake and tea over a marble-topped table. It cost twopence, but it was a feast to me. What matter the poor fare! I was young and free, and my capacity for bright dreams was unlimited. Never was I more happy, and this because I felt so blissfully *alone.* When other boys of my age were playing games and idling away their leisure, I was living in an imaginative world of my own.

''I was never popular at school. I was too much of a lone dog and I disliked games. Only on the football field was I in demand because I weighed ten stone. As centre forward I was valuable in the scrum, but I thought it very stupid spending half the game in a pushing mob. I really preferred Soccer to Rugger. However, we were little snobs and thought the former too plebeian.

''There was much competition to get into the team, so that we who made it were inclined to be cocky. We wore tasselled caps in the school colours. My shorts were very short, and when I walked to the football field I kept my macintosh partly unbuttoned, so that my bare knees might show. I imagined people saying: 'Fine specimen of a lad. No doubt Captain of his school.' Whereas no doubt they were thinking: 'Silly young ass. Thinks himself a puling International.' Maybe I did dramatize myself to some extent. Youth must have its dreams, its vanities. It needs a certain equipment of conceit to affront the realities of life. But the only time I distinguished myself in school football was when I split my shorts, and the opposing team was so convulsed with laughter at the sight of my bare buttocks that they allowed me to run in and score a try.''[1]

Then, as I hung half in, half out of the window, he clutched me by the throat

(From *The Trail of '98* by Robert W. Service. Illustrated by Maynard Dixon.)

1888. After being expelled from Hillhead School for defying his drill master, Service, enchanted by the lure of the sea, began work in a shipping office.

1889-1896. Apprenticed in a bank. During this period Service began experimenting with writing, especially poetry. ''However, my passion for poetry was nearing its end. It had a final flicker when I discovered Bret Harte and Eugene Field and added them to my models. But soon after I developed a fed-up feeling that ended in revolt. I began to dislike poetical words and to prefer blunt Saxon speech. Then I grew sick of the subject matter of verse, such as mythology and nature. Why should poetry concern itself with beauty and not with ugliness, which is just as fascinating? Why should it deal with virtue when vice is more interesting? Why did poets write about flowers and love and the stars? Why not about eating and drinking, and lusts and common people? I was a rebel. Poets, I complained, cared more for the way of saying things than for the thing said. I was tired of ideals and abstractions. Flowery language, words musically arranged and coloured like a garden—no, I did not react to that any more. Poetry farewell!

"But I stuck to verse. Though I turned from nectar I still liked beer. I could rhyme with the best and make verse with facility. But I practised it less and less, and the time came when I confined my efforts to limericks, of which the least said the better.

"So ended my poetical period. It was a happy one and no doubt served me well. Though for years I did not write another line, that early training was not wasted. For when I began again to make verse it came as easy to me as slipping off a log."[1]

Early 1890's. Dabbled in the theatre where he won applause by appearing on stage with his kilt on backwards.

March 31, 1896. Resigned from the Bank of Glasgow; sailed to Canada on a tramp steamer to begin a new life as an itinerant worker. "So I got all the books I could find in the library, and made myself an authority on the Dominion. I translated myself into prairie life. Already I was a sturdy settler, raising cattle and grain, or riding a bronco and roping steers. The last particularly intrigued me, and I dramatized myself wearing chaps and a big stetson. The dingy office faded out. . . . *I was a cowboy singing under the stars as I rode round the sleeping herd. . . . I was playing a guitar by the camp-fire. . . . I was loping into town with my pay to whoop things up. . . .* Cattle ranching; that was the romantic side of farming, and it was romance that was luring me. As I thought of the future, I had no doubts. I would accept the bad with the good. Instinct told me that, in throwing over the traces and staking my fate on the unknown, I was unconquerably right; and I knew a joy that bordered on ecstasy as I thought: 'I, too, will be a cowboy.'

"I was now twice as strong as the ordinary city boy of my height, and I walked with a chip on my shoulder. I tensed my muscles with a joy in their fitness. I gloried in the thought that I would overcome all difficulties. I pitied the poor boys who were following the beaten track. I would cram my life with colour, even if it meant crimson patches. No doubt I was rash, but an instinct told me I was right. Although it is half a century ago I still recall the ardour and enthusiasm of my twentieth year. On, it is fine to be young and strong and to have courage! Yet courage is often ignorance. I have never been brave in my life. I have realized many of my dreams and found the reality a very dull affair. To seek for gold, to explore the wilds, to sail strange seas, all that is simply in the day's work.

"Arrived in Alberta I felt the same reluctance to grapple with grim reality. There the prairie was rolling, but it could not roll too much for me. I was beginning to feel a rolling stone anyhow. It was not that I lacked vitality. Indeed I was keyed up and effervescent with enthusiasm. However, all that did not incline me favourably to the job of making a hard living by the sweat of my brow. On the contrary, the more I voyaged, even though the going was tough, the more I wanted to keep going. Such was my westward impetus that only the barrier of the salt sea could arrest it. And I wondered if that could.

"As I look back, I see myself a feckless young fool without any apprehension for the future. I had never worked hard, and already I felt an aversion for strenuous forms of toil. Perhaps this was why I dallied, putting off the evil day when

I would have to come to grips with reality. So in a spirit of irresponsibility I crossed the Rockies, revelling in the sheer glory of peak and glacier. Here was something greater than my imagination had ever conceived. As I looked awe-struck at rivers roaring through canyon walls, I thought that these moments alone justified my joust at jeopardy. It was so gorgeous I grudged every minute I could not devour the scenery with my eyes, and got up in the first dawn light so that I should miss nothing. But I was alone. None of my companions shared my ecstasies.

"Then we seemed to have left all that behind. I awoke one morning to find we were speeding through a land of forest to the sounding sea. My Nemesis of toil was nearing. I began to be afraid.

"So passed my apprenticeship to farm labour. I acquitted myself well, because there was nothing else I could do. I worked harder than ever in my life; or rather I worked hard for the first time in my life. And from the first I realized that I hated hard work. Yes, with a feeling of horror I now knew that I had made a hideous mistake. For from now on, nothing but hard work lay before me. I had sold myself to serfdom. I had freedom only to serve. I had relinquished my heritage of easy living for the grimmest life I could have chosen. True, farm work was not so gruelling as other forms of labour, but there was no end to it. I had plunged myself into a morass from which I saw no way out."[1]

1897. Left Canada to seek new forms of adventure in California. ". . . I was happy because I belonged to myself again. Freedom was the finest thing in the world. Later I came to think health more important; but in youth liberty is most to be prized. I was as careless as a breeze. I gave the future no thought. When the evil day came I would meet it; in the meantime let me live lyrically. But I would control my destiny. I would never allow myself to be shaped by circumstances.

"Perhaps I might become a writer. The thought was always at the back of my mind. I might commit all kinds of folly but my pen would save me in the end. It may have been that instinctive confidence that made me so jaunty in assurance and challengeful of fate. All this, I thought, was but a preparation. Some day I would get my chance and I would take it. Yet how many like me have dreamed and dawdled on the dreary road to failure! I did not realize how I had been mentally starved during the past six months till I found in the shack a pile of *Harper's Magazines.* It seemed like a treasure to me. I devoured them, and never did I get such delight from the printed page. Avidly I read, finding each word vital, each phrase pregnant.

"We get from a writer what we bring to him, and sometimes we get more than he intended. Our intelligence fuses with his, and his words go deeper than ever he purposed. We may read a passage a dozen times and it leaves us unmoved; then there comes a special mood when it burns like a living flame. We must be hungry to appreciate literary fare. In my case I was famished. I read those magazines from end to end. Nothing in them bored me, much enraptured me. Every page had the pulse of life in it, and many passages had the preciousness of words engraved on brass. But most luminous of all were some articles on Southern California. They dealt with the fruitlands, and had wonderful photographs of groves and orchards. These articles were like a beacon light to me. They gave me a new incentive, a fresh inspiration."[1]

(From the movie "The Shooting of Dan McGrew," starring Lew Cody and Barbara La Marr. Released in 1924.)

Christmas, 1897. Drifted down to Los Angeles where he lived with bums in an evangelical mission.

1898. Toured Southwestern United States as a singing troubadour, lost his guitar and returned to work as a cowman in Canada where an encounter with a black bull left him with cracked ribs.

1899-1903. Position as storekeeper on a ranch. Service returned to school, but fell into deep depression due to his lack of success. "Then one morning the break-down came. I had my usual breakfast of bread and coffee and rose heavily to go to class. It was a radiant morning, but my heart was sad. The sun greeted me with a friendly smile and the sky was blue with hope. I sniffed the fresh breeze from the sea, and I looked wistfully at the pines of the park. So, instead of going to the class-room, I found myself walking wildy in the woods. I was playing truant. I was dismayed at what I was doing, but I could not help myself. I walked round and round the park, walked for hours and hours till I was completely played out. Then I went to a good restaurant, and for the first time in months I had a real meal.

"That night in my room I had a fit of bitter remorse. My books stared so reproachfully at me, I vowed I would go back to school in the morning, yet I knew I never would. I was licked, miserably licked. Nerve-racked and exhausted, I passed a sleepless night, but next morning I found a grim exultation in the thought that never again would I sit in my classes. My university career was over.

"I had enough money to keep me for a week or two, and I pondered what to do. I was indeed a failure. I had tried to storm the citadel of decent society, and been thrown into the ditch. Because I had not enough stamina to be a labourer, I would have to go back to the farm. A hired man at the age of thirty! I had made a nice mess of life. To what shabby fate was I drifting? I tasted the dregs of defeat and felt cast into the outer darkness.

"I answered advertisements, but the mildest rebuff would discourage me for days. Where many would have drowned their despair in drink, I took it out in savage exercise. I walked till I was physically exhausted. Many of these tramps I made by night, preferably by moonlight. Then a certain peace and serenity would come to me, and I would imagine all the jobs I could have enjoyed doing. Here are some of them:

> A ragtime kid in a honky-tonk.
> A rose gardener.
> A Parisian *apache*.
> A librarian.
> A rural delivery postman.
> A herring fisherman.

"Enough to show the futility of my nature. Yes, I was a trifler with life, a minion of the Moon, whose silver emptiness mocked me. What a muck I had made of things, and now I was at the end of my tether."[1]

October 10, 1903. Employed in a Canadian Bank of Commerce in British Colombia.

November 8, 1904. Transferred to a bank in the Yukon. "When the Great Cold came to the Yukon it clamped the land tight as a drum. The transients scurried out, and the residents squatted snugly in. They were the sourdoughs; the land belonged to them; the others were but parasites living on its bounty. This is what we felt as we settled down to the Long Night. It was a comfortable feeling to be shut off from the world with its woes and worries; for we had none of the first and few of the latter. In the High North, winter is long, lonely and cruelly cold, but to the sourdough it is the season best beloved. For then he makes for himself a world of his own, full of happy, helpful people. The Wild brings out virtues we do not find easily in cities—brotherhood, sympathy, high honesty. As if to combat the harshness of nature, human nature makes an effort to be at its best.

"As it was my ambition to be a true sourdough, I welcomed the winter more than most. Its sunny cold exhilarated me. Its below-zero air was as bracing as champagne. Our work in the bank dropped to a quarter of its volume, so that I could take things easy. I joyed to think that for the coming six months I could loaf and dream. For now I realized my dreaming was creative, that from my reveries came thoughts and fancies I might one day put on paper. It was an incubation of all worth while in my life.

"I have never been popular. To be popular is to win the applause of people whose esteem is often not worth the winning. I was polite and pleasant, but leaned back socially. I became notorious as a solitary walker, going off by myself as soon as work was done, into the Great White Silence. My lonely walks were my real life; the sheer joy of them thrilled me. I exulted in my love of nature, and rarely have I been happier."[1]

Autumn, 1906. Wrote *The Shooting of Dan McGrew*, the work which would bring him his first taste of fame. "I was on fire to get started, so I crawled softly down to the dark office. I would work in my teller's cage. But I had not reckoned with the ledger-keeper in the guard room. He woke from a dream in which he had been playing single-handed against two tennis champions, and licking them. Suddenly he heard a noise near the safe. Burglars! Looking through the trap-door he saw a furtive shadow. He gripped his revolver, and closing his eyes, he pointed it at the sulking shade. . . . Fortunately he was a poor shot or the *Shooting of Dan McGrew* might never have been written. No doubt some people will say: 'Unfortunately,' and I sympathize with them. Anyhow, with the sensation of a bullet whizzing past my head, and a detonation ringing in my ears, the ballad was achieved.

"For it came so easily to me in my excited state that I was amazed at my facility. It was as if some one was whispering in my ear. As I wrote stanza after stanza, the story seemed to evolve of itself. It was a marvellous experience. Where I had difficulty in finding a rhyme, I by-passed it, and sometimes when I had my rhyme pat I left the filling out of the line for future consideration. In any case, before I crawled to bed at five in the morning, my ballad was in the bag.

"I did not write anything more for a month, and my second ballad was the result of an accident. One evening I was at a loose end, so thought I would call on a girl friend. When I arrived at the house I found a party in progress. I would have backed out, but was pressed to join the festive band. As an uninvited guest I consented to nibble a nut. Peeved at my position, I was staring gloomily at a fat fellow across the table. He was a big mining man from Dawson, and he scarcely acknowledged his introduction to a little bank clerk. Portly and important, he was smoking a big cigar with a gilt band. Suddenly he said: 'I'll tell you a story Jack London never got.' Then he spun a yarn of a man who cremated his pal. It had a surprise climax which occasioned much laughter. I did not join, for I had a feeling that here was a decisive moment of destiny. I still remember how a great excitement usurped me. Here was a perfect ballad subject. The fat man who ignored me went his way to bankruptcy, but he had pointed me the road to fortune.

"A prey to feverish impatience, I excused myself and took my leave. It was one of those nights of brilliant moonlight that almost goad me to madness. I took the woodland trail, my mind seething with excitement and a strange ecstasy. As I started in: *There are strange things done in the midnight sun*, verse after verse developed with scarce a check. As I clinched my rhymes I tucked the finished stanza away in my head and tackled the next. For six hours I tramped those silver glades, and when I rolled happily into bed, my ballad was cinched. Next day, with scarcely any effort of memory I put it on paper. Word and rhyme came eagerly to heel. My moonlight improvisation was secure and, though I did not know it, 'McGee' was to be the keystone of my success."[1]

1907. First book published—a hundred copies printed at his own expense. Seventeen hundred copies of the book were sold immediately from the galley proofs in Toronto. "My own feelings, when I caressed this bratling of my muse, were, I suppose, like the rapture of a mother over her firstborn. I gazed with awe and emotion at a slim, drab, insignificant volume. Yet it was a part of me, compounded of my ecstasy and anguish. I would rot in my shroud, but it would remain a testimony to my brief breath of being. . . ."[1]

Spring, 1908. Transferred to a bank in Dawson where he hoped to write the essential story of the Yukon. ". . . I wrote something every day, and always on my lonely walks on the trails. I looked forward to them because I knew the Voice would whisper in my ear, and that I would just as surely express my feelings. It was the outlet of the exultant joy that glowed in me. I was so brilliantly happy. Sometimes I thought I would burst with sheer delight. Words and rhymes came to me without any effort. I bubbled verse like an artesian well. I wrote the *Spell of the Yukon, The Law of the Yukon* and many others, a solitary pedestrian pounding out his rhymes from the intense gusto of living.

"And as I finished each poem I filed it away with the others and forgot it. It never occurred to me to set any value on my work. It was just a diversion, maybe a foolish one. The impulse to express my rapture in a world of beauty and gran-

Service's cabin in Dawson. "Its moose horns over the porch were like arms stretched out to me."

deur was stronger than myself, and I did it with no thought of publication.

"But nature was not enough. I wrote of human nature, of the life of a mining camp, of the rough miners and the dance-hall girls. Vice seemed to me a more vital subject for poetry than virtue, more colourful, more dramatic, so I specialized in the Red Light atmosphere. And every day my pile of manuscripts grew higher, and I piled my shirts on them and forgot them. Then, as suddenly as it had begun, the flow of inspiration ceased. My bits of verse lay where I left them, neglected and forgotten for more than a year.

"It was ever thus with me—bursts of creative energy, then lapses into lethargy. Apathy gripped me, so that I loathed the work I had done. A new enthusiasm would seize me and I would drive in another direction. I was temperamental, unpredictable. It might be months before I put pen to paper again; and in the meantime, in a slovenly roll held by an elastic band, my sheaf of verse lay at the bottom of a bureau drawer. . . ."[1]

November 15, 1909. Left the Dawson bank to begin *The Trail of the '98*. "And this . . . is the low-down on my first novel. In the early morning, feeling like a new man, I began a synopsis of my book. Chapter by chapter I planned it out, even to minor details. Every scene was clear, every situation developed. When I had finished I think any one could have written that book from my script. And now, having organized my work, I was able to concentrate on each chapter and give it all I had. I went ahead like wildfire. I must admit it didn't work out according to schedule. Story schemes seldom do. My characters asserted themselves, but on the main they were pretty docile. My synthetic villain proved to be the most credible of all. So, contrary to all canons of storymaking, I won out. For incidentally the book was a best-seller, was made into a movie and made me a modest competence. The 'feel your way' method in my case was a failure, and in future fiction I always wanted to be sure that I had a story before I began to write it.

"I did the first draft in five months, averaging a thousand words a day. There were days I did three thousand words and days I only bit my nails. When the end drew near I became excited and worked like a demon. After a supper of beef-steak and onions, I went home and wound things up. I worked clear through the night till next day. I ran out of copy-books and began to write on typewriter paper, my pencil flying over the sheets. As I finished them I threw them on the floor. Time and again I had to stop because my wrist ached and my fingers were stiff, but my super-excited mind goaded me on. In all I did over twelve thousand words. When with an exhausted sigh I wrote the blessed words THE END, the floor was strewn with sheets of loosely scrawled manuscript. I tiptoed over them to bed, and slept for ten hours, knowing that my book was definitely cinched. No new mother could have been more ecstatic."[1]

Spring, 1910. Vagabond urgings returned—traveled to Toronto, New York and south to New Orleans and Havana.

1910-1911. After visiting with his family whom he had not seen for fifteen years, Service returned to his cabin in Dawson via the long and dangerous Old Edmonton Trail. "In placid peace for days and days I drifted down my river of dreams. Most of my dreams were of Dawson, my cabin and the work I planned to do. On the Mackenzie I had gathered a lot of material that was different. As I paddled I mulled over this and saw ballads in the making. How I longed to get at them!

"I was now committed to this trail. There was no returning. I must go wherever it led. I kept climbing higher and higher, into the hills which now closed behind me shutting out the valley. I had a trapped feeling but hurried on. What worried me was that the path dwindled so rapidly. It became a toe-track that switches from ridge to ridge but ever mounting. Little by little it grew fainter, till at last it failed. In front of me was virgin snow, and I found I was breaking trail. Then at last I realized I was lost.

"The moon seemed unnaturally bright. It was shining down on me in pity. Damn you, Moon! I don't want your pity. I've always been your lover and now you'll gleam over my snow-cold corpse. I, dreamer, joyous liver of life, so grateful for all good things, will lie white under the silver of your spell. . . . My legs were giving under me. Through the frosted collar of my parka I could see the diamond glitter of the moon.

"There comes a time when the spirit can no longer conquer the flesh, when despite the gallant heart the foot fails. This came to me now. My muscles refused to function, my legs crumpled beneath me. I sank on my knees, rose and sank again. And as I kneeled there in the attitude of prayer my Special Providence came to my aid. Or was it the moon that saved me? For it seemed to burn brighter, brighter. It seemed to cry to me: 'Look! Look!' And in answer to the pleading of the moon I looked, and there in the shadow of the woods across a brief gully I saw . . . A CABIN."[1]

Winter, 1911-1912. Worked on his ballads in his Yukon cabin. "I used to write on the coarse rolls of paper used by paper-hangers, pinning them on the wall and printing my verses in big, charcoal letters. Then I would pace back and forth before them, studying them, repeating them, trying to make them perfect. I wanted them to appeal to the eye as well as to the ear. I tried to avoid any literary quality. Verse, not poetry, is what I was after—something the man in the street would take notice of and the sweet old lady would paste in her album; something the schoolboy would spout and the fellow in the pub would quote. Yet I never wrote to please anyone but myself; it just happened I belonged to the

simple folks whom I liked to please." [Carl F. Klinck, *Robert Service: A Biography*, Dodd, 1976.[2]]

1912-1913. Traveled through Europe. Journeyed on the Orient Express, finally settled in Paris to study art.

June 12, 1913. Married Germaine Bourgoin. "In real life I have always hated sentimentality. How can any man say: 'I love you,' to a woman without feeling a silly ass? I may have been precipitate but some instinct told me I was right when I said to the younger sister: 'Say, why don't we take a chance? Columbus took a chance. I've only known you a few weeks but I feel it will work out all right. Let's get hitched. I'm only a poet and as you know poets don't make money, but I guess we can manage to rub along. If you're not scared at the prospect of marrying a poor man let's live in a garret with a loaf of bread and a jug of wine, and we'll sing under the tiles.' . . . And to my amazement she accepted.

"Writing a book is to me an all-time job which excludes other interests. Night and day I brood and bang at my Remington. I go round like a man demented, mumbling to myself with blank unseeing eyes. In such moods I am an impossible person—nervous, inattentive, boorishly silent. It takes a woman nine months to make a baby and it takes me ten to make a book, but my travail is in the first five. Of course, there are calm spells when I enjoy real life again, yet soon I feel the goad and return to that false life I live so intensely. Perhaps artists should never marry: their egotistic antics are so insufferable." [Robert Service, *Harper of Heaven*, Dodd, 1948.[3]]

1915. War correspondent; arrested as a spy near Dunkirk. Service later joined the Ambulance Corps.

1921. Went to Hollywood for film version of *Dan McGrew*.

1923. Suffered cardiac trouble causing his output to decline for a three year period. "'From now on,' I mused, 'my whole life will be transformed. In a twinkling I have been changed from an athlete to an invalid. Never again shall I be a He-man. Flabbiness makes cowards of us all. After punching a bag for half an hour how capable one feels of punching a human jaw! How often have I swaggered up to a chap with a chip on my shoulder (prudently regardful that he was my own weight) and no one has knocked off that chip. Now no one will ever get the chance. From this on I will take lessons in belligerency from a buck rabbit.'

"*Sad reflection:* Forever must I bid adieu to my Sandow self. My proud muscles must melt like snow in the sun. No more will I watch them ripple under the skin or stand out clear like a chart of anatomy. Alas, I must kill the thing I love! For it has taken me three years of effort to bring my exultant body into being. How often have I driven myself to the daily discipline. I have been severe. I have trained myself to a point where exercise is tyranny. . . .

"*Cheering thought:* Now I can relax, take it easy. At fifty have I not the right to slack up? No longer will I be the slave of my muscles, goaded on by a desire for perfection. . . . And after all, there are worse things than heart trouble. Think of cancer, consumption. It's not good form to talk about one's liver, one's kidneys, one's tummy; but the heart's a noble organ and can be discussed even in a drawing room. A *chic* malady, a *chic* death. Go out like a snuffed candle, burning clearly to the end. How lucky I am! If one has to be sick let it be the heart. . . ."[3]

Robert Service in uniform, 1916.

1924. Placed on a strict diet, exercise, and hygiene regime resulted in a "handbook for men" who had reached fifty.

1937-1938. Toured Russia.

1942. Returned to Hollywood for the duration of World War II, where he was offered a bit part in a movie portraying himself. "Such was my precious part in my first and last appearance as a cinema actor—exactly twenty-three words. But you have no idea how much trouble they gave me. The family heard me going around muttering: 'No, not this time, Cherry,' till they took it up themselves, nearly driving me crazy with their applications of it to our daily life. As for me, I tried it in a dozen different intonations, sitting in front of a mirror, with appropriate grimaces. But I couldn't get that simple phrase to sound anything but idiotic. I put emphasis on first one word, then on another. I changed my tone. I modulated my voice. But the more I said: 'No, not this time, Cherry,' the more difficult I found it.

"The dramatic director came to coach me. I must not, he told me, shake my head or make any gesture, while my face must be expressionless. The camera distorts everything, and what one supposes to be a play of emotion on one's mug becomes a grotesque grimace. Pathos is bathos; drama, farce. Cinema acting needs a low-toned technique, and as most stars are wooden-faced anyway it works out all right. But it was driving me distracted. From every corner of the bungalow I heard mocking voices: 'No, not this time, Cherry!' So, going out to the garage, I patted the head of the pup and said: 'No, not this time, Cherry.'"[3]

September 11, 1958. Suffered a fatal heart attack in Brittany, France. "So in the end let us seek a quiet home, and with earth radiant about us, face the setting sun. With thankful eyes and grateful hearts let us rejoice that it has been granted to us to live the length of our years in a world of beauty—to understand much, to divine much, and to come at last through pleasant paths to peace. Peace and understanding!

So with our last gaze let us face the serene sunset, content to have played our parts and saying humbly:

> 'Nature, from whose bosom I come, take me back tenderly, lovingly. Forgive my faults, my failures, and now that my usefulness to you is ended, grant me to rest eternally.'"[3]

FOR MORE INFORMATION SEE: Geoffrey T. Hellman, "How to Disappear for an Hour," *New Yorker,* March 30 and April 6, 1946, and in his *How to Disappear for an Hour,* Dodd, 1947; C. Hamer-Jackson, "Robert W. Service," *Leading Canadian Poets,* edited by W. P. Percival, Ryerson, 1948; Arthur L. Phelps, editor, *Canadian Writers,* McClelland & Stewart, 1951; W. Reyburn, "He Created Dan McGrew and Cremated Sam McGee," *Reader's Digest,* October, 1951; "Talk of the Town," *New Yorker,* January 23, 1954; Carl Klinck, *Robert Service,* Dodd, 1976.

Obituaries: *New York Times,* September 13, 1958; *Illustrated London News,* September 20, 1958; *Newsweek,* September 22, 1958; *Time,* September 22, 1958; *Life,* October 6, 1958; *Publishers Weekly,* October 6, 1958; *Wilson Library Bulletin,* November, 1958; *Americana Annual,* 1959; *Britannica Book of the Year,* 1959.

SMITH, H(arry) Allen   1907-1976

OBITUARY NOTICE: Born December 19, 1907, in McLeansboro, Ill.; died February 24, 1976, in San Francisco, Calif. Author, journalist, humorist. In the course of his journalistic career, H. Allen Smith served as editor of a small Sebring, Florida daily, *The American,* as feature writer for United Press, and as rewrite man for the *New York World-Telegram.* Beginning in 1941, Mr. Smith devoted all of his time to professional writing. Known for his wacky characters, zany humor, and sometimes biting satire, the author wrote and edited dozens of books which made him a great celebrity of the 1940's. *Low Man on the Totem Pole* was his first of many best-sellers. His other titles include *Life in a Putty Knife Factory, Lost in the Horse Latitudes,* and *Rhubarb* which later became a successful movie. *For More Information See: Authors in the News,* Volume 2, Gale, 1976; *Contemporary Authors,* Volume 5-8 revised, Gale, 1969; *Longman Companion to Twentieth Century Literature,* Longman, 1970; *The Reader's Encyclopedia of American Literature,* Crowell, 1962; *Twentieth Century Authors,* 1st supplement, Wilson, 1955. *Obituaries: A B Bookman's Weekly,* April 12, 1976; *Contemporary Authors,* Volume 65-68, Gale, 1977; *Current Biography,* May, 1976; *Detroit Free Press,* February 25, 1976; *New York Times,* February 25, 1976; *Publishers Weekly,* March 22, 1976; *Time,* March 8, 1976; *Washington Post,* February 26, 1976.

SNYDER, Jerome   1916-1976

OBITUARY NOTICE: Born April 20, 1916, in New York, N.Y.; died May 2, 1976, in New York, N.Y. Graphic artist, illustrator, and gourmet-writer. Jerome Snyder became the first art director of *Sports Illustrated* in 1954. He held this post until 1961 when he became art director for *Scientific American.* Widely known for his black-and-white illustrations, Mr. Snyder was the recipient of a number of awards from the Art Directors Club of New York and the Society of

Illustrators. He illustrated several children's books including G. B. Kirtland's *One Day in Elizabethan England,* Robert Silverberg's *Scientists and Scoundrels,* and Benjamin Elkin's *Why the Sun Was Late.* With Milton Glaser he wrote *The Underground Gourmet Cookbook. For More Information See: Illustrators of Books for Young People,* 2nd edition, Scarecrow, 1975; *Illustrators of Children's Books,* 1957-1966, Horn Book, 1968; *Who's Who in Graphic Art,* Amstutz & Herdeg Graphis Press, 1962. *Obituaries: Contemporary Authors,* Volume 65-68, 1977; *New York Times,* May 4, 1976; *Time,* May 17, 1976.

STREANO, Vince(nt Catello) 1945-

PERSONAL: Born December 9, 1945, in Santa Barbara, Calif.; son of Ralph (a music teacher) and Francyl (Cowles) Streano; married Carol Havens (a writer), July 23, 1977. *Education:* San Jose State University, B.A., 1968. *Home and office:* P.O. Box 662, Laguna Beach, Calif. 92652. *Agent:* Paul Reynolds Agency, 12 E. 41st Street, New York, N.Y. 10017.

CAREER: San Jose Mercury, San Jose, Calif., photographer, 1967-68; *Los Angeles Times,* Los Angeles, Calif., photographer, 1968-73; free-lance writer and photographer, 1973—. *Member:* National Press Photographers Association, American Society of Magazine Photographers (ASMP). *Awards, honors:* National Cigar Institute's first prize in photography contest, 1970; named Orange County's photographer of the year, 1973.

WRITINGS: Touching America with Two Wheels (with photographs), Random House, 1974.

Illustrator—All published by Childrens Press: June Behrens, *Look at the Farm Animals,* 1972; June Behrens, *Look at the Desert Animals,* 1973; June Behrens, *How I Feel,* 1973; June Behrens, *Look at the Ocean Animals,* 1975; June Behrens, *Together,* 1975; June Behrens, *My Favorite Thing,* 1977.

Also photographed and co-produced with wife, Carol Havens, a filmstrip series titled *Children of the World,* Barr Films, 1978.

WORK IN PROGRESS: Illustrating a book about hot air ballooning by Carol Havens, *Sky Dancers.*

SIDELIGHTS: "I am a free-lance photojournalist. Because of my occupation I am able to enact many of my dreams and fantasies. If I find something that interests me such as taking a ride in a hot air balloon, or traveling around the world photographing children, I have only to find a buyer for my work, and I'm off.

"My work the past couple of years has primarily been involved with the above two projects. I recently finished a filmstrip project about children of the world where I traveled to eleven different countries photographing how the children work, live and play.

"I found that children, wherever they live, have basically the same wants, needs and desires. It's their environment and culture which sets them apart. I did this project in hopes

VINCE STREANO

that children in the United States would learn about the cultures of other children in the world.

"The ballooning project I mentioned is on-going. My wife, who is a writer, and I have published many magazine articles on the subject. Because of our involvement with the subject we have taken many balloon rides and have traveled throughout the U.S. and Europe chasing balloons.

"From the age of eight I almost always had a camera in my hands. My parents owned a camera store, and while they both worked in the store, I would wander through the town taking pictures of anything that moved. I soon learned that my camera was a passport to adventure.

"One of my fondest memories is of a tractor driver who stopped his huge machine while I was taking a picture, then gave me a ride afterwards. I also remember the time I was taking pictures of a slow moving locomotive in the train yard, and the engineer stopped the train so I could get a better picture, then I got a short ride in the caboose.

"Recently my photographs have been published in many magazines, including *People, Smithsonian, Sports Illustrated, Datsun Discovery,* and *Air California.* My magazine work still enables me to meet many different kinds of people and have interesting experiences.

"In the future I hope to do another project involving children and to continue my traveling in other countries around the world, photographing different cultures."

**The boy I like best is Roger.
We build block houses together.
Roger never knocks down my house.**
■ (From *Together* by June Behrens. Photographs by Vince Streano.)

STREATFEILD, Noel   1897-

PERSONAL: Born December 24, 1897, in Amberley, near Arundel, Sussex, England; daughter of William Champion (the Bishop of Lewes) and Janet Mary (Venn) Streatfeild. *Education:* Attended Laleham in Eastbourne as well as Hastings and St. Leonards College. Studied at the Royal Academy of Dramatic Art, London. *Home:* 51 Elizabeth St., Eaton Square, London SW1, England.

CAREER: Author and editor. Began as an actress with a provincial repertory company in England; later appeared in a variety of theatrical productions in South Africa and Australia; turned to a writing career in 1930; became a book critic for *Elizabethan* magazine; presented book talks for BBC radio. *Awards, honors:* Carnegie Medal, 1938, for *The Circus is Coming; Thursday's Child* was a Junior Literary Guild selection for March, 1971 and *When the Sirens Wailed* for March, 1977; *A Young Person's Guide to the Ballet* was chosen as a Children's Book of the Year by the Child Study

Association for 1975 and a 1976 Children's Book Showcase Title by the Children's Book Council.

WRITINGS—Fiction: *The Whicharts,* Heinemann, 1931, Brentano's, 1932; *Parson's Nine,* Heinemann, 1932, Doubleday, 1933; *Tops and Bottoms,* Doubleday, 1933; *Children's Matinee* (plays; illustrated by Ruth Gervis), Heinemann, 1934; *Shepherdess of Sheep,* Heinemann, 1934, Reynal & Hitchcock, 1935; *Creeping Jenny,* Heinemann, 1936; *It Pays to be Good,* Heinemann, 1936; *Wisdom Teeth* (three-act play), Samuel French, 1936; *Caroline England,* Heinemann, 1937, Reynal & Hitchcock, 1938; *The Circus is Coming* (illustrated by Steven Spurrier), Dent, 1938, revised edition, (illustrated by Clarke Hutton), 1960; *Dennis the Dragon,* Dent, 1939; *Luke,* Heinemann, 1939.

The House in Cornwall (illustrated by D. L. Mays), Dent, 1940; *The Secret of the Lodge* (illustrated by Richard Floethe), Random House, 1940; *The Winter is Past,* Collins, 1940; *The Stranger in Primrose Lane* (illustrated by R.

NOEL STREATFEILD

Floethe), Random House, 1941 (published in England as *Children of Primrose Lane* [illustrated by Marcia Lane Foster], Dent, 1941, reissued, Collins, 1965); *I Ordered a Table for Six*, Collins, 1942; *Harlequinade* (illustrated by C. Hutton), Chatto & Windus, 1943; *Myra Carrel*, Collins, 1944; *Saplings*, Collins, 1945; *Party Frock* (illustrated by Anna Zinkeisen), Collins, 1946; *Grass in Piccadilly*, Collins, 1947.

Mothering Sunday, Coward-McCann, 1950, reissued, Morley-Baker, 1969; *Osbert* (illustrated by Susanne Suba), Rand McNally, 1950; *The Theater Cat* (illustrated by S. Suba), Rand McNally, 1951; *Aunt Clara*, Collins, 1952; (with Roland Pertwee) *Many Happy Returns* (two-act play), English Theatre Guild, 1953; *Judith*, Collins, 1956; *The Grey Family* (illustrated by Pat Marriott), Hamish Hamilton, 1957; *Wintle's Wonders* (illustrated by Richard Kennedy), Collins, 1957; *Bertram* (illustrated by Margery Gill), Hamish Hamilton, 1959; *Christmas with the Chrystals*, Basil Blackwell, 1959.

Look at the Circus (illustrated by Constance Marshall), Hamish Hamilton, 1960; *New Town: A Story About the Bell Family* (illustrated by Shirley Hughes), Collins, 1960, reissued, White Lion, 1976; *The Silent Speaker*, Collins, 1961; *Apple Bough* (illustrated by M. Gill), Collins, 1962; *Lisa Goes to Russia* (illustrated by Geraldine Spence), Collins, 1963; *The Children on the Top Floor* (illustrated by Jillian Willett), Collins, 1964, Random House, 1965, reissued,

White Lion, 1976; *Let's Go Coaching* (illustrated by Peter Warner), Hamish Hamilton, 1965; *The Growing Summer* (illustrated by Edward Ardizzone; Junior Literary Guild selection), Collins, 1966, published in America as *The Magic Summer*, Random House, 1967; *Caldicott Place* (illustrated by Betty Maxey; Junior Literary Guild selection), Collins, 1967, published in America as *The Family at Caldicott Place*, Random House, 1968; *Gemma* (illustrated by B. Maxey), May Fair Books, 1968; *Gemma and Sisters* (illustrated by B. Maxey), May Fair Books, 1968.

Thursday's Child (illustrated by Peggy Fortnum; Junior Literary Guild selection), Random House, 1970; *When the Siren Wailed* (illustrated by M. Gill; Junior Literary Guild selection), Collins, 1974, American edition, illustrated by Judith Gwyn, Random House, 1976; *Ballet Shoes for Anna* (illustrated by Mary Dinsdale), Collins, 1976; *Gran-Nannie* (illustrated by Charles Mozley), M. Joseph, 1976; *Far to Go* (illustrated by Charles Mozley), Collins, 1977.

"Shoes" series: *Ballet Shoes: A Story of Three Children on the Stage* (illustrated by R. Gervis), Dent, 1936, reissued, 1962, published in America as *Ballet Shoes* (illustrated by R. Floethe), Random House, 1937; *Tennis Shoes* (illustrated by D. L. Mays), Dent, 1937, reissued, 1965, American edition, (illustrated by R. Floethe), Random House, 1938; *Circus Shoes* (illustrated by R. Floethe), Random House, 1939; *Curtain Up*, Dent, 1944, reissued, 1963, published in America as *Theater Shoes, or Other People's Shoes* (illustrated by R. Floethe), Random House, 1945; *Party Shoes* (illustrated by A. Zinkeisen), Random House, 1947; *Movie Shoes* (illustrated by S. Suba), Random House, 1949 (published in England as *Painted Garden*, Collins, 1949), new edition, (illustrated by S. Hughes), Penguin, 1961; *Skating Shoes* (illustrated by R. Floethe), Random House, 1951 (published in England as *White Boots*, Collins, 1951), new edition, (illustrated by Milein Cosman), Penguin, 1976; *Family Shoes* (illustrated by R. Floethe), Random House, 1954 (published in England as *The Bell Family* [illustrated by S. Hughes], Collins, 1954); *Dancing Shoes* (illustrated by R. Floethe), Random House, 1958; *New Shoes* (illustrated by Vaike Low), Random House, 1960; *Traveling Shoes* (illustrated by Reisie Lonette), Random House, 1962.

Also author of the "Baby Books" series, published by A. Barker, 1959—.

Nonfiction: *The Picture Story of Britain* (illustrated by Ursula Koering; edited by Helen Hoke), Bell Publishing, 1951; *The Fearless Treasure: A Story of England from Then to Now* (illustrated by Dorothea Braby), M. Joseph, 1953; *The First Book of the Ballet* (illustrated by Moses Soyer), F. Watts, 1953, revised edition, (illustrated by Stanley Houghton and M. Soyer), Edmund Ward, 1963; *The First Book of England* (illustrated by Gioia Fiammenghi), F. Watts, 1958; *Magic and the Magician: E. Nesbit and Her Children's Books*, Abelard, 1958; *Queen Victoria* (illustrated by Robert Frankenberg), Random House, 1958; *The Royal Ballet School*, Collins, 1959.

A Vicarage Family: An Autobiographical Story (illustrated by Charles Mozley), F. Watts, 1963 [another edition illustrated by S. Hughes, Penguin, 1968]; *The Thames: London's River* (illustrated by Kurt Wiese), Garrard, 1964; *Away from the Vicarage* (autobiographical), Collins, 1965; *On Tour: An Autobiographical Novel of the 20's*, F. Watts, 1965; *The First Book of the Opera* (illustrated by Hilary Abrahams), F. Watts, 1966 (published in England as *Enjoying Opera*, Dob-

(From the television movie "Ballet Shoes," starring Sarah Prince. Presented on PBS television, December, 1976.)

son, 1966); *Before Confirmation,* Heinemann, 1967; *The First Book of Shoes* (illustrated by Jacqueline Tomes), F. Watts, 1967; *Beyond the Vicarage* (autobiographical), Collins, 1971, F. Watts, 1972; *The Boy Pharaoh: Tutankhamen,* M. Joseph, 1972; *A Young Person's Guide to the Ballet* (illustrated by Georgette Bordier), Warne, 1975.

Editor: *The Years of Grace,* Evans Brothers, 1950, revised edition, 1956; *By Special Request: New Stories for Girls,* Collins, 1953; *Growing Up Gracefully* (illustrated by John Dugan), A. Barker, 1955; *The Day Before Yesterday: First-hand Stories of Fifty Years Ago* (illustrated by Dick Hart), Collins, 1956; *Confirmation and After,* Heinemann, 1963; Merja Otava, *Priska* (translated by Elizabeth Portch), Benn, 1964; Marlie Brande, *Nicholas* (translated by Elisabeth Boas), Follett, 1968; M. Brande, *Sleepy Nicholas,* Follett, 1970; *The Noel Streatfeild Summer Holiday Book* (illustrated by Sara Silcock), Dent, 1973; *The Noel Streatfeild Easter Holiday Book* (illustrated by S. Silcock), Dent, 1974; *The Noel Streatfeild Birthday Story Book,* Dent, 1977. Also editor of *Noel Streatfeild's Ballet Annual,* 1959—.

ADAPTATIONS—Television: "Ballet Shoes," 1976; "The Bell Family," adapted from *New Town: A Story About the Bell Family,* ran as a television serial.

SIDELIGHTS: **December 24, 1897.** Born in Amberley, Arundel, Sussex, England. Her father, William Champion, was a country vicar who later became the Bishop of Lewes. Her great-great-great grandmother was the famous prison reformer, Elizabeth Fry. "Every living soul has, of course, a story to tell. Other people's lives have a special fascination, either to compare with our own or to lift the curtain on worlds we never knew. To me, delving into my growing-up years is not a new experience. You cannot, I think, write for children unless you can recall your own childhood. For though of course outward conditions change, inward conditions have not changed at all. A child today feels as intensely as his forebears. Joy is as ecstatic and unreasoning, and grief as abysmal.

"The road back into the past, as I have found it, is through the senses. Smell gives a wonderful route. My goodness, that smell of fallen leaves and bonfires, or of bread roasting, or a lavender hedge with the sun beating on it. Sniff a faint hint of an old smell, shut your eyes and you're back—a child.

"Then, of course, there are sounds. Only this last spring when I was in a wood, a cuckoo started to sing. Then I heard rustling and whispering amongst last year's dead leaves, and suddenly it was Good Friday and I was eight, wasting time in a wood when I should have been picking primroses to decorate the church on Easter Sunday.

"Certain chiming clocks have a great effect on my memory. As they chime I am moving back towards a house I stayed in as a child. Then smells come to hurry me along—a certain type of soap used in that house, and an odd smell of old prayer books. Then suddenly I can see, and today is gone and yesterday so close I can almost touch it." [Noel Streatfeild, "The Album and the Artist," *Horn Book,* April, 1964.[1]]

"[I] was the plain one of the family. Instead of [my older sister's] fairness [I] had hair of a colour which [I] described as mid-mouse.

"[My older sister] was a pretty girl with fair hair and clear blue eyes, but she looked, and was, pitifully frail, for [she] was an asthmatic. Her words had a habit of falling over each other for she could not take as deep breaths as other people and so had to try to say more between breaths.

"In the days before the First World War people of a certain standing, however little money they had, kept servants, and where there were children a Nanny or a governess. So, though [my] father was a poor man, for vicars did not earn much money and he had no private means until his father died, there was a cook and a house-parlourmaid and a woman who came in daily for the heavy work, and [a governess].

"All [we] children . . . detested Sundays. But it was an underground detestation never spoken of in front of a grown-up because Daddy must never know. He thought his children loved Sundays just as he had loved them when he was a boy, and this was why [our] Sundays were modelled on Sundays in [our] grandparents' house.

"On Sundays [we] girls were called at seven-thirty by [our governess] who gave each of [us our] prayer-book open at the collect for the day, which had to be learnt by heart before [we] got up at eight. On Sundays breakfast and lunch were eaten in the dining-room which was . . . the one nice thing about Sundays. For breakfast there were always sausages, and for the children crusts of white bread. This was because the Communion bread was made in the house, but before the loaves were taken over to the church all the crust was cut off and, since 'waste not want not' was a family motto, the children ate them and eating them was supposed to be a treat.

"Special clothes belonged to Sundays. They were not necessarily better than those worn on weekdays, but they were newer and supposedly smarter. Even those families with large wardrobes, though they had no clothes labelled 'Sundays,' always wore something good for church.

". . . All through [our] childhood, [we] heard discussions as to whether people were very high, medium high or low church. As the daughters of a vicar of the Church of England [we] knew nobody who was not Church of England. Presumably at [our] school some girls were Roman Catholics and some were chapel, but if this were so [we] never knew about it. Everyone in [our] world was very high, medium high or low Church of England.

"In [our] world, bound as it was within the walls of the vicarage and [our] school, everything was clear-cut. God was in his Heaven; the King on his throne; you voted Conservative; the English were the finest people in the world; there was no grey about it—you were right or you were wrong." [Noel Streatfeild, *A Vicarage Family: An Autobiographical Story,* Franklin Watts, 1963.[2]]

When her father was appointed Vicar of Eastbourne Streatfeild and her sisters continued their education at a school called Laleham. "The vicarage at Eastbourne lay well back, partially hidden amongst trees. It looked from the outside

(From *A Vicarage Family* by Noel Streatfeild. Autolithographs by Charles Mozley.)

dignified, even imposing, for its garden was the boundary for two streets of small houses. When [we] children came to know the neighbourhood well [we] were to learn that the small houses were largely lived in by their owners, many of whom were retired professional people, and all probably better off than their vicar.

"On the day of arrival the vicarage looked like the home of the Lord of the Manor surrounded by his tenants. The house had a gracious air, it was two-storied, long and low. But one glance inside and it was clear it was very much a vicarage. There was the bench just inside the front hall on which, if several people called at once to see the vicar, they could sit while waiting. The hall, since so many would tramp up and down it, was covered from end to end with linoleum."[2]

1913. Given her first encouragement in the field of writing by a teacher at Laleham School. Streatfeild had already shown dramatic talent, often taking part in parish concerts and plays.

1915. A fourth daughter was born into the Streatfeild family. "[Our] mother had given her two elder daughters a shock. She had told [us] she was having a baby. [We] girls had been horribly embarrassed by the news and had never discussed

Anne was also taught to stand on one leg. Before she tried it this seemed so easy that she thought it was ridiculous to have to learn how. ■ (From *The First Book of the Ballet* by Noel Streatfeild. Illustrated by Moses Soyer.)

it. [We] knew—but how dimly—how babies were conceived; and, of course, [we] must have been conceived [our]selves. But that was long ago; a father and mother didn't go *on* doing it—not when the rest of the family were nearly grown up, [we] thought hazily. But facts were facts, and [our sister] was born. What had been [my younger sister's] room had become the nursery, and a Nanny had been installed. Even . . . when the cost of living was rising, people of [our] mother's class did not contemplate looking after their own children.'' [Noel Streatfeild, *On Tour: An Autobiographical Novel of the 20's,* Franklin Watts, 1965.[3]]

1918. After the war, decided to make acting her career and studied at the Royal Academy of Dramatic Art in London. ''Why [I] was accepted by the Academy of Dramatic Art [I] could never guess.

''The new world in which [I] found [my]self, [was] strange and wildly interesting, but not a bit what [I] had expected. It had been generally accepted in the vicarage that life, even for an actress in training, would be a stern fight against the devil and all his works. In actual fact, [I] found [my]self working harder, in a more disciplined atmosphere, than [I] had ever known.

'' 'Oh, my goodness!' [I] thought. 'How I wish I'd bothered in literature classes at school.'

''This thought was triggered off after one day in the Academy. [My] group of beginners was called to an acting class where the play to be studied was *As You Like It.* With so

many students, it was impossible to give anybody more than one scene to study, and the actress who was to produce, knowing nobody's talents, handed out the parts according to appearances. The tallest girls were given scenes of Rosalind's, the dark ones shared Celia, and those left divided up Audrey and Celia.

'' 'Lucky you!' a girl said to [me]. 'I wanted your scene. It's got everything, hasn't it?'

''[I] tried not to look blank, but to [me], Act I, Scene 2 meant nothing at all. [I] tried to sound enthusiastic.

'' 'I suppose it has.'

''Besides the acting classes the students had to learn fencing, miming, which included being able to fall in any position, dancing and, most important of all, elocution, which in the first term was largely breath control. [We] were never idle for a second and, in fact, since classrooms were scattered up and down the two old buildings in which the school was housed, the students usually had to run from class to class. This meant that study of parts had to be done at home.''[3]

After receiving her certificate from the Royal Academy, Streatfeild worked briefly in the chorus of a musical comedy. ''A musical comedy had been on the road trying out for London. Its producers had decided it had no future, however, so it was to finish at the end of its tour. A few girls from the chorus had been sent back to London for another show, and the agent had been directed to send two replacements. Any pretty girls who could sing would do; it was only for five weeks.

''The five weeks were almost unmixed horror for [me]. [I] was an inexperienced nobody who did not even know how to make up, and . . . was treated as such by the London chorus girls. [I] had [my] first experience of theatrical lodgings. [I] always detested them. Used as [I] was to large vicarages, [I] detested back streets, and longed for the days when [I] knew nobody, [I] discovered the lowest form of theatrical digs—the 'combined room:' one room in which [I] ate and slept.''[3]

Accepted under contract for a Shakespearean repertory company for two years. ''Rehearsals were starting almost at once. Proudly [I] went home to the vicarage, hugging [my] complete book of Shakespeare's plays. [I] had in [my] bag a contract which promised to pay [me] three pounds a week. [I] was an actress.

''Though [I] had no idea of it when [I] signed [my] contract, [I] was putting [my] name to an agreement that meant two years of slogging hard work. [I] had supposed that the Academy had taught [me] how to work, but . . . was to discover that [I] had acquired there only the outline of how to work.

There were eight performances a week. And every morning when there was no matinee there were rehearsals of the new plays to be added to the repertory. But there was fun as well as hard work. A Shakespearean company is ideal for a girl, as so many more males than females are required. A few of the older members of the company were married. Mostly the men were bachelors, and young, however, and there was a lot of mild lovemaking. In addition, there were some of those splendid practical jokes that are often part of life in the theatre.''[3]

Held various acting jobs until she was chosen as a member of a company which toured South Africa. "Father and Mother took the news that their daughter was off to South Africa remarkably calmly. They had never traveled themselves, but it didn't seem to worry them that [I] was going so far away with people they did not know. Presumably, having accepted that [I] was to be an actress, they accepted everything that went with it. In fact, it never appeared to cross their minds to interfere."[3]

Later Streatfeild toured Australia with another theatrical company. "Because the play made no demands on [me], mental or physical, [I] threw [my]self into the life of Australia and enjoyed [my]self enormously. [I] liked almost everything. It was midsummer, and [I] had learned in Africa to worship the sun. There were more of Father's introductions than usual, and [I] visited many Australian homes. [I] learned the hard way that an invitation to tea did not mean four o'clock, but eleven in the morning. That 'to have a spell' had nothing to do with witchcraft, but meant to have a rest. [I] saw a forest fire in all its horror. [I] so filled [my] nose with the smell of gum trees that [I] was never to lose the scent. Unendingly [I] watched cricket, for England was fighting the Australians for the Ashes.

"Months later, in Brisbane, the English captain said to [me]: 'Are you as bored watching us play cricket as I am of being taken to see your play?' In spite of coming from a cricketing family who had once had their own eleven who played the rest of Kent, [I] loathed cricket, and [I] answered fervently: 'Bored-er.'

"...[I] read many books about Australia. [I] already knew something about the prison ships that had brought the prisoners over, for [I] had been brought up hearing how [my] great-great-grandmother, Elizabeth Fry, had collected

The first impression of Great-aunt Dymphna was that she was more like an enormous bird than a great-aunt. This was partly because she wore a black cape, which seemed to flap behind her when she moved. ■ (From *The Magic Summer* by Noel Streatfeild. Illustrated by Edward Ardizzone.)

scraps of dress material and had given each woman prisoner a bagful so that she might make a quilt on the journey, to sell on her arrival in Australia. [I] knew too how often the fault for which a prisoner was deported was mere petty pilfering by the hungry."[3]

1929. While on the Australian tour Streatfeild's beloved father, who had become the Bishop of Lewes, died. "One morning toward the end of the season in Sydney [I] woke and went to the door to take in the paper. Back in bed [I] idly turned over the pages. There were terrible accounts of the weather in England. Although it was February there, the weather was the coldest the country had known for years. [My] eye ran down the page for further items of interest. It was then [I] saw it. It was in black headlines and read: ENGLISH BISHOP DROPS DEAD IN TRAIN.

"[I] stared, waiting for the news to sink in. When it did, [I] shoved a corner of the blanket into [my] mouth so that no one should know that [I] was screaming.

"Days passed. [I] went to the theater as usual. Presumably, too, . . . ate and slept, but . . . felt unconscious of anything but grief. Each morning [I] woke to a load of pain, and each evening . . . took it to bed with [me].

"It's not just Father, [I] thought. It's everything. There's Mother, of course . . . but no home anymore. It was those words, 'no home anymore,' that did it. They were a stimulant. [I] repeated them over and over until they really sank in.

"Then out loud [I] said: 'Get on with it . . . You are on your own now.'"[3]

1930. Left the stage to pursue a writing career.

1931. First novel, *The Whicharts* (the title originated from a childhood mispronunciation of the first line of "The Lord's Prayer") was published in England and America and was followed by other adult novels.

1936. First children's book, *Ballet Shoes,* was published. "J. M. Dent, the publishers, had at that time a Miss Carey in charge of their books for children. She was a brilliant woman, always trying to discover new talent and give it a chance to develop. She had read [my] first novel *The Whicharts* and had decided that children would enjoy a book about the theatre, preferably about children in the theatre. So she invited [me] to a meal and over it poured out her idea.

"'I'm certain the world is full of children who would like to read about children actors. Couldn't you write such a book?'

"[I] was stunned at the suggestion.

"'I'm perfectly certain I couldn't. I've never even thought of writing for children.'

"But Mabel Carey pressed on until at last unwillingly [I] agreed to ask Heinemann [the publisher] if they objected. . . . This was a good get-out for [I] was sure Heinemann would mind. However, there [I] was wrong.

"So, cross with [my]self for agreeing to something [I] was convinced [I] could not write, [I] wrote [my] first book for children. The only thing [I] liked about it was that it fulfilled a childhood's dream of [mine] and [my sister's] that [I] would write a book and [she] would illustrate it. [She] was already much in demand for illustrations but ... gladly accepted the offer to illustrate *Ballet Shoes*, which is what [I] called the book.'' [Noel Streatfeild, *Beyond the Vicarage*, Franklin Watts, 1972.⁴]

1937. *Caroline England* was published. Took her first trip to America. From California she wrote to her mother: ''There have been the usual alarms and excursions that happen to all writers out here. There was an idea of my writing on a picture. It has, I think, come to nothing. And as I was expecting it to come to nothing I was not disappointed. I should have been glad of it financially, because if I could have borne writing out here for three months, I should have made enough money not to have to slave so hard at the million odds and ends with which I make my income. On the other hand the thought of coming home makes me sing.''⁴

1938. *The Circus is Coming*, which won the Carnegie Medal as the Best Children's Book of the Year, was published. Streatfeild and illustrator, Stephen Spurrier, spent a period travelling around with a circus to gain the proper background for the book. ''When the time came to say good-bye to the circus [I] decided to go by a slow cargo boat to California writing [my] circus book on the journey. There were still plenty of holes in [my] knowledge but [I] had decided to tell [my] story through the eyes of two children who knew nothing about circuses. [I] also collected a formidable array of books to help [me], most of which seemed to be translated from the German. . . .

'''Then when I come home,' [I] told mother, 'I shall have finished the circus book and can get down to my Aimée Semple McPherson book.'

'''Well, don't stay too long,' Mother advised. 'I don't like the news at all. Come home at once if things get worse.'

'''Don't fuss, I will,' [I] promised. 'But if you ask me there isn't going to be a war.'''⁴

1940. During World War II Streatfeild joined the Women's Volunteer Service in London. ''During the war [I] had, apart from *I Ordered a Table for Six*, written two books for children and one for adults. [My] usual type of children's story proved impossible to write as [I] needed time for research so [I] wrote two thrillers. Children, [I] often said—not today's children particularly but all children, the ones we were and the ones who will be tomorrow—are most rewarding to write for; not just financially—though that is true too—but as readers. Certainly one of those two thrillers written during the war is still in print in many countries and, though today's children cannot imagine a wartime England with wardens' posts and all the rest of it, they apparently still read it quite happily just for the story.''⁴

1946. ''The moment the war in Europe was over [I] had written one more children's book, but that had been handed to [me] on a plate, as it were. It was called *Party Frock* and the foreword describes exactly how [I] came to know the story.

'''During the war my niece, Nicolette, was given a party frock and shoes from America. A lovely frock of the sort that nobody had because of clothes rationing. Blue organdie over a silk slip. It was Nicolette's first long frock and she could hardly wait for the right occasion to put it on. But no occasion turned up. There was at that time almost no transport. So little heating that if it was a winter party something warmer than organdie would have to be worn. Food was

difficult, and every grown-up person too busy to arrange a party of the making-do sort it would have had to have been. The frock hung in the cupboard, and hung in the cupboard. A most depressing place for a first long party frock. Worst of all, Nicolette grew. Even the most optimistic person had to wonder, if there ever was a party, would the frock be too short and too tight?

'''I am glad to say that Nicolette did wear the frock. If it was a bit tight it did not show. She looked exactly as somebody of thirteen ought to look at a party. But I remember the months of anxiety when the frock hung in the cupboard. How awful to have been Nicolette. How many more girls had party frocks and shoes sent them from abroad and no party? So, for Nicolette in England, and the givers of the party frock and shoes in America, I wrote this book.'''⁴

1949. *The Painted Garden*, a children's book with a Hollywood background (collected during Streatfeild's second trip to America at the end of the war) was published. ''By now, of course, [I] was middle-aged; [I] never knew exactly when that began just as [I] did not know when it finished and [I] was old. Other women told [me] how much they loathed being middle-aged, but [I] not only didn't care [I] quite liked it.

''You see, I think being middle-aged sneaked up on me during the war. I started off at the fag end of being youngish—I mean I did all the same things I'd always done—but I came out of the war what people call 'getting on.' I find it rather

"Do you like living in the orphanage, Horatio?" Lady Corkberry asked. ■ (From *Thursday's Child* by Noel Streatfeild. Illustrated by Peggy Fortnum.)

Read *The Tale of Peter Rabbit* and *The Tale of Mrs. Tiggy-Winkle,* you will find it extraordinary—I could scarcely believe it myself—but these five little stories have been woven into a ballet, danced by the Royal Ballet Company. ■ (From *A Young Person's Guide to Ballet* by Noel Streatfeild. Photo courtesy of EMI Film Productions Ltd., London.)

nice. I'd no idea how unutterably bored I was with night clubs. How sick and tired of being taken on somewhere after a theatre. Of all the other stupid boring things the young or would-be young do to be in the swim. Now I say to myself: 'You're middle-aged. You needn't go.' Having accepted being middle-aged, of course, [I] had to find new interests. Travel [I] had always loved and between books fitted in more of it. This was made possible because [my] mother died.

"After the war when [I] was in America [my] mother had a very serious operation. Mother took the operation with the courage of a lion, remarking to [my] Aunt . . . who came to see her and who said she would be back as soon after the operation as was permitted:

"'I'll love to see you but don't forget I may be harping on a cloud.'

"Mother didn't die from the operation but she was never again the same person. Each time [I] went to see her she had a little less hold on life. She still loved her garden but she, who had made it and done all but the heaviest work herself, was capable of very little, even mild weeding tired her. . . . Every day on his way to London—he worked at the Siamese Embassy—[my brother] called on Mother and warned the family she was definitely going downhill, which, of course, [I] could see for [my]self on [my] week-end visits. How hard it is to watch your mother fade away from you. It is not that you would keep her but in some way the natal cord still holds and when she dies some part of you dies with her."[4]

1950-1959. Continued to write children's books. Among them, *The Bell Family*, which ran as a popular serial in the BBC Children's Hour program and was adapted into a television serial. "There were so many pleasures in the 1950s. There was the abiding joy of Pierre. He was such an amusing dog. Being so small he had accepted that he must get his way by other means than force. He was the only dog in [my] life who stamped when thwarted. Refused something he thought he should have and up would come one minute back leg to be thumped on the ground.

". . . The owner of the house in which [I] lived died and so [I] was able to rent the top floor, giving [my]self a maisonette. The space was desperately needed. Manuscripts were piled up in the temporary office downstairs. Now at last the secretary could come up into daylight and steel cabinets would house all the papers, files, manuscripts, radio scripts and all the other cumbersome stuff that is part and parcel of every author's life.

"[My] first secretary who worked in the new office was a young woman who had learnt her trade in the navy during the war. Her mother and [I] had known each other when [we] were young. The Wren was charming but not a born secretary. She was a real product of the navy, keeping copies of every letter written, but with no idea of typing speed and only rudimentary shorthand. But she had other admirable gifts, she was a beautiful proof corrector and splendid at research and, incidentally, a good shopper. Naturally with her looks she did not last long, for as is the way of pretty secretaries she left to be married.

"Oh yes, without doubt the fifties and early sixties were halcyon days. [I] knew the only way to treat such years was to thank God you had them and never to regret them—which is just what [I] did."[4]

1960. *New Town: A Story about the Bell Family* was published. "The 1960s showed [me] a new America. Random House, the publishers of [my] children's books, decided to give a dinner to celebrate the fact that *Ballet Shoes* had been in print and selling for thirty years. Actually the book had been in print and selling for thirty-two years in England but it had passed unnoticed, not only by the publishers but also by [my]self. After the dinner [I] was to be taken for a month's visit to New England by [the head] of the children's department at Random House."[4]

1963. The first book in Streatfeild's autobiographical trilogy, *A Vicarage Family*, was published. "An autobiographer is one who writes his own history. This—as far as my growing-up years are concerned—I have, to the best of my knowledge, done. For I am the Vicky of this book.

"But how does the autobiographer handle a brother and sisters? A father and mother? How they looked, how they appeared to me as persons—yes. But were they like that inside?

"It is because of my awareness that my portraits of the rest of my family are probably faulty that I have used no real names. The thin shield of anonymity helped me to feel unselfconscious in drawing them, and in approaching the facts of my own life."[2]

1965. Two more autobiographical novels, *Away from the Vicarage* and *On Tour: An Autobiographical Novel of the 20's* were published.

1968. ". . . The bad year for [our family]. It started with the death of [our brother]. . . . When he married he got all his happiness from his immediate family—his wife and children. But he remained very much the head of the . . . family and, though it could happen that he did not see his sisters often [worked abroad], they knew he was there in the background ready to help should a need arise. His death was sudden for though he had been ill with a coronary he was shortly coming out of the hospital, in fact the day before he died [I] had a letter from him saying the doctor thought he would be fit by the time the fishing season started. . . . [I] was only just getting used to the idea that [my brother] was dead when [I] was taken very ill. . . . [I] woke up one morning paralysed all down the left side.

"[I] was wonderfully lucky for [I] had splendid nurses both night and day, a miraculous physiotherapist and, most important of all, a brilliant doctor.

"[I] fortunately, was no slouch when it came to getting well. [I] worked like a slave to get [my] body moving again and after two months was able, after a fashion, to walk. [I] remembered very little about the early days of [my] illness. . . . Two things stood out from the haze. The doctor saying: 'If you can't get some movement into that left hand in four days' time I can't help you,' and one letter. A letter [I] read and re-read throughout [my] illness. It was not from a close friend but from a writer with whom [I] served on a committee. He told [me] not to be afraid that [I] would not get well—[I] would. His wife had suffered from the same illness and had completely recovered. That letter acted as a tonic and a challenge. What the writer's wife could do [I] could do."[4]

Besides the tragedy of her brother's death and her own long illness, 1968 saw the deaths of her brother-in-law, a very close friend and companion, and her pet dog, Pierre. "'The moment has arrived,' [I] told [my]self, 'when you start living by your old age code. Don't be afraid, I'm sure you'll find there's a world of interest still to come.'"[4]

1970. Continued to write children's fiction and non-fiction books.

1971. The final volume of Streatfeild's autobiographical trilogy, *Beyond the Vicarage,* was published by Collins. The following year, Franklin Watts, Inc. published the book in the United States.

1974. *The Noel Streatfeild Easter Holiday Book* and *When the Sirens Wailed,* a book for children about World War II, were published. "Today the second world war belongs to that no man's land which exists between modern life and history. Correctly, it should be taught as history, but it has not yet been included in history books. In Great Britain all towns of any size, from the moment war was declared, were ordered to evacuate their children to rural areas, and so a cut was made, lasting for six years, during which the children lived away from their homes often in families with totally different backgrounds from their own. What I have tried to do in *When the Sirens Wailed* is to picture three of these children and through them tell today's children what living in wartime Britain was like.

"The great difficulty of writing such a book is that it is very difficult to tell the story of life as it was without making it sound exciting, so exciting that children of today could say, 'My goodness, didn't the children of that day have fun!' It does sound exciting to work beside the grown-ups planning to deceive the enemy if they arrived. It does sound adventurous to live through air raids. Actually it is not a nice memory at all. It has got bright spots in it, of course, but most of it was uncomfortable, to put it mildly, and often frightening."

1975. *A Young Person's Guide to the Ballet* was published.

1976. *Ballet Shoes for Anna* and *Gran-Nannie* were published when Streatfeild was in her late seventies. "'It's your last chance,' [I] warned [my]self. 'You don't want to reach the next world with the sort of report you got at school—"could do so much better if she would try."'"

"Jotting down notes was a habit of [mine] for they were usually thoughts for books. Amongst these now turned up a queer assortment of suggestions, which in time [I] numbered.

"(1) Never willingly mention your health. People may ask how you are but they don't want to know. If you should be operated upon keep quiet about it.

"(2) When your health and strength fail to such an extent that you can't pull your weight at a party don't go. N.B. People like to laugh.

"(3) Never, never, never criticise those younger than yourself. If tempted remember yourself at their age and blush.

"(4) Go to church regularly even if you don't feel like it. God understands it's tough growing old and will help you to be pleasant about it.

"(5) Make your motto 'Keep right on to the end of the road.'

"Such a simple little list of ideas but, when the time came to put them into practice, very helpful."[4]

Streatfeild has been one of the most popular and successful of contemporary writers for children. Many of her stories have been adapted for radio and television. "Seen in retrospect, a life has a marked resemblance to a patterned carpet. The carpet may at first glance seem a confusing mass of color, but study it and a shape emerges. There is an overall design that runs through the whole."[4]

HOBBIES AND OTHER INTERESTS: Wild flower collecting.

FOR MORE INFORMATION SEE: London *Times Literary Supplement,* November 21, 1936; *Chicago Daily Tribune,* January 9, 1937; *New York Times,* July 30, 1939; *Horn Book,* September, 1939, January-December, 1947, January-December, 1948, October, 1958, February, 1963, December, 1963, April, 1964, December, 1965, June, 1971, October, 1972; Kunitz & Haycraft, editors, *Junior Book of Authors,* second edition, H. W. Wilson, 1951; Noel Streatfeild, *Vicarage Family: An Autobiographical Story,* Watts, 1963; Barbara Ker Wilson, *Noel Streatfeild,* Walck, 1964; Noel Streatfeild, *Away from the Vicarage,* Collins, 1965; Noel Streatfeild, *On Tour: An Autobiographical Novel of the 20's,* Watts, 1965; Brian Doyle, editor, *Who's Who of Children's Literature,* Schocken, 1968; *Saturday Review,* November 9, 1968, May 20, 1972; *Book World,* April 20, 1969; Noel Streatfeild, *Beyond the Vicarage,* Collins, 1971, Watts, 1972; *Bulletin of the Center for Children's Books,* September, 1973; *Publishers Weekly,* May 26, 1975; Margery Fisher, *Who's Who in Children's Books,* Holt, 1975.

ROBYN SUPRANER

SUPRANER, Robyn 1930-
(Erica Frost, Elizabeth Warren, Olive Blake)

PERSONAL: Born September 14, 1930, in New York, N.Y.; daughter of Mortimer (an insurance broker) and Dorothy (Kalmanowitz) Rubenstein; married Leon Supraner (a photographer), December 16, 1950; children: Keith, Scott, Dennis, Lauren. *Education:* Attended Pratt Institute and Parson's School of Design, 1944-48, and Adelphi University, 1948-51. *Politics:* Feminist. *Address:* Bryant Avenue, Roslyn Harbor, N.Y. 11576.

CAREER: Free-lance song writer, 1962-72 (songs have been recorded by popular recording artists, including Chubby Checker, Mel Torme, and Johnny Winter); writer, 1970—. Taught creative dramatics at Roslyn Creative Arts Workshop, 1973-74.

WRITINGS—For children: *Draw Me a Circle*, Simon & Schuster, 1970; *Draw Me a Square*, Simon & Schuster, 1970; *Draw Me a Triangle*, Simon & Schuster, 1970; *Would You Rather Be a Tiger?*, Houghton, 1973; *Think About It, You Might Learn Something*, Houghton, 1973; *It's Not Fair!* (Junior Literary Guild selection), Warne, 1976; *Giggly, Wiggly, Snickety-Snick*, Parents' Magazine Press, 1977; *Sam Sunday and the Strange Disappearance of Chester Cats*, Parents' Magazine Press, 1979.

All published by Troll Associates: *I Can Read About Witches*, 1975; *I Can Read About Weather*, 1975; *I Can Read About Baseball*, 1975; *I Can Read About Seasons*, 1975; *I Can Read About Homonyms: The Mystery of the Hidden Treasure*, 1977; *I Can Read About Synonyms and Antonyms: The Case of Strange Aunt Pickles*, 1977; *The Mystery at the Zoo*, 1979; *Mrs. Wigglesworth's Secret*, 1979; *The Ghost in the Attic*, 1979; *The Mystery of the Witch's Shoes*, 1979; *The Case of the Missing Canary*, 1979; *The Second Troll Talking Dictionary*, 1979; *Happy Halloween: Things to Make and Do*, 1980; *Merry Christmas: Things to Make and Do*, 1980; *Valentine's Day: Things to Make and Do*, 1980; *Rainy Day Surprises You Can Make*, 1980; *Easy Cook Cookbook*, 1980; *Ten Masks to Make*, 1980; *Illusions*, 1980; *Fun With Paper*, 1980; *Science Secrets*, 1980; *Magic Tricks to Make and Do*, 1980; *Nature Crafts*, 1980; (with daughter, Lauren Supraner) *Plenty of Puppets to Make*, 1980.

Under pseudonym Erica Frost—all published by Troll Associates: *I Can Read About Ballet*, 1975; *I Can Read About Good Manners*, 1975; *I Can Read About Ghosts*, 1975; *Harold and the Dinosaur Mystery*, 1979; *The Mystery of the Runaway Sled*, 1979; *The Mystery of the Midnight Visitors*, 1979; *The Case of the Missing Chick*, 1979.

Under pseudonym Elizabeth Warren—all published by Troll Associates: *I Can Read About Trees and Plants*, 1975; *I Can Read About Bats*, 1975; *I Can Read About Indians*, 1975; *I Can Read About Baby Animals*, 1975.

Under pseudonym Olive Blake—all published by Troll Associates: *The Grape Jelly Mystery*, 1979; *The Mystery of the Lost Letter*, 1979; *The Mystery of the Lost Pearl*, 1979.

Author of twelve single-concept learning books for Columbia Broadcasting System (CBS), published by Shelley Graphics, 1971; author of other learning books published by Shelley Graphics, 1972, and of a sixteen-volume dictionary for children and other learning books, published by Educa-

(From *It's Not Fair* by Robyn Supraner. Illustrated by Randall Enos.)

tional Reading Service, 1972—; also author of books with cassette tapes, under pseudonyms Erica Frost and Elizabeth Warren, for Educational Reading Service, 1975.

WORK IN PROGRESS: Six new mysteries for Troll Associates.

SIDELIGHTS: "I was a quiet child, pursued by those fears known only in childhood. One day, Blackie arrived to comfort me. He was a huge, black-panther—strong and sleek. For months, he stayed by my side, accompanying me to school and sleeping at the foot of my bed. Invisible to others, he was my constant and gentle friend—my fierce and loyal protector.

"Pretending was as natural to me as waking up in the morning. When Blackie returned to the world from which he came, I threw myself into other games of make-believe. Each day, I hurried home from school to assume the character of April Showers, a beautiful and clever young woman with an eighteen inch waistline and impossibly long, red fingernails. Audrey Millstein, who lived across the street, played the part of May Flowers. April and May were inseparable. Their adventures were daring—heart-rending and romantic. Like the soap operas they were, they continued from day to day without missing a beat!

"As I grew older, it became necessary to combine my two worlds. Making up stories and writing them down—reading them aloud and acting them out—became a wonderful way to integrate the reality of my daily life with the fantasy I so loved. Many of my books spring from the bewilderments of my childhood. I was a bewildered child, and now, as a parent, I am a bewildered adult.

"I was almost six when my sister was born. I had wanted a brother. When, in spite of my injunctions, my sister arrived,

I wept for my lost place and my parents' cruel disregard. It wasn't fair. Some thirty odd years later, still smarting, I started and completed *It's Not Fair!*

"Now, I live on a wooded hillside in Roslyn Harbor. My house is large and rambling and slowly emptying itself of children who are growing up."

HOBBIES AND OTHER INTERESTS: Rock polishing, writing and reading poetry, gathering shells.

SWIFT, Hildegarde Hoyt   1890(?)-1977

OBITUARY NOTICE: Born about 1890, in Clinton, N.Y.; died January 10, 1977, in Redlands, Calif. Author of books for children. Hildegarde Hoyt Swift wrote several biographies for young readers including *The Railroad to Freedom,* the story of Harriet Tubman which was cited as an honor book for the John Newbery Medal in 1933. Some of her other titles have been named ALA Notable Books including *The Edge of April, From the Eagle's Wing,* and *The Little Red Lighthouse and the Grey Bridge* which is a well-known picture book. *For More Information See: Authors of Books for Young People,* 2nd edition, Scarecrow, 1971; *The Junior Book of Authors,* 2nd revised edition, Wilson, 1951. *Obituaries: A B Bookman's Weekly,* March 14, 1977; *Times,* January 11, 1977; *School Library Journal,* March, 1977.

THOMPSON, Stith   1885-1976

OBITUARY NOTICE: Born March 7, 1885, in Bloomfield, Ky.; died January 10, 1976, in Columbus, Ind. Author, educator, and folklorist. Dr. Thompson, the Distinguished Service Professor of English and Folklore at Indiana University, was the author of several books on subjects ranging from Indian folktales to English composition. The founder of the Indiana University Folklore Department will long be remembered for such works as *The Motif-Index of Folk Literature* and *One Hundred Favorite Folktales. For More Information See: American Authors and Books, 1640 to the Present Day,* 3rd revised edition, Crown, 1972; *Anthology of Children's Literature,* 4th edition, Houghton, 1970; *The Author's and Writer's Who's Who,* 6th edition, Hafner, 1971; *Indiana Authors and Their Books, 1917-1966,* Wabash College, 1974; *The Oxford Companion to Canadian History and Literature,* Oxford University Press, 1967. *Obituaries: Contemporary Authors,* Volume 61-64, Gale, 1976; *New York Times,* January 12, 1976; *Publishers Weekly,* February 23, 1976.

TUDOR, Tasha

PERSONAL: Name was originally Starling Burgess; legally changed; born in Boston, Mass.; daughter of W. Starling Burgess (a yacht designer) and Rosamond Tudor (a portrait painter). *Education:* Studied at the Boston Museum Fine Arts School. *Politics:* "Not at all interested." *Religion:* "Stillwater." *Residence:* Marlboro, Vt.

CAREER: Author and illustrator of children's books since 1938. *Member:* Pembroke Walsh Coral Club, American Primrose Society, American Goat Association, American Lilac Society. *Awards, honors:* Runner-up for the Caldecott

TASHA TUDOR

Medal, 1945, for *Mother Goose,* 1957, for *1 is One;* Regina Medal, 1971; *The Night Before Christmas* was named a "Children's Book of the Year," 1975, by the Child Study Association.

WRITINGS—All self-illustrated and all published by Oxford University Press, except as noted: *Pumpkin Moonshine,* 1938, enlarged edition, Walck, 1962; *Alexander the Gander,* 1939, enlarged edition, Walck, 1961; *The County Fair,* 1940, enlarged edition, Walck, 1964; *A Tale for Easter,* Walck, 1941; *Snow Before Christmas,* 1941; *Dorcas Porkus,* 1942, enlarged edition, Walck, 1963; *The White Goose,* 1943; *Linsey Woolsey,* 1946; *Thistly B,* 1949; *The Dolls' Christmas,* 1950, reissued, Walck, 1972; *Amanda and the Bear,* 1951; *Edgar Allan Crow,* 1953; *A is for Annabelle,* Walck, 1954, reissued, Rand McNally, 1971; *1 is One,* Walck, 1956; *Around the Year,* 1957; *Becky's Birthday,* Viking, 1960; (with others) *My Brimful Book,* edited by Dana Bruce, Platt, 1960; *Becky's Christmas,* Viking, 1961; *First Delights: A Book About the Five Senses,* Platt, 1966; *Corgiville Fair,* Crowell, 1971; *A Time to Keep: The Tasha Tudor Book of Holidays,* Rand McNally, 1977; *Tasha Tudor's Sampler: A Tale for Easter, Pumpkin Moonshine,* [and] *The Dolls' Christmas,* McKay, 1977; *An Advent Calendar,* Rand McNally, 1978; (with Linda Allen) *Tasha Tudor's Favorite Christmas Carols,* McKay, 1978; (with Linda Allen) *Tasha Tudor's Old-Fashioned Christmas Gifts,* McKay, 1979; *A Book of Christmas,* Collins, 1979; *The Springs of Joy,* Rand McNally, 1979.

Illustrator: *Mother Goose, Seventy-Seven Verses*, Walck, 1944; Hans Christian Andersen, *Fairy Tales from Hans Christian Andersen*, Walck, 1945; Robert Louis Stevenson, *Child's Garden of Verses*, Oxford University Press, 1947; Juliana Horatia Ewing, *Jackanapes*, Oxford University Press, 1947; *First Prayers*, Oxford University Press, 1952; Thomas Leighton McCready, Jr., *Biggity Bantam*, Farrar, 1954; T. L. McCready, Jr., *Pekin White*, Farrar, 1955; *First Graces*, Oxford University Press, 1955; T. L. McCready, Jr., *Mr. Stubbs*, Farrar, 1956; T. L. McCready, Jr., *Increase Rabbit* (a Junior Literary Guild selection), Farrar, 1958; *And It Was So*, Westminster Press, 1958; Sara Klein Clark, editor, *The Lord Will Love Thee*, Westminster Press, 1959; T. L. McCready, Jr., *Adventures of a Beagle*, Farrar, 1959; Rumer Godden, *Doll's House* (ALA Notable Book), Viking, 1962, reissued, 1970; Clement C. Moore, *The Night Before Christmas*, St. Onge, 1962, Rand McNally, 1975; Frances H. Burnett, *Secret Garden*, Lippincott, 1962, reissued, Dell, 1970; F. H. Burnett, *Little Princess*, Lippincott, 1963; Louisa May Alcott, *A Round Dozen: Stories*, Viking, 1963; Bible, *The Twenty-Third Psalm*, St. Onge, 1965; Kenneth Grahame, *The Wind in the Willows*, World Publishing, 1966; Henry A. Shute, *The Real Diary of a Real Boy*, R. R. Smith, 1967; *More Prayers*, Walck, 1967; *First Poems of Childhood*, Platt, 1967; H. A. Shute, *Brite and Fair*, Noone House, 1968; Mary M. Campbell, *New England Butt'ry Shelf Cookbook*, World Publishing, 1968; L. M. Alcott, *Little Women*, World Publishing, 1969; Mary M. Campbell, *New England Butt'ry Shelf Almanac*, World Publishing, 1970; Mary M. Campbell, *Betty Crocker's Kitchen Gardens*, Golden Press, 1971; Efner Tudor Holmes, *The Christmas Cat*, Crowell, 1976; Efner Tudor Holmes, *Amy's Goose*, Crowell, 1977; Kate Klimo, editor, *Tasha Tudor's Bedtime Book*, Platt & Munk, 1977. Efner Tudor Holmes, *Carrie's Gift*, Collins, 1978.

Editor: (And illustrator) *The Tasha Tudor Book of Fairy Tales*, Platt, 1961; (and illustrator) *Wings from the Wind: An Anthology of Poems*, Lippincott, 1964; *Tasha Tudor's Favorite Stories*, Lippincott, 1965; *Take Joy! The Tasha Tudor Christmas Book*, Lippincott, 1966.

SIDELIGHTS: Tudor was born in Boston and raised in nearby Marblehead, Massachusetts. She was christened Starling Burgess, but was renamed Natasha by her father, who was very fond of Tolstoy's heroine in *War and Peace*. Eventually, Natasha was shortened to Tasha.

Even as a child Tudor loved to draw. Her mother was a portrait painter and her father was a well known naval architect. She was exposed at an early age to the works of Edmund Dulac, Arthur Rackham, Randolph Caldecott, and Walter Crane, among others.

At the age of nine, Tudor was sent to live with family friends in Redding, Connecticut. Her mother, recently divorced, lived and worked in Greenwich Village in New York. "I was dumped into the most unconventional atmosphere you can imagine. It was the best thing that ever happened to me. We lived on practically nothing but rice and tomatoes, cold cereals and quickly put-together meals, as Aunt Gwen was far too wrapped up in writing plays to have time for elaborate

(From *The Night Before Christmas* by Clement Clarke Moore. Illustrated by Tasha Tudor.)

"A boy, and a fox, and a crow, and two squirrels, and a newborn lamb, are coming to see me this morning. I want them brought upstairs as soon as they come," he said. ■ (From *The Secret Garden* by Frances Hodgson Burnett. Illustrated by Tasha Tudor.)

cooking, yet she often read out loud to us at night—sometimes until ten or eleven o'clock!' [Bethany Tudor, *Drawn from New England: Tasha Tudor*, Collins, 1979.[1]]

Tudor's most memorable educational experiences were spent in Redding, Connecticut with her Aunt Gwen and with her Uncle Henry, who taught in his home. "I didn't start school until the age of seven, and I never got past the eighth grade. I didn't pass a single test and spent most of the time decorating my copybooks. I hated every minute of school, except the few years with Uncle Henry."[1]

As a teenager Tudor spent summers in Redding and winters in Bermuda with her mother, where she taught nursery school. By nineteen she had written and illustrated her first book.

In 1938 Tudor began a long association with Eunice Blake, then editor at Oxford University Press, when the latter accepted *Pumpkin Moonshine* for publication. The same year Tudor married, and the couple settled a few years later on a

450-acre farm in Webster, New Hampshire. The house lacked electricity and running water, and was heated by wood stoves. Here Tudor worked hard at her chores and raised her four children. She continued to spend many hours illustrating and writing books. Her lifestyle was similar to that of the past century—all their food was grown on the farm. "Motivation was the wolf at the door and four small children to raise and educate. I draw almost entirely from my surroundings—the children are either mine or my grandchildren and the animals are all the animals I own or have had the privilege of caring for."

Tasha Tudor claims her love of drawing was inherited from her mother, a portrait painter. As a child, she enjoyed the books of Beatrix Potter, Randolph Caldecott, and Walter Crane, and was influenced by the works of Edmund Dulac, Arthur Rackham, and Hugh Thomson, among others. Her illustrations are done in water color and ink.

Tudor has lived most of her life in the countryside of the northeastern United States. She owns 160 acres in Vermont, living there in the manner of the nineteenth century. Four years ago, her sons, Seth and Tom built a reproduction of an old farmhouse, set in a pine clearing unreachable

The Sea Rat, as soon as his hunger was somewhat assuaged, continued the history of his latest voyage, conducting his simple hearer from port to port of Spain, landing him at Lisbon, Oporto, and Bordeaux. ■ (From *The Wind in the Willows* by Kenneth Grahame. Illustrated by Tasha Tudor.)

by an ordinary car. Electricity was installed in the unpainted, clapboard house two years ago, but water must still be fetched in buckets from the barn. Tasha Tudor raises all of her food, including cheese and butter. She makes her own candles, spins yarn, and weaves cloth made from her own flax. She wears long calico dresses and no shoes, to save on shoe leather. A menagerie of animals live with her—ducks, geese, goats, chickens, dogs, and cats.

Tudor and some of her friends who enjoy the life-style of the nineteenth century have formed a group called the Still-waters. Their aim is to revive the kind of life reminiscent of that era. "We are great venerators of nature," she explained in a recent *New York Times* article, "believe in peaceful living, in live and let live, and discipline for children."

Tasha Tudor raised and educated her children on the money she earned from the sale of her books. Her first book, *Pumpkin Moonshine,* was written as a Christmas gift for a niece. A *New York Times* critique of *Snow before Christmas* included: "The pictures are charming in color and spirit, and Tasha Tudor has succeeded in capturing that feeling of anticipation in which, for the child, lies in the joy of the Christmas season." Commenting on *Dorcas Porkus,* the *New York Times* wrote, "As always in Tasha Tudor's books, the story is simplicity itself, yet it has lively action and eventfulness in line with a little child's interests. The

(From *A Little Princess* by Frances Hodgson Burnett. Illustrated by Tasha Tudor.)

drawings on every page add distinction and atmosphere and make the setting very convincing. . . . These little stories are never dull nor perfunctory, for the artist-author has touched them with the magic of the changing seasons . . . of firelight and candlelight, cozy kitchens and shady orchards, all homely delights which belong by right to childhood and contribute to joy." Of *1 is One,* the *Chicago Sunday Tribune* observed: "All the pictures—alternating black and white with delicate pastel colors—have a warm, old fashioned flavor which will captivate the ages."

Tudor's works are included in the Kerlan Collection at the University of Minnesota.

HOBBIES AND OTHER INTERESTS: "Making a marionette play of *The Rose and the Ring* and making my garden more beautiful than Eden's."

FOR MORE INFORMATION SEE: New York Times, December 14, 1941, October 25, 1942; Bertha E. Mahony and others, compilers, *Illustrators of Children's Books, 1744-1945,* Horn Book, 1945, reprinted, 1970; Stanley J. Kunitz and Howard Haycraft, editors, *Junior Book of Authors,* second edition, revised, H. W. Wilson, 1951; *Chicago Sunday Tribune,* November 11, 1956; B. M. Miller and others, compilers, *Illustrators of Children's Books, 1946-1956,*

O what a joy to clamber there,
 O what a place for play,
With the sweet, the dim, the dusty air,
 The happy hills of hay.
■ (From *A Child's Garden of Verses* by Robert Louis Stevenson. Illustrated by Tasha Tudor.)

Horn Book, 1958; *Horn Book,* February, 1965, December, 1966, October, 1973; Lee Kingman and others, compilers, *Illustrators of Children's Books, 1957-1966,* Horn Book, 1968; *Christian Science,* November, 1971; *N.Y. Times Book Review,* November 7, 1971, April 15, 1973, December 7, 1975; *Publishers Weekly,* February 28, 1977; Angela Taylor, "An Illustrator Who Works at the Art of 19th-Century Living," *New York Times,* July 5, 1977.

VILLIARD, Paul 1910-1974

OBITUARY NOTICE: Born January 16, 1910, in Spokane, Wash., died August 18, 1974, in Saxton, N.Y. Author and photographer. Villiard wrote and illustrated several books on hobbies for adults and children. Villiard's adult titles include *Handy Man's Plumbing and Heating Guide* and *A Manual of Veneering.* For younger readers he wrote *Insects as Pets, Exotic Fish as Pets, The Hidden World,* and many others. *For More Information See: Authors of Books for Young People,* 2nd edition supplement, Scarecrow, 1979; *Contemporary Authors, Permanent Series,* Volume 2, Gale, 1978. *Obituaries: Contemporary Authors,* Volume 53-56, Gale, 1975, *New York Times,* August 24, 1974, *Publishers Weekly,* September 30, 1974.

WALLER, Leslie 1923-

PERSONAL: Born April 1, 1923, in Chicago, Ill.; son of George and Ruth (Elson) Waller; married Patricia Mahen (an actress), September 22, 1967; children: (from a former marriage) Elizabeth, Susan. *Education:* University of Chicago, student, 1939-41, 1945-46; Columbia University, B.A., 1948, M.A. in American Literature, 1950. *Agent:* Anthony M. Furman, Inc., 527 Madison Ave., New York, N.Y. 10022.

CAREER: City News Bureau, Chicago, Ill., reporter-rewrite, 1939-41; Savings Banks Association of New York, N.Y., public relations director, 1952-56; Sydney S. Baron Public Relations Corp., New York, N.Y., director of publicity, 1956-60; Harshe-Rotman-Druck, Inc., public relations agency, New York, N.Y., vice-president, 1960-68; freelance writer, 1968—. *Military service:* U.S. Army Air Force, public relations, 1941-45. *Member:* P.E.N., Mensa.

WRITINGS: Three Day Pass (novel), Viking, 1944; *Show Me the Way* (novel), Viking, 1947; *The Bed She Made,* Dial, 1951; *Phoenix Island,* Lippincott, 1958; (with Louise Waller) *Take Me To Your Leader,* Putnam, 1961; *The Banker,* Doubleday, 1963; *K,* Fawcett, 1963; *Will the Real Toulouse-Lautrec Please Stand Up?,* Doubleday, 1965; *The Family,* Putnam, 1966; *Overdrive,* Holt, 1967; *The American,* Putnam, 1968; *New Sound,* Holt, 1969; *The Mob: The Story of Organized Crime* (non-fiction), Delacorte, 1970; *The Swiss Bank Connection* (non-fiction), New American Library, 1970; *A Change in the Wind* (novel), Bernard Geis, 1971; *Number One,* (novel), Bantam, 1972; *The Coast of Fear* (novel), Doubleday, 1973; *The Swiss Account* (novel), Doubleday, 1975; *Hide in Plain Sight* (non-fiction), Delacorte, 1976; *Trocadero* (novel), Delacorte, 1978; *The Brave and the Free* (novel), Delacorte, 1979.

Juvenile books—All published by Holt: *A Book to Begin on Weather,* 1959, . . . *Time,* 1959, . . . *Numbers,* 1960, . . . *Our Flag,* 1960, . . . *Our American Language,* 1961, . . . *Explor-*

ers, 1961, . . . *Electricity,* 1962, . . . *American Inventions,* 1963, . . . *The American West,* 1966, . . . *Clothing,* 1967.

Juvenile books—All published by Grosset: *A Book to Begin on Plants,* 1967, . . . *Energy,* 1967, . . . *Air and Water,* 1967, . . . *Gems,* 1968, . . . *Light,* 1968, . . . *Birds,* 1968, . . . *Plains and Prairies,* 1968, . . . *Mountains,* 1969.

WORK IN PROGRESS: A new, untitled novel about the events at the turn of the century in New Orleans, for Putnam.

SIDELIGHTS: "While most of my 'easy reader' books for small children deal with such everyday topics as history and science, I have also written for the high-school level what is considered the first text-book on crime and law-enforcement to be used by American schools. It is *The Mob: The Story of Organized Crime,* currently available both in hard cover and paperback. Early experience with crime, as a police reporter, gave me valuable contacts on both sides of the law, which I continue to maintain.

"This material has also been the basis for a series of 'documentary' novels which deal with true events and real people under a fictional guise. In this series, which continues characters from one book to the next, is included *The Banker, The Family, The American* and *The Swiss Account.* Constant research also produces material that can be dealt with as non-fiction, including books on the use to which criminals put the Swiss banking system and the U.S. Department of Justice's 'witness relocation program,' under which informers are given new identities and immunity from their criminal acts. The latter book, *Hide in Plain Sight,* is now an MGM film, released in late 1979.

"Most of my fiction and all of my non-fiction comes out of research, particularly in the daily newspapers and magazines. Since fiction is primarily the story of characters interacting with each other, there is an added dimension to such work in which the people loom much larger than the themes or background material.

"I write rapidly, once research is finished, but the original research itself may take as long as ten years to complete. Because of the way I work, I have come to have a great deal of confidence in our press and responsible journalism in general. Many times over the past decades the determination of the press has been the only shield between what we would want our country to be and what some of our leaders would like to change it into.

"In this respect, as a primary purveyor of information, journalism has become a full partner with education in our time. People for whom the shocks and outrages of current events come as a total surprise are people who simply have not been reading a responsible daily newspaper. No matter how covered up, every event of history has been reported on, often piecemeal, long before it was announced to the world.

"Often that reportage continues to be piecemeal by the nature of the press's daily schedule. Novels and book-length non-fiction upgrade quotidian events by linking them into a cause-and-effect chain. They are, I hope, a valuable documentary aid to this general process by which the public learns the events of its time."

The Leslie Waller Collection was established at Boston University Library in 1966; the collection includes original manuscripts, editions, and memorabilia.

LESLIE WALLER

HOBBIES AND OTHER INTERESTS: Oil paintings, jazz piano, travel writing for R. H. Donnelly *Travel Scene*.

WECHSLER, Herman   1904-1976

OBITUARY NOTICE: Born August 21, 1904, in New York, N.Y.; died January 13, 1976, in New York, N.Y. Author, art gallery owner, lecturer, and consultant on art. Herman Wechsler, the founder, president, and director of the FAR Gallery in New York City, accomplished a great deal in support of the arts during his lifetime. As editor of the "Pocket Book" series on art in the 1940's and 1950's, he brought art to a much wider audience. Titles in this series include *The Pocket Book of Old Masters, Gods and Goddesses in Art and Legend,* and *Lives of Famous French Painters.* He is also the author of such children's books as *The Life and Art of Vincent Van Gogh* and *The French Impressionists.* For *More Information See: Contemporary Authors,* Volume 65-68, Gale, 1977; *Who's Who in American Art,* Bowker, 1973. *Obituaries: A B Bookmans Weekly,* April 12, 1976; *Contemporary Authors,* Volume 61-64, Gale, 1976; *New York Times,* January 14, 1976.

WEGNER, Fritz   1924-

PERSONAL: Born September 15, 1924, in Vienna, Austria; married; children: four. *Education:* Attended St. Martin's School of Art, London, England. *Residence:* London, England.

CAREER: Free-lance illustrator of books and magazines. *Wartime service:* Worked for the War Agricultural Committee during World War II.

ILLUSTRATOR: Frank Swinnerton, *Cats and Rosemary,* H. Hamilton, 1950; Grace A. Hogarth, *The Funny Guy,* Har-

court, Brace, 1955; Rosemary A. Sisson, *Impractical Chimney Sweep,* Watts, 1956; Ivan Turgenev, *First Love,* H. Hamilton, 1956; Dorothy L. Sayers, *Days of Christ's Coming,* Harper, 1960; Frances Wilkins, *Wizards and Witches,* Walck, 1966; William Mayne, *House on Fairmont,* Dutton, 1968; Andre Maurois, *Fattypuffs and Thinifers,* Knopf, 1968; Barbara Willard, compiler, *Hullabaloo! About Naughty Boys and Girls,* Meredith Press, 1969; Joseph Jacobs, *Jack the Giant-Killer,* H. Z. Walck, 1970; Leon Garfield, *The Strange Affair of Adelaide Harris,* Pantheon Books, 1971; Carolyn Sloan, *Carter Is a Painter's Cat,* Simon & Schuster, 1971; Grimm Brothers. *The Story of Snow White and the Seven Dwarfs,* H. Z. Walck, 1973; Janet Barber, *The Voyage of Jim,* Carolrhoda Books, 1973; Ian Serraillier, *The Robin and the Wren,* Kestrel Books, 1974; Mordecai Richler, *Jacob Two-Two Meets the Hooded Fang,* Knopf, 1975; Roger W. Drury, *The Champion of Merrimack Country,* Little, Brown, 1976.

SIDELIGHTS: **September 15, 1924.** Born in Vienna, Austria. "My childhood memories center mainly around school (which I detested) and the hardships encountered by my family during the years of depression and civil war." [Bertha M. Miller and others, compilers, *Illustrators of Children's Books, 1946-1956,* Horn Book, 1958.[1]]

1938. Escaped to England with his family and has lived there ever since. "When I was thirteen years old some of my fam-

But, even as he spoke, a miracle occurred. To everyone's astonishment, the fog began to lift. For the first time within living memory, the sky over the children's prison began to brighten. ■ (From *Jacob Two-Two Meets the Hooded Fang* by Mordecai Richler. Illustrated by Fritz Wegner.)

ily and I were fortunate to escape the Nazi menace, and gratefully received English hospitality and freedom. There was nothing in the world I wanted to do more than to become an artist, and I finally succeeded in obtaining a scholarship to St. Martin's School of Art, Later, I became apprenticed to a designer who initiated me in the professional practice of lettering and design outside the unreality of the school room.''[1]

1941. ''At seventeen I went on the land to work for the War Agricultural Committee, with whom I remained till the end of the war.''[1]

1945. Began a career as a free-lance illustrator. Wegner is married, has four children and lives in London. ''I have been free-lancing as illustrator of books and magazines, and in advertising. I enjoy a variety of media in my work, but the pen remains my favorite. It always intrigues me to interpret the stories I illustrate accurately, and I approach the work in the old fashioned sense of illustrating rather than decorating a book.''[1]

FOR MORE INFORMATION SEE: Bertha M. Miller and others, compilers, *Illustrators of Children's Books: 1946-1956,* Horn Book, 1958.

WELLS, H(erbert) G(eorge)　1866-1946 (Reginald Bliss)

PERSONAL: Born September 21, 1866, in Bromley, Kent, England; died August 13, 1946, in London, England; son of Joseph (a professional cricket player) and Sarah (a housekeeper; maiden name Neal) Wells; married Isabel Mary Wells (his first cousin), 1891 (divorced, 1895); married Amy Catherine Robbins (a writer; died, 1927); children: (second marriage) two sons. *Education:* London University, B.S. (with honors), about 1890. *Politics:* Liberal Democrat. *Home:* Regent's Park, London, England.

CAREER: Novelist and social critic. Early employment included apprenticeships with a draper and a druggist. After graduation from college, he was a private tutor in science and wrote a biology textbook; later turned to journalism and fiction writing. *Member:* Fabian Society, Savile Club.

WRITINGS—Novels: The Time Machine, H. Holt, 1895, reissued, Berkley Publishing, 1975 [other editions illustrated by William A. Dwiggins, Random House, 1931; Joe Mugnaini, Limited Editions, 1964]; *The Wonderful Visit,* Macmillan, 1895; *The Island of Doctor Moreau,* Stone & Kimball, 1896, reissued, Heinemann, 1970; *The Wheels of Chance* (illustrated by J. Ayton Symington), Macmillan, 1896; *The Invisible Man,* Harper, 1897, reissued, Scholastic Book Services, 1972 [another edition illustrated by Charles Mozley, Limited Editions, 1967]; *The War of the Worlds,* Harper, 1898, reissued, Scholastic Book Services, 1974 [other editions illustrated by Edward Gorey, Random House, 1960; J. Mugnaini, Heritage Press, 1964]; *When the Sleeper Wakes,* Harper, 1899, reissued, Ace Books, 1972 (also published as *The Sleeper Awakes,* Collins, 1964); *Love and Mr. Lewisham,* F. A. Stokes, 1899, reissued, Collins, 1972.

The First Men in the Moon (illustrated by E. Hering), Bowen-Merrill, 1901, reissued, Collins, 1970; *The Sea Lady,* D. Appleton, 1902, reissued, Hyperion Press, 1976; *The Food of the Gods, and How It Came to Earth,* Scribner, 1904 [another edition reissued as *The Food of the Gods*

H. G. WELLS

(illustrated by Graham Byfield), Heron Books, 1969]; *Kipps,* Scribner, 1905, reissued, Dell, 1968 [another edition illustrated by David Knight, Heron Books, 1968]; *A Modern Utopia* (illustrated by E. J. Sullivan), Scribner, 1905, reissued, University of Nebraska Press, 1967; *In the Days of the Comet,* Century, 1906, reissued, Collins, 1966; *The War in the Air, and Particularly How Mr. Bert Smallways Fared while It Lasted* (illustrated by Eric Pape), Macmillan, 1908 [another edition illustrated by Michael Jackson, Heron Books, 1968]; *Tono-Bungay,* Duffield, 1908 [other editions include an edition with an introduction by Theodore Dreiser, Duffield, 1927; an edition illustrated by Lynton Lamb, Limited Editions, 1960; and an edition illustrated by Christina Carpenter, Heron Books, 1968]; *Ann Veronica,* Harper, 1909, reissued, Penguin, 1968.

The History of Mr. Polly, T. Nelson, 1910, reissued, Collins, 1966 [another edition illustrated by Ian Ribbons, Folio Society, 1957]; *The New Machiavelli,* Duffield, 1910 [another edition illustrated by Rosemary Neale, Heron Books, 1968]; *Marriage,* Duffield, 1912; *The Passionate Friends,* Harper, 1913 [another edition illustrated by Leonora Box, Heron Books, 1968]; *The Wife of Sir Isaac Harman,* Macmillan, 1914; *Bealby: A Holiday,* Macmillan, 1915 [an abridged edition illustrated by Richard O. Rose, Methuen, 1958]; *The Research Magnificent,* Macmillan, 1915 [another edition illustrated by Anthony Colbert, Heron Books, 1969]; *Mr. Britling Sees It Through,* Macmillan, 1916, reissued as *Mr. Britling,* Heron Books, 1969; *The Soul of a*

Bishop, Macmillan, 1917; *Joan and Peter*, Macmillan, 1918; *The Undying Fire*, Macmillan, 1919.

The Secret Places of the Heart, Macmillan, 1922; *Men like Gods*, Macmillan, 1923, reissued, Leisure Books, 1970 [another edition illustrated by David W. Whitfield, Heron Books, 1969]; *The Dream*, Macmillan, 1924; *Christina Alberta's Father*, Macmillan, 1925; *The World of William Clissold*, Doran, 1926, reprinted, Greenwood Press, 1972; *Meanwhile: The Picture of a Lady*, Doran, 1927, reissued, E. Benn, 1962; *Mr. Blettsworthy on Rampole Island*, Doubleday, Doran, 1928; *The King Who Was a King*, Doubleday, Doran, 1929, reprinted, Greenwood Press, 1972; *The Autocracy of Mr. Parham* (illustrated by David Low), Doubleday, Doran, 1930; *The Bulpington of Blup*, Macmillan, 1933; *Brynhild; or, The Show of Things*, Scribner, 1937 [another edition illustrated by Jutta Ash, Heron Books, 1969]; *The Camford Visitation*, Methuen, 1937; *Star-Begotten*, Viking, 1937, reissued, Manor Books, 1975; *Apropos of Dolores*, Scribner, 1938; *The Holy Terror*, Simon & Schuster, 1939; *All Aboard for Ararat*, Secker & Warburg, 1940, Alliance Book Corp., 1941; *The Desert Daisy*, Beta Phi Mu (Urbana, Ill.), 1957; *The Wealth of Mr. Waddy*, Southern Illinois University Press, 1969.

Short stories: *The Stolen Bacillus, and Other Incidents*, Methuen, 1895; *The Plattner Story, and Others*, Methuen, 1897; *Thirty Strange Stories*, Harper, 1897, reissued, Causeway, 1974; *A Cure for Love*, E. Scott, 1899; *Tales of Space and Time*, Doubleday & McClure, 1899, reprinted, Books for Libraries, 1972; *The Vacant Country*, A. E. Kent, 1899; *Twelve Stories and a Dream*, Macmillan, 1903, reprinted, Books for Libraries, 1971; *The Door in the Wall, and Other Stories* (illustrated by Alvin L. Coburn), M. Kennerley, 1911; *The Country of the Blind, and Other Stories*, T. Nelson, 1911, reprinted, Books for Libraries, 1971; *The World Set Free*, Dutton, 1914, reissued, Leisure Books, 1971; *The Short Stories of H. G. Wells*, E. Benn, 1927, Doubleday, Doran, 1929, reissued as *The Complete Short Stories of H. G. Wells*, St. Martin's Press, 1970; *The Croquet Player*, Chatto & Windus, 1936, Viking, 1937; *The Brothers*, Viking, 1938; *Babes in the Darkling Wood*, Alliance Book Corp., 1940; *You Can't Be Too Careful*, Secker & Warburg, 1941, Putnam, 1942.

Essays: (With R. A. Gregory) *Honours Physiography*, J. Hughes, 1893; *Anticipations of the Reaction of Mechanical and Scientific Progress upon Human Life and Thought*, Harper, 1902; *The Discovery of the Future* (a speech delivered at the Royal Institution, January 24, 1902), T. F. Unwin, 1902; *Mankind in the Making*, Chapman & Hall, 1903, Scribner, 1904; *The Future in America*, Harper, 1906, reprinted, Arno, 1974; *Socialism and the Family*, A. C. Fifield, 1906; *This Misery of Boots*, The Fabian Society, 1907, Ball Publishing, 1908, reprinted, Folcroft, 1973; *New Worlds for Old*, Macmillan, 1908; *The War That Will End War*, Duffield, 1914; *Social Forces in England and America*, Harper, 1914; *The End of the Armament Rings*, World Peace Foundation, 1914; *The Peace of the World*, Daily Chronicle, 1915.

The Elements of Reconstruction, Nisbet, 1916; *What Is Coming? A European Forecast*, Macmillan, 1916; *War and the Future: Italy, France, and Britain at War*, Cassell, 1917 (also published as *Italy, France, and Britain at War*, Macmillan, 1917); *British Nationalism and the League of Nations*, The League of Nations Union, 1918; *In the Fourth Year: Anticipations of a World Peace*, Macmillan, 1918; *The Idea of a League of Nations*, Atlantic Monthly Press,

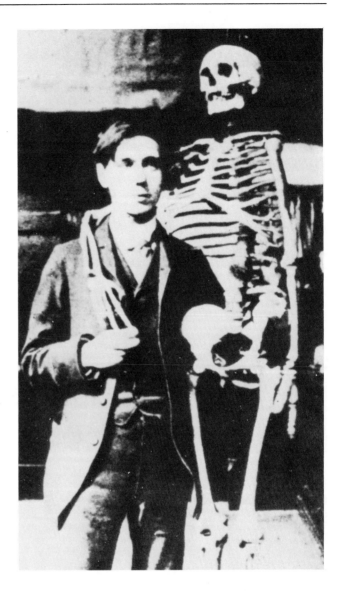

Wells, the science student, 1886.

1919; *Russia in the Shadows*, Hodder & Stoughton, 1920, Doran, 1921, reissued, Hyperion Press, 1973; *The Salvaging of Civilization: The Probable Future of Mankind*, Macmillan, 1921; *Washington and the Riddle of Peace*, Macmillan, 1922 (published in England as *Washington and the Hope of Peace*, Collins, 1922); *A Year of Prophesying*, T. F. Unwin, 1924, Macmillan, 1925.

Mr. Belloc Objects to "The Outline of History," Doran, 1926; *Wells' Social Anticipations*, Vanguard, 1927; *Democracy under Revision*, Doran, 1927; *The Open Conspiracy: Blue Prints for a World Revolution*, Doubleday, Doran, 1928; *What Are We to Do with Our Lives?* (a revised and rewritten edition of *The Open Conspiracy*), Doubleday, Doran, 1931; *The Way the World is Going: Guesses and Forecasts of the Years Ahead*, E. Benn, 1928, Doubleday, Doran, 1929; *Imperialism and the Open Conspiracy*, Faber, 1929; *The Way to World Peace*, E. Benn, 1930; *The Work, Wealth, and Happiness of Mankind*, Doubleday, Doran, 1931, reprinted, Greenwood Press, 1968 (also published as *The Outline of Man's Work and Wealth*, Garden City Publishing, 1936); *After Democracy*, Watts, 1932; *What Should be Done—Now: A Memorandum on the World Situation*,

The Strange Man's arrival ～

(From *The Invisible Man* by H. G. Wells. Illustrated by Charles Mozley.)

Watts, 1932; *The Shape of Things to Come,* Macmillan, 1933, reissued as *Things to Come,* Gregg, 1975 [another edition illustrated by Lisbeth Kneen under the original title, Heron Books, 1969].

The New America, the New World, Macmillan, 1935; *The Anatomy of Frustration,* Macmillan, 1936; *The Idea of a World Encyclopaedia* (a speech delivered at the Royal Institution, November 20, 1936), Hogarth Press, 1936; *World Brain,* Doubleday, Doran, 1938, reprinted, Books for Libraries, 1971; *Travels of a Republican Radical in Search of Hot Water,* Penguin, 1939; *The Fate of Man,* Longmans, Green, 1939, reprinted, Books for Libraries, 1970 (published in England as *The Fate of Homo Sapiens,* Secker & Warburg, 1939); *The Rights of Man; or, What are We Fighting For?,* Penguin, 1940; *The Common Sense of War and Peace: World Revolution or War Unending,* Penguin, 1940; *The New World Order,* A. A. Knopf, 1940, reprinted, Greenwood Press, 1974; *Guide to the New World: A Handbook of Constructive World Revolution,* Gollancz, 1941.

Science and the World Mind, New Europe Publishing, 1942; *The Conquest of Time,* Watts, 1942; *The Outlook for Homo Sapiens* (a combination and revision of *The Fate of Homo Sapiens* and *The New World Order*), Secker & Warburg, 1942; *Phoenix: A Summary of the Inescapable Condi-*

tions of World Reorganisation, Secker & Warburg, 1942; *Crux Ansata: An Indictment of the Roman Catholic Church,* Penguin, 1943, reprinted, Arno, 1972; *'42 to '44: A Contemporary Memoir upon Human Behavior During the Crisis of the World Revolution,* Secker & Warburg, 1944; *Mind at the End of its Tether,* Heinemann, 1945, reissued, Millet Books, 1974 (also published as *The Happy Turning: A Dream of Life,* Heinemann, 1945); *Journalism and Prophecy, 1893-1946: An Anthology,* edited by W. Warren Wagar, Houghton, 1964.

Nonfiction: *Text-Book of Biology,* [London], 1893; *Select Conversations with an Uncle,* Merriam, 1895; *Certain Personal Matters* (autobiographical), Lawrence & Bullen, 1898; *First and Last Things: A Confession of Faith and a Rule of Life,* Putnam, 1908, revised and enlarged edition, Cassell, 1918; *An Englishman Looks at the World,* Cassell, 1914; (under pseudonym Reginald Bliss) *Boon: The Mind of the Race, The Wild Asses of the Devil, and The Last Trump,* Doran, 1915; *God: The Invisible King,* Macmillan, 1917; *The Outline of History, being a Plain History of Life and Mankind,* G. Newnes, 1919-20, Macmillan, 1920, revised edition, Doubleday, 1971; *A Short History of the World,* Macmillan, 1922, revised edition, Collins, 1965; *The Story of a Great Schoolmaster,* Macmillan, 1924; (with Julian S. Huxley and son, G. P. Wells) *The Science of Life*

James F. Sullivan wrote and illustrated *The Island of Dr. Menu* a parody on *The Island of Dr. Moreau.*
■ (From *The H. G. Wells Scrapbook* edited by Peter Haining.)

(also issued in several volumes as *The Science of Life* series), Doubleday, Doran, 1931; *Experiment in Autobiography: Discoveries and Conclusions of a Very Ordinary Brain (since 1866)*, Macmillan, 1934, reprinted, AMS Press, 1976; *The Pocket History of the World*, Pocket Books, 1941.

Other: (For children) *Floor Games* (illustrated by J. R. Sinclair), Small, Maynard, 1912, reprinted, Arno, 1976; (for children) *Little Wars*, Small, Maynard, 1913, reissued, Macmillan, 1970; (author of introduction) Amy Catherine (Robbins) Wells, *The Book of Catherine Wells*, Doubleday, Doran, 1928, reprinted, Books for Libraries, 1971; (for children) *The Adventures of Tommy* (self-illustrated), F. A. Stokes, 1929, reissued, Knopf, 1967; *Man Who Could Work Miracles* (a film by Wells based on the short story of the same title), Macmillan, 1936; *Marxism vs. Liberalism: An Interview between Joseph Stalin and H. G. Wells*, New Century, 1945.

Contributor: "Past and the Great State," in *Socialism and the Great State: Essays by Various Authors*, Harper, 1912; "Apology for a World Utopia," in *Evolution of World Peace*, edited by Francis S. Martin, Oxford University Press, 1921; "Probable Future of Mankind," in *Nineteen Modern Essays*, edited by William A. J. Archbold, Long-

"**But going along the High Street, my old life came back to me for a space, for I met the girl I had known ten years since. Our eyes met.**" ■ (From *The Invisible Man* by H. G. Wells. Illustrated by Charles Mozley.)

mans, Green, 1926; "Fifty Years from Now," in *Challenging Essays in Modern Thought*, second series, edited by Joseph M. Bachelor and Ralph L. Henry, Appleton-Century, 1928-33; "History is One," in *Challenging Essays in Modern Thought*, edited by J. M. Bachelor and R. L. Henry, Appleton-Century, 1928-33; "Aepyornis Island," in *Essays Then and Now*, edited by Alice C. Cooper and David Fallon, Ginn, 1937; "Towards the World-Commonweal," in *Leviathan in Crisis*, edited by Waldo R. Browne, Viking, 1946.

Collections and selections: *Great Thoughts from H. G. Wells*, edited by Marriott Watson, Dodge, 1912; *The Works of H. G. Wells*, 26 volumes, Scribner, 1924; *The Essex Thin-Paper Edition of the Works of H. G. Wells*, 24 volumes, E. Benn, 1926; *A Quartette of Comedies* (includes *Kipps, The History of Mr. Polly, Bealby*, and *Love and Mr. Lewisham*), E. Benn, 1928; *The Scientific Romances of H. G. Wells*, Gollancz, 1933; *Seven Famous Novels*, Knopf, 1934, reissued as *Seven Science Fiction Novels*, Dover, 1950; *The Favorite Short Stories of H. G. Wells*, Doubleday, Doran, 1937, reprinted, American Reprint-Riv-

(From *The Research Magnificent* by H. G. Wells. Illustrated by Anthony Colbert.)

ited by Robert M. Philmus and David Y. Hughes, University of California Press, 1975.

ADAPTATIONS—Movies: "Marriage," Fox Film, 1927; "Island of Lost Souls," adaptation of *The Island of Doctor Moreau,* starring Charles Laughton and Bela Lugosi, Paramount Pictures, 1932; "The Invisible Man," starring Claude Rains, Universal Pictures, 1933; "Things to Come," adaptation of *The Shape of Things to Come,* starring Raymond Massey and Sir Cedric Hardwicke, London Film Productions, 1936; "The Man Who Could Work Miracles," London Film Productions, 1937; "The Invisible Man Returns," starring Sir Cedric Hardwicke and Vincent Price, Universal Pictures, 1940; "Kipps," starring Michael Redgrave, Twentieth Century-Fox, 1941; "Invisible Agent," based on *The Invisible Man,* starring Peter Lorre and Sir Cedric Hardwicke, Universal Pictures, 1942; "The Invisible Man's Revenge," based on *The Invisible Man,* starring John Carradine, Universal Pictures, 1944.

Well's own sketch of what he thought a Martian looked like. ■ (From *H. G. Wells* by Geoffrey West.)

ercity Press, 1976; *The Famous Short Stories of H. G. Wells,* Garden City Publishing, 1938; *The H. G. Wells Papers at the University of Illinois,* edited by Gordon N. Ray, University of Illinois Press, 1958.

Tales of the Unexpected, Collins, 1963; *The War in the Air, In the Days of the Comet, The Food of the Gods: Three Science Fiction Novels,* Dover, 1963; *Tales of Life and Adventure,* Collins, 1965; *The Inexperienced Ghost, and Nine Other Stories,* edited by Hart Day Leavitt, Bantam Books, 1965; *Tales of Wonder,* Collins, 1966; *Best Science Fiction Stories of H. G. Wells,* Dover, 1966; *Works,* 12 volumes, Editio-Service, 1968; *The War of the Worlds, A Dream of Armageddon,* [and] *The Land Ironclads* (illustrated by G. Byfield), Heron Books, 1968; *The Time Machine* [and] *The War of the Worlds* (with an introduction by Isaac Asimov), Fawcett, 1968; *The Last Books of H. G. Wells,* edited by G. P. Wells, H. G. Wells Society, 1968; *The Soul of a Bishop* [and] *The Secret Places of the Heart* (illustrated by Janet Archer), Heron Books, 1969; *The Wheels of Chance* [and] *The World Set Free,* Heron Books, 1969; *The Sleeper Awakes* [and] *Tales of the Unexpected* (illustrated by Pauline Ellison), Heron Books, 1969; *H. G. Wells: Early Writings in Science and Science Fiction,* ed-

Orson Welles narrating the CBS Radio broadcast of "The War of the Worlds," starring the Mercury Players, 1938.

''One Woman's Story,'' adaptation of *The Passionate Friends,* Universal Pictures, 1948; ''The History of Mr. Polly,'' starring John Mills and Sally Ann Howes, Two Cities Films, 1949; ''The Passionate Friends,'' starring Trevor Howard and Claude Rains, Cineguild, 1949; ''Abbott and Costello Meet the Invisible Man,'' starring Bud Abbott and Lou Costello, Universal International Pictures, 1951; ''The War of the Worlds,'' starring Gene Barry, Paramount Pictures, 1953, excerpts from the 1953 motion picture released under the same title (20 min., sound, color, 16 mm.), Films, Inc., 1975; ''The Door in the Wall,'' Associated British and Pathe Films, 1956; ''Daydreams,'' starring Elsa Lanchester and Charles Laughton, Brandon Films, 1958; ''The Time Machine,'' starring Rod Taylor and Yvette Mimieux, Metro-Goldwyn-Mayer, 1960; ''First Men in the Moon,'' Columbia Pictures, 1964; ''Half-A-Sixpence,'' adaptation of *Kipps,* starring Tommy Steele and Cyril Ritchard, Paramount Pictures, 1967.

Plays: Ronald Gow, *Ann Veronica* (two-act comedy), S. French, 1951; Joel Stone, *Horrors of Doctor Moreau* (four-scene; adaptation of *The Island of Doctor Moreau*), S. French, 1972; ''Half-A-Sixpence'' was adapted as a musical play from Wells' novel, *Kipps,* starring Tommy Steele, and

Stephen Lawrence's illustration for *The Island of Dr. Moreau.* ■ (From *The H.G. Wells Scrapbook* edited by Peter Haining.)

was performed in London at the Cambridge Theatre, beginning March 21, 1963, and in New York at the Broadhurst Theatre, beginning April 25, 1965.

Radio and television: ''The War of the Worlds'' (radio drama), adaptation by Orson Welles, starring Welles and the Mercury Company, CBS Radio, October 30, 1938; ''The Invisible Man'' (television series; 30 minutes), syndicated, 1958; ''The Invisible Man,'' (television series; 60 minutes), starring David McCallum, NBC, September 8, 1975-January 19, 1976.

SIDELIGHTS: **September 21, 1866.** Born in Bromley, Kent, England. ''This brain of mine came into existence and began to acquire reflexes and register impressions in a needy shabby home in a little town called Bromley in Kent, which has since become a suburb of London. My consciousness of myself grew by such imperceptible degrees, and for a time each successive impression incorporated what had preceded it so completely, that I have no recollection of any beginning at all. I have a miscellany of early memories, but they are not arranged in any time order. I will do my best however, to recall the conditions amidst which my childish head got its elementary lessons in living. They

''[Orson Welles while narrating 'The War of the Worlds'] kindly gave me access to the rehearsals of those shows and asked me to come to one of his first radio broadcasts. From where I sat that night, safe behind a glass-enclosed booth, it seemed merely a good joke, though it turned out to be the performance in which he scared half the nation out of its skin with the Martian invasion.'' ■ (From *Come One, Come All!* by Don Freeman. Illustrated by the author.)

(From the movie "The Invisible Man Returns," based on the novel *The Invisible Man,* starring Sir Cedric Hardwicke. Produced by Universal Pictures Co., Inc., 1940.)

(From the movie "Invisible Agent," based on the novel *The Invisible Man,* starring Ilona Massey. Copyright 1942 by Universal Pictures Co., Inc.)

(From the movie "The Invisible Man's Revenge," based on the novel *The Invisible Man*, starring John Carradine. Copyright 1944 by Universal Pictures Co., Inc.)

(From the movie "The Invisible Man," starring Claude Rains. Copyright 1933 by Universal Pictures Corp.)

(From the movie "Things to Come," adapted from the novel *The Shape of Things to Come*, starring Ralph Richardson. Copyright 1936 by London Film Productions.)

(From the movie "Island of Lost Souls," adapted from the novel *The Island of Doctor Moreau*, starring Richard Arlen. Copyright 1932 by Paramount Pictures Inc.)

(From the movie "Empire of the Ants," starring Robert Lansing and Joan Collins. Copyright © 1977 by American International Pictures.)

(From the movie "*Time Machine*," starring Rod Taylor. Produced by Metro-Goldwyn-Mayer, 1960.)

seem to me now quite dreadful conditions, but at the time it was the only conceivable world.

"It was then the flaxen head of a podgy little boy with a snub nose and a long infantile upper lip, and along the top his flaxen hair was curled in a longitudinal curl which was finally abolished at his own urgent request. Early photographs record short white socks, bare arms and legs, a petticoat, ribbon bows on the shoulders, and a scowl. That must have been [a] gala costume. I do not remember exactly what everyday clothes I wore until I was getting to be a fairly big boy. I seem to recall a sort of holland pinafore for everyday use very like what small boys still wear in France, except that it was brown instead of black holland.

"The house in which this little boy ran about, clattering up and down the uncarpeted stairs, bawling—family tradition insists on the bawling—and investigating existence, deserves description, not only from the biographical, but from the sociological point of view. It was one of a row of badly built houses upon a narrow section of the High Street. In front upon the ground floor was the shop, filled with crockery, china and glassware and, a special line of goods, cricket bats, balls, stumps, nets and other cricket material. Behind the shop was an extremely small room, the 'parlour,' with a fireplace, a borrowed light and glass-door upon the shop and a larger window upon the yard behind. A murderously narrow staircase with a twist in it led downstairs to a completely subterranean kitchen, lit by a window which derived its light from a grating on the street level, and a bricked scullery, which, since the house was poised on a bank, opened into the yard at the ground level below. In the scullery was a small fireplace, a copper boiler for washing, a provision cupboard, a bread pan, a beer cask, a pump delivering water from a well into a stone sink, and space for coal, our only space for coal, beneath the wooden stairs. This 'coal cellar' held about a ton of coal, and when the supply was renewed it had to be carried in sacks through the shop and 'parlour' and down the staircase by men who were apt to be uncivil about the inconveniences of

the task and still more apt to drop small particles of coal along the route.

". . . There was not a scrap of faded carpet or worn oil-cloth in the house that had not lived a full life of usefulness before it came into our household. Everything was frayed, discoloured and patched. But we had no end of oil lamps because they came out of (and went back into) stock. (My father . . . dealt in lamp-wicks, oil and paraffin.)

"We lived, as I have said, mostly downstairs and underground, more particularly in the winter. We went upstairs to bed. About upstairs I have to add a further particular. The house was infested with bugs. They harboured in the wooden bedsteads and lurked between the layers of wallpaper that peeled from the walls. Slain they avenge themselves by a peculiar penetrating disagreeable smell. That mingles in my early recollections with the more pervasive odour of paraffin, with which my father carried on an inconclusive war against them. Almost every part of my home had its own distinctive smell.

"This was the material setting in which my life began. Let me tell now something of my father and mother, what manner of people they were, and how they got themselves into this queer home from which my two brothers and I were launched into what Sir James Jeans has very properly called, this Mysterious Universe, to make what we could of it.

"My mother was a little blue-eyed, pink-cheeked woman with a large serious innocent face. . . .

"[She] drudged endlessly in that gaunt and impossible home and the years slipped by. Year after year she changed and the prim little lady's-maid, with her simple faith and her definite views about the Holy Sacrament, gave place to a tired woman more and more perplexed by life. Twice more her habitual 'anxiety' was not to be relieved, and God was to incur her jaded and formal gratitude for two more 'dear

They packed the elephant very carefully, (you see they have done his trunk and tail and feet with straw). ■ (From *The Adventures of Tommy* by H. G. Wells. Illustrated by the author.)

(From *The War of the Worlds* by H. G. Wells. Illustrated by Edward Gorey.)

ones.' She feared us terribly before we came and afterwards she loved and slaved for us intensely, beyond reason. She was not clever at her job and I have to tell it; she sometimes did badly by her children through lack of knowledge and flexibility, but nothing could exceed the grit and devotion of her mothering. She wore her fingers to the bone working at our clothes, and she had acquired a fanatical belief in cod liver oil and insisted that we two younger ones should have it at any cost; so that we escaped the vitamin insufficiency that gave my elder brother a pigeon breast and a retarded growth. No one knew about vitamin D in those days, but cod liver oil had been prescribed for my sister Fanny and it had worked magic with her.

"My mother brought my brother Freddy into the world in 1862, and had her great tragedy in 1864, when my sister died of appendicitis. The nature of appendicitis was unknown in those days; it was called 'inflammation of the bowels'; my sister had been to a children's tea party a day or so before her seizure, and my mother in her distress at this sudden blow, leaped to the conclusion that Fanny had been given something unsuitable to eat, and was never quite reconciled to those neighbours, would not speak to them, forbade us to mention them." [H. G. Wells, *Experiment in Autobiography,* (Vol. I), A. P. Watt & Son, J. B. Lippincott & Co., 1934.[1]]

His father, Joseph Wells, when all else failed, was an avid cricket player. "I do not know why my father was unsuccessful as a gardener, but I suspect a certain intractability of temper rather than incapacity. He did not like to be told things and made to do things. He was impatient. Before he married, I gather from an old letter from a friend that has

chanced to be preserved, he was talking of going to the gold diggings in Australia, and again after he left the cottage at Shuckburgh he was looking round for some way out of the galling subordinations and uncertainties of 'service.' He thought again of emigrating, this time to America; there were even two stout boxes made for his belongings, and then his schemes for flight abroad, which perhaps after all were rather half-hearted schemes, were frustrated by the advent of my eldest brother, his second child.

"Perhaps it was as well that he did not attempt pioneering in new lands with my mother. She had been trained as a lady's-maid and not as a housewife and I do not think she had the mental flexibility to rise to new occasions. She was that sort of woman who is an incorrigibly bad cook. By nature and upbringing alike she belonged to that middle-class of dependents who occupied situations, performed strictly defined duties, gave or failed to give satisfaction and had no ideas at all outside that dependence. People of that quality 'saved up for a rainy day' but they were without the slightest trace of primary productive or acquisitive ability. She was that in all innocence, but I perceive that my father might well have had a more efficient helpmate in the struggle for life as it went on in the individualistic nineteenth century.

"He was at any rate a producer, if only as a recalcitrant gardener, but he shared her incapacity for getting and holding things. They were both economic innocents made by and for a social order, a scheme of things, that was falling to pieces all about them. And looking for stability in a world that was already breaking away towards adventure, they presently dropped into that dismal insanitary hole I

(From the movie "Abbott & Costello Meet the Invisible Man," based on the novel *The Invisible Man*, starring Bud Abbott and Lou Costello. Copyright 1951 by Universal-International Pictures.)

(From the movie "One Woman's Story," adapted from the novel *The Passionate Friends*, starring Ann Todd and Claude Rains. Copyright 1949 by Universal Pictures Co., Inc.)

have already described, in which I was born, and from which they were unable to escape for twenty-four dreary years."[1]

1871. Attended Morley's Academy. "I do not remember any teaching at all at school.

". . . We used to draw on our slates, tell one another fantastic stories, trade in stamps, play games with marbles, eat sweets and tarts, and bread and butter, while the process of our education was in active progress." [Geoffrey West, *H. G. Wells*, Folcroft Library Editions, 1972.[2]]

1874. "My leg was broken for me when I was between seven and eight. Probably I am alive to-day and writing this autobiography instead of being a worn-out, dismissed and already dead shop assistant, because my leg was broken. The agent of good fortune was 'young Sutton,' the grown-up son of the landlord of the Bell. I was playing outside the scoring tent in the cricket field and in all friendliness he picked me up and tossed me in the air. 'Whose little kid are you?' he said, and I wriggled, he missed his hold on me and I snapped my tibia across a tent peg. A great fuss of being carried home; a painful setting—for they just set and strapped a broken leg tightly between splints in those days, and the knee and ankle swelled dreadfully—and then for some weeks I found myself enthroned on the sofa in the parlour as the most important thing in the house, consuming unheard-of jellies, fruits, brawn and chicken sent with endless apologies on behalf of her son by Mrs. Sutton, and I could demand and have a fair chance of getting anything that came into my head, books, paper, pencils, and toys—and particularly books.

"I had just taken to reading. I had just discovered the art of leaving my body to sit impassive in a crumpled up attitude in a chair or sofa, while I wandered over the hills and far away in novel company and new scenes. And now my father went round nearly every day to the Literary Institute in Market Square and got one or two books for me, and Mrs. Sutton sent some books, and there was always a fresh book to read. My world began to expand very rapidly, and when presently I could put my foot to the ground, the reading habit had got me securely. Both my parents were doubtful of the healthiness of reading, and did their best to discourage this poring over books as soon as my leg was better."[1]

1880. "Fat fourteen, when so many boys are at a public school, I was precipitated by my father's financial troubles into a driving, systematic, incessant draper's shop, and given so bad a time as to stiffen my naturally indolent, rather slovenly, and far too genial nature into a grim rebellion against the world—a spurt of revolt that enabled me to do wonders of self-education before its force was exhausted. If I had been the son of a prosperous gentleman I should never, I am sure, have done anything at all."[2]

1881. Entered Midhurst School. "I do not know how my mother hit upon the idea of making me a pharmaceutical chemist. But that was the next career towards which I (and my small portmanteau) were now directed. I spent only about a month amidst the neat gilt-inscribed drawers and bottles of Mr. Cowap at Midhurst, rolled a few score antibilious and rhubarb pills, broke a dozen soda-water siphons during a friendly broom fight with the errand boy, learnt to sell patent medicines, dusted the coloured water bottles,

the bust of Hahnemann (indicating homoeopathic remedies) and the white horse (veterinary preparations).

"This broadening out, bucking up and confirmation of my mind by the flood of new experiences at Up Park and Midhurst, were immensely important in my development. I dwell upon this phase because when I look back upon 1880 and early 1881 it seems to me as though these above all others were the years in which the immediate realities about me began to join on in a rational way to that varied world with which books had acquainted me. That larger world came slowly within the reach of my practical imagination. Hitherto it had been rather a dreamland and legend than anything conceivably tangible and attainable.

"I wish I could set down with certainty all the main facts in this phase of my adolescence. Then I should be able to separate the accidental elements, the element of individual luck that is to say, from the normal developmental phases. I realize that I was almost beyond comparison a more solid, pugnacious, wary and alert individual in 1881 than I was in 1879, and as I have already suggested that a large factor in this may have been the nervous and chemical changes that are associated with puberty. So far my experience was the general experience. Puberty is certainly a change in much more than the sexual life. The challenge to authority, the release of initiative, the access of courage are at least equally important. But added to this normal invigoration was the escape from the meagre feeding and depressingly shabby and unlit conditions of Atlas House. There I had a great advantage over my two brothers and I think a quite unusual push forward. I was living in those crucial years under healthier conditions; I was undergoing stimulating changes of environment, and, what is no small matter, eating a more varied and better dietary. Yet even when these more fortunate physical circumstances have been allowed for, there remains over and above them, the influence upon my perplexed and resentful mind for the first time, at its most receptive age, of a sudden irruption of new ideas, ideas of scientific precision and confirmation and ideas of leisure. . . ."[1]

His mother again requested that he pursue a position as a draper's apprentice, as had his brothers. The changes in career ideas and spurts of education continued. "I had reached a vital crisis of my life, I felt extraordinarily desperate and, faced with binding indentures and maternal remonstrances, I behaved very much like a hunted rabbit that turns at last and bites. A hunted rabbit that turned and bit would astonish and defeat most ordinary pursuers. I had discovered what were to be for me for some years the two guiding principles of my life. 'If you want something sufficiently, take it and damn the consequences,' was the first and the second was: 'If life is not good enough for you, change it; never endure a way of life that is dull and dreary, because after all the worst thing that can happen to you, if you fight and go on fighting to get out, is defeat, and that is never certain to the end which is death and the end of everything.'

"Among other things, during that dismal two years, I had thought out some very fundamental problems of conduct. I had really weighed the possibilities of the life before me, and when I used suicide as a threat to shake my mother's opposition to my liberation, it was after a considerable amount of meditation along the Southsea sea front and Portsmouth Hard. I did not think suicide an honourable resort, but it seemed to me a lesser evil than acquiescence.

(From the movie "First Men in the Moon," starring Martha Hyer. Produced by Columbia Pictures, 1964.)

(From the movie "The Food of the Gods," starring Ralph Meeker. Copyright © 1976 by American International Pictures, Inc.)

(From the movie "War of the Worlds." Copyright 1953 by Paramount Pictures Corp.)

(From the movie "The Island of Dr. Moreau," starring Burt Lancaster. Copyright © 1977 by American International Pictures, Inc.)

(From the movie "Half a Sixpence," adapted from the novel *Kipps,* starring Tommy Steele. Copyright © 1967 by Paramount Film Service Ltd. Theater still courtesy of Joseph Abeles Studio.)

(From the movie "Kipps," starring Michael Redgrave. Produced by Twentieth Century-Fox Corp., 1941.)

The cool embrace of swift-running, black deep water on a warm summer night couldn't be as bad as crib hunting or wandering about the streets with the last of one's courage gone. There it was in reserve anyhow. Why should I torture myself to earn a living, any old living? If the living isn't good enough, why live?

"Not perhaps with that much virility did I think at the time, but in that fashion, I was beginning to think. . . .

"All his days my father was a happy and appreciative man with a singular distaste for contention or holding his own in the world. He liked to do clever things with his brain and hands and body, but he was bored beyond endurance by the idea of a continual struggle for existence. So was my elder brother Frank. My brother Fred and I may have the same strain in us, but the world made such ugly, threatening and humiliating gestures at us at the outset that we pulled ourselves together and screwed ourselves up for self-repression and a fight, and we fought and subdued ourselves until we were free. Was that a good thing for us or a bad?

"I am inclined to think bad. The disposition to acquire and keep hold and accumulate, to work for a position, to secure precedences and advantages was alien to all four of us. It isn't in our tradition; it isn't in our blood; it isn't in our race. We can do good work and we are responsive to team play, we can 'play cricket' as the phrase goes, but we cannot sell, bargain, wait, forestall and keep. In a world devoted to private ownership we secure nothing. We get shoved away from opportunity. It was distortion for us to keep our attention on that side of life. I was lucky, as I shall tell, because quite accidentally I suddenly developed extraordinary earning power, which I am still able to exercise, and for thirty years I had my business looked after for me by an extremely competent wife. But I think some very fine possibilities in my brother Fred were diverted to mere saving and shop-keeping.

"In a social order where all the good things go to those who constitutionally and necessarily, watch, grab and clutch all the time, the quality of my father, the rich humour and imagination of my brother Frank, were shoved out of play and wasted altogether. In a world of competitive acquisitiveness the natural lot of my sort of people is to be hustled out of existence by the smarties and pushers. A very strong factor in my developing socialism is and always has been the more or less conscious impulses, an increasingly conscious impulse, to anticipate and disarm the smarty and the pusher and make the world safe for the responsive and candid mind and the authentic, artistic and creative worker. In the *Work, Wealth and Happiness of Mankind* I have written about 'Clever Alec.' He's 'rats' to me and at the smell of him I bristle. I set the highest value on people of my own temperament, which is I suppose, a natural and necessary thing to do, and I believe in the long run our sort will do better than their sort, as men do better than rats. We shall build and what we build will stand at last."[1]

Held various positions as student teacher at small schools. Began writing short stories. After many rejections, one was accepted by the *Family Herald*. His balance sheet read:

		£	s.	d.
Item I Short Story	Sold	1	0	0
Item I Novel. 35,000 words	Burnt	0	0	0
Item I Novel unfinished 25,000	Burnt	0	0	0
Item Much comic poetry	Lost	0	0	0
Item Some comic prose	Sent away, never returned			
Item Humorous essay	*Globe*, did not return			
Item Sundry Stories	Burnt			
Item I Story	Wandering			
Item A Poem	Burnt			
	etc etc			
Total income (untaxed)		£1	0	0

"Some day I shall succeed, I really believe, but it is a weary game."[2]

1887. "I am probably the only completely unsatisfactory student turned out by the Normal School, who did not go the pace there and who yet came up again and made a comparative success in life. I was now nearly of age and able to realize the dangers of my position in the world, and I put up a fight according to my lights. But it was a wild and ill-planned fight, and the real commander of my destinies was a singularly facetious Destiny, which seemed to delight in bowling me over in order to roll me through, kicking and struggling, to some new and quite unsuspected opportunity. I have already explained how I became one of the intelligentsia and was saved from a limited life behind a draper's counter by two broken legs, my own first, and then my father's. I have now to tell how I was guided to mental emancipation and real prosperity by a smashed kidney, a ruptured pulmonary blood vessel, and unsuccessful marriage and an uncontrollable love affair.

"My very obstinate self-conceit was also an important factor in my survival. I shall die, as I have lived, the responsible centre of my world. Occasionally I make inelegant gestures of self-effacement but they deceive nobody, and they do not suit me. I am a typical Cockney without either reverence or a sincere conviction of inferiority to any fellow creature. In building up in my mind a system of self-protection against the invincible fact that I was a failure as a student and manifestly without either the character or the capacity for a proper scientific career, I had convinced myself that I was a remarkable wit and potential writer. There must be compensation somewhere. I went on writing, indeed, as a toy-dog goes on barking. I yapped manuscript, threateningly, at an inattentive world.

"With every desire to be indulgent to myself I am bound to say that every scrap of writing surviving from that period witnesses that the output was copious rubbish, imitative of the worst stuff in the contemporary cheap magazine. There was not a spark of imagination or original observation about it. I made not the slightest use of the very considerable reservoir of scientific and general knowledge already accumulated in my brain. I don't know why. Perhaps I was then so vain that I believed I could write *down* to the public. Or so modest that I thought the better I imitated the better I should succeed. The fact remains that I scribbled vacuous trash. The only writing of any quality at all is to be found in the extremely self-conscious letters I wrote to my friends. Here I really did try to amuse and express myself in my own fashion"[1]

Wells' fragile physical condition was vaguely alluded to as tuberculosis or consumption of the lungs. "Not only were my blood and tissues resisting the suggestion that I was one of those transitory gifted beings too fine and fragile for ordinary life, but my mind also was in active revolt against that idea. I had, I will admit, some beautiful moments of

(From the television pilot "Gemini Man," based on the novel *The Invisible Man*, starring Ben Murphy. Presented by NBC, 1976.)

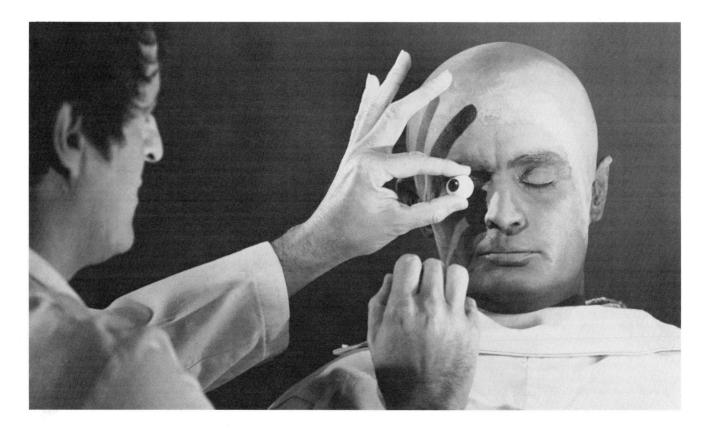

(From the television series "The Invisible Man," starring David McCallum. Presented by NBC Television, 1975.)

exquisite self-pity, tender even to tears, but they were rare. In my bones I disliked the idea of dying, I disliked it hotly and aggressively. I was exasperated not to have become famous; not to have seen the world. . . .

"Here again I can thank my Fate for my sustaining vanity. I posed consistently as the gay consumptive. Indeed I carried it off with Holt [his employer at the time] to the end that I was the invincible Spartan. My letters to those loyal correspondents of mine, were cheerfully fatalist and more blasphemous than ever."[1]

Went to recuperate at the estate, Up Park, where his mother held a position on the hired staff. "I was installed in a room next to my mother's at Up Park and celebrated my arrival by a more serious haemorrhage than any I had had hitherto.

"It chanced that a certain young Dr. Collins was staying in the house and he was summoned to my assistance. I was put upon my back, ice-bags were clapped on my chest and the flow was stopped. I was satisfying all the conventional expectations of a consumptive very completely. I lay still for a day or so and then began to live again in a gentle fashion in a pleasant chintz-furnished, fire-warmed, sunlit room.

"I must have stayed at Up Park for nearly four months. It was an interlude not only of physical recovery but mental opportunity. I read, wrote and thought abundantly. I got better and had relapses, but none were so grave as the breakdown on arriving. Collins was a brilliant young heretic in the medical world of those days, altogether more modern than my Wrexham practitioner, and he rather dashed my pose as a consumptive and encouraged my secret hope of life by refusing to recognize me as a tuberculous case. He held—and events have justified him—that with a year or so of gentle going I might make a complete recovery.

"Spring passed into summer and I grew stronger every day. It became manifest that I could not go on living upon the Burtons indefinitely. One bright afternoon I went out by myself to a little patch of surviving woodland amidst the industrialized country, called 'Trury Woods.' There had been a great outbreak of wild hyacinths that year and I lay down among them to think. It was one of those sun drenched afternoons that are turgid with vitality. Those hyacinths and their upright multitude were braver than an army with banners and more inspiring than trumpets.

"'I have been dying for nearly two-thirds of a year,' I said, 'and I have died enough.'

"I stopped dying then and there!!!"[1]

1889. Took a teaching position at Henley House School.

October 31, 1891. Married his cousin, Elizabeth Healey. "We were married very soberly in Wandsworth Parish Church on October 31st, 1891. My cousin was grave and content but rather anxious about the possibility of children, my aunt was very happy and my elder brother Frank, who had come up for the ceremony, was moved by a confusion of his affections and wept suddenly in the vestry."[1]

Became a tutor at the University Correspondence College. "I did what I could to stifle my fundamental dissatisfaction with life during this period as a correspondence tutor.

There was no one about me whom by any stretch of injustice I could blame for the insufficiencies of my experience, and I tried not to grumble about them even to myself. My correspondence fell away; I had quite enough correspondence without writing personal letters. The zest may have gone out of my interest in myself and there is little or no record of the moods of this time. . . . I was beginning to write again in any scraps of time I could snatch from direct money-earning. I was resuming my general criticism of life."[1]

May, 1893. Unhappy with his job and the mismatched nature of his marriage, his health was again weakened by lecturing, coaching and writing. About this time he became acquainted with a new student, Amy Catherine Robbins, "the embodiment of all the understanding and quality I desired in life. We talked—over our frogs and rabbits. . . . Our friendship grew swiftly beyond the bounds of friendship and I was amazed to find that she could care for me as much as I did for her."[2]

At this same time he was seized by another hemorrhage of his lungs. "No more teaching for me for ever,"[2] he wrote to a friend, and so it was. He recovered and plunged into his own writing with re-enforced vigor. Began enjoying literary successes.

January, 1894. Left his wife and took up lodgings with Catherine Robbins. They later married and two sons were born of this union.

1898. Completed *Love and Mr. Lewisham* and began a new book, *Kipps*.

1899-1900. Began the building of his home, Spade House.

1903. Admitted to the Fabian Society sponsored by George Bernard Shaw. "I did not see very much of him until I went into the Fabian Society, six or seven years later. Then he was a man in the forties and a much more important figure. He was married and he was no longer impecunious. His opinions and attitudes had developed and matured and so had mine. We found ourselves antagonistic on a number of issues and though we were not quite enough in the same field nor near enough in age to be rivals, there was from my side at any rate, a certain emulation between us.

"We were both atheists and socialists; we were both attacking an apparently fixed and invincible social system from the outside; but this much resemblance did not prevent our carrying ourselves with a certain sustained defensiveness towards each other that remains to this day. In conversational intercourse a man's conclusions are of less importance than his training and the way he gets to them, and in this respect chasms of difference yawned between Shaw and myself, wider even than those that separated me from Henry James. I have tried to set out my own formal and informal education in a previous chapter. Shaw had had no such sustained and constructive mental training as I had been through, but on the other hand he had been saturated from his youth up in good music, brilliant conversation and the appreciative treatment of life. Extreme physical sensibility had forced him to adopt an austere teetotal and vegetarian way of living, and early circumstances, of which Ireland was not the least, had inclined him to rebellion and social protest; but otherwise he was as distinctly over against me and on the aesthetic side of life as Henry James.

"To him, I guess, I have always appeared heavily and sometimes formidably facty and close-set; to me his judgments, arrived at by feeling and expression, have always had a flimsiness. I want to get hold of Fact, strip off her inessentials and, if she behaves badly put her in stays and irons; but Shaw dances round her and weaves a wilful veil of confident assurances about her as her true presentment. He thinks one can 'put things over' on Fact and I do not. He philanders with her. I have no delusions about the natural goodness and wisdom of human beings and at bottom I am grimly and desperately educational. But Shaw's conception of education is to let dear old Nature rip. He has got no further in that respect than Rousseau. Then I know, fundamentally, the heartless impartiality of natural causation, but Shaw makes Evolution something brighter and softer, by endowing it with an ultimately benevolent Life Force, acquired, quite uncritically I feel, from his friend and adviser Samuel Butler. We have been fighting this battle with each other all our lives.

"Now here perhaps—if I may deal with Conrad and others and myself as hand specimens—is something rather fundamental for the educationist. I . . . told in my account of my school days . . . how I differed from my schoolmate Sidney Bowkett, in that he felt and heard and saw so much more vividly, so much more emotionally, than I did. That gave him superiorities in many directions, but the very coldness and flatness of my perceptions, gave me a readier apprehension of relationships, put me ahead of him in mathematics and drawing (which after all is a sort of abstraction of form) and made it easier for me later on to grasp general ideas in biology and physics. My education at Kensington was very broad and rapid, I suggest, because I was not dealing with burning and glowing impressions—and when I came to a course where sense impressions were of primary importance, as they were in the course in mineralogy . . . , I gave way to irrepressible boredom and fell down. My mind became what I call an educated mind, that is to say a mind systematically unified, because of my relative defect in brightness of response. I was easy to educate.

"These vivid writers I was now beginning to encounter were, on the contrary, hard to educate—as I use the word educate. They were at an opposite pole to me as regards strength of reception. Their abundant, luminous impressions were vastly more difficult to subdue to a disciplined and co-ordinating relationship than mine. They remained therefore abundant but uneducated brains. Instead of being based on a central philosophy, they started off at a dozen points; they were impulsive, unco-ordinated, wilful. Conrad, you see, I count uneducated, Stephen Crane, Henry James, the larger part of the world of literary artistry. Shaw's education I have already impugned. The science and art of education was not adequate for the taming and full utilization of these more powerfully receptive types and they lapsed into arbitrary inconsistent and dramatized ways of thinking and living. With a more expert and scientific educational process all that might have been different. They lapsed—though retaining their distinctive scale and quality—towards the inner arbitrariness and unreality of the untrained common man.

"Not only was I relatively equipped with a strong bias for rational associations but, also, accident threw me in my receptive years mostly among non-dramatizing systematic-minded people. My mother dramatized herself, indeed, but so artlessly that I rebelled against that. My scientific training and teaching confirmed and equipped all my inherent tendency to get things ruthlessly mapped out and consistent. I suspected any imaginative romancing in conduct. I defended myself against romancing by my continual self-mockery and caricature—what you see in this book therefore as a sort of bloom of little sketches is not really an efflorescence but something very fundamental to this brain-story. I am holding myself down from pretentious impersonations. But they were there, trying to get me. A man is revealed by the nature of his mockeries.

"Such mentalities as my wife, Graham Wallas and the Webbs, and the general Socialist proposition, did much to sustain the educational consolidation that was going on in me. So that by the time I encountered such vigorously dramatizing people as the Blands and such vivid impressionists as Conrad I was already built up and set in the most refractory and comprehensive forms of conviction. I had struggled with a considerable measure of success against the common vice of self-protective assumptions. I had, I have, few 'complexes.' I would almost define education as the prevention of complexes. I was seeing myself as far as possible without pretences, my *persona* was under constant scrutiny, even at the price of private and secret sessions of humiliation, and not only was I trying to avoid posing to myself but I kept up as little pose as possible to the world. I eschewed dignity. I found therefore something as ridiculous in Conrad's *persona* of a romantic adventurous un-mercenary intensely artistic European gentleman carrying an exquisite code of unblemished honour through a universe of baseness as I did in Hubert Bland's man-of-affairs costume and simple Catholic piety.

"When Conrad first met Shaw in my house, Shaw talked with his customary freedoms. 'You know, my dear fellow, your books won't *do*'—for some Shavian reason I have forgotten—and so forth.

"I went out of the room and suddenly found Conrad on my heels, swift and white-faced. 'Does that man want to *insult* me?' he demanded.

"The provocation to say 'Yes' and assist at the subsequent duel was very great, but I overcame it. 'It's humour,' I said, and took Conrad out into the garden to cool. One could always baffle Conrad by saying 'humour.' It was one of our damned English tricks he had never learnt to tackle. . . .

"All this talk that I had with Conrad and Hueffer and James about the just word, the perfect expression, about this or that being 'written' or not written, bothered me, set me interrogating myself, threw me into a heart-searching defensive attitude. I will not pretend that I got it clear all at once, that I was not deflected by their criticisms and that I did not fluctuate and make attempts to come up to their unsystematized, mysterious and elusive standards. But in the end I revolted altogether and refused to play their game. 'I am a journalist,' I declared, 'I refuse to play the "artist." If sometimes I am an artist it is a freak of the gods. I am journalist all the time and what I write *goes now*—and will presently die.'

"I have stuck to that declaration ever since. I write as I walk because I want to get somewhere and I write as straight as I can, just as I walk as straight as I can, because that is the best way to get there. So I came down off the fence between Conrad and Wallas and I remain definitely on the side opposed to the aesthetic valuation of literature.

That valuation is at best a personal response, a floating and indefinable judgment. All these receptive critics pose for their work. They dress their souls before the glass, add a few final touches of make-up and sally forth like old bucks for fresh 'adventures among masterpieces.' I come upon masterpieces by pure chance; they happen to me and I do not worry about what I miss." [*Experiment in Autobiography,* (Vol. II), H. G. Wells, A. P. Watt & Son, J. B. Lippincott & Co., 1934.[3]]

1905. "In 1905 my mother slipped and fell downstairs one evening and was hurt internally and died a few weeks later. In her last illness her mind wandered back to Midhurst and she would fuss about laying the table for her father or counting the stitches as she learnt to crochet. She died a little child again."[1]

"I don't believe a bit more in human immortality because my mother is dead. That event and its circumstances have set up all sorts of trains of thought but I've never let my affections rule my beliefs."[2]

Kipps was a major success.

1906. Went to America to write a series of articles for the *London Tribune*. He met and spoke with Theodore Roosevelt at the White House. "It is a curious thing that as I talked with President Roosevelt in the garden of the White House there came back to me quite forcibly that undertone of doubt that has haunted me throughout this journey. After all, does this magnificent appearance of beginnings, which is America, convey any clear and certain promise of permanence and fulfilment whatever? . . . Is America a giant childhood or a gigantic futility, a mere latest phase of that long succession of experiments which has been and may be for interminable years—may be, indeed, altogether until the end—man's social history? I can't now recall how our discursive talk settled towards this, but it is clear to me that I struck upon a familiar vein of thought in the President's mind. He hadn't, he said, an effectual disproof of a pessimistic interpretation of the future. If one chose to say America must presently lose the impetus of her ascent, that she and all mankind must culminate and pass, he could not conclusively deny that possibility. Only he chose to live as if this were not so.

"That remained in his mind. Presently he reverted to it. He made a sort of apology for his life, against the doubts and scepticisms that, I fear, must be in the background of the thoughts of every modern man who is intellectually alive. He mentioned my *Time Machine*. . . . He became gesticulatory, and his straining voice a note higher in denying the pessimism of that book as a credible interpretation of destiny. With one of those sudden movements of his he knelt forward in a garden-chair—we were standing, before our parting, beneath the colonnade—and addressed me very earnestly over the back, clutching it and then thrusting out his familiar gesture, a hand first partly open and then closed.

"'Suppose, after all,' he said slowly, 'that should prove to be right, and it all ends in your butterflies and morlocks. *That doesn't matter now.* The effort's real. It's worth going on with. It's worth it. It's worth it—even so. . . .'

"I can see him now and hear his unmusical voice saying, 'The effort—the effort's worth it,' and see the gesture of his clenched hand and the—how can I describe it?—the friendly peering snarl of his face, like a man with the sun in

WELLS, 1901

his eyes. He sticks in my mind at that, as a very symbol of the creative will in man, in its limitations, its doubtful adequacy, its valiant persistence, amidst perplexities and confusions. He kneels out, assertive against his setting—and his setting is the White House with a background of all America.

"I could almost write, with a background of all the world; for I know of no other a tithe so representative of the creative purpose, the *goodwill* in men as he. In his undisciplined hastiness, his limitations, his prejudices, his unfairness, his frequent errors, just as much as in his force, his sustained courage, his integrity, his open intelligence, he stands for his people and his kind.

"I might have written that to-day. 'Teddy' was an interesting brain to come up against and it gives a measure of just how much of a constructive plan for the world's affairs there was in the current intelligence of the world twenty-eight years ago. By our modern standards it was scarcely a plan at all. It was a jumble of 'progressive' organization and 'little man' democracy. Afforestation, 'conservation of national resources,' legislation against any 'combination in restraint of trade' were the chief planks of the platform and beyond that 'woosh!' the emotional use of the 'big stick,' a declaration of the satisfying splendour of strenuous effort—which, when one comes to think it over, was, on the intellectual side, not so very strenuous after all.

That I suppose was the most vigorous brain in a conspicuously responsible position in all the world in 1906—when I was turning forty. Radical speculative thought was ahead of this, but that was as far as any ruling figure in the world had gone."[3]

1908. *Tono-Bungay* published.

May, 1909. Sold Spade House and moved to a residence in Hampstead.

October, 1909. *Ann Veronica* published. It was banned, boycotted and generally damned by the press and public.

December 4, 1909. "My book was written primarily to express the resentment and distress which many women feel nowadays at their unavoidable practical dependence upon some individual man not of their deliberate choice, and in full sympathy with the natural but perhaps anarchistic and anti-social idea that it is intolerable for a woman to have sexual relations with a man with whom she is not in love, and natural and desirable and admirable for her to want them and still more so to want children by a man of her own selection. . . .

"Life is filthy with sentimental lying. . . . Every man who would tell of reality does it at his personal cost amidst a chorus of abuse."[2]

1910. Father died.

January, 1914. Travelled to Russia.

1915-1916. *Mr. Britling Sees It Through,* a year's journal published day by day was an account of what the coming War meant to one Englishman. The book as it was published was cherished and quoted and widely read by all English people. He was inundated with correspondence. To one he replied: "I have no sons in the War; my eldest boy is fifteen, but I have seen the tragedy of my friends' sons—many young men friends. . . . I do feel that we owe a kind of altar to all these splendid youths, on which we may offer social service in a great effort to secure the peace of the world. I think for very many years life will now be mainly *world making* (or world mending). If the next ten years are not pitifully disastrous years they may be the greatest years in history."[2]

1926. *The Outline of History* published. It was an unexpected popular and financial success. "One went to bed educational reformer and woke up to find oneself bestseller."[2]

March 15, 1927. Spoke at the Sorbonne in Paris.

April 15, 1929. Addressed the Society for International Discussion at the Reichstag in Berlin on "The Commonsense of World Peace."

1933. *The Shape of Things to Come* published.

1934. Traveled to Russia. Spoke with Stalin and Gorky, where he had years earlier visited with Lenin and Pavlov.

August 13, 1946. Died in London, England. "Personally I have no use at all for life as it is, except as raw material. It bores me to look at things unless there is also the idea of doing something with them: . . . It is always about life being altered that I write, or about people developing schemes for altering life. And I have never once 'presented' life. My apparently most objective books are criticisms and incitements to change."[2]

FOR MORE INFORMATION SEE: John Davys Beresford, *H. G. Wells,* Nisbet, 1915, reprinted, Haskell House, 1972; Van Wyck Brooks, *World of H. G. Wells,* M. Kennerley, 1915, reprinted, Gordon Press, 1973; Sidney Dark, *The Outline of H. G. Wells: The Superman in the Street,* L. Parsons, 1922, reprinted, Folcroft, 1973; Robert Thurston Hopkins, *H. G. Wells: Personality, Character, Topography,* C. Palmer, 1922, reprinted, Folcroft, 1972; Ivor Brown, *H. G. Wells,* Nisbet, 1923, reprinted, Haskell House, 1975; Georges A. Connes, *A Dictionary of the Characters and Scenes in the Novels, Romances, and Short Stories of H. G. Wells,* M. Larantiere, 1926, reprinted, Haskell House, 1971; H. G. Wells, *Experiment in Autobiography: Discoveries and Conclusions of a Very Ordinary Brain (since 1866),* Macmillan, 1934, reprinted, AMS Press, 1976.

George Bernard Shaw, "H. G. Wells Was a Man without Malice," *Scholastic,* November 11, 1946; George Orwell, *Dickens, Dali, and Others: Studies in Popular Culture,* Reynal, 1946; J. B. Coates, *Leaders of Modern Thought,* Longmans, Green, 1947; James A. Salter, *Personality in Politics,* Faber, 1947; Louis Leopold Biancolli, editor, *Book of Great Conversations,* Simon & Schuster, 1948; Antonina Vallentin, *H. G. Wells: Prophet of Our Day,* Day, 1950; Norman Nicholson, *H. G. Wells,* Swallow, 1950, reprinted, Folcroft, 1973; Vincent Brome, *H. G. Wells: A Biography,* Longmans, Green, 1951, reprinted, Books for Libraries, 1972; Montgomery Belgion, *H. G. Wells,* Longmans, Green, 1953; Somerset Maugham, "Remembrances of H. G. Wells," *Saturday Review,* April 11, 1953; Mathilde Marie Meyer, *H. G. Wells and His Family (as I Have Known Them),* International Pubs., 1956; V. Brome, *Six Studies in Quarrelling,* Cresset, 1958; Leon Edel and Gordon N. Ray, editors, *Henry James and H. G. Wells: A Record of Their Friendship, Their Debate on the Art of Fiction, and Their Quarrel,* University of Illinois Press, 1958.

Arnold Bennett, *Arnold Bennett and H. G. Wells: A Record of a Personal and Literary Friendship,* University of Illinois Press, 1960; W. Waren Wagar, *H. G. Wells and the World State,* Yale University Press, 1961; George R. Gissing, *George Gissing and H. G. Wells: Their Friendship and Correspondence,* University of Illinois Press, 1961; Ingvald Raknem, *H. G. Wells and His Critics,* Humanities, 1962; Ilii Iosofovich Kagarlitskii, *Life and Thought of H. G. Wells,* translated from the Russian by Moura Budberg, Barnes & Noble, 1966; Richard H. Costa, *H. G. Wells,* Twayne, 1967; Andre Maurois, *Points of View,* Ungar, 1968; Kenneth B. Newell, *Structure in Four Novels by H. G. Wells,* Humanities, 1968; Lovat Dickson, *H. G. Wells: His Turbulent Life and Times,* Macmillan, 1969.

Patrick Parrinder, *H. G. Wells,* Oliver & Boyd, 1970; William Bellamy, *The Novels of Wells, Bennett, and Galsworthy, 1890-1910,* Routledge & Kegan Paul, 1971; P. Parrinder, editor, *H. G. Wells: The Critical Heritage,* Routledge & Kegan Paul, 1972; Alfred H. Borrello, *H. G. Wells: Author in Agony,* Southern Illinois University Press, 1972; Geoffrey H. Wells, *H. G. Wells: A Sketch for a Portrait,* Folcroft, 1972; Norman Mackenzie and Jeanne Mackenzie, *H. G. Wells: A Biography,* Simon & Schuster, 1973; Jack Williamson, *H. G. Wells: Critic of Progress,* Mirage Press, 1973; Mark R. Hillegas, *The Future as Nightmare: H. G. Wells and the Anti-Utopians,* Southern Illinois University

H. G. WELLS

CAREER: Artist and illustrator. Began as a book illustrator in Germany and turned to magazine illustration when the depression of the 1930's cut the production of illustrated books; left Germany during the Hitler regime and came to the United States, where he has worked in both magazine and book illustration.

WRITINGS—All retold and illustrated by the author: *The Valiant Tailor*, Viking, 1965; *The Cobbler's Dilemma: An Italian Folktale*, McGraw, 1967; *The Monkey, the Lion, and the Snake*, Viking, 1967; *King Thrushbeard*, Viking, 1968; *Lazy Jack*, Viking, 1970; (with Mabel Watts) *Molly and the Giant*, Parents' Magazine Press, 1973.

Illustrator: Rosemary Sprague, *Northward to Albion*, Roy, 1947; Nina Schneider, *Hercules, the Gentle Giant*, Roy, 1947; Alma B. Weber and others, *Coonskin for a General*, Aladdin, 1951; Rosalys Hall, *Merry Miller*, Oxford University Press, 1952; R. Hall, *No Ducks for Dinner*, Oxford University Press, 1953; Phyllis R. Fenner, editor, *Stories of the Sea*, Knopf, 1953; Charlotte Zolotow, *Quiet Mother and the Noisy Little Boy*, Lothrop, 1953; Priscilla Carden, *Aldo's Tower*, Ariel, 1954; Elizabeth Tate, *Little Teddy and the Big Sea*, Lothrop, 1954; Hall, *Baker's Man*, Lippincott, 1954; Pearl Buck, *Beech Tree*, Day, 1955; Blossom Budney, *Huff Puff Hickory Hill*, Longmans, Green, 1955; Dorothy G. Butters, *Papa Dolphin's Table*, Knopf, 1955; Rachel Varble, *Pepys' Boy*, Doubleday, 1955; Helen Kay, *One Mitten Lewis*, Lothrop, 1955.

Vardine R. Moore, *Picnic Pony*, Lothrop, 1956; Ruth L. Holberg, *Tabitha's Hill*, Doubleday, 1956; Joan Windham, *Saints Upon a Time*, Sheed, 1956; Playsted Wood, *Elephant in the Family*, Nelson, 1957; John B. Lewellyn, *Tee Vee Humphrey*, Knopf, 1957; Ruth D. Leinhauser, *Holiday with Eric*, Washburn, 1957; Phyllis McGinley, *Year Without a Santa Claus*, Lippincott, 1957; P. Carden, *Boy on the Sheep Trail*, Nelson, 1957; Hall, *Green as Spring*, Longmans, Green, 1957; Frederick W. Keith, *Danger in the Everglades*, Abelard-Schuman, 1957; Geraldine Ross, *Scat, the Witch's Cat*, McGraw, 1958; Hall, *Seven for Saint Nicholas*, Lippin-

Press, 1974; Kenneth H. Young, *H. G. Wells*, British Book Center, 1975; Darko Suvin and Robert M. Philmus, editors, *H. G. Wells and Modern Science Fiction*, Bucknell University Press, 1976; Robert Bloom, *Anatomies of Egotism: A Reading of the Last Novels of H. G. Wells*, University of Nebraska Press, 1977.

For children: William A. DeWitt, *Illustrated Minute Biographies*, Grosset & Dunlap, 1953; Arthur A. Thomson, *Great Men of Kent*, Bodley Head, 1955; James Playsted Wood, *I Told You So: A Life of H. G. Wells*, Pantheon, 1969; Alan L. Paley, *H. G. Wells: Author of Famous Science Fiction Stories*, SimHar Press, 1973.

Obituaries: *New York Times*, August 14, 1946; *Publishers Weekly*, August 24, 1946; *Christian Century*, August 28, 1946; *Current Biography*, September, 1946; *Wilson Library Bulletin*, October, 1946; *Current Biography Yearbook 1946.*

WERTH, Kurt 1896-

PERSONAL: Born September 21, 1896, in Leipzig, Germany; emigrated to the United States, naturalized a citizen, 1947; married; children: one son. *Education:* Attended the Academy for Graphic Arts, Leipzig, Germany. *Address:* 645 W. 239th St., Bronx, N.Y. 10463.

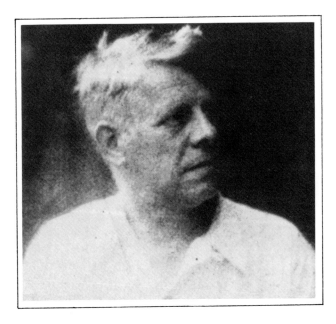

KURT WERTH

**So she looked.
And a mouse hopped out.
And the woman SCREAMED and SQUEALED
and jumped on a chair.**
■ (From *Noodles, Nitwits, and Numskulls* by Maria Leach. Illustrated by Kurt Werth.)

cott, 1958; R. D. Leinhauser, *Aunt Sharon's Wedding Day*, Washburn, 1958; Joanna Johnston, *Great Gravity the Cat*, Knopf, 1958; Rose L. Mincieli, *Tales Merry and Wise*, Holt, 1958; Frances M. Frost, *Little Naturalist*, McGraw, 1959; Constance F. Irwin, *Jonathan D*, Lothrop, 1959; G. Ross, *Stop It, Moppit*, McGraw, 1959; Maria Leach, *Thing at the Foot of the Bed*, Collins, 1959.

Patricia M. Martin, *Happy Piper and the Goat*, Lothrop, 1960; Jane A. Hyndham, *Timid Dragon*, Lothrop, 1960; Lilian Moore, *Bear Trouble*, McGraw, 1960; Shirley Simon, *Molly and the Rooftop Mystery*, Lothrop, 1961; Millicent E. Selsam, *Tony's Birds*, Harper, 1961; Maria Leach, editor, *Noodles, Nitwits, and Numskills*, Collins, 1961; Doris Fos-

ter, *Honker Visits the Island*, Lothrop, 1962; Betty Miles, *Feast on Sullivan Street*, Knopf, 1963; Charlotte Zolotow, *Tiger Called Thomas* (Junior Literary Guild selection), Lothrop, 1963; Helen Copeland, *Meet Miki Takino*, Lothrop, 1963; Polly Curren, *Hear Ye of Boston*, Lothrop, 1964; M. Leach, editor, *The Luck Book*, World Publishing, 1964; Ruth J. Adams, *Mr. Picklepaw's Popcorn*, Lothrop, 1965; H. Wilson, *Herbert's Space Trip*, Knopf, 1965; Roberta S. Feuerlicht, *The Legends of Paul Bunyan*, Macmillan, 1965; W. Mantle, *Chateau Holiday*, Holt, 1965.

Lillian Bason, *Isabelle and the Library Cat*, Lothrop, 1966; Albert S. Fleischman, *McBroom Tells the Truth*, Norton, 1966; Ross, *The Elf Who Didn't Believe in Himself*, Steck-

Vaughn, 1966; A. S. Fleischman, *McBroom and the Big Wind,* Norton, 1967; Maxine W. Kumin, *Faraway Farm,* Norton, 1967; *That Lincoln Boy,* World Publishing, 1967; *The Wind Chasers,* McKay, 1967; Polly Curren, *Hear Ye of Philadelphia,* Lothrop, 1968; John Lewellen, *Tee Vee Humphrey,* Knopf, 1968; Hall, *Miranda's Dragon,* McGraw, 1968; A. S. Fleischman, *McBroom's Ear,* Norton, 1969; Hall, *The Bright and Shining Breadboard,* Lothrop, 1969; Edna M. Preston, *One Dark Night,* Viking, 1969.

Charles M. Daugherty, *Samuel Clemens,* Crowell, 1970; John Hampden, *Endless Treasure: Unfamiliar Tales from the Arabian Nights,* World Publishing, 1970; Earl S. Miers, *That Jefferson Boy,* World Publishing, 1970; Richard Shaw, *Who Are You Today?,* F. Warne, 1970; R. J. Adams and Guy Adams, *Mr. Pickelpaw's Puppy,* Lothrop, 1970; Boris V. Zakhoder, *How a Piglet Crashed the Christmas Party,* Lothrop, 1971; Hazel H. Wilson, *Herbert's Stilts,* Knopf, 1972; Fleischman, *McBroom's Zoo,* Grosset, 1972; Fleischman, *McBroom the Rainmaker,* Grosset, 1973; Eva Moore, *Dick Whittington and His Cat,* Seabury Press, 1974; Joseph Raskin and Edith Raskin, *The Newcomers: Ten Tales of American Immigrants,* Lothrop, 1974; Hall, *The Three Beggar Kings: A Story of Christmas,* Random House, 1974.

Contributor to *Simplicissimus* and *Querschnitt* (German magazines); also illustrator of limited editions of German and Russian classics for several German publishers.

SIDELIGHTS: Werth received his education at Leipzig's Academy for Graphic Arts. After the First World War he began to illustrate books and left Leipzig for Munich where he continued illustrating German and Russian classics for a number of German publishers until the Hitler regime forced him to leave Germany. "The depression in Germany put an end to illustrated books, and I found work in the magazine field, contributing to *Simplicissimus* and *Querschnitt.* The Hitler regime did not allow me to work because of my Jewish wife and we had to leave Germany. So we came to the United States. Here I started from scratch, for the *New York Times,* for a number of anti-Nazi magazines during the war and then back to the book—first textbooks and at last to children's books.

"The development of my work was profoundly inspired by Rembrandt, Daumier and Slevogt. In the past ten years my style has changed to a more expressive and modern approach." [Lee Kingman and others, compilers. *Illustrators of Children's Books: 1957-1966,* Horn Book, 1968.[1]]

Werth lives with his wife in the Bronx section of New York City. They have one son. His works are included in the Kerlan Collection at the University of Minnesota.

FOR MORE INFORMATION SEE: Bertha M. Miller and others, compilers, *Illustrators of Children's Books: 1946-1956,* Horn Book, 1958; Muriel Fuller, editor, *More Junior Authors,* H. W. Wilson, 1963; Lee Kingman and others, compilers, *Illustrators of Children's Books: 1957-1966,* Horn Book, 1968; *Horn Book,* October 1965, December, 1968, October, 1970.

Whitman, age 61.

WHITMAN, Walt(er) 1819-1892

PERSONAL: Born May 31, 1819, in West Hills, near Huntington, Long Island, New York; died March 26, 1892, in Camden, New Jersey; buried in Harleigh Cemetery, Camden, New Jersey; son of Walter (a farmer and carpenter) and Louisa (Van Velsor) Whitman. *Education:* Attended public school in Brooklyn, New York. *Home:* Camden, New Jersey; his home is now a museum in his honor.

CAREER: Poet, journalist, and essayist. Worked as an office boy at the age of eleven; subsequently served as a printer's devil, school teacher, and typesetter, 1832-46; began his journalism career as editor of the *Long Islander,* 1838-39; founded his own paper, the *Freeman,* 1848-49; associated with at least ten other newspapers and magazines in New Orleans and throughout New York, holding various odd jobs in between, and editing his last paper, the Brooklyn *Times,* 1857-59; became a volunteer at military hospitals in Washington, D.C., during the Civil War, supporting himself with a part-time job in the Army Paymaster's Office; obtained a clerkship with the Department of the Interior, 1865, dismissed for writing immoral books, later reinstated with the Office of the Attorney General, 1865-73; forced into semi-retirement after a paralytic stroke, 1873.

I celebrate myself, and sing myself,
And what I assume you shall assume,
For every atom belonging to me as good belongs to you.
I loafe and invite my soul,
I lean and loafe at my ease observing a spear of summer grass.

■ (From *Leaves of Grass* by Walt Whitman. Illustrated by Lewis C. Daniel.)

WRITINGS—All poems, except as noted: *Franklin Evans; or, the Inebriate* (novel), J. Winchester, 1842; *Leaves of Grass*, privately printed, [Brooklyn], 1855, new edition, edited by Sculley Bradley and H. W. Blodgett, Norton, 1973 [nine different collections of poems were published under this title between 1855-92; other editions illustrated by Rockwell Kent, Heritage Press, 1936; John Steuart Curry, Peter Pauper Press, 1943, reissued, 1964; Boardman Robinson (introduction by Carl Sandburg), A. S. Barnes, 1944; John and Clare Romano Ross, Crowell, 1964; James Spanfeller, Hallmark, 1969; excerpts from *Leaves of Grass* published separately—*Passage to India*, Redfield, 1870, reprinted, Haskell House, 1969; *As a Strong Bird on Pinions Free*, S. W. Green, 1872; *Good-bye My Fancy*, McKay, 1891; *Song of Myself*, Roycrofter, 1904, new edition, edited by James E. Miller, Jr., Dodd, 1964].

Drum-Taps, [New York], 1865, reprinted with previously unpublished *Sequel to Drum-Taps*, Scholars' Facsimiles & Reprints, 1959 (contains *O'Captain! My Captain!* and *When Lilacs Last in the Dooryard Bloom'd*); *After All, Not to Create Only*, Roberts Brothers, 1871; *Two Rivulets*, Published by the author, 1876; *November Boughs*, McKay, 1888; *Memories of President Lincoln, and Other Lyrics of the War*, T. B. Mosher, 1906; *The Sleepers: A Poem* (illustrated by Marcel Guillard), 1919, reprinted, Folcroft, 1973; *Songs of Democracy*, McKay, 1919; *Sea Drift*, Jarrold & Son, 1923; *Out of the Cradle Endlessly Rocking*, June House, 1926, new edition, edited by Dominick P. Consolo, Merrill, 1971; *Pictures: An Unpublished Poem of Walt Whitman*, Faber & Gwyer, 1927, reprinted, Folcroft, 1973; *The Half-Breed, and Other Stories* (illustrated by Allen Lewis), Columbia University Press, 1927, reprinted, Folcroft, 1972.

There Was a Child Went Forth (illustrated by Zhenya Gay), Harper, 1943, New edition (illustrated by Gilliam Tyler), Gehenna Press, 1968; *Kentucky: Walt Whitman's Uncompleted Poem*, edited by Harry Warfel, University of Kentucky Library Associates, 1960; *Miracles: Walt Whitman's Beautiful Celebration of Life* (illustrated by Jim Hamil and others), Hallmark, 1973; *Walt Whitman's "I Hear America Singing"* (illustrated by Fernando Krahn), Delacorte, 1975.

Essays and lectures: *Democratic Vistas*, Redfield, 1871, reprinted with other papers, Scholarly Press, 1970; *An American Primer*, edited by Horace Traubel, Small, Maynard, 1904, reissued, Porter, 1972; *Lafayette in Brooklyn*, G. D. Smith, 1905, reprinted, Folcroft, 1973; *Rivulets of Prose: Critical Essays*, edited by Carolyn Wells and Alfred F. Goldsmith, 1928, reprinted, Books for Libraries, 1969; *Walt Whitman's Backward Glances: A Backward Glance o'er Travel'd Roads, and Two Contributory Essays*, edited by Sculley Bradley and John A. Stevenson, University of Pennsylvania Press, 1947, reissued, Books for Libraries, 1968.

Letters and personal narratives: *Memoranda During the War*, published by the author, 1875-76, reissued with the previously unpublished *Death of Abraham Lincoln*, edited by Roy P. Basler, Greenwood Press, 1972; *Specimen Days and Collect*, R. Welsh, 1882-83, reissued, David R. Godine, 1971 (published in England as *Specimen Days in America*, W. Scott, 1887); *Calamus: A Series of Letters Written During the Years 1868-1880*, edited by Richard Maurice Bucks, L. Maynard, 1897, reprinted, Folcroft, 1972; *The Wound Dresser: A Series of Letters Written from the Hospital in Washington*, Small, Maynard, 1898, reprinted, Folcroft, 1975; *Walt Whitman's Diary in Canada*, edited by William Sloane Kennedy, Small, Maynard, 1904, reprinted, Folcroft,

1970; *The Letters of Anne Gilchrist and Walt Whitman*, edited by Thomas B. Harned, Doubleday, 1918, reprinted, Haskell House, 1973; *Whitman and Rolleston: A Correspondence*, edited by Horst Frenz, Indiana University, 1951.

Selections: *Autobiographia; or, The Story of a Life*, Webster, 1892, reprinted, Folcroft, 1972; *Notes and Fragments*, edited by Richard Maurice Bucke, privately printed, 1899, reprinted, Folcroft, 1972; *Walt Whitman*, edited by Mark Van Doren, Viking, 1945, reissued, 1974; (for children) *Poems of Walt Whitman*, edited by Lawrence C. Powell, Crowell, 1964; *Poems of Walt Whitman*, edited by Lawrence C. Powell, Apollo, 1971; *A Most Jubilant Song: Inspiring Writings about the Wonderful World Around Us*, edited by Shifra Stein, Hallmark, 1973; *Walt Whitman's Camden Conversations*, edited by Walter Teller, Rutgers University Press, 1973; *Whitman*, edited by Robert Creeley, Penguin, 1973.

Collected editorials and newspaper articles: *I Sit and Look Out: Editorials from the Brooklyn Daily Times*, edited by Emory Holloway and Vernolian Schwarz, Columbia University Press, 1932, reprinted, AMS Press, 1966; *New York Dissected: A Sheaf of Recently Discovered Newspaper Articles*, R. R. Wilson, 1936, reprinted, Folcroft, 1973; *Walt Whitman Looks at the Schools*, edited by Florence Bernstein Freedman, King's Crown Press, 1950; *Walt Whitman of the New York Aurora: Editor at Twenty-Two*, edited by Joseph Jay Rubin and Charles H. Brown, Bald Eagle Press, 1950, reissued, Greenwood Press, 1972; *Walt Whitman's New York: From Manhattan to Montauk*, edited by Henry M. Christman, Macmillan, 1965, reissued, Books for Libraries, 1972.

Collections: *The Complete Writings of Walt Whitman*, ten volumes, edited by Richard Maurice Bucke and others, Putnam, 1902, reissued, Scholarly Press, 1968; *The Uncollected Poetry and Prose of Walt Whitman*, two volumes, edited by Emory Holloway, Doubleday, 1921, reprinted, Peter Smith, 1972; *Walt Whitman's Workshop: A Collection of Unpublished Manuscripts*, edited by Clifton Joseph Furness, Harvard University Press, 1928, reissued, Russell, 1964 [excerpt from *Walt Whitman's Workshop* published separately—*The Eighteenth Presidency*, edited by Edward F. Grier, University of Kansas Press, 1956].

Walt Whitman and the Civil War, edited by Charles I. Glicksberg, University of Pennsylvania Press, 1933, reissued, A. S. Barnes, 1963; *Faint Clews and Indirections: Manuscripts of Walt Whitman and His Family*, edited by Clarence Gohdes and Rollo G. Silver, Duke University Press, 1949, reprinted, AMS Press, 1971; *The Correspondence*, five volumes, edited by Edwin Haviland Miller, New York University Press, 1961-69; *The Works of Walt Whitman*, two volumes, Funk, 1968; *The Complete Poems*, edited by Francis Murphy, Penguin, 1976.

ADAPTATIONS—Movies and filmstrips: "Poems of Walt Whitman" (motion picture; with teacher's guide; includes *I Hear America Singing, Miracles, When I Heard the Learn'd Astronomer*, and *O Captain! My Captain!*), McGraw-Hill, 1967; "Poems of Walt Whitman: Part 1 and Part 2" (filmstrips; part 1 includes *I Hear America Singing* and *Miracles*, part 2 includes *When I Heard the Learn'd Astronomer* and *O Captain! My Captain!*; each part with phonodisc and teacher's guide), McGraw-Hill, 1967; "Face to Face—Walt Whitman: A Hundred Years Hence" (motion picture; with teacher's guide), adaptation of *Crossing Brooklyn Ferry*, Edinboro State College, 1968.

Whitman, age 35.

"Reading Poetry: O Captain! My Captain!" (motion picture; with study guide), narrated by Efrem Zimbalist, Jr., Oxford Films, 1971; "To the Outsetting Bard" (motion picture), adaptation of *Out of the Cradle Endlessly Rocking*, Edinboro State College; "Walt Whitman's Civil War" (motion picture; with study guide), Churchill Films, 1972; "Whitman" (two filmstrips; excerpts from the poems of Walt Whitman; with phonodisc and teacher's guide), Schloat Productions, 1972.

Other: Paul Hindemith, composer, "When Lilacs Last in the Door-Yard Bloom'd" (piano and vocal score), Associated Music Publishers, New York, 1948.

Movies and filmstrips: "Walt Whitman" (filmstrip), Encyclopaedia Britannica Films, 1954; "Walt Whitman: Background for His Works" (motion picture), Coronet Instructional Films, 1956; "Walt Whitman's Western Journey" (motion picture), Francis R. Line, 1965; "Walt Whitman's Leaves of Grass" (motion picture), Francis R. Line, 1965; "Walt Whitman's World" (motion picture), Coronet Instructional Films, 1966; "Whitman: The American Singer" (filmstrip; with phonodisc), Thomas S. Klise, 1971; "Walt Whitman: Poet for a New Age" (motion picture), Encyclopaedia Britannica Educational Corp., 1971.

Plays: Paul Shyre, "A Whitman Portrait," first produced in New York at Gramercy Arts Theatre, October, 1966; Randolph G. Goodman, *I: Walt Whitman*, Library Associates of Brooklyn College, 1955.

Television specials: "The Night and Morning Worlds of Walt Whitman," produced by Robert Herridte, starring Michael Caine, 1964; "The American Parade: Song of Myself," produced by Robert Markowitz, starring Rip Torn, March 9, 1976.

SIDELIGHTS: **May 31, 1819.** Born at West Hills, Long Island, New York; father, Walter Whitman, was a builder of houses.

"The father, strong, self-sufficient, manly, mean, anger'd, unjust, The blow, the quick loud word, the tight bargain, the crafty lure, . . .

"My old daddy used to say, 'It's some comfort to a man if he must be an ass anyhow to be his own kind of an ass.'" [Henry Seidel Canby, *Walt Whitman an American*, Houghton, 1943.[1]]

His mother, Louisa Van Velsor, was a daughter of "farming folk." "Well-begotten and rais'd by a perfect mother.

"Before I was born out of my mother generations guided me,
My embryo has never been torpid, nothing could overlay it."

[Gay Wilson Allen, *Walt Whitman Handbook*, Packard & Co., 1946.[2]]

"Even as a boy, I had the fancy, the wish, to write a piece, perhaps a poem, about the sea-shore—that suggesting, dividing line, contact, junction, the solid marrying the liquid that curious, lurking something, (as doubtless every objective form finally becomes to the subjective spirit,) which means far more than its mere first sight, grand as that is—blending the real and ideal, and each made portion of the other. Hours, days, in my Long Island youth and early manhood, I haunted the shores of Rockaway or Coney Island, or away east to the Hamptons or Montauk. Once, at the latter place, (by the old lighthouse, nothing but seatossings in sight in every direction as far as the eye could reach,) I remember well, I felt that I must one day write a book expressing this liquid, mystic theme. [Walt Whitman, *Autobiographia; or, The Story of a Life*, Webster, 1892.[3]]

May 27, 1823. Family moved to Brooklyn, New York.

1825. Attended elementary school—which was all the schooling he ever got. Family frequently shifted residences in the city.

1830. Office boy in lawyer's office, then doctor's; presumably quit school at this time.

1831. Left home at age twelve and apprenticed on the newspaper, *Long Island Patriot*.

1832. Worked as a compositor of *Long Island Star*. Became active in debating societies and was a passionate theatre goer.

1836. Began teaching in rural schools on Long Island.

1838. Published his own weekly newspaper, *The Long Islander*, for which he was editor, printer and delivery boy on his horse "Nina."

1840. Campaigned for Van Buren.

February, 1846. Became editor of *The Brooklyn Eagle,* an influential and liberal newspaper. "Living in Brooklyn or New York City from this time forward, my life, then, and still more the following years, was curiously identified with Fulton Ferry, already becoming the greatest of its sort in the world for general importance, volume, variety, rapidity, and picturesqueness. Almost daily, later, ('50 to '60) I cross'd on the boats, often up in the pilot-houses where I could get a full sweep, absorbing shows, accompaniments, surroundings. What oceanic currents, eddies, underneath—the great tides of humanity also, with ever-shifting movements. Indeed, I have always had a passion for ferries; to me they afford inimitable, streaming, never-failing, living poems. The river and bay scenery, all about New York island, any time of a fine day—the hurrying, splashing sea-tides—the changing panorama of steamers, all sizes, often a string of big ones outward bound to distant ports—the myriads of white-sail'd schooners, sloops, skiffs, and the marvellously beautiful yachts—the majestic sound boats as they rounded the Battery and came along towards 5, afternoon, eastward bound—the prospect off towards Staten Island, or down the Narrows, or the other way up the Hudson—what refreshment of spirit such sights and experiences gave me years ago (and many a time since). My old pilot friends, the Balsirs, Johnny Cole, Ira Smith, William White, and my young ferry friend, Tom Gere—how well I remember them all.

"Besides Fulton Ferry, off and on for years, I knew and frequented Broadway—that noted avenue of New York's crowded and mixed humanity, and of so many notables. Here I saw, during those times, Andrew Jackson, Webster, Clay, Seward, Martin Van Buren, filibuster Walker, Kossuth, Fitz-Greene Halleck, Bryant, the Prince of Wales, Charles Dickens, the first Japanese ambassadors, and lots of other celebrities of the time. Always something novel or inspiring; yet mostly to me the hurrying and vast amplitude of those never-ending human currents. I remember seeing James Fenimore Cooper in a court-room in Chambers Street, back of the City Hall, where he was carrying on a law case—(I think it was a charge of libel he had brought against some one.) I also remember seeing Edgar A. Poe, and having a short interview with him, (it must have been in 1845 or '6,) in his office, second story of a corner building, (Duane or Pearl Street.) He was editor and owner or part owner of *The Broadway Journal.* The visit was about a piece of mine he had publish'd. Poe was very cordial, in a quiet way, appear'd well in person, dress, etc. I have a distinct and pleasing remembrance of his looks, voice, manner and matter; very kindly and human, but subdued, perhaps a little jaded. . . .

"One phase of those days must by no means go unrecorded—namely, the Broadway omnibuses, with their drivers. The vehicles still (I write this paragraph in 1881) give a portion of the character of Broadway—the Fifth Avenue, Madison Avenue, and Twenty-Third street lines yet running. But the flush days of the old Broadway stages, characteristic and copious, are over. The Yellow-birds, the Red-birds, the original Broadway, the Fourth Avenue, the Knickerbocker, and a dozen others of twenty or thirty years ago, are all gone. And the men specially identified with them, and giving vitality and meaning to them—the drivers—a strange, natural quick-eyed and wondrous race—(not only Rabelais and Cervantes would have gloated upon them, but Homer and Shakspere [sic] would)—how well I remember them, and must here give a word about them. How many hours, forenoons and afternoons—how many exhilarating night-times I have had—perhaps June or July in cooler air—riding the whole length of Broadway, listening to some yarn, (and the

WALT WHITMAN

most vivid yarns ever spun, and rarest mimicry)—or perhaps I declaiming some stormy passage from Julius Caesar or Richard (you could roar as loudly as you chose in that heavy, dense, uninterrupted streetbass.) Yes, I knew all the drivers then, Broadway Jack, Dressmaker, Balky Bill, George Storms, Old Elephant, his brother Young Elephant, (who came afterward,) Tippy, Pop Rice, Big Frank, Yellow Frank, Yellow Joe, Pete Callahan, Patsey Dee, and dozens more; for there were hundreds. They had immense qualities, largely animal—eating, drinking; women—a great personal pride, in their way—perhaps a few slouches here and there, but I should have trusted the general run of them, in their simple good-will and honor, under all circumstances. Not only for comradeship, and sometimes affection—great studies I found them also. (I suppose the critics will laugh heartily, but the influence of those Broadway omnibus jaunts and drivers and declamations and escapades undoubtedly enter'd into the gestation of *Leaves of Grass.*)

"At the old Park Theatre, just opposite the Astor House, and home of heroic drama, . . . 'young manhood's life' expanded in response to the great art of dramatic communication. Later came music, 'the deep passion of Alboni's contralto,' 'Bettini's pensive and incomparable tenor.' Booth and Forrest played at the Bowery Theatre, which was 'pack'd from ceiling to pit with its audience mainly of alert, well-dress'd, full-blooded young and middle-aged men, the best average of American-born mechanics—the emotional nature of the whole mass arous'd by the power and magnet-

(From *The Magnificent Idler, The Story of Walt Whitman* by Cameron Rogers. Illustrated by Edw. A. Wilson.)

Whitman's house in Camden, New Jersey.

ism of as mighty mimes as ever trod the stage—... tempests of hand-clapping ... from perhaps 2,000 full-sinew'd men.'''[1]

February 11, 1848. Went to New Orleans to join the staff of *The Crescent,* a daily newspaper.

1855. First edition of *Leaves of Grass,* self-published. "*Leaves of Grass* ... is ... the song of a great composite *democratic individual,* male or female. And ... the thread-voice ... of an aggregated ... vast, composite, electric *democratic nationality.*

"I saw that to 'express my own distinctive era,' there 'must be an identical body and soul, a personality—which personality, after many considerations and ponderings, I deliberately settled should be myself—indeed could not be any other.'

"Leaves of Grass ... has mainly been ... an attempt from first to last, to put *a Person,* a human being (myself, in the latter half of the nineteenth century, in America) freely, fully and truly on record. I could not find any similar personal record in current literature that satisfied me.''[1]

"Of all mankind the great poet is the equable man. Not in him but off from him things are grotesque or eccentric or fail of their sanity. Nothing out of its place is good and nothing in its place is bad. He bestows on every object or quality its fit proportions neither more nor less. He is the arbiter of the diverse and he is the key. He is the equalizer of his age and land ... he supplies what wants supplying and checks what wants checking. If peace is the routine out of him speaks the spirit of peace, large, rich, thrifty, building vast and populous cities, encouraging agriculture and the arts and commerce—lighting the study of men, the soul, immortality—federal, state or municipal government, marriage, health, freetrade, intertravel by land and sea ... nothing too close, nothing too far off ... the stars not too far off. In war he is the most deadly force of the war. Who recruits him recruits horse and foot ... he fetches parks of artillery the best that engineer ever knew. If the time becomes slothful and heavy he knows how to arouse it ... he can make every word he speaks draw blood. Whatever stagnates in the flat of custom or obedience or legislation he never stagnates. Obedience does not master him, he masters it. ...

"His brain is the ultimate brain. He is no arguer ... he is judgment. He judges not as the judge judges but as the sun falling around a helpless thing. As he sees the farthest he has the most faith. His thoughts are the hymns of the praise of things. In the talk on the soul and eternity and God off of his equal plane he is silent. He sees eternity less like a play with a prologue and denouement ... he sees eternity in men and women ... he does not see men and women as dreams or dots.

"The greatest poet hardly knows pettiness or triviality. If he breathes into any thing that was before thought small it dilates with the grandeur and life of the universe. He is a seer. ... he is individual ... he is complete in himself. ... the others are as good as he, only he sees it and they do not. He is not one of the chorus. ... he does not stop for any regulation ... he is the president of regulation. What the eyesight does to the rest he does to the rest. ...

"The land and sea, the animals, fishes and birds, the sky of heaven and the orbs, the forests, mountains and rivers, are not small themes ... but folk expect of the poet to indicate more than the beauty and dignity which always attach to dumb real objects. ... they expect him to indicate the path between reality and their souls. ...

"... Love the earth and sun and the animals, despise riches, give alms to every one that asks, stand up for the stupid and crazy, devote your income and labor to others, hate tyrants, argue not concerning God, have patience and indulgence toward the people, take off your hat to nothing known or unknown or to any man or number of men, go freely with powerful uneducated persons and with the young and with the mothers of families, read these leaves in the open air every season of every year of your life, re-examine all you have been told at school or church or in any book, dismiss whatever insults your own soul, and your flesh shall be a great poem and have the richest fluency not only in its words but in the silent lines of its lips and face and between the lashes of your eyes and in every motion and joint of your body. ... The poet shall not spend his time in unneeded work. He shall know that the ground is always ready ploughed and manured. ... others may not know it but he shall. He shall go directly to the creation. His trust shall master the trust of everything he touches. ... and shall master all attachment. [Francis Murphy, editor, *Walt Whitman, The Complete Poems,* Penguin Education, 1975.[4]]

July 21, 1855. A letter from Ralph Waldo Emerson addressed to Whitman—after having received a copy of *Leaves of Grass.* "... I am not blind to the worth of the wonderful gift of *Leaves of Grass.* I find it the most extraordinary piece of wit and wisdom that America has yet contributed. I am very happy in reading it, as great power makes us happy. It meets the demand I am always making of what seems the sterile

Whitman's birthplace at West Hills, 1904.

and stingy nature, as if too much handiwork, or too much lymph in the temperament, were making our Western wits fat and mean. I give you joy of your free and brave thought. I have great joy in it. I find incomparable things said incomparably well, as they must be. I find the courage of treatment that so delights us and which large perception only can inspire.

''I greet you at the beginning of a great career, which yet must have had a long foreground somewhere, for such a start. I rubbed my eyes a little, to see if this sunbeam were no illusion; but the solid sense of the book is a sober certainty. It has the best merits, namely, of fortifying and encouraging.

''I did not know until I last night saw the book advertised in a newspaper that I could trust the name as real and available for a post office. I wish to see my benefactor, and have felt much like striking my tasks and visiting New York to pay you my respects.''[2]

A great flurry of excitement accompanied the publication of *Leaves of Grass:* ''*William Howitt*, the English Quaker poet,

in *The London Dispatch,* reprinted in *Life Illustrated,* April 19, 1856:

'It is of a *genus* so peculiar as to embarrass us, and has an air at once so novel, so audacious, and so strange, as to verge upon absurdity, and yet it would be an injustice to pronounce it so, as the work is saved from this extreme by a certain mastery over diction not very easy of definition.'

''From *The London Leader,* reprinted in *Life Illustrated,* July 19, 1856:

'Walt is one of the most amazing, one of the most startling, one of the most perplexing creatures of the modern American mind; but he is no fool, though abundantly eccentric. . . . The poem is written in wild, irregular, unrhymed, almost unmetrical ''lengths'' . . . by no means seductive, to English ears. . . . It seems to resolve itself into an all-attracting egotism—an external presence of the individual soul of Walt Whitman in all things, yet in such wise that this one soul shall be presented as a type of all human souls whatsoever. . . . Much . . . seems to us purely fantastic and preposterous, . . . disgusting without purpose, and singular without result. There are so many evidences of a noble soul in Whit-man's pages, that we regret these aberrations.'

"*The London Critic*, April 1, 1857:

'Walt Whitman is as unacquainted with art as a hog is with mathematics.'

"*R. W. Griswold*, (Poe's detractor) in *The New York Criterion*, November 10, 1855:

'Thus, then, we leave this gathering of muck to the laws which, certainly, if they fulfil their intent, must have power to suppress such obscenity.... It is entirely destitute of wit.... We do not believe there is a newspaper so vile that would print confirmatory extracts.... We have found it impossible to convey any, even the most faint idea of its style and contents, and of our disgust and detestation of them ... but ... some one should ... undertake a most ... disagreeable ... duty.... Monsters have gone on in impunity, because the exposure of their vileness was attended with too great indelicacy.'

"*Edward Everett Hale*, author of *The Man Without a Country*, in *The North American Review*, January, 1856:

'Walter Whitman, an American—one of the roughs,—no sentimentalist,—no stander above men and women, or apart from them,—no more modest than immodest,—... Everything about the external arrangement of this book is odd and out of the way ... it is well worth going twice to the book-store to buy it ... one reads and enjoys the freshness, simplicity, and reality of what he reads, just as the tired man, lying on the hill-side in summer, enjoys the leaves of grass around him....'

"*Putnam's Monthly*, September, 1855. Written by *Charles Eliot Norton* at the age of twenty-eight:

'Lawless ... poems ... in a sort of excited prose ... a compound of the New England transcendentalist and a New York rowdy. A foreman (of intelligence) might have written this gross yet elevated, this superficial yet profound, this preposterous yet somehow fascinating book.'

"*National Intelligencer*, Washington, D.C., February-March, 1856:

'Walter Whitman is a pantheist, Without, perhaps, ever having read Spinoza, he is a Spinozist. Without, perhaps, much deep insight into Plato the divine, he is a Platonist "in the rough".... The world as he finds it ... is good enough for Walter Whitman who is himself a "kosmos." ... Mr. Whitman thinks ... he would like to turn and live awhile with the animals.... Everyone to his liking, as remarked the venerable dame in the proverb when she kissed her cow.... No one, we may say, however, in all candor, can read this singular prose-poem without being struck by the writer's wonderful power of description and of word-painting. It is only ... his transcendental sinuosities of thought ... which ... become narrower and narrower and at last dwindle to a squirrel path and run up a tree.'"[1]

1856. Second edition of *Leaves of Grass* published by Fowler and Wells.

1857-1859. Edited the Brooklyn *Times*.

1859. Wrote the poem, "Out of the Cradle Endlessly Rocking."

1860. Third edition of *Leaves of Grass* published.

1862-1864. Went to the war front in Virginia to work in field and army hospitals.

His friend, John Burroughs, the naturalist, described his impression of Whitman: "When I came to meet the poet himself, which was in the fall of 1863, I felt less concern about his [egoism and his attitude toward evil] ...; he was so sound and sweet and gentle and attractive as a man, and withal so wise and tolerant, that I soon came to feel the same confidence in the book that I at once placed in its author.... I saw that the work and the man were one, and that the former must be good as the latter was good. There was something in the manner in which both the book and its author carried themselves under the sun, and in the way they confronted America and the present time, that convinced beyond the power of logic or criticism....

"One would see him afar off, in the crowd but not of it,—a large, slow-moving figure, clad in gray, with broad-brimmed hat and gray beard—or, quite as frequently, on the front platform of the street horse-cars with the driver.... There were times during this period when ... the physical man was too pronounced on first glance.... One needed to see the superbly domed head and classic brow crowning the rank physical man....

"Whitman was of large mould in every way, and of bold, far-reaching schemes, and is very sure to fare better at the hands of large men then of small. The first and last impression which his personal presence always made upon one was of a nature wonderfully gentle, tender, and benignant.... I was impressed by the fine grain and clean, fresh quality of the man.... He always had the look of a man who had just taken a bath."[1]

Another friend remarked:—"I marked the countenance, serene, proud, cheerful, florid, grave; the brow seamed with noble wrinkles; the features, massive and handsome, with firm blue eyes; the eyebrows and eyelids especially showing that fulness of arch seldom seen save in the antique busts; the flowing hair and fleecy beard, both very gray, and tempering with a look of age the youthful aspect of one who is but forty-five; the simplicity and purity of his dress, cheap and plain, but spotless, from snowy falling collar to burnished boot, and exhaling faint fragrance; the whole form surrounded with manliness, as with a nimbus, and breathing, in its perfect health and vigor, the august charm of the strong....

"He has been a visitor of prisons; a protector of fugitive slaves; a constant voluntary nurse, night and day, at the hospitals, from the beginning of the war to the present time; a brother and friend through life to the neglected and the forgotten, the poor, the degraded, the criminal, the outcast; turning away from no man for his guilt, nor woman for her vileness."[2]

January 10, 1863. R. W. Emerson wrote: "Mr. Walt Whitman, of New York, writes me that he is seeking employment in the public service in Washington, & perhaps some application on his part has already been made to yourself.

"Will you permit me to say that he is known to me as a man of strong original genius, combining, with marked eccentrici-

My comrade I wrapt in his blanket, envelop'd well his form,
Folded the blanket well, tucking it carefully over head and carefully under feet,
And there and then and bathed by the rising sun, my son in his grave,
    in his rude-dug grave I deposited,
Ending my vigil strange with that, vigil of night and battle-field dim,
Vigil for boy of responding kisses, (never again on earth responding,)
Vigil for comrade swiftly slain, vigil I never forget, how as day brighten'd,
I rose from the chill ground and folded my soldier well in his blanket,
And buried him where he fell.
■ (From "Drum-Taps" in *Leaves of Grass* by Walt Whitman. Illustrated by Rockwell Kent.)

The Singer in the Prison. ■ (From "Autumn Rivulets" in *Leaves of Grass* by Walt Whitman. Illustrated by Rockwell Kent.)

ties, great powers & valuable traits of character: self-relying large-hearted man, much beloved by his friends; entirely patriotic & benevolent in his theory, tastes, & practice. If his writings are in certain points open to criticism, they show extraordinary power, & are more deeply American, democratic, & in the interest of political liberty, then those of any other poet.

"A man of his talents & dispositions will quickly make himself useful, and, if the government has work that he can do, I think it may easily find that it has called to its side more valuable aid than it bargained for." [*Walt Whitman, The Correspondence 1863-1867*, Volume I, edited by Edwin Haviland Miller, New York University Press.[5]]

January 17, 1863. Whitman to Ralph Waldo Emerson: "Your letters from Buffalo have just come to hand. They find me still hanging around here—my plans, wants, ideas, &c gradually getting into shape.

"I go a great deal into the Hospitals. Washington is full of them—both in town and out around the outskirts. Some of the larger ones are towns in themselves. In small and large, all forty to fifty thousand inmates are ministered to, as I hear. Being sent for by a particular soldier, three weeks since, in the Campbell Hospital. I soon fell to going there and elsewhere to like places daily. The first shudder has long passed over, and I must say I find deep things, unreckoned by current print or speech. The Hospital, I do not find it, the repulsive place of sores and fevers, nor the place of querulousness, nor the bad results of morbid years which one avoids like bad s[mells]—at last [not] so is it under the circumstances here—other hospitals may be, but not here.

"I desire and intend to write a little book out of this phase of America, her masculine young manhood, its conduct under most trying of and highest of all exigency, which she, as by

lifting a corner in a curtain, has vouch-safed me to see America, already brought to Hospital in her fair youth—brought and deposited here in this great, white sepulchre of Washington itself—(this union Capital without the first bit of cohesion—this collect of proofs how low and swift a good stock can deteriorate—) Capital to which these deputies most strange arrive from every quarter, concentrating here, well-drest, rotten, meagre, nimble and impotent, full of gab, full always of their thrice-accursed *party*—arrive and skip into the seats of mightiest legislation, and take the seats of judges and high executive seats—while by quaint Providence come also sailed and wagoned hither this other freight of helpless worn and wounded youth, genuine of the soil, of darlings and true heirs to me the first unquestioned and convincing western crop, prophetic of the future, proofs undeniable to all men's ken of perfect beauty, tenderness and pluck that never race yet rivalled.

"But more, a new world here I find as I would show—a world full of its separate action, play, suggestiveness—surely a medium world, advanced between our well-known practised one of body and of mind, and one there may-be somewhere on beyond. We dream of, of the soul."[4]

February 13, 1863. To Thomas Jefferson Whitman, his brother: "... (It is very amusing to hunt for an office—so the thing seems to me just now—even if one don't get it)—I have seen Charles Sumner three times—he says every thing here moves as part of a great machine, and that I must consign myself to the fate of the rest—still [in] an interview I had with him yesterday he talked and acted as though he had life in him, and would exert himself to any reasonable extent for me to get something. Meantime I make about enough to pay my expenses by hacking on the press here, and copying in the paymasters offices, a couple of hours a day—one thing is favorable here, namely, pay for whatever one does is at a high rate. . . .

"... Meantime, I am getting better and better acquainted with office-hunting wisdom, and Washington peculiarities generally.

"I spent several hours in the Capitol the other day—the incredible gorgeousness of some of the rooms, (interior decorations &c)—rooms used perhaps but for merely three or four Committee meetings in the course of the whole year,) is beyond one's flightiest dreams. Costly frescoes of the style of Taylor's Saloon in Broadway, only really the best and choicest of their sort, done by imported French & Italian artists, are the prevailing sorts (imagine the work you see on the fine China vases, in Tiffany's—the paintings of Cupids & goddesses &c. spread recklessly over the arched ceiling and broad panels of a big room—the whole floor underneath paved with tesselated pavement, which is a sort of cross between marble & china, with little figures drab, blue, cream color, &c).

"These things, with heavy, elaborately wrought balustrades, columns, & steps—all of the most beautiful marbles I ever saw, some white as milk, others of all colors, green, spotted, lined, or of our old chocolate color—all these marbles used as freely as if they were common blue flags—with rich door-frames and window-casings of bronze and gold—heavy chandeliers and mantels, and clocks in every room—and indeed by far the richest and gayest, and most un-American and inappropriate ornamenting and finest interior workmanship I ever conceived possible, spread in profusion through scores, hundreds, (and almost thousands) of rooms—such are what I find, or rather would find to interest me, if I devoted time to it—But a few of the rooms are enough for me—the style is without grandeur, and without simplicity—These days, the state our country is in, and especially filled as I am from top to toe, of late with scenes and thoughts of *the hospitals,* (America seems to me now, though only in her youth, but brought *already here* feeble, bandaged and bloody *in hospital*)—*these days* I say, Jeff, all the poppy-show goddesses and all the pretty blue & gold in which the interior Capitol is got up, seem to me out of place beyond any thing I could tell—and I get away from it as quick as I can when that kind of thought comes over me."[5]

March 18, 1863. To his brother: "The Hospitals still engross a large part of my time and feelings—only I don't remain so long and make such exhausting-like visits, the last week—as I have had a bad humming feeling and deafness, stupor-like at times, in my head, which unfits me for continued exertion. It comes from a bad cold, gathering I think in my head. If it were not that some of the soldiers really depend on me to come, and the doctors tell me it is really necessary, I should suspend my visits for two or three days, at least. Poor boys, you have no idea how they cling to one, and how strong the tie that forms between us. Things here are just the same with me, neither better nor worse—(I feel so engrossed with my soldiers, I do not devote that attention to my office-hunting, which is needed for success.)

". . . It is impossible to tell what the government designs to do the coming season, but I suppose they will push on the war. The south is failing fast in many respects—D'Almeida, the Frenchman . . . , told me that he was besieged every where down south to sell (for confederate money) any and every thing he had, his clothes, his boots, his haversack, &c &c. Then their niggers will gradually melt, *certain.* So the fates fight for us, even if our generals do not. Jeff, to see what I see so much of, puts one entirely out of conceit of war—still for all that I am not sure but I go in for fighting on—the choice is hard on either part, but to *cave* in the worst . . ."[5]

April 15, 1863. To his mother he wrote: "Jeff writes he wonders if I am as well and hearty, and I suppose he means as much of a beauty as ever—whether I look the same—well, not only as much, but more so—I believe I weigh about 200 and as to my face, (so scarlet,) and my beard and neck, they are terrible to behold—I fancy the reason I am able to do some good in the hospitals, among the poor languishing & wounded boys, is that I am so large and well—indeed like a great wild buffalo, with much hair—many of the soldiers are from the west, and far north—and they take to a man that has not the bleached shiny & shaved cut of the cities and the east. I spent three to four hours yesterday in Armory Hospital—One of my particular boys there was dying, pneumonia—he wanted me to stop with him awhile—he could not articulate—but the look of his eyes, and the holding on of his hand, was deeply affecting. His case is a relapse—eight days ago, he had recovered, was up, was perhaps a little careless—at any rate took cold, was taken down again and has sunk rapidly. He has no friends or relatives here—Yesterday he labored & panted so for breath, it was terrible—he is a young man from New England, from the country—I expect to see his cot vacated this afternoon or evening, as I shall go down then. Mother, if you or Mat was here a couple of days, you would cry your eyes out. I find I have to restrain myself and keep my composure—I succeed pretty well."[5]

When gorgeous the countless straight stems, the
   forests at the wharves, thicken with colors,
When every ship richly drest carries her flag at the
   peak,
When pennants trail and street-festoons hang from
   the windows,
When Broadway is entirely given up to foot-passengers
   and foot-standers, when the mass is densest,
When the facades of the houses are alive with people,
   when eyes gaze riveted tens of thousands at a time,
When guests from the islands advance, when the
   pageant moves forward visible,
When the summons is made, when the answer that
   waited thousands of years answers,
I too arising, answering, descend to the pavements,
   merge with the crowd, and gaze with them.
■(From "A Broadway Pageant" in *Leaves of Grass* by
Walt Whitman. Illustrated by Rockwell Kent.)

July 7, 1863. "One of the things here always on the go, is long trains of army wagons—sometimes they will stream along all day, it almost seems as if there was nothing else but army wagons & ambulances—they have great camps here in every direction, of army wagons, teamsters, ambulance camps, &c. Some of them are permanent, & have small hospitals—I go to them, (as no one else goes, ladies would not venture)—I sometimes have the luck to give some of the drivers a great deal of comfort & help. Indeed, mother, there are camps here of every thing—I went once or twice to the Contraband Camp, to the Hospital, &c. but I could not bring myself to go again—when I meet black men or boys among my own hospitals, I use them kindly, give them something, &c.—I believe I told you that I do the same to the wounded rebels, too—but as there is a limit to one's sinews & endurance & sympathies, &c. I have got in the way after going lightly as it were all through the wards of a hospital, & trying to give a word of cheer, if nothing else, to every one, then confining my special attentions to the few where the investment seems to tell best, & who want it most—Mother, I have real pride in telling you that I have the consciousness of saving quite a little number of lives by saving them from giving up & being a good deal with them—the men say it is so, & the doctors say it is so—& I will candidly confess I can see it is true, though I say it of myself—I know you will like to hear it, mother, so I tell you—"[5]

September 8, 1863. "Mother, one's heart grows sick of war, after all, when you see what it really is; every once in a while I feel so horrified and disgusted—it seems to me like a great slaughterhouse and the men mutually butchering each other—then I feel how impossible it appears, again, to retire from this contest, until we have carried our points (it is cruel to be so tossed from pillar to post in one's judgment) . . ."[1]

October, 1863. "Well, dear Mother, how the time passes away—to think it will soon be a year I have been away—it has passed away very swiftly somehow to me—O what things I have witnessed during that time—I shall never forget them—& the war is not settled yet, & one does not see any thing at all certain about the settlement yet, but I have finally got for good I think into the feeling that our triumph is assured, whether it be sooner or whether it be later, or whatever roundabout way we are led there, & I find I dont change that conviction from any reverses we meet, or any delays or government blunders—there are blunders enough, heaven knows, but I am thankful things have gone on as well for us as they have—thankful the ship rides safe & sound at all—then I have finally made up my mind that Mr Lincoln has done as good as a human man could do—I still think him a pretty big President—I realize here in Washington that it has been a big thing to have just kept the United States from being thrown down & having its throat cut—& now I have no doubt it will throw down secession & cut its throat—& I have not had any doubt since Gettysburgh—"[5]

". . . I see the President almost every day, as I happen to live where he passes to or from his lodging out of town. He never sleeps at the White House during the hot season, but has quarters at a healthy location some three miles north of the city, the Soldiers home, a United States military establishment. I saw him this morning about 8½ coming into business, riding on Vermont avenue, near L street. He always has a company of twenty-five or thirty cavalry, with sabres drawn and held upright over their shoulders. They say this guard was against his personal wish, but he let his counselors have their way. The party makes no great show in uniform or horses. Mr. Lincoln on the saddle generally rides a good-sized, easy-going gray horse, is dress'd in plain black, somewhat rusty and dusty, wears a black stiff hat, and looks about as ordinary in attire, &c., as the commonest man. A lieutenant, with yellow straps, rides at his left, and following behind, two by two, come the cavalry men, in their yellow-stripped jackets.

"They are generally going at a slow trot, as that is the pace set them by the one they wait upon. The sabres and accountrements clank, and the entirely unornamental *cortége* as it trots towards Lafayette square arouses no sensation, only some curious stranger stops and gazes. I see very plainly ABRAHAM LINCOLN'S dark brown face, with the deep-cut lines, the eyes, always to me with a deep latent sadness in the expression. We have got so that we exchange bows, and very cordial ones. Sometimes the President goes and comes in an open barouche. The cavalry always accompany him, with drawn sabres. Often I notice as he goes out evenings—and sometimes in the morning, when he returns early—he turns off and halts at the large and handsome residence of the Secretary of War, on K street, and holds conference there. If in his barouche, I can see from my window he does not alight, but sits in his vehicle, and Mr. Stanton comes out to attend him.

"Sometimes one of his sons, a boy of ten or twelve, accompanies him, riding at his right on a pony. Earlier in the summer I occasionally saw the President and his wife, toward the latter part of the afternoon, out in a barouche, on a pleasure ride through the city. Mrs. Lincoln was dress'd in complete black, with a long crape veil. The equipage is of the plainest kind, only two horses, and they nothing extra. They pass'd me once very close, and I saw the President in the face fully, as they were moving slowly, and his look, though abstracted, happen'd to be directed steadily in my eye. He bow'd and smiled, but far beneath his smile I noticed well the expression I have alluded to. None of the artists or pictures has caught the deep, though subtle and indirect expression of this man's face. There is something else there. One of the great portrait painters of two or three centuries ago is needed."[3]

November 8-9, 1863. To the soldiers at Hospital: "Well, dear comrades, what shall I tell you to pass away the time? I am going around quite a great deal, more than I really desire to. Two or three nights ago I went to the N Y Academy of Music, to the Italian opera. I suppose you know that is a performance, a play, all in music & singing, in the Italian language, very sweet & beautiful. There is a large company of singers & a large band, altogether two or three hundred. It is in a splendid great house, four or five tiers high, & a broad parquette on the main floor. The opera here now has some of the greatest singers in the world—the principal lady singer (her name is Medori) has a voice that would make you hold your breath with wonder & delight, it is like a miracle—no mocking bird nor the clearest flute can begin with it—besides it is [a] very rich & strong voice—& besides she is a tall & handsome lady, & her actions are so graceful as she moves about the stage, playing her part.

"Boys, I must tell you just one scene in the opera I saw—things have worked so in the piece that this lady is compelled, although she tries very hard to avoid it, to give a cup of poisoned wine to her lover—the king her husband forces her to do it—she pleads hard, but her husband threatens to take both their lives (all this is in singing & music, very fine)—so the lover is brought in as a prisoner, & the king pretends to pardon him & make up, & asks the young man to drink a cup of wine, & orders the lady to pour it out.

The youth lies awake in the cedar-roof'd garret and harks to the musical rain.... ■ (From "Song of Myself" in *Leaves of Grass* by Walt Whitman. Illustrated by Rockwell Kent.)

The lover drinks it, then the king gives her & him a look & smiles & walks off the stage. And now came as good a piece of performance as I ever saw in my life. The lady as soon as she saw that her husband was really gone, she sprang to her lover, clutched him by the arm, & poured out the greatest singing you ever heard—it poured like a raging river more than any thing else I could compare it to—she tells him he is poisoned—he tries to inquire &c and hardly knows what to make of it—she breaks in, trying to pacify him, & explain &c—all this goes on very rapid indeed, & the band accompanying—she quickly draws out from her bosom a little vial, to neutralize the poison, then the young man in his desperation abuses her & tells her perhaps it is to poison him still more as she has already poisoned him once—this puts her in such agony, she begs & pleads with him to take the antidote at once before it is too late—her voice is so wild & high it goes through one like a knife, yet it is delicious—she holds the little vial to his mouth with one hand & with the other springs open a secret door in the wall, for him to escape from the palace—he swallows the antidote, & as she pushes him through the door, the husband returns with some armed guards, but she slams the door to, & stands back up against the door, & her arms spread wide open across it, one fist clenched, & her eyes glaring like a wild cat, so they dare not touch her—& that ends the scene.

"Comrades, recollect all this is in singing & music, & lots of it too, on a big scale, in the band, every instrument you can think of, & the best players in the world, & sometimes the whole band & the whole men's chorus & women's chorus all putting on the steam together—& all in a vast house, light as day, & with a crowded audience of ladies & men. Such singing & strong rich music always give me the greatest pleasure—& so the opera is the only amusement I have gone to, for my own satisfaction, for last ten years."[5]

1864. In correspondence with his mother, he acknowledged that: "I could not keep the tears out of my eyes. Many of the poor young men had to be moved on stretchers, with blankets over them, which soon soaked as wet as water in the rain. Most were sick cases, but some badly wounded. I came up to the nearest hospital and helped. Mother, it was a dreadful night (last Friday night)—pretty dark, the wind gusty, and the rain fell in torrents. One poor boy—this is a sample case out of the 600—he seemed to be quite young, he was quite small (I looked at his body afterwards), he groaned some as the stretcher bearers were carrying him along, and again as they carried him through the hospital gate. They set down the stretcher and examined him, and the poor boy was dead. They took him into the ward, and the doctor came immediately, but it was all of no use. The worst of it is, too, that he is entirely unknown—there was nothing on his clothes, or any one with him to identify him, and he is altogether unknown. Mother, it is enough to rack one's heart—such things. Very likely his folks will never know in the world what has become of him. Poor, poor child, for he appeared as though he could be but 18. I feel lately as though I must have some intermission. I feel well and hearty enough, and was never better, but my feelings are kept in a painful condition a great part of the time. Things get worse and worse, as to the amount and sufferings of the sick, and as I have said before, those who have to do with them are getting more and more callous and indifferent. Mother, when I see the common soldiers, what they go through, and how everybody seems to try to pick upon them, and what humbug there is over them every how, even the dying soldier's money stolen from his body by some scoundrel attendant, or from [the] sick one, even from under his head, which is a common thing, and then the agony I see every day, I get almost frightened at the world."[1]

At the end of the war, he wrote: "And so good-bye to the war. I know not how it may have been, or may be, to others—to me the main interest I found, (and still, on recollection, find,) in the rank and file of the armies, both sides, and in those specimens amid the hospitals, and even the dead on the field. To me the points illustrating the latent personal character and eligibilities of these States, in the two or three millions of American young and middle-aged men, North and South, embodied in those armies—and especially the one-third or one-fourth of their number, stricken by wounds or disease at some time in the course of the contest—were of more significance even than the political interests involved. (As so much of a race depends on how it faces death, and how it stands personal anguish and sickness. As, in the glints of emotions under emergencies, and the indirect traits and asides in Plutarch, we get far profounder clues to the antique world than all its more formal history.)

"Future years will never know the seething hell and the black infernal background of countless minor scenes and interiors, (not the official surface-courteousness of the Generals, not the few great battles) of the Secession war; and it is best they should not—the real war will never get in the books. In the mushy influences of current times, too, the fervid atmosphere and typical events of those years are in danger of being totally forgotten. I have at night watch'd by the side of a sick man in the hospital, one who could not live many hours. I have seen his eyes flash and burn as he raised himself and recurr'd to the cruelties on his surrender'd brother, and mutilations of the corpse afterward.

"Such was the war. It was not a quadrille in a ballroom. Its interior history will not only never be written—its practicality, minutiae of deeds and passions, will never be even suggested. The actual soldier of 1862-'65, North and South, with all his ways, his incredible dauntlessness, habits, practices, tastes, language, his fierce friendship, his appetite, rankness, his superb strength and animality, lawless gait, and a hundred unnamed lights and shades of camp, I say, will never be written—perhaps must not and should not be.

"The preceding notes may furnish a few stray glimpses into that life, and into those lurid interiors, never to be fully convey'd to the future. The hospital part of the drama from '61 to '65, deserves indeed to be recorded. Of that many-threaded drama, with its sudden and strange surprises, its confounding of prophecies, its moments of despair, the dread of foreign interference, the interminable campaigns, the bloody battles, the mighty and cumbrous and green armies, the drafts and bounties—the immense money expenditure, like a heavy-pouring constant rain—with, over the whole land, the last three years of the struggle, an unending, universal mourning-wail of women, parents, orphans—the marrow of the tragedy concentrated in those Army Hospitals—(it seem'd sometimes as if the whole interest of the land, North and South, was one vast central hospital, and all the rest of the affair but flanges)—those forming the untold and unwritten history of the war—infinitely greater (like life's) than the few scraps and distortions that are ever told or written. Think how much, and of importance, will be—how much, civic and military, has already been—buried in the grave, in eternal darkness."[3]

During these years of hospital work Whitman experienced the first physical illness of his life—spells of faintness later thought to be a premature stroke.

January, 1865. Appointed clerk in Indian Bureau for the Department of the Interior.

1867. Fourth edition of *Leaves of Grass* published. "A man's family is the people who love him—the people who comprehend him. You know how for the most part I have always been isolated from my people—in certain senses have been a stranger in their midst: just as we know Tolstoy has been. Who of my family has gone along with me? Who? Do you know? Not one of them . . . They have always missed my intentions. Take my darling dear mother: . . . she had great faith in me—felt sure I would accomplish wonderful things: but *Leaves of Grass*? Who could ever consider *Leaves of Grass* a wonderful thing: who? She would shake her head. God bless her!

She never did. She thought I was a wonderful thing, but the *Leaves?* oh my, hardly the *Leaves!* . . . George is my brother; it may be said that I love him—he loving me, too, in a certain sort of a way. . . . I would say, God bless George my brother: but as to George my interpreter, I would ask God to do something else with him. . . . Nelly and William . . . were my unvarying partisans, my unshakable lovers—my espousers."[1]

January 30, 1872. "My poetry remains yet, in substance, quite unrecognized here in the land for which it was written. The best established magazines & literary authorities (eminencies) quite ignore me & it. It has to this day failed to find an American publisher (as you perhaps know, I have myself printed the successive editions). And though there is a small minority of approval & discipleship, the great majority result continues to bring sneers, contempt & official coolness. My dismissal from moderate employment in 1865 by the Secretary of the Interior, Mr. Harlan, avowedly for the sole reason of my being the author of *Leaves of Grass*, still affords

Caricature of Whitman, 1872.

an indication of one high conventional feeling. The journals are often inveterately grateful. For example, in a letter in the correspondence of a leading New York paper (*Tribune*) from a lady tourist, an authoress of repute, an allusion in the letter to mountain scenery was illustrated by an innocent quotation from, & passing complimentary allusion to me. The letter was all & conspicuously published, except that the editors carefully cut out the lines quoting from & alluding to me, mutilating the text & stultifying the authoress to her great vexation. This to give you a clearer notion—(and I distinctly wish my friends in England writing about my book for print, to describe this state of things here.)

"Of general matters here, I will only say that the country seems to have entirely recuperated from the war. Except in a part of the Southern States, every thing is teeming & busy—more so than ever. Productiveness, wealth, population, improvements, material activity, success, results—beyond all measure, all precedent—& then spreading over such an area—three to four millions square miles—Great debits & offsets, of course—but how grand this oceanic plenitude & ceaselessness of domestic comfort—universal supplies of eating & drinking, houses to live in, farms to till, copious traveling, migratory habits, plenty of money, extravagance even—true there is something meteoric about it, and yet from an over-arching view it is Kosmic & real enough—It gives glow & enjoyment to me, being & moving amid the whirl & din, intensity, material success here—as I am myself sufficiently sluggish & ballasted to stand it—though the best is with reference to its foundation for & bearing on the future. . . ." [Edwin Haviland Miller, editor, *Walt Whitman The Correspondence 1868-1875*, Volume II, New York University Press.[6]]

January 26, 1873. "I have been not well for two or three days, but am better to-day. I have had a slight stroke of paralysis, on my left side, and especially the leg—occurred Thursday night last, & I have been laid up since—I am writing this in my room 535 15th st, as I am not able to get out at present—but the doctor gives me good hopes of being out and at my work in a few days—He says it is nothing but what I shall recover from in a few days—Mother, you must not feel uneasy—though I know you will—but I thought I would write & tell you the *exact truth—neither better nor worse—*"[6]

May 23, 1873. Mother died. "I have the feeling of getting more strength and easier in the head—something like what I was before mother's death. (I cannot be reconciled to that yet: it is the great cloud of my life—nothing that ever happened before has had such an effect on me.)" [Henry Bryan Burns, *A Life of Walt Whitman*, Haskell House Publishers, 1969.[7]]

"I can put up with all but the death of my mother—that is my great sorrow that sticks."[6]

1876. Sixth edition of *Leaves of Grass* published.

April 14, 1879. Gave lecture on Lincoln in New York (given each year for thirteen years).

June 2, 1879. ". . . This is the fourth day of a dark northeast storm, wind and rain. Day before yesterday was my birthday. . . . Every day of the storm, protected by overshoes and a waterproof blanket, I regularly come down to the pond, and ensconce myself under the lee of the great oak; I am here now writing these lines. The dark smoke-color'd clouds roll

in furious silence athwart the sky; the soft green leaves dangle all round me; the wind steadily keeps up its hoarse, soothing music over my head—Nature's mighty whisper. Seated here in solitude I have been musing over my life—connecting events, dates, as links of a chain, neither sadly nor cheerily, but somehow, to-day here under the oak, in the rain, in an unusually matter-of-fact spirit.

"But my great oak—sturdy, vital, green—five feet thick at the butt. I sit a great deal near or under him. Then the tulip tree near by—the Apollo of the woods—tall and graceful, yet robust and sinewy, inimitable in hang of foliage and throwing-out of limb; as if the beauteous, vital, leafy creature could walk, if it only would. (I had a sort of dream-trance the other day, in which I saw my favorite trees step out and promenade up, down and around, very curiously—with a whisper from one, leaning down as he pass'd me. *We do all this on the present occasion, exceptionally, just for you*.)"[3]

April 16, 1881. ". . . A short but pleasant visit to Longfellow, am not one of the calling kind, but as the author of *Evangeline* kindly took the trouble to come and see me three years ago in Camden, where I was ill, I felt not only the impulse of my own pleasure on that occasion, but a duty. He was the

Whitman, age 50.

O to make the most jubilant song!
Full of music-full of manhood, womanhood,
   infancy!
Full of common employments—full of grain and
   trees.

■ (From *Leaves of Grass* by Walt Whitman. Illustrated by Valenti Angelo.)

only particular eminence I called on in Boston, and I shall not soon forget his lit-up face and glowing warmth and courtesy, in the modes of what is called the old school.

"And now just here I feel the impulse to interpolate something about the mighty four who stamp this first American century with its birth-marks of poetic literature. In a late magazine one of my reviewers, who ought to know better, speaks of my 'attitude of contempt and scorn and intolerance' toward the leading poets—of my 'deriding' them, and preaching their 'uselessness.' If anybody cares to know what I think—and have long thought and avow'd—about them, I am entirely willing to propound. I can't imagine any better luck befalling these States for a poetical beginning and initiation than has come from Emerson, Longfellow, Bryant, and Whittier. Emerson, to me, stands unmistakably at the head, but for the others I am at a loss where to give any precedence. Each illustrious, each rounded, each distinctive. Emerson for his sweet, vital-tasting melody, rhym'd philosophy, and poems as amber-clear as the honey of the wild bee he loves to sing. Longfellow for rich color, graceful forms and incidents—all that makes life beautiful and love refined—competing with the singers of Europe on their own ground, and, with one exception, better and finer work than that of any of them. Bryant pulsing the first interior verse-throbs of a mighty world—bard of the river and the wood, every conveying a taste of open air, with scents as from hay-fields, grapes, birch-borders—always lurkingly fond of threnodies—beginning and ending his long career with chants of death, with here and there through all, poems, or passages of poems, touching the highest universal truths, enthusiasms, duties—morals as grim and eternal, if not as stormy and fateful, as anything in Eschylus. While in Whittier, with his special themes—(his outcropping love of heroism and war, for all his Quakerdom, his verses at times like the measur'd stop of Cromwell's old veterans)—in Whittier lives the zeal, the moral energy, that founded New England—the splendid rectitude and ardor of Luther, Milton, George Fox—I must not, dare not, say the willfulness and

narrowness—though doubtless the world needs now, and always will need, almost above all, just such narrowness and willfulness."[3]

1884. Bought a house on Mickle Street in Camden, New Jersey. Here visited by celebrities, disciples and most importantly, by good companions.

"After the supper and talk—after the day is done,
As a friend from friends his final withdrawal prolonging,
Good-bye and Good-bye with emotional lips repeating,
   . . .
E'en at the exit-door turning—charges superfluous
   calling back—e'en as he descends the steps, . . .
Soon to be lost for aye in the darkness—loth, O so loth
   to depart!
Garrulous to the very last."[1]

August 19, 1890. "My life, young manhood, mid-age, times South, &c., have been jolly, bodily, and doubtless open to criticism. Though unmarried I have had six children—two are dead—one living Southern grandchild, fine boy, writes to me occasionally—circumstances (connected with their fortune and benefit) have separated me from intimate relations."[2]

1891. "I used to feel . . . that I was to irradiate or emanate buoyancy and health. But it came to me in time, that I was not to attempt to live to the reputation I had, or to my own idea of what my programme should be; but to give out and express what I really was; and, if I felt like the devil, to say so; and I have become more and more confirmed in this."[7]

March 26, 1892. Died. Buried in Harleigh Cemetery, Camden, New Jersey. "A great poem is for ages and ages in common and for all degrees and complexions and all departments and sects and for a woman as much as a man and a man as much as a woman. A great poem is no finish to a man or woman but rather a beginning."[4]

FOR MORE INFORMATION SEE: John Burroughs, *Notes on Walt Whitman as Poet and Person,* American News, 1867, reprinted, Haskell House, 1971; William Clarke, *Walt Whitman,* Macmillan, 1892, reprinted, Richard West, 1973; Walt Whitman, *Autobiographia; or, the Story of a Life,* Webster, 1892, reprinted, Folcroft, 1972; John A. Symonds, *Walt Whitman,* J. C. Nimmo, 1893, reprinted, Folcroft, 1973; Sadakichi Hartman, *Conversations with Walt Whitman,* 1894, reprinted, Folcroft, 1973; J. Burroughs, *Whitman; A Study,* Houghton, 1896, reprinted, Scholarly Press, 1970; William Sloane Kennedy, *Reminiscences of Walt Whitman,* A. Gardner, 1898, reprinted, Richard West, 1973; W. Whitman, *Walt Whitman at Home,* Critic, 1898, reprinted, Folcroft, 1973; W. Whitman, *The Wound Dresser: A Series of Letters Written from the Hospital in Washington,* Small, Maynard, 1898, reprinted, Folcroft, 1975.

Elizabeth P. Gould, *Anne Gilchrist and Walt Whitman,* McKay, 1900, reprinted, Folcroft, 1972; Mila Maynard, *Walt Whitman: The Poet of the Wider Selfhood,* C. H. Kerr, 1903, reprinted, Folcroft, 1973; Henry Bryan Binns, *Life of Walt Whitman,* Methuen, 1905, reprinted, Haskell House, 1969; Mable M. Irwin, *Whitman: The Poet Liberator of Woman,* privately printed, [New York], 1905, reprinted, Folcroft, 1975; Bliss Perry, *Walt Whitman,* Houghton, 1906, reprinted, Richard West, 1973; George R. Carpenter, *Walt Whitman,* Macmillan, 1909, reprinted, Gale, 1967; James Thomson, *Walt Whitman: The Man and the Poet,* [London], 1910, reprinted, Haskell House, 1971; Basil De Selincourt, *Walt Whitman: A Critical Study*, M. Secker, 1914, reprinted, Folcroft, 1973; H. B. Binns, *Walt Whitman and His Poetry*, Harrap, 1915, reprinted, AMS Press, 1972.

Leon Bazalgette, *Walt Whitman: The Man and His Work*, translated by Ellen Fitzgerald, Doubleday, 1920, reprinted, Cooper Square, 1971; Will Hayes, *Walt Whitman: The Prophet of the New Era*, C. W. Daniel, 1921, reprinted, Folcroft, 1973; Elizabeth Keller, *Walt Whitman in Mickle Street*, M. Kennerley, 1921, reprinted, Haskell House, 1971; Gerald Bullett, *Walt Whitman: A Study and a Selection*, G. Richards, 1924, reprinted, Folcroft, 1976; John C. Bailey, *Walt Whitman*, Macmillan, 1926, reprinted, Scholarly Press, 1970; Maurice O. Johnson, *Walt Whitman As Critic of Literature*, [Lincoln, Nebraska], 1938, reprinted, Haskell House, 1970; Hugh I. Fausset, *Walt Whitman: Poet of Democracy*, Yale University Press, 1942, reprinted, Russell, 1969; Henry Seidel Canby, *Walt Whitman: An American*, Houghton, 1943, reprinted, Greenwood Press, 1970.

Joseph C. Beaver, *Walt Whitman: Poet of Science*, Kings Crown Press, 1951, reprinted, Octagon, 1972; Arthur E. Briggs, *Walt Whitman: Thinker and Artist*, Philosophical Library, 1952, reprinted, Greenwood Press, 1968; Gay W. Allen, *Solitary Singer: A Critical Biography of Walt Whitman*, Macmillan, 1955, reprinted, New York University Press, 1967; G. W. Allen, editor, *Walt Whitman Abroad*, Syracuse University Press, 1955, reprinted, Folcroft, 1975; United States Library of Congress, Reference Department, *Walt Whitman: A Catalogue Based upon the Collection of the Library of Congress*, Library of Congress, 1955, reprinted, Folcroft, 1974; G. W. Allen, *Walt Whitman as Man, Poet, and Legend*, Southern University Illinois Press, 1961, reprinted, Folcroft, 1975; Edwin Haviland Miller, editor, *The Correpondence*, five volumes, New York University Press, 1961-69; E. H. Miller, *Walt Whitman's Poetry: A Psychological Journey*, New York University Press, 1969.

Thomas L. Brasher, *Whitman as Editor of the Brooklyn Daily Eagle*, Wayne State University Press, 1970; Barbara Marinacci, *O Wondrous Singer: An Introduction To Walt Whitman*, Dodd, 1970; Bertha Funnell, *Walt Whitman on Long Island*, Kennikat, 1971; Robert D. Faner, *Walt Whitman and Opera*, Southern Illinois University Press, 1972; Richard H. Rupp, editor, *Critics on Whitman*, University of Miami Press, 1972; Fred E. Carlisle, *The Uncertain Self: Whitman's Drama of Identity*, Michigan State University Press, 1973; Manuel Komroff, *Walt Whitman: The Singer and the Chains*, Folcroft, 1973; Floyd Stovall, *The Foreground of "Leaves of Grass,"* University Press of Virginia, 1974; G. W. Allen, *The New Walt Whitman Handbook*, New York University Press, 1975; Stephen A. Black, *Whitman's Journeys in Chaos: A Psychoanalytic Study in the Poetic Process*, Princeton University Press, 1975; Henry E. Legler, *Walt Whitman: Yesterday and Today*, Haskell House, 1976; Ivan Marki, *The Trial of the Poet: An Interpretation of the First Edition of Leaves of Grass*, Columbia University Press, 1976.

For children: Babette Deutsch, *Walt Whitman: Builder for America*, Messner, 1941; Laura Benét, *Famous American Poets*, Dodd, 1950; Frederick Houk Law, *Great Americans*, Globe Book, 1953; Sarah (Knowles) Bolton, *Famous American Authors*, Crowell, 1954; David Edward Scherman and Rosemarie Redlich, *America: The Land and Its Writers*, Dodd, 1956; Patrick Pringle, *101 Great Lives*, Ward, Lock,

1963; Adrien Stoutenburg and Laura Nelson Baker, *Listen America: A Life of Walt Whitman*, Scribner, 1968; Edmond L. Leipold, *Famous American Poets*, Denison, 1969.

ZONIA, Dhimitri 1921-

PERSONAL: First name is pronounced "*the*-me-tree"; born June 12, 1921, in St. Louis, Mo.; son of Ligor (a steelworker) and Polixenna (Rucho) Zonia; married Margaret C. Wieland (a horticulturist), April 20, 1947; children: Margaret Elizabeth, Susan Catherine, Carolynn Louise, Laura Elaine. *Education:* Independent study in Italy and England. *Home and studio:* 4680 Karamar Drive, St. Louis, Mo. 63128.

CAREER: Artist; illustrator; engraver. St. Louis *Post Dispatch*, St. Louis, Mo., engraver, 1955-1964. *Exhibitions:* Brooks Memorial Museum, Memphis, Tenn.; Albrecht Art Museum (one man show), St. Joseph, Mo.; Traveling Exhibit, Missouri State Council on the Arts; Mid-America, St. Louis City Art Museum; Oklahoma City Art Center, represented Missouri; American painters in Paris, Paris, France; Contemporary Arts Museum, Houston, Texas, University of Missouri, Kansas City, Mo. Works in public collections: Arkansas Art Center, Little Rock, Ark., Oklahoma Art Center, Okla.; Del Mar College, Corpus Christi, Texas; Butler Institute of American Art, Youngstown, Ohio; Albrecht Art Museum, St. Joseph, Mo. Also exhibited at: Nelson Gallery, Kansas City, Mo.; Joslyn Memorial Museum, Omaha, Neb.; Springfield Art Center, Springfield, Mo.; Hilton Galleries, Alcapulco, Mexico. *Military service:* United States Air Force, sargeant, 1940-1945. *Awards, honors:* Portrait Exhibition, first prize, St. Louis Artist's Guild, 1968; Mid-South Exhibit, purchase award, Oklahoma City Art Center, 1971; National Drawing, Robert Pearlman Purchase Award, Corpus Christi, Texas, 1973; Arkansas Art Center, Delta Annual, Little Rock, Ark., 1974; *Stepka and the Magic Fire* received Best Book of the Year Award, Catholic Press Association, 1975; Butler Institute of American Art, Josh Butler Purchase Award, 1975; Drawing America, purchase award, State Council on the Arts, 1975; *Arise My Love* received Best 10 Books in the Mid-West 1975, National Printing Institute, 1976.

ILLUSTRATOR: Dorothy Van Woerkom (reteller), *Stepka and the Magic Fire*, Concordia, 1974; D. Van Woerkom, *Journeys to Bethlehem*, Concordia, 1974; *Arise My Love*, Concordia, 1975.

WORK IN PROGRESS: Two one man shows in London, England and Chicago.

SIDELIGHTS: "When the call from Concordia came, I was just completing a commissioned wall mural—one with nine-foot figures. 'We have a children's book, we'd like you to consider.' said the art director. 'It has a Russian Orthodox setting,' added the editor. 'That should appeal to your Eastern Orthodox background.' 'Wow!' I said.

"The book was *Stepka and the Magic Fire*, a Russian Easter legend retold beautifully by Dorothy Van Woerkom. I took the manuscript home and sat down to give it that first and vitally important concentrated reading. As I read I jotted down my ideas and impressions. If I decided to illustrate the book, I'd be living with it for a long time, but I knew that the art must have a strong initial impact on readers who would be a first-impression audience. Images crowded into my

(From *Journeys to Bethlehem, The Story of the First Christmas* retold by Dorothy Van Woerkom. Art by Dhimitri Zonia.)

DHIMITRI ZONIA

mind, sparked by Mrs. Van Woerkom's colorful words. I decided to take the job.

"My next step was to read the manuscript again and again until it became a part of me and I could recite whole passages of it from memory. Then I tucked it into a corner of my mind and let it age. Soon the faces of Stepka and his children began to emerge, closely followed by stylistic and technical ideas. This stage, when everything is as fresh to me as I want it to be in the final artwork, is my favorite and I always leave it with great reluctance to become a 'working' artist.

"I began to sketch, technical concerns nibbled into the freshness of my first impressions. At this point the notes I'd made during my first reading proved of immense value. I also cornered family and friends and made them give me their first impressions. I tried out character sketches of Stepka and the children on them. I was determined to keep my relation with the book spontaneous.

"The next step was to work my sketches into a dummy. A dummy is a rough version of the final book. It indicates the number of pages, the cover design, the style and placement of art, and the distribution of text. It's also the subject of many meetings with the art director, editor, and printing experts. After I'd incorporated the input from those meetings into a revised dummy for *Stepka*. I received the green light to proceed with the final art.

"The first piece I finished was the cover, because it was needed for prepublication promotion. A cover, I discovered, has a special challenge all its own. It must first invite the adult to buy the book and then the child to read it. The cover must be both aesthetically pleasing and informative.

"Using water color and pen and ink on illustration board, I prepared the art for *Stepka* in the same size as it appears in the final book. I had decided to start at the back and work forward. This gave me a greater consciousness of the current and drift of the plot.

"At last my work was finished. I delivered the art and sat down to consider what I'd done. I'd ventured from what are called the 'fine arts' into children's book illustration. I'd gone from nine-foot wall figures and large canvases to page-size illustration board. It had been a stimulating experience for me. So stimulating, in fact, that when the next two calls came from Concordia, I again said yes.

"As with most contemporary artists we are called upon to execute work in a wide range of art projects. In the varied activities of art that I have been involved in required the following skills: engraver-etcher (print-making), oil and water-color painting (fine arts), drawing and sketching (live television), muralist (church and public building wall painting), drawing for book illustration, art instructor, lecturer, stained glass window designer, Icon painter and audio-visual film making.

"My primary field is in the fine arts, my work is in the 'New Realism' manner. I use contemporary elements in our environment 'hamburgers, television, automobiles, supermarkets and shopping carts, etc., in my work. Many of these works are in the permanent collections of museums and galleries and art centers nationally and in private collections in Europe.

"I am married to an English girl I met in England during World War II, where I served with the 8th Air Force. My parents were Romanian immigrants and I grew up in a strong ethnic community. I speak Romanian and Albanian."

FOR MORE INFORMATION SEE: St. Louis Globe Democrat Sunday Magazine, August 29, 1971; *CPH Commentator,* Winter, 1974; *Today's Art,* December, 1975; *St. Louis Post Dispatch,* January 30, 1976.

CUMULATIVE INDEX TO
ILLUSTRATIONS AND AUTHORS

Illustrations Index

(In the following index, the number of the volume in which an illustrator's work appears is given *before* the colon, and the page on which it appears is given *after* the colon. For example, a drawing by Adams, Adrienne appears in Volume 2 on page 6, another drawing by her appears in Volume 3 on page 80, another drawing in Volume 8 on page 1, and another drawing in Volume 15 on page 107.)

YABC

Index citations including this abbreviation refer to listings appearing in *Yesterday's Authors of Books for Children,* also published by the Gale Research Company, which covers authors who died prior to 1960.

Illustrations Index

Author Index

(In the following index, the number of the volume in which an author's sketch appears is given *before* the colon, and the page on which it appears is given *after* the colon. For example, the sketch of Aardema, Verna, appears in Volume 4 on page 1).

YABC

Index citations including this abbreviation refer to listings appearing in *Yesterday's Authors of Books for Children,* also published by the Gale Research Company, which covers authors who died prior to 1960.

Author Index

D'Amato, Alex, *20:* 24
D'Amato, Janet, *9:* 47
Damrosch, Helen Therese. *See*
  Tee-Van, Helen Damrosch,
  10: 176
D'Andrea, Kate. *See* Steiner,
  Barbara A(nnette), *13:* 213
Dangerfield, Balfour. *See*
  McCloskey, Robert, *2:* 185
Daniel, Anne. *See* Steiner, Barbara
  A(nnette), *13:* 213
Daniel, Hawthorne, *8:* 39
Daniels, Guy, *11:* 64
Darby, J. N. *See* Govan, Christine
  Noble, *9:* 80
Darby, Patricia (Paulsen), *14:* 53
Darby, Ray K., *7:* 59
Daringer, Helen Fern, *1:* 75
Darke, Marjorie, *16:* 68
Darling, Lois M., *3:* 57
Darling, Louis, Jr., *3:* 59
Darling, Kathy. *See* Darling, Mary
  Kathleen, *9:* 48
Darling, Mary Kathleen, *9:* 48
Darrow, Whitney. *See* Darrow,
  Whitney, Jr., *13:* 24
Darrow, Whitney, Jr., *13:* 24
Daugherty, Charles Michael, *16:* 70
Daugherty, James (Henry), *13:* 26
d'Aulaire, Edgar Parin, *5:* 49
d'Aulaire, Ingri (Maartenson Parin)
  5: 50
Daveluy, Paule Cloutier, *11:* 65
Davenport, Spencer. *See*
  Stratemeyer, Edward L.,
  1: 208
David, Jonathan. *See* Ames, Lee
  J., *3:* 11
Davidson, Basil, *13:* 30
Davidson, Jessica, *5:* 52
Davidson, Margaret, *5:* 53
Davidson, Marion. *See* Garis,
  Howard R(oger), *13:* 67
Davidson, Mary R., *9:* 49
Davis, Bette J., *15:* 53
Davis, Burke, *4:* 64
Davis, Christopher, *6:* 57
Davis, Daniel S(heldon), *12:* 68
Davis, Julia, *6:* 58
Davis, Mary L(ee), *9:* 49
Davis, Mary Octavia, *6:* 59
Davis, Paxton, *16:* 71
Davis, Robert, *YABC 1:* 104
Davis, Russell G., *3:* 60
Davis, Verne T., *6:* 60
Dawson, Elmer A. [Collective
  pseudonym], *1:* 76
Dawson, Mary, *11:* 66
Day, Thomas, *YABC 1:* 106
Dazey, Agnes J(ohnston), *2:* 88
Dazey, Frank M., *2:* 88
Deacon, Richard. *See* McCormick,
  (George) Donald (King),
  14: 141
Dean, Anabel, *12:* 69
de Angeli, Marguerite, *1:* 76

DeArmand, Frances Ullmann,
  10: 29
deBanke, Cecile, *11:* 67
De Bruyn, Monica, *13:* 30
de Camp, Catherine C(rook), *12:* 70
DeCamp, L(yon) Sprague, *9:* 49
Decker, Duane, *5:* 53
DeGering, Etta, *7:* 60
de Grummond, Lena Young, *6:* 61
Deiss, Joseph J., *12:* 72
DeJong, David C(ornel), *10:* 29
de Jong, Dola, *7:* 61
De Jong, Meindert, *2:* 89
de Kay, Ormonde, Jr., *7:* 62
de Kiriline, Louise. *See* Lawrence,
  Louise de Kirilene, *13:* 126
deKruif, Paul (Henry) *5:* 54
De Lage, Ida, *11:* 67
de la Mare, Walter, *16:* 73
Delaney, Harry, *3:* 61
Delano, Hugh, *20:* 25
De La Ramée, (Marie) Louise,
  20: 26
Delaune, Lynne, *7:* 63
DeLaurentis, Louise Budde, *12:* 73
Delderfield, Eric R(aymond), *14:* 53
Delderfield, R(onald) F(rederick),
  20: 34
De Leeuw, Adele Louise, *1:* 77
Delmar, Roy. *See* Wexler, Jerome
  (LeRoy), *14:* 243
Delton, Judy, *14:* 54
Delulio, John, *15:* 54
Delving, Michael. *See* Williams,
  Jay, *3:* 256
Demarest, Doug. *See* Barker, Will,
  8: 4
Demas, Vida, *9:* 51
Dennis, Morgan, *18:* 68
Dennis, Wesley, *18:* 70
Denslow, W(illiam) W(allace),
  16: 83
de Paola, Thomas Anthony, *11:* 68
de Paola, Tomie. *See* de Paola,
  Thomas Anthony, *11:* 68
deRegniers, Beatrice Schenk
  (Freedman), *2:* 90
Derleth, August (William) *5:* 54
Derman, Sarah Audrey, *11:* 71
Derry Down Derry. *See* Lear,
  Edward, *18:* 182
Derwent, Lavinia, *14:* 56
De Selincourt, Aubrey, *14:* 56
Desmond, Alice Curtis, *8:* 40
Detine, Padre. *See* Olsen, Ib
  Spang, *6:* 177
Deutsch, Babette, *1:* 79
Devaney, John, *12:* 74
Devereux, Frederick L(eonard),
  Jr., *9:* 51
Devlin, Harry, *11:* 73
Devlin, (Dorothy) Wende, *11:* 74
DeWaard, E. John, *7:* 63
Dewey, Ariane, *7:* 63
Dick, Trella Lamson, *9:* 51
Dickens, Charles, *15:* 55

Dickens, Monica, *4:* 66
Dickinson, Peter, *5:* 55
Dickinson, Susan, *8:* 41
Dickinson, William Croft, *13:* 32
Dickson, Naida, *8:* 41
Dietz, David H(enry), *10:* 30
Dietz, Lew, *11:* 75
Dillard, Annie, *10:* 31
Dillon, Diane, *15:* 98
Dillon, Eilis, *2:* 92
Dillon, Leo, *15:* 99
Dines, Glen, *7:* 65
Dinsdale, Tim, *11:* 76
DiValentin, Maria, *7:* 68
Dixon, Franklin W. [Collective
  pseudonym], *1:* 80. *See also*
  Svenson, Andrew E., *2:*
  238; Stratemeyer, Edward,
  1: 208
Dixon, Peter L., *6:* 62
Doane, Pelagie, *7:* 68
Dobell, I(sabel) M(arian) B(arclay),
  11: 77
Dobler, Lavinia G., *6:* 63
Dobrin, Arnold, *4:* 67
"Dr. A." *See* Silverstein, Alvin,
  8: 188
Dodd, Ed(ward) Benton, *4:* 68
Dodge, Bertha S(anford), *8:* 42
Dodgson, Charles Lutwidge,
  YABC 2: 97
Dodson, Kenneth M(acKenzie),
  11: 77
Doherty, C. H., *6:* 65
Dolson, Hildegarde, *5:* 56
Domanska, Janina, *6:* 65
Donalds, Gordon. *See* Shirreffs,
  Gordon D., *11:* 207
Donna, Natalie, *9:* 52
Doob, Leonard W(illiam), *8:* 44
Dor, Ana. *See* Ceder, Georgiana
  Dorcas, *10:* 21
Doré, (Louis Christophe Paul)
  Gustave, *19:* 92
Dorian, Edith M(cEwen) *5:* 58
Dorian, Harry. *See* Hamilton,
  Charles Harold St. John, *13:* 77
Dorian, Marguerite, *7:* 68
Dorman, Michael, *7:* 68
Doss, Helen (Grigsby), *20:* 37
Doss, Margot Patterson, *6:* 68
Dougherty, Charles, *18:* 74
Douglas, James McM. *See*
  Butterworth, W. E., *5:* 40
Douglas, Kathryn. *See* Ewing,
  Kathryn, *20:* 42
Douglas, Marjory Stoneman, *10:* 33
Douty, Esther M(orris), *8:* 44
Dow, Emily R., *10:* 33
Dowdell, Dorothy (Florence)
  Karns, *12:* 75
Dowden, Anne Ophelia, *7:* 69
Dowdey, Landon Gerald, *11:* 80
Downey, Fairfax, *3:* 61
Downie, Mary Alice, *13:* 32
Draco, F. *See* Davis, Julia, *6:* 58

Farrington, Benjamin, *20:* 45 (Obituary)
Farrington, Selwyn Kip, Jr., *20:* 45
Fassler, Joan (Grace), *11:* 94
Fast, Howard, *7:* 80
Fatchen, Max, *20:* 45
Father Xavier. *See* Hurwood, Bernhardt J., *12:* 107
Fatio, Louise, *6:* 75
Faulhaber, Martha, *7:* 82
Feagles, Anita MacRae, *9:* 63
Feague, Mildred H., *14:* 59
Fecher, Constance, *7:* 83
Feelings, Muriel (Grey), *16:* 104
Feelings, Thomas, *8:* 55
Feelings, Tom. *See* Feelings, Thomas, *8:* 55
Feiffer, Jules, *8:* 57
Feil, Hila, *12:* 81
Feilen, John. *See* May, Julian, *11:* 175
Feldman, Anne (Rodgers), *19:* 121
Fellows, Muriel H., *10:* 41
Felsen, Henry Gregor, *1:* 89
Felton, Harold William, *1:* 90
Felton, Ronald Oliver, *3:* 67
Fenner, Carol, *7:* 84
Fenner, Phyllis R(eid), *1:* 91
Fenten, D. X., *4:* 82
Fenton, Carroll Lane, *5:* 66
Fenton, Edward, *7:* 86
Feravolo, Rocco Vincent, *10:* 42
Ferber, Edna, *7:* 87
Ferguson, Bob. *See* Ferguson, Robert Bruce, *13:* 35
Ferguson, Robert Bruce, *13:* 35
Fergusson, Erna, *5:* 67
Fermi, Laura, *6:* 78
Fern, Eugene A., *10:* 43
Ferris, James Cody [Collective pseudonym], *1:* 92
Fiammenghi, Gioia, *9:* 64
Fiarotta, Noel, *15:* 104
Fiarotta, Phyllis, *15:* 105
Fichter, George S., *7:* 92
Fidler, Kathleen, *3:* 68
Fiedler, Jean, *4:* 83
Field, Edward, *8:* 58
Field, Eugene, *16:* 105
Field, Rachel (Lyman), *15:* 106
Fife, Dale (Odile), *18:* 110
Fighter Pilot, A. *See* Johnston, H(ugh) A(nthony) S(tephen), *14:* 87
Figueroa, Pablo, *9:* 66
Fijan, Carol, *12:* 82
Fillmore, Parker H(oysted), *YABC 1:* 121
Finkel, George (Irvine), *8:* 59
Finlayson, Ann, *8:* 61
Firmin, Peter, *15:* 113
Fischbach, Julius, *10:* 43
Fisher, Aileen (Lucia), *1:* 92
Fisher, Dorothy Canfield, *YABC 1:* 122

Fisher, John (Oswald Hamilton), *15:* 115
Fisher, Laura Harrison, *5:* 67
Fisher, Leonard Everett, *4:* 84
Fisher, Margery (Turner), *20:* 47
Fitch, Clarke. *See* Sinclair, Upton (Beall), *9:* 168
Fitch, John, IV. *See* Cormier, Robert Edmund, *10:* 28
Fitschen, Dale, *20:* 48
Fitzgerald, Captain Hugh. *See* Baum L(yman) Frank, *18:* 7
Fitzgerald, Edward Earl, *20:* 49
Fitzgerald, F(rancis) A(nthony), *15:* 115
Fitzgerald, John D(ennis), *20:* 50
Fitzhardinge, Joan Margaret, *2:* 107
Fitzhugh, Louise, *1:* 94
Flack, Marjorie, *YABC 2:* 123
Flash Flood. *See* Robinson, Jan M., *6:* 194
Fleischman, (Albert) Sid(ney), *8:* 61
Fleming, Alice Mulcahey, *9:* 67
Fleming, Ian (Lancaster), *9:* 67
Fleming, Thomas J(ames), *8:* 64
Fletcher, Charlie May, *3:* 70
Fletcher, Helen Jill, *13:* 36
Flexner, James Thomas, *9:* 70
Flitner, David P., *7:* 92
Floethe, Louise Lee, *4:* 87
Floethe, Richard, *4:* 89
Flood, Flash. *See* Robinson, Jan M., *6:* 194
Flora, James (Royer), *1:* 95
Florian, Douglas, *19:* 122
Flynn, Barbara, *9:* 71
Flynn, Jackson. *See* Shirreffs, Gordon D., *11:* 207
Folsom, Franklin (Brewster), *5:* 67
Forbes, Esther, *2:* 108
Forbes, Graham B. [Collective pseudonym], *1:* 97
Forbes, Kathryn. *See* McLean, Kathryn (Anderson), *9:* 140
Ford, Albert Lee. *See* Stratemeyer, Edward L., *1:* 208
Ford, Elbur. *See* Hibbert, Eleanor, *2:* 134
Ford, Marcia. *See* Radford, Ruby L., *6:* 186
Foreman, Michael, *2:* 110
Forrest, Sybil. *See* Markun, Patricia M(aloney), *15:* 189
Forester, C(ecil) S(cott), *13:* 38
Forman, Brenda, *4:* 90
Forman, James Douglas, *8:* 64
Forsee, (Frances) Aylesa, *1:* 97
Foster, Doris Van Liew, *10:* 44
Foster, E(lizabeth) C(onnell), *9:* 71
Foster, Elizabeth, *10:* 45
Foster, Elizabeth Vincent, *12:* 82
Foster, F. Blanche, *11:* 95
Foster, Genevieve (Stump), *2:* 111
Foster, John T(homas), *8:* 65
Foster, Laura Louise, *6:* 78
Fowke, Edith (Margaret), *14:* 59

Fox, Charles Philip, *12:* 83
Fox, Eleanor. *See* St. John, Wylly Folk, *10:* 132
Fox, Freeman. *See* Hamilton, Charles Harold St. John, *13:* 77
Fox, Lorraine, *11:* 96
Fox, Michael Wilson, *15:* 117
Fox, Paula, *17:* 59
Frances, Miss. *See* Horwich, Frances R., *11:* 142
Franchere, Ruth, *18:* 111
Francis, Dorothy Brenner, *10:* 46
Francis, Pamela (Mary), *11:* 97
Frank, Josette, *10:* 47
Frankau, Mary Evelyn, *4:* 90
Frankel, Bernice, *9:* 72
Franklin, Harold, *13:* 53
Franklin, Steve. *See* Stevens, Franklin, *6:* 206
Franzén, Nils-Olof, *10:* 47
Frasconi, Antonio, *6:* 79
Frazier, Neta Lohnes, *7:* 94
Freedman, Russell (Bruce), *16:* 115
Freeman, Don, *17:* 60
French, Allen, *YABC 1:* 133
French, Dorothy Kayser, *5:* 69
French, Fiona, *6:* 81
French, Paul. *See* Asimov, Isaac, *1:* 15
Frewer, Glyn, *11:* 98
Frick, C. H. *See* Irwin, Constance Frick, *6:* 119
Frick, Constance. *See* Irwin, Constance Frick, *6:* 119
Friedlander, Joanne K(ohn), *9:* 73
Friedman, Estelle, *7:* 95
Friendlich, Dick. *See* Friendlich, Richard, *11:* 99
Friendlich, Richard J., *11:* 99
Friermood, Elisabeth Hamilton, *5:* 69
Friis, Babbis. *See* Friis-Baastad, Babbis, *7:* 95
Friis-Baastad, Babbis, *7:* 95
Friskey, Margaret Richards, *5:* 72
Fritz, Jean (Guttery), *1:* 98
Froman, Elizabeth Hull, *10:* 49
Froman, Robert (Winslow), *8:* 67
Frost, A(rthur) B(urdett), *19:* 122
Frost, Erica. *See* Supraner, Robyn, *20:* 182
Frost, Lesley, *14:* 61
Frost, Robert (Lee), *14:* 63
Fry, Rosalie, *3:* 71
Fuchs, Erich, *6:* 84
Fujita, Tamao, *7:* 98
Fujiwara, Michiko, *15:* 120
Fuller, Catherine L(euthold), *9:* 73
Fuller, Iola. *See* McCoy, Iola Fuller, *3:* 120
Fuller, Lois Hamilton, *11:* 99
Funk, Thompson. *See* Funk, Tom, *7:* 98
Funk, Tom, *7:* 98
Funke, Lewis, *11:* 100

Author Index

Author Index